Macworld® Microsoft®
Office 2001 Bible

Macworld® Microsoft® Office 2001 Bible

Bob LeVitus and Dennis R. Cohen

IDG Books Worldwide, Inc.
An International Data Group Company

Foster City, CA ✦ Chicago, IL ✦ Indianapolis, IN ✦ New York, NY

Macworld® Microsoft® Office 2001 Bible

Published by

IDG Books Worldwide, Inc.

An International Data Group Company
919 E. Hillsdale Blvd., Suite 300
Foster City, CA 94404
www.idgbooks.com (IDG Books Worldwide Web site)

ISBN: 0-7645-3462-9

Printed in the United States of America

10 9 8 7 6 5 4 3 2 1

1B/RR/QR/QR/FC

Distributed in the United States by IDG Books Worldwide, Inc.

Distributed by CDG Books Canada Inc. for Canada; by Transworld Publishers Limited in the United Kingdom; by IDG Norge Books for Norway; by IDG Sweden Books for Sweden; by IDG Books Australia Publishing Corporation Pty. Ltd. for Australia and New Zealand; by TransQuest Publishers Pte Ltd. for Singapore, Malaysia, Thailand, Indonesia, and Hong Kong; by Gotop Information Inc. for Taiwan; by ICG Muse, Inc. for Japan; by Intersoft for South Africa; by Eyrolles for France; by International Thomson Publishing for Germany, Austria, and Switzerland; by Distribuidora Cuspide for Argentina; by LR International for Brazil; by Galileo Libros for Chile; by Ediciones ZETA S.C.R. Ltda. for Peru; by WS Computer Publishing Corporation, Inc., for the Philippines; by Contemporanea de Ediciones for Venezuela; by Express Computer Distributors for the Caribbean and West Indies; by Micronesia Media Distributor, Inc. for Micronesia; by Chips Computadoras S.A. de C.V. for Mexico; by Editorial Norma de Panama S.A. for Panama; by American Bookshops for Finland.

For general information on IDG Books Worldwide's books in the U.S., please call our Consumer Customer Service department at 800-762-2974. For reseller information, including discounts and premium sales, please call our Reseller Customer Service department at 800-434-3422.

For information on where to purchase IDG Books Worldwide's books outside the U.S., please contact our International Sales department at 317-572-3993 or fax 317-572-4002.

For consumer information on foreign language translations, please contact our Customer Service department at 800-434-3422, fax 317-572-4002, or e-mail rights@idgbooks.com.

For information on licensing foreign or domestic rights, please phone +1-650-653-7098.

For sales inquiries and special prices for bulk quantities, please contact our Order Services department at 800-434-3422 or write to the address above.

For information on using IDG Books Worldwide's books in the classroom or for ordering examination copies, please contact our Educational Sales department at 800-434-2086 or fax 317-572-4005.

For press review copies, author interviews, or other publicity information, please contact our Public Relations department at 650-653-7000 or fax 650-653-7500.

For authorization to photocopy items for corporate, personal, or educational use, please contact Copyright Clearance Center, 222 Rosewood Drive, Danvers, MA 01923, or fax 978-750-4470.

Library of Congress Cataloging-in-Publication Data

LeVitus, Bob.
    Macworld Microsoft Office 2001 bible / Bob LeVitus and Dennis R. Cohen.
        p. cm.
    Includes index.
    ISBN 0-7645-3462-9 (alk. paper)
    1. Microsoft Office. 2. Microsoft Word.
3. Microsoft Excel (Computer file) 4. Microsoft Powerpoint (Computer file) 5. Business--Computer programs. 6. Word processing. 7. Electronic spreadsheets. 8. Business presentations--Graphic methods--Computer programs. I. Cohen, Dennis R. II. Title.
HF5548.4.M525 L48   2001
005.369--dc21   00-053994

ABOUT IDG BOOKS WORLDWIDE

Welcome to the world of IDG Books Worldwide.

IDG Books Worldwide, Inc., is a subsidiary of International Data Group, the world's largest publisher of computer-related information and the leading global provider of information services on information technology. IDG was founded more than 30 years ago by Patrick J. McGovern and now employs more than 9,000 people worldwide. IDG publishes more than 290 computer publications in over 75 countries. More than 90 million people read one or more IDG publications each month.

Launched in 1990, IDG Books Worldwide is today the #1 publisher of best-selling computer books in the United States. We are proud to have received eight awards from the Computer Press Association in recognition of editorial excellence and three from Computer Currents' First Annual Readers' Choice Awards. Our best-selling ...For Dummies® series has more than 50 million copies in print with translations in 31 languages. IDG Books Worldwide, through a joint venture with IDG's Hi-Tech Beijing, became the first U.S. publisher to publish a computer book in the People's Republic of China. In record time, IDG Books Worldwide has become the first choice for millions of readers around the world who want to learn how to better manage their businesses.

Our mission is simple: Every one of our books is designed to bring extra value and skill-building instructions to the reader. Our books are written by experts who understand and care about our readers. The knowledge base of our editorial staff comes from years of experience in publishing, education, and journalism — experience we use to produce books to carry us into the new millennium. In short, we care about books, so we attract the best people. We devote special attention to details such as audience, interior design, use of icons, and illustrations. And because we use an efficient process of authoring, editing, and desktop publishing our books electronically, we can spend more time ensuring superior content and less time on the technicalities of making books.

You can count on our commitment to deliver high-quality books at competitive prices on topics you want to read about. At IDG Books Worldwide, we continue in the IDG tradition of delivering quality for more than 30 years. You'll find no better book on a subject than one from IDG Books Worldwide.

John Kilcullen
Chairman and CEO
IDG Books Worldwide, Inc.

Eighth Annual
Computer Press
Awards ≥1992

Ninth Annual
Computer Press
Awards ≥1993

Tenth Annual
Computer Press
Awards ≥1994

Eleventh Annual
Computer Press
Awards ≥1995

IDG is the world's leading IT media, research and exposition company. Founded in 1964, IDG had 1997 revenues of $2.05 billion and has more than 9,000 employees worldwide. IDG offers the widest range of media options that reach IT buyers in 75 countries representing 95% of worldwide IT spending. IDG's diverse product and services portfolio spans six key areas including print publishing, online publishing, expositions and conferences, market research, education and training, and global marketing services. More than 90 million people read one or more of IDG's 290 magazines and newspapers, including IDG's leading global brands — Computerworld, PC World, Network World, Macworld and the Channel World family of publications. IDG Books Worldwide is one of the fastest-growing computer book publishers in the world, with more than 700 titles in 36 languages. The "...For Dummies®" series alone has more than 50 million copies in print. IDG offers online users the largest network of technology-specific Web sites around the world through IDG.net (http://www.idg.net), which comprises more than 225 targeted Web sites in 55 countries worldwide. International Data Corporation (IDC) is the world's largest provider of information technology data, analysis and consulting, with research centers in over 41 countries and more than 400 research analysts worldwide. IDG World Expo is a leading producer of more than 168 globally branded conferences and expositions in 35 countries including E3 (Electronic Entertainment Expo), Macworld Expo, ComNet, Windows World Expo, ICE (Internet Commerce Expo), Agenda, DEMO, and Spotlight. IDG's training subsidiary, ExecuTrain, is the world's largest computer training company, with more than 230 locations worldwide and 785 training courses. IDG Marketing Services helps industry-leading IT companies build international brand recognition by developing global integrated marketing programs via IDG's print, online and exposition products worldwide. Further information about the company can be found at www.idg.com. 1/26/00

Credits

Acquisitions Editors
Tom Heine
Michael Roney

Project Editor
Linda Turnowski

Technical Editor
Jefferson R. Johnson

Copy Editors
Michael D. Welch
Richard H. Adin
Karyn S. DiCastri
Julie Campbell Moss

Proof Editor
Patsy Owens

Project Coordinators
Joe Shines
Danette Nurse

Graphics and Production Specialists
Robert Bihlmayer
Rolly Delrosario
Jude Levinson
Michael Lewis
Victor Pérez-Varela
Ramses Ramirez

Quality Control Technician
Dina F Quan

Book Designer
Drew R. Moore

Illustrators
Gabriele McCann
Ronald Terry
John Greenough

Proofreading and Indexing
York Production Services

Cover Image
Lawrance Huck

About the Authors

Bob LeVitus (pronounced Love-eye-tis) was the editor-in-chief of the wildly popular *MACazine* until its untimely demise in 1988. From 1989 to 1997, he was a contributing editor/columnist for *MacUser* magazine, writing the "Help Folder," "Beating the System," "Personal Best," and "Game Room" columns at various times in his illustrious career. In his spare time, LeVitus has written 36 popular computer books, including *Mac OS 9 For Dummies* and *AppleWorks 6 For Dummies* (also with Dennis Cohen). Always a popular speaker at Macintosh user groups and trade shows, LeVitus has spoken at more than 100 international seminars, presented keynote addresses in several countries, and serves on the Macworld Expo advisory board. He was also the host of "Mac Today," a half-hour television show syndicated in more than 100 markets, which aired in late 1992. Millions in the United States and abroad read his syndicated newspaper column, "Dr. Mac." LeVitus has forgotten more about the Macintosh than most people ever knew. He won the Macworld Expo MacJeopardy World Championship an unbelievable four times before retiring his crown. But most of all, LeVitus is known for his clear, understandable writing, his humorous style, and his ability to translate techie jargon into usable and fun advice for the rest of us. He lives in Austin, Texas, with his wife, two children, and a small pack of dogs.

Dennis R. Cohen coauthored *AppleWorks 6 For Dummies* (with Bob LeVitus), *Macworld AppleWorks 6 Bible* (with Steven Schwartz), and *Teach Yourself WebTV* (with Erica Sadun), in addition to being the technical editor of more than fifty titles, including *Macworld Mac Secrets*, *Teach Yourself Excel 2000*, *Macworld FileMaker Pro 5 Bible (and 3 and 4)*, as well as *Mac OS 9: The Missing Manual*. When Bob runs his Mac trivia contests at various Macworld Expos, he disqualifies Dennis from competing. Dennis has been developing software for the Macintosh since 1984 and for other platforms (Apple III, Lisa, Unix, PCs, VAX, Modcomp, and CPM) before that. A few of the products on which he has worked are ClarisWorks (now called AppleWorks), Claris Resolve, dBASE Mac (and dBASE III for Unix), ClarisImpact, and StuffIt InstallerMaker. He resides in Sunnyvale, California, with his Boston terrier, Spenser. For diversion from computers, he plays bridge, backgammon, golf, and shoots trap.

Preface

Welcome to the *Macworld Microsoft Office 2001 Bible*. This book is your personal guide to the Microsoft Office 2001 applications: Word, Excel, PowerPoint, Entourage, and Internet Explorer. This book tells you all the details you need to learn about any or all of the Microsoft Office applications, regardless of how much you already know about Office. While first and foremost a comprehensive reference, the *Macworld Microsoft Office 2001 Bible* also helps you learn by example. The book gives you special tips and techniques to get the most out of the Office applications, as they stand alone and as they work in conjunction with their fellow applications. All in all, this book helps you integrate the use of the Office applications into your life for maximum efficiency and shows you how to share information among the applications to produce impressive documents and presentations.

Although each chapter is an integral part of the book as a whole, each chapter can also stand on its own. You can read the book in any order you want, skipping from chapter to chapter and from topic to topic. (This book's index is particularly thorough: Rely on the index to find the topics that interest you.)

For each of the major applications — Word, Excel, and PowerPoint — we include chapters that answer the ten most common user questions, based on user feedback to Microsoft. We also include "At Work" chapters that show you how to accomplish common, everyday office tasks with the Office software. In case you've never touched Word, Excel, or PowerPoint, we include appendixes that provide the basics for each application.

Is This Book for You?

If you use (or will soon use) Microsoft Office, this book is for you. As we describe fully in the next section, this book is divided into parts. If you're an Office beginner, start with the first chapter in each part and work to the end. (If you've never used any kind of word processor, spreadsheet, database manager, or presentation graphics program before, start with the appendixes!) If you have some Office experience, at least breeze through the chapters that cover topics you already know. They introduce you to the new features and provide tips and techniques that help you work better with Office.

How We've Organized This Book

We've divided this book into five parts: one part that gives an overview of Office; one part each for Word, Excel, and PowerPoint; and one part that describes the Office Internet tools — Entourage (for e-mail and personal information management) and Internet Explorer (for viewing Web pages).

Part I: Introducing Microsoft Office 2001

This tiny, one-chapter part introduces the tools Office gives you to work more efficiently: Word, Excel, PowerPoint, Internet Explorer, and Entourage.

Part II: Word

Ah, Word: the 800-pound gorilla of word processors. This part tells you what Word can do for you. For example, you will learn how to create and format documents and tables; save your documents as Web pages; and use templates and wizards to create high-quality documents, newsletters, and brochures.

Part III: Excel

This part describes Office's spreadsheet application, Excel. Here you can learn how to create and format spreadsheets, see how to publish them on the Web, and use your data to create charts, graphs, and PivotTables.

Part IV: PowerPoint

This part tells you how to use PowerPoint to create great presentations. Here you will learn how to produce slide presentations, use Auto Fit to automatically size and fit text onto slides, and see how to save your presentation as HTML so that others can view it on the Web.

Part V: The Internet Office

This part tells you about Entourage, Office's Internet messaging and personal information management application, and Internet Explorer, a Web browser that enables you to view Web pages efficiently. In the chapter on Entourage, you will learn how to use the address book, calendar, notes, reminders, and task lists features. In the chapter on Explorer, you will learn how to surf the Web with this browser and use Offline Browsing to read Web pages when you're not connected to the Internet, and much more.

Appendixes

If you haven't installed Office on your Mac yet, check out Appendix A. If you are new to any of the Office applications, visit the appendixes dedicated to the programs that interest you; they will get you going. Here's what to expect in each appendix:

+ **Appendix A** tells you how to install Office 2001 and goes over each of the Value Pack additions you can install.

+ **Appendix B** shows the new Word user how to launch Word, how to create a document, how to open an existing document, how to navigate in a document, how to enter and edit text, and how to print and save a document.

+ **Appendix C** shows the new Excel user how to launch Excel, what a workbook is, how to navigate in a workbook, how to enter and edit data and formulas, how to do basic formatting, and how to save and print a workbook.

+ **Appendix D** shows the new PowerPoint user how to launch PowerPoint, how to create, move around in, and save presentations; and how to enter text and graphics.

+ **Appendix E** shows the new Entourage user how to launch Entourage, how to read and send e-mail, peruse Internet newsgroups, manage the Office Address Book, maintain the Office Calendar, and use the Tasks list.

+ **Appendix F** gives you the full lowdown on how to change your Office menus and toolbars to best fit your own use. This appendix is for after you've worked with any of the applications.

Conventions This Book Uses

We've written a thick book: There's a lot to say about Office! So make the material more accessible, we use several devices that help you find your way.

For starters, you'll see eye-catching icons in the margin from time to time. They alert you to critical information, warn you about problems, tell you where to go for more information, and highlight useful tips.

This icon highlights a special point of interest about the current topic.

This icon helps you work faster by pointing out shortcuts and killer techniques. If you've worked with the Office applications before and want to expand your knowledge quickly, skim the book for these icons.

Sometimes it's important to be aware of potential problems that can develop if you're not aware of them. This icon points out those situations so you can avoid them.

This icon sends you to other places in the book for more information about something we mention.

This icon indicates what's brand new in Microsoft Office 2001 for the Macintosh.

While each Office application stands on its own and does an excellent job, many times having the applications work together increases your productivity. This icon highlights examples where we use more than one Office application to accomplish a task.

Sidebars

We use sidebars to highlight related information, give an example, or discuss an item in greater detail. For example, one sidebar tells you where to get graphics you can add to documents, spreadsheets, and presentations — cool information, but not critical. If you don't want to delve too deeply into a subject, stick to the body of the text and skip the sidebars.

When we write command names, we use a convention that shows you the menus you need to use to execute the command. So, when we want you to choose the Print command from the File menu, we write "choose File ⇨ Print." When we want you to execute the Define command from the Name submenu of the Insert menu, we write "choose Insert ⇨ Name ⇨ Define."

Where Should I Start?

For an overview of Microsoft Office, start with Chapter 1. After that, or if you want to focus on one particular program in the Office suite, dive in as follows:

- ✦ If you want to learn about **Word**, start with Chapter 2. If you've never used a word processor before, read Appendix B first.

- ✦ If you want to work with **Excel**, go to Chapter 15. Appendix C teaches the basics of Excel, for those who've never used a spreadsheet program.

- ✦ If you want to create presentations in **PowerPoint**, start with Chapter 28 (or Appendix D, if you don't know the first thing about presentation-creation software).

- ✦ If you want to use **Entourage**, go to Chapter 36. Appendix E provides the bare necessities in starting to use Entourage.

- ✦ If you want to use **Internet Explorer**, jump to Chapter 37.

Acknowledgments

First, thanks to the folks at IDG Books Worldwide: Michael Roney, for asking us to do this book and for all his work to make it a great experience; Linda Turnowski, for her excellent editing expertise, and the entire staff who make working with IDG Books Worldwide such a pleasure for us writers.

Thanks to some really cool programmers at Microsoft: program manager Irving Kwong for sharing his knowledge and insights as well as keeping us current with Office 2001 development; and engineers Matt Centurion, Bart Chellis, Jud Spencer, and David Cortright for sharing tips and answering questions.

Thanks also to superagent Carole "stop calling me Swifty in the acknowledgments" McClendon of Waterside Productions for her deal-making and coordination beyond the call of duty. Carole, you're the greatest!

Finally, thanks to all the software and hardware makers who provided the tools we used to create this book, including Microsoft, Apple, Adobe, QPS, Ambrosia, Iomega, Aladdin, and others too numerous to mention.

Contents at a Glance

Contents

Part V: The Internet Office   675

Introducing Microsoft Office 2001

This part, with just one chapter, gives you an overview of what you'll find in the Office 2001 package, how to open and save documents, and the general usage of Office 2001 components. This part also points you to places in the book where you can get more information on the various components of Office 2001.

Getting to Know Microsoft Office

This chapter introduces Microsoft Office 2001, explains what comes with Office 2001, and shows you how to install its core components. We introduce the various ways you can launch your Office applications and the basics for opening documents. We also introduce the toolbars and the Office Assistant, your Office Help venue.

Getting to Know Microsoft Office

Microsoft Office is a group of applications that complement each other to accomplish things in a similar way and provide easy access to data shared between the individual applications. Office is designed to make you more productive with fewer hassles. With Microsoft Office, you can create business documents to meet virtually any need, handle complex financial analysis, and produce professional presentations. Microsoft Office includes the following applications:

✦ **Word,** which provides all the power that you need in a word processor along with a range of tools to make complex formatting tasks easier.

✦ **Excel,** which provides you with a spreadsheet that is powerful yet simple to use. In addition to offering powerful spreadsheet capabilities and the ability to work with multiple pages in the same spreadsheet file (the workbook concept), Excel provides powerful charting and graphing features and can readily use spreadsheets that were saved in other popular spreadsheet formats.

✦ **PowerPoint,** which is a presentation graphics program that can provide you with overheads for team meetings, slides for sales meetings, animated special effects for video presentations, and more. PowerPoint's tools, combined with its simple approach, make it easy for you to create presentations that clearly emphasize what you are trying to say.

✦ **Entourage,** which is a personal information and e-mail management program. The personal information features include a basic address book in which you can list names, addresses, numbers, and e-mail and Web information, as well as take notes; a calendar similar to a day planner, in which you can schedule events and have Entourage remind you of them as well as invite others to them; a Tasks list similar to the traditional to-do list, with the addition of reminders and prioritization of the items to be done; and a Notes function, similar to a personal scratch pad. Entourage enables you to send and receive e-mail, participate in Usenet newsgroups, and manage your messages. Filters and actions can be applied to incoming mail. For those of you familiar with Outlook Express (which is included with every Macintosh and copy of the MacOS sold), Entourage is a superset of that program.

✦ **Internet Explorer,** which is a Web browser, an application that brings the pages of the World Wide Web to your screen. Features such as the Favorites list help you bookmark sites of interest for easy access. (Internet Explorer is not a core application. It must be installed separately.)

Office 2001 also includes several "shared" applications that you can access from any of the individual programs. These shared applications are Word Art, Equation Editor, Microsoft Graph, and Microsoft Clip Gallery.

✦ **Word Art** is actually art with words. You type in any text, pick a shape and colors for your text, and in a moment you have decorative text. You can then adjust the text. It can be edited or changed at any time, too. Although Word Art works in any of the core Office applications, we cover Word Art in the PowerPoint section.

✦ The **Equation Editor** enables you to create mathematical equations. Equations can be inserted into Word, Excel, or PowerPoint using the Insert Object command. Equation Editor is part of the Value Pack install.

✦ **Microsoft Graph** enables you to create charts and graphs easily. We show you how to use it in the Word section in Chapter 10.

✦ **Microsoft Clip Gallery** is an extensive collection of clip art, with the capability to search the Internet for even more clip art based on criteria you establish.

Installing Office 2001

Microsoft Office 2001 reprises a wonderful twist, introduced with Office 98, on the original Mac software installation technique. Installation couldn't be simpler. Just insert the CD-ROM and drag the folder called Microsoft Office 2001 onto your hard drive. That's it! The icons for each of the core Office 2001 applications — Word, Entourage, Excel, and PowerPoint — are in this main folder. You don't need to search through buried folders to find and launch any of the applications. Instead, simply double-click the one you want to run to launch it. Each of the Office applications self-install and reinstall themselves as needed. Each time you launch an Office application, it looks to see that all necessary pieces are in your System folder. If you turn off or remove any necessary pieces, the pieces are reinstalled.

The drag install provides all the basics of Microsoft Office 2001; it's commonly called a standard install, and this is what most people want. If you find the drag install is more than you want, you can do a custom install instead by running the Microsoft Office Installer (located inside the Office Custom Install folder on your install CD-ROM). For details, see Appendix A.

Office 2001 also comes with more than what the drag install provides. You can find these additions in the Value Pack folder on your Office CD-ROM. These elements are installed via the Value Pack Installer inside the Value Pack folder. For the lowdown on what's in the Value Pack and installation instructions, see Appendix A.

Should you wish to remove Office 2001 from your hard drive, you can drag the Microsoft Office 2001 folder to the Trash and remove the following files from your System folder hierarchy: in the Extensions folder, remove Microsoft Component Library, Microsoft Hyperlink Library, Microsoft OLE Automation, Microsoft OLE Library, Microsoft Structured Storage, and the Type Libraries folder; from the Preferences folder, remove the Microsoft folder. The previous version of Microsoft Office (Office 98) had an application that removed Office from your hard disk, but it was problematic and, unfortunately, an uninstall program is not part of Office 2001.

As stated previously, Internet Explorer is a separate install. You can install it by dragging the Internet Explorer 5 Folder from your install CD-ROM to your hard disk.

How Does Office Do It?

The Office folder, within the Microsoft Office 2001 folder, contains all the necessary extensions. If Microsoft Office First Run, a document within the Office folder, lists any extensions missing from your active extensions folder, Office invisibly copies what it needs into your extensions folder.

If you happen to disable any necessary extensions, Office places a new copy in your active extensions folder. Therefore, it is possible that you'll end up with duplicate copies of an extension. An extensions manager, such as Conflict Catcher, will notice this duplication and ask whether you want to delete one version. You can delete the disabled version.

The installation performed by dragging the Microsoft Office 2001 folder is the basic installation. Additional Office components, such as the small business templates, and Word Speak are available in the Value Pack on the CD-ROM. For details on these options and their installation, see Appendix A.

Launching Office Applications

As with all Macintosh software, launching an Office application is as easy as double-clicking the application's icon. The standard shortcuts, such as placing an alias on your desktop or in your Apple menu, are also available.

Creating New Documents

When you have any Office application other than Entourage (Word, Excel, or PowerPoint) open, you can use the New Blank Document button to create new documents within that application. Entourage requires that you specify from a submenu the type of Entourage document you wish to create. Of course, you can also use the standard Mac commands, File ➪ New Blank Document or ⌘-N. Microsoft Office 2001 introduces another method: the Project Gallery (File ➪ Project Gallery or Shift-⌘-P) in all Office applications.

Aliases and the Apple Menu

You can save yourself considerable time by adding an alias of each Office icon to your Apple menu.

An alias is a small file that points to, and opens, the actual program, file, disk, or folder that it represents. You can place an alias anywhere on your Mac, but placing it in the Apple menu provides universal access. To create an alias, click the icon to select it, and then choose File ➪ Make Alias (⌘-M). Alternatively, if you're using OS 8 or 9, press ⌘-Option as you click the desired icon and drag the icon to your destination. (These are the standard Mac procedures for creating aliases. See your Mac documentation for more information.) For example, to create an alias of Word, open the Microsoft Office 2001 folder, click the Microsoft Word icon, and then choose File ➪ Make Alias. Alternatively, press ⌘-Option as you click the Microsoft Word icon and drag the icon to your destination.

The point is that if you place an alias of Word, Excel, Entourage, or PowerPoint (or any other application) in the Apple Menu Items folder, you can start that program without bothering to open the hard drive and the application's folder. Instead, you simply select the application's name in the Apple menu. If you place an alias of a file directly in the Apple menu, you can select it from this menu at any time to launch that file easily. If you place an alias of a folder in the Apple menu, you can go down to the folder to open it or slide over to any file within that folder to launch that file.

Don't skip the creation of an alias by dragging the Word, Excel, or PowerPoint icons from the Microsoft Office 2001 folder to your desired location. If you do this, you are literally moving the program file from the application's folder (from which it is designed to work).

You can also place aliases of your Office applications on your desktop. This comes in handy when you want to open a file that was created in another application.

The New Blank Document button directly opens a generic new document (from the Normal template). So does the New document shortcut, ⌘-N. File ⇨ Project Gallery provides more flexibility by taking you to the Project Gallery window, enabling you to use a specialized template or wizard.

In the Project Gallery window, you can peruse the various document choices, categorized in a Finder-like list. For example, if you wanted to create a fax sheet while in Word, you would click the Business Forms triangle and then choose Fax Covers, finally selecting the particular one you want from the catalog of selections (you can also view the choices as a list, but then you have to click each one individually to see its preview). Or, if you want to create a sales presentation using PowerPoint, you might click the Presentations triangle and select one of the sales presentations in the Content catalog. Clicking a template in a List view (which selects it) presents a preview to help you decide which template is right for you. Figure 1-1 shows the Project Gallery window provided by the default install. After you select the template that you want to use, clicking OK opens a new document based upon that template. (Or, if you've selected a wizard, it launches the wizard.) If the template or wizard is for another Office application's document type, that application will be launched for you. You can also open a template in a List view by double-clicking it, rather than clicking it once to select it and then clicking OK. (This works because the OK button is the default selection, as designated by the black ring around it.)

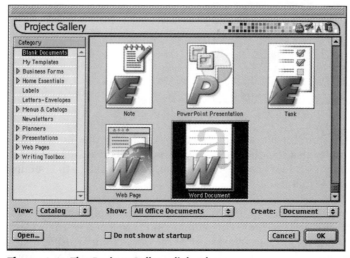

Figure 1-1: The Project Gallery dialog box

Opening Existing Documents

Opening an existing Office document is the same as opening any document on the Mac. From within Word, Excel, Entourage, or PowerPoint, you can use File ⇨ Open. Or, in the Finder, you can directly select your document and open it, which launches the application in which the document was created (if it isn't already running), or brings the application forward (if it is already running).

Using File ⇨ Open from within a Word, Excel, Entourage, or PowerPoint document enables you to open another Word, Excel, Entourage, or PowerPoint document. The Open dialog box is shown in Figure 1-2. You can filter the documents that appear in the open document list by selecting a filter from the Show pop-up box below the file list.

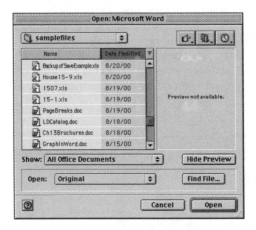

Figure 1-2: The Open dialog box revealing all Office document types

To open a document from the Finder, go directly to the folder that houses the document, and then double-click the document. If you have placed an alias of the document (or the document's folder) in the Apple menu, you can select the document directly from the Apple menu.

You can often open a document created in another, similar application. For example, you can be in Word and use the File ⇨ Open command to select a word processing document that was created in ClarisWorks (or AppleWorks 5) or WordPerfect. Word will translate it for you. Another way to do this is to drag the ClarisWorks/Apple-Works or WordPerfect document onto the Word icon or an alias of the Word icon.

Office 2000, the Windows equivalent of Office 2001, has a feature called the Binder, which enables several Office documents to be bound into one file. If someone gives you an Office 2000 document but you can't open it, the file may be one of these

Binder files. It's easy to separate a Binder file into individual Office documents that you can work with. To do so, you use the Unbinder, a small application installed via the Value Pack Installer.

If you receive a document that has been bound, follow these steps:

1. Launch the Unbinder. After it is installed, it should be located in the Microsoft Office 2001 folder.

2. Select File ➪ Open Binder. Locate the file to unbind and click Open. A dialog box will appear, telling you the name of each file as it unbinds, and also reporting how many files there are in all.

3. The files will appear in the Office 2001 folder. You can double-click any of the files and use them as normal.

Learning About Toolbars

When you activate Word, Excel, or PowerPoint, you will see a gray area containing toolbars — rows full of symbols — across the top of your screen (unless your toolbars were turned off). Toolbars are strips of buttons that you can use to perform common tasks. Word, Excel, and PowerPoint each have a standard toolbar as well as several function-specific toolbars. As you rest your mouse over any button, a little yellow information window pops up, telling you what that button does. Using the toolbars is a great way to accomplish an action with as few motions as possible. This section introduces toolbars so that you can learn to use them comfortably as you work.

Toolbars are highly customizable. You can add or remove buttons as you wish, swap button positions, and customize button icons. In Appendix E, you can learn how to customize your toolbars.

Note　Entourage and Internet Explorer also have toolbars, so you can enjoy the same convenience you are used to in Office. However, these toolbars are not customizable.

Turning toolbars on or off

Toolbars provide great shortcuts; but of course, if you had every toolbar in view, there would be no room onscreen to see your document. Therefore, you can turn each of these toolbars on and off as desired. Turning a toolbar on or off is easy. The toolbar control is under the View menu. Simply click the View menu, and then move down to the Toolbars option and over to the toolbar you want to turn on or off. A checkmark in the menu indicates the menu is on. (Of course, you can also see the menu onscreen.) Office applications often turn on toolbars, as appropriate, when you call upon a function.

Docking, undocking, and moving toolbars

You can change a toolbar's position or undock the toolbars. Rather than keeping your toolbars attached to the top of the screen, you may prefer to move a toolbar to the left or right edge of your monitor. Simply click the resize handle in the lower-right corner and drag to reshape a horizontal toolbar to vertical. Click in the hatched "title bar" area to drag a toolbar to a different location. Note that most toolbars do not have a title in their title bar area.

Toolbars can also float freely as palettes, rather than remaining attached to the top of your screen. Notice that the left side of the toolbar has a couple of rows of dots and a close box. To undock a toolbar, click these dots and drag the toolbar down and away from the docked area. (Actually, you can click any edge of any toolbar to undock it.) Like any window, you can drag this palette anywhere onscreen and resize it. Resizing the palette doesn't add a scrollbar; it rearranges the buttons. To redock the toolbar, drag it back up into the toolbar area until your mouse overlaps the toolbar below which you want it to fall.

Enabling ScreenTips

The little yellow information window that pops up when you rest your mouse over a button is called a ScreenTip. You can turn them on and off at any time. Select Tools ⇨ Customize, and then click the Appearance tab of the Customize dialog box that opens (see Figure 1-3). Click the checkbox to turn on or turn off Show ScreenTips on toolbars. ScreenTips are turned on by default. In Excel, the checkbox for one ScreenTip option, Show shortcut keys in ScreenTips, which shows you a keyboard equivalent to pressing the button (when one exists), is not available. Enabling this feature is a great way to become more familiar with your keyboard shortcuts. Show shortcut keys in ScreenTips is turned off by default.

Figure 1-3: The Appearance tab of the Customize dialog box

By the way, Large icons sets your buttons to a (very) large size.

When you select Tools ➪ Customize, you are likely to be greeted by the Office Assistant. He pops up occasionally to guide you when he feels you may need help (as described in the following section). Because selecting options is so easy, you probably won't need to consult the Office Assistant in this case.

Working with the Office Assistant

The Office Assistant is another element common to the core Office applications (Word, Excel, Entourage, and PowerPoint). The Office Assistant provides you with help, tips, advice, and warnings. You can call it up at any time by pressing the Help key or by selecting ". . . Turn Assistant On" from the Help menu. From time to time, the Assistant pops up on its own, offering to tell you about something you're about to do. It may even pop up to suggest a way to do something easier, for example, by suggesting you use a wizard.

The default Assistant is Max, a classic Mac. Several more are included in the Value Pack. Each has a unique personality and can prove entertaining as it hangs out watching you work, waiting to be useful. By default, the assistants are quiet, but you can program them to speak.

Getting help from your Assistant

To get help, click your Assistant, press the Help key, or select Turn Assistant On from the Help menu. If the Assistant isn't already onscreen, he'll pop up at your beck and call. In a yellow balloon, he'll ask, "What would you like to do?" There's a text area below in which you type your question, and then you click Search. You don't have to place your cursor anywhere. Just type. The Assistant understands plain English, so you can ask it any question. If it doesn't respond with what you need, try removing unnecessary instructions. For example, you don't need to say "Show me . . ." or "Tell me about. . . ." You can experiment with cutting down your questions to phrases. After you type your question, press Return or Enter, or click Search. The Assistant will then present a list of all topics that may meet your needs. Click the blue bullet next to the offering you want. A new window opens, providing details. When appropriate, there will be other symbols to click for more information on a related topic.

If you switch help pages and want to return to one you visited, click the Back button (the left-pointing arrow) as many times as necessary to return to the desired page.

You can copy help text. While on the page, select the desired text by dragging over it and choose Edit ➪ Copy (⌘-C). The formatting and style of the text is not retained, nor are graphics copied. While this process is more natural, it is a significant loss from the clarity in Office 98's Help system, where pressing ⌘-C with a Help window up presented a dialog showing exactly what would be copied.

Tips

A yellow light bulb by the Assistant's head lets you know that a tip is waiting for you. Click the light bulb to view the tip. You can determine whether you see tips and what tip topics are offered. (See "Setting Your Assistant's Behavior," which follows.)

Setting your Assistant's behavior

You can change your Assistant or its behavior at any time. This Assistant and behavior is common throughout each of the core Office applications. When you call up the Assistant, an Options button appears in its dialog box. Click the Options button. Click the Gallery tab (see Figure 1-4) to select a new Assistant (after you've installed alternatives via the Value Pack Installer). The Back and Next buttons move through each installed Assistant. Each Assistant is shown and described. Click the Options tab (see Figure 1-5) to determine what your Assistant will help you with and how.

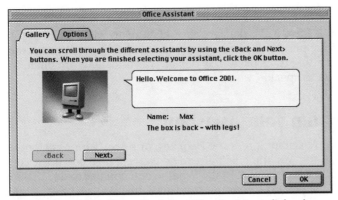

Figure 1-4: The Gallery tab of the Office Assistant dialog box

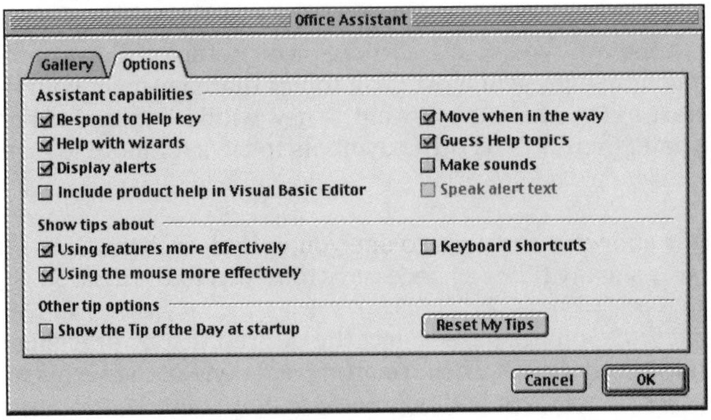

Figure 1-5: The Options tab of the Office Assistant dialog box

The available options are self-explanatory, but a few are worth pointing out. Guess Help Topics is the option that enables the Assistant to anticipate your needs, suggesting help relevant to what you are doing. The Help with wizards option triggers help to come up whenever you start a wizard. The Display alerts option enables the Assistant to deliver alerts. Alerts can also be spoken when the Speak alert text option is checked. When the Display alerts option is not checked, alert messages are shown in an alternative dialog box.

After you have set your Assistant, chosen your options, or both, click OK.

Getting more help

When the Assistant fails to find what you are looking for, you can go to the Help menu and select Contents and Index. You now have three options: You can press the Contents, Index, or Search buttons at the top of the Help window, and then click any item in the left pane of the window.

If you see a subject that looks like what you want, click to expand on the subject, and then click any of the underlined items. As you might gather from this, Office 2001 Help is organized like a Web site, with links from one page to another.

If you don't see your subject, click the Search button at the top. The Assistant will pop back up and ask you what you'd like to do.

Summary

This chapter showed how to access the Microsoft Office applications — via standard Mac methods. You also learned about getting help. This chapter covered these points:

✦ Microsoft Office 2001 includes Word (for word processing), Excel (for spreadsheets), PowerPoint (for presentations), and Entourage (for managing contacts, newsgroups, calendars, to-do lists, and e-mail).

✦ Some Windows users bind their documents. Use the Unbinder to access those documents.

✦ In addition to the standard Mac install, you can install complementary productivity (Value Pack) features. Appendix A covers the Value Pack.

✦ You can customize Word, Excel, or PowerPoint's toolbars. Appendix E shows you how.

✦ The Office Assistant is always standing by to help you. You can ask questions in real English. If the Assistant can't help to answer your question, you can find topics in the Help Index.

✦ The Office Assistant can even anticipate your needs. You can set the Assistant's behavior, which will remain consistent between each core application.

Where to go next

The remainder of this book details how you can get the most out of Microsoft Office.

✦ If you want to work in Word, go to Chapter 2. If you're a Word neophyte, Appendix B gets you started.

✦ If you want to use Excel, go to Chapter 15. Appendix C provides Excel basics for those who have never used a spreadsheet before.

✦ If you want to create presentations in PowerPoint, see Chapter 28. If you are a beginner, see Appendix D for a PowerPoint Quick Start.

✦ If you want to manage personal information or e-mail in Entourage, see Chapter 35. If you are a beginner, see Appendix E.

✦ If you'd like to customize your toolbars, visit Appendix E.

✦ If you'd like to custom install Office, or add Value Pack features, go directly to Appendix A.

✦   ✦   ✦

Word

This part gives you a soup-to-nuts run-through of how to use Microsoft Word 2001 to create effective documents. You'll learn how to add and manipulate graphics, style and format your text, add tables, work with outlines, create and use templates, publish to the World Wide Web, and print your documents. You'll also learn how to automate repetitive tasks and receive an introduction to using Visual Basic for Applications to further automate Word.

Creating and Working with Documents

Because your first step in Word is to create documents, it makes sense for us to cover the basics of creating documents in the first Word chapter. You also need to know about the many techniques you can use to edit the documents you create. These techniques help you fix mistakes in your documents.

Launching the Program

Of course, before you can work with documents in Word, you have to launch the Word application. You can start Word by opening the Microsoft Office 2001 folder and double-clicking the Microsoft Word icon, located directly inside. If you have placed an alias of Word in your Apple menu, you can select the alias there to launch Word. If an alias of Word is on your desktop, you can double-click the alias. If you have another application that enables you to create a shortcut to launch applications, you can assign a shortcut to Word and use the shortcut. If you have a recent-vintage Mac, you can use the Keyboard control panel to set one of the F-Keys (those keys along the top of your keyboard, such as F7 or F12) to launch Word.

If you have a Word document on your hard disk, simply double-click the document. This launches Word automatically as it opens your document.

If Word is already running on your Mac, but it's not the active program, you can bring Word to the front (in other words, make it active) by selecting it in the Application menu at the far right of your menu bar. If Word is already running, all the methods described previously, including opening a Word document, make Word the active application as well.

Creating and Opening Documents

Each time you launch Word, a blank document automatically appears, ready for you to use. It is a common mistake to think that because no document is showing on your screen, Word (or any other application for that matter) is not running. Some people quit Word and relaunch it to have a new document open for them; but this isn't necessary. To create more documents, simply select New from the File menu (⌘-N) or click the New Document button on Word's Standard (top) toolbar.

File ⇨ New opens the New Document dialog box so you can select a template or wizard. ⌘-N or the New Document button provides a generic document based on your default margins, font, and such. (See the next section, "Understanding Templates.") You can create new documents any time Word is the active application.

If you already have a Word document on your hard disk, simply double-click the document. This launches Word automatically as it opens your document.

Understanding Templates

You may not have thought about it before, but when you create a new document in any program, you are, in effect, opening up a template. A template is a collection of settings that determine how the document created from it will look. Templates help you streamline the creation of documents that you produce on a regular basis. In Word, any time you use the New Document button, choose File ⇨ New, or use the ⌘-N shortcut, you are launching a copy of Word's default template, which is named Normal.

New Feature

In Office 98, choosing File ⇨ New presented a New document dialog box from which you could choose the template to use. In Word 2001, File ⇨ New behaves as it does in other applications — you are presented with a new, default document. To let you select from the various templates, Office 2001 introduces the Project Gallery (Shift-⌘-P). The Project Gallery was introduced in Chapter 1.

Word gives you two ways to create documents: You can use the Normal template or a template of your choosing — be it one of Word's specialty templates or one you create yourself. You will probably use both methods in your work.

When Word is first opened, it contains a document with default settings ready for you to use. This is the Normal template (stored in the Templates folder), which contains a set of standard margins and no formatting. Remember that clicking the New button in the Standard toolbar, choosing File ⇨ New, or using the ⌘-N keys always creates a new document based on this Normal template. After you begin to enter text, you can change all these settings.

If you do not want to use the default Normal template, you can use one of the other Word templates that may be better suited to your needs. To open one of these templates, choose Project Gallery from the File menu (Shift-⌘-P). The Project Gallery dialog box appears, in which you can make the selection that is best for your needs (see Figure 2-1). The dialog box contains a list of categories on the left, and each category contains one or more templates (or subcategories) appropriate to a specific task in Word or another Office 2001 application. For example, if most of the documents you create are letters, you can click the Letters-Envelopes category to display a group of templates appropriate for creating letters. (The tab also lists two wizards; see the section "Looking at Template Wizards" a little later in this chapter for information about using wizards.) After you create a document based on a template, the template controls the initial appearance of the document.

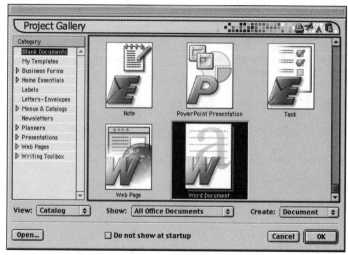

Figure 2-1: The Project Gallery dialog box

Many documents are made up of standard parts. For example, an interoffice memo often contains a company name and address heading; To, From, Date, and Subject headings; and closing information, such as a routing list of persons receiving the memo. Assuming a template is designed for your interoffice memos, the template can contain your boilerplate (or standard) text. You can even design your templates to prompt you for the specific information (such as the recipient's name) needed each time the template is used. (See "About user input" in Chapter 24 for more about this.)

Note
Another benefit of using templates is that in Word, all toolbar, menu, and keyboard customization is stored within the document—in the Normal template, by default. If you want to distribute customized toolbars, menus, or shortcuts, store them in a template and send it along to those who should use those customizations. (See Appendix F for the story on customizing toolbars, menus, and keyboard shortcuts.)

Exploring template categories

Table 2-1 lists the template categories and the templates in each category or sub-category. The name of each template explains its function. You can view the available templates by thumbnail (the default, Catalog view) or by name (called List View). Select your desired view in the pop-up View menu.

Table 2-1 Templates Available in Microsoft Word	
Template Category/Subcategory	**Name of Template or Wizard**
Blank documents	Word document (uses Normal template)
	Web page
Business forms/brochures (all of these are Wizards)	Accessory
	Bar
	Blocks
	Bracket
	Capsule
	Column
	Corners
	Dots
	Dragon
	Elegant
	Forms
	Marquee
	Neutral
	Saucer
	Simple
Business Forms/Fax Covers	Accessory
	Bar
	Capsule
	Circuit
	Corners
	Dots
	Dragon
	Elegant
	Forms
	Marquee
	Neutral
	Simple

Template Category/Subcategory	Name of Template or Wizard
Business forms/invoices	Accessory
	Bar
	Capsule
	Circuit
	Corners
	Dots
	Dragon
	Elegant
	Forms
	Marquee
	Neutral
	Simple
Business forms/letterhead	Accessory
	Bar
	Capsule
	Circuit
	Corners
	Dots
	Dragon
	Elegant
	Forms
	Marquee
	Neutral
	Simple
Home essentials/family medical	Dental record
	Emergency contacts
	Family history
	Hospital-illness record
Home essentials/résumés	Elegant
	Modern
	Rule
	Simple
Labels	Mailing label wizard

Continued

Table 2-1 *(continued)*

Template Category/Subcategory	Name of Template or Wizard
Letters-Envelopes	Cover letter-professional
	Cover letter-simple
	Envelope wizard
	Letter wizard
	Letter-circuit
	Letter-professional
	Letter-whimsy
	Stationery-bold
	Stationery-professional
	Stationery-simple
Menus & catalogs/catalogs (all of these are wizards)	Accessory
	Bar
	Beach
	Blocks
	Capsule
	Corners
	Desert
	Dots
	Dragon
	Elegant
	Forms
	Marquee
	Neutral
	Phosphors
	Saucer
	Simple
Menus & catalogs/menus (all of these are wizards)	Accessory
	Bar
	Beach
	Blocks
	Capsule
	Corners
	Desert
	Dots
	Dragon
	Elegant
	Forms
	Marquee
	Neutral
	Phosphors
	Saucer
	Simple

Template Category/Subcategory	Name of Template or Wizard
Newsletters (all of these are Wizards)	Accessory
	Bar
	Beach
	Blocks
	Capsule
	Column
	Corners
	Dots
	Dragon
	Elegant
	Forms
	Marquee
	Neutral
	Rocket
	Rule
	Simple
Planners/checklists	Emergency preparations
	Home maintenance checklist
	Vehicle details
Planners/Meals-Diets	Diet-allergy
Planners/Shopping Lists	By store
	Grocery list
	Pet supplies
	Pharmacy
Planners/To Do lists	Child's chores
	Daily household
	Weekly housecleaning
Web pages/Cypress	Column with contents
	Frequently Asked Questions
	Left-aligned column
	Personal Web page
	Right-aligned column
	Simple layout
	Table of Contents
Web pages/zero	Column with contents
	Frequently Asked Questions
	Left-aligned column
	Personal Web page
	Right-aligned column
	Simple layout
	Table of Contents

Continued

Table 2-1 (continued)	
Template Category/Subcategory	*Name of Template or Wizard*
Writing toolbox/Journals	Baby Family Writing
Writing toolbox/reports	Book report Essay Term paper

Additional templates and wizards are available through the Value Pack installation (see Appendix A) as well as a number that Microsoft makes available over time on their Web site.

Looking at template wizards

As noted in Table 2-1, Word 2001 includes template wizards that help you create a document when you may not be sure of the document's layout or even its content. To activate any of these wizards, choose File ➪ Project Gallery and select the wizard that best fits the document you want to create.

Use the Envelope Wizard, found in the Letters-Envelopes category, to create professionally formatted envelopes. The Envelope Wizard can create an envelope containing various pieces of information about the sender, recipient, or both; use either your printer's page-size settings or custom envelope sizes; and (optionally) include barcodes. The Envelope Wizard also lets you specify font and positioning information for both the delivery and return addresses and lets you select your address and recipient's address from your Address Book (see Chapter 35 for a discussion of the Address Book). Finally, you can omit any elements of the envelope wizard that you don't want to include.

The Envelope wizard screen is shown in Figure 2-2.

The Envelope Wizard gives you the option of using the Data Merge feature. If you choose the Data Merge option in the dialog box, you see the Data Merge Manager floating palette appear, which aids you in creating envelopes from a mailing list. Data Merge is covered in detail in Chapter 6.

Tip   You might also want to check out the Mailing Label Wizard, located in the Labels category, to create mailing labels for your letters. After you activate this wizard, you have the option of creating a single label or a sheet of mailing labels, or accessing the Data Merge Manager. For additional details about data merges, see Chapter 6.

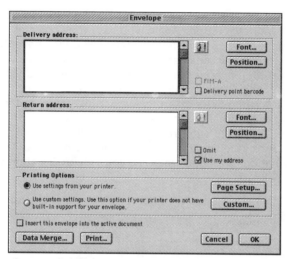

Figure 2-2: The Envelope wizard screen

The Brochure wizards, also collected as a subcategory of business forms, provide 15 colorful brochure styles. The wizards enable you to create brochures in differing styles, with variations such as modern, formal, or decorative styles. Each one of the styles has appropriately themed art for the brochure. Figure 2-3 shows a document created with the Brochure Blocks Wizard.

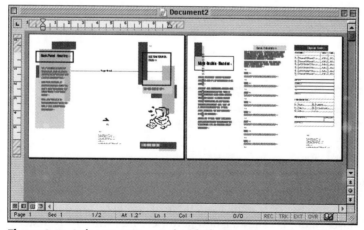

Figure 2-3: A document created with the Brochures Blocks Wizard

The Letter Wizard, located in the Letters-Envelopes category, can create prewritten letters or help in the design of your own letters. Again, you have the choice of creating a letter via a mailing list or just creating a single letter. You then have the option of choosing a page design for your letter using any of the available letter templates. You can also choose different styles for your letters: full block (document left-justified), modified block (paragraphs all left-justified), or semi-block (first line of paragraphs indented). You can tell the wizard you are using preprinted letterhead, and then tell it where the letterhead is located and how much space it needs. The Letter Wizard then asks you to enter recipient information or take this information from the Address Book. A few more handy options are available. The wizard ends with sender information. (Yes, that would be you.) Figure 2-4 shows a letter created using the Letter Wizard.

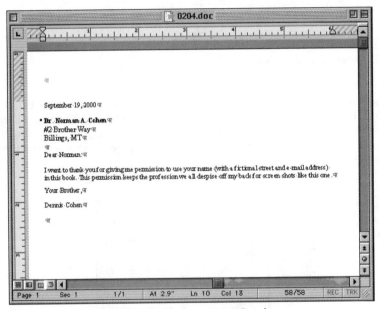

Figure 2-4: A letter created with the Letter Wizard

The Newsletter Wizards (all 16 of them), found in the Newsletters category, help you create an attractive newsletter. You can create the newsletter in professional, contemporary, or elegant style. You can also include the date and volume number. Options, such as the number of columns and table of contents, are determined by the style you choose. Figure 2-5 shows a newsletter created with the Newsletter Wizard called Simple. As you can see, the wizard creates a professional-looking newsletter, and it does so in a short amount of time. The Newsletter Wizards are covered in more detail in Chapter 10.

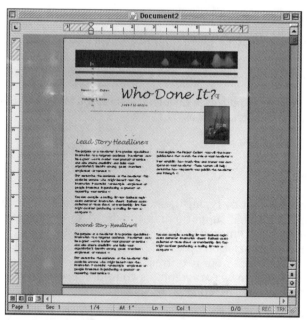

Figure 2-5: A newsletter created with the Newsletter Wizard

Avoiding Bad Typing Habits

If you are upgrading to the world of Word from a very old environment (such as a typewriter or a very early-generation word processor), you need to drop some habits. First, you don't have to press Return at the end of every line, because word processors automatically wrap text.

Second, don't use spaces (inserted with the spacebar) to center or indent text. To center text, use the Center button on the Formatting toolbar (discussed in Chapter 3). To indent, use tabs or indented paragraphs (also discussed in Chapter 3). If you need to create columns, don't use spaces or tabs—use Word's Columns feature (see Chapter 3), or use tables (see Chapter 5).

Finally, when you use a computer to type text, you don't need two spaces at the end of a sentence. Two spaces after a punctuation mark is an old habit that dates back to the manual typewriter days; in today's word-processor world, a single space after a sentence is all that's needed. (This last item isn't really related to Word or Office, but it's a pet peeve of the authors. So, because we were on the subject of bad typing habits already, we thought we'd throw it in.)

Editing templates

You can change the templates so they better fit your needs. We give you the full lowdown on how to create your own templates based on any of Word's templates — after we fill you in on some of the cool stuff you can do to format your documents.

Tip   Look for the details on editing templates in Chapter 8. In fact, you find other information about templates in Chapter 8 as well.

Working with Text

You can get text into your document by typing it, dragging it from another document (even in another application that supports drag-and-drop), or pasting text copied from another source. Text is entered at the right of the insertion point (which we sometimes call the cursor). Don't press Return or Enter at the end of each line — Word automatically wraps your text from line to line. Press the Return key only when you want to create a new paragraph. As you work, previously entered text is moved up to keep the insertion point visible.

Using AutoComplete

From time to time, as you type you may see a yellow box pop up and suggest a word to you. This is Word's AutoComplete feature. If Word recognizes that you may be typing a specific word, it suggests the word inside the pop-up box. If that's your intended word, press Return. Word will completes that word for you so you can go on typing as normal. In this case, pressing Return does not create a new paragraph. (If the suggestion isn't your desired word, just ignore it.)

Word also recognizes AutoText entries (covered in detail later in this chapter).

Copying and pasting

You can paste text from another document into your current document by using the clipboard. In previous versions of Word, the MacOS clipboard, an area of memory that stores temporary information, was used. In Word 98, a multiple undo and redo feature was added, and now, in Word 2001, Microsoft introduces the Office Clipboard (View ➪ Office Clipboard), as shown in Figure 2-6. The Office Clipboard enables you to collect text, graphics, and objects on a clipboard that functions very similarly to the Scrapbook accessory in the MacOS. Edit ➪ Paste (⌘-V) pastes whatever is selected in the Office Clipboard into the current document at the insertion point, or you can drag a selection from the Office Clipboard into position in your document — of course, the Office Clipboard must contain at least one item before you can paste it into your document. Two buttons are also on the bottom left of the Office Clipboard floating window — Paste Selection and Paste All. Actually, four exist, the two on the right of the Paste buttons being Clear Selection and Clear All.

Figure 2-6: The Office Clipboard

To place text into the Office Clipboard, select it, and then choose Edit ➪ Copy (⌘-C), click the Copy button on the Standard toolbar, or drag the selection to the Office Clipboard. Then move the insertion point to the desired position for the text and choose Edit ➪ Paste (⌘-V), click the Paste button on the Standard toolbar, click the Paste Selection button on the Office Clipboard, or drag the selection from the Office Clipboard to your document. The text or graphic stored in the clipboard appears at the insertion point. The Office Clipboard's contents remain there for repeated pasting until you clear them using one of the Clear buttons. This means you can copy parts of your own document and paste them into other parts of the same document or other documents.

You can also use the Office Clipboard to move text from one place in a document to another. Highlight the text you want to move and then use Edit ➪ Cut (⌘-X) or click the Cut button on the Standard toolbar. This places the selection into the Office Clipboard. Move the insertion point to the desired location and use Edit ➪ Paste (⌘-V), click the Paste button on the Standard toolbar, click the Paste Selection button on the Office Clipboard, or drag the selection from the Office Clipboard to the desired new location.

Selecting text

Before you can make any changes to text (or cut or copy it), you need to select it. Clicking and dragging is the most common way to select text. If you're not proficient with a mouse, spend time practicing. In the long run, the time you spend practicing with the mouse saves you hours. The following list contains practical techniques for selecting text:

✦ To select a word, double-click anywhere in the word. You can then select adjacent words by keeping the mouse button pressed after the second click and dragging through the additional words.

✦ To select entire paragraphs, triple-click anywhere within the paragraph.

✦ To select entire lines, move the mouse pointer to the left of the line (where it becomes a right-pointing arrow) and click once. This lets you select lines but not parts of a line.

✦ To select entire sentences, hold down the ⌘ key while you click anywhere in the sentence.

✦ To select the entire document, choose Edit ➪ Select All or press ⌘-A.

✦ To select a large portion of a document, click the start of the portion you want to select. Then move to the end of the desired portion while holding down the Shift key, and click again. Your initial selection determines the type of unit you can select. For example, if your initial selection is one character, you can select by character; if you first select a word, you can select to the end of any word. The same goes for lines or sentences. Use this method in conjunction with the scroll bars or navigation keys to avoid having to drag through your entire document.

If you select too much text, you can even deselect some. Just press Shift again as you click at the place you want your selection to end.

Deleting text

You can delete text (or graphics) in several ways. One method is by using the Delete key. When you use the Delete key, the text to the left of the insertion point is removed. Another method involves using the Forward Delete key, which is marked by an arrow with an X inside, or the characters "Del," and is located under the Help key on an Extended keyboard. The Forward Delete key deletes text that appears to the right of the insertion point. If you are using a PowerBook, an iBook, or the standard USB keyboard which ships with the iMac, Blue & White G3s, or the G4, you won't have a Forward Delete key.

You can also delete blocks of text by selecting (highlighting) the block of text and then pressing Delete.

Inserting Graphics

Word 2001 is rich in graphic abilities. You can create graphic objects within Word, insert existing graphics, and do quite a bit of manipulation to make them look just right. We discuss graphics in Chapter 10 and in Part IV, "PowerPoint." But while we're on the topic of pasting, you can also paste graphics into your document. To paste graphics, first get into the drawing or graphics program that contains the image you want to use in your Word document. Use the selection tool within the drawing or graphics program to select the desired image; choose Edit ➪ Copy (or press ⌘-C) to copy the selection into the clipboard. Leave or quit the drawing or graphics program and click a visible portion of your document to come back to it, or select Word from the Application menu (top right) to make Word the active program. With the insertion point at the desired location, choose Edit ➪ Paste (or press ⌘-V). The graphic appears at the insertion point. If the other application supports drag & drop editing, you can also drag the object from the original application's document and drop it in place in Word 2001.

You can also add graphics to your documents by means of clip art; word includes plenty to get you started. Position the insertion point where you want the clip art to go. Then, simply choose Insert ➪ Picture ➪ Clip Art. This opens Microsoft Clip Gallery, as shown in Figure 2-7. In the Clip Art tab, select the category of graphic you seek. A preview appears in the area to the right. Select the art you want, and click Insert. The clip art appears at the insertion point in your document.

Figure 2-7: Preview the clip-art file before you insert it into your document.

Navigating Within a Document

For basic navigation within a Word document, you can use the arrow keys and the navigation keys on the keyboard. Table 2-2 lists the keyboard combinations that help you move around in your document.

Table 2-2
Navigation Shortcuts

Keyboard Combination	What It Does
⌘-up arrow	Moves the cursor up one paragraph
⌘-down arrow	Moves the cursor down one paragraph
⌘-left arrow	Moves the cursor one word to the left
⌘-right arrow	Moves the cursor one word to the right
Page Up key	Moves the cursor up one screen page
Page Down key	Moves the cursor down one screen page
Home key	Moves the cursor to the beginning of the current line of text
⌘-Home key	Moves the cursor to the beginning of the document
End key	Moves the cursor to the end of the current line of text
⌘-End key	Moves the cursor to the end of the document

You can also scroll through a document. Scroll controls, standard on the Mac, are located at the right side and bottom of every document window. Click the up or down arrow to move in the direction you want to go. Use the left or right arrow to view longer lines of text. As long as you press the mouse button, the document scrolls. To move more quickly, click the scroll box (the rectangle inside the scroll bars) and drag it up or down or left or right to move in the direction you want to go. You can also click within the shaded areas of the scroll bars to scroll more roughly.

If you click the scroll box, drag it, and hold the mouse button down for approximately half a second; a small window appears showing the page number of the document represented by the position of the scroll box. In a large document, this can provide an easy way to reach a desired page quickly.

If you want to jump to a specific page number in a document, press F5 and enter a page number in the dialog box that appears.

Customizing keyboard commands

All Mac applications provide you with keyboard equivalents you can press to invoke a command without going to the menus or dialog boxes. In Word, you can change the keys used. For example, if you are used to a certain key combination from using another program, you can assign that combination the parallel command in Word.

To alter (or just to discover) a keyboard combination, Control-click in any blank spot on a toolbar and select Customize (or select Tools ⇨ Customize). When the Customize dialog box appears, click the Keyboard button to open the Customize Keyboard dialog box. Select the category the command falls under (or select All Commands), and then click the command in the Commands list. If a shortcut already exists, it appears in the Current Keys list.

To add a key combination, after selecting the command from the Commands list, click in the box that aptly says Press new shortcut key, and then type your new combination. A message appears in the dialog box to tell you if this combination is available or already taken and, if so, what command uses it. If these keys are already assigned to some item you want to keep, use the Delete key to delete your combination, and then try a new one. When you are happy with a new key combination, click Assign.

Note A word about locating commands in the Commands list: Built-in menu commands are composed of the name of their menu attached to the name of the command, rather than just the name of the command. For example, the Save command isn't under S for save, but under F for FileSave.

Tip If a key combination makes you crazy and you want to change it, you can, but you have to figure out what that command is called first — and that can be a challenge with Word's mysterious key command names. The trick is to open the Customize Keyboard dialog box, and then click in the Press new shortcut key box and type the keys in question. The dialog box reports that the keys you entered are already in use and tell you the name of the command using them. That's all you need to know. Now you can follow the customization steps listed previously, knowing which command to change.

Using the Document Map view

The Document Map view provides another useful way of navigating in a document. This view is especially useful when you are working with long documents. Document Map analyzes a document, finds the patterns for the headings you have included, and places them in a frame to the left of your document. This gives you a quick view of your entire document without the use of the scroll bar. As you look at the headings, you can click one and move to that heading in your document. To view the Document Map, click the button with a magnifying glass icon in front of a wide document rectangle (it's in the More Buttons add-on to the Standard toolbar) or choose View ⇨ Document Map.

Control-clicking the heading on the right enables a specific level of headings to be shown. This feature is much like the Outline view, which is discussed in detail in Chapter 5.

Tip

Control-clicking is pervasive throughout Office 2001; Control-click menus are called Context-sensitive menus because their contents change based on what or where you've clicked. Control-click a button in a toolbar and you get a set of menu items that relate to that item including a shortcut to change its key combination. Control-click a word with a squiggly line under it in a document (which means, as you learn in a few pages, that it's misspelled), and you see a dictionary menu that enables you to replace it with the properly spelled word instantly. Control-click a properly spelled word and the contextual menu lets you look it up in the dictionary or thesaurus. Control-click a button in a toolbar and the contextual menu includes menu items for editing or getting help with that button, and so on. The point being that Control-clicking is highly recommended, and one of the primary features that makes using Office 2001 easy and convenient.

Saving Your Documents

Saving is a fundamental part of working with documents. (Your documents won't be permanent if you don't save them for later use.) As soon as you begin your document, save it using File ➪ Save. After the initial save, each save makes changes to the existing document. To create a duplicate document under a new name or to save a document under a file format different from Word's native file format (known as Microsoft Word 2001 Document in the Save dialog box's Format pop-up menu), choose File ➪ Save As. In addition to the normal Save and Save As commands that enable you to save a document or change the name, Word 2001 offers additional options for saving documents.

You can choose File ➪ Save as Web Page to save a Word document as an HTML file. (HTML, or Hypertext Markup Language, is the language used to format information on the World Wide Web.) The HTML files you create using Word can be uploaded to a Web server for availability on the Web or to a corporate intranet. These files are actually XML (eXtensible Markup Language, which is a superset of HTML) and contain XML directives that significantly increase the size of the file. However, XML enables more formatting options than HTML, so these files let Word reopen the file and keep some formatting that is not supported by HTML. When you save a Word document as an HTML file, the document is closed by Word and then reopened in HTML format with Word acting as a Web browser. You have the option of either saving the entire file into HTML or just the display information. Here are examples of formatting that would be dropped from a document when you save it as HTML without the display information:

✦ Comments
✦ Paragraph formatting

✦ Tabs

✦ Fields

✦ Tables of contents and authorities

✦ Indexes

✦ Drawing objects

✦ User-defined styles

Note   Saving without the display information makes the generated Web page compatible with more browsers and, due to its significantly smaller size, faster to load. For more specifics on working with Word and the Web, see Chapter 11.

You can also save multiple versions of the same document to a single file. When you choose File ➪ Versions, the Versions dialog box appears. It enables you to save a new version, open a previous version, delete a previous version, or view and edit comments on any previous version. It also displays a listing of the existing versions of the document (if any), the date and time that each version was saved, and the name of the person who saved that version, plus any comments typed when that version was saved. This feature mimics using Save As to create different versions of a document with the advantage of storing all the versions in a single file on your hard disk (with Save As each version would be a separate file and would require a separate name). At least one of your authors uses this feature frequently.

Looking at Word's Views

Word enables you to work with your document in one of five possible views: Normal, Online Layout, Page Layout, Outline, and Master Document. Page Layout is the default view. You can access these views by selecting the appropriate command on the View menu. A checkmark to the left of the command in the View menu indicates your current view. You can also switch among Normal, Online Layout, Page Layout, and Outline views by clicking the View buttons at the bottom-left of your document's window. (The left-most button is Normal, the next button is Online Layout, then Page Layout, and then Outline.) Master Document view is only accessed from the View menu.

Note   If you are using line numbering and wish to see the line numbers, you need to switch to Page Layout view; see Chapter 3.

Use Normal view for basic typing and editing. Normal view shows a simple version of the document and is the best all-purpose view. Should you change views, you can return to Normal view at any time by clicking the Normal View button in the lower-left corner of the document or selecting it from the View menu. On slower Macs, this view feels fastest.

Use Outline view for outlining and organizing a document. Outline view enables you to see only the main headings of a document or the entire document. In this view, you can easily move text over long distances or change the order of your topics, as detailed in Chapter 5. To change to Outline view, choose View Page Layout Outline.

Note   You control how much you see of the document in Outline view by clicking the plus signs located next to the headings for each section. When you double-click a plus sign, the text under the heading is hidden to show only the heading. Double-click again to reveal the hidden information. Chapter 5 discusses outlines in detail.

Use Page Layout view to see the printed page. This view lets you see how the elements of the document appear when printed. To switch to Page Layout view, click the Page Layout View button on the lower-left corner of the document window, or choose View ➪ Page Layout. Many users prefer to do much of their work in the Page Layout view, but if your Mac is older and slower, this view may seem more sluggish to you than the Normal view.

Use the Online Layout view to create your online documents as HTML documents. HTML documents behave differently from standard word processing documents. By default, the Document Map appears to give you an overview of your page and aid you in navigation. Fonts appear larger and text wraps to the document window, Web browser style. Graphics default to inline. Outline elements do not show. Remember, though, this is only a bit of an approximation. If you're creating a document to use online, use Online Layout view. When you browse Web pages directly in Word, this is the view Word uses.

Use Master Document view to work with long documents. This view helps you divide long documents into several shorter documents to make them easier to work with, because you can see all the components of a document when you are in Master Document view. To switch to Master Document view, choose View ➪ Master Document.

Word 2001 also lets you change options in each of the views. To change the default settings, choose Preferences from the Tools menu. The Preferences dialog box appears, from which you can change options for the current view. The Preferences dialog box contains ten tabs, each with its own set of options, as shown in Figure 2-8. Click a tab to bring it to the front of the dialog box so you can view and make changes to its options. When you click OK, the new settings take effect in all the tabs that you have changed.

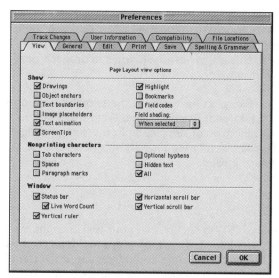

Figure 2-8: The Preferences dialog box

Setting Margins, Tabs, and Line Spacing

The three most elementary aspects of formatting—margins, tabs, and line spacing—can be found even on the most basic typewriters. These elements are very important to setting up your pages appropriately. This section shows you how to apply these formatting elements to all or part of a document. To control page margins, select Format ➪ Document; to set tab stops, select Format ➪ Tabs; and to change line spacing, select Format ➪ Paragraph (Option-⌘-M). However, these commands are not the only ways to change parameters that affect margins, tabs, and line spacing in Word, as is revealed shortly.

Changing margins

When you start a new Word document, default margins are already set at 1 inch for the top and bottom margins and 1.25 inches for the left and right margins. To change the default settings, choose Format ➪ Document. The Document dialog box contains two tabs, Margins and Layout. We discuss the Layout tab in Chapter 3. The Margins tab lets you set the top, bottom, right, and left margins to your desired measurements. You also can click the Mirror Margins checkbox to force the left-facing and right-facing pages to have the same margins between the edge of the text and the center of the binding (or, the edge of the text and the outside edge of the page).

Margins can be changed visually as well. Switch your view to Page Layout. Page Layout view shows your margins as gray bars in the rulers. Position your mouse where the margin (gray) and text area (white) meet. As you do, your cursor becomes a two-headed arrow. With this cursor in effect, you can drag left or right (or up or down) to resize your margin.

Tip　It's possible to create margins that place text outside the printable area of the page. Fortunately, when you try to print the document, Word alerts you to the problem, and then offers you the option of stopping to fix it before printing. You should do this, otherwise the page won't print properly. In our experience most printers require .5 inch margins or greater.

Applying tabs

Tabs are the only way (aside from tables) to ensure that your text lines up. Word has tab stops set to every 0.5 inch by default. These tab stops are depicted by the gray tick marks at the bottom of the ruler. The ruler should appear at the top of your document window. (If the ruler is not on, select View ➪ Ruler. A checkmark appears beside the word "Ruler.") To change the default tab stops, select the Format ➪ Tabs command. In the Tabs dialog box, change the measurement in the Default tab stops box to any desired value. The value is measured in inches, centimeters, picas, or points, depending upon your ruler's units. (This measurement can be changed in the General tab of the Preferences dialog box.)

Tip　Regardless of your ruler's unit settings, you can specify the unit explicitly. For example, if you enter **1 cm** when the units are inches, Word makes the conversion (1 cm is approximately 0.39 inches). Use "in" for inches, "cm" for centimeters, "pi" for picas, or "pt" for points.

Note　Points and picas are units used for measurement, usually in a publishing context. A pica has 12 points, while one inch has 6 picas.

Default tab stops are only a starting point. When you need to move text 2 inches, for example, it's a very bad idea to press tab four times. Instead, you should set a custom tab stop 2 inches in. This setting would be only for the paragraph that needs it. (You can have different ruler settings for each paragraph.) Custom tab stops take precedence over the default tab stops; therefore, whenever you set a custom tab stop, Word clears all default tab stops that occur to the left of the custom tab stop. When you set one or more custom tab stops, these remain in effect until you change the tab setting. When you start a new line, the ruler formatting, including tabs, of the previous paragraph is carried through. Once you begin a new paragraph, you can assign that paragraph its own tab settings.

Understanding the types of tabs

Word has five types of tabs; left, center, right, decimal, and bar. The type of tab you choose controls where the text aligns with the tab. When you use a left tab, the left edge of the text aligns with the tab stop. With right tabs, the right edge of the text aligns with the tab stop. When you use centered tabs, the text centers at the tab stop. Decimal tabs are used when the decimal point in numbers must align with the tab stop. Finally, bar tabs are thin vertical lines that can be used to separate columns created by tabs within a document.

Note   The decimal tab aligns on the character specified for the Decimal separator in your Numbers control panel. This defaults to a period in a US system, but might well be a comma in a European system (French, for example).

Setting custom tabs

You can set custom tabs visually, using your mouse and one of the Tab buttons on the ruler (the easier method) or with the Format ➪ Tabs command. To set tabs with the mouse, first click the Tab button on the ruler (the button to the far left of the ruler) until you get the tab alignment indicator you want, and then click the gray strip just under the ruler at the desired location. For example, to set a center tab at the 2-inch location on the ruler, you would first click the Tab button until the marker for the center tab appears and then click just under or on the 2-inch marker on the ruler. To verify the position of the tab stop numerically, choose Format ➪ Tabs to open the Tabs dialog box (see Figure 2-9).

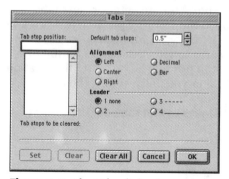

Figure 2-9: The Tabs dialog box

If the 2-inch tab stop isn't in the exact position you want, you can click it and drag it to whatever position you want on the ruler. After you drag it to its new location, verify the new position of the tab stop by opening the Tabs dialog box again. Alternately, you can manually enter a measurement in the Tab stop position text box. The Tabs dialog box gives you unlimited control of how to position the tabs in your documents.

Figure 2-10 shows some of the different tab alignments in Word. In the figure, a left tab stop has been set at the 1-inch position, a center tab at the 2-inch position, a right tab at the 3-inch position, a decimal tab at the 4-inch position, and a bar tab stop at the 5-inch position. Actually, you can have all these tabs on one line. You can place as many custom tab stops on one line as you need. The first time you press Tab, your text jumps to the first tab stop. The next tab character causes the text that comes after it to jump to the second tab stop, and so on. Remember that one tab on your line of text should equal one tab stop on the ruler. The number of tabs in your line of text should be no greater than the number of tabs on the ruler for that line.

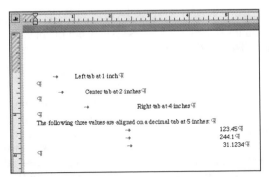

Figure 2-10: The different Tab alignments shown in Word

To set tabs with the Tabs command, choose Format ⇨ Tabs. The Tabs dialog box (refer to Figure 2-9) appears. In this dialog box, you can enter or clear tab stops. Enter the desired location for the tab stop in the Tab stop position text box and then choose the type of tab you want (Left, Center, Right, Decimal, or Bar) from the Alignment options. If you have additional tabs to set, click the Set button to set the current tab, and then go back to the Tab stop position box to enter the location for the next tab and to choose its alignment. After you finish setting the tabs, click OK.

Try experimenting with the tab stop techniques to find the one that suits you best (see Figure 2-11).

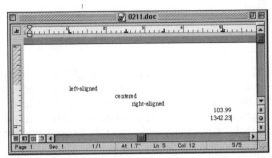

Figure 2-11: A document with different tab stops

You can use the following steps to see the effects of some of the different tab stops you can set in Word:

  1. Create a new document with a left tab at 1.0 inch, a center tab at 2.5 inches, a right tab at 3.5 inches, and a decimal tab at 5.0 inches.

2. Press the Tab key once (to reach the left-aligned tab at the 1 inch mark), and type the words **left-aligned**. Then press Return.

3. Press the Tab key twice (to reach the center tab at the 2.5-inch mark), and type the word **centered**. Notice that as you type, the word remains centered at the tab stop. When done, press Return.

4. Press the Tab key three times (to reach the right-aligned tab at the 3.5-inch mark), and type the words **right-aligned**. Notice that as you type, the words remain right aligned with the tab stop. When done, press Return.

5. Press the Tab key four times (to reach the decimal tab), type the value **103.99**, and press Return.

6. Press the Tab key four times (to reach the decimal tab), type the value **1342.23**, and press Return. Notice that the second number correctly aligns with the first, based on the location of the decimal point.

Moving and clearing tabs

As with setting tabs, you can move tabs and clear tabs using your mouse and the ruler, or with the Format ⇨ Tabs command. Again, the mouse excels in ease of use. To move a tab, simply click the tab and drag it to the desired location. To clear a tab, simply drag the tab up or down off the ruler.

You can also use the Format ⇨ Tabs command to move or clear tabs. The Tab stop position area of the Tabs dialog box displays all tab settings for custom tabs in the document. From the list of tab positions, select the tab you want to delete, and then click Clear. To clear all custom tabs, click Clear All and then click OK. To move a tab stop, select it in the dialog box, click Clear, and then enter a new location for the tab.

Creating leader tabs

Some documents, such as tables of contents, make use of leader tabs — characters that fill the space prior to the tab. To set a leader tab, set the tab as you normally would, and then open the Tabs dialog box with the Format ⇨ Tabs command. Word offers three kinds of leader tabs (other than none): periods, hyphens, and underlines. After you select the desired type of leader, click OK.

Adjusting line spacing

Line spacing affects the amount of space between lines of a paragraph. You can also change the spacing between paragraphs as described later in this chapter. To change the line spacing, place the insertion point anywhere within the desired paragraph and choose Format ⇨ Paragraph (Option-⌘-M). The Paragraph dialog box appears, with the Indents and Spacing tab visible, as shown in Figure 2-12. Use the options in this tab to enter the desired line and paragraph spacing. In the Line spacing pop-up menu, select the kind of spacing you desire: Single, 1.5 lines, Double, At Least, Exactly, or Multiple. You can adjust the preset spacing of these options by clicking the arrows next to the At box. The Exactly option makes the spacing only the specified amount. The At Least choice can be used to set the spacing to a specified amount or greater.

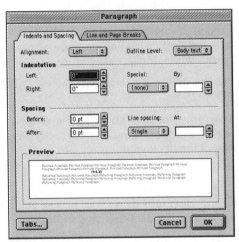

Figure 2-12: The Indents and Spacing tab of the Paragraph dialog box

In the Indentation area, you can specify the amount of indentation you want to apply to the left and right margins of the document. The Special box also allows for the addition of a hanging indent or other custom indent. However, indents are more commonly done on the ruler, which we cover later.

If you don't want to use the default unit of measurements, enter one of the abbreviations for alternate measurements. In the At box to the right of the Line Spacing list box, enter one of the following abbreviations: inches (in.), centimeters (cm.), picas (pi.), points (pt.), or lines (li.). Picas and points are units of measurement used by typesetters: 6 picas equal 1 inch, and 72 points equal 1 inch. If you enter a numeric value alone, Word assumes that value is in points.

To set the three commonly used variations of line spacing, you can use key combinations without entering the dialog box. With the insertion point anywhere in the desired paragraph, press ⌘-1 for single line spacing, ⌘-2 for double line spacing, or ⌘-5 for one-and-a-half line spacing.

Paragraph formatting only applies to the paragraph your cursor is in, or the paragraphs that are selected when you apply the formatting. If you want to apply spacing to a specific paragraph only, click in that paragraph (or select it), and then choose Format ➪ Paragraph. In the Paragraph dialog box, select the desired spacing and click OK. (You can also use the ⌘ key combinations mentioned in the previous paragraph to change the spacing in the paragraph.)

Adjusting paragraph spacing

Word also enables you to control the amount of space that appears before or after paragraphs. In the Paragraph dialog box, you may have noticed the Before and After text boxes in the Spacing area. You can enter numeric values in the Before or After boxes to place additional spacing before or after a paragraph. For example, placing 12 points after a paragraph automatically adds 12 points of space when you press Return. This would be the same as pressing Return an extra time, when your text is 12-point size.

Note   Paragraph spacing is an important part of formatting styles, which we cover in Chapter 8. One reason is that if you have a document in which you've used a style that includes the space-after or space-before settings to control the space between your paragraphs, but then find yourself short on space, you're in luck. All you need to do is place your cursor in one paragraph that contains that style, and then return to the Paragraph dialog box and change the space before or after to 10 or 11 points. Then, with a couple of clicks, you can redefine that style — all the paragraphs that have that style tighten up by a point or two and ideally give you the room you need to fit your document in the desired amount of space. And if you still need more room, you can go back and try 9 points.

As with line spacing, you can enter any value for paragraph spacing that Word understands: inches (in.), centimeters (cm.), picas (pi.), points (pt.), or lines (li.). Word assumes points as a default value of measurement (one point being $\frac{1}{72}$ of an inch).

Moving and Copying Text

The original way to move text or graphics is to use the standard cut (or copy) and paste method. Cutting removes your text or graphic from its place. Copying keeps it there and makes a copy to be used elsewhere.

With this method, you use the menu commands or their keyboard shortcuts to transfer the information to the invisible clipboard as a staging area. This method works best when moving information long distances within a document or between documents — or even applications. To use this method, select your text and either cut it by using Edit ➪ Cut or ⌘-X or copy it by using Edit ➪ Copy or ⌘-C. Then move your cursor to the location where you want the data to end up, and use Edit ➪ Paste or ⌘-V. Word also provides buttons for cutting, copying, and pasting.

If you are moving information from one Word document to another, you can use the Arrange All command under the Window menu to have Word tile your documents for you. Alternately, you can move between open Word documents by selecting any document name from the bottom of the Window menu. Any Word documents you have open appear there. If a desired document is not open yet, use the File ➪ Open command or return to the Finder to locate the document in its folder and double-click it from there.

Tip   Rather than using cut and paste to move text, you can use drag-and-drop. Drag-and-drop has two benefits: it's faster when moving text short distances and it doesn't use the Office Clipboard, so your clipboard's contents don't grow. Notice that when you select text, your cursor becomes an arrow. Immediately click the text and drag it to the desired position in your document. As you drag the selection, the mouse pointer consists of the usual pointer arrow and a dotted small outline denoting the selection; the outline indicates that you are dragging text. You also notice a cursor-type line as you drag. This line indicates where the text lands when you release the mouse. When that line is in the desired position, release the mouse button.

The same method can be used to copy information. Simply select the text you want to copy, and then press Option as you click the selected text and drag it to the new location.

Searching and Replacing Text

As with all full-featured word processors, Word 2001 offers a search-and-replace capability. You find these commands in the Edit menu: Find (⌘-F) and Replace (⌘-H). These commands may offer more search capabilities than you are accustomed to, because you can look for more than just text. You can search for specific formatting as well as for special characters, such as paragraph marks, new-line characters, and tabs.

Searching for regular text

To search for text, choose Edit ⇨ Find. In the Find dialog box (see Figure 2-13), enter the desired word or phrase in the Find What text box. Click the Find Next button, which is the default option, or press Return or Enter. Word finds the first occurrence of the text, starting its search at the position of your cursor. You may continue the search for subsequent occurrences by pressing Return or Enter or clicking Find Next.

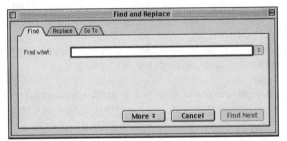

Figure 2-13: The Find tab of the Find and Replace dialog box

Clicking the More button gives you additional search options. The choices in the dialog box are self-explanatory. The Match Case option tells Word you want the search to be case-sensitive. When checked, Word searches for a match that uses the same case as the letters you entered. When the option is not checked, case does not matter during the search. The Use Wildcards option tells Word to let you use wildcards — such as a question mark — for any single character and an asterisk for any combination of characters within the search text.

The Find Whole Words Only option specifies that only whole words matching the search text will be found. For example, if you search for the word *move* in the sample document and the Find Whole Words Only option is not checked, Word finds occurrences of move, moves, and remove in the document. If Find Whole Words only is checked, only occurrences of the word *move* are found. The Sounds Like option finds words that sound like the word entered but are spelled differently. The Find All Word Forms option, when checked, tells Word to locate all matching noun forms or verb tenses. (Word can do this based on logic built into its grammar checking.) The Search list box lets you set the direction of the search. The default choice is All, which tells Word to search through the entire document. If you select Up or Down from this list box, Word begins its search at the current insertion point and searches up or down in the document for the desired search term. If the end of the document is reached and the search term has not been found, Word displays an alert box telling you that a match has not been found.

Searching for special characters

If you want to find special characters, such as paragraph marks or tab characters, you can also use the Find dialog box. Click the Special button to open a pop-up menu (see Figure 2-14) for special characters for which you want to search, and select the desired character from the menu.

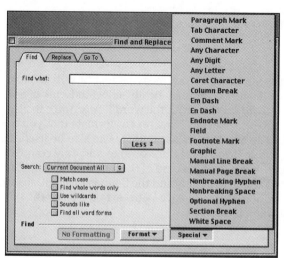

Figure 2-14: The pop-up menu for special characters

If you want to search for a format, click the Format button and select the format you want to find. This option lets you search for fonts, paragraph formats, languages, styles, tabs, frames, and highlighting.

Replacing text

You can use the same search techniques to replace the search text with other text as well. For example, you may want to replace every occurrence of the word *version* with the word *level* throughout a document. Or, you may have a word that is underlined at every occurrence in a document and want to replace it with the same word without the underline. To replace text, you use Edit ➪ Replace (⌘-H), which displays the Replace dialog box, as shown in Figure 2-15. (It's actually the same dialog box as Find, but with the Replace tab in front.)

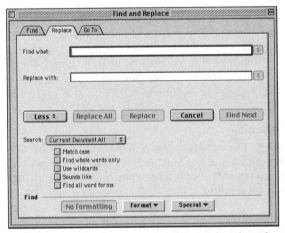

Figure 2-15: The Replace tab of the Find and Replace dialog box

As with searches, you enter the search text in the Find what text box. By default, Word intelligently replaces what it calls "all grammatically inflected forms of a word." For example, Word replaces the word *versions* with the word *levels*. You can also use the Format and Special buttons to find special characters or formats that you want to replace. The Find whole words only and Match Case options can also be used. Turn on the Find whole words only option if you want the search to find only complete words, and turn on the Match Case option if the case of the letters found must match that of the search text. The Use Pattern Matching and the Sounds Like options work just as they do in the Find dialog box. In the Replace With text box, enter the text that should replace the search text when it is found.

After you click the Find Next button, Word stops and asks for confirmation when the first occurrence of the search term is located. Click the Replace button to make the change at this occurrence of the found text. Click Replace All to make all the subsequent changes for you automatically without asking for confirmation. After the changes are made, Word tells you the number of replacements it made.

Caution

Be careful when using the Replace All button because it may make some replacements you do not intend. For example, if you want to replace the word *Figure* with the word *Item*, and you choose Replace All, the phrase "Figure out the answer" also gets changed to "Item out the answer." Or, while changing *go* to *travel*, "I have gone to the store" becomes "I have travelne to the store." Oops! Not exactly what you intended. Therefore, if you are not sure that the word is used only in the one context that you want to replace, click the Replace button to make the first replacement, and then use the Find Next button to find the next occurrence of the text so you can view it and decide if you want to replace it.

If you choose the Replace button, the replacement of the word is made. If you do not care to replace that word, skip it by using the Find Next button. Word then finds the next occurrence of the word and, again, you have the option of replacing it.

Tip

You can search for and replace formatting in the Replace dialog box. For example, you can replace all instances of a word in bold formatting with the same word in italic formatting. With the cursor in the Find What text box, click the Bold button (for bold formatting). Beneath the Find What text box, you see "Format: Bold" appear to reflect the bold formatting you've applied to the search text. Then tab to the Replace with text box and click the Italic button (for italic formatting). Figure 2-16 shows an example of this search procedure. After you click Find Next, Word finds the first occurrence of the word Figure in bold formatting. You can click Replace or Replace All to make the change to italic formatting. (Note that the keyboard commands such as ⌘-B and ⌘-I don't work here.)

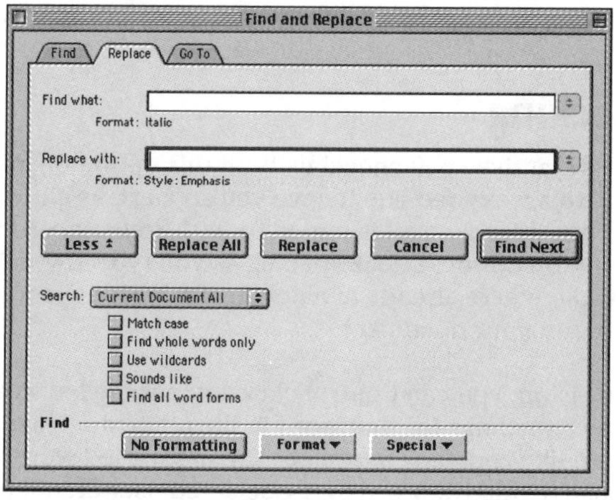

Figure 2-16: Replacing formatting in the Replace dialog box

If you are searching for an occurrence of a word or format by using the Find dialog box, and you decide to change the word or format, simply click the Replace tab, which brings up the Replace dialog box. In the Replace dialog box, you can replace what you are looking for in your search by entering text in the Replace with text box.

Checking Spelling and Grammar

Word's spell-checker and grammar-checker features check your documents for spelling errors and for proper, but real-world, grammatical construction. You can create multiple dictionaries and them depending on the specific type of document. You can check spelling and grammar as you work, or check a word, section, or entire document at any time. As part of the grammar-checking process, Word also checks for grammatical errors — including many commonly confused words. If Word finds an error, it often suggests ways to correct the sentence containing the error. You can make changes based on Word's suggestions, make changes based on your own preferences, or bypass the error altogether (the "error" may be okay as is).

Word's spell- and grammar-checkers use a main dictionary and a custom dictionary to check for potential misspellings. The main dictionary is supplied with the program and cannot be changed. The default supplemental dictionary is called Custom Dictionary. When you add new words to the dictionary (which you can do when the spell-checker finds a word it does not know, but you know is spelled correctly), you are adding them to the Custom Dictionary file unless you specify a different dictionary. Those of you used to earlier versions of Word may be impressed by Word's new vocabulary. Your name and organization, as entered upon registration or edited in Preferences, are now recognized. Additionally, the dictionary now displays definitions for the words so that you can make sure you have the right word in the right context. Many Fortune 1,000 names are now known, as are many new technological terms. Country names and most U.S. cities (with a population of 30,000 or more, to quote the Office Assistant) are recognized. Internet addresses are not only flagged, they can be automatically converted into clickable links to your e-mail program.

Interactive spell-checking

Word 2001 provides excellent interactive spell-checking. With this option on, misspelled words are underlined with a wavy red line to give you an alert, as shown in Figure 2-17. The preference to turn this on or off is under Tools ➪ Preferences in the Spelling & Grammar tab. It is the top option: Check spelling as you type. If you turn on interactive spell-checking while you're already in a document, Word takes a moment to go through and mark up your document.

While interactive spell-checking is on, you can Control-click any misspelled word to reveal a list of possible correct spellings for that word in the contextual menu. Simply drag to the spelling you'd like and click to replace the misspelled word with your choice. You can also choose to add the word to the selected user dictionary, ignore the spelling, or open the spell-checker.

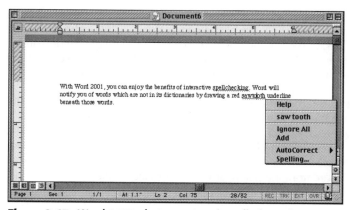

Figure 2-17: Word 2001 alerts you to misspelled words as you type.

Spell-checking manually

When spell-checking manually, you check a selected portion of a document or the entire document. You can check the spelling or grammar in only part of a document by first selecting the part you want checked, and then choosing Tools ⇨ Spelling and Grammar. If no selection has been made, Word assumes you want to check the entire document.

After you choose Tools ⇨ Spelling and Grammar, or you click the Spelling button on the Standard toolbar, Word checks all words and grammar constructions against those in the dictionaries. If a suspected misspelled word or improper use of grammar is found, Word stops, and the Spelling dialog box shown in Figure 2-18 appears. After Word finds a misspelling or misuse of grammar, it tries to provide a number of options for a correct spelling of the word, or offers an alternate grammar construction that can be used.

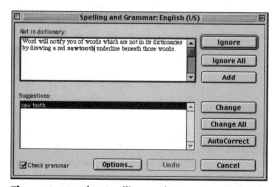

Figure 2-18: The Spelling and Grammar dialog box

Any suggestions for the misspelled word are presented in the Suggestions list below a display of the incorrect word. If one of the suggestions is the desired spelling, select it in the list box, and then click the Change button. The Ignore button lets you leave a word as is; the Cancel button cancels the entire spell-checking operation. The Add button lets you add a word to the selected user dictionary.

Tip   As a shortcut to selecting the Spelling and Grammar command from the Tools menu or clicking the Spelling button on the Standard toolbar, you can press F7 to start checking the spelling of a selection or a document, assuming that you have Word's function keys in control rather than those of MacOS. The same applies for the grammar-checker. If you wish to keep the grammar construction you presently have, choose Ignore from the dialog box, and Word leaves the sentence as it is.

Interactive grammar-checking

As with spell-checking, you can have Word do interactive grammar-checking and underline any questionable grammar. If Word wants to alert you to a potential problem, the words in question get underlined with a wavy green line.

With interactive grammar-checking on, Control-clicking any questionable phrase tells you the error and reveals suggestions. Simply drag to the correction you would like to make and click to replace the error word with your choice. Or, you can open the grammar-checker from this contextual menu.

The preference to turn this on or off is under Tools ➪ Preferences in the Spelling & Grammar tab. It is the top option under Grammar: Check grammar as you type. If you turn on interactive grammar-checking while you're already in a document, Word goes through and marks up your document.

Note   While interactive spelling and grammar are turned on, you can tell the document is being checked by looking at your status bar. As Word is checking, you see a pen writing in the book. When an error is found, an "x" appears over the book and awaits your attention. Double-click this status bar icon and Word points out the potential error, presenting the shortcut menu you'd see if you Control-clicked the error. You can correct the error from the shortcut menu. If no errors are found in your document (or if you've approved all the potential errors), the icon shows a checkmark.

Grammar-checking manually

To check grammar in a document, first select the passage of text you wish to check or make no selection to check the entire document. Then choose Tools ➪ Spelling and Grammar. If an error is found, Word displays the Grammar dialog box and the animated help (if you haven't turned it off as *we* do). A suggestion may appear that explains the error or offers a way to fix it. If you agree with the suggestion to fix the error, click the Change button. You can ignore the error by clicking Ignore.

Sometimes you may want to edit the sentence yourself. Click in the Sentence text box and edit the sentence as you normally would, and then click the Change button. You can also start the grammar-checker by clicking the Standard toolbar's Spelling button.

The Suggestions box contains alternatives to the construction you used in your sentence. Animated help provides you with some explanations as to why the grammar construction is incorrect. The explanation appears in an automated help window, as shown in Figure 2-19. You can ignore this rule in the rest of the grammar-check by clicking the Ignore button in the Grammar dialog box.

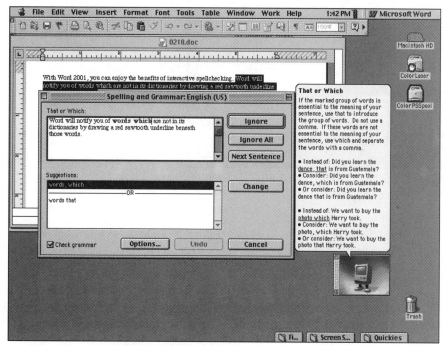

Figure 2-19: The Spelling and Grammar dialog box with an automated help window

Spelling and grammar preferences

To see the options available to you, choose Tools ➪ Preferences, and then select the Spelling & Grammar tab. Alternatively, if you are in the Spelling and Grammar dialog box, click the Options button. Either way, the same Spelling and Grammar preferences appear. The options are fairly self-explanatory. Figure 2-20 shows the contents of the Spelling & Grammar Preferences dialog box as selected from Tools ➪ Preferences. Notice that you can tell Word which grammar rules to follow. The default setting is Standard, but the Writing Style pop-up list enables you to choose the rules group you prefer: casual, formal, technical, or a custom style that you create by removing or changing the settings. To customize the type of grammar checking you want for your documents, click the Settings button.

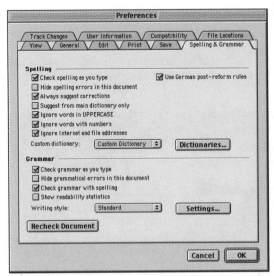

Figure 2-20: The Spelling & Grammar tab of the Preferences dialog box

As mentioned earlier, when you check spelling, Word also checks your grammar by default. If you prefer not to have Word check grammar, turn it off by removing the checkmark from the Check grammar with spelling box on the Spelling & Grammar tab of the Preferences dialog box.

You can also obtain readability statistics on your document. After Word has completed the grammar check, it analyzes the document and provides a summary of readability statistics. These statistics let you evaluate whether an adult reader can easily understand your document. You can turn this analysis on and off through the Grammar tab of the Preferences menu.

Changing dictionaries

As mentioned, Word always uses the main dictionary and at least one supplemental dictionary. You normally add words to the Custom Dictionary when you click the Add button in the Spelling dialog box, but you can also add words to any supplemental dictionary that you have created (or intend to create).

At times you may want to create a new custom dictionary. For example, if you work with many medical terms, you can create a medical dictionary and give it a name such as "Medical Dictionary." Then, you can add the medical words to this new dictionary as they are found in the spell-checker. To create a new dictionary, first click the Options button in the Spelling and Grammar dialog box. When Spelling & Grammar Preferences appears, click the Dictionaries button to bring up the Custom Dictionaries dialog box, shown in Figure 2-21.

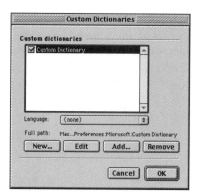

Figure 2-21: The Custom Dictionaries dialog box

Click the New button in the Custom Dictionaries dialog box. You are presented with a save dialog box that says Save Current Dictionary As. (Don't let this throw you. Word isn't saving an existing dictionary; it's creating a new, blank one.) Name your new dictionary and choose a location in which to save it. You may want to save it in the folder along with the provided dictionaries. Just don't forget to copy the dictionary if you ever uninstall Word. Your new dictionary is automatically added to the list of custom dictionaries and checked for immediate use.

Why You Should Use More Than One Custom Dictionary

Many Word users leave Word set to the default Custom Dictionary. But, depending on your needs, you may have good reason to create and use more than one custom dictionary. If you tend to bounce back and forth between projects that involve a good deal of technical lingo or other nonstandard terms, you can make the overall process of spell-checking a bit faster by using different custom dictionaries, with each one specific to the task on which you are working.

Word spends less time searching a smaller, specific custom dictionary than a large custom dictionary that contains terms for many subjects. Just remember to turn on the custom dictionary of your choice when it's needed by using the Spelling & Grammar tab, available through the Edit ⇨ Preferences command.

In case you are provided with an existing supplemental dictionary (for example, from someone in your office), you need to tell Word to recognize it. To do so, click the Options button in the Spelling and Grammar dialog box. The Spelling & Grammar Preferences dialog box appears. In the Custom Dictionaries area, you should see Custom Dictionary, the default, already chosen. Click the Dictionaries button to bring up the Custom Dictionaries dialog box, and then click the Add button. The Add Dictionary dialog box opens (see Figure 2-22). Navigate to the dictionary you want to install, select it, and then click Open. The dictionary appears in the custom dictionaries list as active.

You can also turn a supplemental dictionary on or off at any time by opening the same Custom Dictionaries dialog box and checking or unchecking any dictionary in the list.

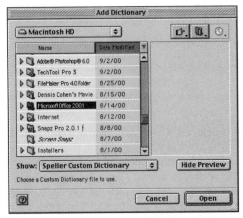

Figure 2-22: The Add Dictionary dialog box

 Note   You can check and edit any custom dictionary from the Custom Dictionaries dialog box by clicking the Edit button. This button opens the dictionary as a Word document in which you can make your changes.

Using AutoCorrect

As with the spell- and grammar-checkers, AutoCorrect works with you to ease your workload. When your fingers get tangled, this feature tries to figure out what you meant to type and automatically repairs the word for you. For example, if you type

wnat, it automatically changes to **want** and **witht he** becomes **with the.** AutoCorrect can also become your shorthand manager. You can tell it which letter combinations to turn into words or phrases.

 Note   AutoCorrect is also available in Excel, Entourage, and PowerPoint. Each Office application shares your AutoCorrect list.

AutoCorrect's features and capabilities

To gain insight into AutoCorrect's features and capabilities, and to customize the Correction and Shorthand list, select Tools ⇨ AutoCorrect. The scrolling list contains all words to be corrected. When you are ready to add a new AutoCorrect entry, type your key combination in the Replace box, and then type the word, phrase, or symbol you want entered in place of the combination in the With box. Finally, click Add. To change an existing AutoCorrect entry, select the correction from the list and enter your change or changes in the Replace or With box. Click Replace. To remove an AutoCorrect entry, select it from the list and click Delete.

By the way, AutoCorrect is intelligent. If you happen to request that jd be replaced by John Doe (your name, of course), when you type jd, Word substitutes John Doe.

Working with AutoText entries

AutoText entries are stored entries of text or graphics (even though it's called AutoText) that you frequently use and want to have handy for easy entry. Phrases such as closings to business or personal letters are candidates for AutoText entries. To store an AutoText entry, type the text you want or import the graphic you want to use, and then select it. Next, choose Insert ⇨ AutoText ⇨ New. The Create AutoText box appears, with the entry as the default name. If you want to keep the suggested name, simply click OK. This is the name as it appears under the AutoText submenu to help you select it later. If you prefer to make changes to the menu listing, do so in the text box before clicking OK. Word then places the entry on the submenu that appears under Insert ⇨ AutoText ⇨ Normal. The Normal submenu doesn't appear unless you have created at least one AutoText entry.

Word provides some default entries, such as common openings and closings to letters, signatures, and filenames. You can view them by choosing Insert ⇨ Auto Text ⇨ Auto Text. This brings up the AutoText tab of the AutoCorrect dialog box shown in Figure 2-23. The AutoText names appear in the top area. Click any AutoText name to view the entire entry in the preview area, below.

To insert an AutoText entry, place your cursor where you want the entry to go and then choose Insert ⇨ AutoText ⇨ AutoText. In the dialog box that appears, double-click the desired AutoText entry from the list box.

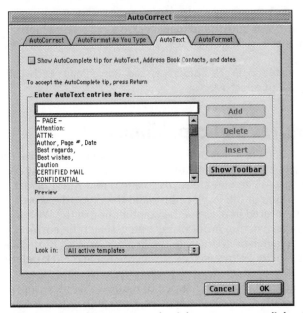

Figure 2-23: The AutoText tab of the AutoCorrect dialog box

Word also gives you the option of assigning an AutoText entry to a toolbar so you can insert the AutoText entry by clicking that toolbar button. If you want to assign an AutoText entry to a toolbar, perform the following steps:

1. Choose View ➪ Toolbars ➪ Customize.

2. In the Customize dialog box, click the Commands tab (see Figure 2-24).

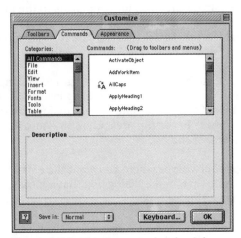

Figure 2-24: The Commands tab of the Customize dialog box

3. In the Categories list box, scroll down to AutoText and click this category. The Commands box now displays the names of all your AutoText entries (and the default entries) in alphabetical order.

4. Click the name of the entry to which you want to assign a button. You see the outline of a toolbar button appear.

5. Click the entry. Your cursor now has a special *x* at its bottom right. Drag the button to the toolbar and position where you want the AutoText button. (The toolbar must be displayed to do this.)

6. The name of the AutoText entry appears as the default name for the button, but you can change the name. With the Customize window open, press ⌘ and Option as you click the button you created, and select Properties from the menu which pops up, and which displays the Command Properties dialog box. To change the text that appears on the button, click in the Name field, and edit the text that appears. To add a default button image, click in the pop-up button in the upper-left part of the dialog box and select the image of your choice, if you like one of them. Otherwise, see Step 7.

7. If you choose to create your own button, select Edit Button Image from the pop-up button to open the Button Editor dialog box (see Figure 2-25). The editor is a miniature paint program for you to redraw your button. You can also paste an image from the clipboard.

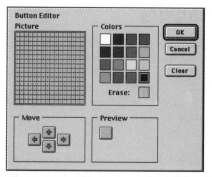

Figure 2-25: The Button Editor dialog box

Changes can be made to an AutoText entry at any time. You might want to begin by placing the AutoText into a document. Edit this text as you desire, and then select the edited text. Create a new entry, but give it the same name as the original. When asked if you want to redefine your existing entry, click Yes.

If you no longer need an AutoText entry, you can delete it. Return to the AutoText tab of the AutoCorrect dialog box (Insert ⇨ AutoText ⇨ AutoText). Select the name of the AutoText entry you want to delete and click the Delete button. The entry is removed.

You can also print your AutoText entries. Select Print from the File menu. The Print dialog box appears. Select Microsoft Word from the pop-up menu that typically says General—if you're using the LaserWriter 8 driver. This presents you with printing options specific to Word. Next, select AutoText entries from the first Print pop-up menu, as shown in Figure 2-26. After you click Print, the AutoText entries print.

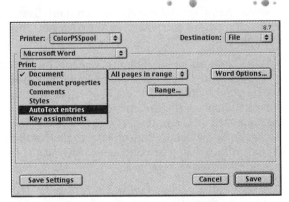

Figure 2-26: Word-specific print options as seen in a laser printer's Print dialog box

Accessing Word's Thesaurus

Word's Thesaurus enables you to find synonyms for specific words in your documents. The fastest way to do so is to move your cursor over the desired word, and then Control-click to bring up the shortcut menu. At the bottom of the menu is a submenu that lists all the synonyms Word can find for your word. Simply drag to the word you desire (if any) and click that word. (In case you are a cross-platform user, we should point out that this method is not available in Office 97 for Windows.)

If you prefer not to Control-click or you want to further explore your synonym options, you can always go the long route. To do so, first select the desired word (remember, you can double-click anywhere in a word to select it) and then choose the Tools ➪ Thesaurus (⌘-Option-R or Shift-F7). The Thesaurus dialog box appears, as shown in Figure 2-27.

The dialog box shows any definitions found for the selected word in the Can Mean list box and each one, when selected, displays possible replacements in the And Has Synonyms list box. To replace the selected word with a synonym, select the desired synonym from the And Has Synonyms list box, placing that choice in the Replace With Synonym text box and then click the Replace button.

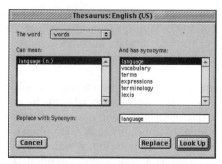

Figure 2-27: The Thesaurus dialog box

In the Can Mean list box, you see one or more definitions for the selected word. The list of available synonyms changes when you select a different meaning. You can use the mouse to move between the And Has Synonyms and the Meanings list boxes. If you want to look up one of the words in the Can Mean list box, simply select the word and click the Look Up button.

New Feature Word 2001 adds an Antonyms choice to the Can Mean list. This enables you to select words with the opposite meaning.

Hyphenating Your Document

Word provides different ways to handle hyphenation, the process of adding hyphens to reduce the ragged appearance of a document's right margin. If the text is justified, hyphens reduce the space between words to fill out a line. In Word, you can add hyphens manually or automatically.

To enter hyphens manually, choose Tools ➪ Hyphenation. This displays the Hyphenation dialog box (see Figure 2-28). After you click the Manual button, Word switches to Page Layout view and stops to let you confirm the desired location for each hyphen. If you don't want to add a hyphen to a word, click No, and the word is skipped untouched.

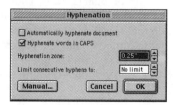

Figure 2-28: The Hyphenation dialog box

With automatic hyphenation, Word adds hyphens automatically, making its best guess as to where hyphenation should occur. In the Hyphenation dialog box, click the Automatically hyphenate document checkbox to activate automatic hyphenation.

If you choose to hyphenate as you type, you can use one of two types of hyphens: optional or nonbreaking. Optional hyphens appear only if the word is at the end of the line. Optional hyphens are the kind Word inserts when you use semiautomatic or automatic hyphenation. To insert an optional hyphen, press ⌘- - (hyphen). Use nonbreaking hyphens (also called hard hyphens) when you do not want a hyphenated word to be broken at the end of a line. To insert a nonbreaking hyphen, press ⌘-Shift- - (hyphen).

Using the AutoFormat Feature

The newest and coolest way to add paragraph numbers or bullets is to use Word's AutoFormat feature. To create a bullet list, simply type an asterisk and a space or a tab, and then type your list text and press Return to begin your next list element. By default, Word automatically converts the asterisk and space (or tab) into a bullet and tab. Word also places the next bullet and tab for you, so all you need to do is type your list text.

To create a numbered list, type your first number and a period or closing parenthesis, then a space or tab, and then type your text and press Return to begin your next list item. Word converts this into a proper numbered list (a number, period, and tab) and places the next number on the page for you. The ever-courteous Office Assistant lets you know when one of these conversions has been made and gives you the option of undoing it. When you are done with your list, press Return twice to end. Should you prefer to deactivate this AutoFormat feature, you can deselect it under Tools ⇨ AutoCorrect in the AutoFormat As You Type tab.

When you add numbers, using either of the fast methods, Word automatically checks the preceding paragraph for its numbering style. If it is numbered, Word uses the same style of numbering for the selected paragraph. If the paragraph is not numbered, Word applies the style of numbering that you selected last. (You select numbering style in the dialog box mentioned next.)

You can also add paragraph numbering or bullets the old-fashioned way. Select the paragraphs or section to which you want to apply the numbering or bullets. Next, choose Format ⇨ Bullets and Numbering. The Bullets and Numbering dialog box appears, from which you can choose from seven different bullet layouts on the Bulleted tab or seven different numbering layouts from the Numbered tab. The Outline Numbered tab lets you create outline-style numbering with numbers and letters. Each bullet or numbering effect is depicted visually. Click the one you want, and then click OK or simply double-click the one you want.

Adding Bullets or Paragraph Numbers

With Word, you can automatically add paragraph numbers to your documents or bullets to each paragraph. This feature can be very useful when you are working with legal documents. Also, documents that are numbered are easy to edit and revise. As you add or delete paragraphs, Word maintains the correct numbering for the paragraphs.

Tip In addition to typing an asterisk and space to create a bulleted list, you can also type one hyphen, two hyphens, a greater-than sign (>), or a hyphen or equal sign followed by a greater than sign. The number followed by a period,), -, or > creates the numbered list with that specific character.

The next-fastest way to add simple bullets or numbers to paragraphs as you type is to use the buttons on the Formatting toolbar. Select the paragraphs or section to which you want to add numbers or bullets, and then click the Bullets button to add bullets or the Numbering button to add numbers.

Note With the advent of the Web, bulleted lists using images rather than bullets or symbols have gained popularity. Word 2001 even has a quick way for you to create this specialized list using AutoFormat. For a bulleted list using a symbol, select Insert ➪ Symbol and choose from either the Symbols or Special Characters tab to insert a symbol, close the Symbol dialog box, type two or more spaces, add your list text, and press Return. For an image as a bullet, insert your image as an inline graphic, type two or more spaces, add your list text, and then press Return. In each case, as with bullets and numbers, Word automatically creates your next line until you press Return twice to end the list. One important rule applies to using an image: The graphic must not be more than 1.5 times the height of the text in that list. (Note that the easiest ways to get the graphic inline is to either use drag and drop to place it at the insertion point or go to its source and copy it. Then use Edit ➪ Paste Special, select Picture from the list, and uncheck Float over Text.)

Collaborating on a Document

Often several people must work together to create a final document. Word offers a full complement of collaboration tools. A Reviewing Toolbar is even present, containing buttons for most of the Tools ➪ Track Changes options to help. To activate this toolbar, select View ➪ Toolbars ➪ Reviewing. This toolbar may also open automatically when you select certain reviewing options. Using the Track Changes feature, you can see what each person suggests, and then accept or reject each change. When you use the Comments feature, each person can add his or her own two cents without messing up the document.

Tracking changes to your document

When two or more people are working together on a document, being able to track the changes (called Revisions in Word 6) is a very handy feature. To begin tracking changes, select Tools ⇨ Track Changes ⇨ Highlight Changes (see Figure 2-29). Then click to place a check by the Track Changes While Editing option. In addition, you can choose to see those changes onscreen while you work by checking Highlight changes on screen. (This means you now see the revision marks.) You can also see those changes printed by checking Highlight changes in printed document. The last two choices are selected by default.

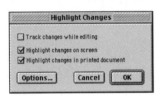

Figure 2-29: The Highlight Changes dialog box

If you choose to highlight the changes onscreen, whenever a change is made to your document, deleted text shows in strikethrough font and new text is underlined. (These are the defaults. You can change the markings.) Each person who edits shows up in a different color. (Word doesn't know you as a person, but it knows it's on a different machine.) To get a feel for how this feature works, from the Highlight Changes dialog box, click Options, or select Tools ⇨ Preferences and select the Track Changes tab. Either way, you end up in the same place. In this Preferences tab, you can determine what changes are tracked. By default, only inserting and deleting text is tracked, but you can also follow formatting changes. Lines with changes on them receive a mark in the outside border, by default, but you can turn that feature off or force the mark to either the left or right border.

As your document is passed around, each person can make the changes visible and see what happened to the document so far. (You may not want to keep the revisions visible most of the time while you are trying to read the document.) After the document has made the rounds, you can decide whether to keep each change. Select Tools ⇨ Track Changes ⇨ Accept or Reject Changes to bring up the dialog box of the same name. You can move through the entire document, change by change, by clicking either Find button. There's a button for moving forward and one to go backward through the document. As you get to each change, you can see it in the document (you may have to move the dialog box window at times). Click Accept or Reject. Or, you can simply view the document with or without changes, decide you love or hate all the changes, and then Accept All or Reject All of the changes.

Tip   Another, fast way to turn Track Changes on and off is to double-click the letters TRK in the status bar. When changes are being tracked, these letters are black. When changes are off, the letters are grayed out (dimmed).

Comparing documents

Perhaps you've kept a copy of a document you created and want to see how it stacks up to the final version. With one version open, select Tools ➪ Track Changes ➪ Compare documents. This opens the Mac's Open dialog box. Locate and open the other copy. Word now goes through and place revision marks so you can see the changes between the two documents.

Creating comments

You can easily create and edit comments—notes regarding your document—as a part of your Word document. Think of comments as annotations added to a document: They are not normally visible in the document, but can easily be seen by choosing View ➪ Comments. Comments are very useful when multiple Word users want to make comments on a proposed document. Because each comment includes the initials of the person making the comment, you can view the comments and contact the persons who have made the comments for help in incorporating the changes. Even when you are working on documents alone, you may find comments useful for reminding yourself about revisions that you plan to make to the document.

To create a comment, place the insertion point at the desired location for the comment and choose Insert ➪ Comment (⌘-Option-A). Word splits the current window and inserts your initials within a bracket at the comment point (see Figure 2-30). In addition to your initials, Word provides an annotation number so you can add more comments later. Each comment is assigned a number in sequential order.

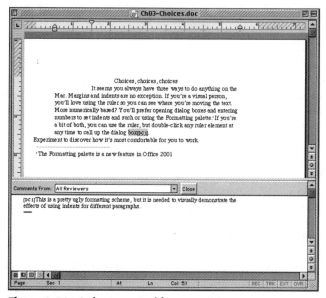

Figure 2-30: A document with comments

The active insertion point is automatically placed in the comments pane—the lower half of the split window. Type any desired comments here, as no limit to the length of an annotation exists. Refer to Figure 2-30 to see a document with a comment added. You can even add sound, which can be especially useful by giving specific instruction that should be delivered with the touch of a human voice. You can do this by clicking the Insert Sound Object button in the comments window. (The Insert Sound Object button is only enabled if you have the Voice Annotation OLE server installed. If Voice Annotation is not in your Value Pack Installer, look for it at Microsoft's Web site.)

When you finish writing the comments, close the comments pane of the window by clicking the Close button on the pane, choosing the View ⇨ Comments command again or by double-clicking the split line. You can also drag the split bar to the bottom of the window.

To view a comment, move your mouse over the highlight that indicates the comment and rest it a moment until the comment pops up. To view all comments that you have added to a document, select View ⇨ Comments. The command is a toggle, so choosing it repeatedly turns comments viewing on or off. To edit the text of an existing comment if the comments pane is not already open, choose View ⇨ Comments, click the Edit Comment button on the Reviewing Toolbar, or Control-click the highlight that indicates a comment in the document and select Edit Comment. This opens the comment pane. Edit the comment text as you would edit any other text.

To delete a comment, go to that comment's marker in the document (the yellow highlight), Control-click the highlighted word and choose Delete Comment from the shortcut menu or click the Delete Comment button on the Reviewing Toolbar. You can also print all the comments in a document by choosing File ⇨ Print, selecting Microsoft Word from the top pop-up menu, and then selecting Comments from the Word-specific pop-up menu.

You can use the Cut and Paste commands to move text from the comments pane into the document or by using drag and drop. This technique is particularly helpful when some of the comments that have been added to your documents by other people should be incorporated into the actual document.

Finding comments

In a large document, you can quickly get to a desired annotation with the Go To command from the Edit menu (F5 or ⌘-G). In the Go To dialog box, choose Comment in the Go to What list on the left. A reviewer's name field appears. Select the name of a specific reviewer by clicking the arrow to the right of the box, or keep the default, Any Reviewer, if you prefer. Click the Next button to go to the first qualifying comment. Each time you click Next, you are moved to the next qualifying annotation.

Locking the document

When multiple persons are commenting on a document, you may find it helpful to lock the document so no one but the author can change the actual document — others can only add or edit comments. If you lock a document and allow comments only, you can safely pass the file around for comments, while ensuring that others cannot make any changes to the document.

To lock a file for comments only, choose File ➪ Save As and click the Options button in the Save As dialog box. In the Save tab (the only one available), enter a password under Password to modify. Those opening the document without this password cannot make changes. You can also restrict the editing of your document by clicking the Read-Only Recommended box. After you've entered your password(s), perform the save. Use the same document name only if you want to replace the current document.

Working with Document Summaries

Document summaries are not exactly an aid to the editing process, but they can be helpful in the long run. If you take the time to fill in a summary, you can later use the information stored in it as a way to search for desired documents.

When you want to open a document but can't recall a filename, you can find the file by searching document summaries. Choose File ➪ Open, and then click Find File. This brings up a basic search dialog box. From here you can search for a document by title, although you can also do that within the Mac OS. More importantly, you can select which hard drive (volume) to search — handy for machines with more than one disk drive or networked computers. Click Advanced Search to present more search criteria (see Figure 2-31). Enter the desired search criteria on any or all of the tabs. Special characters may also be used to create approximate criteria (see "Searching for Special Characters" earlier in this chapter). Click OK to close the Advanced dialog box and click OK again to begin the search.

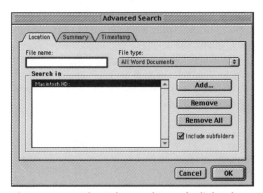

Figure 2-31: The Advanced Search dialog box

Viewing or editing a summary

To view or edit a document summary, make sure the document is open, choose File ➪ Properties. This brings up the Summary tab in the Properties dialog box that opens. The Summary tab is shown in Figure 2-32.

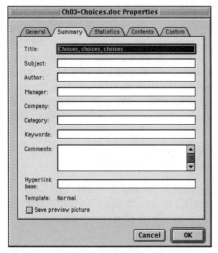

Figure 2-32: The Summary tab of the Properties dialog box

The fields are self-explanatory — you can enter the desired document title, subject, and keywords that may help you identify the document later. Word inserts the author's name, based on the name that is stored in the dialog box on the User Info tab of the Preferences dialog box (accessed from the Edit menu). When you change the author's name in the Summary dialog box, the change takes effect only for the current document.

The Statistics tab in the Properties dialog box can be useful for getting information about the productivity of the document. This tab displays all sorts of useful information regarding your document (see Figure 2-33).

The Statistics tab shows the document's creation date, when it was last saved, how many times it has been revised, the total time you have spent editing it, as well as how many characters, words, and pages are in the document.

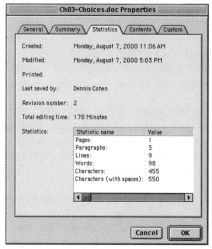

Figure 2-33: The Statistics tab of the Properties dialog box

Using the AutoSummarize feature

AutoSummarize is another feature of Office 2001. This feature enables you to summarize the key points in a document. It analyzes documents and assigns scores to each of the sentences in a document by analyzing the frequency of words in sentences. You can also choose a percentage of the high-scoring sentences that you wish to display in your summary. Figure 2-34 shows the AutoSummarize window that appears when you choose Tools ➪ AutoSummarize.

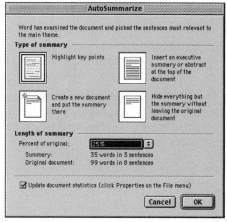

Figure 2-34: The AutoSummarize dialog box

You find that this feature works best with well-structured documents. Also, the use of the Find All Word Forms tool helps produce quality summaries. With your well-structured document, you can add the summary as a highlighted section at the top of your document, in a new document, or hide the original and just show the summary. You do this by making the corresponding choices from the AutoSummarize dialog box.

Next, you need to choose the percentage of the document that you want to summarize, using the options in the Length of Summary section of the AutoSummarize box. There, you have choices between sentences, percentages, or number of words in your document on which you wish to base the summary. This gives you the power to control the length of the summary Word creates for you.

After the summary is created, the results appear, based on the selection you made in the Type of Summary section of the AutoSummarize dialog box. By default, the AutoSummarize box also updates the document statistics automatically.

Summary

This chapter provided you with useful techniques for working with documents in Word. The following points were covered:

✦ Word's File ➪ New command displays a dialog box containing tabs you can use to create new documents. New documents are based on a blank document or on one of Word's predefined templates. You can base your documents on different templates containing certain formatting and, in many cases, boilerplate text.

✦ Word includes a number of wizards that ask you a series of questions and then create a basic document based on your responses.

✦ You can see your document in one of five possible views: Normal, Outline, Online Layout, Page Layout, or Master Document.

✦ You can change your margin settings with the Format ➪ Document command, your tabs with the Format ➪ Tabs command, and your line spacing with the Format ➪ Paragraph command.

✦ You can search for text with the Edit ➪ Find command, or search for and replace text with the Edit ➪ Replace command. Word provides a full-featured search-and-replace capability that lets you search for text, formatting, and special characters such as paragraph marks and tabs.

✦ You can use the spell- and grammar-checkers to find and fix misspellings and/or grammatical errors. Word can do this checking as you type. Word even fixes common spelling or spacing errors automatically, and lets you create your own shorthand to have an entire phrase replace your shorthand combination.

✦ You can mark and track revisions made to your documents.

✦ You can use the Insert ⇨ Comment command to add comments to a document.

Where to go next

✦ Chapter 3 takes you to the next step: formatting documents.

✦ Ready to print your work? Chapter 4 tells you how.

✦ Do you need to create tables, outlines, tables of contents, or indexes? See Chapters 5 and 7 for help.

✦   ✦   ✦

Formatting Documents

As you create and refine your text, you will need to control the appearance of the document. This is where Word's formatting features come in. In the previous chapter, you were introduced to some of the basic ways to format your text. This chapter details formatting as it applies to the pages, sections, paragraphs, and individual characters of your document. We begin by discussing the formatting required for a document as a whole, and then go into the formatting needed for paragraphs and characters. Finally, we talk about *sections*, which are parts of a document that you can format differently from the rest of the document.

Discovering Formatting

Later in this chapter, you'll use many of the options in Word's Format menu and in the Formatting Palette, which offer many of the features that control Word's formatting. In the meantime, the following are some basic points you should know about formatting in Word:

✦ The largest unit in terms of formatting is document formatting. With document formatting, you control the appearance of every page for the entire document. Document formatting affects such settings as page size, default tab stops, numbers of columns, and margins for the document.

New Feature

In Word 2001, collections of these document settings can be saved as Themes. A theme is a collection of backgrounds, fonts, color schemes, lines, margins, and other document-level elements. A theme differs from a template in that it doesn't include such things as macros, menu settings, and toolbars. Themes are shared features in Office and are not specific to Word. This feature is especially useful when creating and previewing documents meant to be published as Web pages. It will be covered in more detail in Chapter 11, where we discuss Word and the Web.

✦ Optionally, you can apply section formatting to entire sections of a document. A document can consist of a single section, as most do, or you can divide a document into multiple sections. When you format a section of a document, you change the formatting for pages within that section. For example, you may want to change the number of columns in a portion of the document, or you may want to change the look of the headers and footers in another section. After you divide a document into sections, you can use many formatting commands to format each section individually. If you're a beginner and won't be creating documents such as newsletters from scratch, you can skip the information about sections.

✦ The next level of formatting is paragraph formatting. With paragraph formatting, the formatting you apply controls the appearance of the text from one paragraph mark to the next. Paragraph marks appear whenever you press the Return key. If you press Return once, type seven lines of text and press Return again, those seven lines of text are one paragraph. After you select paragraphs, you can change the formatting for those particular paragraphs. For example, you can change a paragraph's alignment or its line spacing. To change only one paragraph, you only need to place your cursor within that paragraph.

✦ Because paragraphs consist of characters, it is easy to confuse character and paragraph formatting. It may help to remember that paragraph formatting generally controls the appearance of lines, because a group of lines typically makes up a paragraph. Paragraph formatting controls the alignment of lines, the spacing between lines, the indents in lines, and borders around the paragraph.

✦ The smallest unit of formatting is the character. With character formatting, any formatting you apply affects all the characters within a selected area of text or all the characters you type after you select the formatting. When you select a sentence and click the Bold button in the Formatting palette, you're applying character formatting. Character formatting is often used to make a word or phrase stand out.

Formatting Documents

The broadest degree of formatting you can do applies to your entire document. Document formatting affects such settings as page size, orientation, and page margins for the appearance of each page in your document. In the Macintosh version of Word, two menus work together to provide full document-formatting control. File ➪ Page Setup, a regular feature of every Mac program, offers controls for Paper Size, Orientation, and Scale. Other document formatting options, such as Margins, are accessed from the Format ➪ Document menu item. Most of these settings are also available via the Formatting palette's Document pane. Because the Page Setup dialog box can also be accessed from the Document dialog box, you can just remember that to affect the format of the entire document, choose Format ➪ Document. You can also start with the Page Setup command and access the other document formatting from there.

Changes made within the Document dialog box can apply to the entire document or just from the position of your insertion point onward, as you specify in the Apply To pop-up menu. Accordingly, your choices are: Whole Document or This Point Forward. (By default, This Point Forward creates a section break and moves your cursor into the new section where your changes begin to apply. However, if you want the change to take place within one page, go to the Document dialog box's Layout tab and change the Section start option from New Page to Continuous. (See the "Formatting Sections" section, later in this chapter, for details.) The Preview area provides a visual representation of how the formatting changes appear when applied to the printed page.

Note   If, instead of an insertion point, you have a selection, then Selected Text replaces This Point Forward in the Apply To pop-up menu and choosing it puts section breaks before and after the selection.

Changes made within the Document dialog box apply only to the document in which you are currently working. However, with the Default button, you can make them the default and have these settings apply to all future Word documents. (We're assuming you are using the default Normal template. If you are using any other template, the changes are applied to the template you are using. Templates are explained in detail in Chapter 8.)

Orientation

The first thing to consider about your document's look is the orientation. The default orientation of a Word document is Portrait, the format of most written documents, where the document is considered taller than it is wide. If this suits your needs, as it probably does, you don't need to do anything. You can change the orientation to Landscape, the wide or horizontal format, by choosing File ➪ Page Setup to open the Page Setup dialog box and clicking the image that represents the orientation you want. The Page Setup dialog box for a LaserWriter is shown in Figure 3-1.

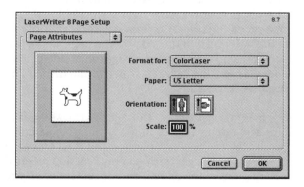

Figure 3-1: The Page Setup dialog box

Orientation can be changed at any point of your work. The default margins for the new orientation take over automatically so your text doesn't get clipped.

Backgrounds

You may notice a command called Background under the Format menu. Adding a background is indeed formatting that can enhance the appearance of your documents. Word enables you to choose a color that you want to appear as the background for the entire document. However, it is viewable only in Online Layout view, as it's a Web-page-creation feature. We cover Word and the Web in Chapter 11.

Page size

The default page size for the U.S. version of Word 2001 is the standard $8^{1}/_{2} \times 11$ inches. If this is appropriate for you, do not adjust anything. If not, select File ➪ Page Setup (or click the Page Setup button from within the Document dialog box) to make your adjustments. In the Paper pop-up menu (refer to Figure 3-1), you can select a desired paper size. The available choices are US Letter, US Letter Small, US Legal, US Legal Small, A4, A4 Small, or B5. You can also create a custom size. To do so, click the pop-up menu at the top of the dialog box and select Microsoft Word. This brings you to another view of the Page Setup dialog box. Here you find a Custom button. Click Custom, and then simply enter any desired width and height for the paper size in the Custom Page Options dialog box that appears, and check the Use custom page size checkbox. (Of course, you need a printer that can handle the size you set up.)

Margins

Now that you have your page's most basic settings down, margins are your next concern. Margins are the distance between the top of the page and the first printed line, between the bottom of the page and the last printed line, and between the printed lines and the paper's right and left edges. You can see your document's margins by looking at the ruler while in Page Layout view. The barber-pole gray on the left reflects the left margin and the barber-pole gray on the right is the right margin. By default, Word uses a 1.25-inch margin on the sides. Corporate letterhead is often printed with only one inch from the letterhead to the sides of the page. If you want your text to align with your letterhead, you may need to change your side margins. Word's default top and bottom margins are one inch. The ruler within the left and top margin areas measures in negative increments.

You can change your document's margins visually via the ruler, in the Margins tab of the Document dialog box (Format ➪ Document), or in the Formatting palette's Document pane. To use the ruler, switch to Page Layout view, and then move your cursor to the place on the ruler where the margin (striped gray) section meets the white (text) section. At this meeting point of the margin and document area, your cursor becomes a double-headed arrow. Simply drag the margin to reduce or enlarge the margin area. This works for all margins: side, top, and bottom.

Figure 3-2 shows you the Document dialog box's Margins tab and the Margins area of the Formatting palette's Document pane. Simply enter the appropriate number in each margin box. You can type the number or use the arrows.

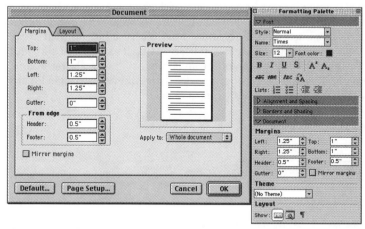

Figure 3-2: The Margins tab of the Document dialog box and the Formatting palette's Document pane

The From edge settings control the distance from the top and bottom edge of the page to the header and footer. Word measures the distance from the top edge of the header and the bottom edge of the footer to the page edges.

A Mirror Margins option also exists. Turn on Mirror margins to have margins on facing pages mirror each other, as you would want to have happen if you printed on both sides of each sheet of paper and then bound the pages into a book. With this option turned on, the right margin of a left-hand (even) page will be the same as the left margin of a right-hand (odd) page, and vice-versa. In fact, the Left and Right margin options change to say Inside and Outside. You can also enter a numeric value to determine the width of an optional *gutter*. What's a gutter? Well, just as the top of a page has white space between the edge of the page and the first line of text and, similarly, the bottom of a page has white space between the last line of text and the bottom of a page, on a left-hand page white space exists between the end of every line of text and the crease of the book. This white space is the gutter. The gutter also refers to the white space between the crease of the book and the start of every line of text on a right-hand page.

Finally, you need to tell Word where to apply your new margin settings. In the Apply to pop-up menu, you can choose to apply the changes to the entire document — Whole document — or apply the changes to all text following the current location of the insertion point — This Point Forward. Whole Document is fine for most common letters.

Formatting Paragraphs

For the most part, documents consist of paragraphs. Therefore, Word lets you apply formatting to words on the paragraph level. Again, remember that Word considers a paragraph to be any text between one paragraph mark and the next. While you are working on formatting your document, it helps to see the paragraph marks. Clicking the Show/Hide button on the Standard toolbar (the button with the paragraph symbol, which resembles a backward P), or using its keyboard shortcut (⌘-8), toggles these marks along with other invisible formatting characters. (A similar command, Reveal Formatting, works a little differently, but is located under the View menu. You might want to try it as well.)

Figure 3-3 shows you what paragraph marks look like.

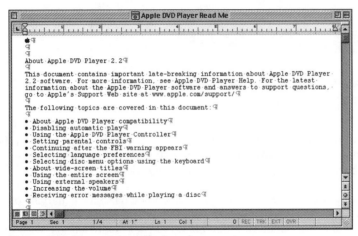

Figure 3-3: Paragraph marks in a document

The most common paragraph formatting is the alignment of lines at the left and right edges, and the indentation of each paragraph's first line. Paragraph formatting also lets you control the length of lines, the space between lines, and the space between paragraphs. You can also control the placement of tab stops and how text is aligned at the tab stops. When deciding where paragraph formatting is necessary, remember that paragraphs are basically collections of lines. Paragraph formatting affects the appearance of a collection of one or more lines that end with a paragraph marker, which appears when you press Return.

Note   At times your paragraph formatting may include automatic space before or after each Return. You may find yourself with a single word oddly hanging out at the end of a line, or prefer to place some words at the start of a new line, and you'll find yourself with unwanted space if you use the Return key to move those words down to a new line. To avoid this space, use a soft return by pressing Shift as you press Return. Word does not consider the soft return character (a left-pointing arrow when you reveal formatting) to be the start of a paragraph.

Carrying Down Formatting

It's very helpful to understand how formatting gets carried down from one paragraph to your next new paragraph. Begin a new document, turn Show Formatting on or press ⌘-8, and then type a few lines of text. Don't press Return. Notice that you can't place your insertion point after the paragraph marker, only before it. (Go ahead and try.) Center that paragraph by going to Format ⇨ Paragraph, then choosing the Indents and Spacing Tab, and then choosing Centered from the Alignment drop-down menu. Each paragraph marker invisibly holds its paragraph's formatting so your marker now holds the code for centering. Now press Return. When you do, the paragraph marker at the end of your first paragraph is carried down or cloned so the new marker carries the identical formatting. This helps you to create consistent documents. (Your second paragraph will now be centered.)

Often, beginners press Return without realizing the repercussions. Each time you press Return you create a marker that contains formatting codes. Each might contain different codes, depending on when you created the Return marker (by pressing Return). Therefore, if you use your mouse (or arrow keys) to move your insertion point in front of another marker, you may end up with a paragraph that looks nothing like the preceding paragraph. People commonly do so, and wonder why each paragraph looks different. Now you know why.

Applying paragraph formatting

You can apply paragraph formatting in different ways. The easiest way is to use the Formatting palette buttons and the indent controls on the ruler. For more in-depth control, you can use Format ⇨ Paragraph to bring up the Paragraph dialog box shown in Figure 3-4. Whichever method you use, remember that the formatting you select will apply to either the paragraph your cursor is in or the paragraphs selected at the time you make the changes. And remember that each paragraph can have its own formatting.

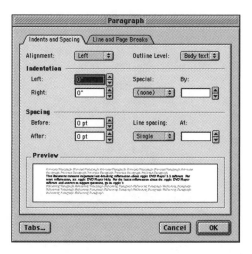

Figure 3-4: The Indents and Spacing tab of the Paragraph dialog box

Tip   If you don't like the Formatting palette, or your screen resolution makes the screen too crowded when the Formatting palette is visible, you might wish to hide it and add the Formatting toolbar instead. The buttons on the Formatting toolbar are a subset of those on the Formatting palette.

Any time you wonder what type of formatting a paragraph contains, you can simply place your insertion point within any paragraph and look at the ruler and Formatting palette (or Formatting toolbar, if you have added it). For example, place your insertion point within any paragraph and look at the alignment buttons (Align Left, Center, Align Right, and Justify). The one that looks pressed reflects the alignment of the paragraph your cursor is in. The positions of the indents and tabs in effect for that paragraph are also evident on the ruler.

The Paragraph dialog box contains two tabs. On the Indents and Spacing tab, you can control the amount of left and right indentation and create a first-line indent or hanging indent (and how much of an indent). This can also be done by dragging the indent controls on the ruler at the top of each document or the buttons and other controls in the Formatting palette's Alignment and Spacing pane. Using the ruler enables you to see the results more quickly and work visually. In the Spacing area, you can choose the amount of spacing above each new paragraph (Before), below each new paragraph (After), and between each line within the paragraph (line spacing). This is best done from the dialog box, the Formatting palette, or with the keyboard shortcuts you learn in Table 3-1. Spacing can't be done with the ruler.

Table 3-1 Shortcut Keys for Paragraph Formatting	
Format	*Shortcut Key*
Left-align text	⌘-L
Center text	⌘-E
Right-align text	⌘-R
Justify text	⌘-J
Indent from left margin	⌘-M
Decrease indent	⌘-Shift-M
Create a hanging indent	⌘-T
Decrease a hanging indent	⌘-Shift-T
Single-space lines	⌘-1
Create 1.5-line spacing	⌘-5
Double-space lines	⌘-2

Format	Shortcut Key
Add/remove 12 points of space before a paragraph	⌘-0 (zero)
Restore default formatting (reapply the Normal style)	⌘-Shift-N
Show/hide formatting (nonprinting) characters	⌘-8

The Line and Page Breaks tab of the Paragraph dialog box (see Figure 3-5) contains options that control how text flows within a paragraph. These controls don't have ruler or button equivalents, although you can add them to your menus or create buttons for them in case you find yourself adjusting the controls often.

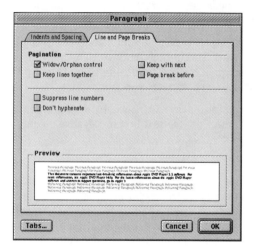

Figure 3-5: The Line and Page Breaks tab of the Paragraph dialog box

You can turn on the following options in the Line and Page Breaks tab:

✦ The Widow/Orphan control option prevents a widow (a single, very short line at the bottom of the page) from appearing by itself at the top of the page, and it prevents an orphan (a single line at the top of a page) from appearing by itself at the top of the page.

✦ The Keep lines together option prevents a page break within the paragraph.

✦ The Keep with next option prevents a page break between the paragraph and the one that follows.

✦ The Page break before option inserts a page break before the paragraph.

✦ The Suppress line numbers option suppresses line numbers for the selected paragraph when line numbering is turned on in a document.

✦ The Don't hyphenate option excludes the paragraph from automatic hyphenation.

What Are First-Line Indents and Hanging Indents?

In some paragraphs, you might want to align the first line of the paragraph differently than the remaining lines.

A *first-line indent* begins a paragraph's first line to the right of the paragraph's margin. You probably remember the two-finger first-line indent you learned in elementary school — this is the high-tech version.

To format a first-line indent, you can either drag the top arrowhead at the left of the ruler (the Screen Tip pops up telling you that it is the first-line indent marker) to the desired point, or you can set the first-line indent in either the Alignment and Spacing pane of the Formatting palette or in the Paragraph dialog box (Format ➪ Paragraph).

A *hanging indent,* sometimes called an outdent, begins a paragraph's first line to the left of the paragraph's margin. You can use a hanging indent to create a bulleted list, for example.

To format a hanging indent, use Format ➪ Paragraph to bring up the Paragraph dialog box. In the Special pop-up menu of the Indents and Spacing tab, choose Hanging. In the By entry, type **.25"**. Click OK. In your document, type a bullet symbol, a tab, and then type the text of the bullet item. The text wraps cleanly along that quarter-inch margin.

If you wish to use the Formatting palette for these indents, reveal the Alignment and Spacing pane, and enter the indent's size in the First line text box (a negative value gives you a hanging indent).

Word also provides what it calls a shortcut menu to do character and paragraph formatting. (As a Mac user, you are more likely to call it a Contextual menu.) To call up this menu, Control-click (press Control as you click) over any location in your paragraph. Figure 3-6 shows the formatting shortcut menu that appears. Here you can choose Cut or Copy (if text is selected); Paste (if something is on the clipboard); or the Font, Paragraph, or Bullets and Numbering dialog boxes. If a single word is selected or your cursor is next to or within a word, you will also have a Define choice and a Synonyms submenu. Choosing Define displays Office's dictionary, open to the word in question. The Synonyms submenu displays that word's synonyms in a submenu from which you can select a replacement or invoke the thesaurus. In addition to those options, you can choose hyperlinks, as discussed in Chapter 11. Depending upon the selection or the location of your cursor, the bottom items will vary.

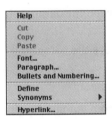

Figure 3-6: The formatting shortcut menu

Indenting paragraphs

Indenting the first line of each paragraph is perhaps the most common formatting effect. However, entire paragraphs can also be indented—on either the left, the right, or both sides (which creates a block quote). For practice, type the following text (or your own words) and follow the steps to experiment with paragraph formatting:

1. Type the following text (not in bold):

   Choices, choices, choices

   It seems you always have three ways to do anything on the Mac. Margins and indents are no exception. If you're a visual person, you'll love using the ruler so you can see where you're moving the text. More numerically based? You'll prefer opening dialog boxes and entering numbers to set indents and such or using the Formatting palette. If you're a bit of both, you can use the ruler, but double-click any ruler element at any time to call up the dialog box.

   Experiment to discover how it's most comfortable for you to work.

2. Center your title. Place the insertion point anywhere on the first line, and click the Center button (on the Formatting palette). Notice the first paragraph ("Choices, choices, choices") takes on a centered alignment. It is actually centered between the left and right margins set for that line.

3. Indent the paragraph from the left. Place the insertion point anywhere within the first full paragraph. (Text does not need to be selected.)

   Visually: Click the rectangle (called the left indent), located below the two left arrowheads on the ruler, and drag it about ½" to the right. This moves both the top and bottom arrows, which affects the indent of both the first line of the paragraph and all following lines. You see the effect when you release the mouse.

   or

   Numerically: In the Formatting palette's Alignment and Spacing pane, enter **0.5** as a value in the Left text box. You'll see the effect as soon as you click anywhere in Word. You can also choose Format ⇨ Paragraph (⌘-Option-M) to open the Paragraph dialog box. In the Indentation area on the Indents and Spacing tab, enter **0.5** as a value in the Left box. You see the effect after you click OK and close the dialog box.

4. Indent the paragraph from the right. (Keep the insertion point within the first paragraph.)

   Visually: Click the triangle at the right on the ruler and drag it about ½" to the left. This brings the end of the line (for this paragraph) inward. Your text will wrap when it reaches that triangle. In effect, you have changed the margin for that paragraph. You see the effect when you release the mouse.

   or

Numerically: Use the Right text box in the Formatting palette or, if you've closed the Paragraph dialog box, open it again (as in Step 3). In the Indentation area, enter **0.5** as a value in the Right box. Click OK. The paragraph appears indented by half an inch on both sides.

5. Indent the first line of the paragraph. Keep your cursor in the same paragraph.

Visually: Click the top arrow on the left side of the ruler and drag it to the 1" mark. When you release the mouse, the first line of the paragraph is indented to that 1" mark.

or

Numerically: Return to the Formatting palette or the Paragraph dialog box and its Indents and Spacing tab. Under Indentation, select First Line (from the pop-up menu under Special, if using the Paragraph dialog box). Enter **1** under By. When you click OK, the first line of the paragraph is now indented by one inch.

Figure 3-7 shows the results of all this paragraph formatting.

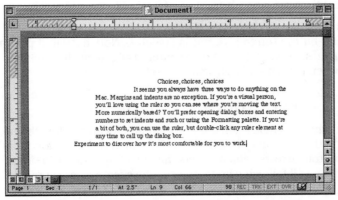

Figure 3-7: Paragraphs after formatting has been applied

If you use the visual method and open the dialog box later, you'll notice that the numbers in the dialog box reflect your ruler movement. Regardless of the method you use, you can change the settings for any paragraph any time. Of course, you can drag the left-indent symbol (the rectangle) back to the zero mark on the ruler to realign the paragraph with the zero marker on the ruler (which is your document's left margin). The first line is indented by one inch unless you drag the first-line indent symbol (top-left triangle) back to the zero mark on the ruler.

When you set indentations on the ruler, remember that the measurement set by the first-line symbol is always relative to that set by the left-indent symbol. Therefore, to indent an entire paragraph by half an inch and the first line by another half an inch, you should drag the left-indent symbol to the right by half an inch and then drag the first-line symbol to the right another half an inch past the left-indent symbol. The best way to do this is to move the entire paragraph first, using the left-indent (rectangle) symbol and then moving the first-line indent marker. To move the first-line symbol independently of the other controls, drag the top triangle.

Note

While we've been using ½" as indents in our examples, ½" isn't necessarily the correct indent to use. The typographic standard is to indent one em space, which is the width of a capital letter M for the font and size you are using. Look closely at books and experiment with your own document to decide what works best for you. The ½" standard is a hold-over from the days of typewriters, but typewriters never had the proper typesetting power that word processing has.

Aligning paragraphs

Paragraphs can be aligned in four ways: left, right, centered, and justified (aligned on both sides). The text you've seen so far in this book is all left-aligned, meaning that the left edge of the paragraph is even and the right edge is ragged. By comparison, there may be times you need justified text (where both edges of the paragraph are aligned) or centered paragraphs (as in titles or headings). In rare instances, you may need to right-align a paragraph; in such cases, the right side aligns flush, and the left edge of the paragraph is ragged. You can change these settings by clicking the alignment buttons on the Formatting palette or from the Alignment pop-up menu of the Paragraph dialog box's Indents and Spacing tab.

To see an example of the available paragraph alignments, open any existing Word document, place the insertion point anywhere within a paragraph, and click each alignment button. Watch how the text moves from left to center to right to justified.

To Justify, or Not to Justify?

Many people consider the look of fully justified text (that is, justified both left and right) to have a professional, typeset quality. Justification also provides an appearance of formality. In multicolumn documents, the justified right edge creates a line that serves as a clear delimiter between columns. On the other hand, if you want your document to appear more friendly or informal, avoid full justification.

Also, note that full justification can cause uneven spacing and vertical rivers of white space within paragraphs. If you don't enable hyphenation, full justification creates some lines that are excessively loose (lots of space between words), and some lines that are excessively tight (too little space between words). If you enable hyphenation when you use full justification, Word hyphenates many words to create evenly spaced lines—far more than if you left the right margin ragged. This effect can be eased somewhat if your font and size allow for kerning, which can be found on the Character Spacing tab of the Font dialog (Format ➪ Font or ⌘-D). Kerning refers to parts of characters projecting beyond their display rectangle—excessive kerning can actually result in adjacent characters overlapping.

Depending on the type of document, the appearance of justified text may be improved by hyphenation. To enable Word to hyphenate automatically, choose Tools ➪ Hyphenation and turn on the Automatically hyphenate document option in the Hyphenation dialog box, and then click OK.

Justified text is most often seen in books and magazines to give them a neater appearance. Justification is accomplished by adjusting the space between words to make the right edge of the line even with the edge of the paragraph.

Applying line spacing

Line spacing affects the amount of space between the lines in a paragraph. To change the line spacing, place the insertion point anywhere within the desired paragraph or, to set several existing paragraphs identically, select all of the paragraphs in which you would like line spacing changed. Choose the desired line spacing by using shortcut keys (see Table 3-1 earlier in this chapter) by clicking the buttons in the Formatting palette, or by setting the Line spacing option in the Indents and Spacing tab of the Paragraph dialog box.

The common choices for line spacing are Single, 1.5 lines (for 1.5-times single spacing), and Double. You can also select At least, Exactly, or Multiple if you are using the Paragraph dialog box. (When you choose any of the last three options, you must enter or select a corresponding amount in the At box.) The At least choice sets a minimum line spacing that Word adjusts, when needed, to allow for larger font sizes or graphics. The Exactly choice sets a fixed line spacing that Word will not adjust. The Multiple choice lets you enter incremental values (such as 1.2) to increase or decrease spacing by a fractional amount. For example, choosing Multiple and entering 1.2 in the At box results in line spacing that is 120 percent of single spacing.

Applying paragraph spacing

Word also lets you control the amount of space that appears before or after paragraphs. This is set in the Formatting palette's Alignment and Spacing pane or within the Spacing area on the Indents and Spacing tab of the Paragraph dialog box. You can enter numeric values in the Before or After boxes to indicate the additional space that you want. As with line spacing, you can enter the value in points (pt.), each point being $\frac{1}{72}$ of an inch.

Applying borders to paragraphs

You may find borders useful for emphasizing a particular portion of text, such as in newsletter layouts, fliers, and data sheets. Borders will appear around any text selected when you choose your border options. You can easily apply a border to paragraphs by clicking the arrow next to the border button in the Formatting palette's Borders and Shading pane. However, for the most control, select

Chapter 3 ✦ **Formatting Documents**   85

Format ⇨ Borders and Shading to use the Borders and Shading dialog box. If you apply borders often, click the Show Toolbar button in the Borders and Shading dialog box. The Tables and Borders toolbar that appears makes adding borders to your documents much easier, although it offers fewer options than the dialog box.

Word offers several border choices:

✦ **Top Border** — a line above the paragraph

✦ **Bottom Border** — a line below the paragraph

✦ **Left Border** — a line to the left of the paragraph

✦ **Right Border** — a line to the right of the paragraph

✦ **Inside Border** — a line within the paragraph

✦ **Outside Border** — lines that surround the paragraph

✦ **Box Border** — a line around all sides of the paragraph

✦ **Shadow Border** — a shadowed line around the paragraph

✦ **3-D** — a 3-D line around the paragraph

✦ **Custom** — a custom line of your choice around the paragraph

✦ **No border**

When using the dialog box, after you select the type of border you want for your paragraph, you still need to tell Word where you want the border to appear. On the right side of the Borders tab in the Preview box, you can click the side of the paragraph on which you want the border to appear. This will give you a general idea of what the border will look like once it is applied to your paragraph.

You can even change the line width and color for the different borders in your document. Both the dialog box and the optional menus make it easy to select a line width or color from the pop-up menus each provides. The default width is ½" and the default color is Automatic (same as the text color). In Figure 3-8, you can see the Width pop-up menu, located in the Style section of the Borders tab (in the Paragraph Borders and Shading dialog box).

Figure 3-8: The Borders tab of the Borders and Shading dialog box

A Word About Styles

Character, paragraph, and page formatting are known as direct formatting options. Another way to control formatting is with styles. When you use styles, you apply a group of formatting settings to an entire document.

As an example, if a certain style defines indented paragraphs, and you apply that style to a document, that document's paragraphs will be indented. Chapter 8 explores the use of styles.

Besides adding borders, you can also apply various kinds of shading to your text. To do this, move to the Shading tab (see Figure 3-9). In the Fill palette, click a shade of gray or another color to select it. You also have the option to apply a pattern to the fill. Just select a percentage from the Style pop-up menu. To have the pattern be a different color, select any color from the Color pop-up menu in the Patterns area. The Style must be something other than Clear for the Color pop-up menu to be enabled. The Preview area to the right will give you a general idea of how that will appear in your document. Click OK to apply the effects.

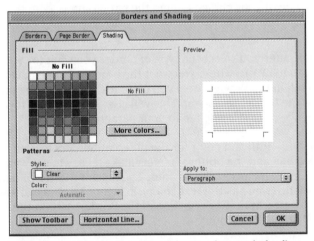

Figure 3-9: The Shading tab of the Borders and Shading dialog box

Formatting Characters

As mentioned earlier, character formatting is the lowest level of formatting. Character formatting — the most common type of formatting — governs how your characters look. When you apply character formatting, you are changing the format for each character. When you look at a newspaper or a book, character formatting is evident. Headlines appear in boldface characters and in large fonts. Secondary headlines, however, are in smaller fonts and may not be bold. The role of character formatting is to emphasize text:

Characters and lines

can be produced

in a number of ways,

even in combination,

TO HELP MAKE

different points.

You can also add color formatting to any characters. Of course, you need a color monitor to see the colors onscreen. To print the colors properly, you need a color printer, too. Colors will show in shades of gray on good laser or ink jet printers.

Using character formatting options

We can further divide character formatting into specific areas that are controlled by the options in the Font dialog box, which appears after you choose Format ⇨ Font. Table 3-2 explains these formatting options.

Table 3-2 **Formatting Options**	
Option	**Description**
Font	A character set with a consistent and identifiable typeface, such as Times, Courier, or Helvetica.
Font style	Defines a style for the chosen font, such as regular, italic, bold, or bold italic.
Size	Specifies what point size to use — essentially, how big the text should be. Strictly speaking, point size measures character height, but characters proportionally increase in width as they increase in height. A point is $\frac{1}{72}$ of an inch, so a 72-point font can take up an inch from top to bottom (not counting descenders, which dangle from the bottom of y, g, q, and so on). This does not mean, however, that a 72-point f is always an inch tall. Each font has other characteristics that determine its actual size. (This is why an f in one font may look bigger than an f in another font, even when they're the same point size.)

Continued

Table 3-2 *(continued)*

Option	Description
Font color	You can select 32 possible colors from the pop-up menu, and you can show more by clicking the More colors button in the pop-up menu.
Underline style	Specifies a type of underlining (none, single, double, dotted, and a myriad of others).
Underline color	If an underline style is selected, this pop-up menu becomes available with the same choices as the Font color pop-up menu.
Effects	Specifies appearance attributes, such as strikethrough, hidden (which means the text does not appear, but is actually still there), superscript, subscript, small caps (in which all letters are in caps, but those created by pressing Shift are slightly larger), and all caps.
Scale	Specifies at what percentage of the Font size you wish the characters displayed. This is under the Character Spacing tab.
Spacing	Controls the amount of space that appears between characters (under the Character Spacing tab). Word places a default amount of space between characters, but you can expand or condense this allowance in the By text box.
Position	The position of the characters on a line. Options are normal, raised (the characters appearing above the baseline by half a line), or lowered (the characters appearing below the baseline by half a line) in the amount specified in the By text box. Position is located on the Character Spacing tab.
Kerning for fonts	Specifies that a scalable (TrueType or Type 1) font's kerning table should be used to determine intercharacter spacing. You set the minimum font size for the kerning table to be in effect. This checkbox is on the Character Spacing tab.
Animation	Controls different animating effects to your document, such as a Las Vegas lights effect with blinking, moving borders. Animation is set under the Animation tab.

The most frequently used character formats are in the Formatting palette. From there, you can choose the font and point size, and then apply bold, italics, underlining, and shadow. Also available are superscript, subscript, two forms of strikethrough, small caps, and all-caps. It is also easy to use the keyboard equivalents for bold (⌘-B), italics (⌘-I), and underline (⌘-U). If you wish to use more formats than are available via the Formatting palette, you can show the Formatting toolbar and add them to it or you can add them to the menus.

To add formatting to the toolbar, you need to select Format ⇨ Font to bring up the Font tab of the Font dialog box. It may also be easier to open this dialog box when you need to change several formats at one time. The Font dialog box reveals many options, as shown in Figure 3-10. Here you can choose a font, select a style, change text color, specify the type and color of underlining you desire, and add effects such as outline, emboss, or engrave.

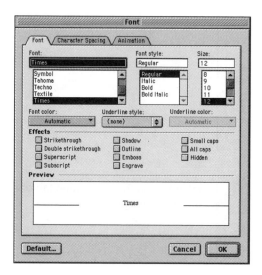

Figure 3-10: The Font tab of the Font dialog box

You can use the options in the Font and Font style list boxes to choose a desired font and font style, and you can choose a desired size in the Size list box. You can select a color for the text in the Font color pop-up menu, a type of underlining (Single, Words Only, Double, Dotted, or a number of others) from the Underline style pop-up menu, and you can select a color for the underlining in the Underline Color pop-up menu, if an Underline style has been selected. In the Effects portion of the tab, you can turn on as many effects at one time as you want.

The Character Spacing tab of the Font dialog box (see Figure 3-11) provides options for how much the text should be scaled from its nominal font size, changing the amount of spacing between characters (Normal, Expanded, or Condensed), the position (whether text appears raised or lowered relative to the baseline of normal text), and kerning (the precise amount of space between characters, as detailed shortly).

The Animation tab of the Font dialog box applies animation to characters in your document. You may find this useful to draw attention to certain words. Select the text you wish to animate, choose Format ⇨ Font to open the Font dialog box, and then click the Animation tab. (The Animation tab is shown in Figure 3-12.) Select the type of animation you wish to apply. The preview box at the bottom of the Animation tab demonstrates the effect. Click OK to apply the selected animation to your text.

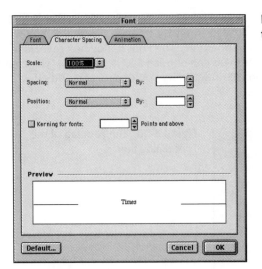

Figure 3-11: The Character Spacing tab of the Font dialog box

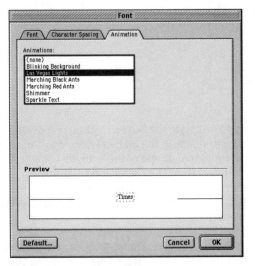

Figure 3-12: The Animation tab of the Font dialog box

To remove or apply character formats, simply select the text you want to affect, or position the cursor where you want to begin typing the formatted characters. Then, click the formatting option in the Formatting palette, or choose Format ➪ Font to choose your options.

Using character formatting shortcuts

You can also apply most of these character formats with shortcut keys, which are sometimes easier to use than the mouse. The shortcut keys act as switches to turn the various Format commands on and off. Table 3-3 contains several shortcut keys that you can use to apply character formatting.

Table 3-3 Shortcut Keys for Character Formatting	
Format	*Shortcut Key*
Bold	⌘-B
Italic	⌘-I
Underline	⌘-U
Word underline	⌘-Shift-W
Double underline	⌘-Shift-D
Subscript (H2O)	⌘-= (equal sign)
Superscript (X2)	⌘-Shift-= (equal sign)
Small caps	⌘-Shift-K
All caps	⌘-Shift-A
Change case of letters, cycling through	Shift-F3
Hidden text	⌘-Shift-H
Remove formats	Control-spacebar
Font	⌘-Shift-F
Symbol font	⌘-Shift-Q
Next larger size	⌘- Shift ->
Next smaller size	⌘- Shift <
Up one point	⌘-]
Down one point	⌘-[

You can turn off all character formatting for a selection — returning to plain text — by pressing Control-spacebar. This is especially useful when you've applied various formatting features to a selection, and you want to return to normal, plain text.

The Hows and Whens of Formatting

You can apply formatting before you enter your text (but you must turn it off when you're done with the effect), or you can enter all the new text in a single format and change the formatting later. The latter enables you to get all of your thoughts out first, without distracting yourself with formatting.

You can also finish a sentence or chunk of text, and then go back and format that section before writing some more. No right or wrong way exists; you can use either method at any time.

Changing character fonts and point sizes

You can use various fonts within any document and see how they look as you work. The font used initially as the default is Times, but you can change this to whatever you wish. Any fonts installed on your Mac (or turned on by a font management program, such as Font Reserve) are available to you. You can use the following steps to change the default font used for your documents:

1. From the menus, choose Format ➪ Font.

2. Click the Font tab in the Font dialog box (if it isn't already visible).

3. Choose the desired font, font style, and size you want to use as the default.

4. Click the Default button in the dialog box.

5. When asked if you really want to change the default font, click Yes.

In addition to choosing appropriate fonts, you can also select various point sizes with the Formatting palette or the Font dialog box. Each point is $\frac{1}{72}$ of an inch, so in a 10-point font size, the characters would be roughly $\frac{10}{72}$ of an inch high. The following lines demonstrate the effects of various point sizes:

This is 12-point Times New Roman.

This is 14-point Times New Roman.

This is 16-point Times New Roman.

This is 18-point Times New Roman.

Caution

With varied fonts and font sizes, you can easily get carried away. A document with too many different fonts and font sizes can take on a busy look and be visually distracting to the reader.

Applying superscript and subscript

You can create superscript (raised) text or subscript (lowered) text by selecting the Superscript or Subscript options on the Font tab of the Font dialog box. Examples of both types of text are as follows:

This is superscript text

This is subscript text.

You can apply super- or subscripting to text by using the Font dialog box, the Formatting palette, or the shortcut keys (see Table 3-3 earlier in this chapter). If you use the Font dialog box or the Formatting palette, you can also change the font size you use for the superscript or subscript while you're there.

Adjusting kerning

You can also control kerning — the adjusting of the space between characters, relative to the specific type of font used. Kerning can give a document a better appearance, although you need a high-resolution printer (usually 600 dpi or better) for the effects of minor changes in kerning to be noticeable. Kerning can be used only with proportionally spaced PostScript or TrueType fonts. This feature is available in the Character Spacing tab of the Font dialog box.

Copying character formatting

If you use a particular type of formatting often in a document (but not in all places), you can save time by copying the format from one place in the document to another. Word makes this simple with the Format Painter button in the Standard toolbar. To copy a character format, first select some text that has the format you want to copy. Next, click the Format Painter button (it's the button with the small brush). A small plus sign appears on your cursor as you click the button. Then select the characters or section to which you want to apply the format. If you are applying it to just one word, simply click the word — no need to select the word first. The formatting is automatically applied to the new characters. This only works to apply the formatting once. If you wish to apply the same formatting to several areas, double-click the Format Painter button initially. The plus sign and format painting will remain in effect until you place the cursor and type.

Formatting Sections

Sections are portions of documents that carry formatting characteristics independent of other sections in the same document. Section formatting isn't required — by default, Word treats an entire document as a single section. By giving you the power to add multiple sections to a document, Word gives you a way to apply different formatting settings to each section. At first, the concept of sections may be difficult to understand. However, knowledge of how sections operate in Word is worth the effort because sections add flexibility to how a document can be formatted. If you have used AppleWorks, older versions of Word or desktop publishing software, such as Adobe PageMaker, the concept of formatting in sections will be more familiar to you. (If you are coming from an old version of Word for DOS, you may be familiar with divisions, which are equivalent to sections.)

Typically, you use section formatting to change the number of columns or the style of page numbering for a section of the document. Changes that affect all pages of a document, such as page margins, are part of page formatting.

Even in a very short document, you are still using sections, although you may not give them any thought. In a short document (such as a one-page memo), the entire document consists of a single section, so you can use Word's section formatting commands to control certain elements of its layout.

If you want to apply a specific set of formatting to a section, select the text and choose Format ⇨ Document. In the Document dialog box, click the Layout tab (see Figure 3-13). In the Apply to pop-up menu, you will see Selected text, the default option. (At times this will say Whole document or Selected sections as the default; it changes to suit what you're doing.) In this tab, you can control the section breaks for a document, headers and footers, and vertical alignment.

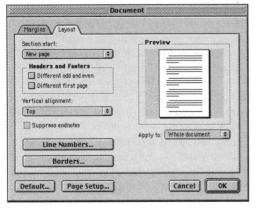

Figure 3-13: The Layout tab of the Document dialog box

To control the section breaks in a document, select an option in the Section start pop-up menu. Here, you can control where you want the section to begin and where the preceding section should end.

✦ **Continuous** causes the selected section to follow the preceding section immediately, without a page or column break.

✦ **New Column** starts printing the selected section's text at the top of the next column.

✦ **New Page** breaks the page at the section break.

✦ **Even Page** starts the selected section at the next even-numbered page.

✦ **Odd Page** starts the selected section at the next odd-numbered page.

The Layout tab also lets you control vertical alignment. Vertical alignment is the spacing of a document from the top to the bottom of the page. The document can be vertically aligned to the top, centered, or justified.

You can also add line numbers by clicking the Line Numbers button and turning on the Add line numbering option in the dialog box that appears (see Figure 3-14). You can apply line numbers to the whole document or only to a selected section.

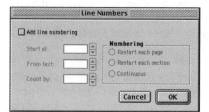

Figure 3-14: The Line Numbers dialog box

You can apply line numbers in various ways. They can start at the beginning of the document and go to the end; they can start at a specified line or section; they can begin from line 1 at the start of each new page; or they can begin at a specified number on the selected page. Line numbers are useful in legal documents where you may need to examine a specific line of a contract or other legal document.

Headers and footers

Word makes it easy to add headers and footers to a document. A header is text or a graphic that is printed at the top of every page in a document; a footer is text or a graphic that is printed at the bottom of every page. Headers and footers can be different for odd and even pages.

You can create headers and footers by choosing the View ➪ Header and Footer command or by double-clicking within the header or footer area. Word switches to Page Layout view, the body of your document grays out, and the cursor activates in the Header area. The Header and Footer toolbar also appears, as shown in Figure 3-15.

You can switch between headers and footers by clicking the Switch Between Header and Footer button (which shows both a header and a footer) on the toolbar, or you can scroll up or down the document with the vertical scroll bar.

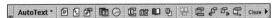

Figure 3-15: The Header and Footer toolbar in Page Layout view

You type and format text in headers and footers the same way you type text in a normal document. You can also enter page numbers, the date, and the time as a header or footer in a document. Click the Page Numbers, Date, and Time buttons on the Header and Footer toolbar. If you want the time, page number, or date centered, you can do so the way you center text in a document.

After entering your header or footer information, click the Close button on the Header and Footer toolbar or double-click in the body area of the document, and Word returns to whatever view you were in. From now on, when you switch to Page Layout view, Word displays the header and footer as dimmed (grayed out) so you can read it but not edit it. (To edit, select View ➪ Header and Footer again or double-click within the header or footer.)

You may want to use a different header or footer for the first page, as in a case where page numbering isn't appropriate. Or, you may want a different header on odd and even pages, as in books. Both options are checkboxes in the Layout tab of the Document dialog box. Just click to select either one.

Deleting a header or footer

Deleting a header or footer is also simple. Choose View ➪ Header and Footer, and then Select All (⌘-A) within the header or footer. Press Delete or use the Cut command (⌘-X), emptying the header or footer. The header or footer area still appears when you choose View ➪ Header and Footer, but when this area is empty, it won't appear in print or in Page Preview. To delete other headers or footers, click the Show Next button on the Header and Footer toolbar to display the next header or footer, and then delete that text.

Adjusting margin settings

Headers and footers are printed inside the top and bottom margins. If the header or footer is too large to fit in the margin, Word adjusts the top or bottom margin so the header or footer fits. If you don't want Word to adjust the margins, choose Format ➪ Document and go to the Margins tab. Enter a hyphen before the Top or Bottom margin setting. However, if the header or footer is too large, it may overwrite the main document.

Positioning headers and footers

You may want to adjust the position of your headers and footers in your document. You can adjust the horizontal position by centering it, running it into the left or right margin, or aligning it with the left or right margin. Two preset tabs exist in the header and footer areas. One is centered between the left and right margins, and one is right aligned at the default right margin. You can use these tabs to place a page number flush right and to center text in the headers and footers. (If you change the margins, you may also want to adjust the tab stops.)

For a left-aligned header or footer, type the text where the cursor first appears in the text box. For a centered header or footer, tab once to the center and begin typing. You may also use the alignment buttons on the Formatting palette or toolbar to center, left align, right align, or justify your headers or footers. If you want to add a negative indent to your header or footer, drag the indent markers on the ruler, use the Indent text box in the Formatting palette, or use the Format ➪ Paragraph command to place a negative indent in your header or footer. (Remember, you need to select the header or footer before using the Paragraph command.)

You can adjust the distance of the footer from the top or bottom of the page. To do so numerically, click the Document Layout button on the Headers and Footers toolbar or select Format ➪ Document. Select the Margins tab. In the From edge section, type or select the distance you want from the edge of the paper. To move the header up or down visually, with the header active, move your pointer to the vertical ruler at the left of your screen and point to the top margin boundary. The header area is the white area on the otherwise gray ruler, so it's easy to see. The pointer becomes a double-headed arrow. Click and drag upward to move the header toward the top of the paper's edge or drag downward to increase the distance. Do the same to move the footer in the footer area but, of course, with the direction reversed.

You can also adjust the space between the header or footer and the main document. This is done visually almost exactly as described previously. To add more space after the header, go to the header you want to adjust. Move your pointer to the vertical ruler at the left of your screen and point to the bottom margin boundary. The header area is the white area on the otherwise gray ruler, so it's easy to see. The pointer becomes a double-headed arrow. Click and drag downward to enlarge the space allotted to the header. You can see the effect whenever you release the mouse. Do the same to add space before the footer in the footer area but, of course, with the direction reversed.

Page numbers

Inserting page numbers is one of the easiest of all formatting jobs.

To add page numbers visually, place your cursor in the header or footer. Type any opening text, such as **Page #** and a space. Then click the Insert Page Number button on the Header and Footer toolbar. Type another space—and, if you want, the word **of**— and then click the Insert Number of Pages button. The result of this would read "Page # 1 of 2" in a two-page document and always reflect the correct page numbering and total page count. A third button, Format Page Number, enables you to change the number format by opening the Page Number Format dialog box (for example, letters instead of numbers or roman numerals). You can also add chapter numbers to your document, but you have to tell Word where a new chapter begins. To indicate where a new chapter begins, use the Chapter starts with style pop-up menu, which causes Word to look for the style that is designated as the chapter heading for each chapter. You also have the option of numbering from a previous section if you don't want to number the entire document. And finally, you can ask Word to start numbering from a specific page.

To add page numbers numerically, choose Insert ⇨ Page Numbers to bring up the Page Numbers dialog box shown in Figure 3-16. In this dialog box, you can use the pop-up menus to position your page numbers in the header or footer and align them. Click the Format button to open the Page Number Format dialog box (also shown in Figure 3-16), which lets you change the number format as mentioned previously.

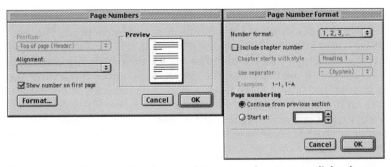

Figure 3-16: The Page Numbers and Page Number Format dialog boxes

Footnotes

Word's capability to display multiple portions of a document simultaneously makes adding footnotes to a Word document a simple matter. You can look at and work with the text of a footnote in a separate pane, while the related portion of your document remains visible. Word, like most word processors, lets you position footnotes either at the bottom of each page or at the end of the document. (When footnotes are placed at the end of a document, they are called endnotes.) However, in Word you can also put a footnote directly beneath the text to which it applies or at the end of a section.

The Place at pop-up menu in the All Footnotes tab enables you to determine the placement of the footnotes. You can choose between Bottom of page or Beneath text. Select Bottom of page to place the footnotes for a given page at the bottom of that page. The Beneath text choice places the footnote directly after the text containing the footnote reference mark.

The Number format pop-up menu enables you to choose the type of numbers you want to use for the footnotes. The Start at box lets you change the starting number for automatically numbered footnotes. If you want Word to restart the automatic numbering each time a new section begins, select the Restart each section radio button in the Numbering area.

Changing footnotes to endnotes

Changing all your footnotes (or just one footnote) to endnotes is easy. Begin in Normal view. Activate the Footnote area by choosing View ➪ Footnotes. In the separator bar above the footnotes, select All Footnotes from the pop-up menu (or All Endnotes if working in reverse). Now that all possible footnotes (or endnotes) are visible, select the footnotes (or endnotes) you want to convert. Control-click the selected footnotes (endnotes) to open the contextual menu. Select Convert to Endnote to convert the footnote to an endnote. Now, to see the kind of note you want, choose it from the Notes box in the footnote window.

You can also copy and move a footnote by using the regular Cut, Copy, and Paste commands or by clicking and dragging it to its new location.

Summary

In this chapter, you have read about all sorts of formatting techniques that you will use often if you work in Word on a regular basis. The chapter covered these points:

✦ In Word, you can apply formatting to paragraphs, characters, or sections of a document.

✦ You can change page formatting in the Format ➪ Document and File ➪ Page Setup dialog boxes as well as on the Formatting palette.

✦ To apply formatting to paragraphs, you can use the various buttons of the Formatting palette and toolbar that apply to paragraph formatting, or you can use the Format ➪ Paragraph command.

✦ You can apply borders and shadings to paragraphs by using the Format ➪ Borders and Shading command or the Borders and Shading pane of the Formatting palette.

✦ To apply formatting to characters, you can use the various buttons of the Formatting palette or toolbar that apply to character formatting, or you can use the Format ➪ Font command.

✦ Section formatting can also be applied through the use of the Format ➪ Document command, by using the options that appear on the Layout tab of the resulting dialog box.

✦ You can add headers and footers to a document with the View ➪ Header and Footer command.

✦ Footnotes and endnotes can be added to a document with the Insert ➪ Footnote command.

Where to go next

✦ Now that you've explored so many aspects of document formatting, you're probably anxious to try printing some examples of your work. Chapter 4 will set you right up.

✦ You can make many common formatting tasks easier by applying styles to portions of your document. Details of this are in Chapter 8.

✦   ✦   ✦

Previewing and Printing Your Documents

This chapter details how to print your documents and how you can preview them prior to printing. Of course, your printer must be connected to your computer and turned on before you can print.

Previewing Documents

Using Print Preview saves trees: you don't waste paper printing draft copies to see if everything looks right. With File ⇨ Print Preview (or the button on the Standard toolbar that looks like a document with a magnifying glass over it — it's usually next to the printer button), you see onscreen what a document will look like when you print it. This includes footnotes, headers (text that's printed at the tops of pages), footers (text that's printed at the bottoms of pages), page numbers, multiple columns, and graphics. You can view more than one page at a time by clicking the Multiple Pages button in the Print Preview toolbar and selecting the number of pages you want to see simultaneously. While in Print Preview mode, you can easily move between pages, change some ruler settings, and even move graphics, and now, in Word 2001, you can edit text.

Learning about the Print Preview toolbar

In Print Preview mode, all toolbars and floating palettes (including the Formatting palette) disappear and the Print Preview toolbar (see Figure 4-1) appears, providing preview-specific options. Click the appropriate button to perform a task, as outlined in Table 4-1.

Figure 4-1: The Print Preview toolbar

Table 4-1	
Print Preview Toolbar Buttons	
Button	***Function***
Print	Brings up the Mac's Print dialog box.
Magnifier	Clicking the preview with the magnifier enlarges the preview so you can read the text better or inspect the document more closely.
One Page	Enables you to see the current page in Print Preview mode.
Multiple Pages	Enables you to see up to six pages at once onscreen. These pages appear so you can see the layout of each page.
Zoom Control	Enables you to control the distance at which you see the pages (magnification) in the Print Preview window.
View Ruler	Toggles the ruler on and off so you can see the sizes and move the margins.
Shrink to Fit	Attempts to shrink your document so it will all fit on one page by reducing the font size. For example, two pages of 10-point text becomes one page of 6-point text.
Full Screen	Takes away all standard window scrolling and controls. Provides a button to click to return you to the traditional window type. (This feature is more commonly used in Windows.)
Close Preview	Closes the preview window and returns you to Normal view.

To leave Print Preview mode and return to your document, you can click the Close button, click the standard close box in the preview window, or press the Esc key.

Many commands from the normal Word menus are not available in Print Preview mode. These commands appear dimmed on the menus. Remember that you cannot open files or change windows while in Print Preview mode.

Adjusting margins

In Print Preview mode, you can move text around. You can also make changes to some aspects of the document, such as the location of page margins, headers, and footers.

To make changes to page margins or indentations, the ruler must be showing. If it's not already on, turn on the ruler using the ruler button in the Print Preview toolbar or choose View ➪ Ruler. When you enter Preview mode, your cursor becomes a magnifier. Click the Magnifier button to switch to a standard cursor.

To change the indentations for a section of text, select the text you wish to change using any typical selection technique. Next, move the triangles (or rectangle) on the ruler until the text starts and ends where you want.

To change the margins for the entire document, move your cursor to the place on the ruler where the gray section of the ruler meets the white section. The gray represents your page margin. Gray appears on the left for the left margin and on the right for the right margin. When your cursor is the meeting point of the margin and document area, it becomes a double-headed arrow. Simply drag the margin left or right to reduce or enlarge the margin area. (You don't need to select any text.)

Tip　When both indents are set at the left margin, you may have trouble positioning so that the cursor becomes the double-arrow box. You might need to temporarily move the indents so that the cursor will change.

To move text around within your document, select the text as you normally would, and then drag it to the new location. Don't forget that you can also Control-click any highlighted text to see a contextual shortcut menu to cut, paste, make font changes, add paragraph modifications, add bullets and numbering, and draw tables.

Adjusting object locations and text wrap

You can also move your graphics while in Print Preview. Again, if your mouse pointer is Preview's default magnifier, you must first switch to a standard cursor by clicking the Magnifier button on the toolbar. Then simply click the graphic and drag it.

You may also want to set your picture apart visually by placing a frame around it. To frame the object while you are in Print Preview, first click the Magnifier button to turn off the magnifier (if it's on) and then either click the picture and click the Format Picture button on the Picture floating window, or control-click the picture you want to frame and choose Format Picture from the shortcut menu. Either of these methods will display the Format Picture dialog box. From the Format Picture dialog box, shown in Figure 4-2, choose the Colors and Lines tab. In the Line area, choose the type of frame lines desired. When you do so, the frame appears around the picture. Note that the Lines section will be disabled for pictures that are Inline with Text on the Layout tab.

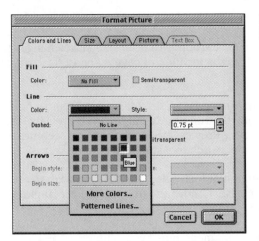

Figure 4-2: Selecting a dark blue border for a graphic object

An object, such as a picture, will sit on top of your text by default. If you want text to wrap around the object, you need to turn on wrapping. Again, either click the picture and then click the Format Picture button in the Picture floating window, or control-click the picture and choose Format Picture from the shortcut menu. Next, choose the Layout tab, as shown in Figure 4-3. Choose the desired type of wrapping from the diagrams and the text will wrap accordingly.

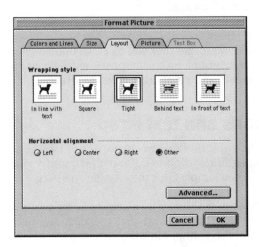

Figure 4-3: Selecting a tight text wrap with a half-inch distance from image to text

Tip

Sometimes it can be difficult to select an object in order to move or set text wrap. You know you've selected the image when the open square handles appear at its corners and the Picture floating window appears. Selecting an object may become easier if you place a frame around the object. If you select a white frame, it won't appear when you print on white paper.

Now, it is time to click the Advanced button. The Advanced Layout dialog box appears. Using the Distance from text section of the Text Wrapping tab, you can control the distance of the text from the picture. Simply adjust the numbers in the Top, Bottom, Left, and Right sections of the Distance from text section.

Printing Documents

Word 2001 isn't limited to simply printing your documents or a range of pages; it enables you to print specifically selected text blocks as well as other related information, such as summary information, annotations, AutoText entries, and style sheets. In the "Formatting Documents" section of Chapter 3, we covered page orientation and page size as they relate to setting up your document. In this chapter, we cover the standard printing options and then introduce Word's unique printing capabilities.

Understanding general (standard) printing options

To print your document, choose File ➪ Print (⌘-P). The standard Print dialog box appears. A pop-up menu typically opens with General and enables you to select the usual Mac printing options. The look of your Print dialog box may be different, depending on the printer you have or the version of the LaserWriter software you have installed on your Mac. However, the options available are basically the same. A typical Print dialog box is shown in Figure 4-4.

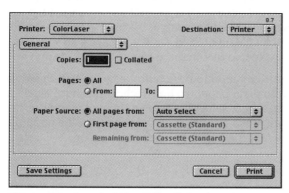

Figure 4-4: A typical Mac Print dialog box (yours may vary)

Here's a rundown of the standard Mac (General) printing options:

✦ **Printer.** This pop-up menu tells you which printer you will print to.

✦ **Destination.** This pop-up menu enables you to tell Word (or any application from which you are printing, such as Excel) to print to a printer or to print to a file. The latter is not commonly used, but is helpful when you don't have a printer handy and want to spool (prepare) the document for printing at a later time. It is also needed if you use Adobe Acrobat's Distiller to create PDF (Portable Document Format) files.

✦ **Copies.** This tells the printer how many copies to print. The default is 1. Notice that the 1 in the Copies field is selected (highlighted), which makes it easy for you to enter the number of copies you wish to print by just typing the number.

✦ **Pages.** With the Pages fields, you can choose which pages of the document you will print. All is the default so your entire document prints. To print only a range of pages, enter the first page to print in the From field and the last page in the To field. For example, to print only Pages 3, 4, and 5, enter **3** in the From field and **5** in the To field. What if you want to begin at Page 3 and print the rest of the document, but don't know exactly how many pages there are? Simply enter **3** in the From box and leave the To field empty. Likewise, you can leave the From field blank and enter a **5** in the To field to print all pages up to Page 5. Of course, you know the document begins on Page 1, but this saves you a keystroke, so what the heck?

✦ **Paper Source.** This feature enables you to control which paper trays you print from—for example, the main tray, a secondary tray (if you have one), or the manual feed. Each tray may hold a different type of paper. Most commonly, you won't change this from the default, which is to print all pages from the main tray. To print onto an envelope or a paper not in the main tray, you would click in the pop-up menu and select Manual Feed. Or, if you have a specialty tray or second main tray, you may keep paper in there and select that tray.

In the corporate world, it is common to print a first page on letterhead and the rest of the document to plain paper. To do so, click the First Page From button and, in that pop-up menu, select the tray containing your letterhead (choose Manual Feed if you need to hand-feed the paper). In the pop-up menu below, Remaining from, select the tray that holds plain paper.

In most cases, these options are all you need to print. After you've set your options (if any are desired), click Print.

Note   On occasion, you may want your document laid out with a horizontal orientation, or in what is known as landscape orientation. This is particularly useful with very wide documents, such as those that contain a table of numbers or documents containing pictures. This is covered in the "Formatting Documents" section in Chapter 3. Page sizing is also covered there.

Word's special printing options

In addition to the usual Mac printing options, Word provides a few more. To access these unique options, you click the pop-up menu that opens with General and drag down to the selection that says Microsoft Word. (This pop-up menu is clear in Figure 4-5 as the pointer is still at the pop-up menu location.)

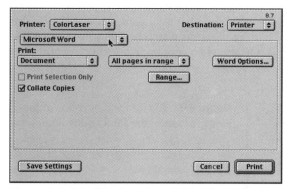

Figure 4-5: The Word section of the Print dialog box

Figure 4-5 shows you one version of the Microsoft Word section of the Print dialog box. The available options in the Print dialog box include printing portions of a document, printing several ranges of full pages, collating a document, printing odd or even pages, printing in reverse order, printing documents containing links, and printing documents containing fields.

Printing portions of a document

Previously, we discussed how to print a range of pages from your document, as opposed to printing the entire document. This is always possible on the Mac and can be set in the print dialog box. However, there may be times when you want to print only a section of a page or one–and-a-half pages. This is easy to do.

Simply select a portion of text you want to print, whether it's part of one page or a selection that spans many pages. You can use any of the usual selection techniques. Then issue the print command as usual (⌘-P or File ➪ Print). Click the pop-up menu that opens with General and drag down to the selection that says Microsoft Word. Click in the checkbox next to Print selection only. (If no text or graphics are selected in the document, this option is grayed out.) When this option is checked, the message "Selected text will be printed" appears below the option. Click Print when all your options are checked and you are ready to print.

Printing several ranges of full pages

At times, you may want to print more than one range of pages. For example, you may want to print pages 3–5, but you also want to print 7 and 9–12. You could issue the Print command four times, naming one range each time, but Word 2001 provides a more convenient way. In the Word section of the Print dialog box, click the Range button to bring up a range-specific dialog box. As shown in Figure 4-6, this box provides very clear instructions. You can fully control your print range or ranges from here. To print several ranges, list the pages in the Pages box. If you want to print consecutive page numbers, separate them with a hyphen. Use a comma to separate nonconsecutive page numbers. For the previous example, you would enter **3-5, 7, 9-12**. Click OK, and then click Print when all your options are checked and you are ready to print.

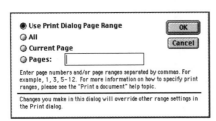

Figure 4-6: The Range dialog box in the Word section of the Print dialog box

Collating a document

Normally, when you print more than one copy of a document, Word prints all copies of Page 1, followed by all copies of Page 2, followed by all copies of Page 3, and so on. The Collate Copies option tells Word to print all the pages of your document once, before it goes on to the next set. This is a true time-saver. To have Word collate as it prints, simply check the Collate Copies box in the Microsoft Word section of the Print dialog box.

Printing odd or even pages

By default, Word prints all the pages in the page range you specify, whether it's the full document, one range, or a series of ranges. You can easily tell Word to print only the odd pages within that range, or only the even pages. You might want to do this for two-sided printing, first print all the odd pages, turn the paper over (possibly reversing the order), and then feed it through printing the even pages. To do so, go to the Word section of the Print dialog box by clicking the General pop-up menu and selecting Microsoft Word. Then click the pop-up menu that reads All pages in range, and select Odd pages or Even pages. That's it! When you've selected all desired options, click Print.

Printing in reverse order

Should you find you want to have Word print your last page first and work forward, rather than beginning with Page 1, you can — easily. In the Word section of the Print

dialog box, click Word Options. This brings up the Print tab of the Preferences dialog (shown in Figure 4-7). By the way, you can also arrive at this tab from Edit ⇨
Preferences. Just click the checkbox next to Reverse print order. While you're there,
select any other printing options, click OK, and then proceed to click Print whenever you're ready.

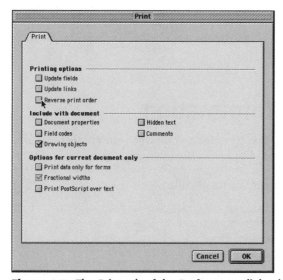

Figure 4-7: The Print tab of the Preferences dialog box

This option is helpful with laser printers that are based on the first-generation Canon
engine (such as the original Hewlett-Packard LaserJet or an Apple LaserWriter where
the paper feeds straight through). You will also find this option very handy with many
inkjet printers, such as the Epson 740. The design of such printers causes printed
pages to come out face up, so a multiple-page document would be stacked with the
last page on top (which is usually not where you want it). The Reverse Print Order
option requests that the printed document end up in the proper order.

Note that Printing options checked in the Preferences dialog box stay with the document and are in effect next time you print (unless you deselect them). In fact, this
option becomes effective for all new documents you create as long as it's checked.

Printing documents containing links

By default, Word updates any links within your document every time the document
is opened. However, a Preference option provides an extra safety to ensure that your
links update before printing. The Update links checkbox is located under the Print
tab of the Preferences dialog box, shown in Figure 4-7. (Select Edit ⇨ Preferences and
click the Print tab, or click Word Options in the Microsoft Word section of the Print
dialog box.) To turn it on, simply check Update links. Once checked, this option is
effective for your current document and all new documents unless you deselect it.

Printing documents containing fields

Fields are placeholders that contain information that is melded into your document in text form. By default, Word updates all fields within your document every time the document is opened. Just to be on the safe side, you can set a preference to ensure fields update before printing. From your document, go to Edit ➪ Preferences, select the Print tab, and then check the option called Update fields. If you are in the Print dialog box, select Microsoft Word from the pop-up menu, and then click the Word Options button to access the same Print preferences tab. As this is a preference, it is effective for your current document and all new documents unless you deselect it.

Printing Document Information

When you go to the Print dialog box, by default you print your current document. However, you can select Microsoft Word from the main pop-up menu, and then use the Print pop-up list to specify what you'd like to print (see Figure 4-8). (This is the pop-up menu that lists the document as its default.)

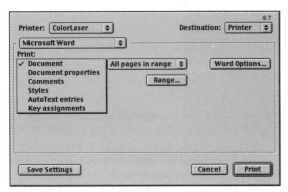

Figure 4-8: The Print choices provided by the Print dialog box

You can print information pertaining to your document, or the comments, styles, or AutoText entries related to your document. Specifically, you can print the following:

✦ **Document properties.** Reports all the information found under File ➪ Properties, including your document's name and location, the template from which it was created, the author's name, keywords and comments you've entered in the document summary, the creation date, last save information, and last date printed. It also includes the total editing time and gives you a page, word, and character count. (You can also set a preference in Word to always print the document properties whenever you print the document.)

✦ **Comments.** Prints the comments stored within the document. Comments are sorted by page number and report the initials of each author. (You can also set Word's preferences to always print the comments whenever you print the document.)

✦ **Styles.** Prints the style sheet for the document.

✦ **AutoText entries.** Prints the AutoText entries belonging to the template you are using.

✦ **Key assignments.** Prints the names and descriptions of macros along with the keys to which they are assigned.

Changing Your Printer

Changing your printer is part of your Mac's operating system, rather than a part of Word. If you are using the Desktop Printer feature, you should have an icon of your printer somewhere on your desktop. If you have several printers available, the printer currently selected should have a black border. To select another printer, simply click the icon of the desired printer and, in the Printing menu that appears, select Set Default Printer or press ⌘-L. (This printer now has the black border.) Alternatively, you can go to the Chooser (in your Apple menu) and click the desired printer.

After you change printers, it's a good idea to go to the File ⇨ Page Setup command. Open the dialog box, double-check your settings, and then click OK. This tells Word the parameters of your chosen printer.

Printing Ancillary Information with Your Document

You can also set Word's preferences to always print certain document information whenever you print the document. These options are found in the Print tab of the Preferences dialog box. You can get to this tab by selecting Edit ⇨ Preferences and clicking the Print tab, or, from the Print dialog box, by clicking Word Options. Remember that these are preferences. Once checked, these preferences are effective for your current document and all new documents you create unless you deselect them.

Use the Include with document options to specify which information should be included with the printed document. If you turn on Document properties, the document properties (as in File ⇨ Properties) sheet is printed along with the document. Turn on Field Codes to print field codes instead of the results of the fields. If you turn on Annotations, Word prints the document and any annotation comments added to the document. Turn on Hidden Text to print the document and any text that you hid with the Hidden option from the Character dialog box. Click the Drawing Objects checkbox to print the drawing objects you may have included in your document.

Printing Envelopes

Word has an envelope-printing feature that makes printing envelopes simple, if your printer can handle envelopes. If you have already created your document, select the addressee's name and address. Then choose Tools ➪ Envelopes to open the Envelope dialog box (see Figure 4-9).

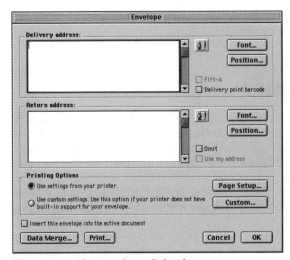

Figure 4-9: The Envelope dialog box

You have two text boxes to use for the delivery and return addresses. If you've selected the addressee's name and address, Word automatically places them in the Delivery address text box. In the Return address area, Word enters the name and address stored under the User Info tab of the Preferences dialog box. (The name is automatically taken from your Mac if you entered it during Mac setup. The address must be hand-entered via the Preferences dialog box.) Both addresses can be hand-edited within these text boxes. You can also manually adjust the positioning of these addresses via the Position buttons and set the character-level formatting options (font, style, size, and so on) by pressing the Font buttons. For the addressee, you also have the option of inserting either the Facing Identification Mark (FIM-A) or POSTNET barcodes.

If you use the Office 2001 Address Book, you can also select a delivery address or return address from the Address Book pop-up menu button to the left of each text box.

Tip If you use Word's Address Book feature, rather than typing an address each time you create a letter, you can select Tools ➪ Envelopes, select a delivery address from the Address Book pop-up menu beside the Delivery address text box, and then click the Add to Document button. This places the selected address into your document for you.

Once your address information is complete, you may want to check or change the kind of envelope on which you are printing. Select the Use settings from your printer radio button and click Page Setup, or select the Use custom settings radio button and click the Custom button to open the Custom Page Options dialog box shown in Figure 4-10.

Figure 4-10: The Custom Page Options dialog box

The Custom Page Options dialog box contains an Envelope size pop-up menu that enables you to change the kind of envelope on which you are printing. It also enables you to control the way envelopes are printed (see Figure 4-10). First, select Face up or Face down. Next, select the icon that represents the way your envelopes feed into your printer. Check or uncheck the Clockwise rotation option to help specify in which direction the text will print.

The Position buttons let you specify the positioning of the delivery and return addresses on your envelope via the Address Position dialog box, as shown in Figure 4-11. All positioning is relative to the top and left edges of the envelope. You can either type the desired values into the text boxes or you can click the little arrows to increase or decrease the values displayed.

If You Have Problems Printing

If your Mac has problems printing, a dialog box should come up and tell you what is wrong. Follow the instructions to solve the problem. You have some basic details to check, such as whether your printer is turned on (don't laugh), and (if you have more than one printer) making sure the right printer is selected. If you are using the Desktop Printer feature, you can easily see which printer is selected as your print destination. (The icon of the printer currently selected to print has a black border.) If the desired printer is already selected, the icon may provide clues about the problem.

For example, if a stop-sign-styled icon with a hand in the middle appears, you have told the printer to stop printing. Simply select Start Print Queue from the Printing menu. If an alert (exclamation point) symbol appears, double-click the printer's icon to open the Print Monitor dialog box and read the messages in this dialog box for clues. If the message says a printer can't be found, check that the cables connecting your Mac to the printer are all firmly connected as are any network connections.

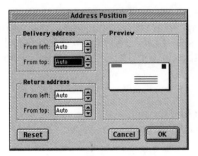

Figure 4-11: The Address Position dialog box

After you have made all the necessary formatting changes, click the Print button in the Envelope dialog box. This calls up your Mac's Print dialog box. Select the appropriate paper tray and then click Print to print your envelope.

Summary

In this chapter, you learned how to examine the appearance of documents before you print them and how to print the documents in Word. The following points were covered:

✦ Choosing File ➪ Print Preview provides a useful way to see what a document looks like before it is printed.

✦ Using Print Preview helps you make changes to margins and indents as well as to move images around in your document.

✦ Using the Microsoft Word view in the Print dialog box, you can print portions of the document, and you can print other items (such as document properties, style sheets, comments, styles, and macro assignments).

✦ Using the Envelope dialog box lets you create and format envelopes by using either the addresses in your document or in your Address Book. Additionally, you can use the Address Book and Envelope dialog box to insert addresses into your documents.

Where to go next

✦ In the next chapter, you learn how to work with tables and outlines in Word.

✦ Macros enable you to automate the printing of documents that you print regularly. Chapter 9 gives you the lowdown on macros.

✦ The appearance of your printed document depends on how your document is formatted. Chapter 3 teaches you how to format your documents.

✦   ✦   ✦

Working with Tables and Outlines

Tables are an excellent way to organize document content and display items grouped by category, and Word makes tables easy to create and highly flexible.

Outlines are another important organizational aid. For many people who work with words, creating an outline is the first step to putting their thoughts on paper. If you've been working with a program less powerful than Word in the past, you may be accustomed to creating outlines by means of tabs and manually numbered headings. Word's automatic outlining enables you to number headings automatically and create tables of contents automatically based on outline headings.

Understanding Tables in Word 2001

A table is any grouping of information arranged in rows and columns, as illustrated in Figure 5-1. Tables have one or more columns and one or more rows. Each box in a table where information can be entered called a cell of the table. If you are familiar with computer spreadsheets, such as Excel, you should easily understand the concept of a cell.

Detective	Book Title	Author
Elvis Cole	Sunset Express	Robert Crais
Phillip Marlowe	The Big Sleep	Raymond Chandler
Sam Spade	The Maltese Falcon	Dashiell Hammett

Figure 5-1: A sample table

CHAPTER

5

◆ ◆ ◆ ◆

In This Chapter

Understanding tables in Word 2001

Creating, editing, and formatting tables

Exploring other uses for tables

Understanding outlines in Word

Changing outline headings

Creating your own outline

Creating tables of contents from outlines

Printing outlines

◆ ◆ ◆ ◆

Before Word's Table feature came along, users typically set up tables using tabs or indented paragraphs. Although this method works if you have a lot of patience, it is cumbersome and awkward. A table set up with tabs gets tricky and becomes ineffi- cient when any cell in the table contains more than one line of text. At that point, any change you make to the table's text also throws off the alignment of the tabs, so you constantly have to add and delete tabs to line up the information in columns. Manually creating a table is more trouble than it is worth.

In comparison, Word's Table feature creates a group of cells that expands as needed to fit all your required text or graphics. The only limit to the size of your table is that a single cell cannot be larger than a page. You can resize columns and cells, you can add rows, columns, and cells, and you can merge cells — that is, combine multiple adjacent cells into a single cell. Word also provides useful commands that make life easier when you need to edit the tables, such as setting a cell's height and width or inserting/deleting cells in the middle of the table. All in all, Word's Table feature is the best way for you to create a table.

By default, a table appears with gridlines surrounding the cells. If you do not see the gridlines surrounding the tables you create, choose Table ➪ Gridlines to turn on the gridlines. Gridlines do not print in your document; they are simply an aid for you to see the boundaries of each cell in a table. You can also add borders (which do appear when printed) to cells or to an entire table (see "Formatting Tables" later in the chapter).

Creating Tables

You have several ways to add a table in Word 2001. You can click and drag, use a dialog box, custom draw a table, or type in a table. Before you begin any table, it helps to place your cursor where you want the table to appear in your document.

To add a table via click-and-drag, place your cursor in the document where you want the table. Then click the Insert Table button on the Standard toolbar and drag down in the pictorial submenu that appears. Drag across until you reach the number of columns you want, and then click your choice. The submenu seems to show a maxi- mum of five columns, but if you drag past that, the submenu grows to accommodate you. Then drag down to define the number of rows, and then click your choice. Don't worry about the number of rows increasing later. You can enter a minimum number of rows, such as two, because your table grows automatically when you get to the last cell in the last row and press Tab. It's even easy to add more rows (or columns) between existing rows (or columns) later.

As stated previously, you can add a table by using a dialog box. To do so, place the cursor where you want the table to appear. Then choose Table ➪ Insert Table, which brings up the Insert Table dialog box shown in Figure 5-2. In the Number of columns text box, enter the desired number of columns for the table. Word proposes 2, but you can enter any value up to 31. If you are not sure how many columns you need, don't worry. You can add columns at any time.

Figure 5-2: The Insert Table dialog box

In the Number of rows text box, enter the desired number of rows for the table. If you are not sure how many rows you need, enter a minimum number of rows, such as two. It's easy to add more rows later. Actually, your table grows automatically when you get to the last cell in the last row and press the Tab key. You can also add rows between existing rows.

In the Column width text box, you can leave the setting at Auto, which is the default, or enter a decimal measurement for the width of the columns. If you use Auto, Word makes all columns an equal width. Later on in this chapter, we discuss how to set different column widths. To add a table via the Insert Table dialog box, follow these steps:

1. Place the insertion point in the document where you want the table placed.

2. Choose Table ⇨ Insert Table or, if the Tables and Borders toolbar is present, click the Insert Table button.

3. Enter the number of columns desired in the Number of columns text box, and enter the number of rows desired in the Number of rows text box.

4. Enter the desired column width in the text box next to the Initial column width radio button (or accept the Auto default). As alternatives, you can select the AutoFit to Contents or AutoFit to Window radio buttons, in which case the text box will be disabled and sizing will be automatic. AutoFit to Contents results in columns that are very narrow until one of their cells contains data. AutoFit to Window results in columns that are a proportional fraction of the space between your page margins.

5. If you want to add borders or other formatting, click the AutoFormat button. In the Table AutoFormat dialog box, you can choose from a wide range of effects. (This is discussed under the "Formatting Tables" section later in this chapter.) You can apply predefined lines, borders, and shading to different sections of the table.

6. When you are finished making your selections, click OK to add the table at the insertion point location. The insertion point automatically waits in the first cell so you can begin typing the desired data.

The Insert Table buttons and dialog box create uniform tables — each row has the same number of columns, each column has the same number of rows, and all rows and columns are equal in their height and width. After you create the table, you can select any two or more cells in a row or column and use the Table ➪ Merge Cells command to create one cell that overlaps the selected columns or rows. (For more information, see the "Merging Cells" section.)

The most flexible way to create a table is by custom drawing it yourself, using Word's intuitive Draw Table feature. Using this method, you can immediately create nonuniform tables without first creating the table and then merging cells.

To create a table using Draw Table, click the Tables and Borders button on the Standard toolbar, which looks like a table (fittingly enough), or choose Table ➪ Draw Table. The mouse pointer then becomes a pencil. Click and drag to draw the outer sides of the table. Next, create the cells within the table by drawing horizontal and vertical lines where desired. Lines do not have to be the full width or length of the table. You can draw a line between individual rows or columns. Again, if you are not sure how many cells you will need, you can always add cells and columns to the table as needed by drawing additional lines or by tabbing at the end to create new rows. If you find after you have drawn the table that you need to remove some of the cells or lines, press and hold the Shift key to turn the pencil into an eraser, and then drag the eraser over the lines that you want to delete. If you use the Draw Table feature, you will not see the Insert Table dialog box shown earlier in Figure 5-2.

Finally, you can take advantage of Word's AutoFormat feature to type in a table. When you type plus sign (+) followed by a hyphen (-) or hyphens and another plus sign, Word creates a table. AutoFormat converts each plus sign to a column border and determines the width of the columns between plus signs by the number of hyphens you type. For example, three plus signs with at least one hyphen between each plus sign translates to two columns. This method provides a one-row table. As with any table in Word, a new row is automatically created when you reach the last cell and press Tab.

New Feature

New in Word 2001 is the ability to *nest* tables. This means that you can now place a table inside a single cell of another table. Nesting tables is a very common method of positioning elements on a Web page, because HTML doesn't allow for such things as tab stops. This material is covered in more detail in Chapter 11.

Navigating within a table

To move forward from cell to cell in the table, press the Tab key; to move in reverse, press Shift-Tab. If you reach the end of a table and press Tab, you add a new row to the table and move into the new row. The arrow keys also move the insertion point around within the table. In addition, the arrow keys move into and out of a table. You can also use the mouse to click in any cell and place the insertion point in that cell. For a complete summary of the keys used for navigation in tables, see Table 5-1.

Table 5-1 Navigation Keys to Use Within Tables	
Key	**Purpose**
Tab	Moves the cursor to the next cell in the table. If the cursor is in the last cell in the table, the Tab key adds a new row and moves the cursor to the first cell of the new row.
Shift-Tab	Moves the cursor to the preceding cell.
Control-Home	Moves the cursor to the first cell in a row.
Control-End	Moves the cursor to the last cell in a row.
Control-PgUp	Moves the cursor to the top cell in a column.
Control-PgDn	Moves the cursor to the bottom cell in a column.
Option-Clear	Selects the entire table.
Shift	Activates the eraser if you used the Draw Table feature, so you can use the eraser to erase unwanted lines.
Arrow keys	Moves the cursor within the text in a cell and between cells. If the insertion point is at the edge of a table, you can use the arrow keys to move in or out of the table.

Navigating inside a table with the mouse works in the same way as navigating in regular text: you point and click in the location where you want to place the insertion point. However, you need to know some additional mouse techniques beyond the obvious ones. Tables provide special selection areas for mouse use. At the left edge of each cell is a selection bar, an area where the mouse pointer changes to an arrow pointing upward and to the right. If you click inside the left edge of a cell while the pointer is shaped like this arrow, you will select the entire cell. You can also double-click in any cell's selection bar to select the entire row of the table, or you can click and drag across cell boundaries to select a group of cells. You will also see the right-pointing arrow cursor when positioned in the margin just to the left of the table. Clicking in the margin when the pointer is so shaped will also select the entire row.

At the top of a table is a column-selection area. If you place the mouse pointer above the border at the top of the table, the pointer changes to the shape of a downward-pointing arrow, which indicates the column-selection mode. If you click while the pointer is shaped like the downward-pointing arrow, you select the entire column below the pointer.

How Can I Type a Tab?

Because you use the Tab key to move around within a table, you can't use the Tab key to enter a Tab character. In some ways, this is good, because tabs inside tables are dangerous. In the first place, you don't often have much horizontal space in the cells to play with.

In the second place, the tabs may mess up the overall formatting for your table. Nevertheless, if you must have a tab character inside a table, you can add one by pressing Option-Tab.

Within a single cell, you can use the same keys that you use to navigate in any Word document. Table 5-1 summarizes the keys that you use to navigate within a table.

As stated previously, if you press Tab while the insertion point is in the last cell of a table, a new row is automatically added, and Word places the insertion point in the first cell of the new row. You can also add new rows by choosing Table ⇨ Insert ⇨ Rows Below, but it is generally easier to add new rows as needed by using the Tab key if they are to be appended to the table.

Creating your own table

To practice setting up a table, entering information, and revising a table, follow along with this next exercise. You can also create your own table with your own data if you want. Follow these steps to create a sample table:

1. Begin a new document by clicking the New button on the Standard toolbar (or typing ⌘-N or choosing File ⇨ New). Type the following phrase:

   `Food arrangements for Herb's visit with us`

2. Press Return to begin a new paragraph.

3. Click the Insert Table button and drag across four columns and down six rows. (You can also use the Draw table method to frame your table, and then add the rows and columns. Or, choose Table ⇨ Insert ⇨ Table and enter **4** in the Number of columns text box and **6** for the number of rows, and then click OK.) The insertion point is in the first cell.

4. Enter the information shown in Figure 5-3. Use the Tab key to advance to each new cell. (Do not press Return or Enter to advance to a new cell—doing so simply creates new paragraphs within the same cell.)

Day	Who	What	Where
Monday	David & Orly	Salads	Orly's Home Cooking Kitchen
Tuesday	Shira & Elysa	Veggies	Mimi's
Wednesday	Donna	Indian	The Curry House by the Sea
Thursday	Rosalie & Herb	Sushi	To be determined.
Friday	Yekutiel & Tani	Pizza	Nagila

Figure 5-3: A sample table containing luncheon arrangements

Notice that as you enter the information shown in the table, the text in the right-most column will often be too long to fit on a single line. When this happens, the cell expands in height automatically. This example illustrates one advantage of Word's Table feature, as stated previously: You do not need to calculate the space you need between rows of a table because Word does this automatically. You can enter as little or as much text as you want in a cell (up to the limit of one page in size).

5. After you have finished entering the information in Step 4, move your cursor into the cell containing the text "To be determined." Press End to get to the end of the existing line of text, and then press Return to begin a new paragraph. Type the following text:

```
(They are looking into a central location.)
```

Notice how Word expands the table downward to accommodate all the necessary information (see Figure 5-4).

Day	Who	What	Where
Monday	David & Orly	Salads	Orly's Home Cooking Kitchen
Tuesday	Shira & Elysa	Veggies	Mimi's
Wednesday	Donna	Indian	The Curry House by the Sea
Thursday	Rosalie & Herb	Sushi	To be determined. (They are looking into a central location.)
Friday	Yekutiel & Tani	Pizza	Nagila

Figure 5-4: Word expands the table to accommodate more information.

Remember that you can insert graphics into the cells of a table. To do so, use the cut-and-paste technique for graphic images detailed in Chapter 10, choose Insert ⇨ Picture, or use drag-and-drop to put them in place.

Cells Can Contain Mucho Texto . . .

As you type within a cell, your text wraps automatically, expanding the height of the cell. This feature alone is useful, but there's more. You can also have more than a single paragraph of text within a cell. In other words, at any time, you can press Return to create a new paragraph and keep right on typing.

Longtime users of Word have often taken advantage of this design trait to create side-by-side columns of unequal size, although newer versions of Word (such as yours) offer specific commands for handling multiple-column documents. You can also format every paragraph in a table just like paragraphs that are not in cells of a table; you can assign your paragraphs indentation settings, alignments, line spacing, and the like.

Editing Tables

After you have created a table, you can add or delete columns and rows, merge the information from more than one cell, and split your table into more than one part. This section looks at how to do all these things.

Before you can edit a table, however, you must know how to select the cells in a table. To select cells in a table, use the same selection methods you use in regular text. Briefly, you can click and drag across text in one or more cells with the mouse, or you can hold down the Shift key while you use the arrow keys. You can also use any of the Option or Control key combinations shown in Table 5-1 in combination with the Shift key. While selecting, as you move the insertion point past the end of text in a particular cell, text in the adjacent cell is selected. If no text is in a cell, the entire cell is selected as you move through it while dragging.

To select an entire column most efficiently, move your cursor just above the table, close to the top of the column to be selected. The cursor becomes a downward-pointing arrow. While the cursor is an arrow, click to select the entire column. This action tells Word that you're specifying columns, not just cells that are next to each other. Therefore, Word provides you with column commands rather than generic cell commands.

To select an entire row most efficiently, move your cursor just to the left of the table, close to the side of the column to be selected, until the cursor becomes a right-pointing arrow. While the cursor is an arrow, click to select the entire row. If you want to select several rows, keep the mouse pressed as you drag up or down to select those rows, too. This tells Word that you're specifying rows, not just cells that are above each other. Therefore, Word provides you with row commands rather than generic cell commands.

Inserting and deleting columns or rows

You can add columns at any time. Select the column or columns as an entire column or columns in the manner described in the previous section — move your mouse to the top of the column until the cursor becomes a downward-pointing arrow. To select one entire column, click above the row. To select more than one column, drag over those columns. Then choose Table ⇨ Insert ⇨ Columns to the Left or Table ⇨ Insert ⇨ Columns to the Right, or click the Insert Columns button on the Standard toolbar to add the new columns in the desired location. (The Insert Table button changes to Insert Columns when a column is selected.) Using the button inserts the new column to the left of the selected column.

To delete an entire column, select it using the arrow pointer, and then select Table ⇨ Delete ⇨ Columns. The column or columns simply disappear, along with any contents.

New rows are added automatically when you get to the last cell in the last row and press the Tab key. You can also insert new rows between existing rows. Choose Table ⇨ Insert ⇨ Rows Above or Table ⇨ Insert ⇨ Rows Below as you wish. The Insert Table button on the Standard toolbar changes to Insert Rows when a row is selected. The new rows are inserted above any row selected when you click the button. If one row was selected, one new row is added. If two rows were selected, two are added, and so on.

To delete an entire row, first select it as a row when the cursor becomes the arrow pointer. Then choose Table ⇨ Delete ⇨ Rows. The rows are removed, along with the data in them.

Inserting and deleting cells

You don't have to add entire rows or columns at a time. You can click in a single cell or select just a few cells in a row or column, and then insert new or delete cells or columns, shifting the already existing ones right or down on an insert, left or up on a deletion.

To add cells, first select the cell(s) you want to add new cells next to, and then choose Table ⇨ Insert ⇨ Cells or click the Insert Cells button on the Standard toolbar. (When a cell is selected, the Insert Table button changes to Insert Cells.) The Insert Cells dialog box, shown in Figure 5-5, asks whether you want to insert an entire row of cells or whether you want only the selected cells to shift after you add them to the table. The dialog box preselects the option Word anticipates you'll want. For example, if you select two cells next to each other, Shift Cells Down is the default option. If you click OK, two new cells land above the selected ones, pushing the selected cells down. The rest of the cells in the row remain in place.

Figure 5-5: The Insert Cells dialog box

When you need to remove rows, columns, or cells from a table, first select the cells that you want to delete. Then choose Table ⇨ Delete ⇨ Cells. The Delete Cells dialog box (see Figure 5-6) lets you shift the cells left after deletion, shift the cells up after deletion, or delete entire rows or columns.

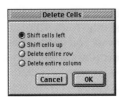

Figure 5-6: The Delete Cells dialog box

How the insertion or deletion of cells affects the table depends on what you delete or add, and whether you choose to shift the cells horizontally or vertically. As an example, Figure 5-7 shows a table measuring 5 rows by 2 columns: 10 cells.

FIRST	SECOND
THIRD	FOURTH
FIFTH	SIXTH
SEVENTH	EIGHTH
NINTH	TENTH

Figure 5-7: A 5 × 2 table

If you select a cell or a group of cells (third and fourth) and not the entire row, choose Table ⇨ Insert ⇨ Cells. Then choose Shift Cells Right in the dialog box, The new cell or group of cells is inserted at the selection location, and the existing cells move to the right, as shown in Figure 5-8.

FIRST	SECOND		
		THIRD	FOURTH
FIFTH	SIXTH		
SEVENTH	EIGHTH		
NINTH	TENTH		

Figure 5-8: The table from Figure 5-7 after choosing Shift Cells Right from the Insert Cells dialog box

If you select a cell or a group of cells (third and fourth) but not the entire row, choose Table ⇨ Insert ⇨ Cells. Then choose Shift Cells Down in the dialog box. The new cell, or group of cells, is inserted at the selection location, and the existing cells move down, as illustrated in Figure 5-9.

FIRST	SECOND
THIRD	FOURTH
FIFTH	SIXTH
SEVENTH	EIGHTH
NINTH	TENTH

Figure 5-9: The table from Figure 5-7 after choosing Shift Cells Down from the Insert Cells dialog box

If you select a cell or a group of cells (not the entire row) and choose Table ⇨ Delete ⇨ Cells, you again have the choice of choosing to shift the cells up or to the left. Figure 5-10 shows the example table if the fifth and seventh cells were selected and the Shift Cells Left option was chosen.

FIRST	SECOND
THIRD	FOURTH
SIXTH	
EIGHTH	
NINTH	TENTH

Figure 5-10: The table from Figure 5-7 after choosing Shift Cells Left from the Insert Cells dialog box

Tip

The quickest way to add one full row is to place your cursor in any cell in the row below where you want the new row to land. Then Control-click and select Insert Rows. You can also quickly delete an entire row by selecting the entire row, Control-clicking, and then selecting Delete rows. If you select less than an entire row, your only delete option is to delete cells, which brings up the Delete Cells dialog box. Remember that, to select a row, you click just to the left of the row (where you have a right-pointing arrow cursor).

Merging cells

Any number of adjacent cells in any one direction can be merged to become one larger cell. This is commonly done to create a header in which text is centered across an entire table. Occasionally, you may also want to merge information from one group of cells into one cell. You have a few ways to merge cells in Word 2001. As an example, consider the simple table shown in Figure 5-11.

Detective	Book Title	Author	Carries Gun?
Elvis Cole	Sunset Express	Robert Crais	Yes
Phillip Marlowe	The Big Sleep	Raymond Chandler	Yes
Sam Spade	The Maltese Falcon	Dashiell Hammett	Yes

Figure 5-11: A table before cells are merged

The traditional way to merge a group of horizontally adjacent cells into a single cell is to first select the cells you want to merge, and then choose Table ➪ Merge Cells. After you choose the command, the information merges into one cell. To achieve the same result, you can also press the Merge Cells button on the Tables and Borders toolbar.

If you were to select the two cells at the right end of the top row of the table and choose Table ➪ Merge Cells, the result would resemble that shown in Figure 5-12, where the adjoining cells are all merged into one cell. Note that any text in the cells is also merged into a single entry, as demonstrated in the figure.

Detective	Book Title	Author Carries Gun?	
Elvis Cole	Sunset Express	Robert Crais	Yes
Phillip Marlowe	The Big Sleep	Raymond Chandler	Yes
Sam Spade	The Maltese Falcon	Dashiell Hammett	Yes

Figure 5-12: The same table after cells are merged

The next, and perhaps easiest, way to merge cells is to select the cells you want to merge, and then Control-click and select Merge Cells from the shortcut menu.

The last way to merge cells is to use the eraser from the Tables and Borders toolbar. If it's not already showing, choose View ➪ Toolbars ➪ Tables and Borders. Then click the Eraser tool so your cursor becomes an eraser. Move the eraser over the line you want to remove and drag over that line. Close the Tables and Borders toolbar window to return to your regular cursor.

If you merge cells and don't like the result, you can undo the operation by immediately choosing Edit ➪ Undo (which will read Undo Merge Cells).

Splitting a table

If a table becomes too intricate or unwieldy, you can split it. When you choose Table ➪ Split Table, the table splits in two just above the insertion point, and Word inserts a paragraph marker between the two tables. Splitting the table makes the groups more visible. Splitting a table is also useful if you want to insert text between the rows of an existing table and you do not want the text to be a part of the table.

Formatting Tables

In Word, you can format the contents of your tables (usually text), and you can format the full table. You can apply formatting to the contents of tables the same way you apply formatting to characters or paragraphs. This means that you can change the text alignment within a cell, rotate the text, highlight the text or change its color, and even make the text in a table part of a numbered or bulleted list. Control-clicking a cell of text gives you an idea of some of the options available. (See Chapter 3 for more on character and paragraph formatting.) For example, if you want to apply bold character formatting to a portion of text in a table, you can select the text and click the Bold button in the Formatting palette, or press ⌘-B to apply the formatting. If you want the text to be vertical within the cell, Control-click and choose Text Direction from the shortcut menu.

If you want to format aspects of the actual table (as opposed to its contents), select Table ⇨ Table AutoFormat to open the Table AutoFormat dialog box (see Figure 5-13). This dialog box has a selection of various formats that you can apply to your table. Choose the format that you want to use, and select the areas to which you want to apply the format by clicking as many checkboxes as you want. The Preview box lets you see what the table will look like after the formatting is complete. When you finish making your selections, click OK to apply the formatting to the table.

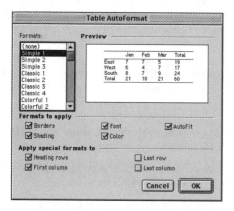

Figure 5-13: The Table AutoFormat dialog box

Setting column widths

Open the Table Cells pane on the Formatting palette (see Figure 5-14). In this pane, you can specify the width of one or more cells of the table. In the Height textbox, you can change the row height. To change the left indentation from and the alignment, use the Alignment and Spacing pane. You can also set the width of the columns in the Table Cells pane.

Figure 5-14: The Formatting palette with the Table Cells pane displayed

Another way to resize cells is to work visually. You can physically drag the gridline between cells or move the gray box on the ruler that corresponds to the gridlines. Move your pointer over the gridline of the desired row or column (or over the gray box on the ruler — you need to be in Page Layout view for the vertical ruler to be visible for row height changes in this manner) until the pointer changes into a two-sided arrow. Then click and drag to the desired height or width.

After you have adjusted the column width, all the columns to the right of the adjusted column are resized in proportion to their previous widths, but the overall width of the table is not changed. The following list contains your options for adjusting your current column:

✦ To adjust the current column and one column to the right, press the Shift key while you drag. The overall table width remains unchanged.

✦ To adjust the current column and make all columns to the right equal in width, press ⌘-Shift as you drag. The overall table width remains unchanged.

✦ To adjust the current column without changing the width of the other columns, hold down the Option and Shift keys while you drag. This changes the overall table width.

To see the actual width measurement on the ruler, add the Option key to any combination as you drag column widths.

Note   Occasionally, using the Draw Table feature to create your tables results in cells or columns that are not the same height. Or, you may find the default cell sizes too big for your needs. In these cases, you can take advantage of the Table ➪ AutoFit ➪ Distribute Rows Evenly or the Table ➪ AutoFit ➪ Distribute Columns Evenly commands. These options even out the sizes of the columns and the rows.

Adjusting the space between columns

You can adjust the default spacing between columns by choosing Table ➪ Table Properties and clicking the Table tab in the Table Properties dialog box, and then clicking the Options button to display the Table Options dialog box. In this dialog box, you can set the default margins Word will use with each cell (the defaults are 0 vertically and .08 inches on both the left and right). If you wish to specify different spacing for specific cells, go to the Cell tab and press its Options button to display the Cell Options dialog box, which is shown in Figure 5-15.

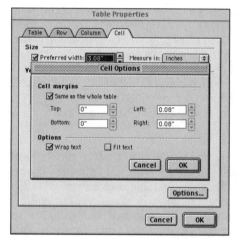

Figure 5-15: The Cell Options dialog box

Making row height adjustments

To set the height of a row, choose Table ➪ Table Properties, and then select the Row tab in the dialog box. Use the Previous Row and Next Row buttons to position yourself in the row whose height you wish to set and then check the Specify height checkbox. By default, this value is set to 0 with the pop-up showing At least. If you choose the At Least option from the Row height in the pop-up menu, Word makes the row at least as tall as the value you enter. If any text within a cell is larger than the minimum height, Word increases the height to accommodate the text. You can also choose the Exactly option from the pop-up menu, which causes Word to make the cell exactly the height that you enter in the box. Using the Exactly option, however, may cause text to be cut off.

Caution

This topic can be confusing if you haven't changed the height setting for the cells from Auto in the Formatting palette. The default dialog box setting is 0, but a Formatting palette setting of Auto will override a setting of 0.

Word 98 had an option to indent specific rows in the Row tab Cell Height and Width dialog box. This particular dialog box doesn't exist in Word 2001. To achieve the same effect, you must select the row or rows you wish to indent, move your cursor into the ruler to cover the hash mark denoting the left-most column's border so that the pointer changes to a box (the Screen Tip will say "Move Table Column"). Now, move in the desired direction to move the row(s) in question.

Aligning a table

To determine the alignment of a table with respect to the page margins, choose from among the Left, Center, or Right options in the Alignment area of the Table tab (Table ⇨ Table Properties). These options are comparable to the ones found in the Paragraph dialog box for text. As with paragraphs, you can left-align, center, or right-align rows horizontally on a page. In fact, you can select the entire table and then use the Alignment buttons on the Formatting palette, as you do with text. By default, the selected table is left-aligned, which causes the left edge of the table to align with the left margin (assuming you have not specified an indentation). Choose Center to center the table or choose Right to align the right edge of the table with the right page margin.

Note   For the Alignment options to have any visible effect, your table must be smaller than the width of the page margins. If you used the default options in the Insert Table dialog box when you created the table, the table is already as wide as the page margins, and choosing an alignment option will have no visible effect. The alignment options are useful when you specify your own widths for the table columns rather than letting Word automatically size the table. They may also be handy after you change your document's margin or if you resize your table.

Remember that adjusting the Alignment options in the dialog box moves the horizontal position of the entire table, not the text within the cells. For example, if you choose the Center option from the Alignment area, Word centers the table within the page margins, but individual text within the cells is not centered. If you want to left-align, center, or right-align text within a cell, select the desired text and then use the alignment options of the Format ⇨ Paragraph command (or the alignment buttons on the Formatting palette). Similarly, if you wish to specify indentations and margins within your cells, use the Formatting palette or the Ruler, just as you would for a column of text.

If you don't select any text to which to apply the text alignment, the alignment you choose applies to the specific cell that contains the insertion point. To apply the alignment to the current table, select the table and then choose one of the alignment buttons on the Formatting palette.

Note   The Borders and Shading dialog box is also available via a button on the Table tab of the Table Properties dialog box.

Applying borders

You can use the various options within the Borders and Shading dialog box (see Figure 5-16) to place borders around a cell or a group of cells in the table. Select one or more cells and open this dialog box by choosing Format ⇨ Borders and Shading while the insertion point is in a table. The borders you create in this dialog box will be printed, unlike the table gridlines that are visible only on the screen. The borders that you specify are added directly on top of the table gridlines.

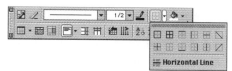

Figure 5-16: The Borders tab of the Borders and Shading dialog box

How Word applies the borders depends on the selections you make in the Borders and Shading dialog box. As with other options in this dialog box, Word applies borders and shading according to the cell or cells you select in the table. Be certain to select Table from the Apply To pop-up menu to apply the shading to the entire table. If Cell is selected, the effects will apply only to the selected cell(s) or to the cell in which the cursor resides. Finally, if Paragraph is selected, the border or shading will be around the paragraph or paragraphs selected, or the paragraph in which the cursor resides, thus nesting borders within the cell's boundaries.

From the Tables and Borders toolbar or the Borders and Shading pane of the Formatting palette, you can also select the Line Style drop-down menu. Doing so gives you a list of choices for line styles that you can use for the table you have created. After selecting the line style in the Tables and Borders toolbar (not in the Formatting palette), the cursor becomes a pencil. Simply draw on the line(s) you want to change the style of, and Word applies the style to the line(s). Press any key when done to revert the cursor and exit this mode. If you decide that you don't like a style after it has been applied, simply Undo (⌘-Z) and the style will be removed.

You can also use Table ⇨ Table AutoFormat to add borders and shading to a table. When you choose this command, Word provides a list of different formats for shading and borders you can use (see the "Formatting Tables" section earlier in this chapter). Simply select the format that you want in the Table AutoFormat dialog box and click OK.

Besides specifying the presence of a border, Word lets you select from among different types of borders. After you choose the desired pictorial button (Outline, Inside, Top, Bottom, Left, or Right, in addition to the two new diagonal line choices) in the Borders and Shading dialog box, you can select the style of borders you want and the width and color to be used for the border.

Converting text to tables

Word's tables certainly provide a lot of flexibility and make it easy to organize your information to look great. But what if you already started using tabs or spaces between columns to create the equivalent of a table? Rest easy. Word converts tab or space-created tables to a Word-formatted table with the Text to Table command (Table ➪ Convert ➪ Convert Text to Table). We recommend this type of conversion because it enables you to take advantage of Word's table formatting and editing features.

You can also use the Convert Text to Table feature to convert data that's been exported from databases in a comma-delimited or tab-delimited format. (See your database documentation for directions on creating comma-delimited or tab-delimited files.) Any text that is separated by either tabs, commas, or paragraph marks can be converted into a table.

To convert text into a table, first select the text and then choose Table ➪ Convert ➪ Convert Text to Table. When the Convert Text to Table dialog box appears, choose one of the following options as a separator of text: Paragraphs, Tabs, or Commas option (based on the text to be converted) from the Separate text area of the dialog box. You can also choose Other and specify a separator character (such as a hyphen). Then click OK. Word will recommend a number of columns and a number of rows. It will see each tab or comma as forming a new column and each paragraph marker as creating a new line. (You can change the recommendations by entering any desired value in the Number of columns text box.) To complete the conversion of the text to a table, click OK.

Note   Word computes the number of rows required from the number of columns you specify. Thus, the Number of rows text box is disabled and the value presented is for informational purposes only.

For example, consider the text shown in Figure 5-17. (You can easily duplicate this example by opening a new document, typing the text shown, pressing Tab once between columns, and pressing Return at the end of each line.)

Detective	Book Title	Author	Carries Gun?
Elvis Cole	Sunset Express	Robert Crais	Yes
Phillip Marlowe	The Big Sleep	Raymond Chandler	Yes
Sam Spade	The Maltese Falcon	Dashiell Hammett	Yes

Figure 5-17: Text separated by tabs can form the basis of a table.

To convert this text into a table, select all three rows of text and choose Table ➪ Convert ➪ Convert Text to Table. In the Convert Text to Table dialog box, accept

Word's suggestions for a table measuring four columns by three rows by clicking OK. The table shown in Figure 5-18 is the result of Word's efforts. (We've added borders to the table in the figure to make the table more easily readable.)

Detective	Book Title	Author	Carries Gun?
Elvis Cole	Sunset Express	Robert Crais	Yes
Phillip Marlowe	The Big Sleep	Raymond Chandler	Yes
Sam Spade	The Maltese Falcon	Dashiell Hammett	Yes

Figure 5-18: A newly created table based on the text in Figure 5-17

Tip

If the makeshift table you are converting contains more than one tab between any two columns in any row, remove the extra tabs. Removing extra tabs keeps everything in the proper columns. If you leave the extra tabs in place, empty cells will be included in the table.

Exploring Other Uses for Tables

You can do more with tables than just create them and enter text. You can use tables to lay out large amounts of textual data in the form of side-by-side paragraphs — for example, you can create a detailed résumé, with information about your place of employment in one paragraph and your job duties in the next one. You can also sort information stored in your tables. Finally, you can use tables to lay out your Web-page designs, because HTML does not support all the formatting that you will find in a word processor such as Word (see Chapter 11 for further discussion on the use of tables in designing Web pages).

Creating side-by-side paragraphs

Word's capability to store up to one page-length of text in any column of a table makes it easy to set up side-by-side paragraphs with the Table feature. (Side-by-side paragraphs are one way to create newspaper-style columns. You can create side-by-side paragraphs in other ways as well, and Chapter 10 provides additional details regarding this and other desktop-publishing topics.) To create side-by-side paragraphs, simply insert a table with two or more columns into your document and use the Table Properties dialog box to size the columns as desired. Remember that you visually set the column widths by clicking the gridlines and dragging them to the appropriate width. Then type as much text as you want in the columns, but keep in mind the rule that a table cannot extend beyond the length of a single page. The table will automatically display the paragraphs of text side-by-side onscreen. You can also add borders to differentiate the text.

Tip   If you are creating a legal pleading page, you'll find a two-column, one-row table useful on Page 1 to format the information about the parties.

Sorting information

Sometimes you may want to arrange a list of data (often within a table) in alphabetical or numerical order. You can use Word's Sort command for this task.

Note   Remember that the Sort command is by no means limited to tables. You can use the Sort command to sort any list of data, whether the information is in a table or in a simple list with paragraph marks separating the lines.

When Word sorts a list, it rearranges the list entries in alphabetical or numerical order. You can choose whether to sort in ascending or descending order or whether to sort by date, text, or number. Follow these steps to sort the data in a table:

1. Select the column, row, or items in the table that you want to sort.

2. Choose Table ➪ Sort. The Sort Text dialog box appears, as shown in Figure 5-19.

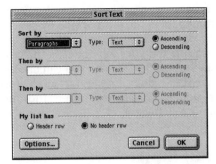

Figure 5-19: The Sort Text dialog box

3. If you have headings that you don't want sorted, click the Header row radio button in the My list has area of the dialog box.

4. In the Sort by area, make your selection for the column by which you want to sort.

5. In the Type pop-up menu of the Sort by area, choose the Text, Number, or Date option, and then click the Ascending or Descending radio button. To choose additional columns to sort by, repeat Steps 4 and 5.

6. Click OK to sort the data.

Understanding Outlines in Word

For many people who work with words, writing an outline is the first step to putting cohesive thoughts down on paper. Even with the earliest word processors, simple outlining was possible using tabs and manually typed headings. Word, however, offers automatic outlining and its significant advantages. In addition to aiding the organizing process, Word's outlining lets you number headings automatically and create a table of contents based on an outline. When you create an outline in Word, you can easily rearrange parts of the outline without worrying about precise formatting by just dragging a topic (or group of topics) from one place to another — Word will do the indenting and numbering for you.

With Word, the only difference between a normal document and an outline is the view you use to examine the document. When you are in Normal view, Online Layout view, or Page Layout view, you are looking at the document in its normal (nonoutline) form. When you turn on Outline view, however, you look at the document in the form of an outline. Figure 5-20 shows an example of a document in outline form (you will duplicate this document in a later exercise).

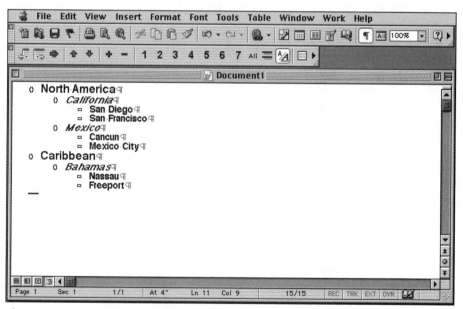

Figure 5-20: A sample document viewed in outline form

Outlines consist of headings and body text. A heading is any paragraph that has been assigned a heading paragraph style. Word provides these styles specifically for the creation of outlines. Eight predefined styles exist, from Heading 1 through Heading 8. The numbers define the importance of headings in an outline: A top-level heading is assigned the Heading 1 style, the next level heading is assigned the Heading 2 style, and so on. Word automatically places all top-level headings at the left margin by default, and each lower-level heading style is successively indented (placed farther to the right than the preceding heading level).

Body text is any text within an outline that hasn't been given a heading style. Word also uses the term subtext to refer to all headings and body text that appear below a particular heading.

Selecting text

When you are in Outline view, selecting text is the same as selecting text in other areas of Word—with one difference. You can select any heading or body text by clicking once in the margin to the left of it. Double-clicking selects not only the heading or subtext, but also all the subtext below it. Alternately, you can press Shift along with the arrow keys to select headings and their subtext.

Changing the structure of an outline

To work with a document in Outline view, choose View ➪ Outline or click the Outline view button at the bottom-left corner of the document window. In Outline view, small icons appear to the left of each paragraph, and character formatting such as bolding appears to differentiate headings levels and subtext. Additionally, the Outlining toolbar appears at the top of your window to help structure the outline. When you rest your mouse over a button, its function appears in a yellow pop-up box, so you don't have to memorize all the functions right away. Figure 5-21 shows the Outlining toolbar and its functions.

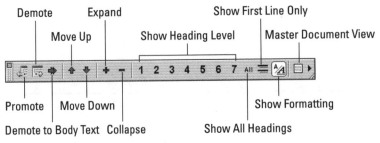

Figure 5-21: The Outlining toolbar

You can use Word's outlining features and benefits at any time. You can create a document and later come back and structure it in outline form, or you can create the document in outline form and then switch to Normal view. You can add additional portions of a document, whether headings or body text, at any time.

At any time, you can promote a paragraph to a higher level or demote it to a lower level of importance. You can also move any element up or down in the order of the document; you can even place it under another heading. Making such changes is simple. All you need to do is drag text from one place to another. (See the next section, "Changing Outline Headings.") In case you're not comfortable dragging, you can select the desired paragraph and click the appropriate button on the Outlining toolbar, or you can use keyboard equivalents. To get an idea of what you can do with outlines, see Table 5-2, which explains the function of the Outlining toolbar's buttons.

Table 5-2
The Outlining Toolbar Buttons and Their Functions

Button	Function
Promote	Promotes a paragraph to a higher level
Demote	Demotes a paragraph to a lower level
Demote to Body Text	Demotes a heading to body text
Move Up and Move Down	Moves a heading up or down to a new location in the outline
Expand	Expands all text after a heading (in other words, all text and subheadings after a heading are visible)
Collapse	Collapses a paragraph so only the heading shows
Show Heading	Controls how many levels of the outline are displayed
All	Expands or collapses the entire outline
Show First Line Only	When All is selected, shows just the first line of body text
Show Formatting	Shows or hides character formatting
Master Document View	Switches to Master Document view

Keyboard equivalents exist for every Outlining toolbar button. Table 5-3 summarizes these equivalents for you.

Table 5-3	
Keyboard Equivalents for the Outlining Toolbar	
Keyboard Combination	*Function*
Control-Shift-left arrow or Shift-Tab	Promotes a paragraph
Control-Shift-right arrow or Tab	Demotes a paragraph
Control-Shift-up arrow	Moves a paragraph up
Control-Shift-down arrow	Moves a paragraph down
Control-Shift-+ (plus sign)	Expands body text (so that body text is visible)
Control-Shift-– (minus sign)	Collapses body text (so that body text is temporarily invisible)
Control-Shift-1 *through* Control-Shift-9	Expands or collapses headings to specified levels (1 through 8), or to show body text (9); only levels 1 through 7 are on the Outlining toolbar by default
Control-Shift-L	When All is selected, shows just the first line of body text

Tip   You can tell Word to include keyboard shortcuts in the screen tips by choosing Tools ⇨ Customize and clicking the corresponding checkbox on the Appearance tab. Then, when you rest your mouse over any button, you not only learn what each button does but also see its keyboard equivalent.

Changing Outline Headings

You can drag, use the Promote and Demote buttons, or use keyboard equivalents to change heading levels, convert body text to headings, or convert headings to body text. To promote a heading level with the mouse, select the heading and drag the heading's icon to the left. Alternatively, select the heading and click the Promote button on the Outlining toolbar. To demote a heading level, select the heading and drag the heading's icon to the right or click the Demote button.

When you promote a heading, it is assigned the next highest heading level, and it moves farther to the left. The opposite happens when you demote a heading: it is assigned the next lower level, and it is indented farther to the right.

Converting body text

To demote a heading to body text, click the double-right arrow in the Outlining toolbar. The appearance of the selected text changes from a heading to regular body text.

You can convert body text to a heading simply by promoting the body text. Select the body text and click the Promote button. When promoted, the body text is converted to a heading that has the same level as the heading above it.

Expanding or collapsing outline headings

As an aid in organizing your thoughts, you can expand or collapse outline headings. As stated previously, when you expand a heading, all the subtext (lower-level headings and body text) below the heading is made visible. On the other hand, when you collapse a heading, all subtext below the heading is hidden from view. Figure 5-22 shows an outline with its body text collapsed; it then shows the same outline with its body text expanded.

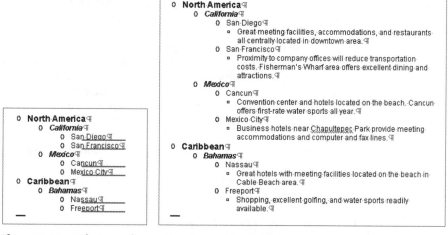

Figure 5-22: *Left:* An outline with collapsed body text
Right: The same outline with body text expanded

To expand or collapse a single heading, simply double-click the heading's symbol. If you prefer, you can also use the buttons. To expand a heading, select the desired heading and then click the Expand button on the Outlining toolbar. To collapse a heading, select the heading and then click the Collapse button.

To collapse or expand an entire outline, use the Show buttons on the Outlining toolbar. The numbered buttons correspond to the possible heading levels within an outline: clicking the 1 button causes level-one headings to be visible; clicking the 2 button causes all level-one and level-two headings to be visible; clicking the 3 button causes all heading levels of 1, 2, and 3 to be visible; and so on. Clicking the All button causes all headings and all body text in an outline to be visible.

Moving headings

Word provides considerable flexibility regarding the movement of headings and associated subtext. You can move headings around in an outline, you can move associated subtext with or without the headings, and you can move multiple headings and associated subtext by selecting more than one heading prior to the move operation.

To move a heading, first select it by moving your cursor to the left of the heading symbol (the hollow plus or minus sign) so your cursor becomes an arrow. When the arrow points to the heading's symbol, click to select that heading. After you have selected the heading you want to move, click the up or down arrow on the Outlining toolbar to move the heading up or down in the outline.

Note that if you select only a heading in an expanded outline (the subtext is visible), Word moves only the heading and leaves the subtext in its current position. If the heading is collapsed, however, any movement of the heading causes the associated subtext to be moved, even if only the heading is selected.

You can also drag headings to new locations. After selecting the heading, move your cursor over the selected text until it becomes an arrow. Then drag as you normally would to move text. It appears as if your selected heading will become part of the line to which you are dragging. The trick is to release the mouse when the dragged heading looks as if it will land between the first word and the symbol of the heading you are placing the dragged heading in front of.

Tip   You can also drag a heading and its subtext, even when showing, by dragging the heading's symbol. The cursor changes to a plus sign with arrowheads on all ends and clicking selects the heading and all subtext at the same time.

Applying numbering to outlines

You may want to apply numbering to the headings of an outline. You can manually number an outline by typing the numbers as you type the headings, but the drawback to this is evident as soon as you rearrange the outline and have to renumber the headings manually. The efficient way to do it is to take advantage of Word's Bullets and Numbering command to apply numbering or bullets to your outline headings. Click either the Numbering button or the Bullets button on the Formatting palette; call up the Bullets and Numbering dialog box by selecting Format ⇨ Bullets and Numbering; or Control-click in the outline and choose Bullets and Numbering from the contextual menu.

To number an outline or make a bulleted list from an outline using the buttons, perform these steps:

1. Select the paragraphs you want to number or apply bullets to. (To number or apply bullets to the entire document, select the entire document — Edit ⇨ Select All or ⌘-A.)

2. Click the Numbering button to apply numbers or the Bullets button to apply bullets. The buttons don't open the dialog box. Instead, they automatically apply whichever format was last selected in the dialog box. (To remove the numbers or bullets, click the button again. If you've deselected the text, select it again and then click.)

To number or bullet an outline with the dialog box, perform these steps:

1. Select the paragraphs you want to number. If you want to number the entire document, select the entire document by choosing Edit ➪ Select All or pressing ⌘-A.

2. Choose Format ➪ Bullets and Numbering or Control-click in the outline and select Bullets and Numbering to open the Bullets and Numbering dialog box.

3. Select the desired tab and effect. You can choose from among seven possible number formats, seven bullet formats, and seven outline numbering formats (not counting the None choices for each).

   If you want to customize the effect, select a choice other than None and click Customize. In the Number format area, type a number as an example for Word to follow. If you don't want the numbers to start with 1, enter a new starting number in the Start at box. You can also align the numbers and set an indent for them.

4. Click OK. Paragraph numbers or bullets appear beside each selected topic in your outline.

You can remove paragraph numbering from the outline at any time by opening the Bullets and Numbering dialog box again and clicking None as the format.

Creating Your Own Outline

To demonstrate the concepts you can use in building outlines, it's best to create an outline of your own on which to experiment. Follow along with this exercise to create an outline.

1. Use any method to create a new document (File ➪ New, ⌘-N, or the New document button).

2. Choose View ➪ Outline or click the Outline View button at the bottom-left corner of the window to switch to Outline view. (Do this now, before you enter the text. If you do it later, your outline will behave a bit differently. More on this soon.)

3. Choose File ➪ Save (⌘-S) to save the document with the name Sample Outline #1. (The sooner you save your document, the less you have to redo if you lose it. Continue saving as you work.)

4. To begin your outline, type the following text and press Return after each line:

```
North America
California
San Diego
San Francisco
Mexico
Cancun
Mexico City
Caribbean
Bahamas
Nassau
Freeport
```

Each of these words is automatically assigned a level-one heading. (If they are not, you didn't begin entering your text while in Outline view. In that case, see the Note that follows Step 6 in this list.)

5. Because California is to be a subheading under North America, you want to create a second level in your outline. Click in the California heading and then click the Demote button. (If any words under California move right along with it, you probably didn't begin entering your text while in Outline view. In that case, see the Note that follows Step 6 in this list.) Repeat this step for the Mexico and Bahamas headings.

6. Because San Diego and San Francisco are categories under California, there should be a third level in your outline. Select San Diego and San Francisco and click the Demote button twice to indent them one step further than California. Repeat this step for the Cancun, Mexico City, Nassau, and Freeport headings.

At this point, the structure of the sample outline is apparent. If you have been following the directions, your outline should resemble the example shown in Figure 5-23.

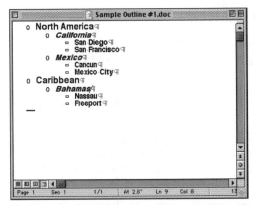

Figure 5-23: The structure of the sample outline

Note

If you enter the text while in Normal view, or decide to make an outline after beginning the document in Normal view, headings act differently when demoted or later promoted. All text may begin as Normal, so you need to begin by promoting the level one headings once to the left. Next, you need to demote the level two headings (California, Mexico, and Bahamas) once. (Look in the Style pop-up box on the Formatting toolbar to see the level of your heading.) As you demote the level two headings, notice that anything under it, up to the next level one heading, moves along with it. As you move a line, rather than that line moving alone, all lines under a line move with it. Lines following the current line are assumed to be part of the current heading, so they are indented below the current heading. Continue to demote or promote your headings until they look like the ones shown in Figures 5-23, 5-24, and 5-25.

Now you can begin adding body text to the various parts of the outline. Remember that Word's flexibility means that you do not necessarily have to create your outlines in this same manner. This example follows the common technique of creating outline headings first and then filling in the details; however, you can create headings and body text as you go along. To add some body text to the sample outline, perform these steps:

1. Move the cursor to the end of the San Diego line. Press Return to begin a new line. Note that the icon aligns with the existing level directly above it; hence, the new line is initially a heading. Before you begin typing, convert this new line to body text.

2. Click the Demote to Body Text button on the Outlining toolbar, and type the following text:

   ```
   Great meeting facilities, accommodations, and restaurants are
   all centrally located in downtown area.
   ```

3. Move the cursor to the end of the San Francisco line. Press Return to begin a new line, and click the Demote to Body Text button on the Outlining toolbar. Then type the following text:

   ```
   Proximity to company offices will reduce transportation
   costs. The Fisherman's Wharf area offers excellent dining and
   attractions.
   ```

4. Move the cursor to the end of the Cancun line. Press Return to begin a new line, and click the Demote to Body Text button on the Outlining toolbar. Then type the following text:

   ```
   Convention center and hotels are located on the beach. Cancun
   offers first-rate water sports all year.
   ```

5. Move the cursor to the end of the Mexico City line. Press Return to begin a new line, and click the Demote to Body Text button on the Outlining toolbar. Then type the following text:

   ```
   Business hotels near Chapultepec Park provide meeting
   accommodations and computer fax lines.
   ```

6. Move the cursor to the end of the Nassau line. Press Return to begin a new line, and click the Demote to Body Text button on the Outlining toolbar. Then type the following text:

```
Great hotels with meeting facilities are located on the beach
in the Cable Beach area.
```

7. Move the cursor to the end of the Freeport line. Press Return to begin a new line, and click the Demote to Body Text button on the Outlining toolbar. Then type the following text:

```
Shopping, excellent golfing, and water sports are readily
available.
```

At this point, your outline should resemble the one shown in Figure 5-24.

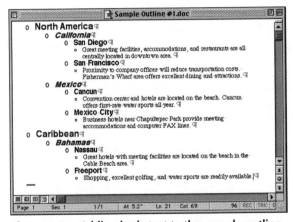

Figure 5-24: Adding body text to the sample outline

Collapsing and expanding the sample outline

As we mentioned earlier, it's often helpful to collapse an outline so you can see the major points without being distracted by the less important points or by the body text. The easiest way to collapse an entire outline is by using the numbered Show buttons on the Outlining toolbar or their keyboard equivalents.

To experiment with collapsing your own outline, open it. (Sample Outline #1, if you followed along.) Click the 1 button on the Outlining toolbar to show only level one headings in your outline. Only the North America and Caribbean lines should be visible. To show the next level of headings, click the 2 button. Now you should also be able to see the California, Mexico, and Bahamas lines. When you click the 3 button, the level three headings (the names of the cities) become visible beneath the level two headings. Finally, click the All button. The body text becomes visible along with all headings of the outline.

Of course, you can also individually expand or collapse headings using the Expand and Collapse buttons on the Outlining toolbar or by double-clicking any heading's symbol. To see how these buttons work, place the cursor anywhere in the Mexico heading, and click the Collapse button. Notice that the Cancun and Mexico City headings collapse underneath and hide the body text. If you click the Expand button, the subheadings expand to reveal the body text underneath. To see how double-clicking works, move your cursor directly over the heading's symbol, causing your cursor to become two crossed, double-headed arrows, and then just double-click. If your heading is expanded, it will collapse.

Changing headings in the sample outline

As stated previously, you can use the Promote and Demote buttons on the Outlining toolbar to promote and demote headings, or you can simply drag any outline part into a new position. Remember that body text for a heading is promoted or demoted along with the heading, but subheadings are not. To see how this concept works using the toolbar's buttons, click in the line of the San Francisco heading and click Promote. Notice that the San Francisco heading is promoted to the same level as the California and Mexico headings. Notice, too, that the text immediately below the San Francisco heading moved along with the heading. With the cursor still in the same line, click the Demote button to demote the heading and subtext back to its original level. Then demote the heading one level further to see the effect.

To try dragging, move your cursor directly over the heading's symbol, causing your cursor to become two crossed, double-headed arrows. Click and begin to drag your cursor left or right. A gray horizontal line appears to help you see how far in or out you are moving the heading. The cursor also changes to indicate the direction in which you are dragging. Stop anywhere you want. How far you go determines the level your dragged header will take on. Dragging has the same effect as using the buttons.

Use the Move Up and Move Down buttons (or their keyboard equivalents) to move headings up or down within an outline. Remember that if any subtext is collapsed, subtext moves with the heading. However, if subtext is not collapsed, then it moves with the heading only if you have selected it with the heading. To demonstrate this concept, click All to give yourself a fresh start and be sure all text is revealed. Then place the cursor in the Mexico City heading and click the Move Up button (Control-Shift-up arrow). The Mexico City heading moves up in the outline. The body text associated with the heading remains in its original location, however. While Mexico City is still the selected paragraph, click the Move Down button (Control-Shift-down arrow) to restore the heading to its proper location.

Next, select the Mexico City heading and the subtext underneath the heading. Click the Move Up button twice. This step moves the heading and its subtext above the Cancun heading and its subtext, as shown in Figure 5-25.

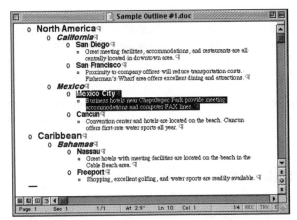

Figure 5-25: Moving the Mexico City heading and subtext

In most cases, you'll want the body text to move with the headings. To make this move easier, first collapse the outline to the level of the heading to be moved (use the numbered Show buttons or their keyboard equivalents). After you have collapsed the outline, you can move headings without worrying about selecting the subtext, because the subtext automatically follows the headings. (If you are using the dragging method to move your text, you don't have to collapse the headings because contents below the heading also move with it.)

It is also possible to promote body text to headline stature at any time.

Creating Tables of Contents from Outlines

The capability to generate a table of contents quickly based on the headings within an outline is a powerful Word feature. Use the Insert ➪ Index and Tables command to insert a table of contents at the location of the insertion point.

After your document exists in outline form, perform these steps to create a table of contents:

1. Place the insertion point where you want to insert the table of contents.

2. Choose Insert ➪ Index and Tables to open the Index and Tables dialog box.

3. Click the Table of Contents tab, and then choose the type of format you want for the table of contents from the Formats list box. The Preview box gives you an idea of how the format will look before you apply the style. Of course, Word provides many customization options. For more on Table of Contents options, see the "Building Tables of Contents" section in Chapter 7.

4. Click OK. Word inserts a table of contents at the insertion point.

It doesn't matter whether you are in Outline view when inserting a table of contents in this manner. All that matters is that your document contains headings. Because it is common to place a table of contents on a page separate from the main content, however, you probably want to switch to Normal view first. This way, you can add a page break above your document's main content, and position the cursor in the new blank page. (You will probably want to put a page break above the table of contents, too, so that you can include a title page to precede it.)

Adding a table of contents

You can see how easy it is to create a table of contents by trying creating one using the sample outline you created earlier. Perform the following steps to add a table of contents to the sample outline or to any existing outline:

1. Choose View ➪ Normal to turn off the Outline view. (In Normal or Page Layout view, you can add a page break to put the table of contents on the first page. You cannot add page breaks while in Outline view.) In previous versions, you could not insert page breaks in Outline view — this capability is present in Word 2001. However, the appearance is more awkward to work with when in Outline view.

2. Scroll to the top of your document (or press ⌘-Home). Press Return once to add a new line, and then press Shift-Enter (not Return) to insert a page break. (Alternatively, you can use Insert ➪ Break ➪ Page Break.) Place your cursor back to the start of the document again. (It appears on the page break's line.) Add the table of contents on what is now Page 1 of the document, with the remainder of the document appearing on Page 2.

3. Choose Insert ➪ Index and Tables, and click the Table of Contents tab.

4. Leave the default options set as they are for now, or select a style from the Formats list.

5. Click OK to have Word create your table of contents.

Because the entire outline is on Page 2, all topics of the outline are shown in the table of contents as being on Page 2. If your sample document was longer, Word would assign the proper page numbers automatically.

Updating a table of contents

Tables of contents (TOC) are not updated automatically. If changing your document's content changes page numbers, you must tell it to update itself. To do so, select the table of contents, issue the Update Fields command (press F9), and tell Word to update the TOC. (The table of contents is based on fields, which is why you're using the Update Fields command.) For more information on fields, see Chapter 6. Word can do a lot more when it comes to tables of contents and indexes. See Chapter 7 for additional details on updating Tables of Contents and indexes.

To update a table of contents, follow these steps:

1. Move your cursor the left of the document so that the cursor turns into an up and right-pointing arrow, like the one that normally selects a line. Point the arrow cursor toward the first line of the table of contents and then click to select the entire TOC.

2. Press F9. This brings up the Update Table of Contents dialog box.

3. Select either Update page numbers only or Update entire table. Then click OK.

Tip You can also tell Word to update the table of contents in the Print dialog box by choosing Microsoft Word from the Print dialog box's unlabeled pop-up menu, clicking the Word Options button, and checking the Update fields checkbox. This can be made an automatic operation by checking this box on the Print tab of your Preferences dialog box.

Printing Outlines

Although you print outlines the same way that you print any other document, remember that what you get as printed output varies, depending on what view you are using when you print. Just as the document looks different onscreen in the various views, the document also prints differently in the different views. If you are in Outline view, the document prints much like it appears onscreen in Outline view. The only items that don't appear on the printed copy are the outline icons. Word uses whatever tabs are in effect for the document to indent the headings and body text.

If you are not in Outline view, Word prints the document somewhat differently. Heading styles are still printed, but all text is printed at the left margin, without any indentation. In short, it prints as it looks onscreen.

Summary

This chapter covered topics related to tables and outlines. Specifically, you learned about the following:

✦ Creating tables using Word's Table feature

✦ Editing the contents of a table and deleting, inserting, and merging cells

✦ Using the tools needed to add borders, control table alignment, and sort table contents

✦ Converting text to a table

✦ Using the Outlining toolbar

✦ Promoting, demoting, and moving headings in an outline

✦ Creating a table of contents from your outline

Where to go next

✦ The next chapter teaches you to work with fields and form letters in Word.

✦ Tables are a routine part of documents that demand a desktop-published appearance. For more tips and techniques on performing desktop-publishing tasks, see Chapter 10.

✦ Tables are an essential feature in laying out attractive Web pages For more tips and techniques on performing Web-design tasks, see Chapter 11.

✦ If you regularly use outlining in complex documents, remember that you can quickly create tables of contents based on your outline. For details on using an outline to create a table of contents, see Chapter 7.

✦   ✦   ✦

Working with Fields

This chapter covers topics related to working with fields — special codes that can be inserted in documents to perform various tasks, such as creating index entries. In this chapter you learn some of the common uses for fields when working in Word and how to create form letters to be used in a Data Merge.

Defining Fields

In Word, a field is a special set of instructions that tells Word to insert certain information at a given location in a document. The basic difference between fields and normal text is that with fields, the computer provides the specific information for you — for example, you may simply ask for the current date to be inserted at a point in your document, and the computer provides the particular month, day, and year. You already may have used fields at various times in your work with Word. For example, when you insert page numbers in a document, you are inserting a certain kind of field. When you create a table of contents, as discussed in Chapter 5, you are also creating fields. Think of fields as special codes that you include in documents. The codes tell Word to insert information at the location where the code appears. The codes can automatically update the text of your document, or you can tell Word to update the information produced by the fields only when you specify. Typically, you use fields to add text or graphics to a document, to update information that changes on a regular basis, and to perform calculations.

Word has dozens of types of fields. Some, like page numbers and the current date, are simple to understand and use. Others are more complex and are beyond the scope of this book. But all fields can be inserted into a document and updated using the same procedures, and this chapter details those actions.

You can effectively work with fields after you learn four skills: how to insert fields in a document, how to update fields so they show the most current results, how to view fields, and how to move between fields.

Using fields

A field consists of three parts: field characters, a field type, and instructions. It is not necessary to know about these components because they are compiled for you when you use the Insert ⇨ Field command or place a field in a document using, for example, Insert Date. In case you are curious, here's an explanation. Consider the following example date field:

```
{Date\@M/d/yy}
```

The field characters are the curly braces that enclose the field. The curly braces indicate the presence of a field in Word to the user. Inside the curly braces, you find the special code or instruction that tells Word what is to appear in this area. Although curly braces are used to indicate the presence of a field, you cannot insert a field in a document by typing curly braces. If you are manually entering your field, you must use the key combination (⌘-F9) specifically designed to insert fields to create the braces and position the cursor for your input. (If you use Insert ⇨ Field to choose a field function, the brackets are automatically placed, along with all the field coding.)

The field type is the first word that appears after the left field character. In the preceding example, the word "date" is the field type; this particular field type tells Word to insert the current date — based on your computer's clock — into the document.

The instructions follow the field type. Instructions are optional, depending on the field type, but most field types have instructions. The instructions tell Word exactly how the information specified by the field type will be displayed. In this example, \@M/d/yy is an instruction that tells Word to display the current date in the American numeric format with the month, day, and last two digits of the year separated by slashes. The contents of the instructions may appear somewhat cryptic, but you need not be concerned with what they mean because Word inserts the proper instructions for you automatically.

Inserting fields

Many commands in Word insert fields indirectly. When you insert page numbers or a table of contents, for example, you are inserting fields to produce the page numbers or the table of contents. But when you specifically want to insert fields into a document, you use Insert ⇨ Field. Follow these steps to use the Field command to insert a field into your document:

1. After placing the insertion point where you want to insert the field, choose Insert ⇨ Field. The Field dialog box appears, as shown in Figure 6-1.

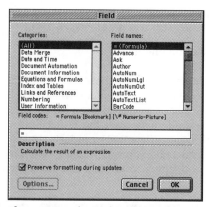

Figure 6-1: The Field dialog box

2. From the Categories list box, select the category for the type of field you want to insert. The All category enables you to see all the fields in alphabetical order in the Field Names list box.

3. From the Field Names list box, select the field you want to insert. The Field codes text box at the bottom of the dialog box displays the field you have selected. (You can also use this text box to enter the name of the desired field; however, it's generally easier to pick the field by name from the Field Names list box.)

4. Click the Options button if you want to add switches to the field. (Switches are options that change the characteristics of a field's results, such as the way a date appears, displaying characters as uppercase, or converting numbers to Roman numerals.) The Field Options dialog box is shown in Figure 6-2. To add switches or formatting, select the desired formatting from the list, and then click the Add to Field button. If you change your mind and decide to remove the formatting or switches, click the Undo Add button.

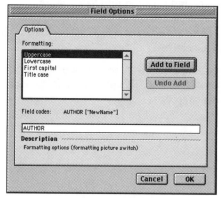

Figure 6-2: The Field Options dialog box

In the Field dialog box, check the Preserve Formatting During Updates option so any formatting you apply to the resulting text won't be lost during updates.

5. Click OK to insert the field into the document.

Tip

Word also provides an Insert Field shortcut key combination (⌘-F9). This shortcut inserts the field characters (curly braces) into the document, which enables you to type the field name and instructions manually. This method for entering fields is typically used by programmers who are familiar with the Visual Basic programming language built into Word and other Office 2001 products. Unless you are familiar with field types and their instructions, you will probably find it much easier to add fields using Insert ⇨ Field and letting Word build your fields for you.

More About Switches

Switches are not an easy topic to tackle. However, this list is provided in case you are interested:

✦ Switches determine the data to be inserted into your field, the order of the data, and even what the data look like. Two kinds of field switches exist. Field-specific switches set certain options for a given field, such as \l for the hyperlink field, and other switches affect formatting. The switches you are most likely to deal with are the ones that affect formatting. These formatting switches serve to enforce the formatting during field updates.

✦ You can tell Word what to put in a switch. Use the Options button from within the Field dialog box when you first insert your field. While you are in the Insert ⇨ Field dialog box, choose your category as normal, and then choose the specific field from the Field Names list. Then click the Options button. Depending upon the field you chose, you will see either a lone Options tab for formatting options in the Field Options dialog box or a pair of tabs: General Switches and Field Specific Switches. When the switches tabs appear, select the General Switches tab for a display of a list of options specific to the category you've chosen. These options are mostly formatting options. Select the format you want and click the Add to Field button. The other tab, Field Specific Switches, offers more options. For each tab, a description appears, telling you about the switch you are considering. When you click OK, the field comes into your document in the form you've selected.

✦ After your field appears in your document, you can manually type another switch to tell Word how to format the results of the field. This procedure is covered in the "Formatting fields" section later in this chapter.

Viewing field codes

When you insert a field, by default you see the results of that field. For example, when you insert a date field, you see the current date. When you are editing documents, however, you may find it useful to see the actual contents of the fields rather than the results. Here's how to see one field's contents, instead of its results:

1. Place the cursor in the field and Control-click to display a shortcut menu.

2. Choose Toggle Field Codes to display the codes for the field. Perform the same steps if you want to turn off the codes again.

If you prefer the keyboard, you can place the insertion pointer anywhere in the desired field and press Shift-F9 to toggle between showing the codes and showing the results.

If you want to see the codes for all fields, choose Tools ⇨ Preferences, click the View tab, check Field codes, and click OK. With this option turned on, the default for all fields inserted with the Insert ⇨ Field command is to see the code immediately, rather than the results.

If you are working with a large document that contains a number of fields, you may find it helpful to split the document into two panes. You can then scroll so the same text shows in both panes, and you can turn on Field codes in one pane while viewing the resulting text in the other. Place your cursor in one pane, and then click Option-F9. If you prefer, you can go to the View tab of Tools ⇨ Preferences and check the Field Codes checkbox, but this may affect both panes identically unless you select all the text (⌘-A) in one pane first. (Note that although Control-clicking while in a field also reveals a Toggle Field Codes command, this command has a different effect than the one suggested in this paragraph. This command affects both panels, toggling each panel from whatever state each was in just as does pressing Shift-F9.)

Updating fields

You can update fields by selecting the text containing the field, Control-clicking the text, and choosing Update Field from the shortcut menu that appears. Some fields, such as those used in page numbering, are automatically updated whenever you print or repaginate a document. Other fields, such as in tables of contents, are not updated until you tell Word to update the fields.

To update fields in the entire document, select the entire document (⌘-A) and Control-click anywhere in the document. Choose Update Field from the shortcut menu that appears.

It is important to realize that when you update a field, it can lose any formatting you apply. To help prevent this, check the Preserve Formatting During Updates option when you insert your fields via the Field dialog box.

Moving between fields

To move to the next field, just click the field you want to move to. If you prefer keyboard commands, use F11 to move to the next field and Shift-F11 to move to a previous field.

Formatting fields

You have two ways to format fields. You can either insert the field and then apply font and paragraph formatting, or set the code of the field to format the field results automatically. As stated previously, the latter method is called adding switches to the field codes.

To format the field if the code is showing, first Control-click the field and choose Toggle Field Codes to display the results. That way you can see your formatting more clearly. Then Control-click the field and choose the desired formatting option from the shortcut menu. (Choose Font to format the fonts used, or choose Paragraph to apply paragraph formatting.)

If you're brave, format the field by manually typing switches: display the code for the field and then manually type the command into the code. Your switch options change certain characteristics of the field results, such as displaying characters as uppercase or converting numbers to Roman numerals. For example, a simple DATE field looks like this:

```
{DATE}
```

However, a field with the DATE code and a switch that tells Word how to display the date looks like this:

```
{DATE\@d-M-yy}
```

Table 6-1 lists some of the general switches and their functions. Be aware that not all switches apply to all fields or field types.

Table 6-1
Commonly Used Switches and Their Functions

Switch	Function
* caps	Capitalizes the initial letter of each word in the result.
* alphabetic	Lists numbers by using lower-case letters.
* ALPHABETIC	Lists numbers by using all capitals.
* firstcap	Capitalizes the initial letter of the first word in the result.
* lower	Makes all letters in the result appear as lowercase.
* upper	Makes all letters in the result appear as uppercase.
* Arabic	Converts a number to Arabic (standard) format, overriding any default set elsewhere in your Mac control panels.
* DollarText	Spells out a number with two decimal places as words with initial capital letters for the numbers that precede and follow the decimal places (suitable for producing checks with currency amounts spelled out).
* roman	Converts a number to lowercase Roman numerals.
* Roman	Converts a number to uppercase Roman numerals.
\@ dddd,MMMM,d,yyyy	Displays a date as spelled out, such as Monday, November 20, 2000.
* mergeformat	Preserves manual formatting in the fields, such as character and paragraph formatting in text, and scaling and cropping dimensions in graphics.
* charformat	Applies the formatting on the first character of the field name to the entire field result.

Locking a field's contents

At times, you may want to prevent the results of a field from being updated. You can lock a field to prevent it from being updated until you unlock it. To lock a field, place the cursor anywhere in the desired field and press ⌘-F11. To unlock the field, place the cursor anywhere in the field and press Shift-⌘-F11.

Note Locking a field does not prevent you from making formatting changes to the field or even deleting the field. This merely prevents the field from being updated until you unlock it.

Using fields in an example

To see how fields can be used within a document, open a new document in the usual manner and perform the following steps:

1. Choose Insert ➪ Field to display the Field dialog box. In the Categories list, select Date and Time. Then click Date in the Field Names list and click OK. The current date, as measured by your Mac's clock, appears at the insertion point. (If you see the actual field type and instructions for the field instead of the current date, choose Tools ➪ Preferences, click the View tab, turn off the Field Codes option, and then click OK.)

2. Press Return twice and type the following words:

    This document was written by

    Add a space after *by*, and then select Insert ➪ Field. In the Categories list of the Field dialog box, choose Document Information. In the Field Names list box, choose Author and then click OK to insert the author's name into the document.

    Word automatically fills in the name that was entered when Word was first installed and launched. This name can be changed in the User Info tab of Word's Preferences (found under the Edit menu).

3. Add a period after the author's name, and then start a new sentence by typing the following:

    The document contains

    Add a space after contains, and then choose Insert ➪ Field. In the Categories list box, choose Document Information. In the Field Names list box, scroll and choose NumWords (an abbreviation for number of words), and then click OK.

4. Add a space after the number that was just inserted, and finish the sentence by typing the following text:

    words, and the time of day is now

5. Add a space after now and choose Insert ➪ Field. In the Insert Categories list, choose Date and Time. In the Field Names list box, choose Time and click OK to place the field.

6. Add a period after the time that was just inserted.

At this point, your document should resemble the one shown in Figure 6-3. Of course, the date and time will be different, the word count may differ, and you may have a different font in use. If you have interactive grammar-checking, you will probably have a green squiggly line beneath the first sentence. This line indicates that Word has a suggestion for better wording of the sentence. If so, you can resolve that issue when you do your spelling and grammar check.

Printing Field Codes

When you print a document containing fields, Word prints the results of the fields by default and does not print the actual field codes themselves. At times, you may want to print the actual field codes so you can get a concrete idea of what codes are used in your documents.

The printing of field codes is a preference set in the Print tab of the Preferences dialog box within Word (Edit ⇨ Preferences). If you are already in the Print dialog box, you can set Word to print the field codes by selecting Microsoft Word from the pop-up menu in the Print dialog box, and then clicking the Word Options button and checking Field Codes.

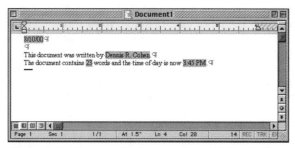

Figure 6-3: The sample document containing fields

Notice that the word count is accurate only to the point that the field for the number of words was inserted. It has not updated to include words added after that field. To update the word count without closing the document, click anywhere on the word count field to select it, and then Control-click and select the Update Field command. Doing so changes the number in this example to 23.

Creating a Data Merge

One way to take advantage of fields in your documents is to use them in data merges to create personalized form letters, mailing labels, legal documents, data sheets, catalogs, and other documents. Data merges let you print multiple copies of a document, where certain information (such as a name or address) changes for each document. Direct-mail letters that you receive are examples of data merges at work.

Data merges combine two kinds of documents: a main document, which contains identical text for each printed copy, and a data source, which contains the text specific to each copy printed. The main document also contains fields that tell Word where to find the information stored in the data source. These fields are referred to as merge fields. As you type the main document, you can insert the fields at any desired location.

In the data source, you type the information Word needs to fill in the fields inserted in the main document. For example, if your main document contains a name field and an address field, your data document should have names and addresses of all the people who should receive the letter. Just like a table in which the first row typically contains labels describing what information follows, the first line of a data document normally contains a header record, a single line that identifies the order in which you place the data in the data document. When you use a table as your data source, the first row becomes your header. When you use a database as your data source, field names become your header.

If you aren't dealing with a ton of names, you can create a data source by typing the desired information into a Word document. This is best done by setting up a table. (You can actually use any word processing document and separate each piece of merge data by a tab or a comma, with a return at the end of each contact; however, that's more confusing to read and takes more time to set up from scratch.) If you are managing a lot of names or contacts, you will find it easier in the long run to use a database (such as FileMaker Pro, ACI US 4th Dimension, or Provue Panorama) or Office's Address Book. You can also store and manage your information in database form within spreadsheet programs. In the section "Creating a data source" later in this chapter, you'll learn how to create a data source by using data stored in an Excel spreadsheet or in a database.

How to finish your data merge

After the data source and main document both exist, you can print multiple copies of the main document, based on the data contained in the data source. When you print the file, Word reads the first record in the data source, inserts the fields of that record into the main document, and sends the information to your printer to print a copy. It repeats this process for as many records as are contained in the data source. If a data source has five entries that each contain the name and address for one of five individuals, a data merge operation would print five copies of the document, each addressed to a different individual.

Specifying a main document

The first step in the process of creating a form letter is to choose your main document. This may be a new blank document, or it may be an existing one, such as letterhead, complete with text and graphics. To choose the main document, perform the following steps:

1. For this exercise, open a new document. Then choose Tools ➪ Data Merge Manager to activate the Data Merge Manager palette shown in Figure 6-4. (The option will be grayed out if you don't have a document open.) The figure displays all of the panes visible. Most will be closed when the palette first appears.

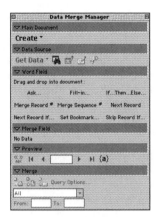

Figure 6-4: The Data Merge Manager palette

2. Select Form Letters from the pop-up Create button. Word will then convert the front-most document to a form letter.

Creating a data source

Now that you have created your main document (the document that will be your actual form letter), you need to designate the source from which you will get the data to be used in the form letter's fields. In this case, you will create one from scratch.

Follow these steps to create a data source:

1. Select New Data Source from the Get Data pop-up button. This activates the Create Data Source dialog box shown in Figure 6-5. This dialog box aids you in the creation of the fields you are going to use in your form letter. The Field Names in Header Row box lists commonly used fields for form letters.

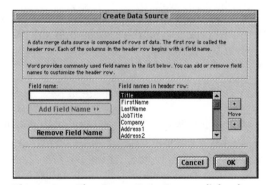

Figure 6-5: The Create Data Source dialog box

2. In the Field Names in Header Row box is a list of all the fields Word includes by default. One by one, highlight the names of the fields you do not need, and then click the Remove Field Name button. If you need a field that is not included in the list, type the name in the Field Name text box (field names cannot contain spaces or punctuation) and click the Add Field Name button, which activates after you enter a name. When the Field Names in Header Row list contain all the fields from which you want to merge data, click OK. The Save As dialog box opens. Enter a name for your data source (note the location where you're saving it) and save it.

3. Word then displays a message telling you that your data source has no data. Click the Edit Data Source button in the Data Merge Manager palette to open a data source into which you can enter information for your data merge. If you have no information for one of the fields, press Return (or Enter) to skip it. Don't enter any spaces in the boxes. (They will print and drive you crazy.) To record the completed information and add a new record, click the Add New button. Repeat this procedure until you have entered all the information needed in your data source, and then click the OK button.

4. Now that you have created your data source, return to your main document by clicking OK.

5. If you later decide that you want to add information to your data source, click the Edit Data Source button on the Data Merge Manager palette (or press Control-Shift-E). Your merge form must be the front-most (active) document when you do this. You go directly to the Data Form you used to enter information in your data source. You can click the Add New button to add a new record.

Adding merge fields to the main document

After you finish creating a data document or opening the one you want to use, you can finish the main document.

First, you can add any text or graphics you want to complete your document. Then you add the fields by inserting a merge field where you want each category of information to appear in printed form. You can format the information any way you want using the Formatting palette. When the information is placed in the main document, it takes on the formatting you applied.

To add merge fields to your main document, follow these steps:

1. Enter the graphics and text that you want in each version of the form letter.

2. Place your cursor where you want the first field to appear. Then drag the merge field you want from the Merge Field pane of the Data Merge Manager palette (see Figure 6-6) to your merge document, dropping it where you wish it to appear. Be sure to add any spaces and punctuation that you want to include between merge fields (for example, a comma and space between a

city name and a state name). You can move your cursor freely and perform any other document creation as you add the merge fields. (You must use the Merge Field panel because a merge field cannot be typed directly into a document.)

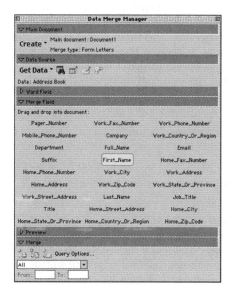

Figure 6-6: The Data Merge Manager with the Office Address Book chosen as the Data source.

3. Save the main document to complete your work.

Merging data

Now it's time to merge the data with the main document. Before continuing, be sure you have done the following:

✦ Entered all the information into the data document

✦ Inserted all the merge fields into the main document

You can use the Data Merge Manager to see the form letter onscreen, enabling you to make sure the records contain everything you want to have in the form letter. Click the View Merged Data button in the Data Merge Manager's Preview pane to see the result of merging the first record. You can scan more records using the forward and reverse arrows in the Preview pane—First record, Previous record, Next record, and Last record. The record number you are viewing appears in the box between them. You can also enter any record number in the box and press Return or Enter to go directly to that record. The final button lets you toggle whether you view the field codes or merged data in your merge document. You can also print the example document by using the Print One button in the Standard toolbar or choosing File ➪ Print (⌘-P).

As you perform your inspection, you can make any changes to your document. When you have completed your inspection, you can print each letter using the Data Merge Manager's Merge to Printer button (Control-Shift-M) in the Merge pane, the left-most button.

Follow these steps to merge the data document with the main document:

1. Make sure the main document is active, and then click the View Merged Data button on the Mail Merge Manager's Preview pane. The information from the first data record appears in the main document. Click the Next Record button on the Mail Merge toolbar to see the information inserted from the next record(s). To see the printed result of one sample page, tell Word to print (File ➪ Print or ⌘-P) as normal. Only the record you are viewing prints.

2. Merge the data document into the main document by doing one of the following:

   • To print the form letters, click the Merge to Printer button (Control-Shift-M). Then select any print options and print as normal.

   • You also have the option of creating a new single document that contains one copy of each document, complete with the merged data. This may be desirable as a historic record of your mailing. You can also use this document to reprint the same document at a later date. To create this historic merged document, click the Merge to New Document button (Control-Shift-N) on the Mail Merge Manager's Merge pane (the second button).

   • New in Word 2001 is the ability to merge the data to e-mail (no, Microsoft did not provide a keyboard shortcut for this one). Click the Merge to E-Mail button (the third button in the Merge pane) to present the Mail Recipient dialog box shown in Figure 6-7. The To: pop-up menu comes preset to an e-mail address or to a field that has e-mail as part of its name, if such a field exists in the data source, but you can also choose any field from the data source as being the source for the e-mail address. Provide a subject for the e-mail in the Subject text box and select to send the data as either the e-mail message body, or as an attachment. When you're ready, click the Data Merge to Outbox button.

Figure 6-7: The Mail Recipient dialog box

Note   You may also perform filtering and sorting operations on the merged data. These options are discussed later under "Printing Mailing Labels."

Printing Envelopes and Mailing Labels

You can also print mailing labels and envelopes using the Data Merge Manager. You can either create a new data document or use an existing one. This feature can prove invaluable: it prevents you from having to address many envelopes by hand.

Printing envelopes

You have two ways to create an envelope merge or label merge. The steps in the first method for printing envelopes and mailing labels are similar to the steps used to create a form letter. Follow these steps for printing envelopes:

1. Set up the main document; in this case, the one representing the face of the envelope. Note that Word uses the information from the currently selected printer. If you want to print on a different printer, go to the Chooser or select a new default Desktop Printer before continuing.

2. Choose Tools ⇨ Data Merge Manager and select Envelopes from the Create pop-up button.

3. In the Envelope dialog box that appears, follow the formatting steps described in Chapter 4's section on printing envelopes for any information that won't change, such as the return address, and set the Page Setup parameters. Click OK.

4. Your main document window will now appear, probably reduced in size to fit on your screen, with a dotted outline around the delivery address area and instructions to drag fields to that box or type text, as shown in Figure 6-8.

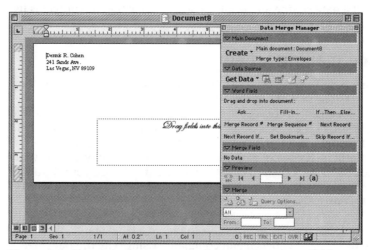

Figure 6-8: The main document window awaiting merge fields

5. For the Data Source, you'll likely want to get existing data if you already printed letters. To do so, choose Open Data Source from the Get Data pop-up button, find your way to your data source, and then click OK. (If your document doesn't show in the Open window, select All Documents from the pop-up menu beside Show.) Then click the Set Up Main Document button.

Your other option is to choose Create Data Source from the Get Data menu. Cull the Field Names in Header Row list box down to only the fields you want merged, and then click OK. Next, name and save the file, and then enter the data and click OK. You now are back in your document window and may drag fields to your document.

6. The envelope is now displayed in Page Layout view. Click the View Merged Data button in the Data Merge Manager's Preview pane to verify that data is in the correct place, if you wish. Make any changes as needed. Finally, click the Merge to Printer button and print as normal.

After your perform all the steps, your printer should turn out one envelope after another.

The other method draws upon the techniques described in Chapter 4, within the section called "Printing Envelopes." Proceed as follows:

1. Create a new document (use the New Document button, File ➪ New, or ⌘-N).

2. Choose Tools ➪ Envelopes. Set your envelope size in the Printing Options area, set the font and positioning for the delivery and return addresses, and, if it is constant, enter the return address in the Return address text box.

3. Click the Data Merge button. You are now in your document and ready to select a data source and print, as described within the previous list during Steps 4 and 5.

Printing mailing labels

You can also use Word to print mailing labels. If you have used the Merge command in earlier versions of Word or the Mail Merge command in Word 98, you can reuse your main document. If this is the first time you are printing labels, or you want to change the size of the labels, select Tools ➪ Labels and set up a new main document. A document is automatically set up for most Avery brand labels, as well as numerous others. If you need to use another brand, specify an Avery label of the same size or specify a custom label. Remember to choose your destination printer (in the Chooser or with the Desktop Printer) before you begin so Word can set up the margins correctly.

As with envelopes, you have two ways to create a label merge. We discuss only the one using the Tools ➪ Labels menu command. Using only the Data Merge Manager is exactly analogous to creating envelopes in that manner. To create mailing labels, perform the following steps:

1. Start a new document, and then choose Tools ➪ Labels.

2. Set the font for the address. Then select the Label type by pressing the Options button if the default label type is not the one you wish, and setting your choices in the Label Options dialog box (shown in Figure 6-9) as described in Step 3.

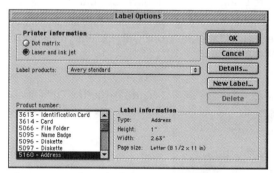

Figure 6-9: The Label Options dialog box

3. Change your printer type from Laser and ink jet to Dot matrix if necessary. In the Label products pop-up menu, select a label type. In the Product number list box, select the product number for the labels you are printing to. (Most label packages have such a designated number code.) The Details button shows you the exact specifications of the label you've selected. You can make alterations to your label layout, seeing the effect as you make the change, and then give it a custom name. The New Label button lets you set up your own custom label size. Press OK in the Label Options dialog and the Data Merge button in the Labels dialog. Word 2001 now displays your document in Page Layout view.

4. In the Data Merge Manager, move down to the Data Source area and click the Get Data pop-up button. In this step you have five options:

- *New Data Source* enables you to create your own data document, as explained previously in the "Creating a Data Merge" section. In the Create Data Source dialog box, remove and add fields as described earlier in "Creating a Data Source."

- *Open Data Source* enables you to locate, select, and open an existing data file via the Open dialog box. This will be the option we assume for the further discussion.

- *Use Office Address Book* enables you to use the Office 2001 Address Book, maintained as a part of Entourage (see Chapter 35 for a discussion of Entourage and the Office Address Book).

- *FileMaker Pro* lets you use FileMaker Pro databases. FileMaker Pro is the leading Macintosh database application. If you're interested in more information about FileMaker Pro, Steven Schwartz's book, *The Macworld FileMaker Pro 5 Bible* (from IDG Books Worldwide), is an excellent reference.

• *Header Options* is for those who use several data sources. Word's built-in help explains the header options under the heading "About using a header source for a mail merge." In the Header Source submenu, you can choose either New Header Source to create a header or Open Header Source to select an already-existing file for use. If you're managing a lot of data, chances are you're using a database. Because your database export can include a header, it's just as well to use that method instead.

5. When you select an existing data file, Word will present you with the Edit Labels dialog box, shown in Figure 6-10.

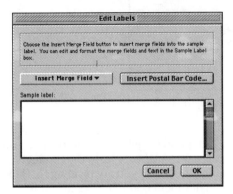

Figure 6-10: The Edit Labels dialog box; this is where you'll lay out your labels

6. Click the Insert Merge Field pop-up menu to select fields to add to the Sample Label area at the current cursor position. You can add text, spacing, and punctuation to format the label. If you click the Insert Postal Bar Code button, you'll be presented with the Insert Postal Bar Code dialog box requesting that you select the field containing the Zip code and the field containing the street address. Word will position the bar code along the top of the label.

7. Click OK when you have the fields laid out as you wish. You're now returned to your Word document in Page Layout view.

8. To print one label for each address in the data file, leave All chosen in the Merge pane's drop-down list. Otherwise, designate a range to print.

9. You can set filtering and sorting options by clicking the Query Options button. The Query Options dialog box has two tabs: Filter Records and Sort Records, as shown in Figure 6-11. Filtering enables you to set up to six levels of comparisons, eliminating records that do not meet your criteria. Sorting enables you to sort your data up to three levels deep.

10. Now, you're ready to perform your merge. Click the type of merge you desire: Merge to Printer (Control-Shift-M), Merge to New Document (Control-Shift-N), or Merge to E-Mail.

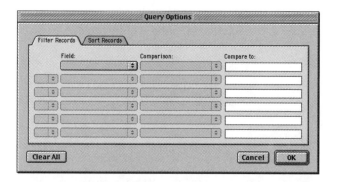

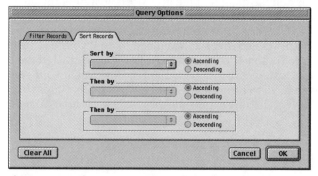

Figure 6-11: The Query Options dialog box: Filtering on top, Sorting on the bottom

Creating Data Documents with Other Software

So far in this chapter, you've sometimes used data documents that were created by typing the data directly into a Word table or the Office Address Book. However, there's a good chance your company or personal contacts are already stored in another software package, such as in a spreadsheet or database. (PIMs, also called Personal Information Managers, such as Palm Organizer, Now Contact, or Symantec's ACT are actually databases. They count here, too.) If this is the case, it's very easy to export your information from there. Every good database or spreadsheet has an export function. The most basic export formats are tab-delimited and comma-delimited. (See your spreadsheet or database manager documentation for details on how to create a tab- or comma-delimited file. There should be an Export command under the File menu. From there you should be able to select a format and determine which fields to export.) FileMaker Pro, the leading database management program on the Macintosh, is so common that direct support for its files as data sources is provided with Microsoft Office.

Tab- or comma-delimited exports result in a simple text file where each chunk of information (field) is separated by a tab or a comma (see Figure 6-12). A paragraph mark is placed between each contact to tell the importing software where to begin a new record/page/envelope/label. Sometimes quotation marks are placed around each field. Word does not need quotation marks, but the software has no problem with them.

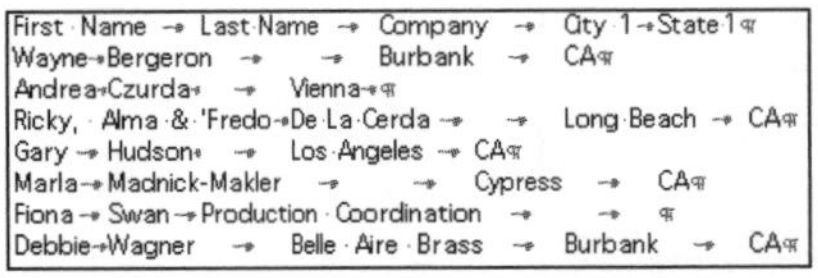

```
First Name → Last Name → Company → City 1 → State 1¶
Wayne → Bergeron → → Burbank → CA¶
Andrea → Czurda → → Vienna → ¶
Ricky, Alma & 'Fredo → De La Cerda → → Long Beach → CA¶
Gary → Hudson → → Los Angeles → CA¶
Marla → Madnick-Makler → → Cypress → CA¶
Fiona → Swan → Production Coordination → → ¶
Debbie → Wagner → Belle Aire Brass → Burbank → CA¶
```

Figure 6-12: A tab-delimited exported file, complete with headers

To bring a tab-delimited or comma-delimited file into Word, just drag the file onto Word's icon, and the file coverts automatically. Then select the text as it appears in Word and use the Convert Text to Table command under the Table menu to turn the newly imported text into a table. That's all you need to do if your end result is a table. If your end result is to be a merged document, after you've created the table, you can merge it as demonstrated earlier in this chapter. However, if your goal is a mail merge, you don't even have to turn the text into a Word table. Simply begin your merge process and select the raw export file as your data source from the Data Merge Manager.

Copying Excel data

You can easily use any data you have stored in Excel to create a table or to create your mail merge documents. When a portion of any Excel worksheet is selected and copied and then pasted into a Word document, the Excel data automatically appears as a table. If the selection includes your column headers, your new Word table is complete with headers. If not, you can add a header and save the table as a Word document. Then you use the Data Merge commands to do the merge.

To transfer data from an Excel worksheet into a Word document, perform the following steps:

1. Start Excel and open the desired worksheet.
2. Using the selection techniques common to Excel (see Chapter 15), select the worksheet range that contains the desired data. If the data is not contiguous to the column names in the first row, press the ⌘ key as you select the data row. Use the same selection method to select any other noncontiguous rows or columns. (In case you miss selecting information, you can always add it as described in the following steps.)
3. Choose Edit ➪ Copy (⌘-C) to copy the selection to the clipboard.
4. Launch (or return to) Word and open a new document.
5. Choose Edit ➪ Paste (⌘-V). The data selected in the Excel document appears as a table in Word.

If for some reason your copy and paste didn't include information such as the column names to create a header row, choose Table ⇨ Insert Rows to add a new row where needed. Then enter or paste the missing information into this row.

After the data exists in table form in Word, you can use the techniques outlined earlier in this chapter to complete the mail merge process.

Cross-Reference

This method is a straight copy and paste. For more flexibility, see the method described in the next section, "Embedding Excel data."

Embedding Excel data

If the data you are using for your merge already exists in Excel, you have a more flexible way to use the data than by copying or exporting/importing it. By establishing a link to existing data in Excel, you gain the advantage of having your mail merge information automatically sorted, filtered, and even updated when the data changes.

If you think you will regularly update the information in your data document, you will want to use the field code method. If you won't be updating the information, insert it directly into the data document. In both cases, follow these steps:

1. Click the Insert Database button on the Database toolbar to open the Database dialog box shown in Figure 6-13.

Figure 6-13: The Database dialog box

2. Click the Get Data button to open the Choose a File dialog box shown in Figure 6-14. This box looks like the standard Open dialog box from the File menu. Choose the data document you want to use. Because you're in Word, the Show pop-up filter might be set to show only Word documents. Select the appropriate filter so you can see your document. If your source is in an Excel version file listed, choose that filter. Otherwise, the link is created using Excel via DDE, which is much slower.

Double-click your Excel worksheet to choose it. (It doesn't matter whether Excel is running or whether the spreadsheet is open.)

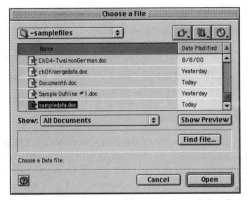

Figure 6-14: The Open Data Source dialog box

The status bar in Word keeps you apprised of what is happening. If necessary, Excel launches and the worksheet opens.

3. In a moment, a dialog box asks what you want to import. Depending on your source, you are asked to choose a specific worksheet from a pop-up menu or if you want to import the entire spreadsheet or a range, in which case you double-click your choice of selection.

Note   Importing an "entire spreadsheet" doesn't include the empty cells. An "entire spreadsheet" simply includes all cells that contain data or a formula. You learn how to further filter your import in a moment.

4. The Database dialog box reappears, so you have the option of performing a query on the information you are importing. Click the Query Options button in the Database dialog box to open the Query Options dialog box. This is the same Query Options dialog box discussed earlier under "Printing Mailing Labels." In here you can filter records by entering conditions in the Filter Records tab, select the fields you want to include using the Select fields tab, or sort records by choosing the desired sort fields in the Sort Records tab.

If your goal is to limit the number of imported records or show only certain records, click the Filter Records tab and choose a field from the pop-up list. Next, move to the Comparison box and select a comparison, such as equal to, not equal to, greater than, less than, and so forth. The final part of the query is to enter a value to which the field can be compared in the Compare to box. You can also enter additional conditions for the filter. On each successive line of the dialog box, select an And or an Or relationship, and then enter the rest of your conditions (refer back to Figure 6-11).

The records can also be sorted to help organize the presentation of your data. Click the Sort Records tab of the Query Options dialog box (refer back to Figure 6-11). Select the primary field by which to sort, and then choose an ascending or descending sort. To have a secondary sort, select a field from the next pop-up menu (Then by) and again choose between ascending or descending. The same goes for a third sort criteria.

After you have finished in the two tabs, click OK. You are again returned to the Database dialog box.

5. Click Table AutoFormat if you want to format the table. The Preview window lets you see what the data will look like after the formatting is applied. After choosing the format you want for the table, click OK.

6. Click the Insert Data button in the Database dialog box. The Insert Data dialog box appears, as shown in Figure 6-15. This dialog box gives you one more opportunity to choose a range for the information being imported; otherwise, retain the default choice—All. Click OK to import the information.

 **Figure 6-15:** The Insert Data dialog box

If you want the information to be linked, check the Insert Data as Field option in the Insert Data dialog box. When information is linked, the data can be updated to reflect changes made to the Excel data. If Insert Data as Field is not checked, automatic updating is not an option, and you'll have to enter any changes manually.

After you click OK, Word and Excel communicate, as reflected by the messages in the status bar, and then your new table appears in Word.

If you have selected the Insert Data as Field option, when the data is updated in Excel, you can tell Word to talk to Excel and update your table in Word. Click the Update Fields button on the Database toolbar, or Control-click in any cell of your table (in Word), and choose Update Fields from the shortcut menu that appears. Word initiates communication to Excel, as reported in the status bar, and then the data within your table changes to match the data in Excel. If you do not choose the Insert Data as Field option, the Update Fields button will have no effect, and you will not see Update Fields in the shortcut menu when you Control-click in a cell in your table.

Embedding data from other sources

You can also use the Get Data button to insert data from other Microsoft sources, such as Outlook Express's contact list (assuming you haven't brought that data into Entourage), the Office Address Book, or FileMaker Pro databases. Doing so is similar to the method for embedding Excel data, except that, depending on the source, different dialog boxes will present appropriate choices. To make this procedure a bit easier, begin by selecting that source's filter in the Show pop-up filter when you are getting the data source.

You may also be able to embed data from other sources. Again, begin with the Get Data button.

Summary

This chapter has detailed the following topics related to working with fields:

- ✦ Fields are instructions that Word uses to insert certain information, such as the current date, into a document.
- ✦ You can insert fields by choosing Insert ➪ Field or using the Insert Field shortcut key combination (⌘-F9).
- ✦ You can update a field's results by Control-clicking the field and choosing Update Fields from the shortcut menu.
- ✦ Fields can be formatted like other text.
- ✦ Fields aid in the creation of form letters, which can be handled with the Data Merge Manager.
- ✦ Fields can also be used in the creation of envelopes and labels.
- ✦ We also covered the creation of data sources in other software applications — useful for large mailing lists or other cases where you need to work with large amounts of data that would be better handled in a database.

Where to go next

- ✦ After you have created your form letters, you want them to look their best. This requires some formatting work. For more information on formatting, see Chapter 3.

✦   ✦   ✦

Building Tables of Contents and Indexes

This chapter covers two elements of a document that are
similar in many ways: tables of contents and indexes. Both
are essentially lists that are arranged in slightly different ways.
A table of contents is a list of the major portions of a document
(such as sections of a report), including the page numbers for
each section. By comparison, an index is a list of important
words or subjects in a document with page numbers where the
subjects can be found.

Word lets you avoid much of the work in preparing both
tables of contents and indexes. With the Insert menu's Index
and Tables command, you can automatically create tables of
contents and similar lists or indexes based on special fields
that you insert while writing your document. Besides saving
you from all that typing and formatting, Index and Tables
enables you to update the table of contents and index easily
to reflect changes you make to the document.

Building Tables of Contents

You can use several methods for building a table of contents.
You can base the table of contents on built-in heading styles or
outline headings; you can change the default styles so Word
creates the table of contents based on your chosen styles; or
you can build the table of contents by using TC fields, a special
type of field that you insert into a document by using the steps
outlined in this chapter. The easiest method for creating a
table of contents — to base it on the styles within your document — requires only that you structure your document with

styles such as headings or that you use an outline form. Figure 7-1 shows an example of a typical table of contents in Word. In this case, the table of contents was generated on the default heading styles used throughout the document.

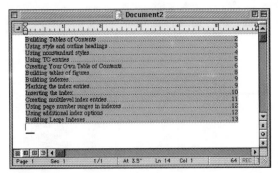

Figure 7-1: A typical table of contents generated in Word

Tip   If you need both a table of contents and an index in the same document, create the index first (use the techniques discussed in the second part of this chapter). This way you can include an entry for the index in your table of contents.

Using style and outline headings

In any document, Word includes the default styles of Normal, Heading 1, Heading 2, Heading 3, and Heading 4. You can apply these styles (or outline headings, if you've added these to your documents) to lines of text in your document to make the creation of tables of contents a simple matter. Follow these steps:

1. Check the headings of your document to be sure they are formatted in one of the heading styles. To do so, simply place your cursor (insertion point) anywhere in the heading text and then note the style reported in the Style box on the Formatting palette. To apply a heading style, with the insertion point anywhere within the heading, click the pop-up arrow to the right of the Style box on the Formatting palette and drag down or up to select any available style. (For more about the use of styles, see Chapter 8.)

2. Move the insertion point to the place where you want the table of contents.

3. Choose Insert ➪ Index and Tables and then click the Table of Contents tab in the Index and Tables dialog box (see Figure 7-2).

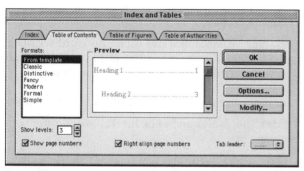

Figure 7-2: The Table of Contents tab of the Index and Tables dialog box

4. In the Formats list box, select the format you want for your table of contents. As you click each format, a representative sample of how the table of contents will look appears in the Preview area of the dialog box.

You can include page numbers, along with the format, by leaving the Show page numbers checkbox turned on. You can also specify the number of heading levels by entering the desired value in the Show levels box. (When you select 1, only Heading 1 styles are included in the table of contents; when you select 2, Heading 1 and Heading 2 styles are included in the table of contents; and so on.) Clicking the Options button displays the Table of Contents Options dialog box that lets you designate styles (other than Word's default heading styles) that Word should use to build the table of contents.

5. After you select the options and settings you want, click OK. Word constructs the table of contents at the insertion point location.

The Funny Codes Dilemma

If you see a series of codes, such as {TOC}, rather than actual text after you generate your table of contents, your table of contents is displaying field codes. If you want to see the actual text of the table of contents, select Edit ➪ Preferences, select the View tab in the Preferences dialog box, and uncheck the Field codes checkbox in the Show area. This displays all the field results instead of the codes.

If you like seeing the codes but want to see page number results in individual instances, place the cursor in the field code and press Shift-F9, or Control-click and select Toggle Field Codes.

Using nonstandard styles

Sometimes you may find that the heading styles built into Word are not the styles you prefer for building your table of contents. If you want to base the table of contents on different styles, you can do so by performing these steps:

1. Position the cursor in the area where you want to insert the table of contents.

2. Choose Insert ➪ Index and Tables and click the Table of Contents tab in the Index and Tables dialog box.

3. In the Formats list box, select the format you want to use. Then click the Options button to open the Table of Contents Options dialog box (see Figure 7-3).

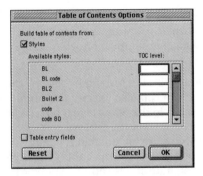

Figure 7-3: The Table of Contents Options dialog box

4. Scroll down in the Available styles list box to find the first style you want to use for the table of contents. In the TOC level list to the right of the style name, type **1**. Notice that a checkmark automatically appeared in the column to the left of the style. This style is now designated as the first level of importance in your table of contents. Continue, entering a **2**, **3**, **4**, and so on, depending on how many styles you'd like to include in your table of contents. You can renumber any style at any time. Styles with no TOC level indicated are not part of the table of contents.

5. Click OK to close the Table of Contents Options dialog box and preview the table of contents in the Index and Tables dialog box.

6. Click OK in the Index and Tables dialog box. Word compiles the table of contents at the insertion point location.

Using TC entries

Another method for building a table of contents involves adding fields called TC entries (an abbreviation for table of contents entries) to your document. This involves manually building the field by using ⌘-F9 to insert field brackets. The overall technique involves two main steps: identifying and marking items to include in the table of contents, and generating the table of contents itself.

You can insert TC entries in a document and generate the table of contents by performing the following steps:

1. Be sure that hidden text is showing on the screen. (If you can see paragraph markers at the end of your paragraphs, hidden text is showing.) If hidden text is not showing, click the Show/Hide ¶ button on the Standard toolbar.

2. Place the insertion point at the location in the document where you want to insert a TC entry. (A good place for TC entries is right after the section titles or headings in your document.)

3. Press ⌘-F9 to insert an empty field. You see the field braces with the insertion point placed between them. The field code resembles the following: {_}.

4. Type the letters **TC** and a space. Then type a quotation mark, the entry that you want to have appear in the table of contents, and then another quotation mark. (The letters TC can be either uppercase or lowercase.) For example, if you want to add a table of contents entry that reads "Unpacking your new lawn mower," your entry would resemble the following:

   ```
   {tc "Unpacking your new lawn mower"}
   ```

5. Repeat Steps 2 through 4 for each table of contents entry you want to add.

6. When all the TC entry fields have been placed in the document, move the insertion point to the place in your document where you would like the table of contents to appear.

7. Choose Insert ⇨ Index and Tables and click the Table of Contents tab. Next click the Options button and, in the dialog box that appears, turn on the Table entry fields checkbox. This action tells Word to base the table of contents on the TC entries that you have added to the document. Click OK.

8. Click OK in the Index and Tables dialog box. Word builds the table of contents at the insertion point location.

 Note

If the Field codes option is turned on in your View Preferences, you see field codes in the table of contents rather than text. You can turn off the field codes by choosing Edit ⇨ Preferences, clicking the View tab in the Preferences dialog box, and turning off the Field codes option. (Another easy way to turn off the field codes is to Control-click in the field code and choose Toggle Field Codes from the shortcut menu that appears.)

Remember that the table of contents is based on a Word field. If changes you make to the document result in changes to the page count, you need to update the table of contents to reflect those changes. To update a table of contents, place the insertion point anywhere within the table of contents and Control-click. Choose Update Field from the shortcut menu that appears.

Similarly, because TC entries are fields, if you want to delete or move a TC entry to another location, select the entire field and move it or delete it as you would move or delete any text.

> ## Formatting on the Fly
>
> Probably the easiest way to make a quick format change to your table of contents or index is to Control-click anywhere within the table of contents or index. Then choose the Font, Paragraph, or Bullets and Numbering command from the shortcut menu that appears.
>
> Depending on which menu option you select, you can then make appropriate changes in the dialog box that appears.

Creating Your Own Table of Contents

To see how to build a table of contents by inserting TC fields, you can follow the steps in the next exercise. Or, if you have a sizable document of your own, you may want to apply these steps to create a table of contents based on your own document:

1. Choose File ➪ New (⌘-N) and then click OK to create a new document and save it right away. (Always save and keep saving.)

2. Type the following lines (press Return after each one) and press Shift-Enter after each line to insert a page break between each line and the next:

   ```
   Principles of Flight
   Aircraft and Engines
   Flight Instruments
   Navigation
   ```

3. If the hidden text option is not turned on, click the Show/Hide button on the Standard toolbar to show the hidden characters.

4. Place the insertion point at the end of the first line of text. Press ⌘-F9 and then type the following inside the brackets:

   ```
   tc "Principles of Flight"
   ```

5. Move the insertion point to the end of the next line of text. Press ⌘-F9 and then type the following inside the brackets:

   ```
   tc "Aircraft and Engines"
   ```

6. Move the insertion point to the end of the next line of text. Press ⌘-F9 and then type the following inside the brackets:

   ```
   tc "Flight Instruments"
   ```

7. Move the insertion point to the end of the next line of text. Press ⌘-F9 and then type the following inside the brackets:

   ```
   tc "Navigation"
   ```

Banishing Strange Codes

By default, TC entries are stored as hidden text. If you cannot see them, though, they are rather difficult to enter because you cannot see what you're typing.

However, if they are visible, the entries may become annoying when you are trying to proofread your text. You can easily toggle this hidden text between visible and invisible by clicking the Show/Hide ¶ button, a backwards fancy P on the Standard toolbar.

You should also ignore when Word's spell-checker flags most field codes, including the `tc` code, as misspelled.

8. Insert your cursor at the beginning of the document (or press ⌘-Home as the shortcut). Press Return once to add a new line, and then press Shift-Enter to insert a page break. Then, with your cursor, the arrows, or ⌘-Home, move back to the start of the document. You add the table of contents on what is now Page 1 of the document, with the remainder of the document appearing on the following four pages.

9. Choose Insert ➪ Index and Tables. Then click the Table of Contents tab in the Index and Tables dialog box.

10. Click the Options button to open the Table of Contents Options dialog box and turn on the Table Entry Fields checkbox. Click OK.

11. Click OK in the Index and Tables dialog box to have Word insert your table of contents. It should look like the one in Figure 7-4.

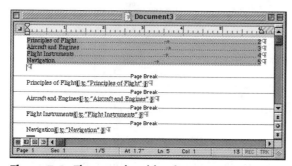

Figure 7-4: The sample table of contents

Building tables of figures

A table of figures is another type of list you can easily create in Word. Like a table of contents and an index, a table of figures is a list of items. In this case, the items are figure (or art) captions, shown in the order in which the figures appear in the document. A table of figures can include such items as illustrations, figures, charts, or graphs. Examples of figure captions appear throughout this book; every figure in this book includes a caption that describes the figure. You can add similar captions to your own Word documents.

All the captions you create in your documents can be easily included in a table of figures that you can place at any location within your document. You have two ways to create a table of figures. You can use the Insert ⇨ Caption command, or you can assign a style to each caption.

To create your table of figures with the Insert ⇨ Caption command, you work on your document as normal, using this command as you come to each caption location. (Or you can create your document, and then go back and insert the captions by choosing Insert ⇨ Caption.) This command brings up the Caption dialog box, which presents you with a field into which you type the name of the caption. You repeat this process for every caption you want to insert.

After inserting all your captions, you can perform the following steps to insert the table of figures:

1. Position the cursor where you want to place the table of figures.

2. Choose Insert ⇨ Index and Tables and click the Table of Figures tab in the Index and Tables dialog box (see Figure 7-5).

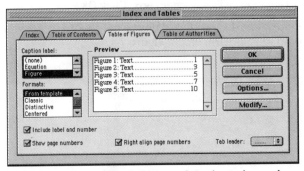

Figure 7-5: The Table of Figures tab in the Index and Tables dialog box

3. Choose the kind of caption label you want for your table of figures.

4. Select the format you want for your table. As with tables of contents, you can choose to build your table of figures from a template or use a Classic, Distinctive, Centered, Formal, or Simple style. (These formats are displayed in the Preview portion of the dialog box.) The Show page numbers option, when checked, causes page numbers to be included with the table of figures. The Right align page numbers option, when checked, causes the page numbers to be aligned with the right margin. The Tab leader pop-up menu lets you select a tab leader from the caption to the page number (or none).

5. After making your choices, click OK to insert the table of figures at the insertion point.

To create your table of figures based on styles, you enter your caption by typing within your document as normal, and then assign a style to each caption. For example, you could type the words, "Figure 7-5: The Table of Figures tab in the Index and Tables dialog box." You could then assign this line a style, such as Caption. (For more information on styles, see Chapter 8.) After all your text is entered, you select Insert ➪ Index and Tables, as with the previously described method. This time, however, click the Options button and click the checkbox next to Style, telling Word to build the table of figures from a style. In the pop-up menu next to the selection, choose the style you used for your captions. We would select Caption as our style because that's the style we assigned to our caption text. Click OK. Then choose your Table of Figures options and click OK to have word build your table.

Building indexes

Word enables you to build indexes in a manner similar to the one for building a table of contents. You insert special fields, called index entries, into the document at locations where you mention the indexed topics. In the case of index entries, Word provides a command just for this purpose, or you can use the Insert ➪ Field command (⌘-F9). After you mark all the index entries, you use Insert ➪ Index and Tables to place the index at the insertion point. As with a table of contents, the index that Word generates is based on a field, which you can easily change by updating the field as the document changes.

Word offers considerable control over the index. You can generate an index for the entire document or for a range of letters in the alphabet. Index entries can all appear flush left in the index, or they can be indented to multiple levels. And you can easily add bold or italics to the page numbers of the index entries.

Marking the index entries

Every item that is to appear in the index must have an index entry. You can mark index entries by performing the following steps:

1. Select the text in the document that you want to use for an index entry or place the insertion point immediately after the text.

2. Choose Insert ➪ Index and Tables, and then click the Index tab. Click the Mark Entry button to reveal the Mark Index Entry dialog box (see Figure 7-6). By default, any selected text appears in the Main entry text box. If you want the text to appear in the index as a subentry (a secondary-level index heading), delete any entry in the Main entry text box and enter the entry in the Subentry text box.

Figure 7-6: The Mark Index Entry dialog box

3. After entering the desired entry, click the Mark button. Word inserts the index entry at the insertion point location. (As with the fields you use to insert a table of contents, index entries are stored as hidden text. You do not see them in the document unless you click the Show/Hide button on the Standard toolbar.)

The Mark Index Entry dialog box contains various options you can use to determine how Word should handle the index entries. In the Cross-reference text box, you can type the text you want to use as a cross-reference for the index entry. You can also specify a range of pages in an index entry by turning on the Page Range option and typing or selecting a bookmark name that you used to mark a range of pages. Finally, the Page number format options apply bold or italic formatting to page numbers in the index.

If you don't like using menus and dialog boxes, an alternative way of inserting index entries exists. Because an index entry is a field, you can use the Insert Field key (⌘-F9) to insert an index entry. To do so, press Insert Field (⌘-F9), type the letters **xe** followed by a space, and then type the index entry surrounded by quotation marks. If you want the page number of the index entry to be in bold or italic, you must also add a \b or \i switch; type \b for bold or \i for italic (you can add both options in the same field). With hidden text showing, a sample index entry may resemble the following:

```
{xe "Adding Oil to the Lawn Mower" \b}
```

Tip   An index entry should follow the topic to which it refers in the text; that is, the index entry should be placed immediately after the sentence that concludes the subject that is indexed. (If you select the text before you use the Index and Tables command—rather than typing the index entry yourself—Word automatically places the index entry immediately after the selection.) This rule of thumb is important because if you place the index entry before the subject being indexed, and the subject is near the bottom of the page, Word may add a page break between the index entry and the text. The result would be an index with an incorrect page number.

Inserting the index

After you mark all the index entries, you can use Insert ⇨ Index and Tables to place the index in the document. To insert the index, perform the following steps:

1. Place the insertion point at the desired location for the index. (With most documents, indexes are customarily placed at the end of the document.)

2. Choose Insert ⇨ Index and Tables and click the Index tab, as shown in Figure 7-7.

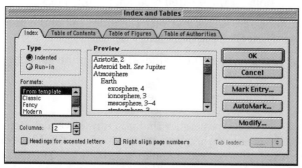

Figure 7-7: The Index tab of the Index and Tables dialog box

3. Choose the type of index (Indented or Run-in) that you want and choose the desired format for the index. As you select among the available formats, a preview of each format appears in the Preview area of the dialog box.

4. After you click OK, Word generates the index. Note that if Field codes is turned on (in your View Preferences), what you see is the fields that built the index and not the index itself. You can turn off the field codes by choosing Edit ⇨ Preferences and clicking the View tab of the Preferences dialog box. Just turn off the Field codes option in the Show area of the tab.

Creating multilevel index entries

You can insert index entries that indicate multiple levels. As an example, the following part of an index is designed with two levels:

```
Data
   Copying, 104
   Definition, 251
   Deleting, 92
   Editing, 91
   Linking, 216
   Reporting, 251
Data Menu, 64, 216
Database
```

```
Attributes of, 251
Creating, 216
Criteria, 230
```

To create an index based on multiple levels, enter the text of the secondary entry in the Subentry text box rather than in the Main entry text box of the Mark Entry dialog box. If you are typing the entries manually, simply add a colon (:) when you type the index entry into the dialog box to separate the levels. You can create a multilevel index by performing the following steps to mark your index entries:

1. Place the insertion point at the desired location for the index.

2. Choose Insert ➪ Index and Tables and click the Index tab of the Index and Tables dialog box. Then click the Mark Entry button.

3. In the Main entry text box, type the first-level entry. In the Subentry text box, type the second-level entry.

4. Click the Mark button to place the index entry.

When you specify multiple levels, remember that you now have a choice of how Word structures a multilevel index when you use the Index and Tables command. You can choose either the Indented or the Run-in type of index. The default is Indented, which results in an index where sublevel entries are indented, as shown in the following example:

```
Database
   Attributes of, 251
   Creating, 216
   Criteria, 230
```

On the other hand, if you choose the Run-in option in the dialog box, Word inserts all sublevel entries in the same paragraph as the main entry in the index. The main entry is separated from the subentries with a colon, and semicolons separate all remaining subentries. The preceding indented example now appears as a run-in example in the following:

```
Database: Attributes of, 251; Creating, 216; Criteria, 230
```

Using page number ranges in indexes

In those cases where a subject covered by an index entry spans several pages in a document, you may want the reference in the index to include the range of pages in the document. In the following example, the entries for the Go To command and Hardware both contain a range of pages:

```
Get Info command, 41
Go To command, 62-65
Gridlines command, 145
Hardware, 19-20
Help menu, 12
```

With the methods described so far for inserting index entries, you get only the first page of the subject referred to by the index, even if you make a selection that spans multiple pages. If you want page numbers that span a range of pages, you must operate a little differently. First you must select the range of text and insert a bookmark that refers to the selection by following these steps:

1. Use your preferred selection method to select the range of text you want to index.

2. Choose Insert ⇨ Bookmark. In the Bookmark dialog box, type a name for the bookmark, and then click Add.

3. Choose Insert ⇨ Index and Tables, click the Index tab, and click Mark Entry. In the Mark Index Entry dialog box, click the Page Range Bookmark radio button and enter the bookmark name in the text box or select it from the pop-up menu that appears when you press the double-arrow button. When you create the index using the steps described earlier in this chapter, your entry includes your specified range of pages.

Using additional index options

Additional switches (programming codes) are available for you to use in Word's index fields to add sophistication to your indexes. These features include changing the separator character used between ranges of page numbers (normally a hyphen) and restricting an index to include only index items that begin with a certain letter. These special index switches are beyond the scope of this book, but Word's Help talks more about them.

Building Large Indexes

If you are generating a large index (one with 4,000 entries or more), Word may run out of memory when you attempt to use the Index and Tables command. Microsoft recommends that you generate indexes for large documents in multiple steps. First, for example, you build an index that contains entries only for the letters A through L, and then you build an index for the letters M through Z. You choose Insert ⇨ Field rather than Insert ⇨ Index and Tables to insert a separate field for each portion of the index after you have marked all the entries that you want in the document.

To create a separate field for each portion of the index, do the following:

1. Place the insertion point at the location in the document where the index is to appear.

2. Choose Insert ⇨ Field or press ⌘-F9.

3. Type the word **index** followed by a space, a backslash, the letter **p**, a space, and a range of letters (such as A–L); for example, **index \p A-L**.

4. Click OK to insert the first index field into the document. If the hidden text option is turned on, the field may resemble the following:

```
{index \p A-L}
```

5. Move the insertion point to the right of the existing index field and press Return to start a new line.

6. Repeat Steps 2 through 5 for each additional range of letters that you need.

Summary

In this chapter, you learned how to use Word's capabilities to generate indexes and tables of contents. The chapter covered the following topics:

✦ Tables of contents can be based on heading styles, outline headings, or TC fields (a special kind of field inserted into a document).

✦ If you use Word's default heading styles or outlining in your document, you can quickly generate a table of contents by choosing Insert ➪ Index and Tables, clicking the Table of Contents tab, and selecting the desired format in the dialog box.

✦ You can create a table of contents based on any text in your document by adding fields called TC fields to your document. After adding these fields, you can generate a table of contents with the Table of Contents tab, which appears in the dialog box when you choose Insert ➪ Index and Tables.

✦ You can create indexes by adding fields called index entries to your document. After adding index entries, you can generate an index with the Index tab, which appears in the dialog box when you choose Insert ➪ Index and Tables.

Where to go next

✦ In the next chapter, you learn how to work effectively with styles and templates to govern the overall appearance of your document in Word.

✦ If you make full use of Word's predefined styles or of outlines in your documents, the creation of a table of contents becomes an easy task. You can find more information on working with Word's predefined styles in Chapter 8. For the lowdown on using outlines in Word, see Chapter 5.

✦ An important part of any complex document is page number formatting, and possibly the inclusion of headers and footers. These topics are detailed in Chapter 3.

✦　　✦　　✦

Working with Styles and Templates

Word provides styles and templates, which are tools that make it easy to mold the appearance of routinely produced or long documents. The first part of this chapter deals with styles; the second part deals with templates. The two concepts are closely related.

Discovering Styles and Templates

Too many users of Word find styles to be an esoteric subject and avoid it. It is easily possible to use Word day after day and never learn about the strength and flexibility of styles. The same can be said for templates, which offer another way to reduce repetitive work while aiding in design consistency. You're doing yourself a disservice if you avoid styles or templates — they can be timesavers.

So, what is a style? A style is a collection of character formatting settings, paragraph formatting settings, or both. Styles save time that you might otherwise spend formatting your documents — and they give your documents a consistent look. For example, you may routinely apply a 0.5-inch left indent, a first-line indent, and Times font to paragraphs in a document. You can define this set of formatting settings as a style. After you define the style, you can apply all these formatting settings to any paragraph in a document in a single operation.

Word has a number of built-in styles. They may be all you need, but you can also create your own. Figure 8-1 shows an essay template that contains a number of different styles. (Here we'll get a jump on the topic of templates by saying that you should think of a template as a pattern for a type of document. A template usually contains several styles.) Notice the names of the styles to the left of the document. (You can display style names at the far left like this, when in Normal or Outline view, by choosing Edit ➪ Preferences, clicking the View tab, and changing the Style Area Width. This is discussed further in the section "Displaying Style Names as You Work.") All available styles appear in the pop-up Style list on the left side of the Formatting toolbar as you create a document.

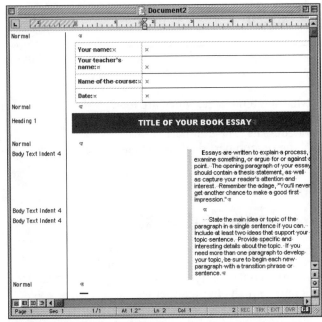

Figure 8-1: An example of an essay template containing various styles

Besides making formatting easier to apply, styles also offer an advantage when you revise document formats. When you change the formatting in the style, all paragraphs that are formatted with this style automatically change. For example, you may decide to apply a border and shading to all paragraphs with a particular style. By changing the definition of the style to include the border and shading, you automatically add the border and shading to all paragraphs that use that particular style.

Word offers two overall kinds of styles — character and paragraph:

✦ **Character styles** apply a variety of formatting to the individual letters and punctuation in a document. Character styles are those that appear in the Font dialog box (Format ➪ Font). This is the formatting that includes font size and style; bold, italics, or underlining; small caps; and other text-related settings. These attributes can be applied with buttons, keyboard commands, or from within the Font dialog box.

✦ **Paragraph styles** govern the overall appearance of the paragraph. You apply paragraph styles with the Format ➪ Paragraph command or from the ruler. Paragraph formatting includes indentation, line spacing, and paragraph alignment. It also includes character formatting. Word normally saves styles along with the active document, but you can easily copy the styles you create to a specific template, which brings us to the strength of templates.

A document template, sometimes called a stationery document on the Mac, is like a blank page of stationery that has your name, address, and logo already printed and waiting to go. For example, in the case of an interoffice memo, you can create a template that already contains the text for a company name, date, to, from, and subject headings. In addition to this boilerplate text, templates can also contain margin settings, headers and footers, styles, macros, and custom keyboard, menu, or toolbar assignments. By storing styles in a template, you make the stored styles available for use whenever you use that template. When you click the drop-down arrow in the Style list on the Formatting palette, the styles you see are all stored in the template that you are using.

By starting with a template you arrive directly at a particular format, rather than having to begin from scratch defining everything from the page margins to the most intricate of styles. The second part of this chapter explains templates in more detail. Because templates include collections of styles, however, it's important to understand styles before you begin working with templates.

Applying Styles

You can apply styles throughout your Word documents in two ways. You can use the pop-up Style list that's in the Formatting palette or you can use keyboard shortcuts.

Using the Formatting palette

Because Word comes with a number of default styles, putting styles to work is as easy as choosing the desired style from the Style list on the Formatting palette. To apply any of the available styles to paragraphs in your document, follow these steps:

1. If the Formatting palette isn't already showing, choose View ➪ Formatting palette. (We recommend that you keep it open at all times, which is the Office 2001 default.)

2. To apply a paragraph style to one paragraph, place the insertion pointer anywhere in that paragraph. To apply the style to more than one paragraph, select at least part of each paragraph.

   To apply a character style, select the desired portion of text.

3. Click the arrow to the right of the Style list in the Formatting palette to reveal the list of available styles (see Figure 8-2) and drag to the style you wish to apply.

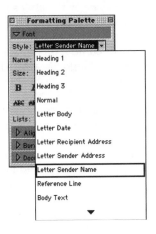

Figure 8-2: The pop-up Style list on the Formatting toolbar

The style list also provides a Style preview to help you select the appropriate style. The style name doubles as a view of any indentation and shows the font size if it's from 8 to 16 points. If the style's font is below 8 points, it is still seen at 8 points. If the style's font is above 16 points, it is still seen at 16 points. The information on the right states the font size of that style, shows you the alignment, and then tells you that style is a character style (with an underlined a) or a paragraph style (with paragraph mark).

Note   To see the Style preview, you must have the WYSIWYG font and style menu preference checked in the General tab of Preferences.

If you don't like the effects of a style you apply, you can undo its effects by immediately choosing Edit ➪ Undo (Style).

Why Is My Style List Different?

If you look at the available styles shown in Figure 8-2 and compare them to the styles shown in your own Style list, you may find the lists don't match. "Where are all these styles?" you may ask. Remember that each template contains a collection of styles. When you look in the Style list, the styles you see are part of the template you are using. If we are using a different template, the styles will be different. For now, remember that you can choose from among different templates in the New dialog box that appears when you select File ➪ New. Each template in the New dialog box has its own list of styles that are useful for that particular type of document.

Why Do Italicized Words Become Normal?

If you apply a style that includes bold or italics to selected text that already contains bold or italic formatting, the existing bold or italicized text in the selection changes to normal text — in other words, neither bold nor italicized.

This change happens because, in Word, bold and italic character formatting is a "switch" that is either on or off for a given selection. Thus, any style-applied bold or italic formatting toggles that switch, removing any bold or italic formatting that had been previously applied to the selection.

Other character styles that switch in this manner are underlining and any of the eleven effects found on the Font dialog box's Font tab.

Using the keyboard

If you are using a document that is based on Word's default (Normal) template, you can use keyboard shortcuts to apply the available styles. Table 8-1 shows the available styles in the Normal template that have keyboard shortcuts and the shortcuts that apply the styles.

Table 8-1
Styles That Have Keyboard Shortcuts

Style Name	Formatting Applied	Keyboard Shortcut
Heading 1	Normal; Helvetica 14 point; Bold; Space Before 12 pts; After 3 pts	⌘-Option-1
Heading 2	Normal; Helvetica 12 point; Bold; Italic; Space Before 12 pts; After 3 pts	⌘-Option-2
Heading 3	Normal; Helvetica 12 point; Space Before 12 pts; After 3 pts	⌘-Option-3

Tip   You can quickly apply the same style to a number of items in your document. After applying the style to the first selection, select the additional text that you want formatted with the same style and press the ⌘ key.

Defining Styles

Word provides two methods for creating (defining) styles. For the first method, you choose Format ➪ Style and click the New button in the Style dialog box. In the New

Style dialog box that appears, enter a name for the new style, and then click the Format pop-up menu to define the style, choosing the characteristics you desire. (Yes, this is a lot to describe in one paragraph, but the next section gives you the complete scoop.)

Styles can also be defined by example. This means that you can format your paragraph until you like the way it looks, and then define a style based on that paragraph. This method is friendlier and easier.

Using the Style command

The more powerful (and, yes, more complex) method of defining a style is using Format ➪ Style. This command opens the Style dialog box shown in Figure 8-3. Click the New button in the dialog box to reveal the New Style dialog box shown in Figure 8-4.

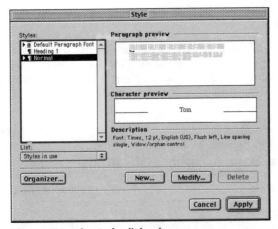

Figure 8-3: The Style dialog box

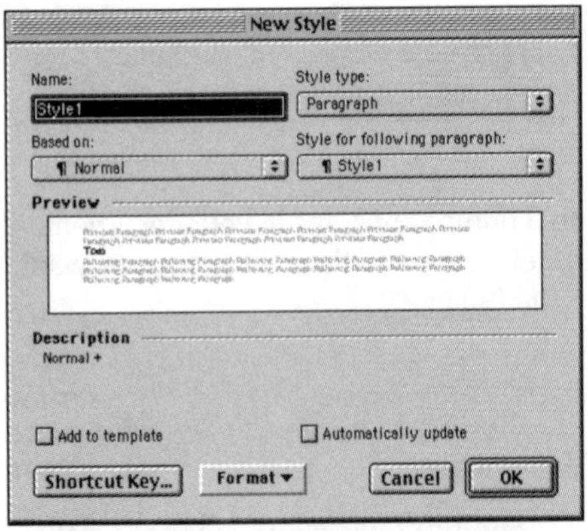

Figure 8-4: The New Style dialog box

You can change the formatting for the style by clicking the Format pop-up menu and selecting the appropriate category to format. Each of the menu choices displayed in the Format list (Font, Paragraph, Tabs, Border, Language, Frame, and Numbering) takes you directly to the dialog box that particular formatting command uses. For example, choosing Font displays the same Font dialog box displayed with Format ⇨ Font; choosing Paragraph displays the same Paragraph dialog box as Format ⇨ Paragraph. The Style Type pop-up menu offers a choice of Character or Paragraph, which is where you indicate whether your new style is a character style or a paragraph style.

Make the desired changes in the respective dialog boxes and then click OK to return to the New Style dialog box. (The only formatting option not covered elsewhere in this text is the one provided by the Language option. This menu option brings up a dialog box that lets you change the language used by the spelling-checker, thesaurus, and grammar-checker.)

You can use the Based On pop-up menu in the New Style dialog box to base the style you are creating on an existing style. (If the style you are defining is not based on any other style, choose "(no style).") To base a new style on an existing one, select it from this pop-up menu. (This technique is covered in more detail in the "Basing a Style on Another Style" section later in this chapter.) The Style for Following Paragraph pop-up menu is enabled when you select Paragraph in the Style Type pop-up. This enables you to specify whether the same style is to continue in effect after a paragraph break or whether a specific new style should be in effect. For example, you will usually put Normal in effect for the paragraph following a Heading style.

You can turn on the Add to Template checkbox at the bottom of the New Styles dialog box if you want to add the style that you've defined to the current template. (If you are using the default Normal template, the style will be added to that template and will be available in all documents that you create in Word.)

After you have made all the desired formatting changes, enter a name for the style in the Name box. Remember that each style name must be unique. It doesn't make sense to have two styles with the same name so Word doesn't let you make this mistake. Because style names are case-sensitive, you can use "Figures" and "figures" as two different style names (although that would confuse most people). Style names can be up to 253 characters in length, and they can use any combination of characters except for the backslash (\), the curly braces ({}), or the semicolon (;).

After giving your style a name, click OK to return to the Style dialog box. From here you can apply the style to the current paragraph or selection by clicking the Apply button. When you do, the dialog box closes and you are back in your document. After the style has been defined, you can apply that style to the desired paragraphs of the document by using the techniques covered in the "Using the Formatting Palette" section earlier in this chapter.

In addition to the Apply button, the Style dialog box contains other interesting buttons. Use the Modify button to change the formatting of an existing style that you have selected in the Styles list box. Use the Delete button to remove an unwanted style from the Styles list box. Click the Organizer button to display the Organizer dialog box, which lets you rename and copy a style (see "Copying, Deleting, and Renaming Styles" later in this chapter).

Defining styles by example

The easy way to define a new style is to base it on an existing paragraph and then use the buttons on the Formatting palette. (This includes starting with Normal as the style as when you've simply typed new text.) To create a new style based on an existing paragraph, follow these steps:

1. Be sure the Formatting palette is displayed. Place the insertion pointer anywhere in the paragraph on which you want to base the style. Of course, it is more efficient to make the changes to the paragraph you really want to change. Make any desired changes to the formatting for that paragraph using the ruler and Formatting palette, the menus, and the dialog boxes. (Any changes made are reflected in the new style.)

2. Click once in the Style text box on the Formatting palette. Yes, you're clicking where the name of the current style is displayed. This selects or highlights the name of the style (see Figure 8-5). Remember that you can always type over selected text. Here you can type a new name.

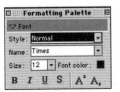

Figure 8-5: A highlighted entry in the Style list box

3. Type a name for the style and press Return or Enter. Word adds the new style name to the list of styles for the document.

Assigning a shortcut key to a style

As a timesaving feature, Word lets you assign shortcut keys to styles. Then, to apply a style you use regularly to selected paragraphs, you just press a key combination. To assign a shortcut key to a style, follow these steps:

1. Choose Format ➪ Style.

2. In the Style dialog box (refer to Figure 8-3), select the desired style and click the Modify button to open the Modify Style dialog box.

3. Click the Shortcut Key button to open the Customize Keyboard dialog box (see Figure 8-6). You assign a shortcut key to your style in this dialog box.

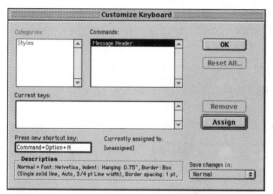

Figure 8-6: The Customize Keyboard dialog box

4. Press the desired shortcut key combination. Your key combination appears in the Press New Shortcut Key box (where the cursor was waiting for you when you got there).

5. To the right of the new shortcut key box, a message appears. This Currently Assigned To message tells you whether the key combination you have chosen is currently selected for another use in Word. If you see an existing description for that particular key combination, you can overwrite the existing key assignment or choose another.

6. Click the Assign button to assign the shortcut key to the style.

Tip

Before you create a large number of styles on your own, take the time to become familiar with the styles that are already in Word's templates. Word may already have a style that will accomplish what you want, or a style may be similar to what you want and you could modify it to suit your needs.

Basing a style on another style

You can base a new style on an existing style. Suppose you have an existing paragraph of text that uses the Normal style. If you indent that paragraph by 0.5 inch, you can define that as a new style based on the way the paragraph now appears. That new style you created is based on the Normal style. If you then change the font used for the Normal style, the font used for your new style would also change. In such a case, the Normal style would be the base style for the new style that you created.

You can see which (if any) style is used as a base style by opening the Style dialog box (Format ➪ Style). As you select any style in the Styles list box at the left, the Description area at the bottom of the dialog box shows whether that style is based on another style. For example, Figure 8-7 shows the Style dialog box with the Body Text style selected. The Description area tells you that the Body Text style is based on the Normal style with 6-point line spacing after paragraphs added.

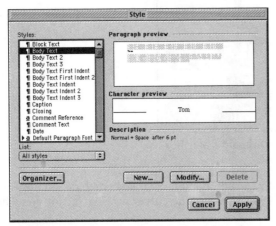

Figure 8-7: The Body Text style is based on the Normal style, according to the Description area in this dialog box.

Caution   Be aware that the capability to base a style on another style can create quite a chain of interdependencies. For example, if the Signature Name style is based on the Signature style, the Signature style is based on the Body Text style, and the Body Text style is based on the Normal style, any change to the Normal style affects all the other named styles.

You can change the base style for any style by using the options found in the Modify Style dialog box. To change a style's base style, follow these steps:

1. Choose Format ➪ Style to display the Style dialog box.

2. In the Styles list box, select the style for which you want to change the base style.

3. Click the Modify button to reveal the Modify Style dialog box, as shown in Figure 8-8. In the Name box, you should see the name of the style that you want to change. In the Based On pop-up menu, you should see the base style that is currently used.

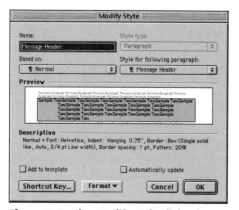

Figure 8-8: The Modify Style dialog box

4. Click the Based On pop-up menu to display all available styles in the document and to find a desired style to serve as the base style. Then click OK.

Tip

If you turn on the Add to Template checkbox before clicking OK, the changes to the base style are recorded in the template that you used to create the document.

Copying, deleting, and renaming styles

Word enables you to copy styles from one document to another. In many cases, this capability helps you to avoid having to create the same style twice. To copy styles from one document to another and to delete and rename styles, follow these steps:

1. Choose Format ⇨ Style.

2. In the Style dialog box, click the Organizer button. Word displays the Organizer dialog box shown in Figure 8-9.

The Dangers of Redefining Normal

Word takes advantage of the fact that styles can be based on other styles by basing many of its built-in styles on the Normal style. Therefore, redefining the Normal style can cause major repercussions elsewhere, including some that may prove undesirable. For example, if you redefine the Normal style to use 12-point Palatino font, every style based on the Normal style will use 12-point Palatino (unless specifically overridden), whether you like it or not.

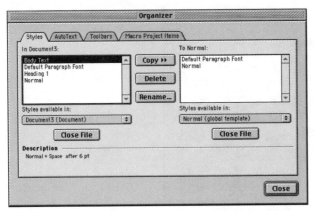

Figure 8-9: The Styles tab of the Organizer dialog box

3. To copy a style to or from a different document or template, click the Close File button (which toggles to Open File) beneath the list for the other file (defaults to Normal) and then click the Open File button to open the desired document or template containing the style. Select the desired style in the list box for that file and click the Copy button to copy the style to the other document or template.

4. To delete a style, click the desired style in the list box and click the Delete button.

Word will not let you delete its built-in styles; you can delete only custom styles.

5. To rename a style, click the desired style in the list box, and then click Rename and enter a new name in the dialog box that appears. Then click Close.

Redefining Styles

As you create your document, you won't always be certain exactly how you'll want every bit of it to look. That's an opportunity to call on the power of styles. For example, assume you're doing a ten-page document, such as a contract. Perhaps you create a style that is 12-point type with 12 points of space after each paragraph. (Does this sound the same as pressing Return an extra time between paragraphs?) What if, after entering all the text, you find the document looks silly with only six lines on the last page? Or what if your boss decides it should be done in a different font and in 10-point type? And, to make it worse, what if your boss doesn't like your half-inch indents at the start of each paragraph? None of this is a problem as long as you've used styles. All you need to do is change one paragraph to the way you want them all to be. Then you just redefine the existing style that's applied to all the paragraphs in question.

To redefine a style, follow these steps:

1. Place the cursor in the paragraph you want to change. Then make your changes.

2. Click in the Style text box (in the Formatting palette), which selects the entire contents of the box. Press Return to bring up the Modify Style dialog box. Note that you haven't made any changes; nothing will happen when you press Return.

   The default choice in this dialog box is to "Update the style to reflect the recent changes." This is the option you want, so you can click OK.

   The other choice is to "Reapply the formatting of the style to the selection." This option removes your changes and returns the paragraph to the way it was before you altered it. At times being able to do this will be handy.

   Checking the Automatically Update the Style From Now On checkbox results in any future changes you make to text in that style being automatically incorporated into the style definition.

Note   Once you have chosen Automatically Update for a given style, you would need to choose Format ⇨ Style, click the Modify button, and make your changes there rather than using the shortcut described in Step 2.

After updating the style, all paragraphs containing the style automatically change to the new look. Just imagine — ten pages can all be changed with so few clicks of the mouse!

Finding Styles When You Need Them

Word provides two ways to find and use styles. Using Word's Help feature, you can display information about your styles as you work, or you can use Format ⇨ Theme and click the Style Gallery button.

Displaying style names as you work

You can see which styles are in effect in your documents in two ways. One is to have the style names appear in Formatting balloons; the other way is to see the style names onscreen in the left margin area of Normal or Outline view.

To have the Formatting balloons appear, select View ⇨ Reveal Formatting. When this feature is on (checked in the menu), your cursor looks like a text balloon. When you click this cursor on any text, a balloon full of style information about that text pops up, as shown in Figure 8-10. Balloons will continue to reveal style information until you return to View ⇨ Reveal Formatting to uncheck the feature or until you begin to type again. (Typing automatically turns off Reveal Formatting.)

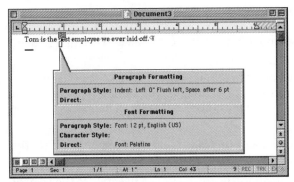

Figure 8-10: A document displaying style information Reveal Formatting balloons

You can see the styles you have used in your document by displaying them onscreen in the left margin area. Referring back to Figure 8-1, you can see the styles displayed in such a manner. To do so, first make sure you are in either Normal or Outline view (you can't show styles in the margin in any of the other views of Word), and then follow these steps:

1. Choose Edit ⇨ Preferences.

2. Click the View tab in the Preferences dialog box.

3. In the Style Area Width box, enter a number or use the arrows to select a desired width. (One inch works well for showing the names of most styles, unless you've added very long style names to your document.)

4. Click OK. The style names in your document appear to the left of the document.

You can easily resize the style area width visually. Move your mouse over the line that divides the style area from the rest of the document until the cursor becomes a line with arrows pointing left and right. When it does, you can click and drag in either direction to enlarge or reduce the style column.

You have two ways to remove the style names from view. One is to return to the Preferences dialog box and change the Style Area Width setting back to zero. The faster way is to use the visual resizing technique and drag the dividing line all the way to the left of your document window.

Using the Style Gallery

With Word's plethora of built-in styles scattered across numerous templates, it can be challenging to find where a useful style is located. To help you find the styles you seek, use Word's Style Gallery dialog box (see Figure 8-11). To open this dialog box, choose Format ⇨ Theme and click the Style Gallery button.

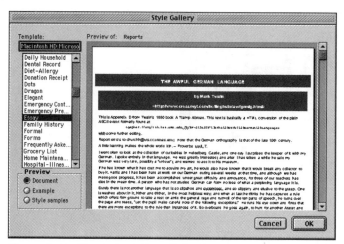

Figure 8-11: The Style Gallery dialog box

Tip

The Template list box contains all the available templates. You can click any template name in the list box to see a preview of your own document as it uses the styles contained in that particular template. At the lower-left corner of the dialog box, you can click the Style Samples radio button to view samples of the different styles, if samples exist, instead of viewing a preview of your document. You can also click the Example radio button to see an example document formatted with the various available styles, if such have been supplied. The Style Gallery is helpful when you're trying to locate a style that will work in a given situation.

Defining and Applying Styles: An Exercise

To try your hand at using the dialog boxes to create and apply a new style to a document, follow these steps:

1. Open any existing document that contains two or more paragraphs and place the insertion point anywhere in the first paragraph.

2. Choose Format ➪ Style command. When the Style dialog box appears, click the New button.

3. In the Name text box, type My Style as a name for the new style.

4. Select Font from the Format pop-up list to display the Font dialog box (see Figure 8-12). In the Font list box, choose any font other than the one you are currently using and then click OK.

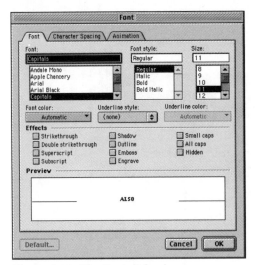

Figure 8-12: The Font dialog box

5. Select Paragraph from the Format pop-up list to display the Paragraph dialog box (see Figure 8-13). In the Indentation area, set the Left value to 0.5 inches, and then click the Special pop-up menu, choose First Line, and set the First-line indentation to 0.5 inches. Set the Line Spacing to 1.5 lines and click OK.

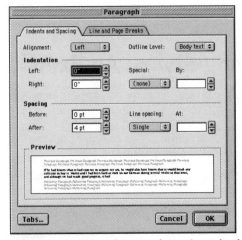

Figure 8-13: The Indents and Spacing tab of the Paragraph dialog box

The Preview box shows your formatting changes, including your selected font, the new paragraph indentations, and the new line spacing.

6. Click OK to add the new style to the list.

7. Click the Apply button to apply the style and close the Style dialog box.

 Note   Remember that the preceding method is one of the two ways to define a style. The other method was described earlier in the section "Defining Styles by Example."

To apply the new style to another paragraph in the document, follow these steps:

1. Place the insertion pointer anywhere in a different paragraph of the document.

2. If the Formatting palette is not visible, choose View ➪ Formatting Palette.

3. Click the arrow to the right of the Styles text box and choose My Style from the list. When you choose the style, the paragraph takes on the style's formatting, as shown in Figure 8-14.

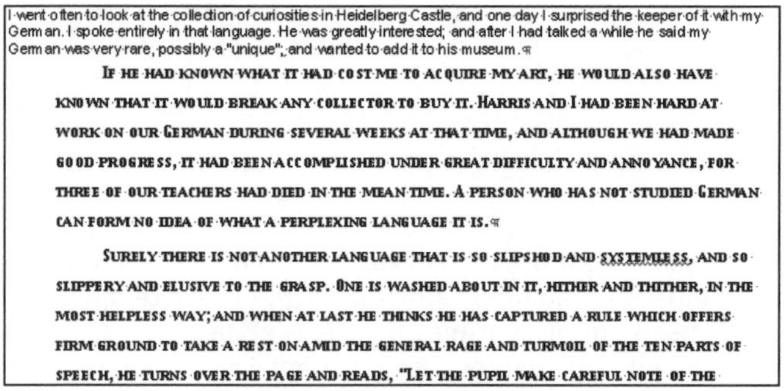

I went often to look at the collection of curiosities in Heidelberg Castle, and one day I surprised the keeper of it with my German. I spoke entirely in that language. He was greatly interested; and after I had talked a while he said my German was very rare, possibly a "unique", and wanted to add it to his museum. ¶

IF HE HAD KNOWN WHAT IT HAD COST ME TO ACQUIRE MY ART, HE WOULD ALSO HAVE KNOWN THAT IT WOULD BREAK ANY COLLECTOR TO BUY IT. HARRIS AND I HAD BEEN HARD AT WORK ON OUR GERMAN DURING SEVERAL WEEKS AT THAT TIME, AND ALTHOUGH WE HAD MADE GOOD PROGRESS, IT HAD BEEN ACCOMPLISHED UNDER GREAT DIFFICULTY AND ANNOYANCE, FOR THREE OF OUR TEACHERS HAD DIED IN THE MEAN TIME. A PERSON WHO HAS NOT STUDIED GERMAN CAN FORM NO IDEA OF WHAT A PERPLEXING LANGUAGE IT IS. ¶

SURELY THERE IS NOT ANOTHER LANGUAGE THAT IS SO SLIPSHOD AND SYSTEMLESS, AND SO SLIPPERY AND ELUSIVE TO THE GRASP. ONE IS WASHED ABOUT IN IT, HITHER AND THITHER, IN THE MOST HELPLESS WAY; AND WHEN AT LAST HE THINKS HE HAS CAPTURED A RULE WHICH OFFERS FIRM GROUND TO TAKE A REST ON AMID THE GENERAL RAGE AND TURMOIL OF THE TEN PARTS OF SPEECH, HE TURNS OVER THE PAGE AND READS, "LET THE PUPIL MAKE CAREFUL NOTE OF THE

Figure 8-14: The results of applying the styles to paragraphs

Understanding Templates

To carry document design consistency even further than character and paragraph formatting, use templates. As mentioned earlier, templates serve as molds for your documents. Templates include such items as margins, text, and page setup in addition to collections of styles.

When you create a new document from the Project Gallery, you specify which template you want to use by selecting from the various categories and subcategories (see Figure 8-15). The categories group Office's predefined templates according to their functions. Any new templates that you create appear under the My Templates category. If you click OK in the Project Gallery without making a category selection, Project Gallery tells Word to use the default Normal template to create the new document.

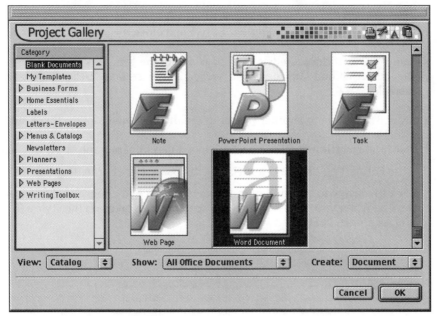

Figure 8-15: The Project Gallery

When you select a template from the Project Gallery, your new document takes on all the features of that template—including any text stored in the template, any character, paragraph, and page-layout formatting, any preset styles, and any new styles that you added to the document. Any macros, AutoText entries, or keyboard, menu, or toolbar definitions stored in the template are also available to the document.

The Easiest Way to Apply a Heading

Word's AutoFormat feature makes it incredibly simple to apply Word's built-in Heading 1 style to text. Simply type your line of text and press Return twice without adding any punctuation to the end of the line.

If you change the style called Heading 1 in any way, those changes will also apply to text that was styled Heading 1 using this method.

Hint: If this autoformatting feature doesn't work for you, make sure the headings are turned on in the AutoFormat tab (click the Options button in the dialog box that appears when you choose Format ⇨ AutoFormat).

New Feature Word 2001 introduces the concept of Themes. Themes are collections of styles, backgrounds, and other graphic adornment that give an overall look or appearance to a document. Almost all of the templates supplied with Word 2001 employ themes — for example, Artsy, Bars, Blends, and so forth. Almost every category in the Project Gallery includes examples of templates by these names — the only substantive difference between the templates in any given category is the theme applied to its contents. You can apply a theme to one of your documents by choosing Format ➪ Theme and selecting from the Theme list box. You can also apply one of a selection of color schemes to that theme. Be aware that it can take Word some time to load the information to display the theme in the Theme dialog box's Sample of Theme box.

You can use any of Word's predefined templates or you can create and save your own. If you take the time to examine the templates provided with Word, you may find many that can be useful in your work. When you click any template (except Normal), Word provides a preview to help you determine whether this template is right for you. Predefined Word template categories include those shown in Table 8-2 (the list is not exhaustive).

Table 8-2 Word Template Categories		
Category	*Subcategories*	*Comments*
Business Forms	Agendas, Brochures, Expense Reports, Fax Covers, Fundraising, Inventories, Invoices, Letterheads, Memos, Press Releases, Purchase Orders, Quotations, Refunds, Reports, Statements, Time-Billing	Themed variations are available in each subcategory except Fundraising, which has six templates, and Reports, which contains just a Business Report template.
Home Essentials	Family Medical, Résumés	Four templates exist in each subcategory.
Labels	(none)	No templates exist as such. A Mailing Label Wizard exists, which walks you through the process of creating your labels and applying a theme to them.
Letters-Envelopes	(none)	Contains eight letter and stationery templates, plus wizards for creating both letters and envelopes.
Menus & Catalogs	Catalogs, Menus	Contains themed variations in each subcategory.

Continued

Table 8-2 (continued)		
Category	*Subcategories*	*Comments*
Newsletters	(none)	Contains themed variations.
Planners	Checklists, Meals-Diets, Shopping Lists, To Do Lists	From one to four templates exist in each subcategory.
Web Pages	Cypress and Zero	Each subcategory includes the same seven templates, but each employs a different theme.

Because a template is a document, you use the same procedure to create and save a template as you use for a document. Word lets you specify whether you want to create a document or a template when you use the Project Gallery. At the lower-right corner of the Project Gallery, simply choose Template from the Create pop-up menu to make the new document a template, and then click OK. When the new document appears onscreen, you can add whatever boilerplate text, formatting, styles, and theme that you want, and then save the file by choosing File ➪ Save.

Note   You can also specify that a file be saved as a template after you have created it. For example, if you have created a boilerplate document, and you want to store that document as a template, you can do so with the File ➪ Save As command. In the Save As dialog box, choose Document Template from the Format pop-up menu. Be sure to name your new template appropriately. By default it will use the name you've previously used. Remember that two documents with the same name will lead to confusion. To have this template accessible from the Project Gallery with the File ➪ Project Gallery command (⌘-Shift-P), be sure to save it in the My Templates subfolder within the Templates subfolder in the Microsoft Office 2001 folder (choosing Document Template from the Format pop-up menu will place you in this directory by default).

Working with Templates

When you need to set standards for more than just the character and paragraph formatting of your documents, you can use templates. Templates can contain styles, boilerplate text or graphics, macros, and even custom menu, keyboard, and toolbar assignments.

Applying templates

To begin a new document using one of Word's templates, simply use the File ➪ Project Gallery command, and then click your desired template and click OK (or double-click the thumbnail depiction of the template). You can also access your own templates from the Project Gallery if you've saved them within the Templates:My Templates folder of the Microsoft Office 2001 folder. Otherwise, you can go directly to your template from the Finder and double-click it to open it, just as you would any other document.

Creating a template

To create a new template for use with Word, follow these steps:

1. From the File menu choose the Project Gallery command.

2. In the Project Gallery dialog box, choose Template from the Create pop-up menu and click OK. (This will start you with the Normal document.)

3. Design your template as desired. Set margins. Add graphics. Add any desired character, paragraph, section, or page-layout formatting, and create any desired styles. Define any desired AutoText entries or desired macros.

4. From the File menu, choose the Save command.

5. In the Name text box, enter a name for the template.

6. Select a folder in which to save your template if you do not wish it to be in the My Templates folder.

7. Click the Save button to save the template.

Tip

If you save your template in the Templates:My Templates folder of the Microsoft Office 2001 folder, it will always be available in the Project Gallery in the My Templates category. (However, you may lose your templates if you ever reinstall your software.) You can also create your own category by simply creating a new folder in the Templates folder. If you save your own templates in your own folder, you will always know which templates are your own, and you will always be able to identify them for saving during a software reinstall. You can even make several personalized folders/tabs.

What's "Normal"?

Some new users of Word get confused about what "Normal" refers to. Word has both a Normal style and a Normal template, and the two don't have the same meaning. The Normal *style* refers to one particular style (available in all Word's default templates) that defines the character and paragraph formatting for ordinary text. The Normal *template*, on the other hand, is a template file (saved as Normal) that contains Word's default styles along with the default keyboard, menu, and toolbar macro assignments. All styles and default keyboard, menu, and toolbar macro assignments that are saved to the Normal template are available for use from anywhere within Word.

Basing a new template on an existing template

You can use a simple variation of the steps in the preceding section to create a new template based on an existing template. In the Project Gallery, choose Template from the Create pop-up menu. Then, click the desired category under which the existing template is stored and choose the thumbnail or name of the template on which you want to base the new template, and click OK. When you save the template, be sure to save it under a different name than the original template.

Tip   To modify an existing template, simply open the template as you would any document, make the desired changes, and save it using an appropriate name.

Changing the default template

Word uses its default template, Normal, to store all of its global settings — those settings that are available no matter what document you are using. Because Normal is the default template, it is worth spending time to customize it so that it meets the needs of your work. The Normal template is a template like all other templates, so you can modify it (and save the changes) as you would any other template. Remember that the Default button present in some dialog boxes also lets you change the default settings in the Normal template. You can change the defaults for the character font, the page setup, and the language used by the proofing tools.

The Normal template is in the Templates folder of the Microsoft Office 2001 folder. Either go there and double-click the document called Normal, or use the File ⇨ Open command (or the Open button in the Project Gallery) to get to it and open it. Here's how to change a few aspects of the Normal template:

✦ **Default font.** To change the default font, choose Format ⇨ Font, select the desired font and point size in the Font dialog box, and then click the Default button. Click Yes in the next dialog box to verify that the changes should be stored in the Normal template.

✦ **Margins.** To change the margins, choose Format ⇨ Document and select the desired options from the Margins tab. Make any other appropriate changes you want in this dialog box. Click the Default button, and then click Yes in the next dialog box to verify that the changes should be stored in Normal. Click OK to close the Document dialog box. (You can also get to the Margins tab from the Word-specific screen of the Page Setup dialog box — File ⇨ Page Setup.)

✦ **Page setup.** To change the default page setup, choose File ⇨ Page Setup and select the desired options in the Page Setup dialog box. To change the orientation and paper size, do so in the first screen that appears by default, and then click the pop-up menu and select Microsoft Word from the list. This brings you to the Word-specific screen. On this screen, click the Default button, and then click Yes in the next dialog box to verify that the changes should be stored in Normal. You can make other page-customizing choices on the Word-specific screen. When you've made all your selections, click the Default button, and then click Yes in the next dialog box to verify that the changes should be stored in Normal.

✦ **Language.** To change the default language used by the proofing tools, choose Tools ⇨ Language to open the Language dialog box shown in Figure 8-16. Select the desired language from the list, click the Default button, and click Yes in the next dialog box to verify that the changes should be stored in Normal. Click OK to close the Language dialog box. (You may need to purchase optional dictionaries to use a language other than the one(s) supplied with the version of Word for your country.)

Figure 8-16: The Language dialog box

When you finish making changes to the Normal template, use the Save command from the File menu to save the changes.

Note

If you find you don't like the changes you've made to your Normal template, you can trash it. If Word can't find the Normal template it creates a new one. To trash it, simply go to the folder it's in, drag it to the Trash, and then empty the Trash. Unless you've assigned a custom location for your Normal template (using the File Locations tab of the Preference dialog box), Word looks for the Normal template directly inside the Templates folder of the Microsoft Office 2001 folder.

Creating and Applying a Template: An Exercise

Create your own business letterhead as a template for practice in creating templates. You can later create documents based on that template and the documents will automatically include your letterhead. To create your own business letterhead as a template, follow these steps:

1. Choose File ⇨ Project Gallery.

2. In the Project Gallery dialog box, choose Template from the Create pop-up menu and then click OK. A blank document appears with the title Template1 (or, if you've already tried this, Template2, Template3, and so on).

3. On the first three lines of the document type your name and address. Add a blank line after the last line of your address.

4. This is a good time to save your document. From the File menu, choose the Save command. Enter Letterhead in the Name text box. Select the Templates folder within the Microsoft Office 2001 folder, and then select the folder whose category you want your letterhead to show under — this defaults to the My Templates folder within the Templates folder, but you're free to select a different location. Click Save to save the template.

5. Select all three lines and click the Center button on the Formatting palette's Alignment and Spacing pane (or press ⌘-E) to center the text.

6. Format your characters. With the three lines still selected, click the arrow next to the Font box on the Formatting palette and drag down to select a font that you like. In the same manner, select the desired point size from the Font Size pop-up list next to the Font list. If you'd like to bold your name and address, click the Bold button next to the Font Size list (or use ⌘-B).

7. Place your cursor at the end of your text (or press ⌘-End) and press Return or Enter twice.

8. Close the document by clicking the close box in the top-left corner of the document window (or use ⌘-W).

You can now create documents based on the template that you saved. Choose File ➪ Project Gallery, select the My Templates category, and then click your Letterhead template to select it. (If you saved it in another folder within the Templates folder, your Letterhead template appears under the category with the name of that folder.) Click OK to open the template. A new document that already contains your letterhead, such as the example shown in Figure 8-17, appears. Notice that this document is not called Letterhead and is unnamed. This is because you've opened a template rather than a regular document. Doing a save will not affect the original template.

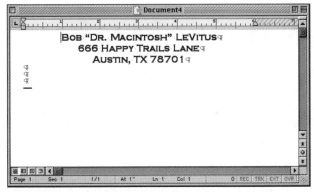

Figure 8-17: A sample letterhead produced with the new template

This chapter gives you a basic idea of what you can do with styles and templates. A detailed discussion of the possibilities could fill a book of its own. You can get more ideas about creating styles and templates of your own by examining the sample templates and themes provided with Word.

Summary

In this chapter, you learned how you can use styles and templates to mold the appearance of your documents to suit your needs and to make document creation easier. These points were discussed:

✦ Styles are collections of character and paragraph formatting decisions; templates are collections of styles, macros, and keyboard and toolbar assignments.

✦ You can choose a variety of styles from the Style list on the Formatting palette.

✦ Themes are collections of styles, backgrounds, fonts, and the other visual components used in a document.

✦ You can easily create new styles and can base new styles on existing styles.

✦ You can copy styles between documents and between templates.

✦ Word provides a number of predefined templates that employ different collections of styles and themes.

✦ All of Word's global settings regarding formatting are stored in the Normal template.

Where to go next

✦ In Chapter 9, you learn how to use macros to automate many of the tasks that you normally perform in Word.

✦ Because styles are, in effect, collections of character and paragraph formatting, it makes sense to be familiar with the mechanics of formatting when you want to put styles to work in your Word documents. You can find more details about those formatting specifics in Chapter 3.

✦ Styles, themes, and templates are useful when you want to do desktop publishing in Word. Chapter 10 has the lowdown on desktop publishing.

✦ Themes and templates are especially important in the design and layout of attractive Web pages. Chapter 11 explores Web publishing in Word.

✦ ✦ ✦

Working with Word Macros

Macros bring to mind scary connotations for some people, whereas other people, such as QuicKeys users, would hate to use a Mac without them. If you're one of the former, you can relax. Word 2001's macros require no programming genius. (If you're still nervous, check out Word 2001's macro feature. You might just be surprised.)

Macros are easy to create, and they can accomplish a great deal by saving time in your everyday work. In this chapter, you learn what macros are and how you can create them. You can then take a look at step-by-step examples that illustrate how you can use macros to automate common Word tasks.

Defining Macros

Macros are recorded combinations of keystrokes and certain mouse actions. Macros can automate many of the tasks that are normally performed manually, keystroke by keystroke, within Word. In a macro, you can record a sequence of keyboard and mouse entries and link them to a single key combination, or to a menu option, or to a toolbar button. Later, you can essentially play back the recorded sequence by pressing a key combination, or clicking a toolbar button, or choosing the menu option that you've assigned to it. When the macro plays back, Word performs as if you had manually executed the operations contained within the macro. When your work involves highly repetitive tasks such as the production of daily reports, or the repeating of certain formatting tasks, you can often save many keystrokes by creating a few macros.

Cross-Reference

At first glance, macros may seem similar to AutoText entries (see Chapter 2), but significant differences do exist. AutoText entries can reproduce text, but macros can do much more than simulate typing. Macros can perform menu and dialog box selections — operations that you cannot perform with AutoText entries. For example, if you routinely print two copies of a certain weekly report, you can create a macro that opens the document, chooses File ➪ Print from the menus, and marks the dialog box options needed to send two copies of the report to the printer.

Word records your macros as instructions in the programming language used by the Microsoft Office applications: Visual Basic for Applications (or VBA for short). Don't panic at the sound of the name (or the implication that you need to learn programming). You can create macros in Word without knowing one iota about Visual Basic for Applications. You can create macros in either of the following two ways:

✦ You can record a series of keyboard and mouse actions (the most commonly used method). This method requires no knowledge of Word's programming language.

✦ You can type a macro directly into a VBA Editor window. This method lets you do some advanced tricks by means of VBA commands that you can't do by recording actions, but it requires that you get your hands dirty with VBA.

You can not only use a macro to combine a sequence of commands that you use regularly, but you can also use a macro to perform routine editing and formatting tasks faster. Additionally, you can create a macro to reach buried dialog boxes more quickly.

Macros are especially useful when you format documents. You may have to change a document's font and spacing, enter heading styles, change margins, and check spelling and grammar. If you make these changes regularly, create a macro so you don't have to invoke the same commands over and over again. The following sections show you how to make your life easier with macros.

Alternatives to Macros

After spending this much time touting the benefits of macros, you should know that sometimes a macro might not be the most effective solution to a specific need. Before you jump into the task of designing macros for a task, consider whether another feature of Word can handle the task with less effort on your part.

If you want to use a macro to apply several character or paragraph formatting options to selected text, consider using a style instead. If you wish to apply extensive style and graphic changes to a document, consider using a Theme. If you want to use a macro to type long, repetitive phrases, consider using AutoCorrect instead to designate an abbreviation of your choice to serve as the phrase. And if you are trying to use a macro to automate the process of filling out a form, consider using fields to make this task easier.

Storing Macros

Where you store macros depends on two factors: the settings in the Template and Add-ins dialog box (which appears when you choose Tools ⇨ Templates and Add-Ins), and whether you are using the default template (Normal). If you are using the default template, macros are stored in Normal.

When you quit Word, you are asked whether you want to store the macros you've created during your session in the Normal template; you can answer Yes to store the macros or No to discard the macros.

When you choose Tools ⇨ Templates and Add-ins, the Templates and Add-ins dialog box appears, as shown in Figure 9-1.

Figure 9-1: The Templates and Add-ins dialog box

If you are using a template different from Normal, the storage location for new macros depends on the settings in the Templates and Add-ins dialog box. If you turn on the checkbox for the template you are using, Word saves macros in that template. You can click the Add button to display all your templates and then navigate to and select any template to add it to the list in the Templates and Add-ins dialog box. In addition to saving macros to templates you've checked in the Templates and Add-ins dialog box, on exit Word asks if you want to save the new macros to the Normal template file. All macros saved to Normal are global in nature, which means that they are available from any document in Word.

Creating Macros

The easiest way to record a macro is to use Word's macro recorder and follow the steps in the dialog boxes that appear. You then perform the desired actions with your keyboard and mouse and tell Word to stop recording. To turn the macro recorder on you can choose Tools ➪ Macro ➪ Record New Macro or you can double-click the letters REC in the status bar at the bottom of your document window. Both provide the same result.

You can also create macros manually by using Visual Basic for Applications, the programming language used with Microsoft Office applications. Using Visual Basic for Applications to write and edit macros is beyond the scope of this chapter, but, in short, you open a window into the VBA Editor and type macro instructions using VBA code. (Word and VBA programming is discussed in greater detail in Chapter 12.)

Note   The macro recorder is limited in an important way: you cannot record mouse actions within a document, such as selecting text with the mouse. If you try to use the mouse within a document, Word just beeps. However, you can use the mouse to select menu options and choose dialog box settings. If you want to select text as part of a macro, use the keyboard. (Hold down the Shift key and use the arrow keys to select large amounts of text; use ⌘-A to select all text in a document.)

Preparing to create your macro

Before you record your macro, you need to make some decisions about how it will be invoked, in what kinds of documents it will be used, and so on. Keep these points in mind when making these decisions:

✦ Give some thought to the overall workspace and how it should appear when the macro runs. You want to organize the workspace in the same manner as it should appear when the macro runs. For example, if you use the macro in a blank document, you should have a blank document onscreen before you begin recording the macro.

✦ Think about all the steps that you need to take to accomplish the task for which you are creating the macro. Write the steps down if this helps you remember them. You don't want to forget an important step as you are recording the macro.

✦ If you want the macro to apply to a selected piece of text, select the text before you begin to record the macro.

✦ Think of a name for the macro that reminds you of the macro's function. For example, if you have a bad habit of typing two periods at the end of a sentence and you want a macro that deletes the extra period, you can call the macro Delete_period.

✦ Decide how you want to invoke your macro. You can assign a key combination to your macro, place it in a menu in the menu bar, or create a button for it in a toolbar.

✦ When you choose to assign a key combination to a macro, you can use Shift, Control, Option, the ⌘ key, or a combination of these modifier keys along with all letters, numbers, and the function keys F2 through F12. Word also lets you use some keys such as the Forward Delete key (assuming your keyboard has one) alone or with a modifier key or keys. If you assign a key combination, you simply press it to execute the macro. If you assign ⌘-Option-P to a macro that prints two copies of the document that's currently open, and then you open a document and press ⌘-Option-P, the newly opened document prints twice.

Caution

While Word may let you assign macros to such keys as the Forward Delete key, it's not a good idea to do so because this disables the normal editing function of that key. (Even if you're aware of the change, your guest-users may not be and this might wreak havoc on your documents.) Also, be aware that Word has several shortcut keys that have already been assigned to execute other functions. You can assign a macro to these preassigned key combinations, but if you do, their preassigned function is lost in documents using those macros. For example, ⌘-B makes typed or selected text appear in bold font. If you assign ⌘-B to a macro, you would not be able to use that key combination to apply bold to any text in the document. Don't worry too much about accidentally overwriting a key combination, however, because Word tells you whether it's already assigned to another function.

Recording the macro

To record a macro, follow these steps:

1. Choose Tools ➪ Macro ➪ Record New Macro (or double-click the letters REC in the status bar) to bring up the Macro dialog box shown in Figure 9-2.

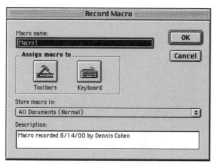

Figure 9-2: The Record Macro dialog box

2. Type a name for your macro in the Macro name text box. (Macro names cannot contain spaces, commas, or periods.) Word creates a new macro and, unless you choose a different template in the Store macro in pop-up menu, saves it in the Normal template, making the macro available to all active templates.

3. If desired, add an optional description in the Description text box. (It may help you later when you can't recall what you did or what you were thinking. See the section "Understanding the Macros Dialog Box.")

4. Click the Toolbars button or the Keyboard button, respectively, to assign the macro to a toolbar button or to a key combination. (The choice is up to you; one isn't necessarily better than the other. People who aren't wild about the use of the mouse generally prefer keyboard shortcuts. People who don't want to memorize tons of commands generally prefer menus or buttons.)

5. After you choose how you want to activate the macro, either the Customize Keyboard dialog box or the Customize dialog box appears.

If you choose to add the macro to a toolbar, click the Toolbars tab of the Customize dialog box (see Figure 9-3). If the desired toolbar isn't already visible onscreen, click the Toolbars tab and click to place a check by it to turn it on. In the Commands tab, drag the name of the macro from the Commands list out of the dialog box to the area on the toolbar where you want to place the button. Your cursor gives you a bold line as feedback to tell you where the new button will land. Release the mouse when the cursor is where you want your button. (You can then control-click the button and choose Properties to edit the button.)

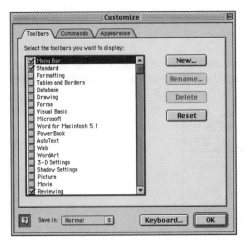

Figure 9-3: The Toolbars tab of the Customize dialog box

If you choose to assign your macro to a key combination, the Customize Keyboard dialog box appears (see Figure 9-4). The cursor is waiting in the Press new shortcut key text box so just press the key combination you want to assign to the macro. If these keys are already assigned to an item that you want to keep, use the Delete key to delete your combination and try a new one. When you are happy with the keys you've chosen, click the Assign button. The keys you've chosen are reported in the Current keys list. You can assign more than one key combination if you'd like.

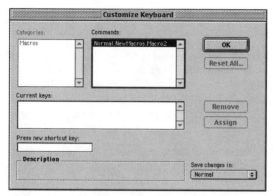

Figure 9-4: The Customize Keyboard dialog box

6. After assigning the activation command(s) click the OK button to start record-ing the macro. The Macro Recorder toolbar appears (see Figure 9-5). This toolbar contains just two buttons: a Stop button (on the left) and a Pause button (on the right).

Figure 9-5: The Macro Recorder toolbar, with the Stop button on the left and the Pause button on the right

7. Perform the steps that you want to record in the macro.

   If you want to pause the recording of the macro while you carry out actions that you don't want recorded, click the Pause button. When you want to start recording again, click the Pause button again.

8. After you finish recording, click the Stop button on the Macro Recorder toolbar. (Alternately, you can choose Tools ➪ Macro ➪ Stop Recording or double-click the letters REC in the status bar.)

Now you can activate the macro in the way you chose in Step 4: either from the toolbar or by pressing the key combination. You can also choose Tools ➪ Macro ➪ Macros, as detailed in the following section.

Note   You have two ways to tell if you are in Record mode. You see the Macro Recorder toolbar, and the letters REC in the status bar are active rather than grayed out.

What's Recorded? What Isn't?

Word's macro recorder doesn't actually record your actions; instead, it records the commands and the keystrokes you enter. Remember that the macro recorder doesn't record mouse movements. If you want to create a macro that depends on selecting text, select the text by using the keyboard and not the mouse. Clicking the OK button in a dialog box while you are recording a macro records the state of every option in the tab that is visible in the dialog box.

If you want to select options in another tab of the same dialog box, you must click OK to accept the options in the first tab and then reopen the dialog box. Click the new tab, select the options in it, and click OK to accept the options in the second tab. You do all these steps while you are recording the macro.

Running Macros

If you assigned your macro to a key combination, menu, or toolbar, you execute the macro by using the chosen method. To run macros with Tools ⇨ Macro ⇨ Macros, follow these steps:

1. Choose Tools ⇨ Macro ⇨ Macros. The Macros dialog box appears, as shown in Figure 9-6.

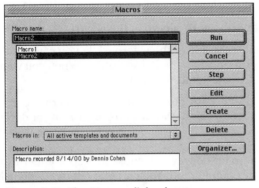

Figure 9-6: The Macros dialog box

2. Choose a macro from the list or type the name of the macro in the Macro name text box.

If the macro you want to execute isn't listed, Word may not be configured to run macros from all active templates. If the Macros in pop-up menu does not say *either* All active templates and documents *or* the name of the template in which you created the macro, select either of those values. This pop-up menu controls available macros based on the templates in which they were created.

3. Click Run. Word executes the chosen macro. (Or, to run the macro, double-click the name of the macro.)

If you try to run a macro and you can't find it, chances are that your document is using a different template from the one to which your macro was originally saved.

Deleting Unwanted Macros

If you create a macro and later decide that you no longer need it, you can delete it. To delete a macro, choose Tools ⇨ Macro ⇨ Macros. In the Macros dialog box that appears, click the unwanted macro to select it and click Delete. Click Yes in the confirmation alert that appears, and the macro is deleted.

Understanding the Macros Dialog Box

As noted earlier, you enter the name of the desired macro in the Macro name text box. After a name is entered (or chosen from the list box), all the buttons at the right side of the dialog box are made available. Also, if you entered a description when you created the macro, the description appears in the Description text box at the bottom of the dialog box. The buttons in the dialog box perform the functions shown in Table 9-1.

Table 9-1 Macro Dialog Box Buttons	
Button	**Purpose**
Run	Runs the selected macro.
Cancel	Closes the dialog box without running the macro
Step	Opens the selected macro in the VBA Editor and runs the macro one step at a time.

Continued

Table 9-1 *(continued)*

Button	Purpose
Edit	Opens the selected macro in the VBA Editor where you can edit the code.
Create	Creates a macro by using the Visual Basic for Applications program code. If a macro of that name already exists, you are asked whether you wish to replace the existing macro with a new macro.
Delete	Deletes the selected macro.
Organizer	Displays the Organizer dialog box, which can be used to copy macros between templates.

Macros can be copied from one template to another, which is very useful when you have created a macro in one template that you want to use in another. This is done by clicking the Organizer button in the Macro dialog box, which selects and displays the Macro Project Items tab of the Organizer dialog box to copy macros from one template to another. To copy a macro from one template to another, follow these steps:

1. Choose Tools ⇨ Macro ⇨ Macros to bring up the Macros dialog box.

2. Click the Organizer button to bring up the Organizer dialog box shown in Figure 9-7. The Macro Project Items tab should be in the front of the dialog box.

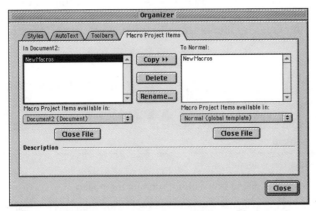

Figure 9-7: The Macro Project Items tab of the Organizer dialog box

3. You may need to close the open file. If so, click the Close File button on the left side of the dialog box. It then toggles to say Open File. Click this Open File button and choose the template in which you created the macro that you want to copy. On the right side of the dialog box do these steps again: Click the Close File button; click the Open File button; choose the template to which you want to copy the macro. If you want to copy macros into the document which was already open on the left, leave it open and just close the right-hand document or template (usually Normal), click the Open File button on the right, and select the file containing the macro. You can then select it on the right and click the Copy button (which now has the arrow pointing to the left).

4. The Copy button now appears active so you can copy the macro to the other template. You can also rename the macro by clicking the Rename button and entering a new name in the Rename dialog box.

Note   Word stores your macros in the Normal default template so you can use them with every document. You can use the Organizer dialog box to sort your macros by putting them into the templates in which you use the macros most often.

Using Macros in an Example

To show you that macros aren't intimidating, I'll let you try your hand at creating the following macro. After following these steps to create the macro, try one of your own.

In this example, assume that you regularly switch to Page Layout view from Normal view so you can see as much of your document as possible. You routinely choose View ➪ Page Layout menu and turn off the ruler. These steps are time-consuming if you do them often in a day, so you can save time by creating a macro to carry out the commands for you. To set the stage, first turn on your ruler (if it is not already on) by choosing View ➪ Ruler and check that you are in Normal view. To record the macro, follow these steps:

1. Choose Tools ➪ Macro ➪ Record New Macro to bring up the Record Macro dialog box.

2. In the Macro name text box, enter MoreSpace as the name for this macro.

3. Click the Keyboard button to assign the macro to a key combination. The Customize Keyboard dialog box appears.

4. Because Word doesn't use Control-. (period) for any other command, it makes a good key combination. Press Control-. (period) and then click the Assign button to assign this key combination to the MoreSpace macro.

5. Click the Close button to begin recording the macro.

6. Choose View ➪ Ruler to turn off the ruler.

7. Choose View ➪ Page Layout to activate this view.

8. Click the Stop button (the one on the left) on the Macro Recorder toolbar to end the recording.

To try out the macro, go back to the Normal view and redisplay the ruler. Then run the macro by pressing Control-.(period). Word turns off the ruler and switches to Page Layout view. Now you can create a macro that switches it back!

Cross-Reference   For another example of a useful Macro, see Chapter 12.

Creating Macros That Run Automatically

Assigning a specific name to a macro causes the macro to run automatically when a certain action is performed. For example, if you want a macro to run whenever you start Word, you would name that macro AutoExec. If you want a macro to run each time that you open a new document, you would name that macro AutoNew. Table 9-2 lists the names that you can assign macros to make them run when you perform the related action.

Table 9-2 Automatic Macros and the Actions That Trigger Them	
Macro Name	*Action That Triggers the Macro*
AutoExec	Launching Word
AutoExit	Quitting Word
AutoOpen	Choosing File ➪ Open
AutoNew	Choosing File ➪ New
AutoClose	Closing the current document

You can have only one AutoExec macro for your copy of Word. However, you can have a different AutoOpen macro for each template. A good use for an AutoOpen macro is to activate a special toolbar that you need in that template or to add a special message to the screen. Note that an AutoClose macro, which runs whenever you close a document, also runs whenever you quit Word before closing a Word document (because Word automatically closes documents when you attempt to quit Word).

Tip

An excellent use for an AutoOpen macro is one that automatically changes to your favorite folder for your Word files. When you create this macro, name it AutoOpen, and during recording use the Open dialog box from the File menu to switch to your favorite folder. After switching folders, click Stop to stop recording the macro. Of course, the utility of this is somewhat lessened by the presence of the Favorites button in the Open and Save dialogs.

Summary

In this chapter on using macros in Word, you learned the following:

✦ Macros are actually Visual Basic for Applications programs, but you don't need to know programming to create a macro. You can record a series of keystrokes and mouse actions as a macro.

✦ Macros can be assigned to toolbar buttons and key combinations.

✦ Some macros can be associated with launching or quitting Word, with creating a file, and with opening or closing a file. Such macros execute automatically when the event occurs.

Where to go next

✦ Macros can perform a number of tasks. Printing is one of them. Chapter 4 has the details about using macros to print.

✦ You may also create macros to format your documents. For some ideas on the different formatting options you have and how you can implement them, see Chapter 3.

✦　　✦　　✦

Desktop Publishing with Word

This chapter explains several techniques for using Word's desktop publishing capabilities. You learn to create documents that contain graphic images, text boxes, frames, and columns. You also learn how to create newsletters and other documents that contain headlines.

Word provides significant drawing and charting tools to create business graphs (also called charts). It is easy to insert into Word documents graphs created with the built-in Microsoft Graph, the popular FastTrack Schedule, or many other programs.

Tip Many programs let you save files in a common format. These saved files can easily be imported into Office documents. For example, Photoshop files can be saved as JPEG, GIF, TIFF, EPS, or PICT (among others) and are an ideal addition to a Word, PowerPoint, or Excel document.

Working with Columns

At times you will want columns in your documents. This section explains how to add columns. You can set your entire document in newspaper-style columns or add columns to just a section of it. Word lets you have up to eight columns in a portrait layout. To insert columns into a document, follow these steps:

1. Select the text that you want to place in columns.

2. Click the Columns button on the Standard toolbar (this button shows two columns of text) and drag to indicate the number of columns that you want for your text, or choose Format ➪ Columns. If you choose the second option, the Columns dialog box appears (see Figure 10-1).

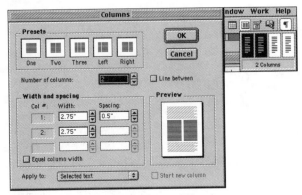

Figure 10-1: *Left:* The Columns dialog box.
Right: The Columns button.

Only four columns show when you click the Columns button, but if you drag right, the selection will grow, enabling you to select up to eight columns. These columns are preset in width. They are adjustable, as explained in the next section.

In the dialog box, you use the arrows next to the Number of columns text box to set up to twelve columns for your document. You can also choose the width of each column. For example, you can have two columns, one column smaller than the other column. The smaller column can be placed on the left or the right side of the page. Adjusting the settings in the Width and spacing area of the dialog box lets you easily set column width and spacing. To place a thin-ruled line between each column, check the Line between checkbox. The Preview area lets you see the document layout with the chosen settings.

Column width can also be adjusted visually in the document itself. This method is useful if you are not sure what width you want the column to be. To change the column width in the document, move the mouse pointer to the column marker on the ruler until the pointer turns into a box with arrows on both sides. Then click and drag to make the columns the desired width.

Using the AutoFormat Command

Automatic formatting is a relatively new feature, first introduced in Word Version 6.0. Word's AutoFormat command provides a quick and easy way to format a document that you have created. AutoFormat makes Word analyze each of the paragraphs in your document to determine how the paragraph is used. Even though you may have formatted the text, the AutoFormat command may change the formatting to improve the overall appearance of the document; however, styles you have applied are not changed unless you permit Word to do so.

So Where Are My Columns?

When you add columns to a document, Word automatically switches to Page Layout view so you can see the columns. If you switch to Normal view, you'll probably wonder what happened to your columns. Don't think you've done something horribly wrong. Columns aren't visible side-by-side in Normal view.

To see your columns side by side (the way they will actually appear when printed), switch from Normal view to Page Layout view (View ➪ Page Layout). Many of Word's desktop publishing features are not evident unless you are in Page Layout view. If you are desktop publishing in Word and prefer to work in Normal view, you may want to switch to Page Layout view after you have entered your basic text.

Note Remember the differences between the AutoFormat button and Format ➪ AutoFormat. To format your document quickly, click the AutoFormat button. If you use this method, however, you are on your own to review the changes and to change things back. If you're at all worried about Word wantonly reformatting your text, and you wish to review each of the changes AutoFormat makes, use Format ➪ AutoFormat and select the AutoFormat and review each change radio button. When Word is finished formatting the document, it presents another dialog box that gives you the opportunity to accept all changes, reject all changes, or review the changes one by one. Simply select the option you want.

AutoFormat removes extra returns or paragraph marks at the end of each line of body text. It also replaces straight quotation marks and apostrophes with "smart" (curly) quotation marks and apostrophes. AutoFormat can also replace hyphens, asterisks, and other characters used in a bulleted list with another kind of bullet character. It indents your paragraphs to replace horizontal spacing that you inserted with the Tab key or the spacebar. It makes e-mail addresses into live mailto links and URLs into Web links. You can program AutoFormat to add copyright ©, trademark ™, and registered trademark ® symbols to a document. It can even add borders and shading for a professional look.

To use AutoFormat, open the desired document and choose Format ➪ AutoFormat for the dialog box, or, if you have added the AutoFormat button to one of your toolbars, you can click it. If you use the AutoFormat button, you will not have the opportunity to review your changes. If you choose Format ➪ AutoFormat, you will see the AutoFormat dialog box, which provides the opportunity to review each change and then accept or reject each change separately.

Cross-Reference The AutoFormat command is very valuable. It can take the monotony out of formatting documents for users who don't do it along the way. See Chapter 8 for more information about the styles Word uses as it formats your document.

You may feel a little nervous about permitting Word to make such global changes to your document. For this reason, you can allow or disallow certain specific changes to be made by choosing Format ➪ AutoFormat, and then clicking the Options button. This brings you to the AutoFormat tab of the AutoCorrect dialog box (see Figure 10-2). The AutoFormat tab lets you control the changes Word makes to your document when you select the AutoFormat command. You can control whether Word preserves the styles that you apply or whether Word applies styles to lists, headings, and other paragraphs. In the Replace area of the AutoFormat tab, you can control the replacements Word makes as it formats. It is a good idea to review these options before you begin the AutoFormat process to prevent unwanted changes.

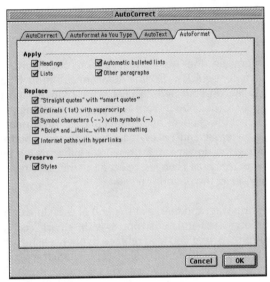

Figure 10-2: The AutoFormat tab

When Not to Use AutoFormat

Word's AutoFormat command shares an interesting trait with that of Excel's: they both work well with documents (in Excel's case, worksheets) that follow a conventional format. If your document is very unusual in terms of how it is structured, you may not like the kind of changes that AutoFormat applies.

If you happen to click the Accept button in the AutoFormat dialog box, and you don't like what Word does to your document, you can reverse the changes by choosing Edit ➪ Undo (⌘-Z).

If you select the option to review the formatting results, when the formatting is complete, a second AutoFormat dialog box appears. It contains the Review Changes button. Click this button to display the Review AutoFormat Changes dialog box (see Figure 10-3), which enables you to review the changes that were made. Using this box, you can review the changes one by one by clicking the right arrow Find button to move forward, or clicking the left arrow Find button to move backward in the document. Each change is explained in the dialog box, as well as highlighted in the document.

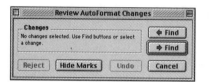

Figure 10-3: The Review AutoFormat Changes dialog box

Tip

If you forget to ask Word to let you review changes, or if you gamble and let Word do its thing but don't like the effect, you can always use the Edit ➪ Undo command to revert your document to its former glory. As another safety measure, save your document before beginning the AutoFormat. That way, in addition to the Undo command, you can simply close your document without saving it, and then reopen it in its pre-AutoFormat form.

Understanding Graphic Images

Word's capability to import graphic images from other software adds much to its desktop publishing capabilities. The basic installation of Word enables you to import any of the image types listed in Table 10-1.

<table>
<tr><td colspan="2" align="center">Table 10-1
Image Types That Are Importable into Word</td></tr>
<tr><td>*File Type*</td><td>*Popular Abbreviation*</td></tr>
<tr><td>Encapsulated PostScript</td><td>EPS</td></tr>
<tr><td>Enhanced Windows Metafile</td><td>EMF</td></tr>
<tr><td>FlashPix</td><td>FPX</td></tr>
<tr><td>[CompuServe] Graphics Interchange Format</td><td>GIF</td></tr>
<tr><td>Joint Photographic Experts Group File Interchange Format</td><td>JPEG</td></tr>
</table>

Continued

Table 10-1 (continued)	
File Type	**Popular Abbreviation**
Macintosh Picture	PICT
Macintosh Paint	PNTG
[Adobe] PhotoShop Document	PSD, 8BPS
Portable Network Graphics	PNG
QuickTime Image Format	QTIF
Silicon Graphics Incorporated	SGI
Tagged Image File Format	TIFF
Targa	TGA, TPIC
Windows Bitmap	BMP
Windows Metafile	WMF

Word uses graphic filters to convert these image file formats to an image that appears in your document. If you try to import a picture (Insert ⇨ Picture) that your copy of Word lacks a filter for, you will have to install the necessary filter. Running the Value Pack Installer easily does this. See Appendix A or your Word documentation for details.

Note   As programs grow in popularity, new graphic filters are added to Word, so your version of Word may be able to import more file types than are listed in Table 10-1. Refer to your Word documentation and the Microsoft Office for the Mac Web pages (www.microsoft.com/macoffice) to determine which file types your version of Word can import.

Two kinds of graphic images exist: bitmapped images, which are created in painting programs, and object (or vector) images, which are created in drawing programs. Because both types of images have definite advantages and disadvantages, you should be familiar with both.

Bitmapped images

Bitmapped images are images composed of dots or pixels. These images are called bitmaps because the image is literally defined within the computer by assigning each onscreen pixel to a storage bit (location) within the computer's memory. You can create your own bitmapped images by using any painting program, such as the Painting environment in AppleWorks or Dabbler 2 (by MetaCreations), or by using clip art (predrawn images). Figure 10-4 shows an example of a bitmapped image (a screen shot) inserted into a Word document.

Figure 10-4: An example of a bitmapped image inserted into a Word document

Photographs are also stored as bitmapped images. If you have access to a scanner, you can scan photographs and store them on disk as bitmapped images by using the directions supplied with your scanner. You can then import the bitmapped image of the photo into your Word document. Note that black-and-white photographs typically scan with greater clarity than color photographs. Digital cameras are also a very common source of bitmapped images. Figure 10-5 shows an example of a digital photograph inserted into a Word document.

Bitmapped images have one major advantage and one major disadvantage. The strength of bitmapped images is that you can easily modify them at a very fine level of detail. Most painting programs enable you to modify existing parts of a bitmapped image by selectively adding or deleting bits. You can zoom in on the image as if it were under a magnifying glass, and you can turn individual pixels black, white, or any one of a range of colors. The disadvantage of bitmapped images is that you typically cannot modify their size by scaling (stretching or shrinking the image in one or more directions) without distorting the image or making it appear jagged.

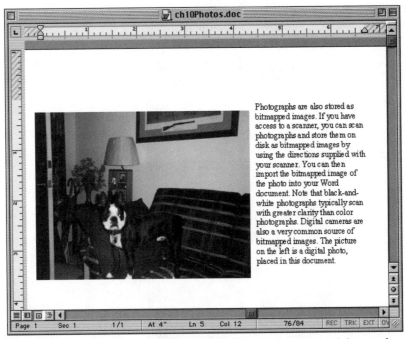

Figure 10-5: A digital photo (of Dennis's Boston terrier, Spenser) inserted as a bitmapped image in a Word document

Object images

Drawing programs, such as Adobe Illustrator or the Draw environment in AppleWorks, create object images. Drawing programs work better than painting programs for creating line drawings (which is typically art that looks as if it were created from lines only—in other words, with no shading) such as company logos, maps, and images of constructed objects (houses, cars, planes, bridges, and so on), especially if you want to view or print them at a number of different sizes. Painting programs work better than drawing programs for projects that you would sketch on paper without using a ruler, such as drawing a person's portrait.

The disadvantage of painting programs becomes the advantage of drawing programs, and vice versa. For example, object images can easily be scaled, which means that you can change the size of the object by stretching it or shrinking it in one or more directions. Because the object is based on a collection of mathematically defined lines and curves, the software simply expands or contracts the lines to expand or contract the entire image. The disadvantage of object images, however, is that you don't easily get a painted look. Paint programs enable you to work pixel by pixel, adding the tiniest of touches.

Getting Some Snazzy Graphics

If you'd like to jazz up your documents with some snazzy graphics but don't happen to be an artist, don't worry. There's no shortage of artwork available. In fact, the default installation of Office 2001 even gives you some to start with. (It's stored in the Clipart folder in the Microsoft Office 2001 folder.) In addition, you can find clipart and stock photos in many inexpensive commercial disk packages.

Plenty of advertisements for specialized packages appear in the back pages of your favorite Mac magazines. Macintosh user groups may also be another good source of clipart. You can also find large quantities of free or shareware art on the Internet, as well as commercial art. Lastly, commercial online services may have shareware clipart online.

Note   You can paste or import a bitmapped image into a PostScript-based drawing program; however, this does not convert the bit-mapped image, which consists of pixels, into an image of PostScript-based lines. Curved lines in a bitmapped image are made up of "stepped" pixels (squares) of light and dark pixels. Bringing a bitmapped image into a PostScript-based program doesn't make the lines perfectly straight. If you bring a bitmapped image into a drawing program and then try to scale the image, the jagged patterns change disproportionately. The result is often a distorted image. Similarly, you can place a PostScript-based image in a painting program. It will probably look fine at its original size, but it is unlikely to enlarge well because the lines will become "stepped."

Using Graphic Images

The addition of graphic images to your desktop publishing documents is very useful. After inserting the images, you will need to perform various tasks to make the object look presentable in your document. This includes tasks such as cropping, or adding borders or callouts to your graphic image. In Chapter 2, we discussed pasting graphics and inserting clipart. In this chapter, we show you how to insert images from other files.

Inserting images into Word

Insert ➪ Picture is used to insert images from a wide range of sources. To insert a picture into your document, follow these steps:

1. Place the insertion pointer where the image is to appear.

2. Choose Insert ➪ Picture ➪ From File to open the Choose a Picture dialog box, as shown in Figure 10-6.

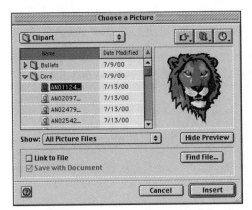

Figure 10-6: The Choose a Picture dialog box

3. Using the normal Mac technique to open a file, select the folder your image is in. By default, all picture files will appear in the list of files within that folder. To make it easier to find the correct image, you can control what type of files you see in the window (although this is not necessary). To see files of a particular type, click the Show pop-up menu and choose your desired file format from the list.

If the preview area is hidden, click the Show Preview button (it changes to Hide Preview). As you select a file, a preview appears. Preview is a great timesaver when searching for an image. If you'd rather not see a preview, click the Hide Preview button.

If you want to link the image in Word to the original graphic file, turn on the Link to File checkbox. Word inserts the image as a field, and you can use the Update Field key (F9) to update the picture if you later make changes to the image. The advantages to this include decreased file size and automatic updating when you change the source image. The disadvantages are that you have to include both files in the correct locations if you give the document to someone else, and that moving the image to a different folder or disk can break the link.

4. Click the Insert button to close the dialog box and to insert the image into your Word document. (You can also double-click the image name, or press Return or Enter to issue the Insert command.) The image appears at the insertion pointer location. Figure 10-7 shows an example of a clipart image pasted into a Word document using this technique.

Normally, you can think of an image that you insert into a document as a single large character, such as a giant letter A. As such, you cannot place text around the image because the image takes up one giant line of text. This is considered an "inline" graphic. However, you can surround the image with a frame (which might be invisible). You can position the frame containing the image anywhere in your document. Using a frame around the image makes available the option of text wrapping; that is, text will automatically reposition itself around the frame. (Wrapped text is visible only in Online Layout and Page Layout views.) See the "Working with Text Boxes" section later in this chapter for details about using frames in Word.

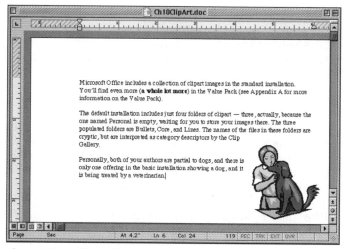

Figure 10-7: Clipart inserted into a Word document

In addition to importing graphics, you can also create graphics directly from Word. To do so, make the Drawing toolbar visible (View ➪ Toolbars ➪ Drawing) if it isn't already. This toolbar contains several tools for creating shapes and images. Some buttons provide pop-up selections of tools to create shapes, while other buttons turn your cursor into a drawing tool so you can draw your own shape directly within your document.

Don't Forget Copy and Paste or Drag and Drop

In addition to using the Insert command to place images in your document, you can paste them in. Just open the image you want, select it, and copy it (Edit ➪ Copy or ⌘-C). Return to Word, place the insertion pointer at the desired location, and paste (Edit ➪ Paste or ⌘-V). You can also drag the icon of a graphic file into your Word document or drag images from other applications that support drag-and-drop into your document.

The image from the other program is placed into your Word document at the insertion point.

Changing the look of the image

An inserted image can be scaled (resized) or cropped (trimmed). It is easier to use the mouse than the keyboard to change the size of the image, but the keyboard gives more precise control. If using the mouse, select the image and drag the sizing handles that appear; with the keyboard, select Format ⇨ Picture, and then enter dimensions in the dialog box that appears.

You can also apply borders to an image by using Format ⇨ Borders and Shading or by clicking the Borders button on the Formatting palette (Borders and Shading pane). You cannot apply shading to an image as you can to a paragraph. Notice that when you select a picture and choose Format ⇨ Borders and Shading, the Shading tab is dimmed in the dialog box.

Scaling an image

To scale an image (in other words, to make it larger or smaller), you must first select it. Instead of dragging over the image, as you do for text, click it. Word selects the image and displays sizing handles. Your cursor also changes to a pointer. (If you're really not into using your mouse, you can select an image by placing the insertion pointer anywhere inside the image, hold down the Shift key and press the right-arrow key once.)

Note   Drawn objects can be scaled by dragging sizing handles or by using the Formatting palette (Size pane), but not by using the Format Picture dialog box.

To scale a graphic visually with the mouse, drag one of the handles until the image reaches the desired size. Dragging the center-left or the center-right handle resizes the width of the image. Dragging the center-top or the center-bottom handle resizes the height of the image. Dragging any of the corner handles resizes both the width and height of the image. To maintain the image's proportions, press the Shift key while you click and drag one of the corner handles. To scale an image numerically, select the image and use the Formatting palette's Size pane or choose Format ⇨ Picture to open the Format Picture dialog box. Then select the Size tab, as shown in Figure 10-8.

The scaling can be changed by either entering a percentage in the Height and Width text boxes in the Scale area (in which case the Size and rotate measurements change accordingly), or by entering a measurement in the Height and Width boxes in the Size and rotate area (in which case the Scale percentages change accordingly). To maintain the image's proportions, use the Scale feature and be sure to enter the same number in the Height and Width boxes. After you have made your desired changes, click OK or press Return.

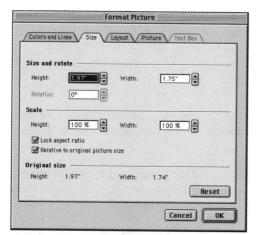

Figure 10-8: The Size tab of the Format Picture dialog box

Tip

Word remembers the original size of an image, regardless of how you scale or crop it, so you can later undo your modifications — even after you've saved and closed your document. Use the Reset button in the Size tab of the Format Picture dialog box to restore an image to its original size.

Cropping an image

To crop a graphic, select the Crop tool (which looks like two corners overlapping) from the Picture toolbar. (This toolbar should activate automatically when you place a picture in your document. If it doesn't turn it on, try selecting it using the View ➪ Toolbars ➪ Picture command.) Your cursor takes on the appearance of the Crop tool. Using this cursor, drag any handle to crop your image.

Dragging a handle on either center side crops the image on that side; dragging a handle on the center top or the center bottom crops the image from the top or the bottom; and dragging any of the corner handles crops from both the side nearest that corner and the top or bottom nearest that corner.

You can also crop a graphic by using a dialog box. Select the image and then choose Format ➪ Picture and make sure you're in the Picture tab. In the Picture dialog box, use the measurement boxes in the Crop from area to enter the amounts by which you want to crop the image. A measurement in the Left and Right text boxes specifies how much the image will be cropped on the left and right sides, and a measurement in the Top and Bottom text boxes specifies how much the image will be cropped on the top and bottom. Use the Reset button to restore the original measurements if you need to start fresh. After you have made your desired changes, click OK (or press Return or Enter). As with scaling, you can always go back and use the Reset button to restore a cropped image to its original size.

Adding borders

You can apply a border to an image using the Drawing toolbar, the Picture toolbar, the Formatting palette, or the Format Picture dialog box. Regardless of method, you must begin by selecting the image.

If you have the Drawing toolbar showing, select the image, and then click either one of the two buttons that look like lines and select the desired line from the menu that pops up. (Each button provides different lines.) To apply a color to your border, click the Line Color button (which looks like a pencil drawing a line) and select your color from the list that pops up. Choosing More Line Colors opens the Mac OS Color Picker; Pick Line Color turns your cursor into an eyedropper and will "pick up" the color at whatever point you click (even outside your Word document); and Patterned Lines will display the Patterned Lines dialog box, from which you can choose a pattern, as well as foreground and background colors for the pattern.

Tip   If you want to create a simple border the full width of your paragraph, you can take advantage of one of Word's many AutoFormat features. Simply type three or more consecutive hyphens (-) or equal signs (=) in a row and press Return. The hyphens create a single line border while the equal signs create a double line border.

If you have the Formatting palette showing, select the image, and then choose the desired line from the Style pop-up in the Lines pane. Selecting More Lines opens the Colors and Lines tab of the Format Picture dialog box.

If you have the Picture toolbar showing, select the image, click the Format Picture button, and select the Colors and Lines tab of the Format Picture dialog box. Now, you can select the type of border you wish, so long as the picture's wrapping style is not Inline with Text.

Alternately, you can choose Format ➪ Borders and Shading. This brings you to the Colors and Lines tab of the Format Picture dialog box. In the Line area, select the type of border you want.

Borders can be applied to text, not just to tables and images. In fact, in Word 2001 you can apply a border to any word or phrase, not just to an entire paragraph. However, borders are applied to text differently than they are to graphics or tables. Select the text to which you want to add the border, and then select Format ➪ Borders and Shading to make your selection. This dialog box is highly visual so you will clearly see the effect before applying it. A quicker way to add a border around selected text is to click the pop-up arrow next to the Type button on the Formatting palette (Borders and Shading pane). This enables you to apply a border to the top, bottom, right, or left (or any combination) of the text. You can also set the color, width, and pattern using the other pop-up buttons in this Formatting palette pane.

Adding Callouts to Your Art

You may want to add callout text to the images you insert in your documents. You have several ways to insert callouts. The most flexible way is to click the Text Box button on the Drawing toolbar, which selects the Text Box tool. Then bring your cursor to the approximate place in your document where you want to place the callout. Your cursor becomes a cross hair (+). Click and drag to define a text box and then release the mouse button. You now have a free-floating text box with a text insertion cursor ready and waiting for you to enter your text. At any time you can click this text box and drag it into the desired position.

The other way is to use Word's Table feature. Add a table with the Table ⇨ Insert ⇨ Table command (or toolbar button) and insert the image into one cell of the table. Then type the text of your callout in an adjacent cell of the table and format the table so the text appears where you want.

Editing images

After you have placed an image into Word, you can edit it. To edit an image, double-click the image, or Control-click and choose Edit Picture from the shortcut menu. Then you can edit the picture by using the Drawing toolbar and the Formatting palette.

After you are finished editing the image, click the Close Picture button located on the tiny free-floating Edit Picture toolbar that has automatically appeared.

Word's drawing capabilities are object-based, so you may get unsatisfactory results if you import a bitmapped image into a Word document and then modify it with the Drawing toolbar.

New Feature

A number of bitmap-level editing tools are available on the Picture toolbar, new to Microsoft Office 2001. These include adjustments for brightness, contrast, red eye, color adjustment, and a variety of selection tools located in the Picture toolbar.

Inserting Graphs into Word

You can insert graphs (also called charts) into Word by using Microsoft Graph, a program designed for creating business graphs. Graphs can also be inserted from spreadsheet programs. To insert a graph from Microsoft Graph, follow these steps:

1. Choose Insert ⇨ Object to open the Object dialog box. In the Object Type list box, select Microsoft Graph 2001 Chart and click OK. This adds a default graph and a Datasheet window. A new set of menus also appears to enable you to work with the chart. In the cells of the datasheet that appears over the graph, you can type the values that you want to use for the graph. Figure 10-9 shows the graph and the Datasheet window in a document.

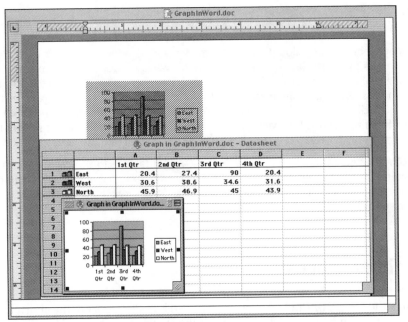

Figure 10-9: A graph and Datasheet window in a Word document

2. The default chart appears in your document, but it is grayed out. Two chart windows appear — one that's a spreadsheet and the other that's the chart you'll edit.

   Enter the desired numeric data into the cells of the Datasheet window. The names of the headings in the cells are used as the categories of the chart. You can change them, too.

3. Choose Chart ➪ Chart Type to select the type of chart you want. In the Chart Type dialog box that appears, choose a chart type from the list box and click the image of the desired chart subtype. Then click OK.

4. Control-click any desired part of the chart to display a shortcut menu that enables you to add any desired titles, legends, gridlines, or other items to the chart by choosing Chart Options.

5. When you are finished making the desired refinements to the chart, select File ➪ Quit and Return to *document name* (⌘-Q). Figure 10-10 shows a document with a chart that's been customized and inserted.

You can make changes to your chart at any time. You can either double-click the chart or Control-click the chart, and then choose Chart Object ➪ Edit. Both actions relaunch Microsoft Graph and call the Datasheet windows back up.

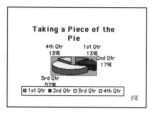

Figure 10-10: The sample document with a pie chart inserted from Microsoft Graph

You can also use Copy and Paste or Drag and Drop to copy graphs from another program to your Word documents. To use Copy and Paste, simply display the graph in a window, select the graph, and choose Edit ⇨ Copy. Then leave or quit that program and switch to Word in the usual manner. Place the insertion pointer at the desired location and choose Edit ⇨ Paste to insert the graph into your document. For Drag and Drop, display and select the graph and drag it to your Word document — a black insertion cursor will appear, tracking where the dragged object will be placed if dropped.

Tip　You can use the clipboard techniques and Drag and Drop to copy information from any other Mac software into a Word document.

Because Microsoft Graph shows a simple bar graph by default whenever it is launched, you can easily use the program to insert a graph into a document. For practice, follow these steps to place a graph in a document using Microsoft Graph:

1. Open a new document and enter this text:

   ```
   Word makes inserting graphs very easy. Many options are
   provided for the formatting of a chart, which will be
   discussed as we move along in the chapter.
   ```

2. Place the insertion pointer at the end of the paragraph and press Return to begin a new line.

3. Choose Insert ⇨ Object and choose Microsoft Graph 2001 Chart from the dialog box that appears. Click OK to open the Microsoft Graph window. (Actually, you can save time by double-clicking your selection — Microsoft Graph 2001 Chart.) A default bar graph appears in the document and two new windows open.

4. In the Data window that contains the spreadsheet, click the cell that contains East, type the name **Karen**, and press Return or Enter. For the cell that contains West, type **Cori**; and for the cell containing North, type **Alex**. Change a few of the numbers using the same methods.

5. Select File ⇨ Quit and Return to Document (⌘-Q).

6. Back in your document, press Return twice to move your cursor down two lines, and then type:

   ```
   Here it is--my first chart.
   ```

You now have a chart containing a bar graph. If you later want to make more changes to the graph's design, you can double-click the graph to switch back to the windows, menus, and toolbar of Microsoft Graph. For now, leave the document open onscreen because you will use it in an upcoming exercise involving frames.

Working with Text Boxes

As you work with text in Word, you will find times when you want to place text into a freestanding container; in Word, this kind of container is called a text box. One common use for a text box is to draw attention to the text within it. Another great reason to use a text box is that you can move it and have other text wrap around it, creating a nice, refined look. However, perhaps the strongest benefit of a text box is that you can link text boxes and have text flow from one to another. This is particularly useful when you have a multipage document such as a newsletter. Text will flow and reflow as you edit the text, resize the text boxes, or make changes to the graphics that your text flows around. Links don't even have to flow forward over pages; text just flows from the first box you create, to the next, and so on. In any case, within the text box, your text can be formatted as usual.

Creating a text box around existing text

You can place a text box around an existing section of text by following these steps:

1. Select the text you wish to create a box for by using your favorite selection method.

2. Choose Insert ⇨ Text Box. Word then inserts a text box around the text you selected and the Fill, Line, Size, and Wrapping panes appear in the Formatting palette. The document switches to Page Layout view if it's not in Page Layout view already.

If all you want is to draw attention to the text in the box or have other text wrap around the box, skip to "Formatting text boxes" and continue from there. If you want to create linked text boxes, continue here, following the steps to insert an empty text box into a document.

Inserting an empty text box into a document

At times you may want to insert an empty text box into a document to serve as a placeholder for text you will be entering later. Such is the case when you plan to link text boxes, or when you are planning your document's layout but don't yet have the text. Wrapping will apply in the text box, so you will not need to press

Return or Enter at the end of your lines. To insert an empty text box, follow these steps:

1. Be sure that no text or object is selected. (For example, if you just created a text box, it is selected so click outside of that text box to deselect it.)

2. Choose Insert ➪ Text Box. The cursor then turns into a crosshair.

3. Click and drag to draw the text box to the size you wish. (You can always resize the text box later.)

You can create as many empty text boxes as you'd like on any pages within your document. If you plan to link the text boxes, don't worry about their order of creation, as it doesn't matter.

Linking text boxes

To link text boxes, first follow the steps in the earlier section "Creating a text box around existing text." Then follow the steps in the section "Inserting an empty text box into a document" (immediately prior to this section). Finally, the floating Text Box toolbar comes into play. If it hasn't appeared, choose View ➪ Toolbars ➪ Text Box. It enables you to link your text boxes. Follow these steps to link text boxes so that text flows from one to another:

1. Click the first text box to select it.

2. Click the Create Text Box Link button on the Text Box toolbar (it's the button that looks like a closed chain). If you happen to close the Text Box toolbar, you can open it again from the View ➪ Toolbars menu. In case you hadn't noticed this toolbar option before, and you're wondering why, it's because the Text Box toolbar can only be activated when you have a text box in your document.

3. Now click inside the text box that you want your text to flow to (if it doesn't fit inside the first text box). This must be an empty, unlinked text box.

4. To link to another box, click the second text box again (because it was the one last linked) and repeat Steps 2 and 3. Clicking the box that was last linked and repeating Steps 2 and 3 can link additional boxes.

Instead of using the Text Box toolbar, you can use the shortcut menu. In Step 1, after you select the first text box, move your cursor to the text box's border so the cursor becomes either a hand or a resizing cursor. Control-click and select Create Text Box Link and then proceed with Step 3.

Text flows in the order of your links regardless of the order in which you created the text boxes or the order in which you dragged them. To unlink text boxes, select the last box you wish to have in the link, and then click the Break Forward Link button (which just happens to look like a broken link).

Linked text boxes may be formatted as any other text boxes so continue on with the rest of the sections on text boxes. The fun of linked text boxes is in resizing them. As you do, your text reflows.

Formatting text boxes

After you have placed the text box(es) in your document, you may want to change the lines and text wrapping that Word uses as defaults. You have the option to change many of the aspects of the text box, such as its location. You can also change whether adjacent text should be permitted to wrap around the text box. All text box movement and most text box formatting can be done using the mouse, by dragging, or by using the ruler, Formatting palette, and toolbars. At times you may prefer to work numerically, or find a setting that can't be done with the mouse (such as setting the top or bottom margin for the text within the box). In this case, you can double-click your text box's frame to open and use the Format Text Box dialog box shown in Figure 10-11. (You can also choose Format ⇨ Text Box to work within the Format Text Box dialog box.)

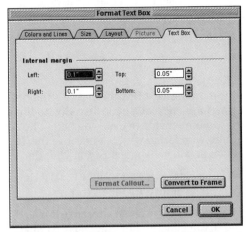

Figure 10-11: The Text Box tab in the Format Text Box dialog box

The Format Text Box dialog box has five tabs. Each of these tabs aids in formatting a text box after you have inserted the text box in your document: The Colors and Lines tab enables you to change the color and line size of the text box. Clicking each option reveals a pop-up list full of choices. Just click and drag to make your selections.

The Size tab is where you manipulate the size of the text box by changing its height and width. This tab even enables you to rotate the box. Scaling the text box is also an option.

The Layout tab controls the wrapping of text around your text box and its horizontal alignment on the page. If you click the Advanced button on this tab, the Advanced Layout dialog box opens, which enables you to control the position of the text box on your document page as well as provides further control over wrapping. The radio buttons, pop-up menus, and text boxes in the Horizontal and Vertical areas change the position of the text box on the page.

When a text box containing a picture is active, the Picture tab can control the cropping, brightness, and contrast of the image.

The Text Box tab determines the internal margins of the text box, enabling you to create space between the frame's border and the text inside the frame. The Convert to Frame button enables you to convert your text box to a frame. Frames are similar to text boxes and do less in the way of text flow, but they are the necessary choice when you want your box to include comment marks, notes, or fields.

Moving text boxes

After you have inserted a text box, you can easily move it to any location in a document. To move a text box visually with the mouse, follow these steps:

1. Choose View ⇨ Page Layout to turn on Page Layout view.

2. Place the insertion pointer on the border of the frame. The mouse pointer changes to a hand when along the edge or a box with two arrows when over a resizing handle. You want the hand cursor.

3. Click and drag the text box to the new location. As you drag the text box, a dotted outline indicates its position. The content of the text box moves to the new location after you release the mouse button.

To move a text box using the dialog box, follow these steps:

1. Choose View ⇨ Page Layout to turn on Page Layout view.

2. Position the insertion pointer inside the frame to move.

3. Choose Format ⇨ Text Box from the menus and select the Layout tab.

4. Click the Advanced button and select the Picture Position tab.

5. Enter the horizontal location you want for the frame in the Horizontal area. Use the pop-up menus on the right to choose whether the measurement that you specify is relative to the margin, the page, or a column.

6. Enter the vertical location you want for the frame in the Vertical area on the Picture Position tab. Use the pop-up menus on the right to choose whether the measurement you specify is relative to the margin, the page, line, or a paragraph.

7. Click OK (or press Return or Enter).

Sizing text boxes

To resize a text box, you can select the text box and drag one of the sizing handles, or you can select the text box and use the Size tab of the Format Text Box dialog box, entering the desired height and width.

To resize a text box using the mouse, follow these steps:

1. Choose View ⇨ Page Layout to turn on Page Layout view.

2. Click anywhere in the text box that you want to resize. Eight hollow sizing handles appear on the edges and corners of the text box.

3. Point to one of the sizing handles so that the mouse pointer becomes a two-headed arrow.

4. Drag the handle to resize the text box.

To resize a text box using the dialog box and keyboard, follow these steps:

1. Choose View ⇨ Page Layout to turn on Page Layout view.

2. Use the arrow keys to position the insertion pointer inside the text box that you want to resize.

3. Choose Format ⇨ Text Box.

4. Click the Size tab of the Format Text Box dialog box, and enter the height and width to apply to the text box.

5. Click OK (or press Return or Enter).

Wrapping text around text boxes

By default Word wraps adjacent text around text boxes. You can turn this trait on or off for a particular text box with the Layout tab of the Format Text Box dialog box. To turn on (or off) text wrapping around text boxes, follow these steps:

1. Choose View ⇨ Page Layout to turn on Page Layout view.

2. Use the mouse or the arrow keys to place the insertion pointer inside the text box.

3. Choose Format ⇨ Text Box to open the Format Text Box dialog box.

4. On the Layout tab of the dialog box, choose one of the options listed. Diagrams will give you an idea of what the text will look like when it is wrapped around the text box. You can also click the Advanced button and select the Text Wrapping tab in the Advanced Layout dialog box for even more choices.

5. You can also make adjustments to the distance the text appears from the text box in the Advanced Layout box's Text Wrapping tab. After you have made your choices, click OK (or press Return or Enter).

Figure 10-12 shows the difference between text wrapping that is on and text wrapping that is off. On the left, the text box containing the graph has been placed in the center of the paragraph, and the surrounding type of wrapping was chosen. Notice how the text wraps around the text box in this figure. On the right, the text box is at the same location, but the text wrapping option has been set to None. As a result, the text does not wrap around the text box that contains the graph. Note that the option applies to the selected text box.

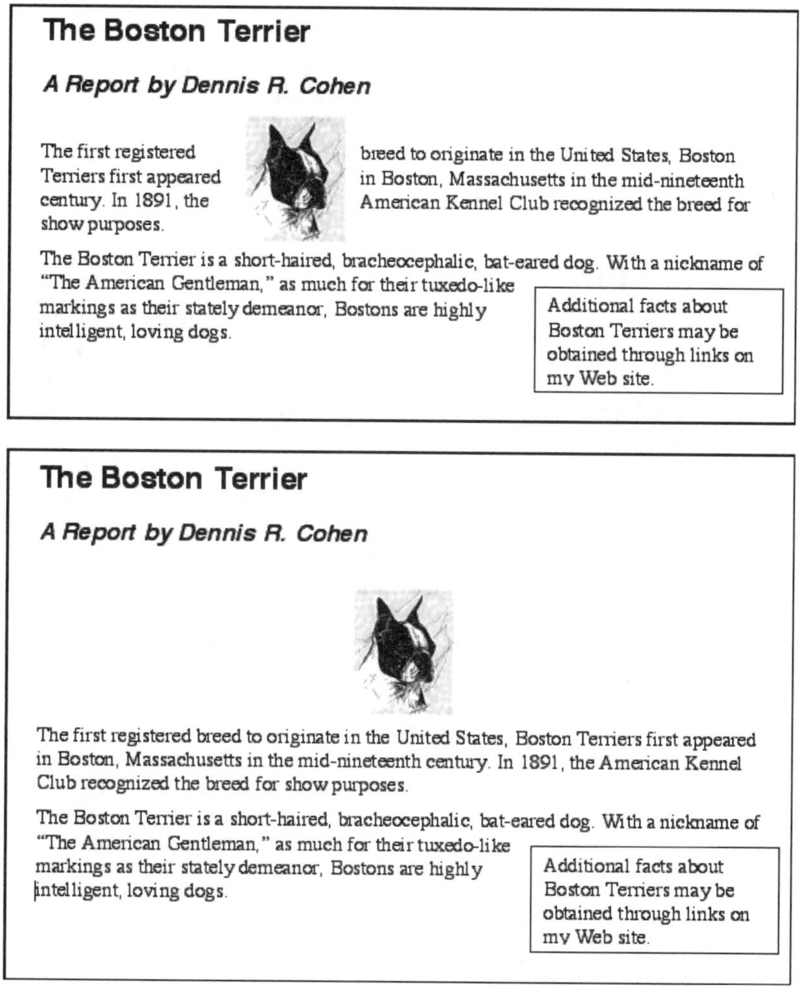

The Boston Terrier

A Report by Dennis R. Cohen

The first registered breed to originate in the United States, Boston
Terriers first appeared in Boston, Massachusetts in the mid-nineteenth
century. In 1891, the American Kennel Club recognized the breed for
show purposes.

The Boston Terrier is a short-haired, bracheocephalic, bat-eared dog. With a nickname of
"The American Gentleman," as much for their tuxedo-like
markings as their stately demeanor, Bostons are highly
intelligent, loving dogs.

Additional facts about
Boston Terriers may be
obtained through links on
my Web site.

The Boston Terrier

A Report by Dennis R. Cohen

The first registered breed to originate in the United States, Boston Terriers first appeared
in Boston, Massachusetts in the mid-nineteenth century. In 1891, the American Kennel
Club recognized the breed for show purposes.

The Boston Terrier is a short-haired, bracheocephalic, bat-eared dog. With a nickname of
"The American Gentleman," as much for their tuxedo-like
markings as their stately demeanor, Bostons are highly
intelligent, loving dogs.

Additional facts about
Boston Terriers may be
obtained through links on
my Web site.

Figure 10-12: *Top:* Text wraps around the graph. *Bottom:* Text wrapping has been turned off.

Applying Organizational Tools

To create a document with a professionally published appearance, use the organizational tools and techniques that Word provides. The combination of these techniques and the use of graphics will turn an ordinary-looking document into a professional-looking document. These organizational tools include such items as columns, gutter margins, headlines and subheads, headers and footers, and the integration of graphics. Later you learn how to use the Newsletter Wizard to create newsletters, another form of desktop publishing.

Before you attempt to apply desktop publishing techniques to any document, you should first sketch out, on paper, exactly how you want the document to look. It is much easier to create a document when you have a good idea of where you're going with it. This step also helps you avoid mistakes that may detract from the appearance of the finished document.

Columns and margins

The layout of your columns comprises a significant part of your design. One- and two-column layouts are the most popular, although you can have more. With text a "visual" limit exists. As the number of columns increases, you will eventually reach the point where readability suffers. Readers don't read individual words; they read phrases or groups of words; therefore, column width has a direct impact on readability. Overly wide columns make it difficult for the reader to follow phrases from line to line. Overly narrow columns can also be hard to read because the eyes must often jump lines before absorbing a complete phrase. The page margins, number of columns, and width between columns all have an impact here. Point size also impacts readability and the number of columns. Small point sizes tend to work better in narrow columns; wide columns generally need larger point sizes. Also, remember that hyphenation helps reduce that jagged-text look that is often prevalent with narrow columns, but too much hyphenation is also distracting.

When working with columns in Word, remember that all the columns do not need to be the same width. Also remember the effect that page margins have on the space available for your columns and on the overall design of your document. Larger margins result in a "lighter" document; smaller margins result in a "denser" appearance. Take a close look at the publications you like or dislike visually and note their designs.

Headlines and subheads

Headlines are vital in calling attention to your message. You can differentiate your headlines from your body text by setting the headlines in larger point sizes and using a sans serif font (such as Helvetica, Franklin Gothic, or Arial). You can also block headlines with borders or shading, or separate them from the body text by means of white space or with rules (vertical or horizontal lines drawn with

Format ➪ Borders and Shading or the Borders and Shading pane of the Formatting palette). Avoid setting your headlines in all uppercase letters, as this reduces readability. Also, keep your headlines short — certainly no more than three lines.

Subheads are a good way to clarify a headline or add information (if the amount of space you have for the headline itself is small). It's often better to use a headline and subhead than wrap a headline onto two (or more) lines. You may also want to use subheads within your text to break large expanses of text into smaller groups. Smaller text blocks tend to be visually easier to follow. Figure 10-13 shows an example of a headline and subhead.

Digital way to speed up: Learn to use all 10 of them!
The cheapest, easiest way to make your Mac faster — learn to type better...

Figure 10-13: A headline with a subheadline

Avoid a common blunder when using subheads to divide your text blocks: Keep your subheads visually tied to the text they introduce by using appropriate spacing. Ideally, you want a bit more space above the subhead than below it. Otherwise, the subhead may be too close to the prior text and not close enough to the text that follows it. In such cases, the subhead appears disconnected from the text it introduces. To position the subhead accurately, place the insertion pointer within the subhead, select Format ➪ Paragraph, and then the Indents and Spacing tab in the Paragraph dialog box. In the Spacing area, set the value of the Before measurement to one that is greater than the value in the After measurement. (Remember that this is measured in points. If your font is 12 points, 12 points of spacing equal one full line.) Alternatively, you could open the Alignment and Spacing pane in the Formatting palette and make the same adjustments there.

Graphic images

By placing graphics in frames, you have a great deal of flexibility when you integrate those graphics into the text. Alternatively, you can place a graphic image in a table cell and use table formatting to control the location of the graphic. No one correct method exists to placing graphics — use whichever method feels the most comfortable and achieves the desired results.

You can use the sizing (scaling) and cropping techniques discussed earlier to add visual interest to many graphics. In some cases, you may be able to add interest to an illustration by purposely stretching it out of proportion. For example, you can use a stretched image of a dollar bill to convey an increase in buying power.

With graphics, the possibilities are endless. Professionally published documents are often a source of inspiration for effective graphics. You can obtain ideas about graphic design by examining publications such as *USA Today*, *Time*, and *Newsweek*, which are abundant in graphics.

Graphs and tables

With Microsoft Graph, you can design business graphs and insert them into your Word documents. With Word's Table feature, you can design tables of data. Use graphs when you want the reader to see a visual representation of the underlying data. Use tables when you want the reader to see the underlying data itself. With tables that display business figures, visually set off any headings or column titles within the table from the remaining contents of the table. You can set the headings apart by formatting the headings or titles or by adding borders or shading.

Informational graphics (such as pie and bar charts) can go a long way in getting business information across to readers. You may want to consider combining clipart or drawings with your charts or graphs.

Using the Newsletter Wizard

Creating newsletters is a common task in many organizations, and one that presents design challenges. Word's Newsletter Wizard greatly reduces the tedium and challenges involved in creating newsletters. It also provides examples of how to use headings, columns, and graphics in a document.

To create a newsletter, choose File ⇨ Project Gallery and select the Newsletters category. Select the design you like and click OK (or simply double-click the thumbnail) to launch it.

The Newsletter Wizard consists of two tabs: Content & Layout, and Theme & Color, as shown in Figure 10-14.

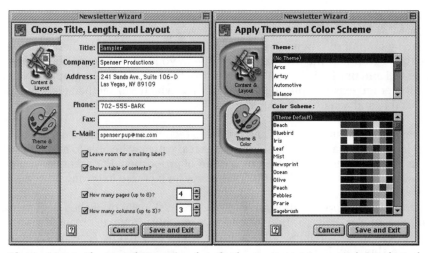

Figure 10-14: The Newsletter Wizard: *Left:* The Content & Layout tab is selected. *Right:* The Theme & Color tab is selected.

In the Content & Layout tab, enter the pertinent information and set your length and layout options. You'll see the changes reflected in the document window.

If you wish to change the theme used, select the Theme & Color tab. In the Theme list box, select the theme you wish to apply. Be aware that it takes Word quite a while to load the Theme data from your disk, so you'll have a fair wait until the changes are reflected in your document. Changing the color scheme is much faster.

Remember that the format the wizard sets can be modified at any time after the newsletter is generated. If you later want to add another column to it, or want to change the look in any way, you can use the normal Word commands and dialogs to do so.

Note   The columns created in the newsletter by the Wizard are not really columns; they are text boxes, both linked and unlinked. You modify the number of columns by changing the size and position of the text boxes and then adding or deleting text boxes to properly fill the space.

After you've set up your newsletter, whether manually or by using the Wizard, it's a good idea to enter your redundant (boilerplate) text, and then save it as a template. This ensures that your future editions will be consistent in their look.

Summary

This chapter provided an overall look at how you can combine the various tools of Word to perform desktop publishing tasks. The chapter discussed these points:

✦ You can set up multiple columns side by side using the Column button or Format ➪ Columns. You can customize the widths of each using Format ➪ Columns.

✦ You can quickly add attractive formatting to a document by using Word's AutoFormat command (in the Format menu).

✦ You can import graphic images of various types into a document.

✦ You can add business graphs to your Word document by pasting them in from other programs or by using Insert ➪ Object. You can create a graph or chart in Microsoft Graph and then insert it into your document.

✦ You can add text boxes or frames to your documents. These frames can contain text or graphics. You can size text boxes or frames and drag them to any location in your document. You can also link text boxes so that text will flow from one to the next.

✦ Word 2001 comes with a number of sample newsletter designs that you can use as starting points for your newsletter. Launching one of these designs invokes the Newsletter Wizard to help you fill in basic information and establish the size and color scheme to be used.

Where to go next

✦ For information on using Word on the World Wide Web, check out the next chapter.

✦ Chapter 13 shows you how to create typical business documents in Word 2001.

✦ Much of what you do in desktop publishing involves the use of Word's different formatting tools. You can find out more about these tools in Chapter 3.

✦ If you desktop publish documents on a regular basis, you'll want to make use of Word's styles and templates. Chapter 8 has the details.

✦   ✦   ✦

Word and the Web

Word 98 differed significantly from its predecessors in that it came with many features for working with the Internet and with intranets. Word 2001 raises the bar significantly higher. Using Word 2001, you can perform a number of Net-related tasks as you work with documents. You can insert hyperlinks in a Word document that link to other Office 2001 documents or to Web sites. When users of the documents click these hyperlinks, they jump directly to that location in the other file or to the Web site. You can also save documents as HTML (Hypertext Markup Language), the publishing lingua franca of the World Wide Web, or as XML (eXtensible Markup Language), a superset of HTML that supports many extra formatting capabilities. Additionally, you can take advantage of a Web Publishing Wizard, as well as a plethora of Web templates, to produce professional-looking Web pages. These topics are discussed in further detail throughout this chapter.

This chapter assumes a familiarity with the basics of Word. If you are familiar with the Web or with intranets but haven't yet learned to work with Word, you should read Chapters 2 through 4 before reading this chapter. You should also be familiar with Chapter 8, which covers styles and templates.

Making the Network Connection

To accomplish many of the tasks described in this chapter, you need to be connected to a network. This can be a dial-up connection to the Internet by means of a commercial Internet service provider (ISP) or by a direct connection through your organization's network. You may be connected directly to a corporate intranet, in which case, you can retrieve or publish data to your company's private network. This chapter doesn't discuss the specifics of making a network connection because that topic is a book in itself. IDG Books publishes several good books on the Internet to help you get connected.

Discovering the Web and the Internet

Because intranets and the Internet may be a newer concept to you than spread-sheets, term explanations are in order. (If you're intimately familiar with the Internet, intranets, and the World Wide Web, you may want to skip this section and the next, and dive right into working with Word and the Web.) First, the Internet is a global collection of computers that are linked by means of telephone, fiber-optic, and microwave lines, and accessible to the public by means of various connections in offices and in homes. The Internet grew out of a research project that originally linked university and government computers in the United States. Since its inception, the Internet has grown to encompass thousands of computers spread throughout dozens of nations. Any personal computer user with an Internet connection (either by means of a phone line, TV cable, or a direct hookup) can connect to the Internet and gain access to the volumes of information located there.

About the World Wide Web

A major component of the Internet is the World Wide Web. The Internet has other parts, but the World Wide Web is the best known part, even if one of the youngest. The World Wide Web is that part of the Internet that makes use of graphical software known as Web browsers and of files stored as HTML. The computers on the Internet that store the HTML files are known as Web servers. When computers connect to the Internet to retrieve this data, they use Web-browser software, which converts the incoming information (encoded in HTML) to graphical pages displayed as a combination of text, graphics, and sometimes audio and video. Commonly used Macintosh Web browsers include Microsoft Internet Explorer, Netscape Communicator, and iCab.

About Internet addresses

Each site on the Internet has a unique address, or Internet address, commonly known by the official name of URL (an acronym for Uniform Resource Locator). When you establish an Internet connection, open a Web browser, and enter an Internet address such as `www.whitehouse.gov`, you are entering the address for the Web server that provides the home page at the entered address (in the example, the office of the President of the United States). Web addresses such as these can be stored in Word documents and displayed as hyperlinks—underlined, blue text that can be clicked to have Word tell your Web browser to display the corresponding URL.

About intranets

Many Internet-related uses of Office 2001 involve making data available on intranets. An intranet is a private network of computers that is available only to the members of a specific organization. Intranets make use of World Wide Web technology—Web servers, network connections, and Web-browser software—to enable members of an organization to share information. Intranets are very popular with corporations because intranets can let employees share work-related information in a confidential manner.

About HTML

HTML is the language used for publishing information to the World Wide Web and to intranets that use World Wide Web technology. HTML is a text-based language that makes use of special codes called tags. These tags are included in the text of the HTML documents. The tags provide instructions to the Web-browser software, which determines how the data appears when the end user views it. Although you don't need to know the nuts and bolts of HTML coding to work with Word and the Web, it's a good idea to be familiar with the concept of saving your data in HTML file format. To publish Word data on the Internet or on an intranet, you need to save that data in HTML format and upload it to your Web server. If you are dealing with an intranet, your company's Webmaster can tell you how to upload the HTML files that Word produces to the company's Web server. If you are managing a Web site on the Internet or on an intranet, you already know how to do this; much of the rest of this chapter deals with getting that Word data ready for uploading to your server.

About the Web toolbar

Word provides a Web toolbar that helps you browse through the resources on an intranet or the Web. Using the Web toolbar, you can quickly open, search, and browse through any document, or through a Web page. You can jump between documents, and you can add sites that you find on the Web to the Favorites folder, enabling you to return quickly to those sites later.

HTML and XML

There have been a number of versions of HTML promulgated by an organization known as the World Wide Web Consortium, or W3C (`www.w3.org`). The current specification (as of this writing) is known as HTML 4.0.1. Shortly after the release of the 4.0.1 specification, W3C released the recommendation for XHTML 1.0, an eXtensible HTML written in XML. XML is the universal format for structured documents and data on the Web.

Because not all the formatting, positioning, and stylistic control that are permitted by powerful word processors such as Microsoft Word are supported in HTML, saving a document as HTML will cause some differences in appearance. Word actually saves Web pages in XML, so that if you wish to later reedit them in Word, the formatting will not be lost. Furthermore, as newer Web browser releases become available, more of the document will be displayable. The downside of this method is that including the extra XML information can significantly increase the size of the file, making your pages slower to open.

Those of you who wish to know more about what Word generates and how to modify the files from outside of Word, a visit to W3C's Web site is time well-spent.

The Web toolbar is displayed in Word by clicking the Web toolbar button in the Standard toolbar or by choosing View ➪ Toolbars ➪ Web. Figure 11-1 shows the Web toolbar.

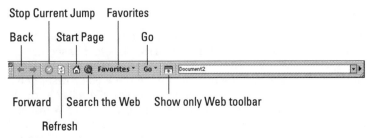

Figure 11-1: The Web toolbar

The Web toolbar is handy when you happen to be in Word and you have a need to go to the Web (or to your company's intranet) for information. For example, you can click the Search the Web button to launch your default Web browser and search the Web, or you can click the Favorites button to open a list of your favorite Web sites. Table 11-1 shows the purpose of the buttons on the Web toolbar.

Table 11-1 The Web Toolbar	
Button	**Purpose**
Back	Moves backward among previously viewed Web pages
Forward	Moves forward among previously viewed Web pages
Stop Current Jump	Halts the current loading of a Web page
Refresh	Refreshes (reloads) the current Web page
Start Page	Jumps to the designated start page, sometimes called a Home page
Search the Web	Jumps to Microsoft's Search page on the World Wide Web
Favorites	Displays a list of favorite sites
Go	Opens the Go menu, which can be used in place of the navigation buttons
Show Only Web Toolbar	Turns off all toolbars except the Web toolbar

Using Word to Open Web Documents

You can open Web pages in Word, effectively using Word as a Web browser.

> **Note** A word of caution here: As a browser, Word can be excruciatingly slow. We also found that Word's choice of font sizes and layout on many pages makes them difficult to read. You'll probably want to resize your window and hide the Formatting palette to give yourself enough working room. Similarly, if you click a link, Word invokes your default Web browser to open the link rather than opening it in Word. If you want to do serious Web surfing, dedicated Web browsers such as Microsoft Internet Explorer and Netscape Communicator are better choices; however, if you just want to view a Web page without leaving Word, you can do so.

To open a Web page in Word, choose File ➪ Open Web Page, enter the URL (it's the same as a Web address) in the dialog box that appears, and click OK. If you've already visited the desired page using Word 2001, instead of typing the URL, you can click the arrows to the right of the address field and select the URL from the pop-up list. If you're on a dial-up connection and you've set your Point-to-Point Protocol (PPP) control panel to enable applications to connect as needed, Word will connect to the Internet or intranet via your default connection and load the Web page. (If not, you'll need to connect to the Internet or intranet before Word can call up the page.)

After you open and navigate among Web pages in Word, the Forward, Back, Stop, and Refresh buttons of the Web toolbar become active. You can use the buttons to navigate forward and backward among Web pages you previously viewed. Also, the Address list box in the Web toolbar keeps a list of the sites you've visited during any Word Web session. To revisit a site, you can open the list and choose the address you want.

As you visit a site, you can add it to the Favorites list of the Web toolbar, so you can quickly go back to it later. While at a Web site, click Favorites on the Web toolbar and choose Add to Favorites.

Creating Hyperlinks in Documents

A significant feature of Word 2001 is its capability to use hyperlinks in documents. You can click hyperlinks to jump to other Office documents stored on your Mac, on your company's network, on a company intranet, or on the Internet. You can also click hyperlinks to trigger a new e-mail message.

Linking to office documents with drag and drop

If you want to create a hyperlink to a location in Word, in an Excel worksheet, or in a PowerPoint presentation, the easiest way is to use drag and drop.

You create a link (this time using Microsoft's OLE technology) to a portion of a Word document by selecting the data to be linked and pressing Ô-Option as you drag the information to the location that is to serve as the link. When you release the mouse button, choose Link Here from the Shortcut menu that appears.

When you perform these steps, Word inserts a link back to the original document at the selected location. You can then click a hyperlink at any time to jump to the linked document or Control-click an OLE link and choose Linked Document Object ➪ Open Link from the shortcut menu to jump to the linked text.

Linking to Web sites or files with Insert Hyperlink

To establish a hyperlink to a Web site on an intranet or on the Internet, follow these steps (you can use these same steps to link to another Office document, but it's easier to use the drag and drop method described earlier):

1. Select the text in the document that will serve as the hyperlink. (Selecting the text is important; Step 3 explains why.)

2. Click the Insert Hyperlink button in the Standard toolbar, or choose Insert ➪ Hyperlink (⌘-K). The Insert Hyperlink dialog box appears, as shown in Figure 11-2.

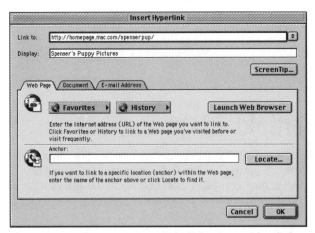

Figure 11-2: The Insert Hyperlink dialog box with a link to Spenser's home page

3. Make sure that you're on the Web Page tab. In the Link to text box, enter the Web address of the destination for the link. If you didn't make a selection before choosing Insert ➪ Hyperlink, the Display text box will be empty and will duplicate the information you enter into the Link to text box. Even if you edit the Display text, the inserted Hyperlink will be the URL. By default, the screen tip that displays as your mouse pointer hovers over the hyperlink will be the URL; however, you can click the ScreenTip button and enter a more meaningful tip.

4. If you want to establish a link to a file, you will do your work on the Document tab. In either case, if you want to jump to a specific location, enter that location in the tab's Anchor text box. (This can be a cell reference or named range in an Excel worksheet, a Word bookmark, or the name of a PowerPoint slide as well as an anchor in a Web page.) If you leave this entry blank, the hyperlink jumps to the beginning of the Web page or file.

5. Click OK to establish the hyperlink.

Publishing Documents on the Web

Word 2001 enables you to create documents and save them as HTML files for Web publication. This is a very simple matter in Word.

 Caution

Before we go on, a word of caution about saving Word documents as HTML files. Many of the formatting features of Word are not supported on conversion to HTML format. Table 11-2, which follows, indicates which formats are retained after conversion to HTML.

The World's Easiest Hyperlinks

Word's AutoFormat feature automatically converts any recognizable Internet address to a hyperlink after you complete the address and press the spacebar, Return, Enter, or Tab. For example, you can type `www.bighit.com`, `lamg@lamg.com`, or `ftp://ftp.somesite.com`, and it will become an active link, ready to start a Web browser and carry anyone who clicks it to the specified site.

Actually, what Word acts on is the identifying part of the address, such as `ftp://ftp`, `http://www`, or any text with the @ symbol between it.

This AutoFormat feature is on by default, but can be turned off by selecting Tools ➪ AutoCorrect, going to the AutoFormat tab, and unchecking the option under Replace that says Internet paths with hyperlinks.

Saving existing Word documents as HTML

You can use the File ➪ Save as Web Page choice to convert existing documents into HTML (again, these are actually XML) files. After you've converted these documents, you can upload them to your Internet or intranet Web server using the procedures applicable to your server.

To save an existing document in HTML format, choose File ➪ Save as Web Page. When you do this, a Save As dialog box opens and Web Page is automatically selected as the format. Two radio buttons exist below the Format pop-up menu: Save entire file into HTML and Save only display information into HTML. If you save the entire file, you will create a much larger Web page, which takes longer to load, but that can later be opened in Word without losing any of the formatting beyond HTML's capabilities. If you choose to save only display information, you end up with a smaller file, but the result might not match the original Word document when reopened. Enter the desired filename and click Save. Word will save the existing document in HTML format. (Don't use the same name as your existing document or you'll replace the existing document with the HTML version. Give the new document a unique name or add the Web standard .html to the document's name.) When saving existing documents as HTML, remember the limitations of HTML documents, as listed in Table 11-2.

Table 11-2 Limitations of Word Conversions to HTML		
Word Formatting	**Supported by HTML?**	**Comments**
Font sizes	See comments	Fonts are converted to the closest HTML font size in browsers that do not support CSS (Cascading Style Sheets)*, that is, browsers whose versions are pre-4.0.
Comments	See comments	Comments don't appear in the document in Internet Explorer, but Netscape Communicator 4.6 and later recognize them.
Emboss, shadow, engrave, caps, small caps, strikethrough, and outline text features	See comments	Double-strikethrough and strikethrough both display as strikethrough; emboss and engrave display as gray text; outline and shadow display as bold text; cap text is case-converted; small cap display will depend upon the browser and its support of CSS.
Patterned or shaded backgrounds	No	Display as solid color backgrounds

Word Formatting	Supported by HTML?	Comments
Decorative border styles around paragraphs	No	Become box borders
Negative paragraph indents	No	Become 0 indent
Fields	See comments	The information in a field is retained but the field will not continue to update; in other words, the field is converted to text.
Tabs	No	Tabs are converted to a sequence of HTML nonbreaking space characters. These appear as spaces in browsers. As an alternative, use indents or a table.
Tables of contents or authorities and indexes	See comments	The information in the tables is converted, but these will not be converted because they are based on field codes. The page numbers are displayed as asterisks that are hyperlinks that readers can click to navigate the Web page. You can replace the asterisks with the text that you want to have displayed.
Drop caps	No	These are removed, but you can increase the size of the letter by increasing the font size and then clicking it in an Online Layout view.
Table widths	See comments	The tables are converted to a fixed width.
Tables	Yes	Tables are converted but the color and width borders settings are not always retained. Their retention depends upon the browser used.
Highlights	See comments	Solid highlight colors are retained, and patterned highlights are converted to solid color highlights.
Page numbering	No	An HTML document is considered a single Web page; therefore, page numbers are lost.
Margins	No	Controlling layout of a page is done via tables.
Page borders	No	No HTML equivalent exists.
Headers and footers	No	No HTML equivalents exist.

Continued

Table 11-2 *(continued)*		
Word Formatting	*Supported by HTML?*	*Comments*
Footnotes	Yes	Inserted as a link, with the footnotes collected at the end of the page.
Newspaper columns	No	For multicolumn effect, use tables in your Web page.
Styles	See comments	User-defined styles are converted to CSS. Browsers that do not support CSS lose user-defined styles. This means that Netscape and Internet Explorer versions prior to 4.0 will probably not recognize your styles.

*Cascading Style Sheets enable a Web page to specify a hierarchy of collective formatting (fonts, sizes, styles, alignments, and so on) to be applied to page elements of various types (such as paragraphs, table cells, list elements, and so on).

Using Web page templates and themes

In Word 2001, support for translation to HTML has been significantly enhanced, so much so that the Web Page Wizard of Word 98 is no longer included in Office 2001; however, the collection of Web page templates is significantly expanded. The belief is that any Word document can be a Web page (within the limits of HTML and the browsers used).

A default installation of Word 2001 will include two subcategories of Web page templates, named Cypress and Zero. No, we don't know why they have those names. Three other oddly named collections of Web page templates exist in the Value Pack: Geared Up, LaVerne, and Radius.

Select one of the template thumbnails and click OK or just double-click the thumbnail.

The Web page that you created then shows up, preformatted. Using it as a starting point, follow the instructions on the template, replacing text and graphics as needed to present the material that you want to have appear on your Web page.

This is where Themes (Format ➪ Theme) really show up to advantage — in Web page creation. Backgrounds are commonly used on the Web and are stored as part of a theme. Remember that to see how your text looks against a background, you need to be in Online Layout view. While you are able to combine any combination of styles, backgrounds, bullet characters, and other graphic document elements to create a theme, some combinations just don't work well — for example, dark colored text against a dark background is difficult to read, as is light text against a light background. Similarly, busy patterns in the background can make text difficult to follow. The themes provided with Word do a decent job of balancing these attributes and provide you with some implicit guidance toward what works. We recommend spending some time studying the things you like and don't like about the supplied themes before you start creating your own.

The following are some tips for creating your own Web pages and Web-page templates:

✦ Make use of contrast such as light colors on a dark background or dark colors on a light background.

✦ You can use a picture as your background, but remember that very busy backgrounds can hinder the readability of text.

✦ Try to avoid fonts that are not commonly in use. Browsers use fonts that are available on the system doing the viewing and will only use the font you specify if the user also has that font installed.

✦ Don't place important information in comments or footnotes — not all browsers will display them.

✦ If you want multicolumn or newspaper-style layout, use tables to position your items.

✦ Create links to other places in your document for cross-referenced information, such as footnotes or endnotes.

✦ If you wish a text to read up-and-down instead of the usual left-to-right, save the information as a graphic and insert the graphic. Web browsers display all text horizontally.

✦ If you want blinking text, you will need to add the <BLINK> tag manually, after saving the Web page.

When creating HTML files based on Word documents, remember that Word has a much wider range of formatting than is possible with HTML. Hypertext Markup Language is a simple formatting language, and if you use some of Word's more unusual features, they may be lost in the translation, or translated in ways that you didn't expect. For example, if you place text in multiple columns on a page, the text will not appear that way on the HTML page. If you place a graphic in a document and save the document as HTML, Word writes the graphic to a .GIF, .JPG, or .PNG file and includes a reference in the HTML code for the graphic. However, the graphic often does not appear (in relation to the paragraph placement) at the same place it was originally stored in the Word document. For example, text-wrapped graphics in Word will be left aligned in a Web browser.

Summary

This chapter discussed the details behind sharing your Word data with Internet/intranet users. In this chapter, you learned the following:

✦ Word 2001 can open files that are stored on the Internet.

✦ Hyperlinks can be added to the text of a document, and that you can store Web addresses or jump locations to other Office documents in Word documents.

✦ You can use the Save as Web Page option of the File menu to save existing Word documents as HTML files for publishing on the Internet or an intranet.

✦ You can use the Web Page templates to quickly create Web pages that use various styles and formats.

✦ Many Word formatting and display options are not supported in HTML, so you should avoid their use in documents intended for the Web.

Where to go next

✦ In the next chapter, you learn how to further extend the power of Word by using Visual Basic for Applications.

✦ Word is just one component of the Web-publishing capabilities provided by Office 2001. Excel and PowerPoint also offer Web publishing and Web interaction features. See Chapter 24 for specifics on Excel and the Web, and Chapter 33 for specifics on PowerPoint and the Web.

✦   ✦   ✦

Word and Visual Basic for Applications

This chapter details the use of Visual Basic for Applications (VBA), the programming language on which Word macros are based. VBA is heavily based on Microsoft's Visual Basic programming language. Because Word macros are based on VBA, you can use VBA to automate common tasks in Word.

VBA can take you much further than simply duplicating keystrokes. VBA gives you full access to all of Word's commands. You can modify Word's own menus by adding your own commands and options; you can create custom dialog boxes to present messages and query users for information, and you can even construct complete applications that users with a limited knowledge of Word can use. To accomplish these kinds of tasks, you need more than a familiarity with the recording and playing of macros — you need a basic understanding of VBA.

Using Macros to Learn VBA

Chapter 9 detailed the basics of using macros, which are sequences of instructions that cause Word to perform a particular task. As Chapter 9 demonstrates, macros can be very handy to use in your work because they can greatly reduce the time you spend performing routine, repetitive tasks. Macros are also an excellent starting point for understanding how VBA works and what you can do with the language. As Word's macro recorder stores all the actions that you perform or the commands that you choose, it translates these actions or commands into statements, or lines of code, using VBA. These statements are automatically placed in a procedure, which is a block of VBA code. Procedures are stored in modules, which you can think of as containers for all VBA code.

To get an idea of how all Word macros use VBA, you should practice with a document and a sample macro. This chapter familiarizes you with Visual Basic code by examining the procedure that results when you record the sample macro. The following exercise produces two printed copies of a document, along with a document summary sheet to accompany each printout. Because you can't print multiple copies of a document with nonstandard options (such as the document summaries) using just the Print icon in the toolbar, this exercise represents a typical task that can be automated by creating a macro.

Follow these steps to create the worksheet and the sample macro:

1. Open an existing document.

2. Choose Tools ⇨ Macro ⇨ Record New Macro.

3. In the Record New Macro dialog box, enter the name **PrintTwo** and then click OK. The Stop Recording toolbar, which you can use to stop recording the macro, appears above the document.

4. Choose File ⇨ Print. The Print dialog box appears, as shown in Figure 12-1.

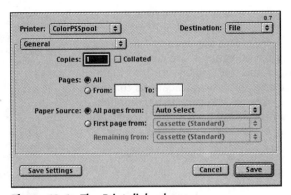

Figure 12-1: The Print dialog box

5. In the Copies portion of the dialog box, change the number of copies to 2.

6. Select Microsoft Word from the top pop-up menu. Then click the Word Options button to open the Print tab of the Preferences dialog box.

7. In the dialog box that appears, turn on the Document Properties checkbox, and then click OK. (If Document Properties is already on, you don't have to do anything.)

8. Click OK to close the Print dialog box and begin printing.

9. *(Optional)* As soon as your Mac finishes the basic printing preparation, select Tools ➪ Preferences. In the Print tab, turn off Document Properties again. (Otherwise, Document Properties is left on whenever you use this macro.)

10. Click the Stop Recording button to stop the recording of the macro.

You can verify the effects of the macro by opening any document, choosing Tools ➪ Macro ➪ Macros, clicking PrintTwo to select the macro, and then clicking the Run button. (You can also just double-click PrintTwo.) Word prints two copies of the current document, along with document summary sheets for each copy.

Understanding VBA Code

Of course, the purpose of the exercise you just completed is not to demonstrate how to create a macro but to show how VBA code works as the basis of any macro. Choose Tools ➪ Macro ➪ Macros to open the Macros dialog box, select the PrintTwo macro, and click Edit. The Visual Basic Editor opens, shown in Figure 12-2. As shown in the figure, the VBA code behind the macro appears in the module window.

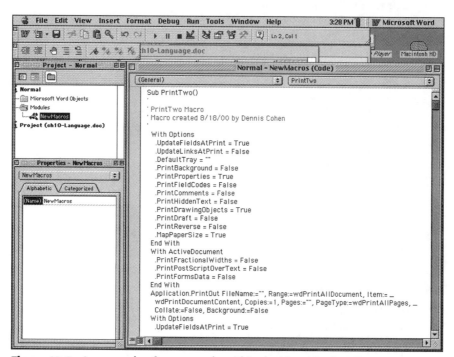

Figure 12-2: An example of macro code within the Visual Basic Editor

Here's the VBA code:

```
Sub PrintTwo()
'
' PrintTwo Macro
' Macro recorded 8/18/00 by Dennis R. Cohen
'
  With Options
    .UpdateFieldsAtPrint = True
    .UpdateLinksAtPrint = False
    .DefaultTray = ""
    .PrintBackground = False
    .PrintProperties = True
    .PrintFieldCodes = False
    .PrintComments = False
    .PrintHiddenText = False
    .PrintDrawingObjects = True
    .PrintDraft = False
    .PrintReverse = False
    .MapPaperSize = True
  End With
  With ActiveDocument
    .PrintFractionalWidths = False
    .PrintPostScriptOverText = False
    .PrintFormsData = False
  End With
  Application.PrintOut FileName:="", Range:=wdPrintAllDocument,
Item:= _
    wdPrintDocumentContent, Copies:=1, Pages:="",
PageType:=wdPrintAllPages, _
    Collate:=False, Background:=False
  With Options
    .UpdateFieldsAtPrint = True
    .UpdateLinksAtPrint = False
    .DefaultTray = ""
    .PrintBackground = False
    .PrintProperties = False
    .PrintFieldCodes = False
    .PrintComments = False
    .PrintHiddenText = False
    .PrintDrawingObjects = True
    .PrintDraft = False
    .PrintReverse = False
    .MapPaperSize = True
  End With
  With ActiveDocument
    .PrintFractionalWidths = False
    .PrintPostScriptOverText = False
    .PrintFormsData = False
  End With
End Sub
```

How VBA Relates to Visual Basic

If you've already worked with Microsoft's Visual Basic as a development language, you'll find Visual Basic for Applications to be a familiar friend; in fact, the term "sibling" is more accurate. VBA is solidly based on Microsoft's Visual Basic programming language. The whole idea in developing VBA was to replace the old macro-based languages, such as Word Basic and Excel's macro language, with a common development language so that developers familiar with applications development in Word could easily develop applications in Excel (or in Access, if using Windows) and vice versa.

Microsoft uses Visual Basic as the base language, and it has added extensions to the language as implemented in the other Office applications. All the commands, functions, methods, procedures, and program structures used in Visual Basic can be used in VBA for Word, Excel, and PowerPoint (and Access, if using Windows). If you are a Visual Basic programmer, you're on very familiar ground.

The main thing you need to remember if your code could be run on either Mac or Windows is to not use platform-specific references for such things as file paths.

Each of the steps you took during the recording of this procedure resulted in the addition of one or more lines of Visual Basic code in the module. The code appears in color — comments are displayed in green, key words of the Visual Basic language appear in blue, and all other code appears in black. When you run this (or any) macro, you are in effect running the Visual Basic for Applications code contained in the module recorded by the macro recorder. As the module runs, each line of Visual Basic code executes in turn, and Word performs an appropriate action as a result.

About comments

You can include comments (lines not acted upon by Word when the code runs) by preceding the text with a single quotation mark. In the sample procedure, you can see that the second and third lines are comments:

```
' PrintTwo Macro
' Macro recorded 8/18/00 by Dennis R. Cohen'
```

In this case, Word added the comments based on the entries in the Macro Name and Description text boxes of the Record Macro dialog box, but you can place comments wherever you desire in your Visual Basic code by typing a single quote mark followed by the text of the comment. Comments can be quite helpful in your more complex procedures because they can help you remember what's going on at a specific point in the procedure. Comments can occupy an entire line, or you can put them at the end of a valid line of code by starting the comment with a single quotation mark. When the procedure runs, everything that follows the single quotation mark is ignored until Word finds a new line of code.

About headers and footers

If you look just above the comments, you see that the first line of the procedure reads:

```
Sub PrintTwo()
```

The matching last line reads:

```
End sub
```

Think of these lines as the header and footer for the procedure. Every VBA procedure starts with a header that begins with Sub or Function and ends with a footer that says End Sub or End Function. VBA supports two types of procedures: function procedures and subprocedures. Function procedures accept a value (or values), act on the data, and return a value. Subprocedures do not return a value (although you can pass values from within a subprocedure using statements inside the procedure). Any arguments used by a function procedure are placed inside the parentheses of the header. The footer tells Word that it has reached the end of the procedure. When Word reaches the footer in the module, it passes program control back to any other VBA procedure that called this procedure. If the procedure was not called by another procedure, Word returns control from the procedure to Word itself.

About VBA code

The code between the Sub and the End Sub lines makes up the actual procedure that does all the work. In this example, many of the lines are assignment statements; these lines assign a value to a property in Word. For example, the following line of code tells Word to include the document properties with the printout:

```
.PrintProperties = True
```

Also included in the VBA code are statements that perform direct actions within Word. For example, the following statement tells Word to print the document:

```
Application.Printout Filename:=
```

Because this macro first tells Word to set the printing options to include document properties and then later tells Word to turn off this option, you will see the full list of preferences (with options and with active document) appear once to set the preferences, and then another time to reset them.

About displaying dialog boxes

One reason you may want to do some Visual Basic programming yourself (rather than using only the macro recorder) is that you can do some custom programming—such as displaying dialog boxes—that you cannot do with recorded macros. To display a dialog box onscreen that contains a message with custom text, you use VBA's MsgBox function. The syntax of the statement is simple: you add a line of code that reads `MsgBox("your custom text")`. Put your desired text between the double quotation marks.

If you duplicated the example earlier in the chapter, go to the end of the line prior to where the macro resets the printing preferences, and place your insertion point there. The text to follow is Background:=False, which is right above the second occurrence of the text Background:=False.

Press Return to add a new, blank line. With the insertion point at the start of the blank line, enter the following:

```
MsgBox("Now printing two copies with document summaries.")
```

After typing this code, choose File ➪ Close and Return to Word (⌘-Q) to exit the Visual Basic Editor. When you are back in the document, choose Tools ➪ Macro ➪ Macros. In the Macros dialog box, select the PrintTwo macro and click Run. When the macro completes this time, you see the dialog box shown in Figure 12-3. Dialog boxes such as this one can inform users about tasks the user needs to perform. After Word displays this dialog box, it continues on to reset your preferences to turn off the document properties printout.

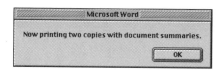

Figure 12-3: The dialog box presented by the MsgBox function

When entering code, it's important to have smart quotes turned off (or to copy and paste a straight quote from somewhere else in the code window). Use of a smart quotation mark results in a compilation error, and your script won't run. To turn off smart quotes, select Tools ➪ AutoCorrect, and then choose the AutoFormat As You Type tab. Under Replace as you type, deselect (clear) the Straight quotes with smart quotes checkbox.

Editing VBA Code

When you open a module, you can enter program code just like you type text in any word processor. You don't have to know the mechanics of entering text and correcting mistakes. You can use the same text-entry and editing techniques (including cutting and pasting) that you use in any Mac word processor.

Although you are in the Visual Basic Editor, you can also insert text from another file into your existing program code. If you want to insert text into the program code, place the insertion point at the location in the module where you want to insert the code and choose Insert ⇨ File. In the File dialog box, select the file that contains the text you want to insert. Click OK to transfer the text into the file.

Printing Visual Basic Code

You can print the code contained in your Visual Basic modules. Open the module that contains the desired code by choosing Tools ⇨ Macro ⇨ Macros, selecting the desired macro, and clicking the Edit button. Then choose File ⇨ Print.

About the Visual Basic Toolbar

If you do a lot of work in VBA programming, you'll find the Visual Basic toolbar (see Figure 12-4) to be useful. You can activate the Visual Basic toolbar by Control-clicking the toolbar area and choosing Visual Basic from the shortcut menu. (Or select View ⇨ Toolbars ⇨ Visual Basic.)

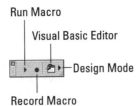

Run Macro

Visual Basic Editor

Design Mode

Record Macro

Figure 12-4: The Visual Basic toolbar

Table 12-1 describes the different buttons on the Visual Basic toolbar.

Table 12-1 Buttons on the Visual Basic Toolbar	
Name	**Function**
Run Macro	Opens the Run Macro dialog box, in which you can run, delete, or modify a selected macro.
Record Macro	Opens the Record Macro dialog box, in which you can fill in the desired options used to begin recording a macro.
Visual Basic Editor	Opens the Visual Basic Editor, in which you can create, edit, and step through macros using Visual Basic.

Just a Beginning . . .

Make no mistake about it, using VBA falls well into the realm of programming. (If you're completely new to programming, you should be congratulated for pressing this deeply into what is, for many readers, a subject of mystifying complexity.) Not only have you learned how VBA lies at the heart of everything you do with macros, you've also learned how you can extend the power of your macros by adding your own Visual Basic code to provide items such as dialog boxes and customized prompts. Still, you've only scratched the surface of what you can do with this language. VBA is a full-featured programming language you can use to automate or customize virtually any conceivable task that can be done with Word. If the challenges of programming catch your fancy, you should look into additional resources for learning about Visual Basic programming. It's a subject about which entire books have been written.

Summary

This chapter provided an introduction to programming using Visual Basic for Applications, the underlying language behind Word macros. The chapter covered the following points:

✦ Every Word macro exists as a series of Visual Basic program statements.

✦ The Visual Basic statements are stored in procedures, and one or more procedures are placed in modules.

✦ Visual Basic procedures can be either function procedures or subprocedures. Function procedures accept a value(s), act on the data, and return a value. Subprocedures do not return a value (although you can pass values from within a subprocedure using statements inside the procedure).

✦ You can modify the Visual Basic code that Word's macro recorder creates to add special features, such as dialog boxes and custom prompts.

Where to go next

✦ The next chapter shows how you can put Word to work. It demonstrates how you can create and use various documents for common business tasks.

✦ Because Visual Basic for Applications lies at the heart of macros you create in Word, you should also be intimately familiar with the use of macros before getting deeply involved with Visual Basic for Applications. See Chapter 9.

✦   ✦   ✦

Word at Work

In this chapter, you find two step-by-step exercises you can follow to put Word 2001 to work quickly. These exercises use two of Word's wizards, which enable you to produce professional-looking documents with ease.

Designing a Brochure

Figure 13-1 shows an example of a brochure you can quickly create using Word's Brochure Wizard.

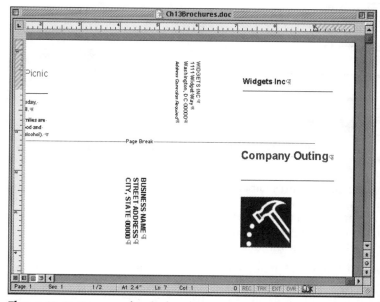

Figure 13-1: An example of a brochure

To create a fax cover sheet, perform the following steps:

1. Choose File ➪ Project Gallery (⌘-Shift-P). The Project Gallery appears.

2. Select the Brochures subcategory under Business Forms and then double-click one of the thumbnail designs — we chose to use Neutral. In a moment, a document window opens with the Brochure Wizard in front, as shown in Figure 13-2.

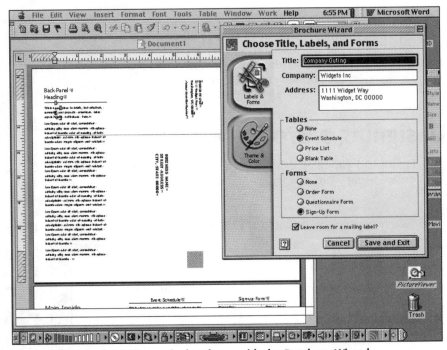

Figure 13-2: The beginnings of a brochure, with the Brochure Wizard

3. On the Brochure Wizard's Labels & Forms tab, enter a title for the brochure, list the company name and address, determine whether you want to include a table, a form, or both (and for whatever you do want, also include what kind), and, finally, check the Leave room for a mailing label checkbox if you are going to mail them out without envelopes.

4. *(Optional)* If you would prefer a different theme or a different color scheme for the theme chosen, select the Theme & Color tab and make your choices from the two list boxes, as shown in Figure 13-3. Selecting a new theme can take a while, but when it is done loading, you will see the results in the document window.

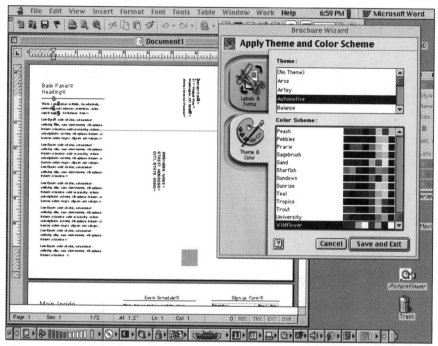

Figure 13-3: The Brochure Wizard's Theme & Color tab

5. Click the Save and Exit button and start to replace the boilerplate text in the template with the text you want.

   You will notice that, unless you have a very large monitor set to a high resolution, the document window is zoomed to a smaller percentage. Unless you feel comfortable working at that resolution (we don't), you'll need to zoom out to 100 percent (or more) and do a fair amount of scrolling.

After creating your brochure, save and print it.

Tip For documents such as brochures (and catalogs, covered in the next section), you're probably going to want to make use of colors, and that means color printing. While you can get a decent draft of your brochure on inkjet printers or color lasers, sending the output to a commercial printer for final output is the more likely scenario. Creating a desktop printer which is a Desktop Translator (created with the Desktop Printer Utility in your Apple Extras: Apple LaserWriter Software folder) is a great way to go about it. This way, you can have a pseudo-printer that is a Color Laserwriter and you can easily send the PostScript output to that printer. You're even better off if you have Adobe's Acrobat Distiller, because you can tell the printer to generate a PDF file, something service bureaus really like. Make sure that you embed all the fonts in your document (preferably Type 1 fonts) if you're creating a PostScript or PDF file.

Creating a Catalog

Figure 13-4 shows an example of a product catalog. You can easily produce a catalog like this with Word's Catalog Wizard and templates. Catalogs are always a multiple of four pages in length, because they are produced as booklets, where each folded sheet of paper results in four pages.

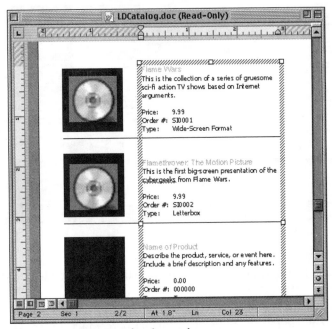

Figure 13-4: An example of a catalog

To create a catalog, follow these steps:

1. Choose File ➪ Project Gallery. The Project Gallery dialog box appears.

2. In the Categories list, click Menus & Catalogs, click Catalogs, and then choose the thumbnail of one of the catalog templates, which creates a document based upon that template and present the Catalog Wizard.

3. The Catalog Wizard has three tabs: Layout & Title, Page Content, and Theme & Color (see Figure 13-5). In the Layout & Title tab, fill in the blanks and set your layout options.

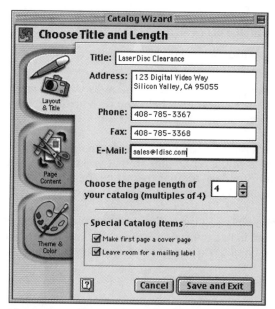

Figure 13-5: The Catalog Wizard's Layout & Title tab

4. Select the Page Content tab. For each page that will be in your catalog, choose from the Choose Page Number pop-up menu and then select the radio button that corresponds to the type of content you want on that page, as shown in Figure 13-6.

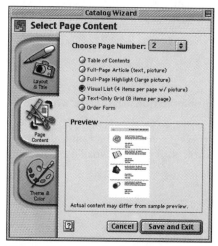

Figure 13-6: The Catalog Wizard's Page Content tab — deciding what goes where

5. The final tab in the Catalog Wizard is the Theme & Color tab, which is exactly as described earlier in Step 4 of "Designing a Brochure."

6. Click the Save and Exit button when you have all your content and parameters set.

7. After the catalog appears, you can edit the content as you edit any text. Word's Assistant pops up, suggesting it help you with further refinements or processes unless, like us, you turn the Assistant off.

As is customary with Wizard-created documents, the document window will probably be zoomed until the text is all but a tiny blur so that you can see the full layout. Click the zoom control in the Standard toolbar to change the magnification to something where you can actually work—usually at least 100 percent.

Now comes the tedious part, replacing the boilerplate and placeholders with your text and graphics. The reward is in a consistently formatted, well-designed catalog where the only real work you had to do was in providing the content.

Summary

This chapter has provided a step-by-step look at what's involved in using two of Word 2001's wizards to create typical business documents. You can use the different templates and wizards to ease the drudgery of creating many common types of documents:

✦ Use the Brochure Wizard to create a brochure or flyer.

✦ Use the Catalog Wizard to create an attractive product catalog, complete with order form, descriptive text, illustrative figures, and product descriptions.

Where to go next

✦ The next chapter answers common questions that arise when you use Word 2001.

✦ The examples demonstrated in this chapter use the templates that come with Word. Chapter 8 tells the whole story about working with templates.

✦　✦　✦

The Word Top Ten

This chapter answers ten common Word 2001 questions. These questions are based on inquiries to Microsoft Technical Support.

1. I have a document that was created with another word-processing program. Can I work on this file in Word?

For the most part, Word converts files that have been created in other programs when you open them using the File ➪ Open command or the Open button in the Project Gallery, or when you drag and drop the document onto Word's icon. If you use the File ➪ Open method (⌘-O) and don't see the desired document in the Open dialog box, select All Documents from the List Files of Type pop-up menu so that you can be sure it isn't being filtered out.

Note, too, that Word uses file converters when it opens files created by other programs. If you did the default (drag the folder) installation of Word, the most common Microsoft converters were installed. However, you may need to add the converters by running the Value Pack Installer. Quit any running Office applications, and then perform these steps to add converters:

1. Insert the Office CD-ROM, open the Value Pack folder, and double-click the Shared Applications folder.

2. Drag the desired converter(s) to the Text Converters folder within your Microsoft Office 2001:Shared Applications folder.

Word comes with these converters when drag-installed:

✦ AppleWorks 5.0

✦ Microsoft Excel 2.*x*–9.0

✦ Recover Text Converter

✦ RTF — Rich Text Format

✦ Word 4.*x* and 5.*x* for the Macintosh

✦ Word 6.0/95 Export

✦ Word 6.0/95 Export JPN

✦ Word 6.0/95 Import

✦ Word 97–2001 Import

The Value Pack Installer offers these converters:

✦ WordPerfect 5.*x*

✦ WordPerfect Graphics

✦ Works 4.0 for the Macintosh

✦ Word 97–2001 Converter Installer (for use by people with Word 6.0 and Word 98 users to open Word 2001 documents)

Note   MacLink Plus from DataViz is a collection of translators for a variety of additional formats that you might also seek out.

2. Why do addresses print on envelopes in the wrong position?

Envelope printing can be tricky to set up, but once you've figured out the setting for your printer, it's a cinch. The problem is that each printer feeds envelopes differently. Some place the envelope in the center of the feed tray; others place the envelope to the left or the right. Some printers need the envelope to be fed face down, while others want face up. If you're using a laser printer, chances are good that the paper tray and manual feeds require different positions. Ink-jet printers usually have an icon somewhere inside the lid to show you how your envelope should feed. On laser printers, there should be an icon on the manual feed tray. You're on your own with the paper tray, so you may have to resort to your printer manual. Another thing to consider is that business envelopes and personal letter envelopes are different sizes.

To print an envelope, follow these steps:

1. *(Optional)* In your document, select the addressee information. (If you don't, Word will guess at the address for you by copying the top several lines of your document.)

2. Choose Tools ➪ Envelopes to present the Envelopes dialog box (shown in Figure 14-1). If you selected the addressee information before opening this dialog box, you see the address in the Delivery address text box. If not, you see

Word's guess or an empty text box. You can edit this guess or any text in the Delivery address text box. Alternatively, you can select an addressee from the Address Book pop-up button or type in the delivery address. The Return address text box will either be empty or contain the information you entered during your initial user setup.

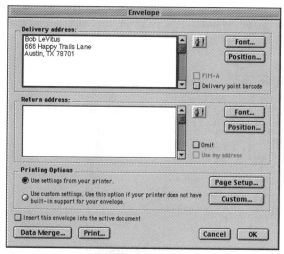

Figure 14-1: The Envelope dialog box

3. To change the envelope size, click the Page Setup button if your printer has a default paper size for the new envelope size; otherwise, click the Custom button in the Printing Options area. This opens the Custom Page Options dialog box. Here you can change the size of the envelope and the envelope feeding method.

4. To change the feed orientation—which is the tricky part that you'll need to experiment with—the Feed method icons represent all the various possibilities, as long as you recognize and take advantage of the Face up/Face down option and properly check or uncheck the Clockwise rotation option. The icons change as you select these options. Click the icon that finally represents the way your envelope looks in its printer tray.

5. In the Envelopes dialog box, you have Position buttons for both the Delivery and Return addresses. These buttons bring up the Address Position dialog box, enabling you to specify offsets from both the left and the top for each address. The Envelope dialog box is a little difficult because you really need to specify the Envelope size (near the bottom of the dialog) before going back to the upper parts to position the addresses.

6. To print the envelope, click Print.

3. How can I prevent page breaks from appearing in my document where I don't want them?

Unwanted page breaks can occur for any number of reasons. You may have applied paragraph formats that affect line and page breaks, or you may have inserted a "hard" page break or a section break that begins a new page. The following paragraphs should help you solve the problem. Your problem may not be an unwanted page break but one of Word's automatic paginations that simply falls in an inconvenient place. This problem is addressed in this chapter, too. Figure 14-2 demonstrates the look of some different kinds of breaks.

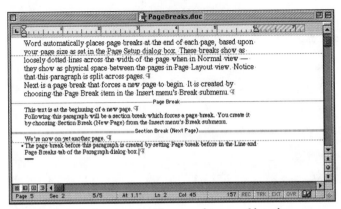

Figure 14-2: A document with several types of breaks

You may have a page break in your document. As you work, Word automatically paginates your document for you, placing page breaks determined by your margin settings. In Normal view, these breaks show as loosely dotted lines across the width of your pages. However, people sometimes want to ensure that a new page will fall at a certain area, and therefore place a hard page break at that point. These breaks often end up falling in undesirable places as you add or delete text or change font size or line spacing. To remove a hard page break, place your insertion point immediately after the break — basically at the start of the text following the break. Then use the Delete key to remove it as you remove any unwanted character. (You'll know the hard page break from Word's automatic soft break because the hard break is labeled "page break" at the break point.)

Similarly, you may have a section break in your document. A section break can be one within a page or one that creates a new page. (It will say "section break, next page" at the break point.) You can remove this break the same way you remove a page break — by placing the cursor in the section immediately after the section break and pressing Delete.

To discover paragraph formatting that produces unwanted page breaks, select the paragraph immediately following the page break, choose Format ➪ Paragraph, and go to the Line and Page Breaks tab. In the Pagination section, you see which options you have checked and can uncheck the culprit. (The options are Keep lines together, Keep with next, or Page break before.) These breaks look like Word's automatic breaks.

You may also have a table in Word that is divided in the middle of a cell. If the entire table does not have to be on the same page, your solution is simple. Place your insertion pointer anywhere on the row that is being split. Choose Table ➪ Table Properties. In the dialog box, click the Row tab, and clear the Allow Row to Break Across Pages checkbox. (If the table has to fit on one page, you have no choice but to rearrange adjoining text to make the table fit.)

If your problem is that Word's automatic pagination leaves you with a few lines of a paragraph moved over to the following page in a document, you will see the loosely dotted page break line dividing the paragraph. To keep the entire paragraph on one page, your best options are to make your margins smaller or to reduce the space between paragraphs. Both options allow more text per page so that the extra lines can move up to the first page. To adjust the margins, switch to Print Preview and, in the ruler, move each margin area closer to the paper's edge. Alternatively, you can use the Format ➪ Document command. You have two ways to reduce the space between paragraphs: If you have used styles, place the cursor within one paragraph, choose Format ➪ Paragraph, select the Indents and Spacing tab, lessen the Space before or Space after, and then redefine the style. (For more on styles, see Chapter 8.) If you pressed Return to create space between paragraphs, reducing space between lines is more tedious. Showing the paragraph markers, select one marker character and make it a smaller font size. Then copy that marker and paste it, one by one, over all other markers that provide your space between paragraphs. A third option is to make your entire font size smaller. Finally, you can let Word reduce the document size for you. In Print Preview, click the Shrink to Fit button on the Print Preview toolbar.

4. Why doesn't Word print the gridlines in my table?

A table's gridlines appear only onscreen. If you want to add lines to your table printouts, you need to apply borders to the table. You can use the Table ➪ Table AutoFormat command to select from predefined borders and shading. Figure 14-3 shows the Table AutoFormat dialog box.

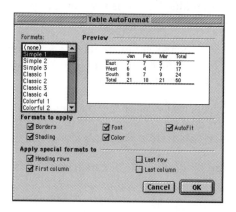

Figure 14-3: The Table AutoFormat dialog box

If you want to make a custom border, however, choose Format ⇨ Borders and Shading to bring up the Borders and Shading dialog box, as shown in Figure 14-4 (or use the Borders and Shading pane in the Formatting palette). In the dialog box, you can apply formatting to the table gridlines or to the text paragraph within a cell. If you want to apply formatting to the gridlines, be sure that you select the end-of-cell mark in the table.

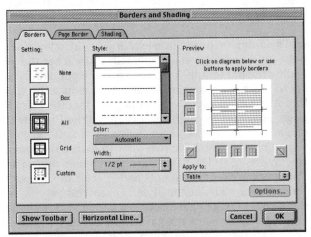

Figure 14-4: The Borders and Shading dialog box

Another option is to turn on the Tables and Borders toolbar and work from there.

5. Can I run Word 2001 and an earlier version of Word on the same computer, or do I need to remove my earlier version(s) in order to run Word 2001?

You can run two or three versions of Word on your computer simultaneously. Just keep each program in the folder in which it was installed.

When you install Word 5.1a, it creates its own folder. Keep this version in that folder. When you install Word 6, it installs two folders: one called Microsoft and one called Microsoft Word 6. Keep this version in those folders. Word 98 is installed in the folder called Microsoft Office 98. Keep all Office 98 components where they were installed, too. Word 2001 is installed in the Microsoft Office 2001 folder. You should also keep all Office 2001 components where they were installed.

To ensure that a document will open in the desired version, keep an alias of each version (clearly named by version) on your desktop, in your Apple menu, or in a pop-up folder and drag your document onto the desired version's icon.

You can launch the desired version of Word by double-clicking its icon or alias.

6. Can I delete Word documents while Word is running?

As is standard on the Mac, you can delete any document that is not open at the time you delete. To delete a document, first close it by clicking the close box on the top left of the document's window. Then click the desktop to return to the Finder (or select Finder in the Applications menu). In the Finder, double-click your hard drive icon, locate the file, and drag it to the trash.

7. Why can't my associate using Word 4, 5, 6, or 98 read my Word 2001 documents?

When Word 4, 5, 6, and 98 were created, Word 2001 didn't exist. No programmer can write software to accommodate things that don't exist. However, because Word programmers know about older software while writing new programs, they can make the newer software "downwardly compatible" with the older software. Therefore, your solution is to work in your newer software (Word 2001), but after saving a version as the normal Word 2001 format, do a Save As and select the older format from the Format pop-up menu by following these steps:

1. In Word 2001, open the document that you want to save in the earlier Word format.

2. Choose File ➪ Save As to open the Save As dialog box.

3. In the Format pop-up menu, select Word 4, Word 5, Word 5.1, or Word 6, as appropriate. Make any desired change to the file's name, specify the folder in which you want to store the file, and then click OK.

4. If your associate is using Word 98, present your associate with a copy of the Word 97–2001 Converter Installer from your Value Pack—that's what it's there for.

8. Why aren't all my changes saved in a document, even with AutoRecover turned on?

AutoRecover is not the same as the AutoSave feature—it does not automatically save your files. No substitute exists for using the Save command each time you do something that you want to be sure to keep. AutoRecover is designed to recover work after a power outage or system crash. AutoRecover periodically makes a copy of your document. If Word or your Mac freezes while you have documents open, Word automatically opens the saved recovery document when you restart and relaunch Word. The recovery files are temporary. They are erased when your document is saved and are deleted when you close the file.

If you want to turn on the AutoRecover feature or adjust the time intervals on the saves, choose Edit ➪ Preferences and select the Save tab (see Figure 14-5). Enter the desired time interval in the Save AutoRecover info every x minutes text box.

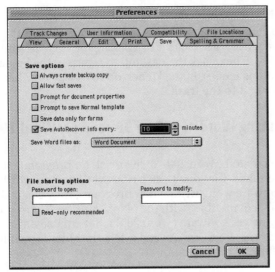

Figure 14-5: The Save Tab of the Preferences dialog box

Caution   Don't put more faith in AutoRecover than it deserves; it is not a substitute for proper saving or backup habits. The best defense is always to back up important work to another media source (such as a floppy, Zip, or Jaz disk) regularly. Backing up final versions (archiving) to a recordable CD-ROM is also a very good practice.

9. How can I set a different font (or font size or style) as the default?

You may want to use a font different from the default font Word uses in the Normal template. Fortunately, changing that font is a piece of cake. Open the Font dialog box by choosing Format ⇨ Font. In the dialog box, select the desired font, font style, and font size. Then click the Default button. Word displays a dialog box asking you to confirm the change to the default font; click OK in this dialog box to put the change into effect.

10. How can I create a bulleted or numbered list?

Word offers an easy way to create a bulleted or numbered list, to add the bullets or numbers quickly, and to apply a hanging indent to each of the paragraphs. To add bullets or numbers to a list, select all the paragraphs in the list and click either the Numbering button in the Formatting palette (to add numbers) or the Bullets button (to add bullets). If the Formatting palette isn't visible, choose View ⇨ Formatting palette.

Tip   Word's AutoFormat technology helps you automatically create bulleted and numbered lists. If you begin typing using a number, asterisk, or another form of bullet, Word will keep that format after the second bullet or number is entered. From then on, Word will automatically add the number or bullet followed by the space with which you began the first two lines of text. When you are done typing bulleted or numbered paragraphs, start a new paragraph and use the Delete key to delete the bullet. Word stops adding the bullets or numbers to successive paragraphs.

Summary

This chapter provided answers to some of the most common Word questions.

This chapter concludes the Word part of the book. The following part deals with Microsoft Excel, the spreadsheet package provided with Office 2001.

Where to go next

✦ Printing is a task you will find yourself doing on a regular basis. For more information on the particulars of printing in Word, see Chapter 4.

✦ Formatting question are also common in Word. For answers to your formatting questions, see Chapter 3.

✦   ✦   ✦

Excel

This part covers using Excel to manage, format, and present data, chart the data, manage lists of information, perform data analysis, and publish your results either on paper or on the Web. You'll also learn how to create and use Excel macros and Visual Basic for Applications to automate cumbersome and repetitive tasks.

Making the Most of Workbooks

This chapter covers topics related to working with Excel
workbooks, which are collections of worksheet pages
saved to the same disk file. Before you can effectively work
with Excel, you need to be familiar with workbooks.

Understanding Excel Workbooks

Excel uses the workbook concept, which means that multiple
pages (each page containing a worksheet) are placed inside of
a "notebook" (or, workbook, in Excel lingo). Excel's designers
assumed that most people who use spreadsheets have different but related groups of number-based data that would best
occupy different pages of the same workbook. If you worked
with numbers to earn a living before the advent of the computer, you would have had different pieces of paper on your
desk, each with related number-based information about a
particular project. At the day's end, all the pages would go
back into a file folder that was stored in your desk. In Excel,
each of these pages becomes a separate worksheet, with a tab
at the bottom of the workbook identifying each worksheet.

Before spreadsheet designers implemented the workbook concept, spreadsheets first accommodated a user's desire for more
power by providing increasingly larger spreadsheets in the
form of a single page. Finding information, however, became
quite a challenge, as spreadsheet pages approached the physical size of small houses. The next step in spreadsheet design
was to give users the capability to base formulas in one spreadsheet on cells of another. This capability partially solved the
organizational problem, but you had to remember to open all
the spreadsheet files that you needed. The workbook concept
overcomes the limitations of earlier spreadsheet designs by
placing all your information in an easily accessible notebook.

When You Need More Worksheets

By default, each workbook has three worksheet tabs. You can copy, add, or delete worksheets at any time. However, you might find it worthwhile to change this default if it is more convenient to begin your workbooks with more (or fewer) worksheets.

To change the default number of worksheets, select Edit ⇨ Preferences, and then select the General tab. In this tab, click the up or down arrows next to the Sheets in new workbook field (or select the existing number and enter a new number).

With the workbook concept, you can easily find information by navigating among the multiple pages of the workbook. Moreover, you can name the tabs that indicate each page (worksheet) of the workbook so that the tabs represent what is stored in each worksheet. Figure 15-1 shows a typical workbook in Excel, with the House Sales worksheet page of the workbook currently active.

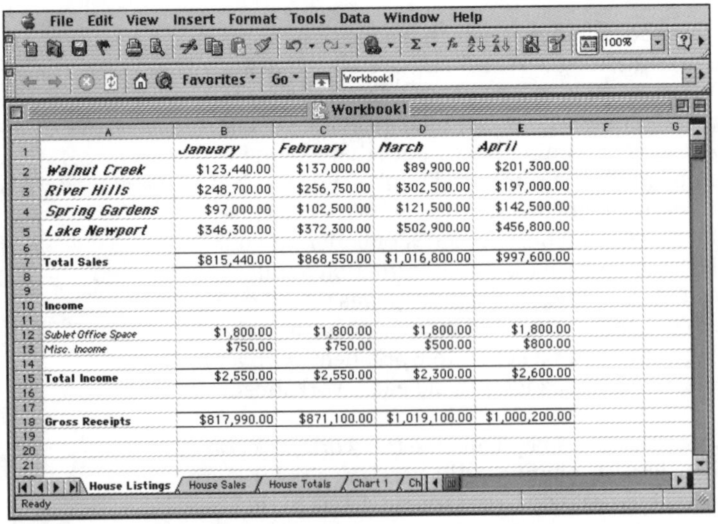

Figure 15-1: A typical Excel workbook

Each workbook can contain up to 255 separate worksheet pages. Each worksheet can have up to 65,536 rows (it went up from 16,384 to 65,536 in Excel 98) and 256 columns — more than you should ever need on a single page. Each intersection of a row and column comprises a cell. Row and column coordinates identify cells (for example, A1 is the cell in the upper-left corner of the worksheet). To make row and column coordinates easy to see, the row header and column header become highlighted when you select a cell. In addition to containing worksheet pages, an

Excel workbook can also contain chart sheets (used to store charts), macros, and modules (collections of program code written in Visual Basic for Applications (VBA), the programming language used by Excel and other Microsoft Office products).

Opening a new workbook

When you launch Excel, it opens a new workbook, and you can begin entering your information. If you want to create a new workbook at any time, click the New Blank Document button on the Standard toolbar, or choose File ➪ New (⌘-N).

Opening an existing workbook

You open an existing workbook the same way that you open any document on the Mac (see Chapter 1 for details). Basically, your options are to double-click the file that you want to open, select the file from the Apple menu if you stored it there, or choose File ➪ Open to select the file from the Open dialog box, as shown in Figure 15-2. You can also launch the file by pressing the Open button in the Project Gallery when Excel first launches (the Open button only appears in the Project Gallery at that time).

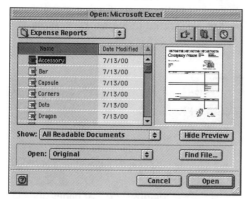

Figure 15-2: The Open dialog box

You may also be able to open a recently worked with workbook by selecting it from the File menu. By default, Excel remembers the last four files that you worked with and lists them at the bottom of the File menu. If the list of recently used workbooks is not displayed in your File menu, the option for displaying them has been turned off. To turn it back on, choose Edit ➪ Preferences, and then click the General tab in the Preferences dialog box. Click the Recently used file list checkbox to activate the option, and then enter a number of files to be remembered. (Up to nine files can be listed.) Click OK.

The More Workbooks, the Merrier

You can have more than one workbook file open at a time. The number of workbooks you keep open at once is only limited by the memory you allot to Excel. Each workbook you open is in its own document window. You can move and size the windows containing your workbooks by using standard Mac moving and sizing techniques. To work with a specific workbook, bring it to the front.

As with any Mac document, if you see even the tiniest edge of a worksheet on your desktop, you can simply click it to bring it forward. Therefore, if you size the windows so that they don't take up the entire screen, you can navigate among multiple windows by using the mouse to make any desired window the active window. You can bring the worksheet to the front by selecting its name from the Window menu. Pressing Control-F6 also rotates through all open worksheets. Control-Tab will take you to the next workbook, and Control-Shift-Tab will take you to the previous workbook.

Working with Worksheets

As you work with Excel worksheets, you use various techniques to move around in the sheet and to select areas of the sheet in which to perform common operations. First, though, it makes sense to become familiar with the parts of a worksheet. The parts of a worksheet window are illustrated in Figure 15-3; Table 15-1 describes the parts.

<table>
<tr><td colspan="2" align="center">Table 15-1
Parts of a Worksheet</td></tr>
<tr><td>**Worksheet Part**</td><td>**Purpose**</td></tr>
<tr><td>Scroll bars</td><td>Use these to view sections of the worksheet that are not currently visible by clicking the arrows or by dragging the scroll box.</td></tr>
<tr><td>Split bars</td><td>Use these to split the worksheet window into two panes horizontally and/or two panes vertically to view different portions of the worksheet. To split the window, move the pointer to the thick line by the up or right arrows and drag when the cursor becomes a two-headed arrow.</td></tr>
<tr><td>Row headers</td><td>Use these to identify each row and to select rows (by clicking the headers).</td></tr>
<tr><td>Column headers</td><td>Use these to identify each column and to select columns (by clicking the headers).</td></tr>
<tr><td>Cursor</td><td>Use these to indicate the currently selected (or active) cell.</td></tr>
</table>

Worksheet Part	Purpose
Tabs	Use these to select each worksheet in the workbook.
Standard toolbar	Provides buttons to access common operations, such as opening and saving files, and cutting, copying, and pasting data.
Web toolbar	Provides buttons to interact with the Web.
Formula bar	Displays the contents of the active cell.
Status bar	Displays various messages as you use Excel.
Scroll buttons	Scrolls among the worksheet tabs in a workbook.

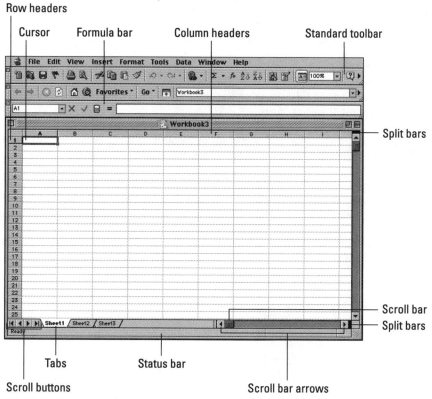

Figure 15-3: The parts of a worksheet

Navigating within your worksheet

Using the mouse is the primary method of navigating within a worksheet. As you move the mouse pointer around the worksheet, the pointer changes shape depending on its location. In most areas of the worksheet, the pointer resembles a plus sign. In most areas outside of the worksheet or over the scroll bars, the pointer changes shape to resemble an arrow. You can scroll the worksheet one row or one column at a time by pointing to the arrows at the ends of the scroll bars and clicking them with the mouse button. As always with the Mac, the longer you press the mouse, the further you travel within your document. You can also drag the scroll box, the square block in each scroll bar area. As you drag, a yellow pop-up box tells you the row or column you will be at when you release the mouse. By pressing Shift as you drag the scroll box, you scroll huge distances at a time.

Note   We're traditionalists and have used the Mac since its birth. Thus, we use the traditional scroll bars and scroll arrows. It is possible that you might have both arrows at one end of the scroll bar and that the scroll box (some of us call it the thumb) is proportionally sized to reflect what percentage of your worksheet is visible.

The Tab and Return keys, used alone or in combination with the Shift key, also move the cursor. Pressing Tab moves the cursor to the right; pressing Shift-Tab moves the cursor to the left; pressing Return moves the cursor down; pressing Shift-Return moves the cursor up.

Tip   If you've lost the cursor and you want to locate it quickly, press Control-Delete. This causes the window to scroll as needed to reveal the active cell.

You can also use Edit ⇨ Go To (F5) to move quickly within a worksheet if you know your destination cell. Press F5 to open the Go To dialog box, as shown in Figure 15-4. In the Reference text box, enter the name or address of the cell you want to go to and click OK, or press Return or Enter. Excel jumps you to that cell. For example, if you enter **AZ400** into the Reference text box and press Return or Enter, the cursor moves to cell AZ400.

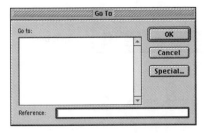

Figure 15-4: The Go To dialog box

Cross-Reference   If you're curious, you can use the Go To list box to select a named range to go to in a worksheet. Chapter 16 provides details about working with named ranges.

You can also navigate within your worksheet by using arrow keys. As you reach the right side or the bottom row of the worksheet, pressing the same cursor key once more causes the worksheet to scroll, which brings an additional row or column into view.

Remember that the part of the worksheet that you can see is just a small part of the entire sheet. Table 15-2 shows various other key combinations that you may find useful for moving around in an Excel worksheet.

Table 15-2 Useful Keys for Worksheet Navigation	
Key	**Function**
Arrow keys	Move the cursor in direction of the arrow.
Control-↑ or Control-↓	Moves the cursor to the top or bottom of a region of data.
Control-← or Control-→	Moves the cursor to the left-most or right-most region of data.
Page Up or Page Down	Moves the cursor up or down one screen.
Control-Page Up or Control-Page Down	Moves the cursor to the preceding or the following worksheet.
Home	Moves the cursor to the first cell in a row.
Control-Home	Moves the cursor to the upper-left corner of the worksheet.
Option-End	Moves the cursor to the last cell in a row that contains data.
Control-End	Moves the cursor to the last cell in the used area of a worksheet.

Caution Certain keyboards, particularly those that require you to hold down an *fn* key to access function keys, page up, and so forth, can be problematic with some of the keyboard shortcuts.

Moving among worksheets

To move among the individual worksheets of the workbook, click the worksheets' tabs at the bottom of the workbook. At the lower-left corner of the worksheet (refer to Figure 15-1) are scroll buttons that enable you to scroll among all the worksheet tabs. If a tab is not visible, click the buttons to scroll the tab into view. Clicking the left- or right-arrow button scrolls you by one tab to the left or right. Clicking the left-end or right-end button (the one with the line to the left or right of the arrow) scrolls you to the first or last tab in the worksheet. By default, new workbooks in Excel have 3 worksheets, but you can add more (up to the limit of 255 worksheets per workbook) by inserting new worksheets, a topic covered later in this chapter.

Tip Remember that you can use the Control-Page Up command to move to the prior worksheet or Control-Page Down to move to the next worksheet.

Scrolling among the tabs works well if your workbook contains relatively few worksheets, but if your workbook is fairly large (for example, 4 years' worth of projected budgets stored on 48 worksheets), there's an easier way to get around the worksheets: You can use Edit ➪ Go To (F5). When the Go To dialog box appears, enter the name of the tab followed by an exclamation point and the cell you want to go to. Follow these steps to use the Go To key:

1. Press F5 to open the Go To dialog box.

2. In the Reference text box, enter the tab name, an exclamation point, and the cell reference. Then click OK.

   For example, to jump to the first cell in the sixth worksheet, you would press F5 and enter **Sheet6!A1** in the Reference text box.

Unfortunately, this technique doesn't work when your tab names include spaces, such as "House Sales." In this case, Excel interprets the first word you type in the Reference text box as a named range, and when Excel can't find a range by that name, it displays an error message. The only way around this problem (if you want to be able to jump across pages with the Go To key) is to rename the tab, removing spaces, or to create named ranges in the other worksheets so Excel can find the named range.

Renaming the worksheet tabs

As you work with different worksheets within a workbook, you may find it helpful to rename the tabs to something meaningful. Face it, Sheet4 means a lot less to most people than May 2001 Slush Fund. You can easily rename the tabs to whatever you want by Control-clicking the desired tab and choosing Rename from the shortcut menu. This highlights the existing name within the tab, ready for you to type a replacement name. Excel doesn't limit what you call your tabs, but keeping tab names short enables you to view the most tabs at the bottom of the workbook. You can also select a sheet's name for editing by double-clicking the name.

Selecting multiple worksheets

For many common operations (such as inserting or deleting sheets or applying formatting), you need a way to select more than one worksheet at a time. You can Shift-click to select multiple adjacent sheets (directly beside one another) by performing these steps:

1. Use the scroll buttons to bring the first tab that you want to select into view, and click the tab to select that worksheet.

2. Use the scroll buttons (if needed) to bring the last tab of the group that you want to select into view. Press the Shift key and click the last tab.

To select multiple nonadjacent sheets, perform the following steps:

1. Use the scroll buttons to bring the first tab that you want to select into view and click the tab to select that worksheet.

2. Use the scroll buttons (if needed) to bring the next tab that you want to select into view. Press the ⌘ key and click the desired tab.

3. Repeat Steps 1 and 2 for each additional tab that you want to select.

Selecting a range of cells

Many operations require selecting large areas of cells, or ranges of cells. To select all cells from A1 to F6, for example, you would click in cell A1, hold down the mouse button, and drag down to cell F6 (see Figure 15-5). As you select the A1:F6 cell range, the first cell does not appear in your highlight color, as the others do; nevertheless, it is one of the selected cells. By placing the cursor at any cell and clicking and dragging the mouse, you can select any range of cells.

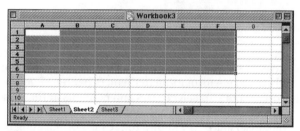

Figure 15-5: Selecting a range of cells in an Excel worksheet

Rather than drag over a large selection, you can Shift-click. Simply click in the first cell of the range, and then press Shift while you click in the last cell of the range. This selects the entire range, leaving the first cell that you selected as the active cell. For example, if you click in cell B2, press Shift, and click in cell E15, the entire range from B2 to E15 is selected, and the active cell becomes cell B2.

To select a very large range of cells, you can combine Shift-clicking and the Go To command to make your selection process faster. Follow these steps:

1. Select the first cell in the range that you want to select.

2. Press F5 to open the Go To dialog box.

3. In the Reference text box, enter the cell reference for the last cell in the range.

4. Press Shift while you click OK.

Other methods can also be used to select a range of cells. Clicking a row header at the left edge of the worksheet selects an entire row, while clicking the column header at the top of the column selects an entire column. To select more than one complete row or column of a worksheet, click and drag across a series of column headers or down a series of row headers. For example, to select all cells in rows 4, 5, and 6, click the row 4 header and drag across rows 5 and 6.

You can also select noncontiguous ranges, or nonadjacent areas. For example, you can select A1:C4 and then select F3:G8. To make this selection, select the first range in any usual manner. Then press the ⌘ key and select the second range by clicking and dragging. Excel selects the second area without deselecting the first. Figure 15-6 shows the result of selecting these two ranges.

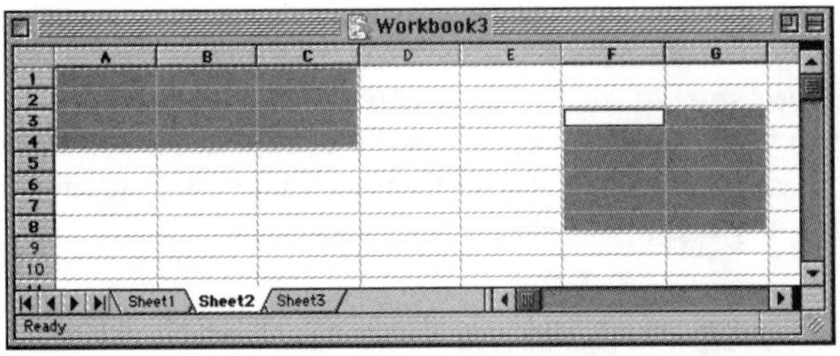

Figure 15-6: A selection of noncontiguous cells

You may also find it helpful to select multiple ranges, such as both rows and columns, as one unit so that you can apply the same formatting to them. (Chapter 17 goes into more detail about formatting worksheets.) To select rows and columns at the same time, select the first row(s) or column(s) that you want and hold down the ⌘ key as you select the other rows or columns. Figure 15-7 shows the results of selecting rows 1 and 2 and columns A and B with this technique.

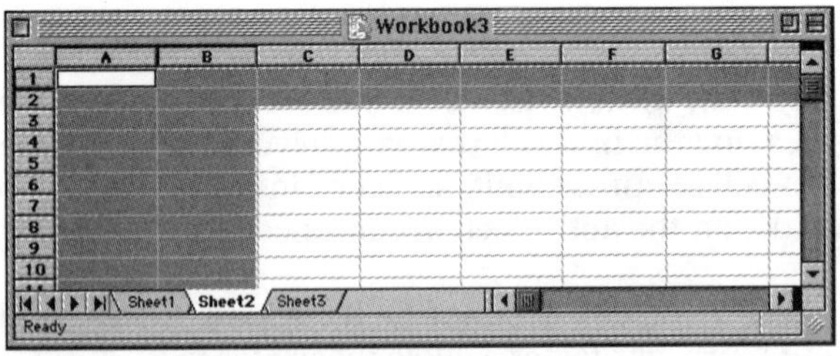

Figure 15-7: The result of selecting rows and columns as one unit

Adding and deleting worksheets

As you work in an Excel workbook, you may have to rearrange the worksheets within it. Control-clicking one of the worksheet tabs causes a shortcut menu to open. You can use this shortcut menu to add, delete, or move your worksheets.

Follow these steps to add a worksheet to a workbook:

1. Control-click the tab of the worksheet that is to appear after the worksheet you want to add.

2. Choose Insert from the shortcut menu to open the Project Gallery with Blank Documents displayed, as shown in Figure 15-8. The Show pop-up menu will be restricted to Excel documents and disabled so that you cannot change the type of document shown.

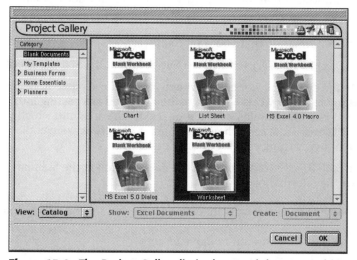

Figure 15-8: The Project Gallery limited to Excel document choices

3. Click the Worksheet thumbnail to insert a new worksheet and click OK (or double-click the Worksheet icon).

You can also delete a worksheet by using the shortcut menu. Select the tab of the sheet that you want to delete, Control-click it, choose Delete, and click OK to confirm the deletion.

Moving and copying information in worksheets

You can move or copy information within worksheets and between workbooks in a variety of ways. To copy information from any worksheet to another, perform these steps:

1. Select the information that you want to copy.

2. Choose Edit ➪ Copy (⌘-C) or click the Copy button in the Standard toolbar.

3. Move to the cell (in any worksheet) where you want to begin the insertion of the information. If you are pasting to a new worksheet, go to Step 4. If you are pasting into a worksheet that already contains information, select the area into which you will paste. This area must have the same number of cells as were copied in order to prevent overwriting existing information.

4. Press Enter (not Return) to place the information in the worksheet. Of course, you can also choose Edit ⇨ Paste (⌘-V), or you can click the Paste button in the Standard toolbar to place the information in the worksheet.

You can move information in the same worksheet or to another worksheet or workbook by following these steps:

1. Select the information that you want to move.

2. Choose Edit ⇨ Cut (⌘-X), or click the Cut button in the Standard toolbar.

3. Move to the cell in the worksheet where you want the paste to begin. If you are pasting to a new worksheet, go to Step 4. If you are pasting into a worksheet that already contains information, select the area into which you will paste. This area must have the same number of cells as were copied in order to prevent overwriting existing information.

4. Choose Edit ⇨ Paste (⌘-V), or click the Paste button in the Standard toolbar, to insert the information.

Moving and copying an entire worksheet is also easy to do. Follow these steps:

1. Select the tab that you want to move or copy.

2. Control-click the tab of the sheet and choose Move or Copy from the shortcut menu. This opens the Move or Copy dialog box. Identify the workbook to which you want to move or copy your worksheet. All available workbooks appear in the To Book pop-up list. You can also move or copy to a new workbook by selecting the (new book) option.

3. In the Before sheet portion of the Move or Copy dialog box select the tab you want your worksheet to land in front of, or select (move to end).

4. If you just want to move the worksheet, leave the Create a copy checkbox empty. To keep the worksheet in place but to also copy it to the new location, check the copy option.

5. Click OK.

Remember that this moves or copies the entire worksheet, not just a part of it, even if only a part of it is selected when you begin.

Viewing as Much as Possible

Toolbars, the formula bar, and the status bar are very handy. However, they take up room on your screen and at times you may need to dedicate every inch to viewing your spreadsheet. You have two options to help you with this. One is to turn off each of the toolbars, the formula bar, and the status bar. However, to turn off each element requires several steps (regardless of whether you do this from the View menu or by Control-clicking any visible toolbar). Later, turning each element back on requires the same actions again.

Your other option is to use Excel's Full Screen command, available on the View menu. Simply select View ➪ Full Screen and the worksheet expands to fit the entire screen, removing all status, the Formatting palette, and toolbars. While in Full Screen mode, a small floating button bar appears, providing a button to Close Full Screen and return to normal mode. You probably don't need this button taking up screen space; you can return to the View menu any time to turn off Full Screen mode.

Splitting the worksheet window

With large worksheets, you may find it helpful to view entirely different parts of the worksheet at the same time by splitting the worksheet window into different panes (see Figure 15-9). To split a worksheet window, drag one of the split bars. You can also select a row where you want the window to split and choose Window ➪ Split. (If you select a cell and choose Window ➪ Split, the panes will split both horizontally and vertically.)

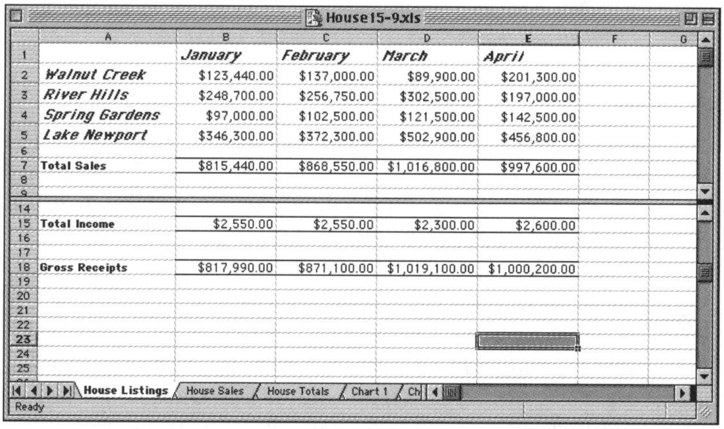

Figure 15-9: A worksheet window split into multiple panes

You can drag the split bar at the top right of the window to create a horizontal split, or drag the split bar at the bottom right of the window to create a vertical split, or both. You can then switch between panes by clicking in the pane where you want to work. You can reposition your splits any time. When you are finished using multiple panes, double-click the split to close it. (Or drag the split bar back to the right or bottom of the window, or choose Window ⇨ Remove Split.)

While a window is split, you can keep the top or left pane from scrolling by choosing Window ⇨ Freeze Panes. This menu option freezes the windowpanes above and to the left of the split.

Working with Excel's Toolbars

As with the other Office applications, Excel provides several toolbars for accomplishing common tasks. By default, Excel displays the Standard and the Web toolbars, shown earlier in Figure 15-3. In addition, Excel has several other toolbars. Figure 15-10 shows the rest of the Excel toolbars.

To turn a toolbar on or off, choose View ⇨ Toolbars, and then select the toolbar name. To learn what a button does, rest your mouse pointer over the button. In a moment, a yellow rectangle pops up, telling you what that button does. If this rectangle doesn't appear, ScreenTips have been turned off. (Toolbars and ScreenTips were introduced in Chapter 1.)

You can change a toolbar's position, change the buttons that appear, and change the buttons' order. Moreover, you can create your own toolbar. Toolbar customization is covered in detail in Appendix F.

The formula bar

Below the toolbars is the formula bar, unless it has been turned off. To turn the formula bar on or off, select View ⇨ Formula Bar. The formula bar is where you enter data and formulas. It also shows you any formula contained in a cell. The formula bar is key to Excel and will be discussed in many places in this section.

The status bar

At the bottom of your screen, you will find a status bar, unless it has been turned off. To turn the status bar on or off, select View ⇨ Status Bar. Occasionally, the status bar displays pertinent messages about what Excel is doing or gives you tips about how to do something.

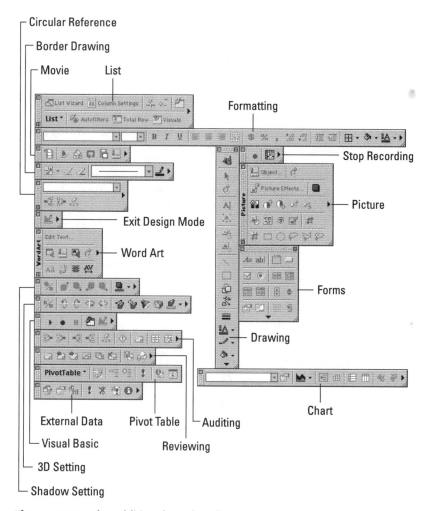

Circular Reference
Border Drawing
Movie   List
Formatting
Stop Recording
Picture
Exit Design Mode
Word Art
Forms
Drawing
External Data   Pivot Table   Auditing
Visual Basic   Reviewing
3D Setting
Shadow Setting
Chart

Figure 15-10: The additional Excel toolbars

Another cool thing the status bar shows is the result of Excel's AutoCalculate feature. When you select any range of cell within your spreadsheet, the sum of those cells appears to the right of the status bar, showing "Sum=" followed by the sum.

Note

If you launch Excel and open a new document, but either the Formula or Status bar is not showing, you should check your Preferences. Both the Formula bar and Status Bar have checkbox preference settings on the Preferences dialog box's View tab (Edit ➪ Preferences).

Saving and Closing a Workbook

Until you save a workbook, it exists only in the temporary memory of your Mac. It's a good idea to save your workbook (and any document) as soon as you create something you wouldn't want to have to re-create.

To save a workbook, use the standard Mac save command, File ⇨ Save (⌘-S). You can also click the Save button on the Standard toolbar. In the Save dialog box that opens, name your workbook. Notice where your workbook is being saved and use the pop-up menu at the top of the dialog box to switch folders as desired. Check Append file extension to automatically include a three-letter file-type extension to the end of the name if you intend to share the file with others who might be using the Windows version. To password-protect the workbook, click the Options button, as shown in Figure 15-11. The Save Options dialog box (see Figure 15-12) appears. Here, you can add a password for opening the workbook, or a modify-only password for making changes. You can also check the Read-only recommended checkbox to make the workbook read-only, so no edits can be added. Checking Always create backup saves the preceding version of the worksheet to a backup file each time you save the latest version. (See the "Creating a Backup File" section later in this chapter.) Click OK to close the Save Options dialog box. Finally, click OK in the Save dialog box to perform the save.

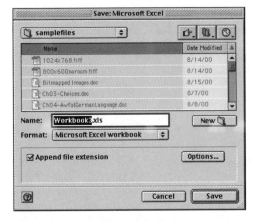

Figure 15-11: The Save dialog box

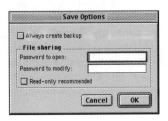

Figure 15-12: The Save Options dialog box

After a file has been saved, you won't see the dialog box again (because you already assigned a name). If you forget to name your document when saving, the document receives the default name, such as Workbook1. You can close the workbook, locate it in the Finder, and then rename it. Never rename a file while it is open.

You can add a password at any time, even after you've saved your workbook. Select File ⇨ Save As. This takes you to the same Save dialog box as when you first saved, providing you with the same Options button mentioned previously. Click the Options button, enter your password in the Save Options dialog box, and then click OK. Back in the Save dialog box, either give your document a new name or keep the same name. By keeping the same name and saving the document to the same place, you replace the former version with the new password-protected version.

You can set a specific folder as the default folder that opens in the Open and Save/ Save As dialog boxes. To set a default folder, follow these steps:

1. Select Tools ⇨ Preferences, and then click the General tab.

2. Click Select, which is next to the Default file location field, and select your folder. The path name appears in the field.

   If you are so inclined, you can type the path for the folder that you want displayed as the default working folder, instead. For example, type **Macintosh HD:accounts**. If, for some reason, your default folder is directly on your desktop, add **Desktop Folder** to the path. In this example, if the Accounts folder is on the desktop, type **Macintosh HD:Desktop Folder:accounts**. (We don't endorse folders on your desktop; we advise keeping folders within the Hard Drive icon and placing aliases of the folders on your desktop — or, better yet, in your Apple menu.)

Adding summary information to your workbook

As part of the information saved with your workbook, you can include details such as a title, author name, key words, and comments about the workbook. You can view and edit this information by choosing File ⇨ Properties, which brings up the Properties dialog box. If it's not already in front, click the Summary tab (see Figure 15-13) and add whatever information you want. The information you enter can later help you locate files for which you may need to search.

Using the AutoSave feature

Excel's AutoSave option can protect you from losing significant amounts of work in case of a power failure or system crash. (It is not infallible, however.)

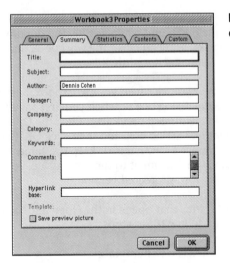

Figure 15-13: The Summary tab of the Properties dialog box

To enable AutoSave, choose Tools ⇨ AutoSave. (If you don't see this menu option, skip to the next paragraph.) In the AutoSave dialog box, check the Automatic Save Every checkbox, and enter the time interval you want Excel to use for the AutoSave. Then choose whether you want AutoSave to save only the active workbook or all open workbooks and whether you want to be prompted before each AutoSave.

If you don't see the AutoSave option on the Tools menu, choose Tools ⇨ Add-Ins to bring up the Add-Ins dialog box, as shown in Figure 15-14. This dialog box contains additional Excel options that you can activate. Check the box by the AutoSave option to make the option available on the Tools menu. Then follow the steps in the preceding paragraph to turn on the AutoSave option.

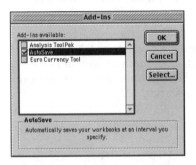

Figure 15-14: The Add-Ins dialog box

The AutoSave add-in is part of the normal Office drag-install so it should be listed in the Add-Ins dialog box. If the feature is not there, you should drag it from the Add-Ins folder within the Office folder of the Microsoft Office 2001 folder on your installation CD-ROM.

Creating a backup file

Another way to protect your work from being lost after a crash or power failure is to create a backup file for each "parent file" you are working with. The backup file minimizes the chances of losing your work.

You can take advantage of this option during your initial save or at any time after. During your first save, click Options to open the Save Options dialog box. If you have already saved your document, choose File ➪ Save As to open the Save dialog box, and then click Options to open the Save Options dialog box. In the Save Options dialog box, check the Always create backup checkbox. Then click OK to close the Save Options dialog box. During your first save, continue with the normal save process. If you are doing a Save As, make sure to keep the same document name and save it to the file's original location. That way the new file that you created by doing a Save As replaces the original, avoiding the confusion of duplicate documents.

After you activate the backup option, Excel creates a file named "Backup of . . ." whenever you save. This gives you what is referred to as *one generation* of backup.

Tip

If you wish to automatically maintain a longer history for your file(s), Aladdin Systems (www.aladdinsys.com) sells a product named Flashback that can provide this capability. Flashback runs in the background and for each file you register in it, it will maintain a version history from which it can recreate any generation of that document.

Saving in other file formats

You often need to save files in formats other than that used by your current version of Excel. Other users may be using earlier versions of Excel, or they may be using other spreadsheets, and you need to provide them with spreadsheet data they can work with. Saving files in other formats is relatively simple if you follow these steps:

1. Choose File ➪ Save As to open the Save As dialog box.

2. In the Format pop-up menu, select the format in which you want to save the file.

3. After selecting the file type, enter a name for the file or accept the default. (You may want to add the new file type as part of the name, or, more conveniently, check the Append file extension box and let Excel do it for you.)

4. Click Save to save the file.

If you save files in a format that is not the native Excel format, some features of the worksheet may be lost if they are not supported by the other program's file format. For example, if you save a file in an Excel 4.0 (or older) format, only the current page of the workbook will be saved to a worksheet file because that version of

Excel did not support workbooks with multiple sheets. The Office Assistant will remind you of this when you save a workbook as Excel 4.0 or older (unless, like us, you turn the Assistant off). It will advise you to save each sheet separately by making each sheet active and then saving it.

Saving Excel data as HTML

Significantly enhanced in Excel 2001 is the ability to save your Excel data as a Web page, generating the HTML files that can be displayed by Web browsers. The HTML files you create using Excel can be uploaded to a Web server for availability on the Web, or to a corporate intranet.

When you choose File ➪ Save as Web Page, Excel displays a slightly different Save dialog box, which is shown in Figure 15-15. See Chapter 23 for additional details on saving worksheet and chart data as HTML, and on publishing Excel data on the Web.

Figure 15-15: The Save as Web Page dialog box has a couple of different buttons.

The Automate button presents a dialog box in which you can set how frequently the document should be saved as a Web page. The Web Options button presents (surprise) the Web Options dialog box in which you can set display characteristics in four categories for the Web page you'll be creating.

Saving a workspace file

If you work with more than one workbook simultaneously on a regular basis, you may grow tired of opening the same workbooks day in and day out. With Excel's workspace file feature, you can avoid this monotony. You can use this workspace file to save the workbooks you are working on, the order they are in, and the sheets that are open at the time. The next time you need to work with these same workbooks, you can open the workspace file and all the workbooks open in the same position they were in when you created the workspace file. Follow these steps to create a workspace file:

1. Open the workbooks that you want to include in the workspace file and arrange them the way that you want them to be when you open the workspace file.

2. Choose File ⇨ Save Workspace to open the Save Workspace dialog box, as shown in Figure 15-16.

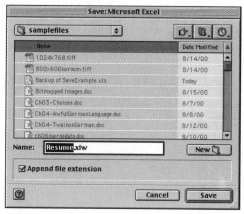

Figure 15-16: The Save Workspace dialog box

3. Enter a name for the workspace file and click OK.

The workspace file keeps track of the arrangement of your work area and opens your files when you double-click it, but you still need to save your changes to the workbook files.

Closing a workbook and exiting Excel

You close a workbook the same way you close any Mac document or window — by clicking the close box in the top-left corner of the document window or choosing File ⇨ Close (⌘-W). If you made any changes to the workbook that were not saved, Excel asks whether you want to save the changes. (This safeguard is provided to avoid your exiting Excel without saving your work.)

You quit Excel as you quit any Mac program — File ⇨ Quit (⌘-Q). If you have any unsaved work, Excel asks whether you want to save the changes and waits for your response before continuing. To make quitting easier, Excel 2001 includes a Save All option. If you have more than one unsaved worksheet when you quit, the dialog box includes a button to save all changed worksheets with one click.

Finding Workbooks

In case the Mac Sherlock (or Sherlock 2) feature isn't enough for you to locate a misplaced file, you can use Excel's Find feature — if you have diligently filled in the Summary tab of the Properties dialog box for your worksheets. This same search system is in Word and PowerPoint, so you can search for files created in either application from here, and vice versa. (It also means that you can refer back here if you need help searching from Word or PowerPoint.) Entourage does not have a generic Open dialog, and thus does not include this feature.

To do a search, select File ➪ Open (⌘-O), and then click the Find File button. This brings up the Search dialog box shown in Figure 15-17. In this dialog box, you can enter a file name for which to search. However, this dialog box offers far less searching capacity than the Mac's Sherlock feature and is not nearly as fast.

Figure 15-17: The Search dialog box

To perform an advanced search, click the Advanced Search button. This opens the Advanced Search dialog box shown in Figure 15-18. This dialog box enables you to search based upon any Summary information you have entered for any Excel, Word, or PowerPoint document.

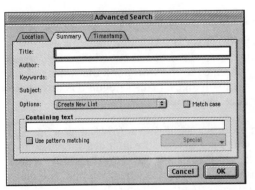

Figure 15-18: The Summary tab of the Advanced Search dialog box

To do an advanced search, follow these steps:

1. Select File ➪ Open (⌘-O), and then click the Find File button to open the Search dialog box.

2. Clear any existing searches by clicking the Clear button.

3. Click Advanced Search to open the Advanced Search dialog box, and then select the Summary tab.

   This is where you can perform searches based on the different sections of the Summary tab of the Properties dialog box. This is the information — file name, author name, or other elements of the document — that you enter when you save a file for the first time.

4. Enter any word on which you want to search. For example, if seeking a keyword, enter that word in the Keywords field.

5. Check the Match case option if you want to search only on words that are capitalized or not capitalized, exactly as you've entered the words in the search fields.

6. If you are looking for a file containing particular text, enter that text in the Containing Text text box. Checking Use Pattern Matching enables the Special bevel button, letting you choose pattern criteria from the pop-up list.

7. Click the Location tab to specify where you want to search. To add more locations to search, click Add. In the dialog box that opens, navigate to the location you want and click Select at the bottom of the dialog box.

8. Make an entry in the Value text box to work with your property and condition choices. For example, if you choose Ends with in the Conditions list box, enter the ending value in this field.

9. To specify a date range to search, such as the date created or date last modified, click the Timestamp tab, and then enter the dates. You can also enter the name of the person who modified the document.

After you have set the criteria for your search and specified the location in which you want to look, you can click OK to search for your file.

You can name and save your search in case you want to use it again later. Click the Save Search As button, and then give it a name. Later, select the name of the search you want to activate from the Saved searches pop-up menu. As time goes on, your saved searches may become old and you may want to get rid of them. To remove an old search, select the name of the search and click Delete Search.

Organizing Your Files

The best way to find your work when you need it is to save it to a logical place. Good organization has no substitute. As you begin a project, create a folder for it on your hard drive. Then save that project's worksheets to that folder. If you have begun the Save procedure and realize you don't have a folder for your current project yet, just make a new folder from the Save dialog box. The Mac makes it easy.

If you create a folder for each project, you can save all project-related files to it — not just Excel files. The same folder can contain a FileMaker Pro database, letters in Word, a PageMaker file, art done in Illustrator and PhotoShop, and so on.

There is no right or wrong way to organize your files as long as your organization makes sense to you. The one thing you should not do is save your Excel files to the Microsoft Office 2001 folder. That folder should only contain the files needed to run the applications.

Summary

This chapter covered topics related to making good use of workbooks. You learned many different techniques that you can use for working with workbooks. This chapter discussed these topics:

✦ Excel uses the workbook concept, in which each file contains a workbook of one or more worksheets occupying separate, tabbed pages. You can store related information in the different worksheets of the workbook, and the worksheets are saved to a single file name.

✦ You can open one or more workbooks, and in each workbook, you can move among the worksheets by using the worksheet tabs.

✦ You can save groups of workbooks in a Workspace.

✦ Excel provides a variety of methods for navigating throughout a worksheet and for moving among worksheets.

✦ You can add and delete sheets in a workbook, and you can move sheets from one location to another in a workbook.

✦ You can save files to Excel format or to a variety of other file formats.

✦ Excel has a Find File feature that enables you to search for a specific workbook based on certain search parameters that you can enter in a dialog box.

Where to go next

✦ Now that you are familiar with workbooks, the next step is to learn the best ways to handle data entry and editing in Excel. See Chapter 16 for more information on entering data.

✦   ✦   ✦

Getting Information into Excel

In this chapter, you learn how to put data into your work-sheets, how to insert cells, and how to add and delete selected ranges, columns, and rows. This chapter also describes great features such as AutoSum, which sums a row or column of numbers at the click of a button; AutoFill, which can fill a range with successive numbers or dates; and the Function Wizard, which quickly helps you find a needed function. The chapter wraps up by explaining how to use formulas and named ranges in your worksheets.

Entering Data

A spreadsheet is nothing without data, so learning how to enter data is the best place to begin. You can enter either a value or a formula in any cell of an Excel worksheet.

Values are exactly that — constant amounts or sets of characters, dates, or times; for example, 234.78, 5/23/95, 9:35 PM, or John Doe. Formulas are combinations of values, cell references, and operators that Excel uses to calculate a result. For more information about formulas, see "Creating and Working with Formulas" later in this chapter.

When you place the cursor in a given cell and begin typing, your entry appears in the formula bar at the top of the window, as shown in Figure 16-1. In the formula bar, the insertion pointer (the flashing vertical bar) indicates where the characters you type will appear. As you type an entry, a Check (Accept) button and an X (Cancel) button appear enabled in the formula bar. You can click the Check button when you finish typing the entry to accept the entry, or just press Enter or Return. If you decide you don't want to use an entry, you can either click the X button in the formula bar or press the Esc key.

Names List Box

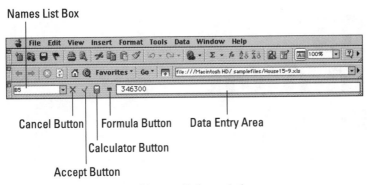

Cancel Button | Formula Button   Data Entry Area

Calculator Button

Accept Button

Figure 16-1: Data entered in Excel's formula bar

You may notice a Names list box (to the left of the X button). The Names list box displays the name or cell reference of the currently active cell. Use the pop-up arrow next to the Names list box to view a list of named ranges for the current workbook (after you've named some ranges, of course). See "Working with Named Ranges" and "Using the Function Wizard" later in this chapter for more information.

You can also enter data directly into the cells of a worksheet by turning on Excel's Edit Directly in Cell option and following these steps:

1. Choose Edit ➪ Preferences. In the Preferences dialog box that appears, select the Edit tab (shown in Figure 16-2).

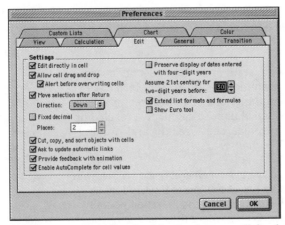

Figure 16-2: The Edit tab of the Preferences dialog box

2. Turn on the Edit directly in cell checkbox. (This may already be on by default.)

3. Click OK.

When the Edit directly in cell option has been turned on, you can double-click the cell in which you want to enter the data—which places the insertion point directly in the cell—and then begin typing. To abort an entry, press the Esc key.

A cell can hold up to 32,000 characters (increased from 255 in versions before Excel 98); however, not all characters will display unless you widen the column. (See Chapter 17 for information on formatting.)

Entering numbers

You can enter numbers into your spreadsheet in several ways. When a number is entered, Excel tries to figure out how the number will be used. This prevents you from having to format each cell for each number. The worksheet in Figure 16-3 shows some of the ways you can enter numbers in Excel.

Figure 16-3: Cells with numbers entered in various formats

To enter a number, click or double-click in the target cell to select the cell, type the number, and then press Enter or click the Check button. (You can also press Return, but when using a spreadsheet, it's better to get used to using the Enter key, which is on the numeric keypad, if you have one, or to the right of the space bar, if you don't.) You can enter numbers as integers (226), as integer fractions (1/8 or 13/5), as decimal fractions (987.326 or 43.65), or in scientific notation (2.5849E+8). Table 16-1 shows some number entries and how Excel formats them.

Table 16-1	
How Excel Formats Number Entries	
Number Entered	**Format Chosen by Excel**
97.9%	Number, percentage format
9705 Becker Ct.	Text, left aligned
$200.00	Number, currency format
7862	Number, general
144,000	Number, thousands format
–27	Negative number
(27)	Negative number
0 4/5	Fraction
2 4/5	Fraction

What the Heck Is ######?

If you're new to Excel, you're likely to be unpleasantly surprised at some point by the dramatic appearance of the dreaded ###### in one or more of your cells. Don't panic; Excel has not suddenly absorbed all of your data into some mystical black hole. The #s tell you that the cell is too narrow to display your data or your formula's results. After you resize the cell to fit the entire value, your number will appear.

To change the width of the column to see the value, move your cursor to the column's header (A, B, C . . .) and over the line that divides the cell in question from the next cell. When your pointer becomes double-headed, click and drag. If you don't like the idea of changing the column's width, you can try reducing the size of the font used to display the data. Select the cells containing the data, and then either use the Font section of the Formatting palette to choose a different font, a different font size, or both; or, alternatively, select Format ➪ Cells (⌘-1), or Control-click the selection and choose Format Cells from the shortcut menu that appears. When the Format Cells dialog box appears, click the Font tab and choose a smaller font size.

 Note   As you can see, even in cases in which the numbers are mixed with text, Excel detects what needs to be stored as text. This feature makes a big difference when you're entering database information such as street addresses.

One key point to remember is that you need to enter an integer in order to enter a fraction. If, as in the next-to-last example in Table 16-1, you need only the fractional part of a number, you must enter a zero and a space before that fraction; otherwise, Excel interprets the number as a date, and you can't use it in calculations.

Entering text

Your text entries can be any combination of letters, numbers, or other special characters. To enter text, select the desired cell and start typing, just like entering numbers. When you finish with the entry, press Enter or click the Check button in the formula bar. (Remember that a single cell can hold a maximum of 32,000 characters.) By default, Excel aligns text at the left side of the cell. The fastest way to change the alignment used for text, or any cell, is by selecting the cell and clicking the Center or Align Right buttons in the Formatting palette (Text Alignment pane). You can also use the other formatting techniques covered in Chapter 17.

Using the AutoComplete feature

Recognizing that you often end up entering some words repeatedly, Excel 98 introduced AutoComplete, and Excel 2001 has significantly enhanced AutoComplete's capabilities. For example, you are keeping a worksheet of family records and repeatedly need to enter the same names: Steven, Stacey, and Amy. The first time you type

To Format, or Not to Format?

Excel automatically formats a cell upon data entry—when you provide clues by means of how you enter the data. For example, when you enter a percent sign, Excel formats the cell as a percentage so that you don't have to call up Format ⇨ Cells. But you might not always want to use such clues in the data-entry process. It depends on how much data you have to enter.

For example, typing a dollar sign in front of an amount tells Excel to format the entry as currency. If you're faced with typing 200 entries, however, putting a dollar sign in front of each currency amount is a lot of added work. It's easier to enter all the numbers, letting Excel accept them as a general format, and then go back, select all the entries, and apply a formatting change to the entire range of cells to format it as currency. (Chapter 17 gives details on formatting a range of cells in your worksheet.)

Steven, Excel silently notes it. The second time it pays more attention. When you begin to type the name the fourth or fifth time, Excel gives you a hand by completing the word for you. If Steven is the only word you've entered several times that begins with the letter S, all you need to type is an **S**, and Excel finishes Steven for you. If you've been typing Stacey, too, Excel 2001 presents a menu that narrows down as you type more letters. Therefore, when you type **Sta**, the entire name Stacey will pop in automatically, and **Ste** will give you Steven; but if you type just **St**, you can choose one or the other from the menu. The more characters you type, the shorter the menu becomes; as you backspace, the menu expands.

There's a bit more to this. If you type **Stacey**, and then type **St** in the next row under "Stacey," Excel guesses that you want to type Stacey and supplies you with that name. If you type **St** under Steven, Excel gives you Steven. This is because Excel looks at what was last typed in that row or column and guesses that pattern. If you've just typed **Amy** a few times, just typing **A** completes Amy, even though the letter a is common and even a word by itself. AutoComplete works for all words, not only with names.

Cross-Reference By the way, if the names used with the AutoComplete feature in the previous example were to be used repeatedly in precise order, you could use the Custom Fill option to enter them. For more information on this feature, see "Copying data with Fill and AutoFill" later in this chapter.

Of course, AutoComplete also has a downside. Once Excel offers the choices, you're forced to use the mouse to approve the selection or to click back into the cell or the Formula bar's entry area to continue typing. Many of us find that this annoyance outweighs the value and utility of AutoComplete—try it out yourself and see whether turning AutoComplete off (Edit ⇨ Preferences, Edit tab, Enable AutoComplete for cell values) is your choice.

Tip   Sometimes, you may need to enter a number and have Excel accept it as text rather than as a numeric value. You can do so by preceding the value with a foot mark (single quote) character. For example, if you enter **"2758"** in a cell of a worksheet, Excel stores the entry as a text string made up of the characters 2758, and not as a numeric value.

Entering dates and times

You can also store dates and times within an Excel worksheet (see Figure 16-4). This can be useful for recording chronological data, such as employee dates of hire or the time spent on billable tasks.

Figure 16-4: Cells with dates and times entered in various formats

Dates and times entered in acceptable date and time formats are recognized by Excel as valid date or time values. Excel converts the times and dates that you enter to serial numbers, with dates being the number of days from January 1, 1904, until the date value you entered. Excel sees a time entry as a decimal fraction of a 24-hour day. If Excel recognizes the entry as a valid date or time, it properly displays the date or time on the screen. If you look in the formula bar for any cell that contains a date you entered, you'll see that all dates appear in the Date & Time control panel's (m/dd/yyyy by default) short date format, regardless of how you entered them. Time entries all appear in the formula bar in Date & Time control panel's (AM/PM by default) format with seconds displayed, regardless of how you enter them.

Oops? Whaddaya Mean, Oops?

As you enter data into Excel, keep in mind how useful Undo is. Undo can get you out of just about anything you can do to a worksheet. (However, some actions, such as saving files, can't be undone.) There's the Edit ➪ Undo menu command, ⌘-Z, and an Undo button on the Standard toolbar. Excel 2001 provides multiple undo capability, and you can undo up to the last 16 actions. To undo multiple steps, click the arrow next to the left-pointing arrow on the Standard toolbar, drag down to the action you want to undo, and then click. A status message below the action list reports the number of actions you are undoing.

If you undo something in haste, you can use Edit ➪ Redo to correct that, too. You can redo up to 16 actions. The right arrow lists your redo options and functions, the same as the Undo arrow button.

The following examples show ways that Excel can accept valid date entries. You can use a slash, a hyphen, or a space to separate the different parts of the entry:

7/3/97

3/Jul/97

3/Jul (the current year according to your Mac's clock is used)

Jul/97

07/03/1997

Time values can be entered in these forms:

7:50

7:50 AM

15:23

15:23:22

3:23 PM

3:23:22 PM

11/13/97 15:23

 Tip You can enter both the current date and time using shortcut keys. To enter the current date, press Control-; (semicolon). To insert the current time, press Control-Shift-; (semicolon) or ⌘-; (semicolon). To produce the combined date and time, press Control-; and Control-Shift-; in succession — either order will work.

You can display time using a 12- or 24-hour clock, depending on how you enter your times. If you decide to use a 24-hour format, you don't need to use AM or PM. If you decide to use a 12-hour time entry, be sure to place a space before AM or PM (or A or P). If you choose to store dates and times within the same cell, the dates and times should be separated by a space.

Excel's capability to handle dates and times as real values is a significant benefit in some applications, because you can use Excel's computational capabilities to perform math on dates and times. For example, Excel can subtract one date from another to provide the number of days between the two dates.

Displayed values versus underlying values

Excel displays values according to precise rules that depend on what formats you've applied to the cells in a worksheet.

Here's an example. In a blank worksheet with no formatting applied, try entering the following data exactly as shown in the cells listed.

In This Cell	Enter
A1	1234567890.1234
A2	$100.5575
A3	2.1459E10

The results appear as displayed values, as shown in the worksheet in Figure 16-5.

Figure 16-5: A worksheet with displayed values

As you move the cursor between the cells containing the data and note the contents of each cell in the formula bar, you will notice that Excel may display data differently than it is actually stored. For example, notice cell A2 in Figure 16-5.

Excel stores the data as you enter it, but it displays the data according to the formatting rules you establish (or according to the rules of the General format if you applied no formatting). Because the entries in cells A2 and A3 of the example include symbols, Excel formats those cells and displays their contents according to the formats dictated by those symbols. (You can also assign formats using menu commands; Chapter 17 covers this topic in more detail.) In the case of cell A1, because the value is so large, Excel displayed the whole number with two decimal places only.

In each case, what appears in the cell is the displayed value. What appears in the formula bar is the underlying value. Excel always uses the underlying value when calculating your formulas, unless you tell it otherwise. Be aware of the possible differences between underlying values and displayed values.

Adding Comments to Cells

To make collaboration on a project easier, Excel enables you to add comments to any cell of a worksheet. Comments are like little yellow sticky notes — except neater. Comments replace Notes that were available in earlier versions of Excel (pre-Excel 98). (Sound Notes, which provided the capability to add sounds to notes in Excel 4.0 for Mac and Excel 7.0 for Windows, are no longer available.)

To attach a comment, Control-click the desired cell and select Insert Comment from the shortcut list that pops up. Alternatively, you can place the cursor in the desired cell and choose Insert ➪ Comment. Either way, a comment for the cell opens. The user's name is automatically placed in the comment with a colon, and the insertion point waits after the colon, as shown in Figure 16-6. You can enter the desired text directly in the comment.

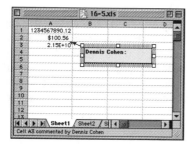

Figure 16-6: A comment added to a cell

A cell with a comment attached includes a tiny red triangle in the upper-right corner — a nondistracting visible indication of the comment. You can read the comment's contents by moving your mouse pointer over the cell containing the comment. When you do this, a window like the one shown in Figure 16-7 appears with the text of the comment.

Figure 16-7: The contents of a comment displayed within a worksheet

After a comment exists for a cell, the Insert ➪ Comment command in the menu bar becomes Insert ➪ Edit Comment. To edit an existing comment, select the cell containing the comment, and then select the Insert ➪ Edit Comment command. You can also Control-click the cell containing the note and then select Edit Comment.

You can review all the comments in a workbook by choosing View ➪ Comments. All comments are made visible, and the Reviewing toolbar becomes visible. In the Reviewing toolbar are Previous Comment and Next Comment buttons that enable you to move between comments. Moving between comments enables you to perform a sequential review of the comments, ensuring that you don't miss any during collaboration. Choosing View ➪ Comment again hides the comments.

To remove a comment, Control-click the cell containing the note, and then select Delete Comment, or click the Delete Comment button on the Reviewing toolbar.

Editing Data

Excel gives you two ways to make changes to cells. One way is to edit the entry within the formula bar; the other is to perform editing within the cell itself.

If you're a spreadsheet user from way back, you may prefer to type your entry into the formula bar as you have in the past. However, if you have a worksheet set up like a database of sorts, with a large amount of data to edit, you may prefer to use the edit-in-cell method. (If you find you cannot edit in the cell, you need to turn on Edit directly in cell. It's an option in the Edit tab under Edit ⇨ Preferences.) Instructions for both methods follow. By the way, a formula can contain up to 1,024 characters.

Editing using the formula bar

When you want to use the formula bar to edit a cell that already contains data:

1. Click in the cell containing the data you want to edit.

2. Move the mouse pointer to the area over the formula bar. (As you do so, the pointer takes on the shape of an I-beam as in Word's word processing.)

3. Place the I-beam at the location where you want to start editing, and then click. As with word processing, the flashing insertion pointer in the formula bar indicates where your editing will occur. Simply edit your text as you would any other text.

If the cell you are entering text into does not contain text, you don't need to click in the formula bar at all. Simply select the cell and then begin typing. The text should automatically land in the formula bar.

Using in-cell editing

To edit using in-cell editing, follow these steps:

1. Double-click the desired cell. This action causes the insertion point to appear directly within the cell.

2. Edit your text as you normally do when word-processing. Use the arrow keys to move the insertion point around within the cell.

3. Make your edits and then press Enter.

Clearing Data from Cells

Excel provides several ways to clear — erase — the contents of existing cells. The most obvious way is to select the cell or range of cells and press the Delete key. Pressing Delete does indeed clear the cell of its contents — any values or formulas entered in the cell — but you can clear a cell of formatting and comments as well.

To clear the contents of a cell and remove more than just the data entered, first select the cell or range of cells you want to clear. Then choose Clear from the Edit menu and select the appropriate choice from the submenu. Table 16-2 lists the Clear menu's suboptions.

Table 16-2 Edit ➪ Clear Submenu Options	
Option	**What It Does**
All	Clears everything from the selected cells, including formatting, the contents of the cell, and any notes attached to the cell. Formatting for the cell returns to the General format.
Formats	Clears formatting only. Formatting for the cell returns to the General format.
Contents	Clears the formulas or values entered in the cell but leaves formatting and notes untouched. (This is the functional equivalent of making a selection and pressing the Delete key.)
Comments	Clears any comments that were attached to the cell but does not change the cell's contents or its formatting.

Excel's Edit menu contains two commands that remove the contents of cells: the Clear command and the Delete command. If you want to clear the contents in cells, stick with Edit ➪ Clear; the Edit ➪ Delete command does more than just clear cells. (For specifics, see the sidebar "Edit ➪ Clear and Edit ➪ Delete: Understanding the Difference" later in this chapter.)

You can also clear the contents of a cell by Control-clicking the cell and selecting Clear Contents from the shortcut menu that appears.

Copying and Moving Cells

As your work with Excel becomes more complex, you'll find yourself regularly needing to move and copy entire portions of worksheets from one area to another. (How often does the boss make a request such as "Oh, could we also see last quarter's sales, too?" after you've spent hours getting your worksheet just right?)

Sometimes you can make the changes you need by inserting or deleting entire blank rows and columns. In many cases, however, you'll want to leave the overall structure of a worksheet alone and copy or move selected areas of the worksheet around.

Excel lets you copy or move data from place to place using either of two methods. You can use the Cut, Copy, and Paste commands (the menus, keyboard commands, or buttons on the Standard toolbar), or you can use drag-and-drop to move and copy data. The two methods work equally well. Generally, keyboard fans prefer using the Cut, Copy, and Paste commands, whereas mouse fans usually lean toward the drag-and-drop techniques. If you are moving data a long way, using cut, copy, and paste works better. Over a short distance, dragging is faster and easier on your hands.

You can use any of the techniques detailed in the following paragraphs to copy data across worksheets, as well as within the same worksheet. When you want to copy across worksheets, first select the desired data, as detailed in the following steps in the next section. Then go to the worksheet where you want to place the copy, and continue with the steps outlined in the next section.

Copying and moving data with cut, copy, and paste

To copy cells using the copy and paste method, perform these steps:

1. Select the cell or cells that you want to copy, and choose Edit ➪ Copy (⌘-C), or click the Copy button on the Standard toolbar, or Control-click the selection and choose Copy. The cells to be copied will be marked with a dotted-line border, as shown in Figure 16-8.

Figure 16-8: Cells in a worksheet marked for copying

2. Click the cell or select the cells that are the destination for the cell or cells you copied in Step 1. (You can move to cells in a different worksheet, if you want.)

3. Choose Edit ➪ Paste (⌘-V), click the Paste button (on the Standard toolbar), or Control-click in the destination cell or selection and choose Paste from the shortcut menu. All three methods place the copied information into the chosen cell or cells.

While the highlight is still visible around the source cells, you can copy the cells again if you wish by repeating Steps 2 and 3, or you can press the Esc key to remove the highlight.

Copying information keeps it in the original location while making a copy you can paste any number of times into any number of places. If you want to actually remove the data from its original location, use the Cut command rather than the Copy command. The steps are the same; just substitute cut (⌘-X) for copy.

Copying and moving data with drag-and-drop

At times, using the drag-and-drop technique is easier for moving or copying data between cells or ranges. Follow these steps:

1. Select the cell or group of cells that you want to move.

2. Move your mouse pointer so that it points to the border of the selected cell(s). The pointer turns from the plus sign into a hand. When it changes, click once and hold down the mouse button.

3. Drag your cells to the new location. As you drag, an outline of the selected area appears, and a yellow box tells you the address of the cell range (top-left and bottom-right cells) your cell(s) will land in. Figure 16-9 demonstrates. (Don't forget that if you move cells over others that contain information, these other cells will be overwritten.)

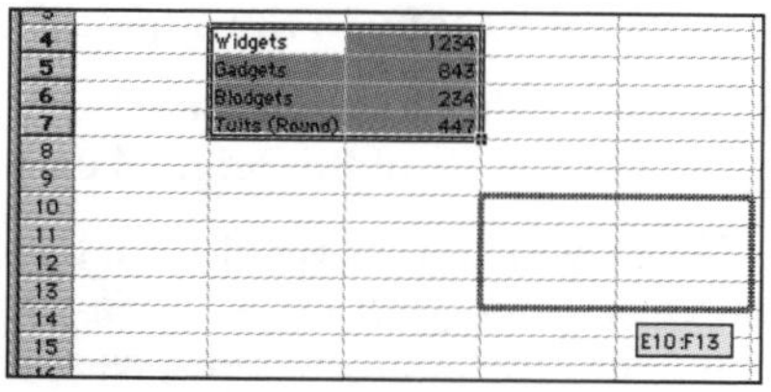

Figure 16-9: The outline of selected cells and their destination when you drag data

4. Release the mouse button.

The same steps can be used to copy a cell or a range of cells. The one difference is that when you want to copy the selection instead of just moving it, you need to press Option as you drag and drop.

Copying data with Fill and AutoFill

Excel offers two features that help you quickly fill cells with data: Fill and AutoFill. The Fill feature fills the range of cells you select with the data in the original cell. The AutoFill feature recognizes patterns or items that traditionally are entered in a pattern (such as months and days), and it fills in a range of cells intelligently, incrementing each successive cell. For example, if you enter January in a cell and then use AutoFill to fill the next 11 cells to the right, Excel fills in the names of the successive months. Actually, it would fill in any number of cells following the month pattern. You can Fill or AutoFill toward the left, right, up, or down. You can Fill or AutoFill using just the mouse, or you can use menu commands.

Note   Excel even tells you what text will land in any cell as you drag over it during a Fill or AutoFill.

You can copy any existing data from a cell into adjacent cells using the Fill feature by performing these steps:

1. Move the cursor into the cell that you want to copy to the adjacent cells.

2. Point the mouse pointer to the Fill handle — the tiny rectangle at the lower-right corner of the selected cell. As you do, your cursor becomes a thin black plus sign. With this cursor active, drag in either a horizontal or vertical direction over all cells that are to receive this data. As you drag, a yellow information box shows you the value being copied. Release the mouse button to copy the data into the cells.

If you prefer using menu commands, perform the following steps to complete Fill:

1. Move the cursor into the cell that you want to copy to the adjacent cells.

2. Place the mouse pointer over the selected cell. Click in the center of that cell and drag over all the cells that should get a copy of the original cell.

3. Choose Edit ⇨ Fill, and then select Up, Down, Left, or Right from the submenu. (Choose the direction in which you've selected your cells. When you make the submenu selection, the data is copied into the adjacent cells, as shown in Figure 16-10.)

Figure 16-10: The results of using the Edit ⇨ Fill ⇨ Right command

It's possible to copy data across worksheets with the Fill command, as well. First, select both the worksheet that you want to copy from and the worksheet you that want to copy to by holding down the Shift key while clicking both worksheet tabs. Next, select the cells to be copied, choose Edit ⇨ Fill ⇨ Across Worksheets. In the dialog box that appears, choose what you want to copy (All, Contents, or Formats) and click OK.

The AutoFill feature saves you time and keystrokes by providing intelligent copying. By default, AutoFill fills in days of the week and months of the year. You can also add your own custom lists to AutoFill so that it can handle other requirements that you have on a regular basis.

To use AutoFill to fill in dates, type the desired day of the week or month of the year into a cell. Next drag the Fill handle (the tiny rectangle at the lower-right corner of the selected cell) to highlight the cells in which you want AutoFill to add the data.

When you release the mouse button, the successive days of the week or months of the year appear. Figure 16-11 shows the results of AutoFill when January is entered into a cell and the Fill Handle is dragged across the next five cells.

Figure 16-11: The results of using AutoFill

If you AutoFill into more cells than the length of the list used by AutoFill, Excel repeats the AutoFill pattern until all selected cells are filled. To prevent the list from repeating, you can watch the yellow information box that reports the fill data as you drag to AutoFill. (Or you can count the number of entries and the number of cells you are dragging over.)

If you regularly fill in a list of your own, you can add it to the lists that AutoFill generates. Choose Edit ➪ Preferences. In the dialog box that appears, click the Custom Lists tab (shown in Figure 16-12). Click the words NEW LIST at the left side of the dialog box (even though they're already selected). An insertion point appears in the List entries box at the right. Type your own list in the List entries box, separating each entry with a Return. (In Figure 16-12, a custom list of book titles has been entered in the List entries box.) When you finish, click Add to add the list, and click OK. From then on, you can type any entry in your list into a cell and use AutoFill to fill in the successive entries based on your own list. This list can also be edited later. (We'll get to that shortly.)

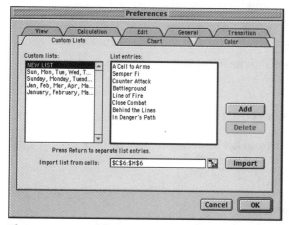

Figure 16-12: Adding a custom list via the Custom Lists tab of the Preferences dialog box

Perhaps you've already gone through the trouble of entering your text into your spreadsheet. You can turn this cell data into a custom AutoFill list without having to retype the data. To turn your cell data into a custom AutoFill list, follow these steps:

1. Select the cells that contain the data you want to turn into an AutoFill list.

2. Choose Edit ⇨ Preferences, and then select the Custom Lists tab.

    The range of cells you have selected should be reported in the field at the bottom of the tab (Import list from cells). (A cell range is reported as the first cell address, followed by a colon, and then the last cell address.)

 Cross-Reference The dollar signs you see in the cell address make it what is called an *absolute address*. If the dollar signs were missing, you would have a *relative address*. These are discussed later in this chapter in the sidebar "References: Relative versus Absolute."

3. Click Import.

    The first words in your list appear as the name of the list in the Custom Lists area. On the right are the elements of your list.

4. Click OK.

Making changes to the custom lists used by AutoFill is a simple matter. If you want to edit one of your custom lists, follow these steps:

1. Choose Edit ⇨ Preferences, and then select the Custom Lists tab.

2. Click the name of your list in the Custom Lists area of the Custom Lists tab. The elements of your list appear in the List entries side of the tab.

3. Click any list entries and make the necessary changes to the list.

4. Click OK.

To delete a custom list that you've created, follow these steps:

1. Choose the name of the custom list from the Custom Lists box of the Custom Lists tab.

2. Click Delete to delete the list.

When making your list, remember:

✦ Error values and formulas are ignored.

✦ Each list entry can contain up to 80 characters.

✦ Lists cannot start with a number. (If you want an increasing or decreasing series of numbers, use the Series command, which is described in the following section.)

✦ A custom list can contain a maximum of 2,000 characters.

Building series

Although AutoFill does wonders with simple and straightforward lists, sometimes you need more flexibility in generating a list of values that change across some kind of series. For those occasions, you can use the Edit menu's Fill Series command.

Excel can work with four types of series:

✦ Linear, which simply increases a number by its step value, such as 1, 2, 3, 4, 5, 6, and so on, where the start value is 1 and the step value is 1; or 5, 10, 15, 20, 25, and so on, where the start value is 5 and the step value is 5.

✦ Growth, which multiplies the previous number by a specific value, such as 5, 10, 20, 40, 80, and so on, where the start value is 5 and the step value is 2.

✦ Date-based, such as 1995, 1996, 1997, 1998, and so on.

✦ AutoFill, as based on the lists entered in the Custom List tab of the Preferences dialog box.

Create a series of values in a range of cells by following these steps:

1. Enter a value in a cell. (The value you enter serves as the starting or ending value in the series.)

2. Starting with the cell containing your value, select the cells into which you want to extend the series.

3. Choose Edit ⇨ Fill ⇨ Series. The Series dialog box appears, as shown in Figure 16-13.

Figure 16-13: The Series dialog box

4. In the Series in field of the dialog box, make sure the Rows or Columns selection matches the type of range you want to fill.

5. If you want the selected values to be replaced by values for a linear or exponential best fit, turn on the Trend checkbox. (If you do this, your options in Step 6 are limited to Linear and Growth.)

6. In the Type field of the dialog box, choose the appropriate Type option:

   • **Linear** adds the step value to the number that preceded the current cell in the series. When you select Trend, the trend values become a linear trend.

   • **Growth** multiplies the step value by the number that preceded the current cell in the series.

   • **Date** is used with date values; it lets you set the Date Unit options to Day, Week, Month, or Year choices.

   • **AutoFill** creates a series automatically, based on entries in the Custom List tab of the Options dialog box (choose Edit ➪ Preferences to get there).

   If you choose AutoFill, Excel fills the selected range based on the entries in the Custom List tab of the Options dialog box.

   If you choose Linear or Growth, continue with the following steps up to Step 9 to finish generating your series. (If you choose Date, go to Step 10.)

7. Enter a step value. The step value is the number by which the entries change from cell to cell. For example, a step value of 2 causes numbers to increment by two, such as 2, 4, 6, 8, and so on.

8. If you don't want the entries to exceed a certain number, you can enter a stop value. (If you leave this blank, Excel continues until it fills the selected range.)

9. Click OK.

   Excel stops either at the stop value or when it reaches the end of the selected cells. If the step value is negative and you enter a stop value, the stop value needs to be less than your starting value. Dates and times can be entered in any date or time format Excel understands.

   If you chose to enter a series of dates by choosing Date in Step 6, continue with these steps.

10. Choose Day, Weekday, Month, or Year from the Date unit field of the Series dialog box to apply the step value to the chosen entry type in the Date unit area.

11. Enter the step value to specify an increment. (For example, if you chose Month as the date unit, the entries increase in the month amount by the step value.) Again, a stop value may be entered if you think you have chosen too many cells.

12. Choose OK.

Using Paste Special

Sometimes, after copying cells, you may want to invoke special options when you paste the cells. You can do this using the Paste Special command.

To see these special options, choose any cell in a worksheet, copy it (⌘-C), move the cursor to another cell, and choose Edit ➪ Paste Special. You see the Paste Special dialog box shown in Figure 16-14.

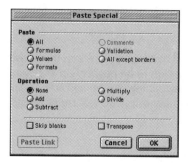

Figure 16-14: The Paste Special dialog box

You can choose any one of the options in the Paste portion of the Paste Special dialog box to select the information to be pasted. For example, if you want to copy only a cell's format, you would choose the Formats radio button, which copies only the cell's format, so you don't have to format the new cell.

You can also combine the contents of the copy and paste areas. First, select Formulas or Values in the Paste portion of the Paste Special dialog box. Next, under the Operation portion of the dialog box, select the operation you want. This combines the copy and paste areas by performing the chosen operation. For example, if cell A6 contains the formula =SUM(A1:A5), and you want to add this formula to the contents of cell D6, first select cell A6 and then choose the Copy command. Next, choose Edit ➪ Paste Special; choose Formulas in the Paste portion of the Paste Special dialog box; and choose Add under the Operation portion of the same dialog box. The result is that the formula is copied in the new cell with the new cell references. (Formulas are discussed in "Creating and Using Formulas" later in this chapter.)

The Paste Special dialog box also enables you to transpose copied rows and columns by selecting the Transpose option. This option is used to transfer information entered in rows to columns, and vice versa.

The Skip blanks option prevents the copying of blank cells from the copy area to the paste area; this way, a blank cell will not delete existing cell data in the paste area.

The Paste Link button is also a useful option for pasting and establishing a link with the source of the data pasted into the selected cells. (The source has to be a single cell or a range.) In cases in which the source is more than one cell, an array—a collection of cells that takes on a single value in relation to a formula—is posted. When the paste area is a single cell, the cell becomes the upper-left corner of the paste area, with the rest of the range filled in accordingly.

Working with Cells, Rows, and Columns

Another important aspect of manipulating existing data in worksheets is inserting and deleting cells and adding or deleting entire rows and columns. The first three options that Excel provides on the Insert menu let you insert cells, rows, or columns into an existing worksheet.

 Caution Before you perform major insertions, be warned that inserting cells in the midst of existing data causes cells in the area of the insertion to be pushed either down or to the right. If your worksheet contains formulas that rely on the absolute location of cells, and you move those cells by inserting new cells, you will create errors in your worksheet's calculations.

Inserting cells, rows, and columns

To insert cells, rows, or columns, follow these steps:

1. Select the cell or range of cells in which the new cells must be inserted, or select any cells in the rows or columns in which the new rows or columns are to be inserted.

   With rows and columns, note that a new row or column is inserted for each row or column cell you select. If you drag across three columns and then choose to insert columns, you insert three new columns.

2. Choose Insert ⇨ Cells, or Control-click the selection and choose Insert from the shortcut menu, to reveal the Insert dialog box (see Figure 16-15).

Figure 16-15: The Insert dialog box

3. To insert cells, choose either Shift cells right or Shift cells down to move existing cells in the direction you want. To insert entire rows or columns, choose Entire row or Entire column.

4. Click OK.

To insert only rows or columns, just select the number of rows or columns to insert at the point of insertion. For example, say you want to insert two columns ahead of column D. Click and drag across the headers for columns D and E, open the Insert menu, and then choose either Rows or Columns — both of these have a keyboard shortcut of Control-I.

 Caution For those of you upgrading from an earlier version of Excel, the keyboard shortcuts have been changed. ⌘-I now italicizes.

Deleting cells, rows, and columns

To delete cells, rows, or columns, follow these steps:

1. Select the cell or range of cells in which the cells must be deleted, or select any cells in the rows or columns in which the rows or columns are to be deleted.

   Note that a row or column will be deleted for each row or column cell you select. If you drag across three columns and then choose to delete columns, you will delete three columns.

2. Choose Edit ⇨ Delete (Control-K), or Control-click the selection and choose Delete from the shortcut menu to reveal the Delete dialog box, shown in Figure 16-16. (If you select an entire row or column, you won't see this dialog box; Excel assumes that you want to delete the entire row or the entire column, and it does so. If the deletion of a row or column was not what you had in mind, choose Edit ⇨ Undo.)

   **Figure 16-16:** The Delete dialog box

3. If you're deleting cells, choose either Shift cells left or Shift cells up to move existing cells to fill in the space left by the deletion. If you want to delete entire rows or columns, choose Entire row or Entire column.

4. Click OK.

Edit ⇨ Clear and Edit ⇨ Delete: Understanding the Difference

In Excel, there's a fundamental difference between the way Edit ⇨ Clear and Edit ⇨ Delete work. The two commands may appear to do the same task when applied to a range of blank cells with no adjacent data nearby, but in reality they behave very differently.

Edit ⇨ Clear clears the selected cells of the information in them but does not move cells out of the worksheet. Edit ⇨ Delete, on the other hand, removes the cells completely; other cells must take the place of the removed cells, even if the new cells are blank.

Compare the results of Edit ⇨ Delete to pulling out toy blocks from a wall made of those blocks; other blocks must be moved into the empty spaces, or the wall becomes unstable. Likewise, understanding how Edit ⇨ Delete works ensures the stability of the remaining areas of your worksheet.

If you want to delete one entire row or column, the fastest ways are to click the row or column header and press Control-K, or to Control-click the row header or column header and select Delete from the shortcut menu. To delete more than one entire row or column quickly, select the rows or columns by dragging across the row or column headers (rather than selecting cells in the rows or columns). Then choose Edit ⇨ Delete Control-K). Excel annihilates your selections, no questions asked.

Working with Named Ranges

Names are always friendlier to use and easier to remember than numbers. Therefore, Excel lets you refer to a cell or group of cells by a name instead of by a cell reference, and lets you use these names in your formulas. For example, you could name row 1 of a worksheet Income, and call row 3 Expenses. A formula in cell B5 that computes net profits could then read =Income–Expenses rather than =B1–B3. (Formulas are discussed in "Creating and Using Formulas" later in this chapter.)

To assign a name to a cell or group of cells, follow these steps:

1. Select the range of cells you want to name. (You can select an entire row or an entire column by clicking the row or column header.)

2. Choose Insert ⇨ Name ⇨ Define, or press Control-L. The Define Name dialog box appears, as shown in Figure 16-17.

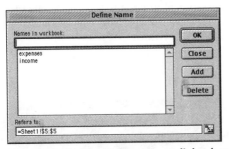

Figure 16-17: The Define Name dialog box

3. In the text box at the top of the dialog box, either type a name for the range or accept any default. (Don't use spaces in a range name; see the Note at the end of this section.)

   When Excel sees a heading at the top of a row or at the left of a column of cells you've selected, it uses the text of that heading as a default range name.

4. Click Add to add the new name to the list, and then click Close. (Or just click Close, or press Return or Enter.)

Figure 16-18 shows an example of named ranges in a worksheet. In this worksheet, columns B, C, D, and E have been assigned the names of the months, at the top of the respective columns, as named ranges. As shown in the formula bar, column F uses formulas such as =January+February+March+April to calculate the totals.

	A	B	C	D	E	F
1		January	February	March	April	Total
2	Walnut Creek	$123,440.00	$137,000.00	$89,900.00	$201,300.00	$551,640.00
3	River Hills	$248,700.00	$256,750.00	$302,500.00	$197,000.00	$1,004,950.00
4	Spring Gardens	$97,000.00	$102,500.00	$121,500.00	$142,500.00	$463,500.00
5	Lake Newport	$346,300.00	$372,300.00	$502,900.00	$456,800.00	$1,678,300.00
6						
7	Total Sales	$815,440.00	$868,550.00	$1,016,800.00	$997,600.00	$3,698,390.00
8						

F7 = =January+February+March+April

House15-9.xls

House Listings / House Sales / House Totals / Chart 1 / Ch

Figure 16-18: An example of named ranges in a worksheet

Tip

You can also create named ranges by selecting the cells comprising the range, clicking in the Named range text box in the Formula bar, and typing in the name you wish to use. This saves the step of displaying the dialog box.

After you've performed the preceding steps, you can refer to the range in your formulas by typing its name rather than using its cells' addresses.

Note

The names you use for ranges can be up to 255 characters in length, and they can include letters, numbers, periods, or underscores, but not spaces.

Creating and Using Formulas

In addition to entering values, you will use formulas throughout your worksheets. Excel uses the formulas you enter to perform calculations based on the values in other cells of your worksheets. Formulas let you perform common math operations (addition, subtraction, multiplication, and division) using the values in the worksheet cells.

For example, say you want to add the values in cells B1 and B2 and display the sum in cell B5. You can do so by placing the cursor in cell B5 and entering the simple formula =B1+B2.

With Excel, you build a formula by indicating which values should be used and which calculations should apply to these values. Remember that formulas always begin with an equal symbol. Figure 16-19 shows examples of various formulas within a typical worksheet.

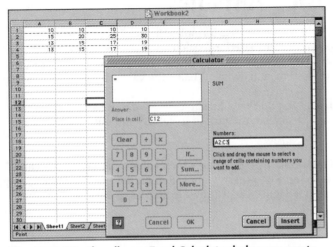

Figure 16-19: Examples of formulas within a worksheet

Excel 2001 added a new feature to help beginning formula creators get a start — the Calculator. Click the Calculator button on the formula bar to open the Calculator dialog box. You can start using the buttons and selecting cells or ranges to create the formula, as shown in Figure 16-20. The Sum button expands the dialog so that you can select the range to be summed and check it before inserting the Sum formulation into the main formula box for the Calculator. The More button will present the Paste Function dialog box (discussed later under "Using the Function Wizard") so that you may create more complex formulas using the built-in Excel functions.

Figure 16-20: The all-new Excel Calculator helps you create formulas more easily.

In the formula bar or with Edit directly in cell

If you place the cursor in any cell and type an equal symbol, the symbol and a flashing cursor appear in the formula bar. As you enter the formula, it appears within the formula bar. When you press Enter, Excel performs the calculation based on the formula and then displays, in the cell, the results of the calculation. If you've turned on Edit directly in cell as described earlier in the chapter, you can double-click the cell and type the formula directly into the cell.

Creating formulas by pointing

One handy way to enter the cell references that make up a major part of formulas is to click the cells that make up the formula. Typing the entire formula manually invites mistakes you can avoid by entering the cell references this way:

1. Place the cursor in the cell in which you want to enter the formula.

2. Click the equal sign (=) that appears in the formula bar. This starts the formula. Alternatively, you can type an equal sign (=).

3. Point to the cell you want as the first cell reference and click. (Alternatively, you can move the cursor there with the arrow keys and then click.)

4. Type an operator (such as a plus or minus symbol) or other character to continue the desired formula.

5. Point to the next cell you want to use as a cell reference and click (or move the cursor there with the arrow keys).

6. Repeat Steps 4 and 5 as needed to complete the formula.

Tip
While using the pointing technique to create formulas, you can enter cell ranges as references. Just click and drag from the starting cell in the range to the ending cell (or hold down the Shift key as you move the cursor from the starting cell to the ending cell).

Allowed elements

Formulas are used to calculate a value based on a combination of other values. These other values can be numbers, cell references, operators (+, −, *, /), or other formulas. Formulas can also include names of other areas in the worksheet, as well as cell references in other worksheets. Individual cells are referred to by their coordinates (such as B5), and ranges of cells are referred to by the starting cell reference, followed by a colon, followed by the ending cell reference (such as D10:D18). Cells in other worksheets are referred to by the name of the worksheet, followed by an exclamation point, followed by the cell reference (such as Sheet2!E5).

References: Relative versus Absolute

In Excel, you can have absolute or relative cell references. An absolute cell reference does not change when the cell containing the formula is copied to another location. A relative cell reference changes when the cell containing the formula is copied to another location.

You determine whether a cell reference will be relative or absolute by placing a dollar sign in front of the row and/or column references. The presence of a dollar sign tells Excel not to muck around with your cell reference, no matter what. For example, perhaps cell B5 of a worksheet contains the formula =B3+B4. If you copy that cell's contents to cell D5, Excel adjusts the references, and the formula in cell D5 reads =D3+D4.

In most cases, you want Excel to adjust references when you copy formulas elsewhere, but in some cases, you don't. You can make cell references absolute by adding the dollar sign in front of the letter and number that make up the cell address. With the preceding example of a formula in cell B5, if the formula were entered as =$B$3+$B$4, the formula could be copied anywhere in the worksheet — and it would still refer back to cells B3 and B4. Note that you can make the row relative and column absolute (for example, B$3) or the row absolute and the column relative (for example, $B3) as well.

You use math operators within your formulas to produce numeric results. Table 16-3 lists the math operators.

Table 16-3
Arithmetic Operators

Operator	Function
+	Addition
–	Subtraction
*	Multiplication
/	Division
^	Exponentiation (for example, 3^2 is 3 squared, or 9)
%	Percentage

In addition to the math operators, Excel accepts an ampersand (&) as a text operator for strings of text. The ampersand is used to combine text strings — a process known as concatenation. For example, if cell B12 contains John followed by a space, and cell B13 contains Smith, the formula B12 & B13 would yield John Smith.

Comparison operators are used to compare values and provide a logical value (true or false) based on the comparison. Table 16-4 describes the comparison operators.

Operator	Function
	Table 16-4
	Comparison Operators
<	Less than
>	Greater than
=	Equal to
<>	Not equal to
<=	Less than or equal to
>=	Greater than or equal to

In a cell, the simple comparison = 6 < 7 would result in a value of true because 6 is less than 7. The result of = 6 < Number depends on the value of Number.

Typically, you use comparison operators with cell references to determine whether a desired result is true or false. For example, consider the worksheet shown in Figure 16-21. In this example, the formulas in cells C2 through C5 are based on a comparison. Cell C2 contains the formula =B2<48000. Cells C3, C4, and C5 contain similar formulas. The comparison translates to this: If the value in B2 is less than 48,000, then display a value of true in C2; otherwise, display a value of false in C2.

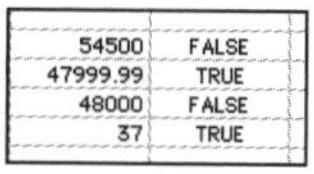

54500	FALSE
47999.99	TRUE
48000	FALSE
37	TRUE

Figure 16-21: Use of comparison operators in formulas of a worksheet

Excel has the following precise order of precedence in building formulas:

1. – (unary minus or negation)
2. % (percent)
3. ^ (exponentiation)
4. * or / (multiplication or division)
5. + or – (addition or subtraction)
6. & (text operator)
7. < > = (comparison operators)

Depending on how you structure your formulas, you may want to alter the preceding order of precedence. For example, if you want to add the contents of cells B2 and B3 and divide the resulting total by five, you cannot use the simple formula =B2 + B3 / 5 because Excel performs division before addition in its order of precedence. If you used this formula, the value in B3 would be divided by five, and that value would be added to the value of B2, producing an erroneous result, at least with respect to the question you meant to ask. To change the order of precedence, insert parentheses around calculations that are to be performed first. Calculations surrounded by parentheses are always performed first, no matter where they fall in the order of precedence. In this example, the formula =(B2 + B3) / 5 yields the desired result. Excel would calculate the expression within the parentheses first and then divide that figure by the constant (in this example, 5).

Displaying and editing formulas

By default, Excel shows the results of the formulas entered in cells and not the actual formulas. (Of course, you can examine any formula by clicking the cell that contains it and looking in the formula bar.) You can also see all the formulas in your worksheet. Choose Edit ⇨ Preferences, and then click the View tab in the Preferences dialog box. Under Window Options, turn on the Formulas checkbox and click OK. Your worksheet then shows all your formulas in the cells, rather than showing the results of the formula. By the way, Excel automatically widens the columns to provide room to view the formulas.

You can edit formulas just as you'd edit any other contents of a cell. Select the desired cell, click in the formula bar, and do your editing there; or double-click the cell and edit the formula within the cell itself.

Changing the recalculation options

By default, Excel recalculates all dependent formulas in your worksheet each time you make a change to a cell. In a large worksheet, recalculation can adversely affect performance, because Excel has to do a lot of calculating every time you change an entry in a cell. You may prefer to turn off Excel's automatic recalculation and let the worksheet recalculate only when you tell it to.

You can change the recalculation options used by Excel through the Calculation tab of the (yes, you guessed it) Edit ⇨ Preferences command. Choose Edit ⇨ Preferences, and then click the Calculation tab in the Preferences dialog box that appears. Under Calculation, choose Manual. Excel now recalculates only when you tell it to by pressing the Calc Now key (either ⌘-= or F9).

Don't forget that you have turned off automatic recalculation, or things may get confusing. Things that appear to be errors may really be changes made when automatic recalculation was turned off and left off. Some operations (including opening and printing a worksheet) will force a recalculation, even if automatic recalculation has been turned off.

What, Me, Make a Mistake?

A frustrating aspect of building complex worksheets is the possibility of errors in your formulas. Watching out for common causes of formula errors can help.

Watch out for these causes in particular:

✦ Attempts to divide by zero

✦ References to blank cells

✦ Leaving out commas between arguments

✦ Deleting cells being used by formulas elsewhere in the worksheet

The codes Excel displays in the cell when an error occurs give you a clue to what's wrong. The code #DIV/0! says your formula is trying to divide by zero. The code #N/A! means that data needed to perform the calculation is not available, and #NAME? means that Excel thinks you're referring to a name that doesn't exist. The code #NUM says Excel has a problem with a numeric argument that you've supplied; #REF says that a cell reference is incorrect; and #VALUE! indicates that a supplied value isn't the type of value the formula expected for that argument.

Using Functions

Typing each cell reference is fine when you're adding a short column of numbers, but doing this with larger columns can be time-consuming. Fortunately, Excel offers functions to be used in your formulas.

You can think of functions as ready-to-run tools that take a group of values and perform some sort of specialized calculation on those values. For example, the commonly used SUM function adds a range of values. Instead of having to enter a formula such as =B2+B3+B4+B5+B6+B7+B8, you could enter the much simpler formula of =SUM(B2:B8).

 Tip

Another benefit of using a function such as SUM and naming a range becomes evident when you add a new column between those involved in the formula. If you hand-typed each cell (=B2+B3+B4+B5+B6+B7+B8), the new cell won't be included. However, if you used the cell range (B2:B8), the new column is included in the range.

Besides making for less typing, functions can perform specialized calculations that would take some digging on your part if you needed to duplicate the calculations manually. For example, you can use the PMT (payment) function to calculate the monthly principal and interest on a mortgage. (Few of us carry the logic for that sort of calculation around in our heads.) Excel's functions can make use of range references (such as A2:A10), named ranges (such as January Sales), or actual numeric values. Figure 16-22 shows examples of the use of functions in a worksheet.

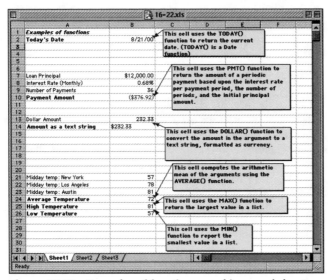

Figure 16-22: Examples of functions used in a worksheet

Every function consists of two parts:

✦ The function name — such as SUM, PMT, or AVERAGE — indicates what the function does.

✦ The argument — such as B2:B12 — tells Excel what cell address(es) to apply to the function. (Although the argument in this example is a range of cells, arguments can also be references to single cells, to a group of single cells, or to actual values.)

You can enter functions just as you enter values — by typing them directly into the formula bar or into the cell. You can also use the AutoSum tool and Paste Function (both discussed shortly) to find help with the entry of your functions.

Excel has many different functions for tasks that range from calculating the square root of a number to finding the future value of an investment. You should know about some statistical functions commonly used in spreadsheet work: the AVERAGE, MAXIMUM, MINIMUM, and SUM functions.

Average, Maximum, Minimum, and Sum

The AVERAGE function calculates the arithmetic mean of a series of values. This function may be expressed as:

```
=AVERAGE(1st value, 2nd value, 3rd value...last value)
```

As an example, the expression =AVERAGE(6,12,15,18) yields 12.75. Similarly, the expression =AVERAGE(B10:B15) averages the values from cells B10 through B15.

The MAX and MIN functions provide the maximum and minimum values, respectively, of all values in the specified range or list of numbers. These functions may be expressed as:

```
=MAX(1st value, 2nd value, 3rd value...last value)
=MIN(1st value, 2nd value, 3rd value...last value)
```

For example, consider the worksheet shown earlier in Figure 16-19. The formula in cell B22 is =MIN(B3:B5). The value that results from this formula is the smallest value in the range of cells from B2 through B5. The formula in cell B23, which is =MAX(B2:B5), produces precisely the opposite effect — the largest value of those found in the specified range of cells is displayed.

The SUM function is used to provide a sum of a list of values, commonly indicated by referencing a range of cells. For example, the SUM function =SUM(5,10,12) would provide a value of 27. The formula =SUM(B5:B60) would provide the sum of all numeric values contained in the range of cells from B5 to B60. The SUM function is an easy way to add a column of numbers; you can most easily use it when using AutoSum.

Using AutoSum

Because the SUM function is the most commonly used function in Excel, a toolbar button is dedicated to the SUM function's use — the AutoSum tool. Using AutoSum is simple:

1. Place the cursor in the cell below or to the right of the column or row you want to sum.

2. Click the AutoSum button on the Standard toolbar — it contains the Greek letter Σ (capital sigma).

When you do this, Excel makes its best guess about what you would like summed, based on the current cell's location relative to the row or column. (If Excel guesses wrong, you can edit the formula to your liking.) When you click the AutoSum button, Excel outlines the area it thinks you want summed, and it places the appropriate formula using the SUM function in the current cell, as shown in Figure 16-23. If you don't like the range that Excel selected, you can click and drag to a different range, and Excel changes the formula accordingly. When you're happy with the formula, press Enter to accept it.

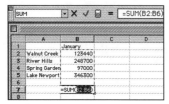

Figure 16-23: Using the AutoSum button

Using the Function Wizard

One of Excel's most useful features is Paste Function. With the help of Paste Function, you can do serious work in Excel without keeping a reference dictionary of functions handy or constantly looking in the help screens to see how particular functions should be used.

Paste Function steps you through the process of inserting a function into the formula you're building. To use Paste Function, follow these steps:

1. Click in the cell in which you want to insert the function. (If you want to insert the function into an existing formula, you can click in the formula bar at the point where the function should go to place the pointer there.)

2. Click the Paste Function button (which contains the letters *fx*) on the Standard toolbar, or choose Insert ➪ Function. The Paste Function dialog box appears, as shown in Figure 16-24.

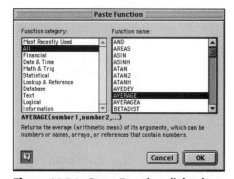

Figure 16-24: Paste Function dialog box

3. In the Function category list box at the left, click a category of functions to choose it. All the functions in the selected category appear in the Function name list box at the right. (You can leave the category set to All, but viewing all the functions can make it difficult to find your function from among Excel's hundreds of functions.)

4. From the Function name list, click the function that you want to insert into your formula. A description of the function appears below the list to aid you in your decision. Click OK to place the selected function. If you are certain of the function that you want and don't need to see the description, you can double-click the desired function to select it and place it.

5. The next dialog box appears below the function bar, asking for values appropriate to that function. Enter the necessary values or cell ranges for the arguments needed by the function in the dialog box. You can enter the values by

   - Typing your values

   - Clicking the cells you need to refer to

   - Dragging across the cells in the range you need to refer to

   - Clicking the row or column header to select an entire row or column

   - Dragging across several row or column headers

   - Typing the names of the ranges, if you have named ranges

Note   For any of the preceding clicking or dragging choices, you might need to click the range button to the right of the text box, collapsing the window and exposing more of your worksheet to view.

6. Finally, click OK in the dialog box to add the function to your formula. Click Cancel, or the X in the function bar, if you don't want to add that function to your formula.

Instead of Step 2, you can also take a longer route. Click the equals (=) sign to begin your formula, and then click the down arrow on the formula bar, adjacent to where you normally see Named ranges. (Because you've begun a formula, the arrow's list contains formulas rather than the named ranges it normally lists.) The last functions you've used appear in this function list. If the function you desire is in view on the list that pops up, drag to select it. If not, select More functions from the bottom of the list to bring up the Paste Function dialog box (refer to Figure 16-24).

The Office Assistant can be helpful if you aren't familiar with the formulas, or if you don't happen to know which formula you need. For function help, while you are in the Paste Function dialog box, click the Help icon (question mark) or press the Help key.

The Office Assistant appears and asks, "What kind of help would you like?" and offers three choices: "Help with this feature," "Help with something else," or "No, don't provide Help now." Accept Help with this feature. The Assistant next either offers help with the currently selected function or invites you to type a brief description of what you want to do. After you enter a description, the suggested function becomes selected in the Paste Function dialog box. Again, you have the opportunity to get help with the currently selected function. Choosing Help with the currently selected function brings up the details of the function, complete with examples and tips.

Validating Your Data

Sometimes it is imperative that data fall within certain confines. For example, if you are tracking sales records for the year 2000, the date in the Date Sold field has to be within the year 2000. Excel 2001 lets you set up data validation to totally prevent data entry unless it falls within your specifications, or just to provide a warning but enable the user to enter the incorrect data if so desired. To set up data validation, follow these steps:

1. Select the cells that are to have your data validation.

2. Choose Data ➪ Validation, and click the Settings tab (see Figure 16-25).

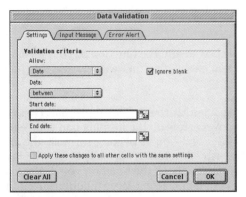

Figure 16-25: The Settings tab of the Data Validation dialog box

3. From the Allow pop-up menu, choose your validation criteria. Depending on your choice of criteria, more text boxes will appear so you can specify the acceptable data.

4. Click the Input Message tab (see Figure 16-26) to control whether the user will see a guiding message.

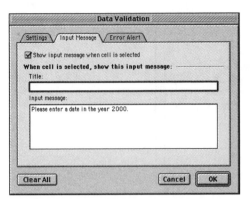

Figure 16-26: The Input Message tab of the Data Validation dialog box

5. The default option, Show input message when cell is selected, is checked. If you don't want a guiding message, uncheck this option. (Error validation will still be in effect.) When the cell is clicked with this option on, any text you type in the Title and Input message fields appears in a yellow pop-up box when the Office Assistant isn't onscreen or in the Office Assistant's balloon (if the Assistant is turned on). Figure 16-27 shows an example of a custom message entered in this tab.

Figure 16-27: The result of an input message — guiding the user

6. Enter the text for your title and input message in the appropriate fields. In the example shown in Figure 16-27, no title text exists, and the input message text entered is "Please enter a date in the year 2000."

7. Click the Error Alert tab, shown in Figure 16-28, to control what happens when the data entered doesn't meet the criteria you set up in the Settings tab.

8. From the Style pop-up menu, select the results that you want:

   • **Stop** prevents the user from overriding your criteria. The user's only choice is to click Retry or Cancel. Clicking in another cell only causes a beep.

   • **Warning** asks if the user wants to continue and lets the user click Yes, No, or Cancel.

   • **Information** asks if the user wants to continue and lets the user click Yes or Cancel. In both Warning and Information, Yes lets the data remain in the cell even if it doesn't meet the criteria.

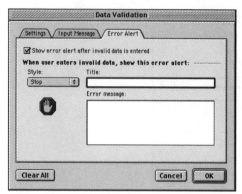

Figure 16-28: The Error Alert tab of the Data Validation dialog box

9. Enter your custom Alert message of up to 225 characters in the Error message field. To start a new line within the message, press Return. If you leave this message box empty, the default message ("The value you entered is not valid. A user has restricted values that can be entered into this cell.") is displayed. The title and error message appear in the Office Assistant's balloon. If the Assistant isn't onscreen, the error message appears (without the title) in a plain alert box.

In the example shown in Figure 16-29, the text typed in the Title field is "Bad date." The text in the Error message field is "The data entered was not a date in the year 2000."

Figure 16-29: The result of an error message — preventing invalid data entry

 Caution   Data validation only works for hand-typed data. If data is entered via a macro or as the result of a formula, invalid data will be accepted. For more info on this topic, click the Office Assistant and enter **data validation**.

Making Your Own Pop-Up List

You can even create a pop-up list of your own so that users see pop-up arrows and click them to select an acceptable value. First, type your list values into a column or row in your worksheet. Then, in Step 3 (in the section on validating your data), select List as your criteria. (Make sure In-cell drop-down is checked.)

To define the list, click in the Source field (shown previously in Figure 16-25), and then click in the worksheet, and drag to select the values you pre-entered. Press Enter to return to the dialog box and continue.

Using Find and Replace

Just as in the word-processing world, you can search and replace with Edit ⇨ Find and Edit ⇨ Replace. As with their counterparts in Word, these commands search for data and, optionally, replace that data with other data. The data you search for can be stored as values, as part or all of a formula, or as a cell note.

Finding data

To search for data in a worksheet using Edit ⇨ Find, follow these steps:

1. Select the cells you want to search. If you want to search the entire worksheet, select any single cell.

2. Choose Edit ⇨ Find (⌘-F). You'll see the Find dialog box, as shown in Figure 16-30.

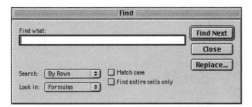

Figure 16-30: The Find dialog box

3. In the Find what text box, enter your search term. If you are not certain what you are searching for, use an asterisk (*) as a wildcard to indicate any combination of characters, or a question mark to indicate any single character.

4. From the Search pop-up menu, choose By Rows if you want to search across rows starting with the current cell, or By Columns to search across columns starting at the current cell.

5. From the Look in pop-up menu, choose Formulas to search through formulas, Values to search through values stored in cells, or Comments to search all comments attached to cells.

6. If you want your search to be case sensitive, check the Match case checkbox. (This means when you search for weekdays, you will not find Weekdays.)

7. Check the Find entire cells only checkbox if you want the entire cell's contents to match your search term. If you leave this option turned off, Excel will find matches where either part or all of the cells' contents match the search term.

8. Click the Find Next button to find the next occurrence of the search term. (You can also press Return or Enter because Find Next is the default button.) When you finish searching, click Close.

When you have entered the parameters for a search in the Find dialog box, you can close the dialog box and press Shift-F4 rather than clicking Find Next to continue searching for the same data.

Finding and replacing data

Use the Replace command of the Edit menu to search for data in a worksheet and replace it with other data. The process is similar to using Edit ➪ Find (in fact, the dialog box you see is nearly identical). Here are the steps:

1. Select the cells that you want to search. To search the entire worksheet, select any single cell.

2. Choose Edit ➪ Replace (⌘-H). The Replace dialog box appears, as shown in Figure 16-31.

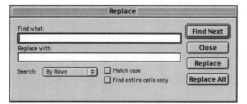

Figure 16-31: The Replace dialog box

3. In the Find what text box, enter your search term. Use an asterisk (*) to indicate any combination of characters. Use the question mark (?) to indicate any single character when you are unsure of the spelling of a word you seek or of the elements for which you are searching.

4. In the Replace with text box, type the replacement text.

5. From the Search pop-up list, choose By Rows if you want to search across rows starting with the current cell. Choose By Columns to search across columns starting at the current cell.

6. For a case-sensitive search, check the Match case checkbox.

7. Check the Find entire cells only box if you want the entire cell's contents to match your search term. If you leave this option off, Excel replaces data where either part or all of the cell's content matches the search term.

8. Click the Replace All button if you want to find and replace all occurrences of the search term with your new term. A more cautious approach is to click Find Next to find the next match in the worksheet, and, after examining it, click the Replace button to replace only that match. When you're finished making your replacements, click Close.

Edit ➪ Undo (⌘-Z) rolls back the effects of a replace operation.

Correcting Your Spelling

Despite the best-looking document and most meticulously laid-out numbers, you're in for embarrassment if you're caught with spelling errors in your worksheet. Excel 2001 does a lot to save you from such errors.

In Office 2001, Word, Excel, Entourage, and PowerPoint share the same AutoCorrect lists and dictionaries, so you don't have to enter custom words multiple times. The spelling interface for each is also shared, except that Word includes grammar checking.

AutoCorrect

How many times have your fingers typed a word incorrectly as you race to get your data into your spreadsheet? You know how to spell the word but your fingers are just not always cooperative. Word 6 introduced autocorrection. The good news is that AutoCorrect is in Excel 2001 — and it's simple. To see for yourself, type **teh** and watch it turn into "the" in a flash, as you continue to work without missing a step.

The AutoCorrect list that Excel refers to as it watches your typing is the same list as Word uses. In fact, PowerPoint and Entourage also have the AutoCorrect feature and share the same list from Word 2001. You are bound to regularly mistype words that Microsoft hasn't thought of, so you can add any forms of a word that you want. You can also remove words from the default list.

AutoCorrect can do more than just fix your typos. It can act as a shorthand translator for you by automatically typing full words, symbols, or phrases when you type the key combination of your choice. For example, you can set up AutoCorrect so that typing **mye** types your e-mail address, saving you from finger-twisting combinations.

Cross-Reference   To learn how to customize your AutoCorrect list, see Chapter 2.

Checking spelling

You can save yourself from possibly embarrassing blunders by checking your worksheet's spelling before you pass out those copies at the annual board meeting. You can check any part of a selection (even a single word) or the entire worksheet, including any embedded charts. You can also add words to your own custom dictionaries in order to handle specialized words you use often (such as medical and legal terms).

To spell-check a worksheet, follow these steps:

1. Select the cells that you want to spell-check. If you want to check the spelling of the entire worksheet, select any single cell.

2. Choose Tools ➪ Spelling, or click the Spelling button (ABC-checkmark) on the Standard toolbar (it might be in the More Buttons pop-up). Excel checks the spelling in the worksheet. If it finds what it thinks is a misspelled word, you'll see the Spelling dialog box, as shown in Figure 16-32.

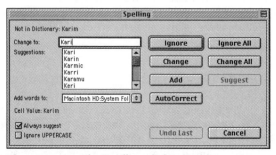

Figure 16-32: The Spelling dialog box

When Excel finds a misspelling, it tries to provide several options for a correct spelling of the word. If the Always suggest checkbox is turned on, Excel suggests proper spellings whenever it can. In the Change to text box, enter the correct spelling, or click one of the suggested spellings in the Suggestions list box, which places that spelling in the Change to box.

If the Always suggest checkbox is turned off, click the Suggest button (which enables) to see a list of possible spellings in the Suggestions list box. If one of the suggestions is the spelling that you want, select it in the list box and click

Change. The Ignore button lets you leave a word as is. Cancel cancels the entire spell-checking operation. Clicking Ignore All tells Excel to ignore all suspected misspellings of the term in question. Change All tells Excel to change all misspellings of the work in question to the entry in the Change to box. The Add button lets you add a word to the selected custom dictionary. When the Ignore UPPERCASE checkbox is turned on, Excel skips words composed of all uppercase letters.

During the spell-checking process, Excel takes a little extra time to suggest corrections to misspelled words. You can speed the process slightly by turning off the Always suggest checkbox and using the Suggest button to ask for help when you need it.

Adding a custom dictionary

If you make regular use of specialized terms (such as medical or legal terms) in your worksheets, the spell-checking capability will be useless unless it can work with those terms as part of Excel's dictionaries. You can add words to Excel's default custom dictionary, but another option is to create additional custom dictionaries. Follow these steps:

1. Place the cursor in any worksheet containing some of your custom terms. (This way, the spell-check operation will find them.)

2. Choose Tools ➪ Spelling. When Excel stops at the first word it doesn't recognize, the Spelling dialog box appears, as shown earlier in Figure 16-32.

3. To begin a new custom dictionary, click in the Add words to box and type a name for the new dictionary that you want to create. If you already created one in Word, it will be offered as the default choice.

4. Click the Add button to add the current word to the dictionary. If Excel displays a dialog box asking if you want to create a new dictionary, click Yes.

   From this point on, you can use the dictionary by choosing from the Add words to pop-up list.

Summary

This chapter examined the many different ways in which you can enter data into an Excel worksheet and manipulate that data. The chapter covered these points:

✦ You can enter values or formulas into cells of a worksheet. Values can be numbers, text, dates, or times.

✦ You can attach notes to cells by using the Insert menu's Comment command. When a note is attached, the Comment command changes to Edit Comment so you can make changes to the note. You can also control-click and choose from the contextual menu.

✦ You can move and copy data from place to place on a worksheet or between worksheets.

✦ Excel's Fill, AutoFill, and Series features can fill ranges of cells with data.

✦ You can insert and delete ranges of cells, as well as entire rows and columns.

✦ Formulas manage the calculations within your worksheets.

✦ Excel 2001 adds a Calculator to further simplify the process of creating formulas. The Calculator button is to the left of the = button in the Formula bar.

✦ Excel provides hundreds of functions, which you can think of as tools for performing specific types of calculations.

✦ Excel's Function Wizard can help you quickly find and properly enter the correct function for a specific task.

✦ You can use the Edit ➪ Find and Edit ➪ Replace commands to search for data and to replace that data with other data.

✦ You can use the Tools ➪ Spelling command to correct the spelling of text in a worksheet.

Where to go next

✦ The next chapter tells you how to format your worksheets so they look good.

✦ You'll soon want to print what you've created. You find the complete scoop on printing in Chapter 20.

✦   ✦   ✦

Excel Formatting

Most spreadsheet users know that a spreadsheet is more than just a collection of raw numbers. Since the days of the first spreadsheets, users have resorted to formatting tricks to enhance the appearance of the numbers presented. (How many seasoned spreadsheet pros remember filling rows of cells with characters such as asterisks or hyphens to enclose information within crude borders?) Excel offers many ways to format worksheets to give them the most effective visual impact possible. You can change the fonts, font sizes, styles, and colors of the characters within your worksheets. You can also control the alignment of text within cells, both vertically and horizontally. You can change row heights and column widths, add borders to selected cells, and use Excel's powerful AutoFormat feature to enhance the appearance of part or all of a worksheet quickly—without the need to use any formatting commands!

Using the AutoFormat Feature

The easiest way to whip your Excel spreadsheet into shape is by using AutoFormat. This relatively new feature applies automatic formatting from a number of well-thought-out styles. You activate the AutoFormat feature by choosing Format ⇨ AutoFormat to call up the AutoFormat dialog box. From the dialog box, you view and select a sample format. With AutoFormat, nice-looking documents are only a few clicks away—even if you know little or nothing about formatting. Figures 17-1, 17-2, and 17-3 show some of the AutoFormat looks available. In Figure 17-1, the Classic 1 style of Auto-Format uses traditional accounting-style fonts and simple borderlines to separate the data visually.

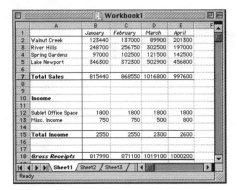

Figure 17-1: The Classic 1 style AutoFormat

In Figure 17-2, the Colorful 1 style of AutoFormat makes extensive use of various background choices to highlight the worksheet data.

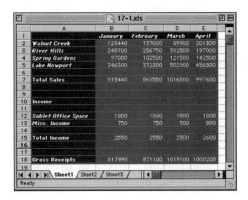

Figure 17-2: The Colorful 1 style AutoFormat

In Figure 17-3, the List 1 style of AutoFormat uses shading in alternate rows of the worksheet.

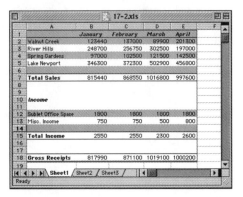

Figure 17-3: The List 1 style AutoFormat

Excel examines the current range to determine levels of summary and detail. It also looks for text, values, and formulas, and then applies formats accordingly. AutoFormats are combinations of several different elements: number, alignment, font, border, pattern, column, and row formats. To apply AutoFormat to your worksheet, follow these steps:

1. Select the range of cells to which you want to apply the format. If you want to select the entire worksheet, click the row and column header intersection at the upper-left corner of the worksheet.

2. Choose Format ⇨ AutoFormat to open the AutoFormat dialog box shown in Figure 17-4.

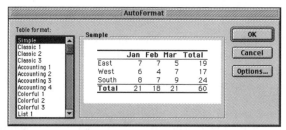

Figure 17-4: The AutoFormat dialog box

3. From the Table format list, click a format name to see a preview of it in the Sample window or to choose the desired format.

4. If you want more control over what formatting will be applied, click the Options button. This expands the dialog box to reveal checkboxes for Number, Border, Font, Patterns, Alignment, and Width/Height (see Figure 17-5). By default, all the boxes are turned on. You can turn off any formatting.

5. Click OK to apply the formatting to the selection.

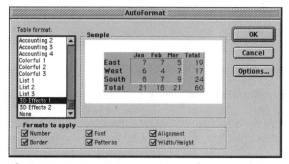

Figure 17-5: AutoFormat options — the expanded AutoFormat dialog box

When to Stay Away from AutoFormat

As helpful a feature as AutoFormat is, it has its limits. Excel has to make judgment calls when it applies AutoFormat to your worksheet. For example, Excel tries to determine which parts of the selection contain column headings so that it can apply a pleasing format to those headings. AutoFormat is designed to work well with worksheets that follow a traditional row-and-column format.

If your worksheet doesn't follow tradition — perhaps it contains a large number of scientific formulas laid out more like a flowchart — AutoFormat may not give you the results you'd like. In these cases, apply your desired formats manually using the formatting techniques discussed later in this chapter.

If you don't like the effects of the AutoFormat command, choose Edit ➪ Undo (⌘-Z). Or, if you have performed other tasks since applying the AutoFormat to the selection, don't worry. You can simply select the range, choose Format ➪ Auto-Format, and select None from the bottom of the list of styles.

You don't have to settle for Excel's default formatting selections in its AutoFormats. You can mix and match styles or mix an AutoFormat style with your own by using the Options button in the AutoFormat dialog box to accept or reject certain AutoFormatting. For example, if you spent a great deal of time formatting different ranges of numeric values with different fonts, you might not want AutoFormat to mess with the fonts. Turn off the Font checkbox in the Formats to apply area of the AutoFormat dialog box. Then when you apply AutoFormat to the selection, Excel won't override the already applied fonts.

You can turn off one formatting option or several formatting options depending on the selection and formatting that you want applied. After turning off the desired options, you can choose the format that you want from the Table format list and click OK to apply it to your selection. Options you turn off in this manner aren't carried over to the next time you use AutoFormat. You'll need to turn off any unwanted options each time you use AutoFormat.

Changing Widths and Heights

Excel does a good job of automatically adjusting row height to accommodate wrapped text and large fonts, so you may never need to make such an adjustment. However, you will probably need to adjust your columns from time to time. For maximum flexibility, Excel enables you to adjust column width and row height at any time.

Column widths

You can adjust the standard width setting of the columns, or you can change only a few columns. You have two ways to adjust column width. The first method, clicking and dragging the column to size it, is easier and enables you to size your columns visually. The second method is numerically accurate but requires the use of commands and dialog boxes.

To use the mouse to adjust the size of the columns, follow these steps:

1. Move the mouse pointer to the heading of the column you want to adjust and move it over the right edge of the column so that the pointer becomes a double-headed arrow.

2. Drag the column-heading border to size it manually to the desired width. You can also double-click the column header instead, which automatically sizes the column to the width of the widest entry in all the selected rows.

If you know the exact column width that you want, or if you want to make several columns exactly the same size, you can use a dialog box. Control-click a column header and choose Column Width or choose Format ➪ Column ➪ Width, and enter a numeric value in the Width dialog box that appears. Control-clicking also offers other choices because Format ➪ Column offers other submenus. For example, you can choose the Standard Width command, and then accept the standard width that appears in the Standard Width dialog box. The AutoFit Selection command in the submenu automatically sizes a column to accommodate the largest entry in the column.

The AutoFit Selection command applies its magic only to selected cells, so you must first make a selection for the command to have the desired effect. If you leave the mouse cursor in a blank cell, using AutoFit Selection accomplishes nothing. Usually, it's a good idea to select the entire column before using AutoFit Selection. (To select a column, click the column header.)

Row heights

A row can range in height from 0 points to 409 points. When it comes to adjusting row height, you again have two choices: clicking and dragging or the Format menu options. To use the click-and-drag method, follow these steps:

1. Move the pointer over the bottom border of the row heading so that the pointer becomes a double-headed arrow.

2. Drag the bottom border of the row heading until the row reaches the desired size.

You can also AutoSize a row's height by double-clicking the bottom border of a row header. This adjusts the row to fit the tallest entry. If you want to AutoSize a number of rows, first select the desired row and then double-click the bottom border of any of the selected rows.

As with columns, you can numerically adjust row height by Control-clicking in a row heading and selecting a command, or by choosing Format ⇨ Row and selecting a command from the submenu. To set the row height, for example, choose Height and enter a value for the height in the Row Height dialog box (see Figure 17-6), or choose AutoFit to adjust the row height to the largest entry in the row.

Figure 17-6: The Row Height dialog box

Hiding and Unhiding Elements

You can hide selected columns or rows from view, and later reveal rows or columns that have been previously hidden. You may want to hide rows or columns so that they don't appear in printed copies of the worksheets, or you may want to hide rows or columns so that a viewer's attention is focused on important parts of the worksheet. For example, you may need to compare the data in columns B and D. With column C between B and D the data is difficult to analyze. If you hide column C, however, the data appear side by side and are easy to compare.

Hiding columns

To hide a column, Control-click the column header and select Hide from the shortcut menu, or click in the column header to select the column and choose Format ⇨ Column ⇨ Hide. To bring the column back, select the two columns (that are now next to each other) that surround the hidden column, Control-click the column headers, and select Unhide from the shortcut menu. Alternatively, choose Edit ⇨ Go To (F5), enter the address of any cell in that column, and click OK. Then, choose Format ⇨ Column ⇨ Unhide.

Hiding rows

Hiding rows is similar to hiding columns. Select the desired row and choose Format ⇨ Row ⇨ Hide. To bring the row back, select the two rows (which are now next to each other) that surround the hidden row, Control-click the row headers, and select Unhide from the shortcut menu. Alternatively, choose Edit ⇨ Go To (F5), enter the address of any cell in that row, and click OK. Then choose Format ⇨ Row ⇨ Unhide.

Note You might run into a conflict with the Hot Function Keys assignments in your Keyboard control panel. If you do, uncheck the box in the control panel that turns on Hot Function Keys.

Hiding gridlines

With some worksheets, you may not want the gridlines that are normally displayed to appear. To hide the gridlines, first activate the worksheet page, and then choose Tools ⇨ Preferences. In the Preferences dialog box, click the View tab, turn off the Gridlines option, and click OK. The gridlines disappear from the current worksheet.

The Gridlines option affects only the current worksheet in a workbook. To turn off gridlines for another worksheet, repeat the preceding steps. You can also turn off the gridlines for multiple worksheets at one time by selecting each of the worksheets before choosing Tools ⇨ Preferences and before turning off the Gridlines. To select several worksheets, press Shift as you click each worksheet tab that you want included in the selection.

Changing Alignments

In your quest to give your worksheet a more professional and refined look, you may want to change the alignment of data in your cells. By default, the following alignment applies to cells: right aligned for numbers, left aligned for text, and centered for logical and error values. Changing the alignment of text in a cell is especially important because what works with text in one area of your worksheet may not work in another area. You may want to enhance the appearance of certain parts of your worksheet by right-aligning or centering text, for example.

To change the alignment of the cells, first select the range of cells to which you want to apply the new alignment. Then you can choose between two methods to change the alignment. The fastest way — clicking the buttons on the Formatting toolbar — provides basic alignment. The other way, which presents more advanced options, is to select Format ⇨ Cells to open the Format Cells dialog box, and then click the Alignment tab to bring up your alignment options. (You can also open the Format Cells dialog box by Control-clicking the selection and choosing Format Cells from the shortcut menu.) Figure 17-7 shows the Alignment tab of the Format Cells dialog box.

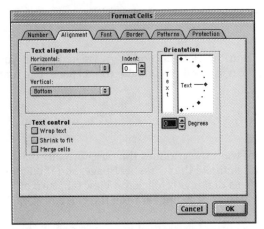

Figure 17-7: The Alignment tab of the Format Cells dialog box

In the Horizontal pop-up menu, you can choose the Left, Center, or Right alignment options. (You can also use the Wrap text and Justify options with text that occupies multiple lines of a cell.) If you've changed the row height of a cell so that the cell is much taller than the text entry, the options in the Vertical list box of the dialog box become equally useful. You can align the text to the top, bottom, or center of the cell, and you can vertically justify it. You can also use the Orientation portion of the dialog box to change the alignment of the entry within the cell.

In the Text control portion of the dialog box, turning on Wrap text makes a long entry wrap within a cell. The Shrink to fit option, when turned on, reduces the font of an entry as needed to fit within a cell. You can use the Merge cells option to merge any selection of cells within a row or column into a single cell.

To use the Formatting toolbar buttons to change the basic alignment of data in cells, follow these steps:

1. Select the cells in which you want to change the alignment.

2. Click the Align Left button to left align the selection, the Center button to center entries in the selection, and the Align Right button to right align the selection.

The disadvantage of using the Formatting toolbar is that it does not offer the range of options that the Format Cells dialog box offers. You can't vertically align text from the toolbar, and you can't use the wrap and justify options, but you can center text across columns, as detailed in the next section.

Formatting Text

As you build worksheets with lots of text headings, you'll discover that you need to center headings across a series of multiple cells. Spreadsheet pros from way back centered titles across multiple columns through trial and error. Excel sends this technique back to the Stone Age where it belongs with the Merge and Center button on the Formatting toolbar and the corresponding Center across selection option on the Alignment tab of the Format Cells dialog box. Figure 17-8 shows the Projected Sales title before and after it was centered across the selected range of cells.

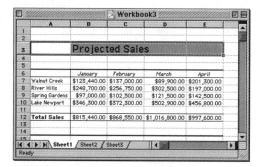

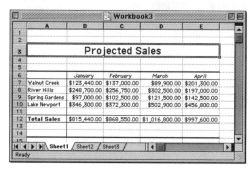

Figure 17-8: *Top:* A title before centering across a range of cells. *Bottom:* The title after centering across a range of cells.

Centering text

To center the contents of a cell across a selection of blank cells, follow these steps:

1. Select the cells the text is to be centered across. (For proper results, the left-most cell in the selection should contain the text to be centered across the range of cells.)

2. Click the Merge and Center button in the Formatting toolbar.

Alternatively, you can make the selection, Control-click it, and choose Format Cells from the shortcut menu that appears. In the Alignment tab of the Format Cells dialog box, choose Center across selection from the Horizontal pop-up menu. However, unless you've turned off the display of the Formatting toolbar, it's generally easier to use the toolbar button.

Wrapping text

When you make lengthy text entries within cells, you can tell Excel to wrap the text so that it fits into an attractive paragraph inside the cell. When text is wrapped, Excel automatically adjusts the row height so that all of the text fits within the width of the cell. Figure 17-9 shows the before-and-after effects of using the Wrap text option. In the figure, both cells containing text contain the same information. In the upper cell that contains text, the Wrap text option has not been turned on; in the lower cell that contains text, Wrap text has been turned on.

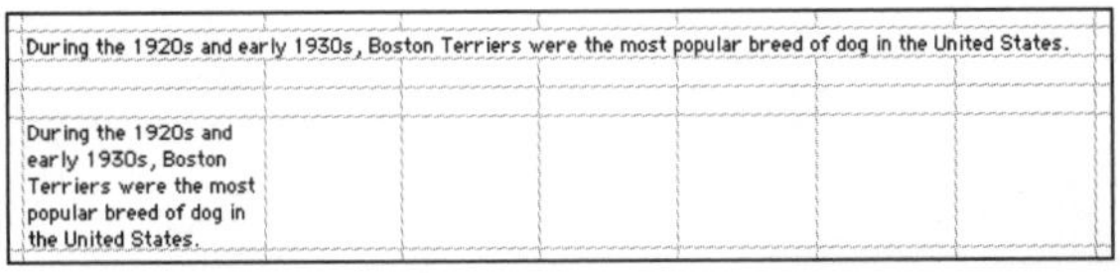

Figure 17-9: Examples of using Wrap text in a worksheet

To wrap text in a cell, follow these steps:

1. Make any desired change to the column width.
2. Select the cell(s) containing the text that you want to wrap.
3. Choose Format ⇨ Cells.
4. Check Wrap text in the Text control portion of the dialog box.

Justifying text

Occasionally, you may want to justify your text so that every line of a paragraph (except the last if it is too short to fill a line) is aligned on both sides. For example, you may want a smooth look after you turn on text Wrap. (A cell has to contain at least two lines of text for justification to have any effect.) Figure 17-10 shows the before and after effects of using text alignment in a worksheet. In the figure, the text in the top cell is not justified (it is left aligned); the lower cell shows the text after applying the Justify option.

Figure 17-10: *Top:* Left-aligned (right-ragged text) text.
Bottom: Left- and right-aligned (justified) text.

To justify entries in selected cells, follow these steps:

1. Select the cell(s) whose text you want to justify.

2. Choose Format ➪ Cells. (You can use the menu bar or the shortcut menu.)

3. Select Justify from the Horizontal pop-up menu. The text is automatically justified. (The effect is only noticed if it contains two or more lines.)

Rotating text

Occasionally, you will need to cram tons of data on a single page and need to save every bit of space possible. The capability to rotate text certainly is handy in such a case. For example, in Figure 17-11, long cell headings would waste space if they were not rotated.

Figure 17-11: Rotated text saves valuable column space.

To rotate text, follow these steps:

1. Select the cell(s) whose text you want to rotate.

2. Choose Format ➪ Cells, and then click the Alignment tab shown in Figure 17-12. (You can Control-click and select Format Cells from the shortcut menu.)

3. At the right side of the dialog box there is a diagram that shows you the angle of the text. (It says Text and has a line following it.) Click the word Text and drag it to the angle you want for your text. If you prefer, you can click the up or down arrows where the degrees of the angle are reported (below the diagram), or type a number into the degrees field. Click OK, or press Return or Enter, when you've set the angle.

After rotating your text, you may want to adjust the height and width of the cells.

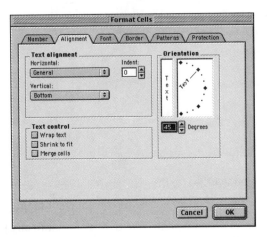

Figure 17-12: Rotating text in the Format Cells dialog box

Applying fonts and style formats

Just as in Word, you can apply different fonts to your entries. Applying fonts in Excel is as simple as it is in Word. Just select the cells that you want to change, and choose the font that you want to apply from the pop-up Font menu on the Formatting toolbar. (Excel doesn't have a Font menu.) You can also choose a font size from the toolbar, and you can use the Bold, Italic, and Underline buttons to apply these types of formatting to the characters in the selected cells. Alternatively, you can use the Format Cells dialog box. Select the cells, Control-click the selection, and choose Format Cells from the shortcut menu, or select the cells and choose Format ⇨ Cells. In the Format Cells dialog box, click the Font tab to display your font choices, as shown in Figure 17-13.

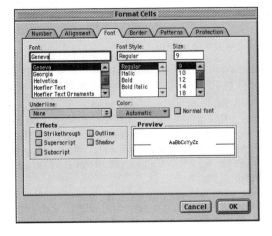

Figure 17-13: The Font tab of the Format Cells dialog box

You can use the options in the Font and Font style lists on the Font tab to choose a desired font and font style, and you can choose a point size from the Size list. You can select a type of underlining (Single, Double, Single Accounting, or Double Accounting) from the Underline pop-up list, and a text color from the pop-up Color menu. In the Effects area, you can turn on special effects (Strikethrough, Superscript, Subscript, Outline, and Shadow).

Note   You don't have to apply styles or fonts to the entire contents of a cell. You can choose to apply formatting to just some of the characters. To accomplish this, place the cursor in the cell that contains the text that you want to change so that the text appears in the formula bar. In the formula bar, click and drag to select the characters that you want to change. Next, use the Formatting toolbar to apply your formatting. Otherwise, choose Format ⇨ Cells to bring up the Format Cells dialog box (which now displays only the Font tab). Here you can choose the Font that you want for those characters, along with the character size and style. Make the desired selections and click OK to apply them. (In case you're wondering, you can also double-click the cell whose text you want to edit and do the character selection directly in the cell.)

Applying Borders, Patterns, and Colors

Excel provides plenty of border types for your visual pleasure. Each border type has different widths, patterns, and colors. You can use these choices to make your worksheets more attractive and easier to read. To apply a border to a selection, follow these steps:

1. Select the cells to which you want to add the border.

2. Click the down arrow to the right of the Borders button on the Formatting palette and drag to the border of your choice from the menu that pops up (see Figure 17-14). The border you choose is applied to the selected cells.

You can also quickly apply shading to a selection by clicking the down arrow to the right of the Fill Color buttons on the Formatting palette and choosing a desired color from the box of colors that appears.

For fuller control over your borders, such as color and line styles, use the Format Cells dialog box. As with the button, select the cells to which you want to add the border. Choose Format ⇨ Cells, or Control-click the selected cells to open the Format Cells dialog box, and click the Border tab, which is shown in Figure 17-15. You can use the options within this tab to apply your border to the selected cells. The left side of this tab provides the same options as the button. The right side enables you to select a line style and color.

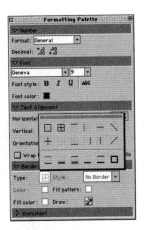

Figure 17-14: The border pop-up menu

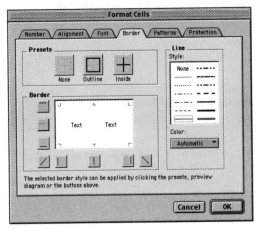

Figure 17-15: The Border tab of the Format Cells dialog box

You can also add colors and patterns to the cells you have selected. To apply a color or a pattern, select the desired cells, Control-click the selection, and choose Format Cells from the shortcut menu, or chose Format ➪ Cells. When the Format Cells dialog box appears, click the Patterns tab to bring it to the front, as shown in Figure 17-16.

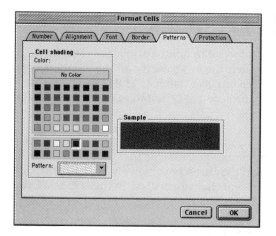

Figure 17-16: The Patterns tab of the Format Cells dialog box

In the Cell shading area of the dialog box, click the desired color or shade of gray to apply it. Then click the Pattern pop-up list and choose a pattern from the choices that appear. After you make your desired color and pattern selections, click OK to close the Format Cells dialog box and to apply your choices.

When applied, some patterns can make cell entries very difficult to read. Remember that you can use Edit ➪ Undo (⌘-Z) if you don't like the looks of your selection.

Sometimes you may want to apply a color to the characters that you enter rather than to the background of the cell. Applying color to the characters can make a specific number or title stand out. To make the total earnings for the year stand out, for example, you can apply orange formatting to the characters in that cell if the earnings were less than the previous year.

To apply a color to the characters in your worksheet quickly, select the characters to which you want to apply the color and then click the down arrow to the right of the Font Color button on the Formatting palette to reveal the color selection box. Choose a color to apply to the characters. (You can also open the Format Cells dialog box and go to the Font tab.)

Note   With both the Font Color and the regular (cell) Color buttons, you can apply the color that was last chosen to another selection by simply clicking the button. This is a great shortcut feature.

Working with Number Formats

By default, Excel applies the General format to numbers in a cell. This format displays up to 11 digits if the entry exceeds the cell's width. All the numbers entered in the General format are displayed as integers (such as 21,947 or 12,382), decimal numbers (such as 21.57 or 3.14159), or in scientific notation (such as 9.43E+7 or 21.212E–5).

When you enter a numeric value in a cell, Excel tries to find the number format that is most appropriate for your entry number and assigns that format to the number. If you enter nothing but numbers and they aren't excessively large or small, Excel is pretty much clueless as to how you want them formatted. In these cases, Excel settles for the General format for the cell.

You can, however, give Excel clues as to how you want it to format an entry by including symbols with your numeric entries. For example, if you enter a dollar amount and precede it with a dollar sign, Excel automatically formats the entry as a currency value. If you want the entry formatted as a percent, you can follow the entry with a percent sign. You can enter scientific notation directly into the cell. For example, if you enter 17.409E+10 in a cell, Excel stores the value of 174,090,000,000,000 in the cell and displays 1.74E+14 in the cell.

If you've already entered your values, using the Formatting toolbar is the simplest way to apply the most commonly used number formats. After selecting the entry that you want to change, click one of the number formatting buttons to apply the format. Table 17-1 lists the number formatting buttons and their functions.

Table 17-1	
Number Formatting Buttons on the Formatting Toolbar	
Button	*Function*
Currency Style	Changes the cell to a currency format
Percent Style	Changes the cell to a percent format
Comma Style	Changes the cell to a comma format
Increase Decimal	Increases the decimal place of the number
Decrease Decimal	Decreases the decimal place of the number

You can also apply number formats via the Number tab of the Format Cells dialog box. To activate the Format Cells dialog box, choose Format ➪ Cells (or Control-click the selection and choose Format Cells from the shortcut menu). Click the Number tab to display the Format Cells dialog box shown in Figure 17-17.

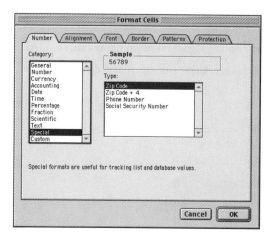

Figure 17-17: The Number tab of the Format Cells dialog box

To apply number formats by using the Number tab of the Format Cells dialog box, follow these steps:

1. Select the cells to format.

2. Choose Format ⇨ Cells or Control-click the selection and choose Format Cells from the shortcut menu.

3. Click the Number tab.

4. In the Category list on the left of the tab, click the category your number falls into.

5. If a list of Types appears to the right, choose the specific way you want your number to appear. As you click a format, a sample appears above the list. (Some categories, such as Text and Accounting, don't offer a list box of types.)

6. Click OK to apply the formatting.

Remember that occasions may arise when you want to format numbers as text. You can do so as you enter the value in a cell of the worksheet by entering an apostrophe before the number. You can also select the cell, choose Format ⇨ Cells, click the Number tab of the Format Cells dialog box, and choose Text from the Category list.

Date and time formats

If you enter data in an acceptable date or time format, Excel stores the value as a date or time value. For example, if you type **7/3/57** into a cell, Excel stores the entry as a date value of July 3, 1957. Excel also recognizes a value such as 3-Feb-98 as a valid date. Similarly, with an entry of **9:45 PM**, Excel stores a time value representing that time. (Chapter 16 provides additional specifics on the entry of dates and times in a worksheet.)

To change the format that Excel uses to display dates and times, follow these steps:

1. Select the cell or range of cells containing the date or time values.

2. Choose Format ➪ Cells, or Control-click the selection and choose Format Cells from the shortcut menu.

3. Click the Number tab.

4. In the Category list, choose Date or Time as desired. Figure 17-18 shows the Date category selected.

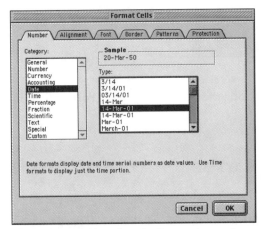

Figure 17-18: Choosing the Date category in the Number tab

5. In the Type list, choose the desired date or time format and click OK.

When you enter a date or time in a format that Excel recognizes, Excel displays the value on the right side of the cell by default. If a value appears on the left side of the cell, Excel has not recognized it as an acceptable date or time value and has instead formatted the entry as text. You should re-enter the value in an acceptable format to get the correct date or time into the cell.

Custom number formats

Besides using the variety of built-in standard formats, you can design your own custom formats. Custom formats are useful for specialized financial or scientific displays of values, or for handling such information as phone numbers, part numbers, or other data that has to appear in a specific format. Figure 17-19 shows some examples of custom formats in columns A, B, and, C.

Data Entered	Custom Format Used	New Data Appears
1505.99596	#.####	1505.996
24562.7678	$#,##0.0000	$24,562.7678
0.15852	0.00%	15.85%
11/19/98 7:40	d-mmm-yy h:mm:ss AM/PM	19-Nov-98 7:40:00 AM
17025551212	#-(###) ###-####	1-(702) 555-1212
21435	"Part number" ##-###	Part number 21-435

Figure 17-19: Examples of custom formats

When working with custom formats, it helps to understand the number format codes that Excel uses. These formats are automatically stored in the correct number format category. Whenever you want to access them, open the Format Cells dialog box and choose Custom from the Category list in the Number tab. Table 17-2 explains the function of the most common symbols you use to make custom formats.

Table 17-2
Symbols Used in Custom Formats

Symbol	Function
?	Acts as a placeholder for digits in much the same way as zeros. Zeros that are not important are removed and spaces are inserted to keep alignment together.
/	Denotes that the slash symbol is to be used after the integer portion with fractional custom formats. This causes the number to appear as a fractional value, such as 5 2/3.
0	Acts as a placeholder. You can use this number to display a zero when no number is entered. Also, decimal fractions are rounded up to the number of zeros that appear to the right of the decimal.
#	Acts as a placeholder for digits, just as the 0 does. The difference between # and 0 as placeholders is that if a number is not entered, no number is displayed. Decimal fractions are rounded up to the number of #s that appear to the right of the value.
General	Denotes the default format for cells that are not formatted.
, (comma)	Marks the thousands position. (Only one comma is needed to specify the use of commas.)
. (decimal)	Marks the decimal point position. For a leading zero, enter a zero to the left of the decimal.
_(underscore)	Followed by the character of your choice, inserts a space the size of the character that follows the underscore before the character itself appears. As an example, if you enter _) (underscore + right parenthesis) to end a positive format, a blank space the size of the parenthesis is inserted. This lets you align a positive number with a negative one that's surrounded by parentheses.

Continued

Table 17-2 *(continued)*

Symbol	Function
:$_+()	These characters are displayed in the same positions in which they are entered in the number code.
E_E+e_e+	Displays a number in scientific notation. The zeroes or values to the right of the e denotes the power of the exponent.
%	The entry is multiplied by 100 and displayed as a percentage.
@	Takes the role of a format code to indicate where text typed by the user appears in a custom format.
*character	Fills the remainder of the column width with the character that follows the asterisk.
"text"	Displays the text between the quotation marks.
[color]	Indicates that the cell is formatted with the specified color.
\ (backslash)	When this precedes an entry, it indicates a single character or symbol.

Format codes include three sections for numbers and one for text. Semicolons separate the sections. The first section is the format for positive numbers; the second section is the format for negative numbers; the third section is the format for zeros; the fourth section is the format for text.

The section you include in your custom format determines the format for positive numbers, negative numbers, zeros, and text, in that order. If you include only two sections, the first section is used for positive numbers and zeros, and the second section is used for negative numbers. If you include only one number section, all the numbers use that format.

The text format section, if it is there, is always last. If you have text that you always want to include, enter it in double quotation marks. If your format has no text section, the text you enter in the cell is not affected by the formatting.

To create your own custom format, follow these steps:

1. Make a selection and choose Format ➪ Cells, or Control-click the selection and choose Format Cells from the shortcut menu.

2. In the Format Cells dialog box, select the Number tab.

3. Choose Custom from the Category box. From the Type list (see Figure 17-20), choose a custom format that is closest to the one you want. (You can modify it to meet your needs. See Step 4.) You could also just select Custom from the Format list box in the Formatting palette's Number pane to present the Number tab of the Format Cells dialog, but the other tabs would not be available.

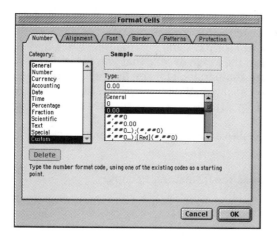

Figure 17-20: The Type list box with the Custom entries

4. Make the desired changes to the format by editing the entry in the Type text box. As you do, if you have anything entered in the selected cell, the sample will reflect that data, giving you feedback as to how your formatting is taking shape in "real life."

5. Click the OK button to save the custom number format.

Remember these points when you create custom formats:

✦ Excel uses zeros and number signs as digit placeholders. If you use a zero, the digit is always displayed, and the number sign suppresses the nonsignificant zeros.

✦ If you follow an underscore by a character, Excel creates a space the width of the character. For example, if you follow an underscore with a right parenthesis, positive numbers will line up correctly with negative numbers that are enclosed in parentheses.

✦ To set a color for a section of the format, type the name of the color in square brackets in the section. An example is available in the custom format starters.

✦ Add commas to your format so that the displayed numbers appear in multiples of 1,000. (The commas that are not surrounded by digit placeholders can be used to scale the numbers by thousands.)

Using the Format Painter

If you've already spent time and effort creating formats in certain areas of a worksheet and want to use them elsewhere, you can easily do so with the format painter. As its name implies, the format painter lets you take an existing format and literally "paint" that format across any other cells in a worksheet. (The same feature is also available in Word.) When you use the format painter, you copy all formatting—including text, number, alignment formats, and cell shading, color, and borders—from the currently active cell to the range of cells that you paint. The format painter is accessible from the Standard toolbar; look for the button with the paintbrush. Use the format painter to copy the formatting information from one cell to another cell or to a range of cells, or from a range of cells to another range of cells.

To copy formatting from one cell to another cell or to a range of cells, follow these steps:

1. Select the cell that contains the formatting to copy.

2. Click the Format Painter button on the Standard toolbar. Your cursor gains a paintbrush beside it.

3. Click and drag across the range of cells that are to receive the format. (If copying to only one cell, just click that cell.) When you release the mouse button, the format of the original cell is applied to the selected range and your cursor is back to normal.

To copy formatting from a range of cells to another range of cells, follow these steps:

1. Select the entire range of cells that contains the formatting to copy. (Yes, each cell may have different formatting.)

2. Click the Format Painter button on the Formatting toolbar. A paintbrush now appears beside the usual mouse pointer.

3. Click the upper-left cell in the range of cells that should receive the format. When you release the mouse button, the format of the original range of cells is applied to a range of cells of the same size as the original range.

   You can copy the format to a larger number of cells. The formatting pattern will simply repeat after the original number of cells. Rather than clicking the upper-left cell, click and drag over all the cells you want to receive the formatting.

Creating Your Own Styles

As this chapter emphasizes, Excel's formatting options give you the power to apply formatting to your worksheets in just about every conceivable manner. If you find yourself applying the same formatting choices repeatedly to different parts of a worksheet, it makes sense to save your formatting choices as a style so that you can easily apply the formatting to a selection of cells. In Excel, a style is a collection of formatting options that you apply to a cell or a range of cells.

The nice aspect of styles is that if you apply them to your worksheets and subsequently decide to change some aspect of the style, all the parts of your worksheet that use that style will automatically change. For example, if you create a style, use it in half a dozen worksheets, and later change the font used by that style, the font will automatically change in those worksheets.

(If you are accustomed to working with styles in Word, you will find the concept of Excel styles to be similar. However, in Excel you can't format the cells first, and then define the style based on those cells.)

You can easily define your own styles by choosing Format ⇨ Style. To define the style, follow these steps:

1. Choose Format ⇨ Style. (No shortcut exists for this command.) The Style dialog box appears, as shown in Figure 17-21.

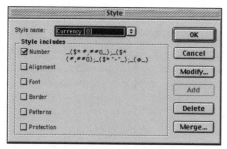

Figure 17-21: The Style dialog box

2. In the Style name box, enter a name for your new style and click the Add button that appears to add the new style to the list.

3. Turn off the checkboxes for any of the attributes that you don't want included in the style.

4. If you want to change any of the attributes for the format settings shown in the list, click Modify to bring up the Format Cells dialog box.

   Click any of the tabs in the Format Cells dialog box and change the settings for the formats.

5. When you are finished setting the formats in the Format Cells dialog box, click OK to return to the Style dialog box.

6. Click OK to save the new style.

After your custom style exists, using it is simple. Just select the range of cells to which you want to apply the style and choose Format ⇨ Style. In the Style dialog box, click the arrow to the right of the Style name box and drag to the name of your custom style. Click OK to apply the style to the selected range of cells.

Protecting Your Formatting Changes

You can protect cells so their formats and other data cannot be changed. (By default, the cells of a worksheet have protection turned on, but the protection does not take effect until you choose Tools ⇨ Protection and choose Protect Workbook from the resulting dialog box.) To make sure that the cells of a worksheet are protected when you turn on overall protection for the workbook, follow these steps:

1. Choose any range of cells that should not be protected. Because the default setting for the cells is to be protected, you want to turn off protection for any cells that you want to retain the ability to change.

2. Choose Format ⇨ Cells.

3. Click the Protection tab of the Format Cells dialog box (see Figure 17-22).

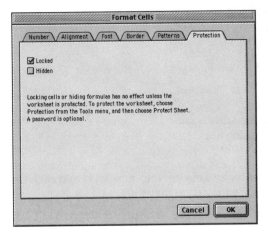

Figure 17-22: The Protection tab of the Format Cells dialog box

4. Uncheck the Locked checkbox if you want the selected cells to remain unprotected. You can also turn on the Hidden checkbox to specify that the selected cells' contents do not appear in the formula bar.

5. Click OK and repeat Steps 1 through 4 for every range of cells that should remain unprotected.

6. Choose Tools ⇨ Protection ⇨ Protect Workbook.

7. In the Protect Workbook dialog box, enter a password, if one is desired. If you omit the password, you can still protect the workbook, but others can remove the protection without the use of a password. (Please read the sidebar "Fair Warning.") Also, check the Windows checkbox if you want to protect the windows in the workbook from being moved or resized.

8. Click OK to implement the protection.

Fair Warning

If you protect a workbook with a password, *do not, do not, do not* (did we repeat that enough?) forget the password! If you forget the password, you may as well start re-creating the workbook from scratch.

Even the technical support people at Microsoft cannot help you get into a workbook that is password-protected when you don't have the password.

Passwords that you enter to protect a workbook are case sensitive.

After you have protected the contents of a workbook, you can remove the protection by choosing Tools ➪ Protection ➪ Unprotect Workbook. If you entered a password during the protection process, you are asked for the password before Excel will unprotect the document.

Summary

This chapter covered formatting your worksheets. You learned how to use formatting to give a worksheet a more appealing look and to enhance its appearance. We discussed these topics:

✦ You can quickly give a worksheet a professional look by selecting a worksheet range, choosing Format ➪ AutoFormat, and selecting the desired options.

✦ You can easily change row heights and column widths to accommodate your entries by clicking and dragging the column or row header edges, or by choosing the Column or Row commands (as appropriate) from the Format menu.

✦ You can apply specific fonts, font sizes, styles, borders, patterns, and colors to a group of cells or to characters within a cell by choosing Format ➪ Cells and using the options in various tabs of the Format Cells dialog box.

✦ In addition to the variety of standard formats provided with Excel, you can create custom formats for the values you enter in your worksheets.

Where to go next

✦ In the next chapter, you learn to add graphic objects to your worksheets and your charts.

✦ You can make charts out of the data in your worksheet. Chapter 19 has the details.

✦ ✦ ✦

Adding Graphics to Worksheets

Worksheets can be far more than just tables of numbers with a chart added here and there. You can emphasize the points expressed by those numbers, add visual information, and (by means of macro buttons) literally make your worksheets easier for others to use. You can draw lines, circles, rectangles, and squares, and you can add text boxes for anything from short titles to multiple paragraphs of text. You can also make use of clip art, which is professionally drawn artwork, from other programs. If you have an artistic personality (or if your worksheets are facing a demanding audience and you need all the help you can get), you can really get carried away with Excel's graphics.

Discovering a Need for Graphics

Perhaps you hadn't thought of Excel and graphics together. Because Excel is a spreadsheet package, many Excel users crunch numbers with it and leave graphics entirely to drawing programs and artists. If you don't use Excel's graphic capabilities, however, you miss out on some of Excel's best power. From its humble origin years ago as a Macintosh product, Excel provided spreadsheet capability with built-in flexible graphics. Excel 2001 really packs a graphics punch with the power to add visual oomph to your work. Figure 18-1 is an example.

In the Figure 18-1 worksheet, the gridlines were turned off and a text box with an arrow was added to describe the point that the numbers in the worksheet are attempting to get across. WordArt was used to create the title. Clip art was added, and a button that runs a macro ("Click here for sales," which displays another worksheet) was drawn. You can add all these effects and more with Excel's graphics features.

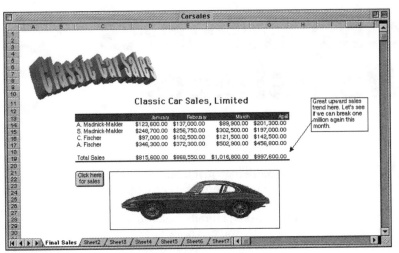

Figure 18-1: A worksheet jazzed up with graphics

Inserting Graphics into Worksheets

You can insert graphics into an Excel worksheet using drag-and-drop, copy and paste, or the Insert ⟹ Picture command.

Drag-and-drop is probably the easiest way to insert graphics into a worksheet. Open the folder the graphic is in, drag it into place in the Excel worksheet, and release the mouse button. You can also store your graphics in the Mac's Scrapbook and drag them from there into your worksheet.

Another way to insert graphic files into an Excel worksheet is to use the Insert ⟹ Picture command. This lets you pull graphic pictures from files created in other programs without opening the file's folder in the Finder. To insert graphics with the Picture command, follow these steps:

1. Place the insertion pointer in the cell where you want the upper-left corner of the picture to appear.

2. Choose Insert ⟹ Picture ⟹ From File. The Choose a Picture dialog box appears (see Figure 18-2).

3. In the dialog box, navigate to the folder that contains the clipart or graphics file you want to insert, as shown in Figure 18-2.

4. Click Insert to place the graphic into the worksheet. You can then use the normal sizing and moving methods to change the size or location of the graphic.

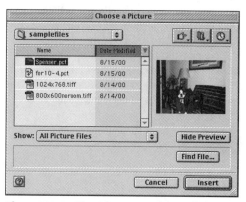

Figure 18-2: The Choose a Picture dialog box

To use the copy and paste method, you need to have the program the graphic was originally created in (or some other program that will open that graphic file type) and to follow these steps:

1. Double-click the graphic's file to open the graphic in the program it was created in and select the graphic.

2. Choose Edit ⇨ Copy (⌘-C).

3. Bring your Excel worksheet forward (launching it if it is not already running). Select the cell or the object where you want the upper-left corner of the graphic to appear.

4. Choose Edit ⇨ Paste (⌘-V). The graphic appears in the worksheet. You can then use the normal sizing and moving methods to change the size or location of the graphic.1

Tip

If you receive graphics from numerous sources in a variety of file formats, attempting to purchase and use all of the creating programs could put quite a dent in your checking account and in your available disk space. An excellent shareware utility, GraphicConverter (www.lemkesoft.de), opens and converts between an enormous number of graphic file formats—Mac, Windows, Unix, and other platform formats. A much more expensive commercial application that does the same job is DeBabelizer (www.equilibrium.com), but its list of supported formats is shorter than that of GraphicConverter.

Working with Graphic Objects

With the tools on the Drawing toolbar (see Figure 18-3) you can create your own graphic objects in Excel. If the Drawing toolbar is not displayed, choose View ➪ Toolbars ➪ Drawing. Another way to open the Drawing toolbar is to Control-click any open toolbar and choose Drawing from the shortcut menu that appears. After the Drawing toolbar is displayed, you can move it by clicking any blank area of the toolbar and dragging the toolbar to a desired location, just as you would move any toolbar. By default, the Drawing toolbar appears as a vertical stack of buttons, but we prefer horizontal toolbars and reshaped it as shown in Figure 18-3.

Figure 18-3: The Drawing toolbar

The Excel Drawing toolbar has a variety of drawing tools to help you enhance your worksheets. You can create items from lines, polygons, arrows, WordArt, and even 3D shapes. Table 18-1 gives the name of each tool and its function, from left to right.

<table>
<tr><th colspan="2">Table 18-1
The Drawing Toolbar's Tools</th></tr>
<tr><th>Tool Name</th><th>Function</th></tr>
<tr><td>Draw</td><td>Opens a menu of additional commands for drawing-related tasks</td></tr>
<tr><td>Select Objects</td><td>Selection pointer used to select objects</td></tr>
<tr><td>Free Rotate</td><td>Rotates a selected object to any degree</td></tr>
<tr><td>Text Box</td><td>Creates a text box for word-wrapped text</td></tr>
<tr><td>WordArt</td><td>Creates a WordArt object</td></tr>
<tr><td>Insert ClipArt</td><td>Opens the Clip Gallery</td></tr>
<tr><td>Insert Picture from File</td><td>Displays the Insert Picture dialog box</td></tr>
<tr><td>Line</td><td>Draws straight lines</td></tr>
<tr><td>Rectangle</td><td>Draws rectangles or squares</td></tr>
<tr><td>AutoShapes</td><td>Opens a menu used to add AutoShape graphic objects</td></tr>
<tr><td>Lines</td><td>Draws straight lines, lines with arrowheads, curved lines, freeform figures, and scribbles</td></tr>
<tr><td>Line Style</td><td>Used to change the style of the selected solid line</td></tr>
<tr><td>Font Color</td><td>Changes the font color for an object</td></tr>
</table>

Tool Name	Function
Fill Color	Changes the fill color for an object
Line Color	Changes the line color for an object
More Buttons	Pop-up displaying the following additional buttons
Arrow	Creates a line with an arrowhead
Oval	Draws ovals or circles
Dash Style	Used to change the style of the selected dashed line
Arrow Style	Used to change the style of the selected arrow
Shadow	Adds a variety of shadow effects to the selected object
3-D	Adds a variety of three-dimensional effects to the selected object
Nudge	Move the selected object(s) in small increments
Change AutoShape	Enables you to select from a variety of shapes as the AutoShape default

For a real timesaver, use the shortcut menus while you are working with objects. The shortcut menu that is displayed when you Control-click an object is shown in Figure 18-4. These shortcut menus provide the Cut, Copy, and Paste commands, as well as other commands related to formatting the object.

Figure 18-4: An object shortcut menu

Inserting AutoShapes

One of Excel 2001's capabilities enables you to add AutoShapes as graphics to your spreadsheets. AutoShapes are groups of ready-made shapes, including lines, rectangles, ovals, circles, arrows, flowchart symbols, and callouts. (If you're curious as to where the freeform and freehand tools of earlier Excel versions vanished, they are now part of the AutoShapes collection of graphics.) The worksheet shown in Figure 18-5 contains several graphics created with the AutoShapes menu in the Graphics toolbar.

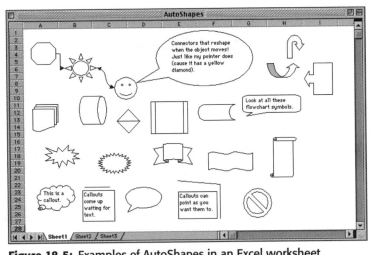

Figure 18-5: Examples of AutoShapes in an Excel worksheet

What Graphic Files Can I Import?

Excel's graphic filters let you import graphic files that have been saved in any of these file formats:

File Type	File Name Extension
Macintosh Picture	PICT
Macintosh MacPaint	PNTG
Tagged Image File Format	TIFF
Encapsulated PostScript	EPS
Graphics Interchange Format	GIF
FlashPix	FPix
PhotoShop Document	PSD, 8BPS
JPEG Filter	JPEG, JFIF
QuickTime Interchange Format	QTIF
Silicon Graphics Incorporated	SGI
Targa	TGA, TPIC
Portable Network Graphics	PNG
Windows Metafile	WMF
Enhanced Windows Metafile	EMF
Windows Bitmap	BMP

To add an AutoShapes graphic to a chart, follow these steps:

1. If the Drawing toolbar isn't visible, Control-click any visible toolbar and select Drawing from the shortcut menu (or choose View ⇨ Toolbars ⇨ Drawing) to display the toolbar.

   By the way, we didn't forget the hotkey for "Drawing." For whatever reason, Microsoft didn't add hotkeys for any of the toolbar menu options.

2. On the Drawing toolbar, click AutoShapes and move your mouse to the name of the desired category of shapes to see the shape. Click the desired shape. Your cursor becomes a crosshair.

3. To add a shape in a preset size, click the worksheet or chart where you want to add the shape. To make the shape your own size, click and drag the shape to the desired size.

You can align a shape with the gridlines of cells by holding the ⌘ (Command) key while dragging the shape. You can set the shape in perfect proportion by pressing the Shift key while dragging the shape by a corner handle.

When the AutoShapes menu opens, you are presented with six options: connectors, basic shapes, block arrows, flowcharts, stars and banners, and callouts. Figure 18-6 shows the shapes that are available under each of these menu choices. In Excel 98, there was a seventh option, Lines, but that now has its own button right after the AutoShapes button.

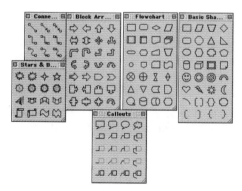

Figure 18-6: Available AutoShapes

Tip

Given that well over 100 shapes are provided, to describe how to place each shape in detail would take more text than you'd likely care to read. However, you can easily view a help screen specific to the use of any AutoShape tools. Press Shift-F1 to bring up the help balloon mode, and then point to a shape in the AutoShapes menu. A help balloon that explains how to draw or manipulate the chosen shape appears.

Drawing lines, arcs, ellipses, and rectangles

The Drawing toolbar lets you create lines, arcs, ellipses (Microsoft calls them Ovals, but they're really ellipses), and rectangles easily. You can combine these basic drawing elements to create more complex shapes. You draw an object by clicking the desired tool to select it, and then clicking and dragging in the worksheet to place the item.

While drawing lines, ellipses, and arcs, press Shift as you drag to keep the lines vertical, at a 45° angle, or horizontal. You can also hold down the ⌘ (Command) key to align the corners of the object with a cell's gridlines.

Tip   When you click a tool to select it, that tool is effective only while you draw one shape with it. If you plan to create multiple shapes with a tool, double-click it to select it. A double-click-selected tool remains effective until you select another tool.

Lines

To draw a line, click the Line tool to select it, click the beginning location for the line, and then drag to the ending location. To draw a line with an arrowhead, click the Arrow tool, click the point where the line should begin, and drag to the point where the arrowhead should appear. After you've drawn your arrow, with it still selected, you can click the Arrow Style list and select an arrow style. Your arrow will take on that style. You can turn any line or arrow into any arrow style by selecting it and choosing a style.

Squares and rectangles

To draw a square or a rectangle, click the Rectangle tool to select it, click a corner of the rectangle, and drag to size the rectangle as desired. To draw a square, press Shift while you drag to size the square.

Ovals (ellipses) and circles

To draw an Oval (ellipse), click the Oval tool to select it, click an edge of the ellipse, and drag to size the ellipse as desired. To draw a circle, press the Shift key while you drag to size the circle.

Filled objects

To fill an object, click the desired object to select it, click the down arrow to the right of the Fill Color button (in the Drawing toolbar), and choose a desired fill color. You can also apply a fancy line to an object. Again, select the object and choose a style from the pop-up Line Style or Dash Style buttons.

Arcs

To draw an arc, open the AutoShapes menu on the Drawing toolbar, choose Basic Shapes, and select the arc tool. Next, click and drag to create the arc where you want it on the worksheet. Drag the yellow handles on the arc to create more or less of the arc shape.

Tip   Many shapes are customizable. Look for yellow diamond-shaped handles, and then drag the handles to experiment and discover what you can do.

Selecting and grouping objects

Most of the items that you add while drawing are considered objects. This includes text boxes, graphics brought in from other sources, and shapes that you draw. Selecting an object is the key to working with it. Once you select it, you can easily manipulate it. You can have as many objects as you want in a worksheet, and you can manipulate as many as are selected.

To select the object that you want to work with, click it when the cursor turns into a hand. You can then change the object's orientation, shape, color, or pattern by using the Drawing toolbar's Color, Style, Shadow, and 3D tools. You can also select a single object by Control-clicking the object, which calls up the shortcut menu so you can choose Format AutoShape. In the Format AutoShape dialog box, select a tab and assign attributes.

To select multiple objects, press Shift while you select each object. To unselect an object, press Shift and click the object again. Even after you've let go of the Shift key, you can press it again to select or deselect another object.

Don't Let Others Mess with Your Graphics

If you want to keep others from changing your graphics, you can protect them by protecting cell contents and scenarios.

By default, all graphics are protected when you turn on cell protection. However, you can exclude individual graphics from protection. To do so, before turning on protection, Control-click a graphic, choose Format AutoShape (or Format WordArt) from the shortcut menu, and click the Protection tab. (To affect several graphics at once, first press Shift as you click each graphic, and then Control-click any one of the selected graphics.) In the Protection tab, uncheck Locked and click OK.

After you have excluded any graphics that you don't want to protect, select Tools ➪ Protection ➪ Protect Worksheet (or Protect Workbook). Make sure Graphics is checked. While in the Protection dialog box, you can also choose to protect the data within all the cells and to protect your scenarios. You can also enter a password, if desired. If you leave the password text box blank, the worksheet will be protected from changes, but you won't need a password to turn off the protection. If you do enter a password, don't forget it! (Or be prepared to re-create the work when you want to make changes.) Click OK to enable the chosen protection. Of course, you can always go back and select Tools ➪ Protection ➪ Unprotect Sheet (or Unprotect Workbook).

By the way, you can also exclude cells from protection the same way you exclude graphics: select the cells, Control-click, and select Format Cells to uncheck Locked in the Protection tab. ⌘-1 is the keyboard shortcut for Format ➪ Cells. Then protect the entire sheet or workbook.

You can also group objects together, which is useful when you want to change the colors for a group of objects or move or align them as a group. All the objects that you include in the group act as one object; if you perform an action on one of the items, the action affects all the items in the group. To group objects, follow these steps:

1. Select the objects that you want to group. Remember to press Shift as you select each object.

2. Control-click any one of the selected objects and choose Grouping ⇨ Group from the shortcut menu that appears.

Using Bring to Front and Send to Back

Each object you draw is drawn on a layer on top of the last object. As you draw and position multiple objects, you may need to place one object on top of another (for example, a company logo may consist of a circle on top of a rectangle). If the wrong object appears on top, you can adjust its placement by using the Bring Forward, Bring to Front, Send Backward, or Send to Back options, which are available from the object's shortcut menu. Control-click the desired object and choose Arrange ⇨ Bring to Front to make the object appear on top of all other objects. You can also Control-click the object and choose Arrange ⇨ Send to Back to make the selected object appear underneath all other objects. You can use the Bring Forward and Send Backward options on the same menu to move a selected object one step closer to the top or to the bottom of a stack of selected objects. Figure 18-7 shows the effects of using the Bring to Front and Send to Back tools.

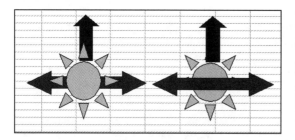

Figure 18-7: *Left:* The original layers. *Right:* Send to Back sends the sun to the back and Bring to Front brings the two-headed arrow to the front (in front of the one-headed arrow, layer-wise).

Moving and copying objects

As you work, you may need to move or copy objects. You have two options to move or copy objects: you can either cut or copy and then paste, or you can click and drag.

To move or copy objects with the Cut or Copy commands, follow these steps:

1. Select the object(s) that you want to move or copy.

2. Choose Edit ⇨ Cut (⌘-X) or click the Cut button on the Standard toolbar to remove the object and place it on the clipboard. Choose Edit ⇨ Copy (⌘-C) if you prefer to leave the existing object intact while copying it to a new location.

3. Move the cursor to the location where you want to place the object.

4. Choose Edit ⇨ Paste (⌘-V) or click the Paste button on the Standard toolbar to place the clipboard information in the worksheet. The cell that contains the insertion pointer becomes the upper-left corner of the entry.

The click-and-drag method for moving objects is equally simple. Simply click the object and (while holding down the mouse button) drag it to the area where you want it placed. Release the mouse button to place the object. This is the equivalent of cutting and pasting the object. You can copy an object by pressing Option as you click and drag it.

To remove an object, select it and press Delete, or choose Edit ⇨ Clear.

Resizing objects

You resize objects in Excel in the same way that you resize objects in other programs. First, select the object that you want to resize. You will see small squares, called handles, appear around the object. To resize the object's width, drag one of the side handles to the desired width. (The arrows on the cursor are a clue as to what you can do.) To change the height of the object, drag a top or bottom handle. If you want to resize the length and width of the object simultaneously, drag a corner handle. However, be aware that these resizing techniques distort your object. To resize without distortion, press Shift as you resize. This constrains the object to its original proportions.

Formatting objects

You can apply a variety of formatting options to an object by selecting it and then applying the Color, Style, Shadow, or 3-D options from the Drawing toolbar. You can accomplish the same result by Control-clicking the object, choosing Format ⇨ AutoShape, and using the various options on the Colors and Lines tabs of the dialog box.

Formatting colors

To change the color of an object, click the object to select it and click the arrow to the right of the Fill Color button in the Drawing toolbar. A Colors tear-off palette appears (see Figure 18-8) and you can choose the desired color.

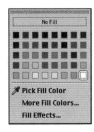

Figure 18-8: The Colors tear-off palette

If you want to change the patterns or the effects for the color, click Fill Effects at the bottom of the palette to open the Fill Effects dialog box shown in Figure 18-9.

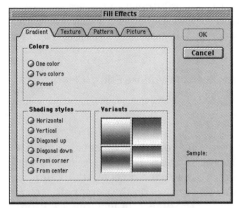

Figure 18-9: The Fill Effects dialog box

Using the tabs of this dialog box, you can change the colors and shading used for the gradient, the texture of the colors (to produce a tiled effect, for example), the pattern, and whether a picture should be used as a fill. Under the Gradient tab, you can select the number of colors (one, two, or preset), the gradient style, and a gradient variant. Using the Texture tab, you can select one of 24 possible preset textures, or you can click the Other Texture button and choose an image file, which appears for use as a texture, in an Open dialog box. Using the Pattern tab, you can choose from one of 48 possible patterns, specifying both the foreground and background colors via the drop-down palettes at the bottom of this tab. In addition, the Picture tab lets you choose an image file to serve as a picture contained within the object. After you make the desired selections in the Fill Effects dialog box and click OK, the changes are applied to the object.

Note   The difference between using a picture as a texture and a picture as a fill is that when used as a texture, the graphic is tiled or cropped to fit the object, and when it is used as a fill, it is scaled (and possibly distorted) to fit the dimensions of the object.

Formatting lines

You can change the style, thickness, and colors of lines using either of two methods. You can select the object and use the Line Color, Line Style, Dash Style, and Arrow Style buttons of the Drawing toolbar. Each button reveals a menu of possible colors or styles from which you can select the desired option.

You can also Control-click the desired object and choose Format ⇨ AutoShape from the menu. In the Format AutoShape dialog box that appears, click Colors and Lines. Figure 18-10 shows what the Colors and Lines tab looks like when an arrow is selected. Double-clicking a drawing object also presents the Format AutoShape dialog box.

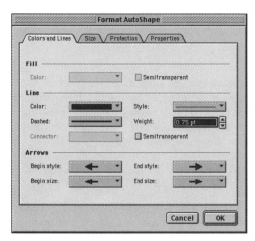

Figure 18-10: The Colors and Lines tab of the Format AutoShape dialog box when you select an arrow

In the Fill Area of the dialog box, you can choose a fill color for enclosed objects such as rectangles and ovals. However, the Fill Color toolbar button (discussed earlier) offers more options including the capability to change patterns and gradients.

Hiding Objects for Better Spreadsheet Performance

If you have many graphic objects in your worksheet, Excel is forced to redraw the graphics as you scroll within the worksheet. This extra effort can slow your system's speed, especially on hardware that meets only the minimum configuration for Excel.

You can speed worksheet display by hiding the graphic objects from view or by displaying them as graphic placeholders. Choose Edit ⇨ Preferences and click the View tab. In the Objects area of the dialog box, turn on the Show Placeholders option to show the graphic objects as placeholders (empty white rectangles), or turn on the Hide All option to hide the graphic objects. When you need to see the objects again, you can return to this dialog box and turn on the Show All option.

In the Line area of the dialog box, you can change line colors, styles, weight (the thickness of the line), and whether the line should be dashed or solid. In the Arrows portion of the dialog box, you can choose styles and sizes for the arrowheads. After you make the desired selections within the dialog box, click OK to apply them to the arrow.

Adding shadows and 3-D Effects

You can use the Shadow and 3-D Effects buttons of the Drawing toolbar (More Buttons pop-up) to add shadows or three-dimensional effects to graphic objects. To do so, click the desired object to select it, click the Shadow or 3-D button on the Drawing toolbar, and then select the desired effect from the submenu that pops up.

Adding Text Boxes

Excel lets you place text boxes in your worksheets. Text boxes make excellent titles for worksheets because they float in a layer over the worksheet. Therefore, you can position a title of any size without affecting worksheet row or column positions. You can edit and format text in these boxes using typical word processing techniques. To add a text box to your worksheet, follow these steps:

1. In the Drawing toolbar, click the Text Box button. Notice that the mouse pointer changes to a thin arrow.

2. Click and drag to form the box in which you will enter the text. To create a square text box, press Shift as you drag. If you want a box aligned with the grid, hold down the ⌘ (Command) key as you drag. When the text box reaches the desired size, release the mouse button.

3. The insertion pointer now appears inside the text box (see Figure 18-11), which permits you to begin entering text. You can continue typing until the end of the text box. As you type, the text scrolls up so part of it is hidden. To make all the text visible, select the text box and drag a handle to make the box larger to accommodate the extra text.

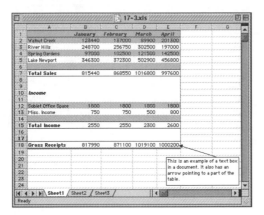

Figure 18-11: A text box added to a worksheet

Editing text

To edit text within a text box, use the normal navigation methods. To move the cursor, use the arrow keys or the mouse. Select any text to format it or type over it. Use the Delete key to delete any unwanted entry.

Formatting text

You can also format the text within a text box just as you format any other text in Excel, PowerPoint, Entourage, or Word. You can select the entire text or select individual characters. After selecting the text or characters, use the buttons and lists available on the Formatting palette, or use Control-click and choose Format Text Box from the shortcut menu. If you Control-click the box without any text selected, you affect the entire contents of the box. Double-clicking the border of a text box will also call up the Format Text Box dialog box, affecting the entire contents. If you first select characters within the text box and then Control-click, your changes only affect the selected text. When you use Control-click, the dialog box contains only the Font tab, as shown in Figure 18-12. Using the options on this tab, you can change your font, font style, and font size, as well as turn on special effects such as underlining, bold, italics, strikethrough, superscript, subscript, outline, and shadow. With the Color menu, you can also change the font's color. Remember, however, that this dialog box changes the font, not the text box's background. The Fill Color button on the Drawing toolbar affects the background.

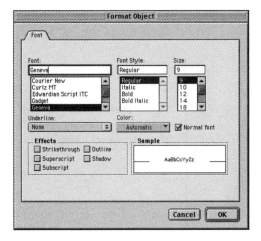

Figure 18-12: The Font tab of the Format Text Box dialog box

Rotating text

Excel also lets you rotate text within a text box, but to a lesser extent than you can rotate text within a cell. Figure 18-13 shows how text in a text box can rotate in Excel.

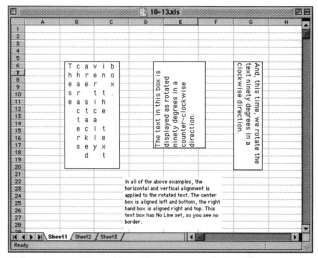

Figure 18-13: Examples of rotated text in boxes

To rotate text in a text box, follow these steps:

1. After creating the text box and entering the text, select the text box, Control-click the edge of the box (not the text within the box), and then choose Format Text Box to open the Format Text Box dialog box.

2. Choose the Alignment tab (see Figure 18-14). The Text Alignment area lets you control both the horizontal and vertical alignment of the text within the text box.

3. In the Orientation area, click the desired orientation for the box.

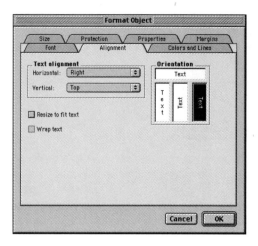

Figure 18-14: Changing text alignment in the Alignment tab after you select a text box

Alternatively, you can select the rotation in the Formatting palette's Text Alignment pane, on the Orientation row. Only the permissible orientations are enabled.

You can use the Resize to fit text option in the Alignment tab to size your entries automatically. If you choose this option, the Wrap text checkbox also becomes available.

Using WordArt

Microsoft WordArt is an applet (actually, it is an object linking and embedding (OLE) application) that lets you create special effects using text. You can enter any text and then bend and stretch the text, or fit the text into a variety of different shapes. You can also add three-dimensional effects. This text, or WordArt, is inserted in your document as a graphic. Figure 18-15 shows an example of what you can do with WordArt.

Figure 18-15: Examples of WordArt

To add WordArt to a worksheet, first make the Drawing toolbar visible (if it isn't already) by Control-clicking any visible toolbar and selecting Drawing or by choosing View ➪ Toolbars ➪ Drawing. In the Drawing toolbar, click the WordArt button to call up the WordArt Gallery dialog box, which is shown in Figure 18-16.

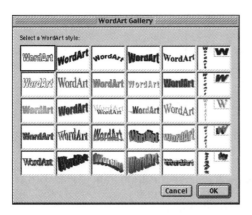

Figure 18-16: The WordArt Gallery dialog box shows the available styles of WordArt.

Click a desired style to select it and then click OK. The Edit WordArt Text dialog box shown in Figure 18-17 appears.

Figure 18-17: The Edit WordArt Text dialog box displays the WordArt text.

Replace the default text with your own text by typing over this preselected message. Select a font and font size from the pop-up menus at the top of the dialog box. If you want bold or italic applied to the text, click their respective buttons. Returns are included as paragraph breaks in the text. Pressing Enter is the same as clicking OK.

Note   Changes that you make to the selected font will override the chosen selection in the WordArt Gallery dialog box. You can always reopen the dialog box by clicking the Gallery button on the WordArt toolbar.

Click OK in the Edit WordArt Text dialog box to place the completed WordArt into your worksheet. The WordArt toolbar appears, as shown in Figure 18-18.

Figure 18-18: WordArt added to a worksheet

As with other graphic objects, you can move and size WordArt using standard techniques.

Additionally, the WordArt toolbar lets you change the appearance of a WordArt object in several ways. Figure 18-19 shows the parts of the WordArt toolbar and Table 18-2 gives the name of each tool and its function.

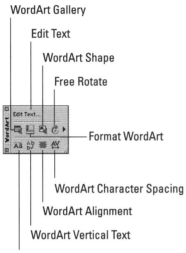

WordArt Gallery
Edit Text
WordArt Shape
Free Rotate
Format WordArt
WordArt Character Spacing
WordArt Alignment
WordArt Vertical Text
WordArt Same Letter Heights

Figure 18-19: The parts of the WordArt toolbar

Table 18-2
The WordArt Toolbar's Tools

Tool Name	Function
Edit Text	Displays the Edit WordArt Text dialog box so that you can change the text.
WordArt Gallery	Displays the WordArt Gallery dialog box so that you can change the overall shape and effect.
Format WordArt	Displays the Format WordArt dialog box.
WordArt Shape	Displays a pop-up menu of available WordArt shapes.
Free Rotate	Rotates the selected WordArt object to any degree.
WordArt Same Letter Heights	Sets all letters in WordArt to the same height; click again to toggle the text height back.
WordArt Vertical Text	Stacks text in the WordArt object vertically.
WordArt Alignment	Presents a pop-up menu of available alignment choices within the dimensions of the WordArt object.
WordArt Character Spacing	Displays a pop-up menu of the character spacing and kerning choices that may be applied to the text of the WordArt object.

The WordArt toolbar performs many WordArt tasks. You can change the shape and rotation, modify the character spacing, and display the text vertically.

Changing colors and sizes

The Format WordArt button opens the Format WordArt dialog box shown in Figure 18-20. Here you can change the text colors and modify the size and rotation of the object.

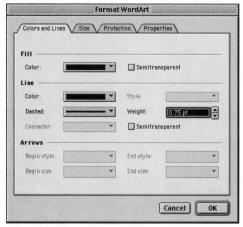

Figure 18-20: The Format WordArt dialog box with the Colors and Lines tab visible

The Fill color affects the color of the letters, whereas the Line color affects the color of the letter shading. In the Size tab, you can change the size and rotation of the object. Note, however, that it is easier to change the size by selecting and dragging the object and the rotation by using the WordArt toolbar's Free Rotate button.

Changing shapes

You can change the overall shape of a WordArt object. To do so, click the WordArt Shape button in the WordArt toolbar. When you do this, a menu of shapes appears, as shown in Figure 18-21.

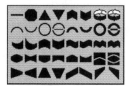

Figure 18-21: A dialog box containing the available WordArt shapes

The different shapes that you see here represent the way the WordArt text will appear in the worksheet. As you select, the effect is immediately applied to the text.

You will also note that one or more handles of a WordArt object are yellow diamonds. You can drag a diamond to change perspective and coverage of the chosen shape.

Rotating objects

Finally, you can use the Free Rotate tool to rotate a selected object to any degree. Select the desired WordArt object, click the Free Rotate button in the WordArt toolbar, and then click and drag a corner of the WordArt object in the direction in which you want it to rotate.

Summary

In this chapter, you learned about using Excel's graphics capabilities to add pictures and other graphic objects to a worksheet. The following points were discussed:

✦ You can insert graphics in a worksheet with the Insert menu's Picture submenu commands.

✦ You can use a variety of tools from Excel's Drawing toolbar to draw different shapes in a worksheet.

✦ You can select multiple objects to manipulate them as a group and to apply formatting, color, or other design choices.

✦ You can add text boxes to worksheets by using the Text Box tool on the Drawing toolbar.

✦ You can add highly ornamental text to your document using WordArt.

Where to go next

✦ For adding visual oomph to your worksheet-based presentations, graphics and charts often go hand in hand. Chapter 19 discusses charts in detail.

✦   ✦   ✦

Working with Excel Charts

◆　◆　◆　◆

◆　◆　◆　◆

This chapter details Excel's powerful capabilities for displaying and printing charts. You can create charts that emphasize numeric trends, support data analysis, and help supply presentation-quality reports. Excel provides a rich assortment of formatting features and options for changing and enhancing the appearance of your charts.

Learning About Charts

Charts graphically represent worksheet data. A collection of values from worksheet cells you select can be illustrated in charts as columns, lines, bars, pie slices, or other types of markers. Figure 19-1 shows some examples of typical charts. The appearance of the markers that are used to represent the data varies depending on the type of marker you choose. In a bar or column chart, the markers appear as columns; in a line chart, the markers appear as lines composed of small symbols. The markers in a pie chart appear as wedges of the pie.

Most charts (with the exception of pie charts) have two axes: a horizontal axis called the category axis, and a vertical axis called the value axis. Three-dimensional charts add a third axis (called the series axis). Figure 19-2 shows an example of a three-dimensional chart.

Charts also contain gridlines, which provide a frame of reference for the values displayed on the value axis. You can add descriptive text to a chart, such as a title, and you can place the text in different locations. Your charts can also contain legends, which indicate which data are represented by the markers of the chart.

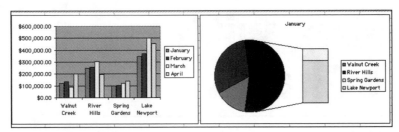

Figure 19-1: Two examples of typical charts — a column chart on the left and a pie chart on the right

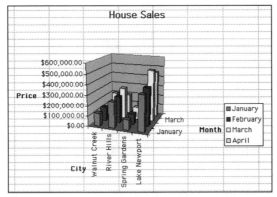

Figure 19-2: An example of a 3D chart

Excel makes adding charts simple. The Office Assistant offers to provide a Chart Wizard whenever you add a new chart to a worksheet. If you accept the help, the Chart Wizard, as with all Office wizards, produces the desired results by asking a series of questions. During each step of the wizard process, the dialog box displays a sample of the chart so you can see how your choices in the dialog box affect the final result.

Embedding Charts and Chart Sheets

You can add charts to Excel worksheets in one of two ways: as embedded charts or as chart sheets. Embedded charts are inserted into an existing worksheet page; hence, the page can show worksheet data with the chart. Figure 19-3 shows an embedded chart.

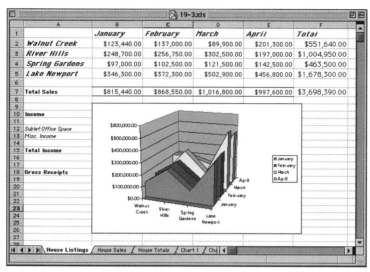

Figure 19-3: An embedded chart

Chart sheets, on the other hand, are charts that are placed on separate sheets of a workbook, apart from any worksheet data. Figure 19-4 shows a chart added as a chart sheet.

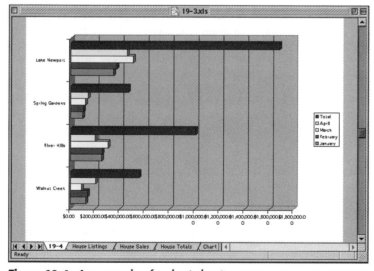

Figure 19-4: An example of a chart sheet

Embedded charts work best when you need to display or print the chart along with worksheet data; chart sheets work best when all you want to show is the chart. Whether you use embedded charts or chart sheets, the data used to produce the chart is always linked to the worksheet. Therefore, as you change the data in the underlying worksheet, the chart changes to reflect the new data.

Creating an embedded chart or chart sheet

You can add an embedded chart to an existing worksheet page or create a chart that resides separately on a chart sheet by performing the following steps:

1. In the worksheet, select the data you want to chart. Include any labels that should be used as legends in the chart.

2. Select Insert ➪ Chart or click the Chart Wizard button on the Standard toolbar. When you do this, your Office Assistant appears (if turned on) and asks whether you'd like help with this feature. Along with the Assistant, the first Chart Wizard dialog box appears showing the available chart types. If you say yes to the help, the Assistant tells you about the Chart Wizard. If you decline, the Assistant leaves you with the Chart Wizard.

3. Choose a desired chart type, click the Next button, and follow the directions in the successive Chart Wizard dialog boxes to specify the data range, the chart's format, and the desired options for category labels and for the legend text. (The Chart Wizard dialog boxes are described in detail in "Using the Chart Wizard," the next section of this chapter.)

4. The last Chart Wizard dialog box (labeled Step 4 of 4) is where you choose to embed your chart or have it appear on a new sheet. The default is As object in, which embeds the chart. By default, Excel expects to place the chart on the sheet that contains the charting data. However, you can choose any other existing sheet from the pop-up list.

   To place the chart on a separate worksheet, select As new sheet and name the new sheet in the text box provided. If you choose the name of an existing sheet, Excel will ask whether you wish to place the chart as an embedded object on that sheet.

5. Click Finish.

Using the Chart Wizard

With either method of adding a chart, the Chart Wizard displays a series of dialog boxes that help you define precisely how the chart will appear. The first Chart Wizard dialog box appears, as shown in Figure 19-5.

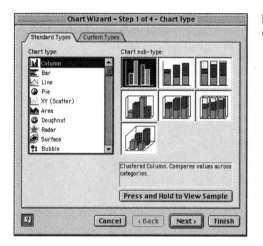

Figure 19-5: The first Chart Wizard dialog box

In this dialog box, you can select the chart type that you want from one of the 14 available chart types. For each chart type selected in the Chart-type list box (at the left side of the dialog box), you can choose any of the available sub-types from the right side of the dialog box.

Tip   To help you decide upon a chart type, you can easily preview the potential chart. Just select the type and sub-type, and then click the Press and Hold to View Sample button (at the lower-right corner of the dialog box).

If none of the dozens of standard type and sub-type combinations suit your taste, you can click the Custom Types tab and choose from 1 of 20 available built-in custom chart types. (For more specifics on the available chart types, see "Working with Chart Types" later in the chapter.)

After you've selected the desired chart type and sub-type, click Next to proceed.

After you click the Next button, the second dialog box, shown in Figure 19-6, appears. You can use this dialog box to define the range of cells within the worksheet that is used as the underlying data for the chart. When you select a range in the worksheet and then use the Chart Wizard, the range automatically appears in the dialog box, as shown in Figure 19-6. If for any reason you want to change the range, you can do so by typing a different range.

You can use the Series in option to determine whether the data series appears as rows or columns in the chart, and you can click the Series tab to add or remove a data series from the chart. (For more specifics on how you can use data series in charts, see "Understanding How Excel Plots a Chart" later in the chapter.) When done choosing the desired data range and series options, click Next to proceed.

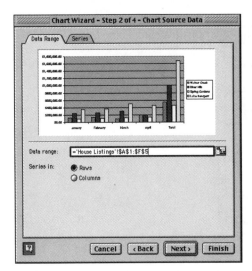

Figure 19-6: The second Chart Wizard dialog box asks for the range of cells to be plotted.

The third Chart Wizard dialog box appears, as shown in Figure 19-7. In this dialog box, you can turn on or off a variety of options for the chart you've selected. The dialog box is divided into six tabs: Titles, Axes, Gridlines, Legend, Data Labels, and Data Table. (If the terminology used throughout this dialog box is unfamiliar to you, you'll learn more about these terms throughout the remainder of this chapter.) You can use the Titles tab to specify titles for the chart, for the category axis, for the value axis of the chart, and (if a 3-D chart) the series axis. For many charts, you'll can also specify secondary category and value axis titles. On the Axis tab, you can turn on or off the display of the category axis and the value axis, or specify a type of category display. On the Gridlines tab, you can specify whether gridlines are added to each axis of the chart, and define the granularity of the gridlines. The Legend tab lets you show and position the chart's legend. The Data Labels tab lets you add labels to the data points plotted by the chart, as well as placing the legend key next to the labels you add; the Data Table tab lets you add an optional data table below the chart (with or without legend keys displayed in the data table). As you change these various settings, you can look at the preview of the chart that is visible in the dialog box, to make sure you obtain the desired look for the chart. When you are done selecting the desired chart options, click Next to proceed.

The fourth Chart Wizard dialog box appears, as shown in Figure 19-8. Here you specify whether the chart should be inserted as an embedded chart in the existing worksheet or placed into a separate chart sheet. If you click the As new sheet button, you can enter a name for the new sheet or accept the default name (Chart1, Chart2, and so on). If you click the As object in button, you can then choose the desired sheet where the chart should be placed by name from the pop-up menu; the default is the same worksheet where you selected the chart data. Click Finish, and your desired chart appears in the chosen location. Remember that, if you embed the chart in an existing worksheet, you can select the entire chart and drag it to any location in that worksheet.

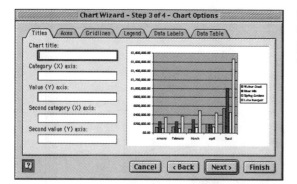

Figure 19-7: The third Chart Wizard dialog box provides various formatting options for the chart.

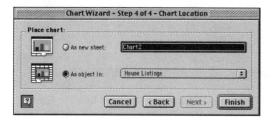

Figure 19-8: The fourth Chart Wizard dialog box asks where the chart should be placed.

After a chart exists, you can run the Chart Wizard on this chart at any time by clicking the chart to select it, and then clicking the Chart Wizard button on the Standard toolbar.

Creating a Sample Chart

The examples shown throughout this chapter make use of the Houses workbook, which you can find at the IDG Books Worldwide's Web site (www.idgbooks.com). You can use the House Sales page to generate the charts shown throughout this chapter, and you can duplicate the examples by opening the Houses workbook in Excel. Figure 19-9 shows the House Sales+Chart page of the Houses workbook.

After you open the workbook and move to the House Totals worksheet, follow these steps to see how easily you can create charts within Excel:

1. Click in cell A1 and drag to cell D5 to select the range that contains the house sales for all four developments for January, February, and March.

2. Choose Insert ➪ Chart. The first Chart Wizard dialog box appears (shown earlier, in Figure 19-5).

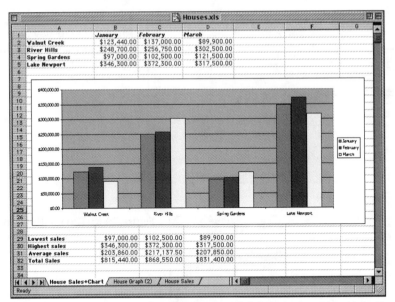

Figure 19-9: The House Sales+Chart page of the Houses workbook in Excel

3. This dialog box asks for a desired format for the chart. Leave the desired chart type selected as Column, choose the first sub-type shown in the dialog box and then click Next. In a moment, the second Chart Wizard dialog box appears (shown earlier, in Figure 19-6).

4. Because the range matches the cells that you selected in the worksheet, there's nothing to do here except to make sure that columns is selected for the series. Click Next in the dialog box to display the third Chart Wizard dialog box (shown earlier, in Figure 19-7). Click Next to accept all the default options for the chart.

5. (In this case, you insert a chart as a separate sheet; you can just as easily insert the chart onto the existing worksheet page.) In the last dialog box (shown earlier, in Figure 19-8), click As new sheet, enter **House Chart** in the text box, and then click Finish to create the chart and add it to the workbook. Your sample chart should resemble the one shown in Figure 19-10.

Saving and Printing Charts

Because charts are stored with worksheet pages, saving and printing charts is no different from saving and printing worksheets. When you save the worksheet by choosing File ➪ Save (⌘-S), the chart is saved along with the worksheet. You can print the chart by activating the page that contains the chart and choosing File ➪ Print (⌘-P). The Print dialog box that appears contains the same options you have for printing worksheets.

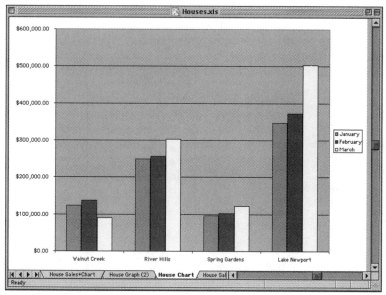

Figure 19-10: The House Chart worksheet

To print pie charts in the proper proportion to fit a single sheet of paper, first choose File ➪ Page Setup, and then click the Chart tab of the dialog box that appears. Turn on the Scale to Fit Page option.

Understanding the Parts of a Chart

Before you explore the options that Excel offers for creating charts, you should know the parts of a chart and the terminology used to describe these parts. Figure 19-11 shows the parts of a two-dimensional chart.

Three-dimensional charts have an additional axis that two-dimensional charts do not have. Three-dimensional charts also have a wall, a floor, and corners. The additional parts of a three-dimensional chart are shown in Figure 19-12.

The following parts can be found on two- and three-dimensional charts:

✦ **Chart.** The chart is the entire area contained within the chart sheet (on charts placed in separate sheets) or in the chart frame in an embedded chart.

✦ **Plot area.** The plot area contains the chart's essential data: the value axis, the category axis, and all the markers that indicate the relative values of your data.

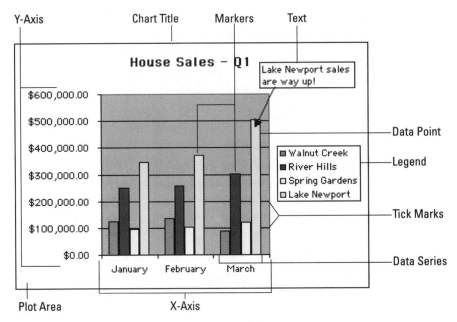

Figure 19-11: The parts of a two-dimensional chart

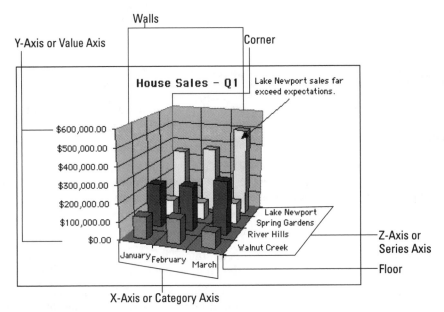

Figure 19-12: The parts of a three-dimensional chart

✦ **Markers.** Markers are the bars, lines, points, or pie wedges that represent the actual data in the chart. The form of the markers depends on the type of chart you choose. In a pie chart, the markers are wedges, or slices, of the pie. In a line chart, the markers are solid lines; although at some sharp angles, the lines may appear jagged or broken due to the limitations of screen resolution. In a column chart, such as the one shown earlier in Figure 19-11, the markers appear as columns.

Note Each set of markers in the chart represents a set of values within the worksheet. The set of values represented by the markers is referred to as a data series. If a chart displays data from more than one data series, then a different pattern or symbol represents each data series. In Figure 19-12, for example, the Walnut Creek data is one data series, and the River Hills data is another. Data series are further differentiated by the patterns of shadings of the columns.

If you selected a range in the worksheet that contains just one row or column of data, the resulting chart contains just one data series. In a chart with a single data series, Excel takes any label in the extreme left column or top row of the selected range and automatically suggests that name as a title for the chart by default.

✦ **Chart title.** The title is a text label that Excel places as a title within the chart.

✦ **Axis.** An axis is the horizontal or vertical frame of reference that appears in all types of charts except pie charts. In two-dimensional charts, the horizontal X-axis is called the category axis because categories of data are normally plotted along this line. The vertical Y-axis is called the value axis because values are normally shown along this line. With three-dimensional charts, a diagonal series axis is added to show multiple data series within the chart.

✦ **Tick marks.** Tick marks are reference marks that separate the scales of the value axis and the categories of the category axis.

✦ **Text.** Excel lets you create text labels as titles and as data labels (associated with data points). You can have unattached, or free-floating, text that you can place anywhere in the chart.

✦ **Data series.** A data series is a collection of data points, such as one month's sales for a housing development.

✦ **Data point.** A data point is a single piece of information inside any data series. In the example shown earlier in Figure 19-11, one month's sales for a specific housing development is a single data point.

✦ **Series name.** You can assign a series name to each series of data contained within a chart. Excel automatically assigns default series names based on headings entered within your worksheets.

✦ **Gridlines.** Gridlines are reference lines that extend the tick marks across the entire area of the graph.

✦ **Legends.** A legend defines the patterns or shadings that are used by the chart markers. A legend consists of a sample of the pattern followed by the series name (or the category name, if the chart displays only one data series). If you include labels as series names in the top row or the left column of the selected worksheet range, Excel can use these names in the legend.

✦ **Arrows.** These are lines with arrowheads that can be moved and sized as desired.

Working with Charts

Excel charts are object-oriented. This means that when you need to change the appearance of an object within a chart, the easiest way to do so is to have the Chart toolbar showing where you select the desired part from the Chart Objects drop-down list and click the Format button. Almost as easy is to Control-click the object and choose the desired options from the dialog box or menu that appears. You can also double-click any part of a chart and be taken directly to the chart's formatting options. Users of older versions of Excel may notice a significant change in the ways in which you make modifications to charts. In older versions, you would double-click the chart, and Excel's menus would change to reflect specialized chart options.

Selecting parts of a chart

It's simple to change the parts of a chart. If you have the Chart toolbar showing, just select from the Chart Objects drop-down list. If you don't have the Chart tool-bar showing, you can just double-click the part to bring up the relevant dialog box, and then make the changes. Or, you can Control-click any part, and then make your choices from the object-specific shortcut list that appears. In most cases, the choices from the shortcut menu open up the same dialog box that double-clicking the object brings up, so double-clicking the chart part is the more efficient way to go. Either control-clicking or double-clicking runs into the problem, especially in crowded charts, of clicking in just the right place to get the part you want.

If, for some reason you don't want to use the mouse to select parts of your chart, you can use the arrow keys. The left-arrow and right-arrow keys first move you among items in the same class of objects (such as markers) and then from class to class (such as from the markers to the legend to the axis and so on). When you select an object, it is marked with square handles. While the object is selected, the name of the object also appears on the left side of the formula bar. Figure 19-13 shows a set of markers selected in a chart — the marker name would also be seen in the formula bar.

Working with the Chart toolbar

You can make use of the Chart toolbar to add new charts or to change existing charts. Figure 19-14 shows the Chart toolbar. If the Chart toolbar is not visible, you can bring it into view by Control-clicking any visible menu and selecting Chart or by choosing View ⇨ Toolbars ⇨ Chart. Table 19-1 describes this toolbar's buttons.

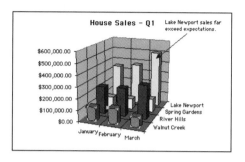

Figure 19-13: A set of markers selected in a chart

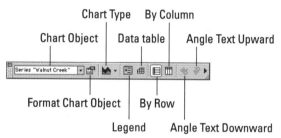

Figure 19-14: The Chart toolbar

Table 19-1	
Chart Toolbar Buttons	

Button	Function
Chart Objects	Lets you select any part of the chart by choosing it from the list box.
Format Chart Objects	Displays the Format dialog box for the object selected in the Chart Objects box.
Chart Type	Selects a chart type for the chart.
Legend	Adds or removes the legend from the chart.
Data Table	Adds a data table to the chart.
By Row	Arranges the series data by row.
By Column	Arranges the series data by column.
Angle Text Downward	Arranges selected text object downward.
Angle Text Upward	Arranges selected text object upward.

Adding titles

Text boxes containing titles are typically used with charts to help describe the purpose of the chart or to clarify the purpose of the various chart axes. You can add titles to a chart by performing the following steps:

1. Control-click the chart and select Chart Options from the shortcut menu that appears, and then click the Titles tab (see Figure 19-15).

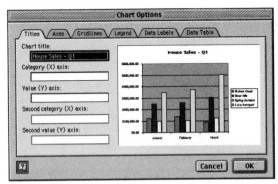

Figure 19-15: The Titles tab of the Chart Options dialog box

2. In the dialog box, shown in Figure 19-15, enter the desired titles in the text boxes and then click OK. Excel inserts text boxes for each title you add, and you can format the text by using the steps under the "Formatting text" section, later in this chapter.

Adding unattached text

At times, you may want to add text that is not attached to a title or to a specific axis. Such text is referred to as unattached text. You can add unattached text to a chart by displaying the Drawing toolbar, clicking the Text Box button, and then clicking and dragging in the chart to create a text box of the desired size. The area you drag over defines the text area. When you release the mouse, an insertion point appears in the text box, and you can type the desired text. You can always resize the text box later by dragging its handles or using any of the other text box formatting techniques described in Chapter 18.

Formatting text

With all the text you can have in text boxes, you may want to change the formatting properties — the fonts and styles used — to something other than the default text formats.

You can format the text in your charts by performing the following steps:

1. Control-click the text you want to format and choose Format Chart Title (for titles), Format Legend (for legends), or Format Text Box (for unattached text) from the shortcut menu.

   Alternatively, you can select from the Chart Objects drop-down list in the Chart toolbar and then click the Format button (its name changes dependent upon what is selected in the Chart Objects list).

2. In the dialog box that appears, click the Font tab to reveal the options shown in Figure 19-16. We chose Format Axis from the Chart Objects drop-down list box.

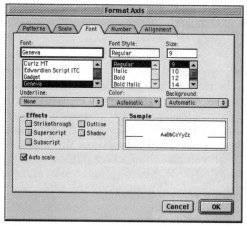

Figure 19-16: The Font tab of the Format Axis dialog box

3. Choose the desired font, font style, and font size by clicking each. You can also choose underlining, color, and background. For special text effects you can select strikethrough, superscript, subscript, outline, and/or shadow. When you are finished selecting the desired options, click OK to place them into effect.

Formatting chart axes

Excel lets you enhance the appearance of the various axes that you use in your charts. You can change the font and modify the scale. You change the format of any chart axis by choosing it in the Chart Objects drop-down list and clicking the Format button or by Control-clicking the axis that you want to format and choosing Format Axis from the shortcut menu. The Format Axis dialog box appears, as shown in Figure 19-17.

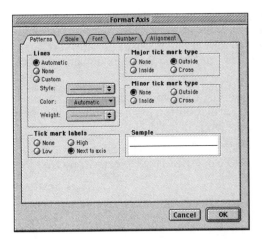

Figure 19-17: The Patterns tab of the Format Axis dialog box

The resulting dialog box contains five tabs, which you can use to change various formatting aspects of the axis. Use the options in the Patterns tab to change the patterns you use for the axis, the tick mark labels, and the types of tick marks. The Scale tab options enable you to change the values that you use to create the axis scale, where the X- and Y-axes intersect, whether units are displayed, and whether the axis uses a linear or logarithmic scale. The Font tab contains options to modify the font of the axis. The Number tab contains number formatting by category so you can choose the desired formatting for numbers along an axis, and the Alignment tab lets you choose an orientation for the text along the axis.

Adding legends

If a chart does not have a legend by default, you can add one at any time by clicking the Legend button on the Chart toolbar or by Control-clicking the chart, choosing Chart Options, clicking the Legend tab, and checking Show Legend. After you add a legend to the chart, you can change its appearance by choosing Legend from the Chart Objects drop-down list and clicking the Format button or by double-clicking the legend or by Control-clicking the Legend and choosing Format Legend from the shortcut menu. Either method brings up the Format Legend dialog box, which contains tabs for Patterns, Font, and Placement of the legend. Use the options on the Patterns tab to change the patterns the legend uses to identify the markers in the chart. The Font tab contains options to modify the legend's fonts. The Placement tab lets you specify where in the chart the legend appears (top, bottom, left, right, center, or corner). Actually, because the legend is just another object in the chart, you can also move the legend by dragging it to any desired location within the chart.

Adding gridlines

To add gridlines to an existing chart, Control-click the chart, choose Chart Options from the shortcut menu, and then select the Gridlines tab in the Chart Options dialog box that appears. In the Gridlines tab, you can choose from major and/or minor gridlines along either the category axis or the value axis. Major gridlines are heavier lines, widely spaced. Minor gridlines are fine lines, closely spaced. After you make the desired options and click OK, the gridlines appear within the selected chart.

Customizing a chart's area

You can add visual pizzazz to a chart by customizing the default settings for the chart's area. You can change the background colors, the borders, and the fonts used throughout the chart. Choose Chart Area from the Chart Options drop-down list and click the Format button, or Control-click in any blank area of the chart and choose Format Chart Area from the shortcut menu. Alternatively, click in any blank area of the chart to select the entire chart (handles appear around the entire chart), and then choose Format ⇨ Selected Chart Area (⌘-1). The Format Chart Area dialog box appears, as shown in Figure 19-18. The dialog box has multiple tabs from which you can choose all sorts of options. (If the chart is embedded, you see three tabs labeled Patterns, Font, and Properties. If the chart is on a separate sheet, you see two tabs labeled Patterns and Font.)

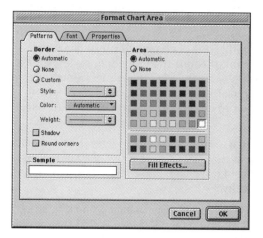

Figure 19-18: The Patterns tab of the Format Chart Area dialog box

In the Patterns tab of the Format Chart Area dialog box, you can click the Custom radio button to choose your own style, color, and weight for the border. Checking the Shadow option adds a shadow to the border and Round corners gives you Mac button-like rounded corners so your border looks less boxy. In the Area section of the Patterns tab, you can choose a background color. Selecting Automatic sets the color to the default, which is usually white. Selecting None establishes no background color. To add color, click one of the Color boxes. To add a fancier background, such as a pattern, texture, or gradient, click Fill Effects, and then choose a desired pattern or effect from the tabs in the Fill Effects dialog box.

This Font tab sets your font for the entire chart (which is overridden when you custom-select a font for a specific chart area). Choose a font, font style, and font size. Select underlining, color, and background if you want. Then select any special font effects, such as strikethrough, superscript, subscript, outline, and/or shadow.

On the Properties tab (which appears if the chart is embedded), you can select options that determine whether the chart will move and resize with the underlying cells; whether the chart should print when the worksheet prints; and whether the chart should be locked (protected against changes) if the worksheet is locked.

After you finish selecting the desired options, click OK and the chart takes on the chosen effects.

Working with chart types

Excel offers several different chart types. Each of these chart types has sub-types that you can also select. The following list describes the types of charts, and how they can best be used.

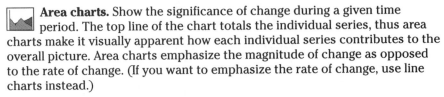 **Area charts.** Show the significance of change during a given time period. The top line of the chart totals the individual series, thus area charts make it visually apparent how each individual series contributes to the overall picture. Area charts emphasize the magnitude of change as opposed to the rate of change. (If you want to emphasize the rate of change, use line charts instead.)

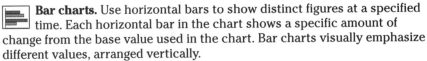 **Bar charts.** Use horizontal bars to show distinct figures at a specified time. Each horizontal bar in the chart shows a specific amount of change from the base value used in the chart. Bar charts visually emphasize different values, arranged vertically.

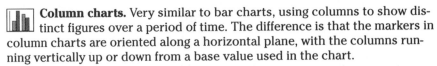 **Column charts.** Very similar to bar charts, using columns to show distinct figures over a period of time. The difference is that the markers in column charts are oriented along a horizontal plane, with the columns running vertically up or down from a base value used in the chart.

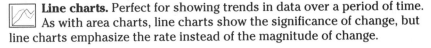 **Line charts.** Perfect for showing trends in data over a period of time. As with area charts, line charts show the significance of change, but line charts emphasize the rate instead of the magnitude of change.

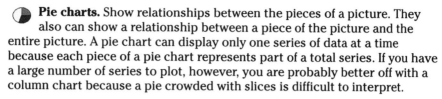

Pie charts. Show relationships between the pieces of a picture. They also can show a relationship between a piece of the picture and the entire picture. A pie chart can display only one series of data at a time because each piece of a pie chart represents part of a total series. If you have a large number of series to plot, however, you are probably better off with a column chart because a pie crowded with slices is difficult to interpret.

Doughnut charts. Show relationships between pieces of a picture, as do pie charts. The difference is that the doughnut chart has a hollow center.

Radar charts. Show the changes or frequencies of a data series in relation to a central point and to each other. (Every category has an axis value that radiates from a center point. Lines connect all data in the same series.) Radar charts can be difficult to interpret, unless you're accustomed to working with them.

(XY) Scatter charts. Show relationships between different points of data, to compare trends across uneven time periods, or to show patterns as a set of X and Y coordinates. These charts are commonly used to plot scientific data.

Surface charts. Show trends in values across two dimensions in a continuous curve.

Bubble charts. Compare sets of three values. In appearance, these are similar to scatter charts, with the third value interpreted by the size of the bubbles.

Stock charts. Also known as open-hi-lo-close charts. They are used to display the day-to-day values of stocks, commodities, or other financial market data. Stock charts require series containing four values to plot the four points (open, high, low, and close).

Cylinder charts. Column charts with the columns appearing as cylindrical shapes.

Cone charts. Column charts with the columns appearing as cone shapes.

Pyramid charts. Column charts with the columns appearing as pyramid shapes.

An important decision for you to make is which type of chart will work best to get the desired point across. Excel offers the 14 different chart types described earlier. All the available chart types can be two-dimensional, and nine of the available chart types can be three-dimensional. When you create a chart by using the Chart Wizard, Excel asks you which chart type you want to use.

You also may want to change the chart type of an existing chart. Follow these steps when you want to change the type of an existing chart:

1. Control-click in an empty space on the chart and choose Chart Type from the shortcut menu. Or, if you prefer not to Control-click, select the chart and choose Chart ⇨ Chart Type. Either way, the Chart Type dialog box appears, as shown in Figure 19-19.

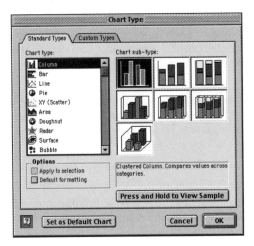

Figure 19-19: The Standard Types tab of the Chart Type dialog box

2. In the Chart type list at the left, choose the desired chart type.

3. In the Chart sub-type area at the right, choose a desired sub-type. To preview the sub-type, click the button that aptly says Press and Hold to View Sample.

4. After you have made your final type and sub-type selection, click OK.

The exact appearance of the sub-type pane will vary, depending on which type you select. Figure 19-20 shows the available sub-types that appear when you choose a pie chart.

In the Chart Type dialog box shown in Figure 19-20, note the presence of the Apply to selection option in the lower-left corner. By default, the chart type you've selected applies to the entire chart. If you select a single data series before selecting the Chart Type command, you will have the option of applying the chart type to the selected data series as opposed to the entire chart.

Tip   You can create combination charts of your own by applying different chart types to different data series. You can also use the Chart Wizard to select a Combination chart type, but you gain more flexibility by selecting each series and applying the types individually.

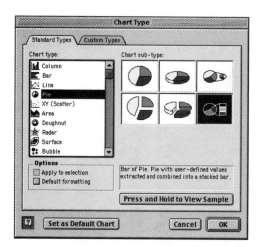

Figure 19-20: The available sub-types for a pie chart

If you need to change the type of chart but not the chart sub-type, you can also use the Chart toolbar. To display the Chart toolbar, Control-click a visible toolbar and select Chart, or choose View ➪ Toolbars ➪ Chart. Click the Chart Type arrow button to pop up a palette of chart types, and then click a chart type in the palette. This palette may be torn off to float and be available separately. If you select an individual data series before using the Chart Type list box in the Chart toolbar, your selection is applied to the individual data series.

How Excel plots a chart

When you select a group of cells and create a new chart, Excel follows specific steps to plot the chart. It first organizes the values contained within the selected range into a data series, based on the responses that you gave in the Chart Wizard dialog boxes. Then it plots the data series in the chart.

As an example, consider the chart shown in Figure 19-21. In this chart, the blue markers are based on one series of data, the sales for January. The red (darker) markers are based on another series of data, the sales for February. The yellow (lightest) markers represent March sales. In the same chart, dollar amounts are plotted along the value (Y) axis, and subdivision names are plotted along the category (X) axis. The chart values appear as dollars because the worksheet values are formatted in dollars. Excel obtains the category axis labels from cells A2 through A5 of the worksheet shown earlier in Figure 19-9, which contains the names of the subdivisions.

The chart shown in Figure 19-21 is actually the same chart that you created earlier (which is the one in Figure 19-10). If it isn't still open, either open it or replot the chart. (Select cells A1 through D5 in the House Totals worksheet. Then choose Insert ➪ Chart. Click Finish in the first Chart Wizard dialog box to accept the default options.)

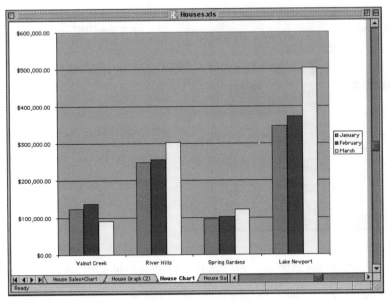

Figure 19-21: A chart based on three data series

The exact points that Excel uses to graph the data are contained in a series formula that Excel builds for you. A series formula is similar to other formulas in that you can edit it from within the formula bar. To see the formula, select the chart marker by clicking the desired group of markers (or by pressing the left- or right-arrow key until the group is selected). Selecting one marker selects all the markers in that group. When you select a group of markers, Excel places small rectangles inside them.

As an exercise, select the markers representing January by clicking any of the markers for January. When the markers are selected, the series formula appears in the formula bar, as shown in Figure 19-22.

Excel uses a special function called the series function to build the data series for each set of markers in the chart. If you click the second set of markers in the chart, the series formula in the formula bar changes to reflect the points that Excel uses for the second data series.

Tip Excel can use named ranges from a worksheet rather than absolute cell references. If you create a chart that uses absolute references and later insert rows or columns in the worksheet so the data referred to by the chart is no longer in the same location, the chart will be unable to plot the data. The result will be a chart with zero values, or, even worse, incorrect data. If you use named ranges in the series formula for the chart, Excel can find the data even if you insert rows or columns in the worksheet.

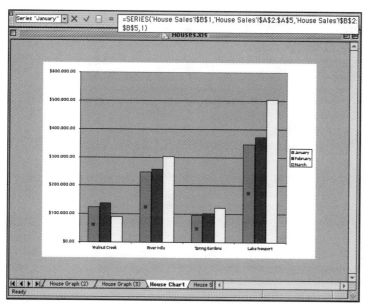

Figure 19-22: The series formula for January sales

It is important to understand how Excel builds a chart automatically because, in some cases, Excel's assumptions may not be what you want, and you can make changes to adjust for those assumptions. For example, when you tell Excel to create a chart and you accept the default entries regarding the data series in the Chart Wizard dialog boxes, Excel plots the data based on certain default assumptions. One significant decision that Excel makes is whether a data series should be based on the contents of rows or columns. Excel assumes that a chart should contain fewer data series than data points within each series. When you tell Excel to create the chart, Excel examines your selected range of cells. If the selected range is wider than it is tall, Excel organizes the data series based on the contents of rows. On the other hand, if the selected range is taller than it is wide, Excel organizes the data series based on the contents of the columns. If the selection is square, Excel will default to rows.

To illustrate this operation, consider the worksheet shown in Figure 19-23. In this example, the selected range of cells to be plotted is wider than it is tall. With this type of selection, Excel uses any text found in the left-most columns as series names. Text labels in the top row are used as categories, and each row becomes a data series in the chart.

On the other hand, if the selected range is taller than it is wide and you accept the default Chart Wizard options, Excel orients the chart differently. In such cases, the text in the top row is used as the series names, text entries appearing in the left columns are used as categories, and each column becomes a data series. This type of worksheet, and the chart resulting from it, is shown in Figure 19-24.

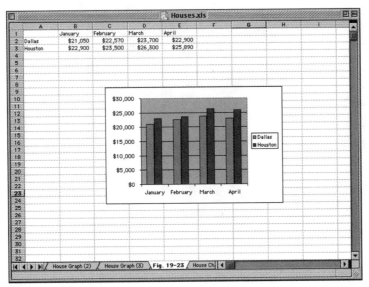

Figure 19-23: A row-oriented chart

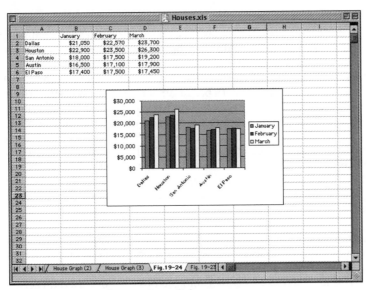

Figure 19-24: A column-oriented chart

You can change the method Excel uses to plot the data series by changing the selection in the Data Range tab of the second Chart Wizard dialog box. With an existing chart, make the chart active. (If it's embedded, click the chart; if it's a sheet, make it the active worksheet.) Then click the Chart Wizard button on the Chart toolbar to bring up the Chart Wizard dialog box. After you click Next to bypass the first dialog box, you can change the data series in the Data Range tab by choosing Series in Rows or Series in Columns.

Summary

In this chapter, you learned how to create charts, how to change the appearance and the basis for the charts, and how to add such items as titles, legends, and text to your charts. The following points were covered:

✦ You can add a chart as an embedded chart (included in an existing worksheet page) or as a chart sheet (included on its own worksheet page).

✦ You can easily add charts to a worksheet by selecting the range of data and selecting Insert ➪ Chart, or by clicking the Chart Wizard button on the Standard toolbar. In each case, you can accept or decline help from the Office Assistant, and then follow the instructions in the Chart Wizard dialog boxes.

✦ You can modify most aspects of a chart by double-clicking a specific area or object in the chart to bring up the appropriate dialog box. You can also Control-click, and then choose the appropriate format command from the shortcut menu that appears. Finally, you can use the Chart toolbar and select the object you wish from the Chart Objects drop-down list, and then click the Format button.

Where to go next

✦ In the next chapter, you learn about the various printing options in Excel, which provide you with different ways to produce your work.

✦ You may want to embellish your charts by adding graphics, such as clip art or callouts. For tips on working with graphics, see Chapter 18.

✦   ✦   ✦

Printing and Page Setup

As with word processing, you have full control over various aspects of printing that affect the appearance of a worksheet, such as margins, page orientation, horizontal and vertical alignment, and the use of headers and footers. You can print entire workbooks, individual sheets from a workbook, or a section in a worksheet. As with any Mac application, the print command is File ➪ Print (⌘-P). As with the other Office applications, Excel also provides a Print button on the Standard toolbar.

Learning Printing Basics

Printing the active page of a worksheet is the most common event, so Excel makes it the default. Printing is as simple as choosing File ➪ Print, or clicking the Print button and then clicking Print (or pressing Return or Enter).

Printing worksheets

To print, follow these steps:

1. To print all the data in one full worksheet, make that worksheet active.

    To print only a portion of a worksheet, select the area you want to print.

    To print multiple worksheets within a workbook, select the worksheets by pressing ⌘ (Command) as you click each desired tab. (If you select a worksheet in error, press ⌘ and click again on its tab to deselect that tab.)

2. Choose File ⇨ Print (⌘-P) to open the Print dialog box, as shown in Figure 20-1. (Depending on your printer and printer software version, your dialog box may look slightly different. Your system and the printer driver you've chosen determine this dialog box, not Excel. We're using the LaserWriter 8 driver, which is shipped as part of Mac OS 9.)

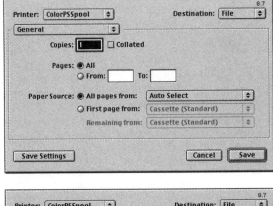

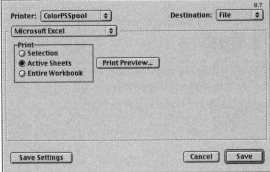

Figure 20-1: *Top:* the Print dialog box's main screen. *Bottom:* the Excel options screen.

3. The default prints all of the data in the current worksheet. If this is your intention, skip to Step 4.

To print a specific selection of the worksheet, or to print more worksheets within the workbook, select the Microsoft Excel options from the pop-up menu at the top of the dialog box. Then select the appropriate radio button (Selection, Active Sheets, or Entire Workbook) in the Excel options dialog box. (Note that if you have a chart selected, the only option is to print Selected Chart.)

To see a preview of what will be printed, click the Preview button. Use the forward and backward arrows to see the entire preview.

4. Click Print to begin printing.

You can also print multiple selections from your spreadsheet or even print selections from several pages, all with one issue of the print command. To do so, utilize the Sheet tab of the Page Setup dialog box. To learn how, see "Setting Print Ranges" later in this chapter.

About the Print dialog box

When you select File ⇨ Print, you call up the standard Mac Print dialog box. The first piece of information in the Print dialog box is the name of the printer you currently have selected in the Chooser or with your Desktop Printer. If you don't see the correct printer named there, click Cancel, select the correct printer, and issue the print command (⌘-P) again. The Destination reported should also say Printer if you are going directly to the printer, or File if (like us) you're creating a PostScript or PDF file for later printing. The next pop-up menu most likely says General. This is the default, common LaserWriter print dialog page.

Your first decision is to set the number of copies (of each page) that you want to print. By default, a 1 appears in that box, so one copy will print. To print one copy, leave it set at the default. Notice the Copies box is preselected. To print more than one copy, just type the new number. This is the same as any printing done on the Mac.

The Pages area looks the same as any Print dialog box on the Mac, with one difference. Rather than determining which pages of your entire document will print, this area only affects the current worksheet. The All option (default) prints all of the pages of the current worksheet. The From and To boxes tell Excel which pages of the current worksheet to print. For example, if a worksheet produces a 12-page printout and you need only Pages 4 through 8, you can enter 4 in the From box and 8 in the To box. As a shortcut, if you want to begin printing from Page 1, you can leave the From box blank and only enter the last page you want to print in the To box. The same works in reverse, so you can leave the To box blank if you want to print from a specific page to the last page.

In the Paper Source area, you tell the printer which paper trays you print from: the main tray, a secondary tray (if you have one), or the manual feed. Often, you don't have to do anything here because the default, Auto Select, prints from the main tray. To use a different paper or an envelope, you can place it in the manual feed tray and select Manual Feed from the pop-up. If your printer has an extra print tray, you would keep another commonly used paper there and select that tray from the pop-up menu as needed. You can also print the first page from one tray and the remainder from another tray. To do so, click the First page from button, and then, in that pop-up, select the tray containing the paper on which you want the first page printed (if it is to be hand-fed, choose Manual Feed). In the pop-up menu below, Remaining from, select the tray that holds the rest of the sheets.

If you want to print only a portion of your current worksheet, or print multiple pages of your worksheet, your next visit is to the Excel-specific options page of the Print dialog box. If you have preselected a portion of your current worksheet and only want to print that area, click the radio button next to Selection. If you have preselected more than one worksheet and want to print all of the sheets you've selected, click the radio button by Active Sheets. To print the entire workbook, select Entire Workbook.

Tip   You can also designate a portion of your worksheet as the *Print Area* by choosing File ⇨ Print Area ⇨ Set Print Area after selecting the cells that you want to make the print area for this sheet. This print area remains the print area for your worksheet in this and subsequent sessions, until you choose File ⇨ Print Area ⇨ Clear Print Area.

At times you may want to save paper by printing smaller versions of your worksheet pages; that is, by printing two or more worksheet pages per paper page. To do so, select the Layout page from the pop-up menu at the top of your dialog box. Here you can select the number of pages per page to print and also, optionally, place a border around each page.

The Print dialog box has more standard Mac printing options. You can explore them by selecting the various options pages from the pop-up menu from which you selected Microsoft Excel or Layout.

Setting Up Your Pages

You have several ways to customize the look of your printed page. You can set margins, add headers and footers, print gridlines, turn column and row headings on or off, scale your pages, change the print orientation and more. All of these page-printing decisions are Page Setup commands.

Select File ⇨ Page Setup to access the Page Setup dialog box. This dialog box, shown in Figure 20-2, contains four tabs: Page, Margins, Header/Footer, and Sheet. In addition to the tabs, the dialog box contains Print and Print Preview buttons. After making the desired changes to the settings, you can click the Print button to begin printing or the Print Preview button to see the worksheet in Print Preview mode. Here's a description of each of the four tabs:

✦ **Page tab.** The first tab in the Page Setup dialog box is the Page tab (see Figure 20-2). In this tab, you control print-related settings that affect all the pages of your print job such as page orientation, scaling, paper size, and print quality. This section looks at the printing controls found on the Page tab or the Page Setup dialog box. Clicking the Options button in this tab will present your printer's Page Setup dialog box.

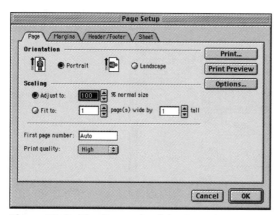

Figure 20-2: The Page tab of the Page Setup dialog box

✦ **Margins tab.** Margins, as you probably know, are the white or unprinted area of each page. In Excel, you set the margins similarly to the way you set them in a word processing program. However, the setting dialog box looks different than it does in a program such as Word (see Figure 20-3).

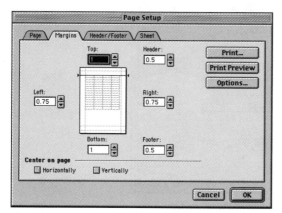

Figure 20-3: The Margins tab of the Page Setup dialog box

✦ **Header/Footer tab.** The Header/Footer tab's options control the appearance and placement of headers and footers printed on your worksheet pages. If you click the Header/Footer tab of the Page Setup dialog box, you see the options shown in Figure 20-4.

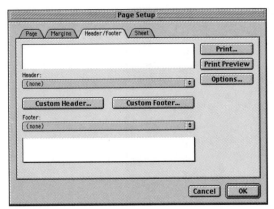

Figure 20-4: The Header/Footer tab of the Page Setup dialog box

✦ **Sheet tab.** The Sheet tab's options control various print-related settings that affect individual worksheets. If you click the Sheet tab of the Page Setup dialog box, you see the options shown in Figure 20-5.

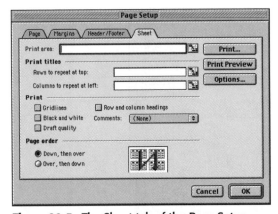

Figure 20-5: The Sheet tab of the Page Setup dialog box

Each of the options available in these tabs is explained in detail in the sections that follow.

Paper size

One of the most basic print choices is the paper size to which you print. The default paper size is Letter size (8.5 × 11 inches). To change the paper size, select

File ➪ Page Setup, and then click the Options button. This takes you to a printer setup dialog box. In the pop-up menu next to the word Paper, select the desired paper size.

Orientation

Orientation is the direction in which text is printed across the paper. Most text documents such as letters are printed so they are taller up and down, which is called a Portrait orientation. Think of a photograph: a portrait is taller than it is wide, whereas a picture of a beautiful mountain scene is wider than it is tall. So it goes with printing: portrait orientation prints lengthwise (like the pages of this book), whereas landscape orientation prints widthwise. If your spreadsheet has a lot of columns, you are likely to want to print across the width of the paper in order to fit more of the columns on one page.

Changing the orientation in which your document will print is very easy. On the Page tab or the Page Setup dialog box (File ➪ Page Setup), simply click the radio button for Portrait or Landscape orientation.

Scaling

Scaling enables you to reduce or enlarge your worksheets. This is useful for making a worksheet that is slightly too big for a page fit on a single page. You can choose a specific percentage to scale to, or you can try to force the spreadsheet data to fit a specific number of pages. Scaling is set on the Page tab or the Page Setup dialog box (File ➪ Page Setup).

To choose a specific percentage, enter a number smaller or larger than 100 in the Adjust to box or use the arrows next to the box to select a larger or smaller number. To take the other approach, use the Fit to option to fit the printed worksheet to a specific number of pages wide by a specific number of pages tall. Enter the dimensions, by pages, in the boxes to the right of the option, or use the up and down arrows to arrive at your desired number.

What Happened to the Sheet Tab?

Have you selected File ➪ Page Setup and seen the Page, Margins, and Header/Footer tabs but found a Chart tab where you expected the Sheet tab to be? Confusing, isn't it? This happens when you have a chart selected in your worksheet when you select File ➪ Page Setup.

To get the Sheet tab back, close the Page Setup dialog box. In your worksheet, deselect the chart by clicking an empty cell, and then select File ➪ Page Setup again.

First page number

As is common in documents, Excel assumes that the page number of the first page to be printed is 1. This is the number assumed by the Auto default, located on the Page tab of the Page Setup dialog box (File ➪ Page Setup). You can start page numbering at any page number by selecting the word Auto and entering any page number in its place.

Print quality

By default the Print Quality for your document is set to high. There may be no reason for you to change this but you can set the level if you want. The higher the setting, the nicer the appearance. If your printer prints at 600 dots per inch (dpi), keep the default high as the print setting. If your printer is only capable of printing at 300 dpi, you can choose 300 dpi without seeing any difference. A lower dpi may speed up printing but may affect the quality of the printed output. To set Print Quality, select File ➪ Page Setup, and then the Page tab of the Page Setup dialog box.

Another print quality option also exists, which is to print in draft quality. This mode ignores most formatting and graphics. To do so, select File ➪ Page Setup, and then the Sheet tab. Then simply check the box by the Draft quality option.

Another somewhat related print setting is the choice to print only in black and white. Without this option selected on a black-and-white printer, colors are printed in shades of gray. When this option is selected, no shades of gray exist; color fonts and borders print in black instead.

Margins

Margins are the distance from each edge of the paper to where printing begins. The amount of space you leave between your text and the paper's edge has a great visual impact. You'll need to balance the need for white space and the need to fit all your data on the page(s). Three margin controls are described here. (You can refer back to Figure 20-3 to see these controls.)

> ✦ **Top, Bottom, Left, and Right.** You can set each margin independent of the others. Use the Top, Bottom, Left, and Right options to specify a distance from the edge of the paper for its respective margin. Note that many printers will not print closer than 0.5 inches from the edge of the paper; however, with some laser printers and inkjet printers, you can go down to 0.3 inches.
>
> ✦ **Header and Footer.** The Header and Footer settings determine how far headers or footers print from the top or bottom edges. By default, the header begins 0.5 inches from the top of the page and extends down as low as it must to accommodate your header text. Similarly, the footer begins 0.5 inches from the bottom of the page and extends up as high as it must to accommodate your footer text.

✦ **Center on Page.** The Center on Page option determines whether printing should be centered horizontally (between the left and right margins) and/or vertically (between the top and bottom margins) on the page.

You can also modify the margins of your document visually while in Print Preview mode. See the Print Preview section for details.

Headers and footers

Excel lets you place headers and footers in a worksheet or workbook when you print. A header, for example, might be a title that appears at the top of every page. A footer appears at the bottom of every page and might include a page number or the current date. Adding headers and footers is relatively simple and painless. They can be very effective in giving a document a more refined and professional look.

To add a header or footer to a worksheet, follow these steps:

1. Choose File ➪ Page Setup.

2. Choose the Header/Footer tab from the Page Setup dialog box (refer back to Figure 20-4).

3. In this tab, you can select a header or footer, or create a custom header or footer. One pop-up menu contains several headers from which you can choose, while the other contains footers. Several generic choices are available by default, such as combinations that include your name and page information. If you have titled the tab of your worksheet, it will appear in the list as a choice for a header or footer. If you want more control over your header or footer, you can create your own.

   To add a custom header or footer to your worksheet, click the corresponding Custom button: Custom Header or Custom Footer.

4. In the next dialog box, enter the header or footer text. The Header dialog box is pictured in Figure 20-6.

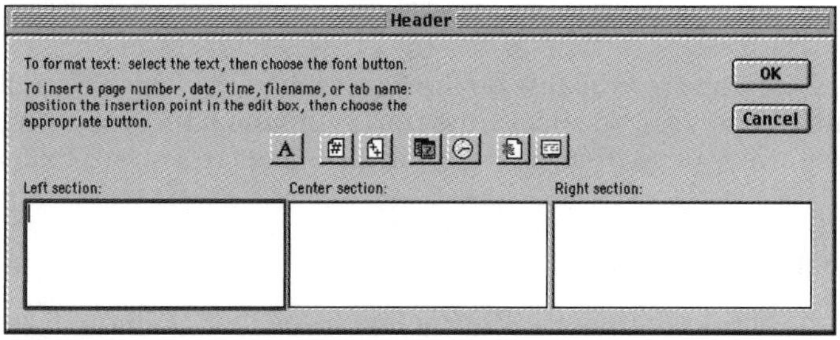

Figure 20-6: The Header dialog box

5. In the Left Section, Center Section, or Right Section portion of the dialog box, enter the desired header or footer text. Use the buttons in the dialog box to add items, insert page numbers, insert the date or time, or change the font.

Table 20-1 explains the custom header and footer buttons that appear in the dialog box after you click either the Custom Header or Custom Footer button on the Header/Footer tab.

6. Click OK.

Table 20-1
Header/Footer Buttons and Their Functions

Button	Function
Font	Opens the Font dialog box from which you can change the header or footer's font.
Page Number	Inserts the page number.
Total Pages	Inserts the total number of pages in the active worksheet.
Date	Inserts the system date.
Time	Inserts the system time.
Filename	Inserts the active workbook's filename.
Sheet Name	Inserts the active worksheet's name.

Print titles

Titles are the words you place in a row or column to identify the content of the rows or columns to follow. Printing the titles on every page of your printout makes it easier to read, particularly in a long worksheet. If you don't select any titles to print, and a column or row carries on to a second or third page, your readers won't have any heading to know what the numbers refer to. Print titles lets your headings repeat on all secondary pages.

The Print titles options are available on the Sheet tab of the Page Setup dialog box. In the Print titles area, you can specify the row(s) or column(s) you would like to see repeated on every page. To print a title on each page of a sheet, follow these steps:

1. Choose File ⇨ Page Setup.

2. Choose the Sheet tab from the Page Setup dialog box. (Refer to Figure 20-5 for an image of this tab.)

3. Place the insertion point in the Rows to repeat at top text box or the Columns to repeat at left text box.

4. Click the worksheet and drag to select the rows or columns that you want to repeat. You may have to move the dialog box if it covers the cells you need to select. (Remember that multiple rows and columns must be adjacent.)

5. Click OK.

If you change your mind and want to delete the entries that you have made as titles, simply return to the Sheet tab of the Page Setup dialog box and delete the cell references from the Rows to repeat at top and Columns to repeat at left text boxes.

Row and column headings

In addition to printing titles, you may want to print the row and column headings, which are the letters that identify the columns and the numbers that identify the rows. By default these headings don't print. If you prefer that they do print, you can turn them on. Select File ➪ Page Setup, and select the Sheet tab. Then simply check the box by the Row and column headings option.

Printing gridlines

By default the gridlines you see onscreen don't print on paper. However, if you prefer, you can turn them on so they do print. Select File ➪ Page Setup, and select the Sheet tab. Then simply check the box by the Gridlines option.

Printing comments

At times it may be helpful to have your comments appear in print. You have two such options: that comments print at the end of your document or that they print where they actually appear on your worksheet. Either way, to have comments print, select File ➪ Page Setup, and select the Sheet tab. Then choose your option from the pop-up list next to the Comments label.

Setting Print Ranges

When you tell Excel to print a worksheet, it prints the entire worksheet unless you tell it otherwise. When you want to print a specific portion of a worksheet, you first need to tell Excel what area of the worksheet you want printed. If you only want to print one area of cells from one worksheet you have two choices. The first way is described at the beginning of this chapter in the section on the basics of printing.

The second option is to specify the portion of the worksheet by choosing File ➪ Page Setup and using the Print Area option of the Sheet tab. This method also enables you to select multiple ranges to print at the same time.

To define one print range using the second method, follow these steps:

1. Choose File ➪ Page Setup. In the Page Setup dialog box that appears, click the Sheet tab.

2. Click in the Print Area text box to place the insertion pointer there.

3. Click your worksheet and select the range of cells that you want to print. When you click in the worksheet, the dialog box is reduced to this single field so you can see the selection you need to make. As you select the range, a dotted line appears around it and the coordinates for the range appear in the Print Area text box. When you release the mouse after making your selection, the entire Page Setup dialog box reappears.

   In case you're wondering, the Print Area text box is blank by default. When it's blank, you print all cells up to the last cell at the bottom-right corner that contains data in the current sheet.

4. While in the Page Setup dialog box, you can continue to set the other page setup options. If you are ready to print, you can click the Print button from the Page Setup dialog box.

You can also print multiple selections from your spreadsheet with one print command. Each range is printed on its own sheet and each can be printed with titles. Printing multiple worksheet page ranges is similar to setting a print range as in the preceding section. To set multiple print ranges, follow these steps (which are similar to Steps 1 to 3 of printing a print range):

1. Choose File ➪ Page Setup to open the Page Setup dialog box and select the Sheet tab as shown in Figure 20-5.

2. Click in the Print Area box to place the insertion pointer there.

3. In the document, click and drag to select the first range you want to print. When you click in the worksheet, the dialog box is reduced to this single field so you can see the selection you need to make. As you select the range, a dotted line appears around it, and the coordinates for the range appear in the Print Area text box. When you release the mouse after making your selection, the entire Page Setup dialog box reappears and your insertion pointer is once again in the Print Area text box.

4. Enter a colon in the Print Area text box.

5. Click in the document and select the next area you want to print. Again, the dialog box is reduced while you make your selection, and you are returned to the Print Area text box when you release the mouse.

6. Repeat Steps 4 and 5 until you select all the areas that you want to print. The areas are printed in the order that you selected them, and they are printed on separate pages.

Whether printing one range or several, to cancel the effects of the selection and return to printing the complete worksheet, return to File ➪ Page Setup, click the Sheet tab, delete the coordinates of the selected range, and click OK.

Setting a Page Order

You can specify whether printing of multiple-page worksheets should occur from top to bottom and then from left to right, or from left to right and then from top to bottom. To do so select File ➪ Page Setup, select the Sheet tab, and click the desired radio button at the bottom of the dialog box. A diagram shows you the result of your choice.

This page order affects page numbering. If you print downward first, Page 2 is the page that falls below Page 1 (the top-left page). If you print across first, Page 2 is the page to the right of Page 1.

Previewing Print Jobs

By previewing your work before you print, you can see how your layout looks and make any changes before wasting paper. In addition, by using the preview's Zoom feature, you can take a closer look at the document and its contents.

To preview a worksheet, choose File ➪ Print Preview, or click the Print Preview button on the Standard toolbar. Figure 20-7 shows an example of a document in Print Preview mode. From Print Preview mode, you can also access the Page Setup dialog box to make modifications as needed. Conversely, you can access Print Preview from the Page Setup dialog box.

You can modify the margins of your document in Print Preview by clicking the Margins button at the top of the screen. Clicking the Margins button activates the "margin grid" (see Figure 20-8). The margin lines can be moved using the mouse. The margin grid feature is helpful because it lets you see the document as it is being adjusted, and you can see whether the document will fit on a single page. Setting margins in Print Preview is easier if you use the Zoom feature so you can see the page in better detail. Click the Zoom button at the top of the Print Preview window to move in closer for detail.

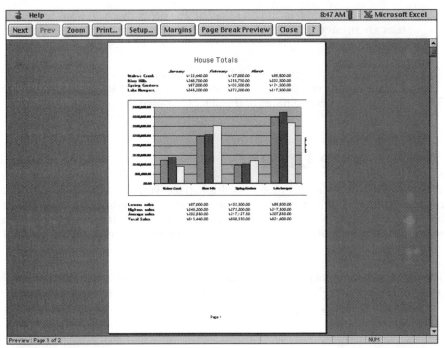

Figure 20-7: Excel's Print Preview mode

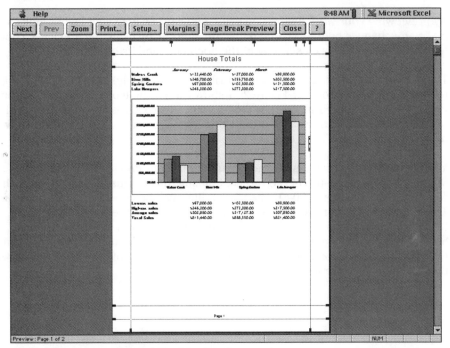

Figure 20-8: The margin grid in Print Preview mode

Controlling Page Breaks

Sometimes automatic page breaks, which are based on paper size, margins, and other settings in the Page Setup dialog box, come at inconvenient places, especially in larger worksheets. When a page breaks at a bad location, you can fix the break by inserting a manual page break. Manual page breaks are especially useful when you want to print one section per page. To insert manual page breaks, follow these steps:

1. In your worksheet, place the insertion point below and to the right of the place where you want to insert the page break.

2. Choose Insert ⇨ Page Break. The page break appears onscreen and is indicated by lines with dashes.

The page breaks you insert remain in the same location until you remove them. The automatic page breaks are also repositioned after the insertion of a manual page break. If you want to remove a page break you have inserted, return to the cell in which you entered the page break and choose Insert ⇨ Remove Page Break. You can also select the entire document and choose Insert ⇨ Remove Page Break to remove all manual page breaks in the worksheet.

You can also set page breaks horizontally and vertically. To do so, select the column or row where you want the page break to appear and click in its header. Next choose Insert ⇨ Page Break. The page break is set horizontally or vertically as you specified.

Tip At times you will want to view your manual page breaks. These page breaks can be difficult to see, though, because of the gridlines in your worksheet. To turn off the gridlines so you can see the manual page breaks, choose Edit ⇨ Preferences. Click the View tab and uncheck the Gridlines checkbox. Then click OK to remove the gridlines.

E-mailing a File

Excel makes it simple to e-mail your workbook. To send a workbook over the network by e-mail, follow these steps:

1. Open the workbook you want to send.

2. Select File ⇨ Send To ⇨ Mail Recipient. This opens your designated default e-mail program, probably Entourage (which comes with Office 2001), or Outlook Express, Claris Emailer, or Eudora. A new e-mail document is started and your workbook is automatically attached to the new e-mail. Figure 20-9 depicts a spreadsheet called Houses that is attached to e-mail and ready to be sent.

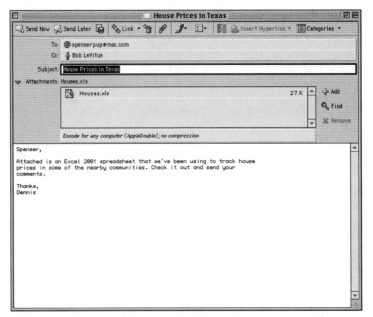

Figure 20-9: A spreadsheet attached to an Entourage e-mail document

3. Proceed to complete your message as normal by entering a recipient and writing a note. When done, send your message as normal.

Summary

This chapter detailed the features that Excel offers to help you get your facts and figures on paper. The chapter discussed these points:

✦ You can print a selected area of the current worksheet, selected sheets, or the entire workbook by choosing File ➪ Print (⌘-P).

✦ By choosing File ➪ Page Setup, you reveal the Page Setup dialog box, which lets you change various settings for printing, such as orientation, paper size, margins, headers, and footers.

✦ Excel's Print Preview feature can be very useful in helping find errors in a document's layout before printing occurs.

✦ You can use the File ➪ Send To command to e-mail your workbook within your current e-mail program's capabilities.

Where to go next

✦ The next chapter explains how to create and work with databases in Excel.

✦ If you find yourself doing a lot of repetitive printing on a regular basis, you'll want to automate your printing by putting the power of macros to work. Chapter 22 tells you how.

✦ Your document's printed appearance is greatly affected by how you format it. Formatting specifics are covered in Chapter 17.

✦ To find out more about using Entourage to send e-mail, see Chapter 35.

✦   ✦   ✦

Working with Excel Database Lists

This chapter details the use of databases (also called lists) that are stored in Excel worksheets. Whether or not you were aware of it at the time, you have probably used databases on numerous occasions. Any time you reference a list of business contacts, or a Rolodex file, or something as familiar as the Yellow Pages, you are working with a database. You can use Excel to manage data in a database, and this chapter shows you how.

Learning About Databases

A database is any system in which information is cataloged, stored, and used; that is, a collection of related information that is stored as a single item. Figure 21-1 shows an example of a simple database. Metal filing cabinets containing customer records, a card file of names and telephone numbers, and even a notebook filled with a handwritten list of store inventory are all databases. The physical container — the filing cabinet or the notebook, for example — is not the database. The database is the contents of the container and the way the information is organized. Objects such as cabinets and notebooks are only tools for organizing information. Excel is one such tool for storing information.

Information in a database is usually organized and stored in a table by rows and columns. Figure 21-1, for example, is an employee list in database form. Each row contains a name, a job title, and an extension. Because the list is a collection of information arranged in a specific order it is a database.

	A	B	C	D	E
	First Name	Last Name	Job Title	Extension	
1		Employee Information Database			
3	First Name	Last Name	Job Title	Extension	
4	Allison	Labrador	Soccer Coach	0350	
5	Jacob	Labrador	Soccer Coach	0351	
6	Dexter	Collie	Mac Support	0352	
7	Alma	Poodle	Mac Support	0353	
8	Ricky	Poodle	Art Director	0354	
9	Alfredo	Poodle	Mac Support	0355	
10	Elysa	Shepherd	Social Director	0356	
11	Shira	Shepherd	Basketball Coach	0357	
12	Corinne	Corgi	Teacher	0358	
13	Alex	Corgi	Fireman	0359	
14	Caleb	Pinscher	PC Support	0360	
15	Naomi	Boxer	Orchestra Leader	0361	
16	Rachael	Boxer	Orchestra Leader	0362	
17	Spenser	Boston-Terrier	Mascot	0363	

Figure 21-1: A typical database in Excel

Rows in a database file are called records, and columns are called fields. Figure 21-2 illustrates this idea by showing an address filing system kept on file cards. Each card in the box is a single record, and each category of information on that card is a field. Fields can contain any type of information that can be categorized. In the card box, each record contains five fields: name, address, city, state, and zip code. Because every card in the box contains the same type of information, the information in the card box is a database.

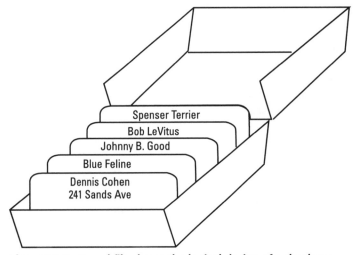

Figure 21-2: A card file shows the logical design of a database.

In Excel, you design a database by following this row-and-column analogy: each column of the spreadsheet contains a different field and each row contains an additional record. Data is organized by devoting a specific column to each specific category (field) of data. You must enter each specific chunk of data in a separate cell of the worksheet. For example, in the worksheet shown in Figure 21-1, a person's first name goes into a cell of the First Name column, the person's last name goes into a cell of the Last Name column, and so on. You begin the design of any database by placing the cursor at the top of the worksheet and entering labels for the names of your fields in successive columns.

Introducing the List Manager

Microsoft's surveys indicated that almost 60 percent of its users' worksheets are simple lists: customer information, compact disc and video collections, inventories, and so forth. To cater to that portion of its market, Microsoft added a new List Manager to assist in the organizing, formatting, sorting, filtering, summarizing, and printing of the lists.

Although you can do anything with your data manually that you can do with the List Manager, doing it manually is usually more work and requires you to remember more details. During the remainder of this chapter, we work on the assumption that you're using the List Manager to manage your data, but we'll also tell you what you need to do to obtain the same results without the List Manager. This will enable you to decide for yourself which approach is more appropriate for the task at hand.

Fortunately, using the List Manager versus using traditional methods is not an irrevocable choice—you can switch between the two states easily. Going from a range in a traditional method to a list is just a matter of selecting the range and choosing Insert ⇨ List, and then (after verifying that the range you selected, and which the List Wizard, described later in this chapter, is displaying, is what you wanted) clicking Finish in the List Wizard. Changing a list to a range is even easier—click anywhere within the list and choose Convert to Range from the List toolbar's List pop-up menu, and then click OK in the alert that asks whether you're sure.

 Caution Any lists in workbooks that you share with users of Excel versions earlier than Excel 2001 will be ranges of data for those users. If they make any changes or additions to the data, the saved workbooks will lose the List Manager control over those ranges.

Creating a Database

To create a database from scratch in an Excel worksheet, follow these steps:

1. In a blank row of the worksheet, enter the desired names of the fields.

2. In each cell of a row, directly underneath the field names, type the desired entries for that field into the cell. Don't leave an empty row between the field names and the data because Excel will have problems recognizing where your database begins.

3. To add entries consisting of numbers that really should be stored as text (such as zip codes), begin the entry with an apostrophe or format the cells as text (more on this very shortly).

When you finish adding records to your database, you'll have an organized collection of row-and-column data in a format somewhat like our example shown in Figure 21-1.

After you've entered a few records, Excel will present a dialog (shown in Figure 21-3) saying that it looks like you're creating a list and asking whether you would like to convert the data to a list object. You can click Yes to make the conversion, click No to continue on as you were, or check the Don't ask me this again box and then click either button. The More info button invokes MS Excel Help, displaying the Guidelines for creating a list by using the List Manager topic.

Figure 21-3: Would you like to convert the data entered to a list?

If you answer Yes to the question posed in this dialog box, your data area will be framed, the information will be reformatted for a consistent appearance, and the List toolbar (shown in Figure 21-4) will appear. Double-clicking any column header is equivalent to positioning your cursor in a column and clicking the Column Settings button on the List toolbar.

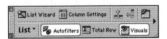

Figure 21-4: The List toolbar

If you need to enter a large number of entries that comprise numbers that should be stored as text (such as zip codes or telephone numbers), format the column containing that field as text. Control-click the header for that column (which automatically selects the entire column), and choose Format Cells from the shortcut menu that appears. Click the Number tab of the Format Cells dialog box. Next, click the Text option in the Category list and then click OK. If you don't use this trick, or if you don't begin each entry with an apostrophe, zip codes that begin with zeroes (such as 00742) will appear without the zeroes.

Your database work will be easier for you to handle if you have only one database per worksheet. To store more than one database in a single worksheet, you need to define database ranges for each database, which adds an unnecessary layer of complexity. Instead, place each database on a different worksheet tab. (Each worksheet can contain up to 255 tabs.) You'll also avoid long-term organizational problems if you don't put other data below your database in the same worksheet. As the database grows, new rows are added to the bottom of the list. If other spreadsheet data exists below the list, you run the risk of overwriting the existing data.

As you work with databases in Excel, remember that the database must have its row of field names at the top of the list and you can't have any blank lines between the row containing the field names and the data. Also, each field name should be unique (having two fields named Date, for example, would be confusing). You can have other rows above the list if you want, but Excel only recognizes the row immediately above the data as the row containing field names. Field names can include 255 characters, although for readability reasons you'll probably want to keep your field names relatively short.

Avoid putting other important data (such as formulas) to the left or to the right of your database because if you later use Excel's AutoFilter capability to filter the data in the database, the other data may be hidden.

A New Approach to Excel Databases

If you've worked with databases in previous versions of Excel, you'll recall the procedures as being considerably more complex. In the past, for example, you had to define a specific range for your data to occupy (called a database range). When you wanted to retrieve specific data, you had to tell Excel what data you wanted by setting up a criteria range and an extract range.

Excel 98 (and Excel 97, the Windows equivalent) introduced a new, much easier approach. Excel now makes intelligent guesses regarding your database range (the size of the database). Additionally, it provides a data form for data entry and basic searches, and provides an AutoFilter for intricate data retrieval.

Excel 2001 takes this much further with the List Manager. List Manager incorporates all of the advances brought by Excel 97/98, and introduces the List toolbar, List Wizard, and a number of other tools to facilitate your database management needs.

Creating a Database Using the List Wizard

As you can see, manually setting up a database takes a lot of work. Excel 2001 List Wizard makes this chore less onerous. If you have the List toolbar showing, you can just click the List Wizard button to start the process; if the toolbar isn't showing, you can choose Insert ⇨ List. In either case, you'll be presented with the first of three List Wizard screens, as shown in Figure 21-5.

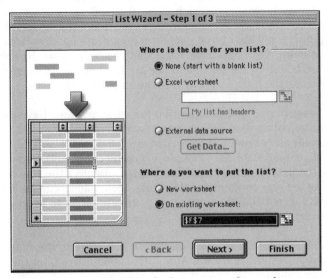

Figure 21-5: The List Wizard's first screen — from whence to where

On this screen, you need to answer two questions. The first question is if/where the data for the list exists. If you are starting from scratch, click None. If your data exists in this or another Excel worksheet, click Excel worksheet and specify the sheet and range, also letting Excel know whether column headers (field names) exist. Finally, if your data is in an external data source, you will need to have installed Microsoft Query from the Value Pack (see Appendix A for more information on the Value Pack) to access it. The second question is where you want Excel to place your list: on a new worksheet or on an existing worksheet (in which case you specify which sheet and where the top-left cell to be used is located). When you've answered these questions, click the Next button and you'll be presented with the second List Wizard screen, shown in Figure 21-6.

This is where you'll name your columns (fields) and specify their data types. Once the fields exist, either because you're converting existing data or because you've created the field, you can click select it in the Columns list and click the Settings button to set formatting or validation criteria. After you've created your fields, click Next and proceed to the final List Wizard screen, shown in Figure 21-7.

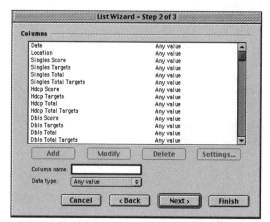

Figure 21-6: The second List Wizard screen — data definition time

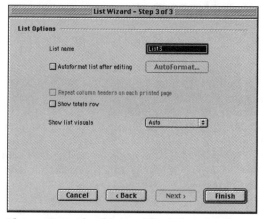

Figure 21-7: The third and final List Wizard screen — wrapping things up

On this screen, you can name the list and set AutoFormat criteria. Click Finish when done here and you'll be returned to Excel with your newly created list active, as shown in Figure 21-8.

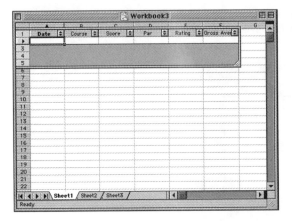

Figure 21-8: A simple list that tracks golf scores

Notice the frame, which is almost identical to a window's frame, that surrounds your list. This is the visual indicator that the list is active; when inactive, your list is surrounded by a blue border.

Working with Database Records

You can add and edit records by typing the desired data directly into the cells. One convenience provided by the List Manager is that, if your database is under List Manager control, the List Manager will take care of continuing any formatting conventions you've applied to a field (column) into new records. You can delete rows by selecting the unwanted row and choosing Edit ⇨ Delete Row or by choosing Delete ⇨ Row from the List pop-up menu in the List toolbar. Most users, however, find basic data entry and editing easier when they use a data form, a convenient form that Excel provides for you to enter and display data. To display a data form onscreen, place the cursor in any cell of your database and choose Data ⇨ Form or choose Form from the List toolbar's List pop-up menu. A data form, such as the one shown in Figure 21-9, containing the fields of your database appears.

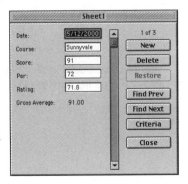

Figure 21-9: A sample data form for a database

You will only have text boxes for those fields that can accept data entry. A calculated column (such as Gross Average in Figure 21-9) will just display the value it contains, and will recompute when you make changes that affect the computation. If you click the Criteria button, the button will change to Form and you will be looking at what appears to be a blank record, but it isn't. This is a database search form. You can put criteria in one or more fields and click Find Next or Find Prev. For example, you could enter <90 in the Score text box and click Find Next and Find Prev to step through all records where you shot a score better than a 90. Criteria are discussed in more detail later in this chapter, under "Finding Data by Using Criteria."

Adding new records

To add a record, click the New button in the data form. A new record data form with blank fields for the new information appears. Repeat this process for each record that you want to add to the database. You can also click the Insert Row button in the List toolbar.

If you're adding new records to an existing database, don't be concerned about the order of the records in the database. You can always sort the database to put the records in any order that you want (see "Sorting a Database" later in the chapter).

Editing records

You can also edit a record by using the data form. To get to the record you need to edit, use the Find Next or Find Prev buttons, use the data form's scroll bars, or press the up- and down-arrow keys to scroll through the records. In a large database, you can use the Criteria button to perform a search. When the desired record appears, click in the appropriate fields and make the desired edits.

Deleting records

To delete a record by using the data form, first locate the desired record. Again, you can use the Find Next or Find Prev buttons, the scroll bar, or the up- and down-arrow keys. When the record appears, click Delete in the data form. Alternatively, you could choose Edit ➪ Delete Row, or, from the List toolbar's List pop-up menu, choose Delete ➪ Row

Tip   If you have a large number of records to delete, it may be faster not to use a data form. Instead, use Excel's AutoFilter capability (discussed later in this chapter) to display all the records that you want to delete. Then drag across the row headers to select the records. With all the desired rows selected, choose the Delete ➪ Row from the List toolbar's List pop-up menu.

Providing summary information

The List Manager provides an easy way to provide summary information for the various columns in your database—the Total Row. You display the Total Row by clicking the Total Row button in the List toolbar.

For each column on the Total Row, you can select whether to display summary information. Click in the Total Row, in the column for which you want to display summary information, click the button that appears, and choose the summary information that you wish from the pop-up list. The summary information is a formula and can be a sum, average, count, count of number values, maximum value, minimum value, or subtotal (listed as Other).

Finding data by using criteria

Another way to locate data in a database is to specify a search criterion in a data form. The criterion identifies the specific data you want to find. For example, in a large database of names and addresses, you may want to locate all records in a particular city. Excel also lets you make use of a computed criterion to find records that pass certain tests based on the contents of a formula. By using a computed criterion with a database of expenses, for example, you can find all expenses that exceed $500 by entering >500. When you specify a computed criterion in a data form, you make use of Excel's comparison operators (the same operators that you can use as part of formulas in the cells of a worksheet). Table 21-1 lists the comparison operators you can use.

Table 21-1 Comparison Operators	
Operator	*Function*
<	Less than
>	Greater than
=	Equal to
<>	Not equal to
<=	Less than or equal to
>=	Greater than or equal to

To use criteria to find individual records in a database, follow these steps:

1. Place the cursor anywhere in the database.

2. Choose Data ⇨ Form to bring up a data form dialog box.

3. Click Criteria in the data form. When you do this, the data form changes in appearance to resemble the one shown in Figure 21-10. The data form now says Criteria in the upper-right corner, the Criteria button on the data form changes into the Form button, and the fields are all blank.

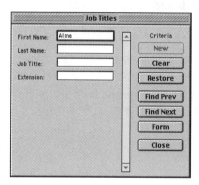

Figure 21-10: The Criteria mode of the data form

4. Enter the desired criteria in the appropriate fields. You need to fill in only the fields on which you want to base the search. For example, if you want to search for all San Francisco records, you would enter San Francisco in the City field of the form. In Figure 21-10, a search by first name is being entered.

5. Press Return or Enter, or click the Form button to find the first record that meets the search criterion.

6. Use the Find Next and Find Prev buttons in the data form to locate the records that match the desired criterion. (Using the scroll bars or arrow keys takes you through all the records, not just the matches.)

7. When you are finished examining the records, click the Close button.

You can also use wildcards to represent characters in your criterion. Use the question mark to represent a single character or the asterisk (*) to represent multiple characters. As an example, the criteria H?ll in a Name field would locate names such as Hall, Hill, and Hull. The criterion entry *der would locate all strings of text ending with the letters der, such as chowder and loader.

How to Get a Report

How can you get a printed copy of all records that meet a certain criterion? You can't use the data form to isolate and print a group of records, but you can filter the data in a database by using the AutoFilter command.

After you filter the records to show the ones you want, you can print the worksheet to produce a report. For details, see "Using the AutoFilter Command" later in this chapter.

Tip

If you're familiar with databases in general, you may be wondering how you can perform searches based on multiple criteria, where you find records based on more than a single argument. In some cases, you'll want to find records by using and-based criteria, where one condition and another condition meet certain requirements. You can easily search using multiple criteria by entering multiple conditions in the different fields of the data form while in Criteria mode. For example, in a table of names and addresses, you may want to find any employee whose first name begins with an A and whose job is Mac Support. Figure 21-11 shows a data form that is set up to search on these criteria.

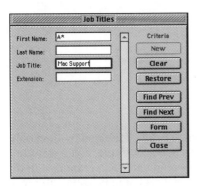

Figure 21-11: The data form set up in Criteria mode to search for multiple criteria

A search for or-based criteria is a little more complex. Or-based criteria describe those cases in which the contents of a field meet one criterion or another criterion. For example, you may want to find records where the City field contains either San Francisco or San Diego. Unfortunately, you can't do searches with or-based criteria by using a data form, but you can use the AutoFilter command.

Using the AutoFormat Command

You can quickly improve the appearance of your database by using Excel's Auto Format command. To apply automatic formatting to a list, place the cursor anywhere within the list, and then choose Format ⇨ AutoFormat or click the AutoFormat button on the List toolbar. In the AutoFormat dialog box, choose one of the available formats, check out the sample, and click OK to apply the formatting. If you don't like the effects of the formatting, you can always remove it with the Undo command (⌘-Z), which will say Edit ⇨ Undo AutoFormat.

Cross-Reference

As detailed in Chapter 17, AutoFormat applies automatic formatting to parts or all of your worksheet to give the worksheet a presentation-quality appearance quickly.

Sorting a Database

At times, you may want your data arranged in a more effective manner. You can do this by sorting the data by field information, which changes the order of the records. When Excel sorts a database, it rearranges all records in the database according to a specified order. If you sort a database of names alphabetically, the sorted database contains all the same records, but the names are arranged in alphabetical order.

Caution   When you sort fields that contain dates or times, Excel sorts correctly if the data is in an acceptable date or time format. If you use some format of your own devising that Excel doesn't recognize to store dates or times, the data will sort as text, and you probably won't get the results that you want.

How it works

When Excel sorts a database in ascending order, it sorts by numbers first, followed by text, and then the logical values True or False. Excel is not case-sensitive; it ignores both case and accent marks while sorting. Blank cells appear at the end of the sort, whether you are sorting in ascending or descending order. To sort, you choose a field, called the key field, which is the field by which the data is sorted. In some cases, you may need to sort a database on more than one field. For example, if you sort a database alphabetically by using Last Name as the key field, you get groups of records with the last names arranged alphabetically but with the first names in random order. In such a case, you can sort the database by using Last Name as the first key field and First Name as the secondary key field. To sort a database, use Data ⇨ Sort. If you are only going to sort on one field, you can just click the Sort and Filter arrows beside the field name in your list, and then choose Sort Ascending or Sort Descending from the pop-up menu.

Tip   Sorting involves a major rearrangement of data so that there's always a possibility you'll make a selection that causes your data to sort in a way that you didn't expect. If you have any doubts about how a sort will turn out, save the workbook under a different name before sorting. (Choose File ⇨ Save As and enter a different name for the workbook file in the Save As dialog box.) Then if you perform a sort that produces undesirable results and you're unable to undo the sort (⌘-Z), you can always reload the original file to get your original data back.

To sort your database, follow these steps:

1. To sort a specific number of rows in your database, select those rows by dragging across the row headers. To sort the entire database, place the cursor anywhere within the database. If your database is an Excel list, to sort a specific set of rows, you need to convert to a range, perform the sort as described, and then convert back to a list. Alternatively, you can define a filter to select that range (as described later in this chapter) and then sort the filtered data.

2. Choose List ⇨ Sort (from the List toolbar) or Data ⇨ Sort to open the Sort dialog box (see Figure 21-12).

Figure 21-12: The Sort dialog box as a second sort field is being selected

3. Click the arrows next to the Sort by (top) field of the dialog box, to choose the field you want to sort by. Then select Ascending or Descending to specify the direction of the sort.

4. If you want to use additional fields as the basis for the sort, select a secondary field from the available fields in the Then by list as in Step 3. When you sort on multiple fields, the Sort by field takes first priority, followed by the first Then by field, and then the second Then by field.

5. If you are not using the List Manager and did not select a range of rows to sort, make sure that the Header row radio button at the bottom of the dialog box remains selected. This tells Excel that there's a header row that contains the field names that are not to be included in the sort.

6. Click OK to perform the sort.

Figure 21-13 shows the effects of sorting. At the top, you see a database that contains records entered in random order. Below it is the same database but sorted by Last Name and, where Last Name values are equal, by First Name fields.

Tip   You can quickly sort a List Manager database on any single field in ascending or descending order by placing the cursor in any desired field and clicking the Sort Ascending or Sort Descending button on the Standard toolbar. If you use the buttons on a database that is not under List Manager aegis, the header will be sorted as data.

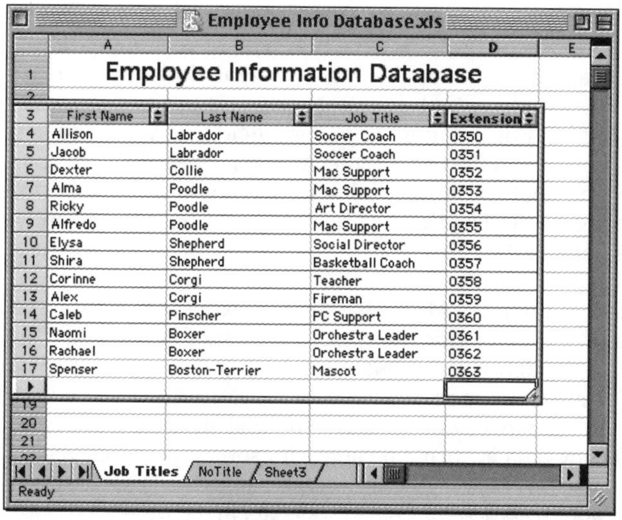

First Name	Last Name	Job Title	Extension
Allison	Labrador	Soccer Coach	0350
Jacob	Labrador	Soccer Coach	0351
Dexter	Collie	Mac Support	0352
Alma	Poodle	Mac Support	0353
Ricky	Poodle	Art Director	0354
Alfredo	Poodle	Mac Support	0355
Elysa	Shepherd	Social Director	0356
Shira	Shepherd	Basketball Coach	0357
Corinne	Corgi	Teacher	0358
Alex	Corgi	Fireman	0359
Caleb	Pinscher	PC Support	0360
Naomi	Boxer	Orchestra Leader	0361
Rachael	Boxer	Orchestra Leader	0362
Spenser	Boston-Terrier	Mascot	0363

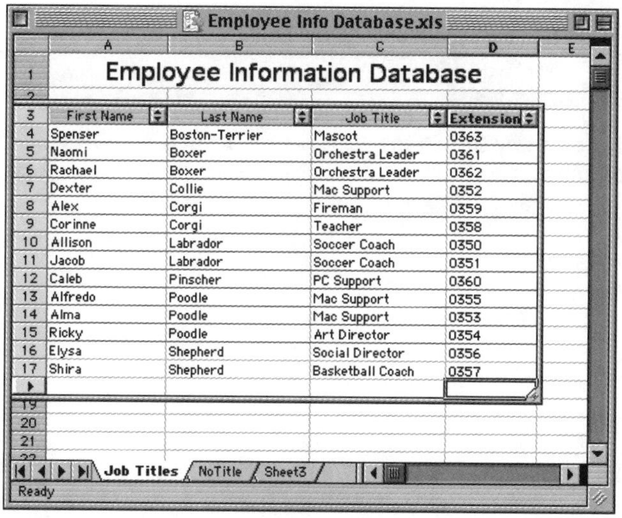

First Name	Last Name	Job Title	Extension
Spenser	Boston-Terrier	Mascot	0363
Naomi	Boxer	Orchestra Leader	0361
Rachael	Boxer	Orchestra Leader	0362
Dexter	Collie	Mac Support	0352
Alex	Corgi	Fireman	0359
Corinne	Corgi	Teacher	0358
Allison	Labrador	Soccer Coach	0350
Jacob	Labrador	Soccer Coach	0351
Caleb	Pinscher	PC Support	0360
Alfredo	Poodle	Mac Support	0355
Alma	Poodle	Mac Support	0353
Ricky	Poodle	Art Director	0354
Elysa	Shepherd	Social Director	0356
Shira	Shepherd	Basketball Coach	0357

Figure 21-13: *Top:* A database containing records in random order. *Bottom:* The same database containing records sorted by Last Name and First Name fields.

Occasionally you may need to sort a database on more than three fields. Suppose that you have a large mailing list in Excel, and you want to sort the database by State, then by City within each state, then by Last Name within each city, and then by First Name within each group of last names. Because Excel provides only three fields from which to select in the Sort dialog box, this type of sort appears to be impossible. In fact, Excel can handle such a task if you break down the job into multiple sorts. Begin with the least important group of sorts and progress toward the most important group of sorts. Put the most important field first within each group of sorts. In the example, you would first sort by using the Last Name field as the first field and the First Name field as the second field. Then you would perform another sort by using the State field as the first field, the City field as the second field, and the Last Name field as the third field.

Tip   If you make a selection in a non-List Manager database before sorting (as opposed to sorting the entire list by just placing the cursor anywhere within the list), make sure that you select all the data that you want sorted. If you select most columns and leave some adjacent columns containing data unselected, the sort will affect only the data in the selected columns. The result will be a seriously garbled database. When selecting data in such a database for sorting purposes, the safest method is to drag across row headings, which selects all of the fields for that row (record). In this way, you're assured of selecting all data in the rows.

Sorting Bizarre Numbers

What happens when you need to sort by something such as product part numbers that are made up of alphanumeric combinations of varying widths? For example, consider a list of such part numbers with entries such as the following:

1R9

4R32

12P182

67S2024

109P182

If you did a sort based on those values, your results would not be what you really want. 12P182 would fall above 1R9, even though in the company's grand scheme, 1R9 is a lower part number than 12P182. This is because the part numbers actually consist of three components: a number of one or more digits, followed by a letter, followed by another multi-digit number. In such a list, all parts beginning with the number 1 appear first in the sorted list, followed by all parts beginning with the number 2, and then all parts beginning with the number 3, and so on.

You can correctly sort this type of a list by breaking the codes into their component parts and using a separate cell for each part. Storing each of these components in a separate cell and sorting based on all three cells solves the problem. If you don't like the idea of entering the data in three cells, you could enter the data as previously described and create formulas (calculated columns) for the component parts, and then define your sort based on the calculated columns.

Can You Undo the Effects of a Sort? Maybe.

If you sort a database and then go on to do other tasks with the data, you cannot later undo the effects of the sort. (The Undo command works only if you perform it as the first action after the sort.) If you want to retain your database in the manner in which the records were originally entered, you have two options. You can save a copy of the database worksheet under another worksheet tab or save the entire workbook under another file name by using Save As. The Save As copy of the worksheet can then be recalled if you want to see how the database was originally organized. However, it is difficult to keep two databases containing the same data updated.

A better approach, at least for a non-List Manager database, is to add a column of record numbers to the database. The first record entered becomes record 1; the second record entered becomes record 2; and so on. That way, to reorganize the database in the order that the records were originally entered, you simply sort on the field that contains the record numbers. It's easy to fill a column with sequential numbers. See Chapter 16 for details. In a List Manager database, you'll end up with a lot of empty records after filling the column, which could affect future sorts, especially those done in descending order.

Custom sort orders

In addition to sorting in ascending or descending order, you can have your primary sort field sort by the date or month custom orders Excel provides, or create your own custom order to sort by. For example, you may need to sort a list by manager or teacher's names, but not alphabetically. Or you may need to sort by priority or by location.

To create your own sort order, follow these steps:

1. Select Edit ➪ Preferences, and then select the Custom Lists tab.

2. If you have not entered the text to sort by in your spreadsheet, click in the List entries box and type the word (letters, numbers, or combination) that you want to have first in the sort order. Press Return or Enter and type the second sort word. Repeat until you have entered all your sort elements. Then click Add.

   If you have already entered the text to sort by in your spreadsheet, select the list before selecting Edit ➪ Preferences and the Custom Lists tab. Then click Import.

   If you have already entered the text but haven't preselected the text, you can click the button attached to the Import list from cells text box. This collapses the dialog box to reveal your worksheet. In the worksheet, drag to select the cells that contain your sort data, and then press Return or Enter. Back in the dialog box, click Import.

3. Click OK.

Custom sort lists can also be deleted. Just click the list name in the Custom lists and click Delete.

If you read "Copying Data with Fill and AutoFill" in Chapter 16, these instructions may sound familiar. In fact, the custom lists you create in your Preferences dialog box are the same lists you use to automatically complete a data series entry when using AutoFill.

To put your custom sort order into effect, follow these steps:

1. Select List ⇨ Sort from the List toolbar or Data ⇨ Sort and choose a field to sort on (from the pop-up list).

2. Click Options to bring up the Sort Options dialog box. Here you'll find a pop-up menu that lets you choose a custom order to sort your first sort field by. Simply select an order from the pop-up menu.

   By default the two date options and the two month options that Excel provides are in this list. Any custom orders that you create in the Preferences dialog box also appear in this pop-up list.

3. *(Optional)* Case Sensitive enables you to include the case of your text in the sort criteria. Check it if it makes a difference whether or not a word is capitalized. For example, do you want low, medium, high, Low, Medium, High or low, Low, medium, Medium, high, High. The first sort is case-sensitive, whereas the second is not.

4. Click a radio button to determine whether the sort will be from top to bottom or bottom to top.

5. Click OK.

Remember that a custom list can mix text and numbers and sort it however you want. Just make sure you format the cells as text before you enter the sort data.

Using the AutoFilter Command

Excel's AutoFilter enables you to define criteria to filter your database so that only records meeting the specified criteria appear. AutoFilter capability comes into play to set more complex retrieval criteria than is possible with the data form (and to print reports based on the selected data).

The AutoFilter command is a toggle, which means that after you turn it on, it's on until you turn it off. AutoFilter gives you three clues that it is on. You see a pop-up list next to each field name in the worksheet or list, the AutoFilter button will be highlighted in the List toolbar, and the AutoFilter submenu under Data ⇨ Filter is checked. Turn AutoFilter off to clear the previous filters and then turn it on again to use AutoFilter on your database.

To put an AutoFilter in effect on a database, follow these steps:

1. Place the cursor anywhere in the database.

2. Click the AutoFilter button in the List toolbar, or choose Data ➪ Filter ➪ AutoFilter.

3. A pop-up menu button appears next to each field name in the database (see Figure 21-14). You can use these lists to choose a sort or to filter out rows that don't match specified criteria.

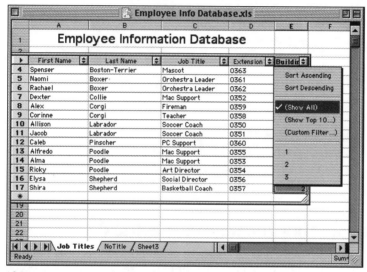

Figure 21-14: Pop-up menu buttons for using AutoFilter

4. Click the pop-up menu for the field you want to filter and choose the entry you want as the filter. You can also select the Custom option from the pop-up menu to create more complex criteria, as described later in this section.

Keeping a Filtered Copy Handy

You may find it useful to keep a copy of the filtered data. For example, perhaps you know that during the week you'll need to refer to a listing of records that meet a certain condition several times. First use AutoFilter to filter the desired records, and then select all the records and choose Edit ➪ Copy (⌘-C). Move to another worksheet and paste a copy of the filtered data there using Edit ➪ Paste (⌘-V).

Just remember that if you make changes to one set of data, the other set isn't automatically updated and won't fully match the changed set.

As you make your selections from the pop-up menu, Excel filters the records per your selections. You can create and-based criteria by choosing filters from more than one field. For example, in Figure 21-15, a Mac Support filter is selected in the Job Title field, and the number 1 is filtering the Building field. In this case, choosing Mac Support in the Job Title field is not enough because records would appear for all Mac Support staff, not just those working in building 1. If you choose multiple conditions, records must meet all of the conditions before they will be visible in the database when the AutoFilter is in effect.

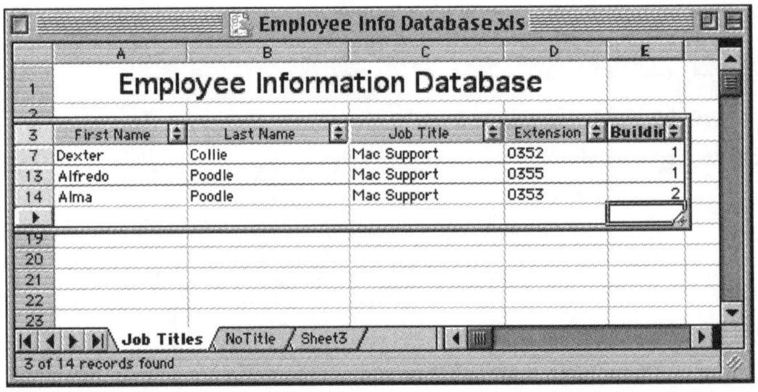

Figure 21-15: An example of AutoFilter used on two fields of a database

Printing a report based on specific data

The AutoFilter capability makes it easy to get a report of records that meet a specified condition. After you have filtered your database using AutoFilter, you can print the visible records by choosing File ➪ Print (⌘-P) or by clicking the Print button on the Standard toolbar. Before the addition of AutoFilter, you would have had to use some of Excel's advanced database features to declare a criterion range and an extract range to manage the same sort of task. That process is no longer necessary, except in very specialized cases, so we won't bore you with the sordid details here. If you're curious, check out the specifics in Excel's Help files.

Using complex criteria with AutoFilter

You can also set more complex criteria (such as records falling within a certain range, records that use computed criteria, or records meeting or-based conditions) with AutoFilter. To do so, select Custom from the pop-up lists. This calls up the Custom AutoFilter dialog box, shown in Figure 21-16.

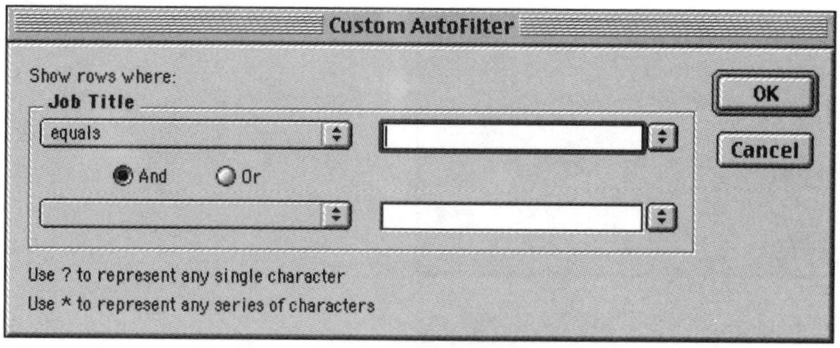

Figure 21-16: The Custom AutoFilter dialog box

Use the options in this dialog box to specify ranges of acceptable data and to specify or-based criteria (such as all records with a State value of CA or TX). Choose a desired comparison operator from the first pop-up list and enter a desired value in the text box to its right. To add a second comparison, select the And or the Or radio button as desired, and use the second pop-up list and text box for the other desired value.

You can see examples of the use of complex criteria by examining the dialog boxes shown in Figure 21-17. At the top, the expressions greater than or equal to M and less than or equal to Zz are used to retrieve all last names that start with M through Z. Note the addition of the second z. If this z was omitted, the criterion would actually find all names beginning with M through the letter Z alone, but would find no names of more than one character beginning with Z. In the middle dialog box, the expression greater than 2 retrieves all records with a value over 2 (but not equal to 2) in the Building field of the Employee Info database. At the bottom, the expression equals Mac Support or equals PC Support retrieve all entries with either of these job descriptions.

Remember that you can use the Custom option in more than one field. By specifying Custom options in multiple fields, you can filter data based on complex criteria. To clear the effects of a Custom option, choose Show All from the pop-up list.

The Top 10 option

Another option you have when using the AutoFilter is to filter your lists to show only the top or bottom 10 values in your list. It's called Top 10, but you can show any number of values. It's easy. To show the Top 10 values, follow these steps:

1. Select Top 10 from the AutoFilter pop-up menu to bring up the Top 10 AutoFilter dialog box.

2. Select Top or Bottom. Enter a number of top or bottom values to show. Then select Items or Percent. Finally, click OK to perform the filtering.

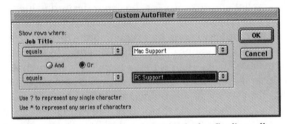

Figure 21-17: *Top:* Complex criteria for finding all records with last names starting with M through Zz. *Middle:* Complex criteria for finding all records with a value greater than 2 in the Building field. *Bottom:* Complex criteria for finding all records that say Mac Support or PC Support in the Job Title field.

Turning off the effects of AutoFilter

When you're finished working with a filtered subset of records, remember to turn off the AutoFilter command by clicking the AutoFilter button in the List toolbar or by choosing Data ➪ Filter ➪ AutoFilter. Alternatively, you can click the pop-up list for any filters you have set and choose Show All from each of the lists for which you've set a filter.

Outgrowing Excel

At what point do your database needs outgrow Excel? If you cross that point and stick with Excel as your database, you're making unnecessary work for yourself. As an obvious example, consider this simple list of sales data for a small mail-order operation:

Date	Name	Phone	Item	Cost
6/15/95	Smith, R.	723-1020	calendar	18.00
6/15/95	Williams, E.	853-6723	calendar	18.00
6/15/95	Smith, R.	723-1020	portfolio	21.00
6/15/95	Smith, R.	723-1020	calendar	18.00

What may look like a simple, effective list in reality is (to a professional database developer's eye) the beginnings of a logistical nightmare. When you find yourself repeatedly entering any kind of data—the same employee names, customer names, item numbers, or descriptions—you're using the wrong product for your database. This kind of data cries out for normalization, the separation of data into individual tables, with relationships established between the tables to avoid redundancy. This is something that isn't possible with Excel but that is within the power of a relational database such as FileMaker Pro or ACI US's 4th Dimension. (Go for FileMaker Pro if you're setting up the database yourself. If you're hiring a developer, both FileMaker and 4th Dimension are terrific, so go with the professional's recommendation.)

Another time to move up from Excel is when your database grows to thousands of records, putting unusual demands on the database power of a spreadsheet.

Yet another time when you'll want to move from Excel is when you need to use your database to print specially formatted forms and reports.

Performing a Data Merge

If you have names and addresses stored in an Excel database, you can combine the power of Excel and Word to create mail merge documents and generate form letters and envelopes. To generate form letters by using a mailing list stored in Excel, follow these steps:

1. Use AutoFilter, if necessary, to show only those records for which you want to print a merged document.

2. Select the entire range of data that contains the records.

3. Open the Word document into which you are merging your data (or create a new document with the desired text).

4. Still in Word, choose Tools ⇨ Data Merge Manager to display the Data Merge Manager floating window.

5. Proceed as described in Chapter 6 to create your form and select your data source. When you specify a data source, choose Open Data Source from the Get Data button pop-up menu, select the Excel workbook file, select the worksheet within the workbook that contains your database, and (if necessary) specify the data range (which you selected in Step 2).

 Cross-Reference Mail merge is more specific to Word, so we give it much a more detailed discussion in the Word section of this book (see Chapter 6).

If you outgrow Excel as a database and move into a relational database, don't worry about still being able to use the Data Merge Manager. Data Merge Manager supports FileMaker Pro directly and it's also very easy to use this feature with any application that can export data in simple tab-delimited form — as all databases can.

Designing Databases

Planning is vital to effective database management. All too often, users create a database and begin storing data only to discover that the database doesn't provide all the necessary information. Correcting mistakes you make during the design of a database, or later trying to compensate for design shortcomings, can be tedious.

Think about how the data should be stored and about how you and others will ask for the data. Outline the business's needs, which Excel's database capabilities can help solve. Just as you would not haphazardly toss a bunch of files into a filing cabinet without designing some type of filing system, you should not place information in a database without first designing the database. As you design the database, you must define the kinds of information to be stored in it.

About data and attributes

Data and attributes are two important terms in database design. Data is the information that goes into your database. Attributes are the types of data that make up the database. For example, an individual's last name is data. An attribute, on the other hand, is another name for a field, so an entire group of last names is considered an attribute. Names, telephone numbers, customer numbers, descriptions, locations, and stock numbers are all common examples of attributes that your database may contain.

In addition to thinking about what kinds of information should go into the database, consider the ways in which Excel will retrieve the information. Information comes from a database in the form of reports. A report is a summary of information. Whether

Excel displays a single row of data through a data form or dozens of rows by means of a list and an AutoFilter, Excel is providing a report based on the data contained within the database file.

Steps in database design

Designing a database in Excel, regardless of its purpose, involves two major parts:

✦ Data definition (analyzing existing data)

✦ Data refinement (refining necessary data)

During the first phase—data definition—list (on paper) all the important attributes that are involved in your application. To do this, examine your needs carefully to determine exactly what kind of information must be stored in the database. List all possible attributes of your database even though they may not actually be needed by your particular application. You can eliminate unnecessary attributes during the data refinement stage.

During data refinement, refine your initial list of attributes so that the list forms an accurate description of the types of data you will need. At this stage, it is vital to include suggestions from as many other users of the database as possible. The people who use the database are likely to know what kinds of information they will need from it. What kinds of reports do they need? What kinds of queries will employees ask of the database? By continually asking these types of questions, you begin to think in terms of your database. This thought process helps you determine what is important and what is not important.

Tip

An example is the best way to demonstrate what we mean by considering usage and queries. Consider addresses: If you are going to store addresses, rather than creating one field called Address, break the address into its components so that you have separate fields for street, city, state, zip code, and the plus-4 zip extension. This way you can sort or filter by city or state, or find common zips for bulk-rate mailing. Now consider names. Break names into first name and last name— even middle name. Create separate fields for name titles such as Dr., Mr., Ms., and so on. That way you can send a letter to Ms. Smith or to Jane. If the entire name was in one field, you'd be stuck saying "Dear Jane Smith." Using the text operator, concatenate (&), you can easily join text fields together. This is far easier than breaking up a name.

Of course, even after you begin using your database, you can change it. If you follow the systematic approach of database design for your specific application, however, the chances are better that you won't create a database that fails to provide the information you need, and you will avoid extensive redesign.

By inserting rows and columns as needed, you can change the design of a database at any time; however, such changes are often inconvenient to make after the database is designed. For example, if you created a database to handle a customer mailing list, you might include fields for names, addresses, cities, states, and zip codes. At first glance, these fields seem sufficient. Gradually, you build a sizable mailing list. But if your company later decides to begin telemarketing by using the same mailing list, the database you designed is inadequate because it does not include a field for telephone numbers. Although a field for telephone numbers can easily be added by inserting a new column, you still have the task of going back and adding a telephone number for every name currently in the mailing list. If this information had been entered as you developed the mailing list, there wouldn't be the inconvenience of having to enter the telephone numbers as a separate operation. Careful planning during the database design process can help avoid such pitfalls.

Summary

In this chapter, you learned how to work with databases stored within Excel worksheets. The chapter discussed these topics:

✦ In Excel, a database is a list of data that is organized into columns of data directly underneath a row of field names.

✦ You can add data to a database by typing it directly into the cells below the field names or by using a data form.

✦ In addition to adding data, you can use data forms to find specific records and to edit or delete records.

✦ Data ➪ Sort enables you to sort the data in a database. You can even create your own sorting orders.

✦ You can use Excel's AutoFilter to filter a database so that only records meeting certain criteria appear. You can then copy these records to a different area of the worksheet or to a different worksheet, or you can print the records.

Where to go next

✦ In the next chapter, you learn how you can put macros to work to automate many routine tasks within Excel.

✦ A major part of setting up and maintaining a database is the tedious, but necessary, task of data entry. Chapter 16 has some tips and techniques that you can use to make data entry easier.

✦ After you've entered data into your database, you'll want to make the most of Excel's printing capabilities to generate reports. Chapter 20 has the story.

✦   ✦   ✦

Using Excel PivotTables

Your data is in an Excel database, and you know how to filter it, sort it, and print it. That's fine and will meet most basic needs for list management. Excel also provides an extremely flexible and potent tool for summarizing and analyzing your data — the PivotTable. With Excel's Chart features, PivotTables enable you to reorganize, analyze, and display your data in a myriad of ways.

You've all seen PivotTables, quite likely without realizing what they were. They're in the newspapers and in magazine articles all the time, summarizing statistical collections. For example, when you see a breakdown of average home costs by year for different cities, you're looking at a PivotTable.

Basically, a PivotTable is a summary of the information in a list. Using the sorting, filtering, validation, and subtotaling capabilities described in Chapter 21, PivotTables enable you to quickly create summaries of your data from a variety of perspectives. Suppose you have a table of sales data, including salesperson, territory, date, and product. With a Pivot-Table, you could view your data sorted by salesperson by month for each territory with a product breakdown.

Creating a PivotTable

Even though you could create a PivotTable that summarizes textual or date information, most summaries are numerical at their root and so are most PivotTables. You can perform many calculations on numeric data, such as averaging, totaling, counting, taking standard deviations, and so forth, whereas with textual information you can't do much more than count it.

Where Does a PivotTable Really Shine?

When your database has a number of fields that vary over a relatively constrained set of values (say ten to twenty) in a large number of records, you can achieve great results using a PivotTable.

When the field values are almost all distinct, you can't make much use of the PivotTable's aggregate capability, but you could make use of the grouping features described later in this chapter ("Grouping Data and Controlling Detail").

An example of a nonnumerically based PivotTable might be one in a company's human resources department. You might want a breakdown by department for each job title or category. A related numeric example could be finding the average salary in each job classification in each department.

Most of the examples we've used in our coverage of Excel have been business oriented or targeted at personal finance. Excel can also be used for fun tasks — such as tracking major league baseball statistics. Imagine a database with fields named Player, Team, Position, At Bats, Hits, Doubles, Triples, Home Runs, and so on. You could sort this database by Team and create subtotal information for each of the batting statistics. Similarly, you could apply a filter to extract only those players with more than a minimum number of at-bats. Neither of these approaches is as fast or informative as a PivotTable applied to the same data. At a glance, you could see each team's batting average, batting averages by player position, and batting average for players in each group of home run totals (such as less than 10, 10 but less than 20, and so on). You'll further see the batting average for each position within each team, the batting average for each home run class within each position, and so forth.

Note   For baseball fans, www.baseball1.com is a really good Web site that has a wealth of baseball statistics going back to the nineteenth century (1871). The data is available in Microsoft Access (Windows-only) format and what they call Generic (comma-separated values). Excel 2001 can open and convert the generic file.

For this example, shown in Figure 22-1, we're using the batting statistics for 1960–1969. The database is in descending order of number of at-bats for each year. Each player has 18 batting/base-running statistics, and we've added a 19th: a calculated column (I) for the batting average. We used the formula IF(F2>100, H2/F2, 0) to avoid any divide-by-zero errors for players who never came to bat that season and also zeroed any averages for players with 100 or fewer at-bats so they wouldn't be considered for high average on the team.

	A	B	C	D	E	F	G	H	I	J	K	L	M	N	O	P	Q	R	S	T	U	S
1	LahmanID	Year	Team	Lg	G	AB	R	H	Avg.	TB	2B	3B	HR	RBI	SH	SF	SB	CS	BB	IBB	HBP	S
2	pinsova01	1960	CIN	N	154	652	107	187	0.287	308	37	12	20	61	1	1	32	12	47	3	5	
3	brutobi01	1960	MIL	N	151	629	112	180	0.286	269	27	13	12	54	1	4	22	13	41	1	2	
4	foxne01	1960	CHI	A	150	605	85	175	0.289	225	24	10	2	59	14	5	2	4	50	2	10	
5	aparilu01	1960	CHI	A	153	600	86	166	0.277	206	20	7	2	61	20	6	51	8	43	3	1	
6	bankser01	1960	CHI	N	156	597	94	162	0.271	331	32	7	41	117	0	6	1	3	71	28	4	
7	mayswi01	1960	SF	N	153	595	107	190	0.319	330	29	12	29	103	0	9	25	10	61	11	4	
8	robinbr01	1960	BAL	A	152	595	74	175	0.294	262	27	9	14	88	13	8	2	2	35	0	0	
9	malzofr01	1960	BOS	A	152	595	60	161	0.271	237	30	2	14	79	4	8	2	3	36	4	4	
10	gardnbi02	1960	WAS	A	145	592	71	152	0.257	215	26	5	9	56	7	1	0	4	43	0	6	
11	minosmi01	1960	CHI	A	154	591	89	184	0.311	284	32	4	20	105	5	9	17	13	52	2	13	
12	aaronha01	1960	MIL	N	153	590	102	172	0.292	334	20	11	40	126	0	12	16	7	60	13	2	
13	powervi01	1960	CLE	A	147	580	69	167	0.288	229	26	3	10	84	14	7	9	5	24	5	0	
14	lumpeje01	1960	KC	A	146	574	69	156	0.272	205	19	3	8	53	4	4	1	1	48	1	0	
15	groatdi01	1960	PIT	N	138	573	85	186	0.325	226	26	4	2	50	12	1	0	2	39	0	4	
16	skinnbo01	1960	PIT	N	145	571	83	156	0.273	246	33	6	15	86	5	4	11	8	59	11	1	
17	clemero01	1960	PIT	N	144	570	89	179	0.314	261	22	6	16	94	4	5	4	5	39	4	2	
18	cepedor01	1960	SF	N	151	569	81	169	0.297	283	36	3	24	96	0	4	15	6	34	9	8	
19	kubekto01	1960	NY	A	147	568	77	155	0.273	228	25	3	14	62	12	4	3	0	31	5	3	
20	tuttlbi01	1960	KC	A	151	559	75	143	0.256	194	21	3	8	40	7	1	1	5	66	2	2	
21	gillijo01	1960	LA	N	151	557	96	138	0.248	177	20	2	5	40	9	4	12	9	96	1	3	
22	colavro01	1960	DET	A	145	555	67	138	0.249	263	18	1	35	87	1	3	3	6	53	4	4	
23	whitebi03	1960	STL	N	144	554	81	157	0.283	252	27	10	16	79	5	3	12	6	42	1	2	
24	hoakdo01	1960	PIT	N	155	553	97	156	0.282	246	24	9	16	79	4	4	3	2	74	9	1	
25	boyerke01	1960	STL	N	151	552	95	168	0.304	310	26	10	32	97	0	4	8	7	56	10	4	
26	kalinal01	1960	DET	A	147	551	77	153	0.278	235	29	4	15	68	5	5	19	4	65	3	3	
27	breedma01	1960	BAL	A	152	551	69	147	0.267	185	25	2	3	43	2	3	10	4	35	2	3	
28	matheed01	1960	MIL	N	153	548	108	152	0.277	302	19	7	39	124	4	6	7	3	111	3	2	
29	ashburi01	1960	CHI	N	151	547	99	159	0.291	185	16	5	0	40	7	1	16	4	116	1	1	
30	francti01	1960	CLE	A	147	544	84	159	0.292	250	36	2	17	79	3	5	4	1	67	7	5	

PivotTable1 / 60s Batting

Figure 22-1: The batting averages database

The first summary we would like to see is a breakdown by league, and then by team for each year, displaying the highest batting average. Performing this task with a PivotTable is a straightforward exercise, as follows:

1. Place your cursor anywhere in your table, and choose Data ⇨ PivotTable Report to present the PivotTable Wizard dialog box shown in Figure 22-2.

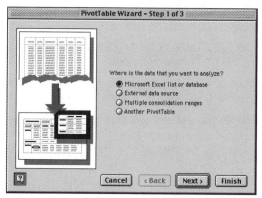

Figure 22-2: The first PivotTable Wizard box:
Where's your data coming from?

2. Click Next to go to the second PivotTable Wizard box, where you see your table's range, as shown in Figure 22-3.

Figure 22-3: The second PivotTable Wizard box: What data makes up your database?

3. Click Next to go to the third PivotTable Wizard dialog box, shown in Figure 22-4. We're going to specify that the PivotTable be placed in a new worksheet rather than the Existing worksheet shown in the figure.

Figure 22-4: The third PivotTable Wizard box: What do you want and where do you want it?

4. Click Layout to display the PivotTable Wizard – Layout dialog box shown in Figure 22-5. This is where the real work gets done.

5. Drag Lg (league) to the Page area, Team to the Row area, Year to the Column area, and Avg (average) to the Data area, as shown in Figure 22-6.

6. As you see, for numeric fields the default action is to sum the values. This is not what we want for average, we want a maximum. To change the operation, double-click the Sum of Avg box, presenting the PivotTable Field dialog box shown in Figure 22-7.

7. Select Max from the Summarize by list and then click Number, presenting our old friend the Format Cells dialog box, showing just the Number tab. Select Number from the list and enter 3 for the number of decimal places, and then click OK. Click OK in the PivotTable Field dialog box. The Name changes to Max of Avg, and we're almost ready to go. Click OK in the PivotTable Wizard – Layout dialog box, and Finish in the PivotTable Wizard – Step 3 of 3 dialog box to display the PivotTable shown in Figure 22-8.

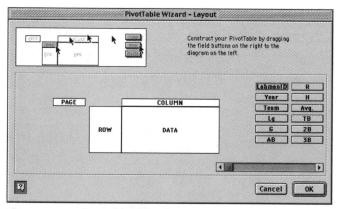

Figure 22-5: PivotTable Wizard – Layout dialog box

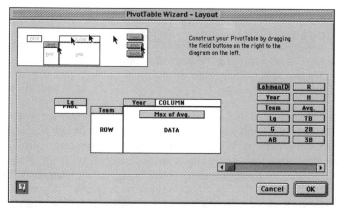

Figure 22-6: Set up your summary by dragging fields into the different areas.

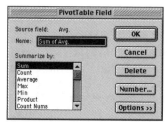

Figure 22-7: The PivotTable Field dialog box—change the summary type here

Team	1960	1961	1962	1963	1964	1965	1966	1967	196
Lg (Show All)									
Max of Avg. Year									
MON									
ATL							0.327	0.307	0.31
BAL	0.294	0.302	0.305	0.295	0.317	0.297	0.316	0.311	0.28
BOS	0.320	0.317	0.326	0.321	0.293	0.312	0.292	0.326	0.30
CAL						0.278	0.288	0.313	0.29
CHI	0.315	0.310	0.318	0.338	0.313	0.315	0.312	0.300	0.29
CIN	0.297	0.343	0.342	0.313	0.306	0.319	0.313	0.301	0.33
CLE	0.308	0.322	0.280	0.292	0.307	0.301	0.279	0.287	0.28
DET	0.286	0.361	0.324	0.312	0.300	0.288	0.289	0.308	0.28
HOU			0.286	0.281	0.280	0.275	0.301	0.333	0.29
KC	0.288	0.296	0.308	0.294	0.281	0.312	0.292	0.305	
LA	0.323	0.328	0.346	0.326	0.314	0.300	0.313	0.277	0.28
MIL	0.300	0.327	0.323	0.319	0.330	0.318			
MIN		0.302	0.298	0.307	0.323	0.321	0.307	0.292	0.28
NY	0.309	0.348	0.321	0.314	0.313	0.279	0.288	0.348	0.29
OAK									0.29
PHI	0.299	0.303	0.310	0.306	0.318	0.303	0.317	0.339	0.27
PIT	0.333	0.351	0.328	0.320	0.339	0.329	0.342	0.357	0.33
SD									
SEA									
SF	0.319	0.311	0.316	0.316	0.304	0.317	0.295	0.292	0.29
STL	0.304	0.329	0.330	0.319	0.348	0.310	0.303	0.335	0.30
WAS	0.294	0.313	0.310	0.274	0.274	0.289	0.278	0.256	0.27
Grand Total	0.333	0.361	0.346	0.338	0.348	0.329	0.342	0.357	0.33

Figure 22-8: The PivotTable displaying the highest batting average on each team for each year in the 1960s

You should note the (Show All) item next to Lg. If you click the arrows adjoining it, you're offered the choice of just showing American League (A) or National League (N) teams in the drop-down list. When you do this, you'll see one of the flaws in putting Lg in the Page area (and not coming up with separate Team designators for different teams that play in the same city) — the Dodgers' and Angels' numbers were combined for the years they both played in Los Angeles (LA), as were the Yankees' and Mets' statistics (NY). Additionally, the Royals figures are still in the same line with those of the Athletics for their Kansas City days (KC).

Laying Out a PivotTable

Notice the difference in the PivotTable shown in Figure 22-9 when compared with that in Figure 22-8. We've moved the Lg field down to the Row area, outside of that of the Team field. As with most details in Office 2001, you have more than one way to accomplish this. You can reinvoke the PivotTable Wizard (in the PivotTable tool-bar, either click the PivotTable Wizard button or choose Wizard in the PivotTable drop-down menu) or you can just drag the fieldname in your PivotTable.

A PivotTable has four basic areas: the Page, Row, Column, and Data. In the Page area, you place filtering fields. For example, when you want to contrast men's pay with women's pay for the same work, using a salary database you might put the employee's gender in the Page area. Now, without creating separate PivotTables, you can see a breakdown of all salaries, all men's salaries, or all women's salaries just by choosing from the pop-up menu. The Row area (or axis) is where you place the fields by which you want to sort. The Column area is where you place fields by which you want to further breakdown the row fields. In our example, that is by year. You can move fields from the Column area to the Row area or vice versa, changing the manner in which you look at the same data. This is where the *Pivot* in PivotTable comes from. The Data area is where you place the fields you want to summarize. Referring back to Figure 22-9, League is the *outer row field*, the row field furthest from the Data area. All other row fields are called *inner row fields*. Similarly, the leftmost column field is the outer field and all others are inner. If you select an outer field and click the Hide Detail button on the PivotTable toolbar, the inner field(s) disappear. To bring them back into view, you need to reselect the outer field and click the Show Detail button.

Max of Avg.		Year										
Lg	Team	1960	1961	1962	1963	1964	1965	1966	1967	1968	1969	Grand Total
A	BAL	0.294	0.302	0.305	0.295	0.317	0.297	0.316	0.311	0.282	0.308	0.317
	BOS	0.320	0.317	0.326	0.321	0.293	0.312	0.292	0.326	0.301	0.309	0.326
	CAL						0.278	0.288	0.313	0.298	0.270	0.313
	CHI	0.315	0.310	0.312	0.295	0.301	0.296	0.273	0.261	0.284	0.304	0.315
	CLE	0.308	0.322	0.280	0.292	0.307	0.301	0.279	0.287	0.281	0.287	0.322
	DET	0.286	0.361	0.324	0.312	0.300	0.288	0.289	0.308	0.287	0.295	0.361
	KC	0.288	0.296	0.308	0.294	0.281	0.312	0.292	0.305		0.282	0.312
	LA		0.288	0.291	0.307	0.314						0.314
	MIN		0.302	0.298	0.307	0.323	0.321	0.307	0.292	0.289	0.332	0.332
	NY	0.309	0.348	0.321	0.314	0.313	0.279	0.288	0.272	0.267	0.290	0.348
	OAK									0.290	0.281	0.290
	SEA										0.309	0.309
	WAS	0.294	0.313	0.310	0.274	0.274	0.289	0.278	0.256	0.274	0.296	0.313
A Total		0.320	0.361	0.326	0.321	0.323	0.321	0.316	0.326	0.301	0.332	0.361
N	MON										0.302	0.302
	ATL							0.327	0.307	0.317	0.342	0.342
	CHI	0.294	0.303	0.318	0.338	0.313	0.315	0.312	0.300	0.294	0.312	0.338
	CIN	0.297	0.343	0.342	0.313	0.306	0.319	0.313	0.301	0.335	0.348	0.348
	HOU			0.286	0.281	0.280	0.275	0.301	0.333	0.291	0.308	0.333
	LA	0.323	0.328	0.346	0.326	0.294	0.300	0.313	0.277	0.285	0.323	0.346
	MIL	0.300	0.327	0.323	0.319	0.330	0.318					0.330
	NY			0.306	0.302	0.311	0.253	0.288	0.348	0.297	0.340	0.348
	PHI	0.299	0.303	0.310	0.306	0.318	0.303	0.317	0.339	0.275	0.288	0.339
	PIT	0.333	0.351	0.328	0.320	0.339	0.329	0.342	0.357	0.332	0.348	0.357
	SD										0.264	0.264
	SF	0.319	0.311	0.316	0.316	0.304	0.317	0.295	0.292	0.293	0.320	0.320
	STL	0.304	0.329	0.330	0.319	0.348	0.310	0.303	0.335	0.301	0.298	0.348
N Total		0.333	0.351	0.346	0.338	0.348	0.329	0.342	0.357	0.335	0.348	0.357
Grand Total		0.333	0.361	0.346	0.338	0.348	0.329	0.342	0.357	0.335	0.348	0.361

Figure 22-9: The same PivotTable with the league in the Row area instead of the Page area

Note   Numeric fields default to being summed and nonnumeric fields default to being counted when placed in the Data area.

Most PivotTable examples will have one or more fields in both the Row and Column areas, but it is quite possible and sometimes desirable to have no fields in one of these areas.

Tip   PivotTables reflect the underlying data, but updating is not automatic. You need to click the Refresh button on the PivotTable toolbar (or Control-click in the table and choose Refresh from the shortcut menu).

Grouping Data and Controlling Detail

In the 1960s, the National League's Braves played in two cites: Milwaukee and Atlanta. We would like to combine those statistics, and PivotTable Grouping is the tool. The first step to take is to select those two entries, and then Control-click one of them, choosing Group and Outline ⇨ Group from the shortcut menu. Looking at Figure 22-10, you can see that a new outer field, Team2, has an entry for Group1 that breaks down into Atlanta and Milwaukee. Click in the field, and change the name to Braves. Select the Team2 header, and click the Hide Detail button on the PivotTable toolbar. Now, the values are grouped and the details are hidden. These are the same techniques you would use in a Sales summary where you might want to group the information for multiple states into a region. Similarly, you could group monthly figures into quarters.

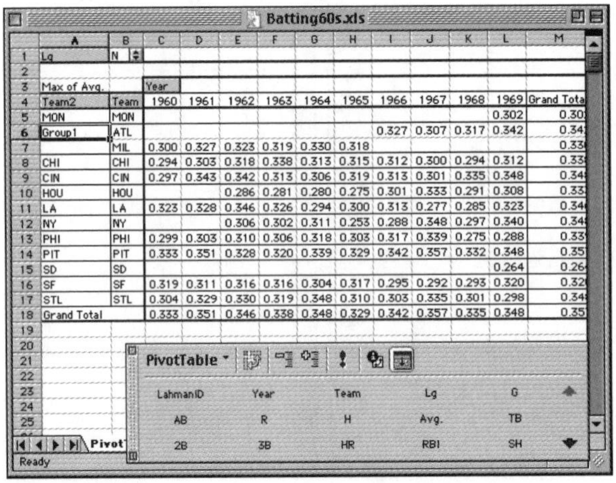

A	B	1960	1961	1962	1963	1964	1965	1966	1967	1968	1969	Grand Total
Lg	N											
Max of Avg.		Year										
Team2	Team	1960	1961	1962	1963	1964	1965	1966	1967	1968	1969	Grand Total
MON	MON									0.302		0.30
Group1	ATL							0.327	0.307	0.317	0.342	0.34
	MIL	0.300	0.327	0.323	0.319	0.330	0.318					0.33
CHI	CHI	0.294	0.303	0.318	0.338	0.313	0.315	0.312	0.300	0.294	0.312	0.33
CIN	CIN	0.297	0.343	0.342	0.313	0.306	0.319	0.313	0.301	0.335	0.348	0.34
HOU	HOU			0.286	0.281	0.280	0.275	0.301	0.333	0.291	0.308	0.33
LA	LA	0.323	0.328	0.346	0.326	0.294	0.300	0.313	0.277	0.285	0.323	0.34
NY	NY			0.306	0.302	0.311	0.253	0.288	0.348	0.297	0.340	0.34
PHI	PHI	0.299	0.303	0.310	0.306	0.318	0.303	0.317	0.339	0.275	0.288	0.33
PIT	PIT	0.333	0.351	0.328	0.320	0.339	0.329	0.342	0.357	0.332	0.348	0.35
SD	SD										0.264	0.26
SF	SF	0.319	0.311	0.316	0.316	0.304	0.317	0.295	0.292	0.293	0.320	0.32
STL	STL	0.304	0.329	0.330	0.319	0.348	0.310	0.303	0.335	0.301	0.298	0.34
Grand Total		0.333	0.351	0.346	0.338	0.348	0.329	0.342	0.357	0.335	0.348	0.35

PivotTable fields: LahmanID, Year, Team, Lg, G, AB, R, H, Avg., TB, 2B, 3B, HR, RBI, SH

Figure 22-10: Grouping the two Braves entries

Creating data groups

Suppose that you wanted to see how many home runs were hit by the batters with the top three averages on each team, each year. Follow these steps:

1. Move Year to the Page area.

2. Drag HR from the PivotTable toolbar to become the innermost field in the Row area.

3. Click the Field Settings button in the PivotTable toolbar (or double-click the HR fieldname) to display the PivotTable Field dialog box, and click the Advanced button to display the PivotTable Field Advanced Options dialog box, shown in Figure 22-11.

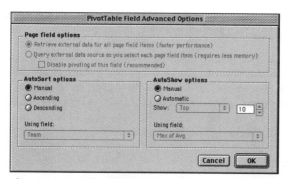

Figure 22-11: The PivotTable Field Advanced Options dialog box

4. In the AutoSort options area, click Descending and choose Max of Avg from the Using field pop-up menu. In the AutoShow options area, click Automatic. Because the Show pop-up menu already is set for Top, type **3** in the text box (or use the up and down arrows).

Note

When you have more than one field in the Data area, you choose which field's top or bottom group to show in the Using field pop-up.

5. Click OK for each of the dialog boxes to return to your PivotTable. Select a year from the Page area pop-up to see the top three averages on each team in the data area, accompanied by the number of home runs hit by that player in the HR column.

When a field contains a number of numeric values, such as Year in our example, you can group the data into ranges. Control-click the Row or Column field you wish to group, and choose Group and Outline ➪ Group from the shortcut menu. The Grouping dialog box, shown in Figure 22-12, appears telling you the minimum and maximum values and suggesting a grouping factor in the By text box. If you wish to subset your data, you could exclude minimal values by setting a higher Starting at value and/or exclude maximal values by reducing the Ending at suggestion. Of course, you can always adjust the granularity of the report by changing the grouping factor.

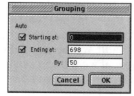

Figure 22-12: The Grouping dialog box show all or a subset and define your ranges here

Some PivotTable Options

Earlier in this chapter, we brushed right past one of the buttons in the third Wizard dialog box—the Options button. Although you can set your options there, we generally find it more helpful to do so after we've seen and worked with the table a bit. Once you have created your PivotTable, you can Control-click anywhere within it and choose Table Options from the shortcut menu or choose PivotTable ⇨ Table Options in the PivotTable toolbar to display the same PivotTable Options dialog box, shown here.

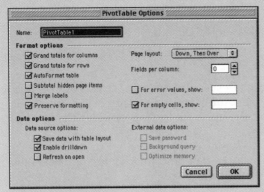

The PivotTable Options dialog box

First, you can name your PivotTable.

In the Format options area, you determine whether the PivotTable will reflect totals across rows and/or columns, whether the table should be autoformatted, and a host of other possibilities.

Probably the most interesting option is in the Data options—Enable drilldown. When Enable drilldown is on (the default), double-clicking in a Data area cell or choosing Group and Outline ⇨ Show Details on a data cell or cells will create a new worksheet in your workbook that displays the underlying data for the selected cell(s).

Breaking your data into separate tables

If you have a field (or fields) in the Page area and you want to explode the table into separate tables for each entry, choose PivotTable ⇨ Show Pages in the PivotTable toolbar (or Control-click and choose Show Pages in the shortcut menu). Select the field you want broken out, and a separate sheet and PivotTable will be created for each entry in the pop-up menu. Using our baseball example, if we wanted separate pages for each league, we would choose Show Pages and would have two new sheets: one for the American League and one for the National League.

Displaying PivotTable Data in a PivotChart

Almost every PivotTable you see in a newspaper has a chart next to it. Creating a chart based upon your PivotTable is a trivial exercise in Excel 2001. Click anywhere in your PivotTable and press F11 — voilà, you're in a new sheet with a column chart of your PivotTable. Using the Chart toolbar as covered in Chapter 19, you can change the kind of chart displayed and further customize its appearance.

If you're more comfortable using the Chart Wizard, you can choose Insert ➪ Chart and continue as covered in Chapter 19.

In Figure 22-13, we show a chart of the PivotTable after grouping years by 5. By default, each column field comprises a series (Y-axis) in the chart and each row field constitutes a category (X-axis) when charted.

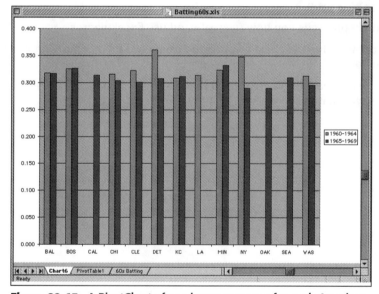

Figure 22-13: A PivotChart of maximum averages for each American League team across five-year periods

Note   Although Excel 2001 has many new and useful features that are not yet available in Excel for Windows, PivotCharts are one area where Microsoft has left Mac users at a disadvantage when compared to users of Excel 2000 on Windows. In Excel 2000, the PivotChart fields can be manipulated, grouped, and so forth exactly as in the PivotTable; however, on the Mac you must do your grouping and arranging in the PivotTable.

Summary

This chapter has shown you that you can use PivotTables to produce summaries, analyze data, and present consolidated information simply and quickly.

✦ You can use a PivotTable to quickly hide and show levels of detail in a database summary.

✦ You can use PivotTables to report total sales by product category, average salary per job classification, number of employees per department, and so forth.

✦ You can use a PivotTable as an intermediate step to breaking a large table out into separate, smaller tables.

Where to go next

✦ The next chapter tells you how to create and use Excel macros

✦ If you want to refine the chart you created from your PivotTable, Chapter 19 tells you how.

✦ Chapter 20 tells you about creating and managing lists in Excel. These lists are the underlying data used when creating a PivotTable.

✦   ✦   ✦

Working with Excel Macros

Macros are combinations of keystrokes that automate
many of the tasks you normally perform manually.
Macros enable you to record a sequence of actions that you
can assign to a keystroke combination, a graphic object, a
toolbar button, or a button on the screen. Later, you can play
back the sequence by pressing the keys, clicking the button,
or selecting the menu command assigned to the macro. When
you run the macro, Excel performs the steps as if you had just
typed the characters, made the menu choices, or performed
whatever actions you recorded for that macro. If you produce
daily reports or perform repetitive tasks, macros can save you
many keystrokes and a lot of time.

You don't have to be a programmer to create macros. All
you have to do is turn on the macro recorder and perform
the Excel steps in your worksheet as you normally do, and
then turn off the macro recorder.

Understanding Macro Types

Excel provides two types of macros:

✦ **Command macros** carry out a series of commands. For
example, you can create a command macro that marks a
specific range of worksheet cells and chooses File ⇨ Print
to begin printing. You can also create a macro that applies
a preferred format to an entire worksheet. Command
macros can range from simple to extremely complex.

✦ **Function macros** are similar to Excel's functions
because they act on values by performing calculations
and returning a value. For example, you can create a
macro that takes the dimensions of an area in feet and
returns the area in square yards.

Command macros are similar to commands because they perform tasks. Function macros are similar to functions because they are stored in formulas and accept and return a value. You can create command macros using the macro recorder. To create function macros, you must write Visual Basic for Applications code (see Chapter 25).

Creating a Macro

To create a macro, first perform every action that you don't want to include in the macro, such as opening a worksheet or moving to a specific location in the worksheet. By performing these actions first, you won't include unnecessary steps in the macro. As soon as you begin recording the macro, everything you do will be included in it.

Some steps shouldn't be included in a macro. For example, although you may always want to gather redundant data, you may not always want the data to land in the same worksheet. In this case, it is better to have the user manually go to the worksheet location prior to running the macro.

To begin creating a macro, choose Tools ⇨ Macro ⇨ Record New Macro. The Record Macro dialog box prompts you for the name and description of your new macro (see Figure 23-1).

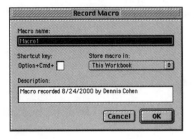

Figure 23-1: The Record Macro dialog box

Name your macro descriptively so that you know what it is and what it does when you need to assign it to a button or menu, or when you need to call on its actions. You can give the macro any name, as long as the first character of the macro name is a letter and you don't include spaces. Letters, numbers, and underscore characters are fair game. An underscore or hyphen works well in lieu of a space to separate words.

In the Description area, you can enter a description of the macro. A description can be helpful, reminding you what the macro does somewhere down the line when you are less likely to remember. You can assign a keystroke combination to your macro by entering a key to add to the ⌘-Option combination assigned by default. Just click in the Shortcut key text field and press the desired key.

When Do I Really Need Macros?

The kinds of macros that you can record with Excel's macro recorder are best at eliminating any kind of redundant work that you perform regularly. The kinds of tasks for which you can create macros to save yourself time and effort include:

✦ Selecting several ranges on one or more sheets of a workbook and printing those selected ranges

✦ Opening a new workbook, entering titles, formatting different ranges in the worksheet, and adjusting row heights and column widths

✦ Opening a database, sorting it in a desired order, applying a filter to the data, and printing the result

By default, the macro expects to be stored in your current workbook—This Workbook. This option places the macro in a module sheet that appears at the end of the workbook. Click the pop-up menu to choose where you want to store the new macro. The Personal Macro Workbook option makes the macro available to all open worksheets by attaching the macro to a hidden notebook that opens each time you launch Excel. If you need to see the macro sheet, choose Window ⇨ Unhide. (This option is only available after you've saved a macro to the Personal Macro Workbook.) The New Workbook option opens a new workbook and attaches the new module sheet to it.

After you complete the information in this dialog box and click OK, a small floating button bar appears to provide a Stop button. You are now in record mode, and any actions you perform are recorded.

Stopping the macro recorder isn't too difficult—click the Stop Recording button. This button appears onscreen when you begin to record a macro. Alternatively, you can choose Tools ⇨ Macro ⇨ Stop Recording.

You can also use the Visual Basic toolbar to record macros. To activate the Visual Basic toolbar, choose View ⇨ Toolbars ⇨ Visual Basic, or Control-click in any visible toolbar area and choose Visual Basic from the shortcut menu. You can then click the Record button on the Visual Basic toolbar to begin recording a macro. For everyday use of macros outside the world of programming, only two buttons on the Visual Basic toolbar will be of any interest to you—Record Macro and Run Macro. For an explanation of the remaining buttons, see Chapter 24, which provides details on programming in Visual Basic for Applications.

Now that you have had a general look at creating macros, you need to see how the specifics work. The following steps show you how to create a macro that selects a range in one of your worksheets and prints that range:

1. Open the worksheet to which you want to apply the macro.

2. Choose Tools ➪ Macro ➪ Record New Macro.

3. In the Record New Macro dialog box, enter **ReportIt** in the Macro name text box.

4. Click in the Shortcut key field and enter any letter key that you want to use (when combined with the ⌘-Option keys) to activate the macro.

5. After you click OK, you are ready to perform the macro steps. In this case, that means making the choices you need to print the range.

6. Select a range of data from your worksheet. Then choose File ➪ Print (⌘-P) to open the Print dialog box, as shown in Figure 23-2.

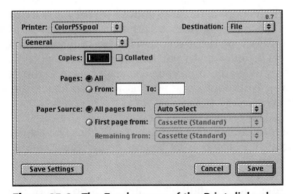

Figure 23-2: The Excel screen of the Print dialog box

7. In the pop-up menu (located below the printer name), select Microsoft Excel. On the Excel screen, click the radio button for Selection. Then click Print (or Save, if you are printing to a file) to print the selected part of your worksheet.

8. Click the Stop Recording button or choose Tools ➪ Macro ➪ Stop Recording to stop recording the macro.

From this point on, you can repeatedly select and print the same range of worksheets just by running the macro. To see how this works, press the keystroke combination that you assigned to the macro. If you didn't assign a key, or if you don't recall the key, you can select Tools ➪ Macro ➪ Macros and then double-click the ReportIt macro name in the Macro dialog box (or click the name once and click Run). With either method, the macro runs and the worksheet range is again printed. That's the beauty of macros — you can automate any task that you perform regularly.

The macros you create will differ because you will have different tasks to automate. By the way, in this exercise, you may need to change the orientation to Landscape so that the selection fits on one page. To do so, after selecting your range of data in the worksheet, select File ⇨ Page Setup, click Landscape (perhaps selecting High for the Print quality) and OK, and then go on to the Print command.

Cross-Reference For another exercise in creating a useful macro see the first exercise — a time sheet — in Chapter 25.

Assigning Macros

By assigning a macro to a button placed on a worksheet, a graphic object, a toolbar button, or a menu, you can probably provide the ultimate in user ease. The following sections cover each of these possibilities in detail.

Tip Using the same techniques described in this chapter, you can even assign the macro to a topic in a Help file.

Assigning macros to a worksheet button

Assigning a macro to a button — within reach, within sight, reminding you that the macro is available — can be very handy when you are working in a worksheet. One such macro button might be set up to open another worksheet page from the current worksheet page. While you look at one set of data, the macro button provides an easy way to access the other relative data.

Placing the button

To place a button in your spreadsheet and attach a macro to it, you can use the Button tool on the Forms toolbar. You activate the macro by clicking the button.

To add a macro button to a worksheet, follow these steps:

1. Turn on the Forms toolbar by choosing View ⇨ Toolbars ⇨ Forms.

2. Click the Button tool in the Forms toolbar.

3. In the worksheet, click and drag to place your button and define its size.

4. When you release the mouse button, the macro button and the Assign Macro dialog box appear, as shown in Figure 23-3.

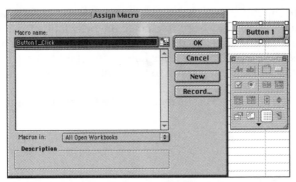

Figure 23-3: The new button and the Assign Macro dialog box (also shows the Forms toolbar)

5. In the Macro name list, double-click the macro that you want to assign to the button, or click the macro name once to select it and then click OK.

If you haven't already created your macro, you can create the button and then record the macro at the same time. Create the button and then click the Record button in the Assign Macro dialog box. In the Record New Macro dialog box, enter a name (optional), description, and key combination (optional) for the macro you will record. Then click OK and perform your macro steps, as described earlier.

Changing the button assignment

Excel also lets you assign a macro to a completed button or change the macro you have assigned to the button. You can perform these tasks by following these steps:

1. Control-click the button and choose Assign Macro from the shortcut menu to bring up the Assign Macro dialog box.

2. If you want to assign an existing macro, double-click the name in the Macro name list (or click the name once and then click OK).

3. If you want to record a macro, type the name for the new macro in the Macro name text box and click the Record button (which becomes active after you type the new macro name). Then use the standard macro recording procedures detailed earlier in the chapter.

Naming Buttons

When you create a button, it is assigned a default name, such as Button 1 or Button 2. Of course, you can change this name. Before the name has been assigned to a macro, it's a plain object, so you can simply select the text and edit and format it as you do with any text. After the text has been assigned to a button, you need to Control-click the button and select Edit Text from the shortcut menu. This provides the text cursor so you can edit the text and format it using the buttons on the Formatting toolbar. To change the formatting, you can also Control-click the button and select Format Control from the shortcut menu.

Assigning macros to graphic objects

You can get visually creative and make your spreadsheets more appealing by assigning a macro to a graphic object. The visual clues of the graphic can make your macro easier to remember. The procedure for adding a macro to a graphic object is much the same as the procedure for adding a macro to a toolbar button. Figure 23-4 is an example of a macro assigned to a graphic. In the figure, a macro that prints a report is attached to a picture of a car. To print the report, the user clicks the car.

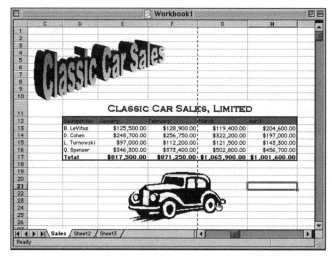

Figure 23-4: A macro attached to a graphic object (the car) in a worksheet

Note

When a graphic object, such as the car clip art in Figure 23-4, has a macro assigned, your cursor will change to a pointing hand cursor when it crosses over the object. This indicates that the object is either a link or acting as a button.

Follow these steps to assign a macro to a graphic object:

1. Add the graphic object to your worksheet using the steps outlined in Chapter 18.

2. Control-click the graphic. This automatically selects the graphic object (selection handles appear on its borders) as it reveals the shortcut menu.

   If the object currently has another macro assigned to it, Control-clicking may cause the macro to run. Instead, try holding down the ⌘ key as you select the object.

3. Select Assign Macro from the shortcut menu. In a moment, the Assign Macro dialog box appears.

The Old Way versus the New Way

If you've upgraded to Excel 2001 from Version 4.0 or 5.0 (Excel 95 on Windows), and you've used macros and the Excel macro language, you'll discover that many details have changed. In earlier versions of Excel, you recorded macros in Excel's macro language, a language with some similarities to (and a lot of differences from) Visual Basic for Applications.

Programs were known as macros and were recorded on macro sheets. In Excel 98 and Excel 2001 each individual program (written in Visual Basic for Applications) is a procedure, and procedures are stored in modules. Each workbook can have a virtually unlimited number of modules and procedures.

The languages also differ significantly. For example, Visual Basic for Applications brings object-oriented techniques into the picture, something that just didn't exist in the old Excel macro language.

You don't have to throw away all those macros you wrote in Excel 4.0. You can run an old macro from Excel 2001 the same way you run a new macro, or you can use the following Visual Basic for Applications statement in the Module tab of the macro:

```
RUN("macrosheetname!macroname")
```

In this statement, *macrosheetname* is the name of the old macro sheet, and *macroname* is the name of the macro you want to run. For more specifics on using Visual Basic for Applications code in your macros, refer to Chapter 25.

4. If you want to assign an existing macro to the object, double-click the name of the macro in the Macro name list, or click the name once to select it and then click OK.

5. If you want to create a new macro to the graphic object, name the macro, click Record, and then perform the steps to create a macro.

Assigning macros to toolbar buttons

Macros can also be assigned to buttons on the toolbar. This can prove useful if you perform certain tasks on a regular basis or create task-specific or job-specific toolbars for your office staff. Typically, people create a custom button to assign a macro to, but you can also assign a macro to an existing toolbar button, which cancels the previous function. To assign a macro to a toolbar button, perform these steps:

1. Choose Tools ➪ Customize.

2. If the toolbar that contains the desired button isn't visible, click the Toolbars tab of the dialog box and check the checkbox beside the toolbar name.

3. To assign a macro to an existing toolbar button, skip to Step 4. If you want to run the macro from a button not on a toolbar, click the Commands tab, and then click Macros in the Categories list. In the Commands list that appears, drag the Custom button onto a toolbar.

4. Control-click the toolbar button that is to receive the macro command, and choose Assign Macro from the shortcut menu.

5. In the Macro name text box, double-click the name of an existing macro in the Macro name list (or record a new macro by entering a name for the new macro, clicking Record, and then performing the macro steps).

6. By default, the name of any new button is Custom Button, which is not highly descriptive. It is easiest to change the name right way, while the Customize dialog box is still open and the button is still selected. Just click the Customize dialog box's Modify Selection button. When a menu pops up, move your mouse up to the Name field. Click in this field, select the existing text, type in your new button name, and press Enter. When the mouse pauses over the button, this name appears as the ScreenTip to inform you (and your users) as to its function.

7. Close the Customize dialog box.

You can change the name of your buttons any time. First select Tools ⇨ Customize because the toolbar cannot be modified without this Customize dialog box open. Then Control-click the button that you want to change, move to the Name field, select the existing text, and enter your new button name.

Assigning macros to menus

Macros can also be assigned to menus. You can place the macro command on an existing menu or create a specialized menu. If you are creating the worksheet for office use, creating task-specific or job-specific menus can be helpful. Adding commands to the menu is covered in detail in Appendix F. However, we'll go over it briefly here as well. To assign a macro to a menu, follow these steps:

1. Choose Tools ⇨ Customize.

2. On the Toolbars tab, check Worksheet Menu Bar. A customizable copy of the menu bar opens, located at the top of your screen below the normal menu bar and any docked toolbars you have displayed.

    (Optional) If you want to create a new custom menu, click the Commands tab, and then click New Menu in the Categories list. In the Commands list that appears, click New Menu and drag the words into place as desired on the customizable menu bar. Control-click the entry on the customizable menu bar and choose Properties from the shortcut menu, edit the command name to your liking, and then click OK. If you place this custom menu in the menu bar, it will appear on your main menu bar; however, you can also place the menu inside one of the existing menus, creating a custom submenu.

3. Click the Commands tab, and then click Macros in the Categories list. In the Commands list that appears, click Custom Menu Item and drag it onto the customizable menu bar. The menu drops down and reveals the menu's commands, and your cursor gains a field and a plus sign. Move your cursor (pointer) to the exact location on the menu where you want the new command to fall. A horizontal black line will show you where the command is due to fall as you release the mouse button. Release the mouse button when the command will fall where you want it.

4. In the customizable menu bar, click the menu in which you've placed the command, and Control-click the newly placed Custom Menu Item command, choosing Properties from the shortcut menu. Edit the name to your liking, and click OK. Then click Close to close the Customize dialog box.

5. You still have to assign the macro to the menu item. Choose the menu item. The Assign Macro dialog box appears, listing all available macros and asking you to assign a macro. Click the macro you want to assign and click OK. Alternatively, you could have assigned the macro before closing the Customize dialog box by Control-clicking the custom item you added, choosing Assign Macro from the shortcut menu, and proceeding as stated in the Assign Macro dialog box.

For more on naming, renaming, and customizing menus, see Appendix F.

Running a Macro

You have several ways to run a macro. After reading this section, you can decide for yourself which method is best for you.

The method always available to you for running a macro is to choose Tools ➪ Macro ➪ Macros and then double-click the name of the macro in the Macro dialog box. Or, if you want to read the macro's description, click the macro's name once to see a description (if you or the creator entered one), and then click the Run button.

Another method for running macros is to use the keyboard combination you assign to a macro in the Record New Macro dialog box. Keyboard combinations easily coexist with buttons, so you can use the combination or click any button you may have assigned to your macro.

You can also run the macro from the menu if you've placed it there. Last, if you've created any type of button for a macro, you can click the button.

Changing Macro Options

After recording a macro, you may have to change its description or the keyboard combination that runs it. You can also change the name of the macro as it appears in a menu or on a button. (See "Assigning macros to toolbar buttons" or "Assigning macros to menus" in this chapter, and Appendix F for more information on this subject.)

Perform these steps to change the options for an existing macro:

1. Choose Tools ➪ Macro ➪ Macros to open the Macro dialog box.

2. In the Macro name list box, select the name of the macro with the options you want to change.

3. Click the Options button to open the Macro Options dialog box, as shown in Figure 23-5.

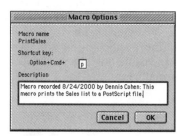

Figure 23-5: The Macro Options dialog box

4. Make the changes you want for the different options, and click OK.

Making Macros Available

You can store macros in a few different places, which directly affects the availability of the macro. You can store a macro in the Personal Macro Workbook, in the active workbook, or in a new workbook.

If you want to make a macro available at all times, store it in the Personal Macro Workbook, which is an invisible workbook that is always open, unless you specify otherwise. The Personal Macro Workbook is like the repository for workbooks you use in a variety of areas throughout Excel. Because this workbook is always open, the macros are all always available, which lets you use them with all worksheets you have open. You might think of this as Excel's equivalent to Word's Normal template.

The first time you quit Excel after the first time you save a macro to your Personal Macro Workbook, you are asked if you want to save the Personal Macro Workbook. Choose Yes. The Personal Macro Workbook is stored in the Excel folder (Microsoft Office 2001\Office\Startup\Excel). It will not exist until you have stored at least one macro in it.

To control where you store your macro, choose Tools ➪ Macro ➪ Record New Macro. In the Store macro in list box, choose the Personal Macro Workbook option to store this and successive macros in that workbook. This option remains in effect for all macros until you change it. In addition to placing the macros in the Personal Macro Workbook, you can also put them in the current workbook or in a new workbook.

The Personal Macro Workbook is similar to other workbooks, with the exception that it begins with one worksheet in which all the macros you specify are stored. If you are into Visual Basic for Applications (VBA), you may want to add other VBA module items to the Personal Macro Workbook.

To display the Personal Macro Workbook (after you have created it by saving a macro to it), choose Window ➪ Unhide and choose Personal Macro Workbook from the dialog box that appears. Figure 23-6 shows what the code stored in the Personal Macro Workbook looks like when the Visual Basic for Applications Editor is opened, using the Visual Basic toolbar. (For more specifics on VBA, see Chapter 25.) Remember that the Unhide menu option is visible only if a worksheet has been hidden (as the Personal Macro Workbook normally is).

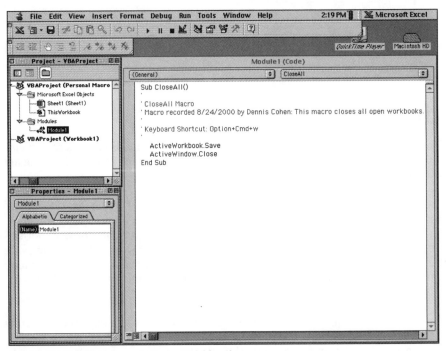

Figure 23-6: The Personal Macro Workbook

Summary

This chapter covered different topics related to macros. Now, you have the tools you need to record macros efficiently and put them to use for yourself. We covered the following areas related to macros:

✦ Excel provides two different types of macros: command and function.

✦ You can easily create macros with Excel's macro recorder.

✦ You can run macros by choosing Tools ➪ Macro ➪ Macros and selecting the desired macro in the dialog box that appears.

✦ You can attach macros to keyboard combinations, menu options, toolbar buttons, custom buttons, and graphic images.

✦ Macros are recorded in Visual Basic for Applications code, the underlying programming language of Office 2001.

Where to go next

✦ Macros can take much of the repetitive drudgery out of formatting and printing tasks. For an explanation of the kinds of formatting tasks you can automate, see Chapter 17. For specifics on printing in Excel, refer to Chapter 20.

✦ Excel macros are the key to learning Visual Basic for Applications. Chapter 25 delves more deeply into Visual Basic for Applications programming.

✦   ✦   ✦

Excel and the Web

Excel 2001 introduces numerous enhancements for working with the Internet and with intranets. Excel 2001 enables you to attach hyperlinks to other Office 2001 documents or to Web sites. The tablelike structure of a spreadsheet makes it easy for you to publish Web pages in table form. You can easily export worksheets or charts in Hypertext Markup Language (HTML) / Extensible Markup language (XML) format, ready for inclusion on your Web pages.

Working with Excel 2001 on the Web

Figure 24-1 shows data in an Excel workbook, published as a Web page on a corporate intranet and viewed using Microsoft Internet Explorer 5.0, a popular Web browser that is included with Microsoft Office 2001. You can also place hyperlink fields in the cells of a worksheet, and you can use these cells to display links in other Web pages on an intranet or on the Internet. If you need to retrieve or publish worksheet data across the Internet, Excel 2001 can be a powerful tool for accomplishing such a task.

 Caution   Many Web pages produced by Excel 2001, such as the one shown in Figure 24-1, are not displayed properly in Web browsers other than Internet Explorer 5.0 or newer. This is particularly true of pages that also contain figures and charts. If it is not guaranteed that your viewing audience will be using Internet Explorer 5.0 or later, you would be well advised to test your pages in other browsers before uploading them to your server.

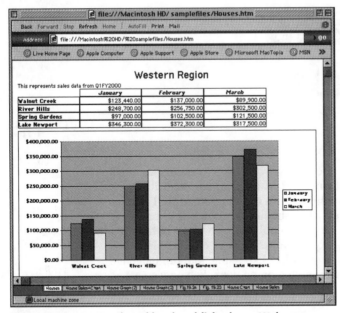

Figure 24-1: An Excel workbook published as a Web page;
the tabs at the bottom will take you to the other worksheets.

To accomplish most of the tasks described in this chapter, you'll need to be connected to the Internet or an intranet. You can obtain a dial-up connection to the Internet by means of a commercial Internet service provider. Your connection can also be a direct connection through your organization's local area network; you may be connected directly to a corporate intranet, in which case you'll be able to retrieve or publish data to your company's private network. This chapter won't go into specifics on getting connected, as that topic is a book in itself. IDG Books Worldwide publishes many great books covering all aspects of the Web.

This chapter also assumes a familiarity with the basics of Excel. If you are familiar with the World Wide Web or with intranets but haven't yet learned to work with Excel, you should peruse Chapters 15 through 20 before proceeding with this chapter.

Excel 2001 lets you perform a number of Internet-related tasks as you work with worksheets and charts. You can format text or objects in Excel worksheet cells as hyperlinks that link to other Office 2001 documents or to Web sites. (Your Web site can be on the Internet or on your company intranet.) When users of the worksheets click in these cells, they can jump directly to that location in the other file or to a specified Web site. You can open workbooks that are stored on the Internet, and you can save worksheet data as HTML, the publishing language of the Web. These topics are covered in more detail throughout this chapter.

Learning the Ropes

Because intranets and the Internet are new concepts to many readers, an explanation of terms may be in order. (If you're intimately familiar with the Internet, intranets, and the Web, you may want to skip this section and the next and dive right into working with Excel and the Web.) First, the Internet is a global collection of computers linked together by means of telephone and microwave lines and accessible to the public by means of various connections in offices and in homes. The Internet grew out of a research project in the 1970s that linked university and government computers in the United States. Since its inception, the Internet has grown to encompass millions of computers spread throughout dozens of nations. Any computer user with an Internet connection (either by means of a phone line or a direct hookup) can connect to the Internet and gain access to the volumes of information located there.

The World Wide Web

A major component of the Internet is the World Wide Web. The Internet has other parts, but the World Wide Web made the Internet fun and caught the public's eye. The World Wide Web is that part of the Internet that makes use of graphical software, known as Web browsers, and of files stored as HTML (which the browsers can read). The computers on the Internet that store the HTML files are called Web servers. When computers connect to the Internet to retrieve this data, they use Web-browser software, which converts the incoming information (encoded in HTML) to graphical pages displayed as a combination of text, graphics, and, in some cases, audio and video. On the Mac, Mosaic was the first Web browser. Then came Netscape Communicator, followed by Microsoft Internet Explorer. (These latter two browsers are the two most popular browsers on both the Mac and Windows platforms.) America Online and Prodigy also provide versions of Web browsers built into their software, generally customized versions of either Netscape Communicator or Internet Explorer. iCab and Opera are two other browsers that are becoming available for the Mac at the time we're writing this book.

The Internet

Each site on the Internet has a unique address, known as a URL (Uniform Resource Locator). When you establish an Internet connection, open a Web browser, and enter an Internet address, you are entering the address that tells the Web server to send you Web pages stored on the server at that address. For example, `www.whitehouse.gov` connects you to the Web server that provides the pages for the White House. If the address you enter specifies a page after the domain name (some examples of domain names are `whitehouse.gov` or `bighit.com`, and some examples of pages listed after domain names are `www.whitehouse.gov/index.html` and `homepage.mac.com/spenserpup/mybed.htm`), that page is served to you. Otherwise, the server brings you to the page designated as the default for the domain name you entered (the president's page, in this example). Web addresses such as these can be stored in Excel worksheets and displayed as hyperlinks.

About intranets

Office 2001 helps you make data available on intranets. An intranet is a private network of computers that is available only to the members of a specific organization. Intranets make use of World Wide Web technology — Web servers, network connections, and Web browser software — to enable members of an organization to share information. Intranets are very popular with corporations, as intranets let employees share work-related information in a confidential manner.

About HTML

As mentioned earlier, HTML is the language used for publishing information to the World Wide Web and to intranets that use World Wide Web technology. HTML is a text-based language that makes use of special codes called tags. These tags are included in the text of the HTML documents and provide instructions to the Web browser software, determining how the data appears when viewed by the end-user. You don't need to know the nuts and bolts of HTML coding to work with Excel and the Web; Excel does the coding for you. You just need to be familiar with the concept of saving your data in HTML file format. To publish Excel data on the Internet or on an intranet, you save that data as a Web Page, and then upload it to your Web server. If you are dealing with a corporate intranet, your company's Webmaster can tell you how to upload the HTML files (that Excel produces) to your company's Web server. If you are renting space on a commercial server, your site host can give you directions. If you are managing a Web site on the Internet or on an intranet, you already know how to do this; the rest of this chapter will deal mostly with getting that Excel data ready for uploading to your server. There might also be a folder of associated files that needs to be uploaded with your HTML file; there certainly will be if you have any graphics on your page, or if you save a workbook rather than just one worksheet.

About the Web toolbar

As with all the core Office 2001 applications, Excel provides the Web toolbar to help you browse through the resources on an intranet or on the Web. Using the Web toolbar, you can quickly open, search, and browse through any document or through a Web page. You can jump between documents, and you can add favorite sites you find on the Web to the Favorites folder, enabling you to go back to those sites later.

In Excel, you can display the Web toolbar by choosing View ➪ Toolbars ➪ Web or by clicking the Web toolbar button in the Standard toolbar, if it is not already visible. Figure 24-2 shows the Web toolbar.

Figure 24-2: The Web toolbar

You may find the Web toolbar handy when you are in Excel and need to get to the Web (or to your company's intranet) for information. For example, you can click the Search the Web button to launch your default Web browser and search the Web, or click the Favorites button to select a destination from a list of your favorite Web sites. For more specifics on the Web toolbar, see Chapter 11. That chapter provides a description of how you can use the Web toolbar and how Word 2001 can serve as a Web browser if you aren't using Microsoft Internet Explorer or Netscape Communicator.

Creating Hyperlinks

A significant feature of Excel 2001 is its capability to use hyperlinks in worksheets. You can create hyperlinks to jump to other Office documents stored on your Mac, on your company's network, on a company intranet, or on the Internet. You can also turn the text in a cell or a graphic into a hyperlink.

Linking to Office documents with copy and paste

Creating a hyperlink from cells in Excel to other cells in Excel, to a Word document, or to a PowerPoint presentation is as easy as copy and paste (actually Paste Hyperlink, in this case). To create a link to another Office document, follow these steps:

1. Select the cells that you want to have hold the hyperlink and choose Insert ➪ Hyperlink (⌘-K).

2. Display the Document tab of the Insert Hyperlink dialog box and click the Select button aligned with the Favorites and Recent Documents pop-up menus. Navigate in the Choose a File dialog box to locate the Office document to which you wish to link and click Open. The file name is now displayed in both the Link to and Display text boxes.

3. *(Optional)* If you wish to link to a specific location within the file, click the Locate button in the Anchor area to select your location.

4. *(Optional)* If you wish to have a screen tip other than the file name appear as the mouse pointer passes over the link, click the ScreenTip button, and supply the text that you wish to appear in the dialog box presented.

5. Click OK and the cell contents are now in blue and underlined, indicating a link.

Tip If you wish the contents of the linked cell or cell range to be something other than the file name of the document to which you're linking, you need to enter that information in the cell before performing Step 1.

From this point on, any time you click the hyperlink, you jump to the linked document.

To create a link from one Excel worksheet to the next, follow these steps:

1. Go to the worksheet containing the cell(s) where you want the link to appear and enter the link text in the cell (by that we mean the text that will be underlined as the actual link).

   Note that links connect to an entire cell or cells, not just to a few characters within any cell.

2. Choose Insert ➪ Hyperlink (⌘-K)

3. Proceed as described previously, selecting the workbook containing the target sheet (even if it is the current workbook).

4. Click Locate to display the Select Place in Document dialog box, as shown in Figure 24-3. Either enter a cell reference or select one from the list box. Click Ok in each dialog box.

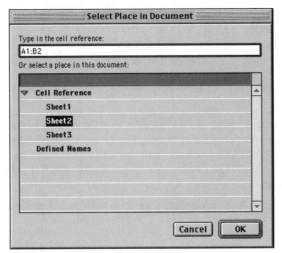

Figure 24-3: Select Place in Document dialog box; specify the location to which you wish to link

Your link will now jump you to the linked document and location.

Linking to Web sites with Insert Hyperlink

If you need to establish a hyperlink to a Web site on an intranet or on the Internet, you can use the following steps to do so:

1. Select the cell(s) that will serve as the hyperlink—if you want a label other than the URL as the link, enter it before proceeding to Step 2.

2. Click the Insert Hyperlink button in the Standard toolbar, or choose Insert ➪ Hyperlink (⌘-K). When you do this, the Insert Hyperlink dialog box appears, as shown in Figure 24-4. If the Web Page tab isn't already displayed, select it now.

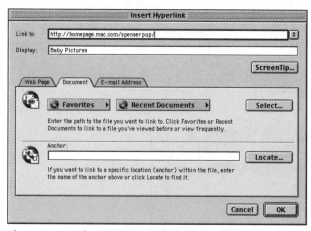

Figure 24-4: The Insert Hyperlink dialog box

3. To tell Excel to link to a Web destination, manually enter the Web address of the destination for the link in the Link to text box. A number of recent URLs will be available to choose from in the pop-up menu activated by clicking the button next to the Link to text box. You can also select from your Favorites list or your History list. Finally, you can click the Launch Web Browser to locate the desired URL.

4. Click OK to establish the hyperlink.

When you rest your cursor over a hyperlink, a ScreenTip appears and tells you the link's destination.

Publishing Worksheets and Charts

Excel 2001 makes it easy to convert worksheet ranges or Excel charts to HTML format, so that you can publish the data on the Internet or on an intranet. You can produce static Web pages; these appear on Web sites as fixed, unchanging data. If you change the data in your worksheet, the data will not automatically change on the Web page. Or, you can create a dynamic Web page, one that updates every time you save or on a fixed schedule.

Tip   Excel 2001 has a Web Page Preview choice in the File menu. Before you save the workbook as a Web page, you can choose File ➪ Web Page Preview to see your document as a Web page in your default Web browser.

When you select File ➪ Save as Web Page, you get a Save dialog box. Use the following steps to produce Web-ready files based on your worksheets or charts in Excel:

1. Choose File ➪ Save as Web Page. In a moment, the Save dialog box appears, as shown in Figure 24-5.

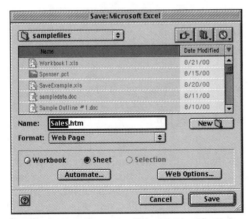

Figure 24-5: The Save dialog box with Web Page options

2. In the dialog box, specify whether you wish to save the workbook, the current worksheet, or the current selection as a Web page. If you wish to create a dynamic Web page, click Automate to display the Automate dialog box, as shown in Figure 24-6.

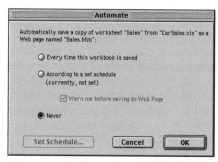

Figure 24-6: The Automate dialog box

3. Here, you can specify whether you want to create an update every time you save, create an update on a fixed schedule, or eliminate dynamic saves. Make your desired selection and click OK.

4. The Web Options button will present (surprise!) the Web Options dialog box (see Figure 24-7) letting you set additional information pertinent to Web browsers. The Web page title appears as the window name. Web page keywords are stored as META information for search engines to access. You can also specify a target monitor size on the Pictures tab, as well as a target resolution. The Files tab has only one option — whether links are automatically updated on a Save. The Encoding tab lets you specify an encoding to use (the default is Western European (Macintosh)). Click OK when you have these options the way you want them.

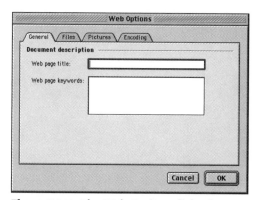

Figure 24-7: The Web Options dialog box

Summary

This chapter covered the details involved in sharing your Excel data with Internet/intranet users. The following points were covered in this chapter:

✦ Hyperlinks can be added to the cells of a worksheet, and you can store Web addresses or jump locations to other locations in the current document or other Office documents in those fields, as well as specifying e-mail links, or links to Web pages on the Internet or an intranet.

✦ Use File ⇨ Save as Web Page to convert ranges of worksheets or charts to HTML files for publishing on the Internet or on an intranet.

Where to go next

✦ Excel is just one component of the Web-publishing capabilities provided by Office 2001. Word and PowerPoint also offer Web publishing and Web interaction features. For specifics on Word and the Web, see Chapter 11; for PowerPoint and the Web, see Chapter 33.

✦ In the next chapter, you learn to further extend the power of Excel by using Visual Basic for Applications.

✦   ✦   ✦

Excel and Visual Basic for Applications

CHAPTER

25

This chapter details the use of Visual Basic for Applications (VBA), the programming language that is the basis for Excel macros. VBA is heavily based on Microsoft's Visual Basic programming language. Because Excel macros are stored as VBA, you can use VBA to automate common tasks in Excel.

VBA can take you much further than simply duplicating keystrokes; it gives you full access to all of Excel's commands. You can modify Excel's menus by adding your own commands and options, you can create custom dialog boxes to present messages and query users for information, and you can even construct complete applications for users with a limited knowledge of Excel. To accomplish these kinds of tasks, you need more than a familiarity with the recording and playing of macros; you need a basic understanding of VBA.

Learning VBA with Macros

Macros are an excellent starting point for understanding how VBA works and what you can do with the language. As Excel's Macro recorder stores all the actions you perform or the commands you choose, it interprets these actions or commands into statements, or lines of code, by using VBA. These statements are automatically placed in a procedure, which is a block of VBA code. Procedures are stored in modules, which you can think of as containers for all VBA code.

Cross-Reference Chapter 22 detailed the basics of using macros, which are sequences of instructions that cause Excel to perform a particular task. As that chapter demonstrated, macros greatly reduce the time you spend performing routine, repetitive tasks.

To give you an idea of how all Excel macros use VBA, you should practice on an example. This chapter familiarizes you with Visual Basic code by examining the procedure that results when you record this sample macro. The following steps create the simple time sheet shown in Figure 25-1. Because time sheets are typically created weekly, this procedure represents a common task that can be automated by creating a macro.

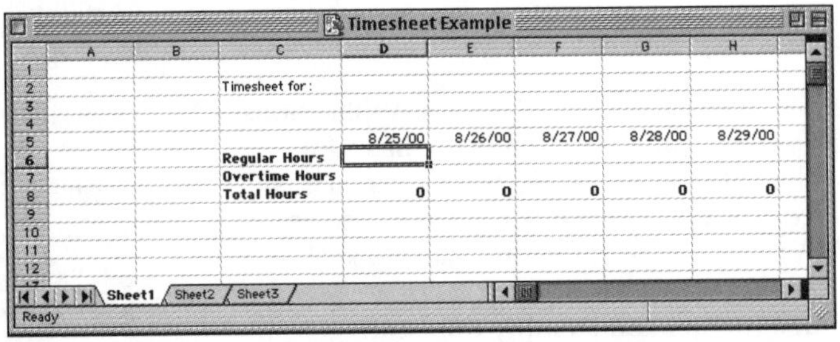

	A	B	C	D	E	F	G	H
1								
2			Timesheet for :					
3								
4								
5				8/25/00	8/26/00	8/27/00	8/28/00	8/29/00
6			Regular Hours					
7			Overtime Hours					
8			Total Hours	0	0	0	0	0
9								
10								
11								
12								

Timesheet Example — Sheet1 / Sheet2 / Sheet3 — Ready

Figure 25-1: A time sheet that results from creating the sample macro

Follow these steps to create the worksheet and the sample macro:

1. Open a new workbook, save it, and name the workbook ("Timesheet Example," for instance).

2. Choose Tools ➪ Macro ➪ Record New Macro.

3. In the Record New Macro dialog box, enter the name **TimeEntry** and click OK. The Stop Macro button, which you can use to stop recording the macro, appears in the Macro toolbar. This button may be floating above the worksheet in its own toolbar or may appear in the Macro toolbar, wherever it was last used.

4. Click in cell C2 and enter **Timesheet for:**.

5. Click in cell D5, enter **=Today()**, and press Enter to end the entry within that cell.

6. Click in the center of D5 and drag from cell D5 to H5 to select D5 and the next four cells to the right.

7. Choose Edit ➪ Fill ➪ Series.

8. In the Series dialog box, click OK to accept the default options.

9. Click in cell C6 and enter **Regular Hours**.

10. Click in cell C7 and enter **Overtime Hours**.

11. Click in cell C8, enter **Total Hours**, and press Enter.

12. Select the range of cells from C6 to C8, and click the Bold button on the Formatting palette to add bold formatting.

13. In the column header, click the border between cells C and D and drag to widen column C until it is wide enough to display the longest text in the column.

14. Click in cell D8. Click the equal sign, and then click in cell D6 and click in D7 to create the formula =D6+D7 (or manually enter the formula **=D6+D7** in the cell). Then click OK to enter the formula.

15. Click in the center of D8 and drag from cells D8 to H8 to select cell D8 and the four cells to the right of it.

16. Choose Edit ➪ Fill ➪ Right (⌘-R).

17. Click the Bold button on the Formatting palette to apply bold formatting to the selected cells.

18. Click in cell D6 (this repositions the cursor to prepare the worksheet for data entry).

19. Click the Stop Macro button (on the floating Macro toolbar) or select Tools ➪ Macro ➪ Stop Recording to stop recording the macro.

20. Save your worksheet again — as you should do frequently.

You can verify the effects of the macro by moving to a blank worksheet, choosing Tools ➪ Macro ➪ Macros, double-clicking TimeEntry to run it (or click once on TimeEntry to select it and click the Run button). The time sheet duplicates in the blank worksheet.

The Similarities of VBA and Visual Basic

If you've already worked with Microsoft's Visual Basic as a development language, you'll find Visual Basic for Applications similar. Visual Basic for Applications is solidly based on Microsoft's Visual Basic programming language. Visual Basic for Applications replaces the old macro-based languages, such as Excel's old macro language (pre-Excel 5), with a common development language. Developers now need only learn one language to develop in all Office applications (except Entourage) easily, on both the Mac and in Windows.

Microsoft uses Visual Basic as the base language and has added extensions to the language as implemented in the other Office applications. The commands, functions, methods, procedures, and program structures used in Visual Basic can all be used in Visual Basic for Applications for Word, Excel, and PowerPoint. So if you're a Visual Basic programmer, you're on very familiar ground.

Understanding VBA Code

Of course, the purpose of the exercise you just completed is not to demonstrate how to create a macro but to show how Visual Basic for Applications code works as the basis of any macro.

To open the Macro so you can edit it, follow these steps:

1. If the macro is stored in the Personal Macro Workbook, this workbook must be unhidden before you can edit it. Select Window ➪ Unhide. In the Unhide dialog box that appears, double-click Personal Macro Workbook. (If you are not sure whether you need to perform this step, you can try skipping it. The Office Assistant lets you know if you need to go back.)

2. Choose Tools ➪ Macro ➪ Macros to open the Macro dialog box. (If you stored your macro in the Personal Macro Workbook and unhid it, you can do this while the worksheet you created the macro in is the active document or while the Personal Macro Workbook is the active window.)

3. Select the TimeEntry macro, and click Edit. This opens the Visual Basic Editor, shown in Figure 25-2. As shown in the figure, the VBA code behind the macro appears in the Module window at the right.

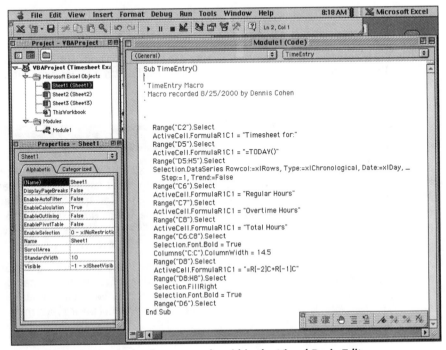

Figure 25-2: An example of macro code within the Visual Basic Editor

The code looks like this:

```
Sub TimeEntry()
'
' TimeEntry Macro
' Macro recorded 8/25/2000 by Dennis Cohen
'

    '
    Range("C2").Select
    ActiveCell.FormulaR1C1 = "Timesheet for:"
    Range("D5").Select
    ActiveCell.FormulaR1C1 = "=TODAY()"
    Range("D5:H5").Select
    Selection.DataSeries Rowcol:=xlRows, Type:=xlChronological,
Date:=xlDay, _
        Step:=1, Trend:=False
    Range("C6").Select
    ActiveCell.FormulaR1C1 = "Regular Hours"
    Range("C7").Select
    ActiveCell.FormulaR1C1 = "Overtime Hours"
    Range("C8").Select
    ActiveCell.FormulaR1C1 = "Total Hours"
    Range("C6:C8").Select
    Selection.Font.Bold = True
    Columns("C:C").ColumnWidth = 14.5
    Range("D8").Select
    ActiveCell.FormulaR1C1 = "=R[-2]C+R[-1]C"
    Range("D8:H8").Select
    Selection.FillRight
    Selection.Font.Bold = True
    Range("D6").Select
End Sub
```

Each step you took during the recording of this procedure resulted in the addition of one or more lines of Visual Basic code in the module. The code appears in color: comments are displayed in green; key words of the Visual Basic language appear in blue; and all other code appears in black. When you run this (or any) macro, you are in effect running the Visual Basic for Applications code that is contained in the module that was recorded by the macro recorder. As the module runs, each line of Visual Basic code is executed in turn, and Excel performs an appropriate action as a result.

About comments

You can include comments (lines that aren't acted upon by Excel when the code runs) by preceding the text with a single quotation mark. In the sample procedure, you can see that the first two lines are comments:

```
' TimeEntry Macro
' Macro recorded 8/25/2000 by Dennis Cohen
```

In this case, Excel added the comments based on the entries in the Macro name and Description text boxes of the Record Macro dialog box. If you assigned a keyboard command, the command appears as a comment there, too. You can place comments wherever you desire in your Visual Basic code by typing a single quote mark followed by the text of the comment. Comments can be quite helpful in your more complex procedures to help you remember what's going on at any specific point in the procedure. They can occupy an entire line, or you can put them at the end of a valid line of code by starting the comment with a single quotation mark. When the procedure runs, whatever follows the single quotation mark is ignored until Excel finds a new line of code.

About headers and footers

The macro begins with an introductory header to the procedure.

```
Sub TimeEntry()
```

The matching footer (last line) reads:

```
End sub
```

Every VBA procedure starts with a header that begins with Sub or Function and ends with a footer that says End Sub or End Function. VBA supports two types of procedures: function procedures and subprocedures. Function procedures are like Excel's built-in functions. They accept a value(s), act on the data, and return a value(s). Subprocedures do not return a value (although you can pass values from within a subprocedure through the use of statements inside the procedure). Any arguments used by a function procedure are placed inside the parentheses of the header. The footer tells Excel that it has reached the end of the procedure. When Excel reaches the footer in the module, it passes program control back to any other VBA procedure that called this one. If the procedure was not called by another procedure, Excel returns control from the procedure to Excel itself.

About selecting and entering data

Following the header statement are two lines of code that select cell C2 and insert a text entry into that cell. The Visual Basic code for these two lines is:

```
Range("C2").Select
ActiveCell.FormulaR1C1 = "Timesheet for:"
```

The Range statement tells Excel to select a range. Because only one cell's address is given (cell C2), Excel selects only that cell. The next statement tells Excel to enter a text value (in this case, the words Timesheet for:) in the active cell of the worksheet, which is now cell C2.

About control statements

Besides containing lines of code that cause cursor movement and data entry in the worksheet, various lines of code within the program control certain characteristics of the worksheet in Excel. For example, when you apply bold formatting to a selection, the following code results:

```
Selection.Font.Bold = True
```

This line of code, when executed, takes the current selection and turns on bold character formatting. The following lines of code result from opening the Series dialog box (after choosing Edit ➪ Fill ➪ Series) and accepting the default options in the dialog box:

```
Selection.DataSeries Rowcol:=xlRows, Type:=xlChronological,
Date:=xlDay, _
        Step:=1, Trend:=False
```

While examining this line, you should also notice the presence of the continuation character used in VBA. The underscore at the end of the first line is the continuation character, and it denotes that a line of program code is to be continued onto the line that follows. (Without this character, VBA considers any single line to be a complete program statement.)

As you grow accustomed to working in VBA, you'll find that you can accomplish a great deal of useful work by means of the various cell selection and control statements that the language supports.

About displaying dialog boxes

One of the reasons you may actually want to do some Visual Basic programming yourself (rather than using only the macro recorder) is that you can do some custom programming—such as displaying dialog boxes—that you cannot do with recorded macros. To display a dialog box onscreen that contains a message with custom text, you can use VBA's MsgBox function. The syntax of the statement is simple—you add a line of code that reads MsgBox("your custom text"), where you put your desired text between the double quotation marks.

If you duplicated the example earlier in the chapter, go to the end of the line prior to the End Sub and press Return to add a new, blank line to the very end of the procedure. With the insertion point at the start of the blank line, enter the following:

```
MsgBox("Enter your week's time and save under a new name.")
```

Choose File ➪ Close and Return to Microsoft Excel (⌘-Q) to quit the Visual Basic Editor. Go to a blank worksheet page and choose Tools ➪ Macro ➪ Macros. In the Macro dialog box, select the TimeEntry macro and click Run. This time, when the macro completes, you see the dialog box shown in Figure 25-3. Dialog boxes such as this one can serve to inform users, providing needed guidance about tasks the user needs to perform.

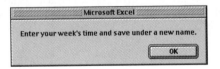

Figure 25-3: The dialog box presented by the MsgBox function

About user input

Another useful task that you can handle by adding your own Visual Basic code is prompting users for information and acting on a user's response. The InputBox function acts in a manner similar to the MsgBox function, but with InputBox, a text box appears within the dialog box. The value that the user enters in the text box is returned by the function.

You can try using the InputBox function by getting back into the module that you created as part of this exercise. Choose Tools ➪ Macro ➪ Macros to open the Macro dialog box. Click the TimeEntry macro, and click Edit to open the Visual Basic Editor. Find the following line:

```
ActiveCell.FormulaR1C1 = "Timesheet for:"
```

Place the cursor at the end of the line, and press Return to add a new line underneath this one. Enter the following two lines as new code in the procedure:

```
Range("D2").Select
ActiveCell.FormulaR1C1 = InputBox("Employee Name:")
```

(It's okay to copy and paste text in the Editor to save time and ensure the proper code. In this case, you can actually copy the line that says `Range("D5").Select` the line, paste it into the new space, and then change the 5 to a 2.)

Choose File ➪ Close and Return to Microsoft Excel (⌘-Q) to quit the Visual Basic Editor. Move to a blank worksheet and run the macro again. (Choose Tools ➪ Macro ➪ Macros. In the Macro dialog box, double-click the TimeEntry macro.) When the macro runs, a dialog box such as the one shown in Figure 25-4 appears, asking for an employee name. After you enter a name, the macro stores that name in cell D2 of the worksheet.

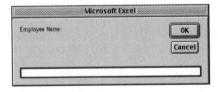

Figure 25-4: The dialog box presented by the InputBox function

Learn By Example

If you really want to do VBA programming, one of the best ways to learn the language is to examine working applications and macros ranging from simple to complex. Microsoft provides examples. To install them, use the Value Pack Installer, open the Programmability option, and then select Excel Sample VBA Code. You should also install VBA Help, so that the Assistant (or Help menu) has the Help files present to answer your questions about VBA.

After they are installed, you find the samples in the Examples folder within the Sample Files folder directly within the Microsoft Office 2001 folder. Double-click this worksheet to open it, or use the File ➪ Open command.

Editing VBA Code

When you click a module tab, select a macro in the Macro dialog box and click Edit to open the Visual Basic Editor, you can enter program code just like you type text in any word processor. You don't have to know the mechanics of entering text and correcting mistakes; you can use the same text entry and editing techniques — including cutting and pasting — that you can use in any Mac word processor.

 Tip In text or spreadsheet documents, it is nice to use smart quotes, which curl inward toward quoted text rather than the straight tick marks typewriters used. In Visual Basic code, you must use the old-fashioned tick marks, so if you've pasted in text that contains the curly-style quotes, delete them and retype the quote marks.

Printing Visual Basic Code

You can print the code that is contained in your Visual Basic modules. To print the code, open the module that contains the desired code by choosing Tools ➪ Macro ➪ Macros, selecting the desired macro, and clicking Edit to reveal the code. Then choose the File ➪ Print (⌘-P) to bring up a simple Print VBA Project dialog box. There may be several macro modules on the page. By default the current one (the one you selected to edit) is printed. You can choose to print all modules in the project if you want.

Using the Visual Basic Toolbar

If you do much work in Visual Basic for Applications programming, you find the Visual Basic toolbar (see Figure 25-5) useful. You can activate the Visual Basic toolbar by Control-clicking the toolbar area and choosing Visual Basic from the shortcut menu, or by selecting View ➪ Toolbars ➪ Visual Basic.

Figure 25-5: The Visual Basic toolbar

Table 25-1 provides an explanation for the different buttons on the Visual Basic toolbar.

Table 25-1	
Buttons on the Visual Basic Toolbar	
Name	*Function*
Run Macro	Opens the Run Macro dialog box, where you can run, delete, or edit any macro you select.
Record Macro	Opens the Record Macro dialog box, where you can fill in the desired options used to begin recording a macro.
Pause/Resume Macro	Resumes playing a macro that you have paused.
Visual Basic Editor	Opens the Visual Basic Editor, where you can create, edit, and step through macros using Visual Basic.
Design Mode	Switch in and out of Design mode.

Because you may likely create macros in each of the Office applications, you should know that the Visual Basic toolbar in Word does not include the Pause/Resume button or the Design Mode button, while PowerPoint simply has the Run Macro and Visual Basic Editor buttons.

Going Forward

Make no mistake about it, using Visual Basic for Applications falls well into the realm of programming. (If you're completely new to programming, you should be congratulated for pressing this deeply into what, for many readers, is a subject of mystifying complexity.) You've not only learned how VBA lies at the heart of all that you do with macros, you've also learned how you can extend the power of your macros by adding your own Visual Basic code to provide items such as dialog boxes and customized prompts.

Still, you've only scratched the surface of what you can do with this language. VBA is a full-featured programming language that you can use to automate or customize virtually any conceivable task that can be done with Excel. If you're encouraged (dare we even say excited?) by the challenges of programming, you should look into additional resources for learning about Visual Basic programming. It's a subject about which entire books have been written.

Summary

This chapter has provided an introduction to programming using Visual Basic for Applications, the underlying language behind Excel macros, and covered the following points:

✦ Every Excel macro exists as a series of Visual Basic for Applications program statements.

✦ The VBA statements are stored in procedures, and one or more procedures are placed in modules. Modules are part of the workbook, edited through the Visual Basic Editor. (They don't show up as sheets in the workbook.)

✦ VBA procedures can be subprocedures or function procedures. Function procedures are like Excel's built-in functions because they accept a value or values, act on the data, and return a value. Subprocedures do not return a value (although you can pass values from within a subprocedure through the use of statements inside the procedure).

✦ You can modify the VBA code that Excel's macro recorder creates to add special features such as dialog boxes and custom prompts.

Where to go next

✦ The next chapter shows how you can use Excel to create and use worksheets for common business tasks.

✦ Because Visual Basic for Applications lies at the heart of macros that you create in Excel, you should be familiar with the use of macros before getting involved with Visual Basic for Applications. See Chapter 22.

✦ ✦ ✦

Excel at Work

This chapter gets you started on your own applications by providing some examples and step-by-step instructions that you can use to build models of worksheets for various tasks.

Managing Cash Flow

Managing cash flow, or your accounts receivable and accounts payable, is a basic job that virtually every modern business faces. The following cash-flow worksheet is relatively simple to set up and keeps a clear "picture" of available funds. The worksheet is patterned after the common single-entry debits and credits bookkeeping system. You enter a starting balance into cell H4. Use column A to record the dates of each transaction, whether a credit or a debit. Use columns B, C, and D to record credits by listing the creditor, the description, and the amount. Use columns E, F, and G to record debits by listing to whom the amount is paid, the description, and the amount. Column H contains the formulas you use to keep a running total of the cash on hand. You compute the total by taking the preceding entry's running balance, adding the credits, and subtracting the debits. You can maintain this type of system by creating a separate worksheet for each month. At the end of the year, you can consolidate the totals into another worksheet to show yearly figures for cash flow. The worksheet is shown in Figure 26-1.

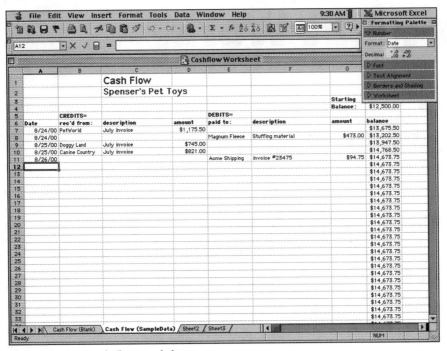

Figure 26-1: A cash flow worksheet

To build the worksheet, enter the following labels and formulas into the cells as shown:

Cell	Entry
A6	Date
B5	CREDITS=
B6	rec'd from:
C1	Cash Flow
C6	description
D6	amount
E5	DEBITS=
E6	paid to:
F6	description
G3	Starting
G4	Balance:

Cell	Entry
G6	amount
H6	balance
H7	=H4+D7−G7
H8	=H7+D8−G8

In the area below cell C1, you may want to add the name of your company or organization. In the example, we used Spenser's Pet Toys.

To copy the formula into successive cells in column H, select the range of cells from H8 to H40. Choose Edit ⇨ Fill ⇨ Down, or select H8 and, when the cursor is over the lower-right corner, drag down through H40. To format the cells in column H, select the range of cells from H4 to H40. Then choose the Currency option in the Formatting palette's Number Format drop-down list. Using the same steps, choose the same currency format for the cells from D7 to D40 and from G7 to G40. To format a range of cells to display dates, select the range of cells from A7 to A40, choose Format ⇨ Cells (⌘-1) to open the Format Cells dialog box, click the Number tab, click the Date option in the Category list, and select the second date format (3/14/01).

At this point, the worksheet is ready to use. Size the columns and format the text as you'd like. Although you may want to use your own figures, to jog your memory Figure 26-1 shows part of the cash-flow worksheet that has been filled in with figures from a hypothetical small business.

Performing Break-Even Analysis

A common what-if scenario for almost any firm is the break-even analysis, which determines how many units of a given product must be sold before the producer shows a profit. A break-even analysis requires the juggling of two groups of figures: fixed costs and variable costs. Fixed costs do not directly increase with each unit sold. Such costs include the rental of the manufacturing plant, utilities to power the production line, and advertising expenses. Variable costs directly increase with each unit sold. Such costs include the cost of the materials to assemble each unit, labor costs per unit, packaging costs, and shipping costs.

A typical break-even analysis performs a one-time deduction of the fixed costs and then calculates the per-unit costs for each unit produced. These negative amounts are balanced against the net profits (the net sales cost times the number of units sold). As the number of units sold increases, a break-even point is reached where the total profit equals the negative fixed and variable costs. Figure 26-2 shows an example of a break-even analysis worksheet illustrating the break-even point for a child's bicycle.

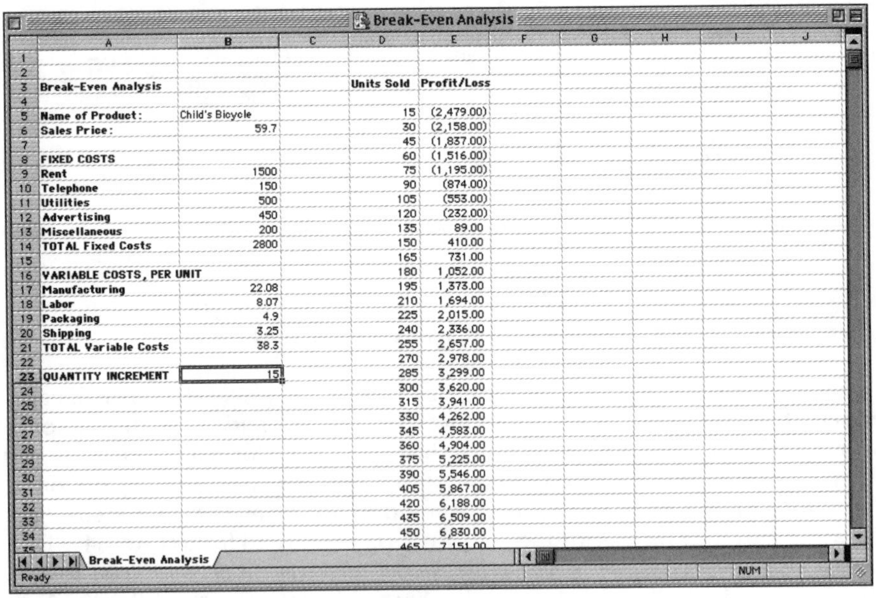

Figure 26-2: A break-even analysis worksheet

To build the model, open a new worksheet. Widen column A to roughly three times its default width and widen column B to roughly twice its default width. The other columns can remain at the default widths. Enter the following formulas in the cells as shown:

Cell	Entry
A3	Break-Even Analysis
A5	Name of Product:
A6	Sales Price:
A8	FIXED COSTS
A9	Rent
A10	Telephone
A11	Utilities
A12	Advertising
A13	Miscellaneous

Cell	Entry
A14	Total Fixed Costs
A16	Variable costs, per unit
A17	Manufacturing
A18	Labor
A19	Packaging
A20	Shipping
A21	Total Variable Costs
A23	Quantity Increment
B5	Child's bicycle
B6	59.7
B9	1500
B10	150
B11	500
B12	450
B13	200
B14	=SUM(B9:B13)
B17	22.08
B18	8.07
B19	4.9
B20	3.25
B21	=SUM(B17:B20)
B23	15
D3	Units Sold
D5	=B23
D6	=D5+$B$23

You can create the remaining formulas in column D quickly by selecting the range from D6 to D41. Then choose Edit ⇨ Fill ⇨ Down, or select D6 and, when the cursor is over the lower-right corner, drag down through D41.

Cell	Entry
D7	=D6+$B$23
D8	=D7+$B$23
D9	=D8+$B$23
D10	=D9+$B$23
D11	=D10+$B$23
D12	=D11+$B$23
D13	=D12+$B$23
D14	=D13+$B$23
D15	=D14+$B$23
D16	=D15+$B$23
D17	=D16+$B$23
D18	=D17+$B$23
D19	=D18+$B$23
D20	=D19+$B$23
D21	=D20+$B$23
D22	=D21+$B$23
D23	=D22+$B$23
D24	=D23+$B$23
D25	=D24+$B$23
D26	=D25+$B$23
D27	=D26+$B$23
D28	=D27+$B$23
D29	=D28+$B$23
D30	=D29+$B$23
D31	=D30+$B$23
D32	=D31+$B$23
D33	=D32+$B$23
D34	=D33+$B$23
D35	=D34+$B$23
D36	=D35+$B$23
D37	=D36+$B$23
D38	=D37+$B$23

Cell	Entry
D39	=D38+$B$23
D40	=D39+$B$23
D41	=D40+$B$23

In column E, enter the following values and formulas:

Cell	Entry
E3	Profit/Loss
E5	=D5*$B$6−($B$14+($B$21*D5))

You can create the remaining formulas in column E quickly by selecting the range from E5 to E41. Then choose Edit ➪ Fill ➪ Down, or select E5 and, when the cursor is over the lower-right corner, drag down through E41.

Cell	Entry
E6	=D6*$B$6−($B$14+($B$21*D6))
E7	=D7*$B$6−($B$14+($B$21*D7))
E8	=D8*$B$6−($B$14+($B$21*D8))
E9	=D9*$B$6−($B$14+($B$21*D9))
E10	=D10*$B$6−($B$14+($B$21*D10))
E11	=D11*$B$6−($B$14+($B$21*D11))
E12	=D12*$B$6−($B$14+($B$21*D12))
E13	=D13*$B$6−($B$14+($B$21*D13))
E14	=D14*$B$6−($B$14+($B$21*D14))
E15	=D15*$B$6−($B$14+($B$21*D15))
E16	=D16*$B$6−($B$14+($B$21*D16))
E17	=D17*$B$6−($B$14+($B$21*D17))
E18	=D18*$B$6−($B$14+($B$21*D18))
E19	=D19*$B$6−($B$14+($B$21*D19))
E20	=D20*$B$6−($B$14+($B$21*D20))

Continued

Cell	Entry
E21	=D21*$B$6–($B$14+($B$21*D21))
E22	=D22*$B$6–($B$14+($B$21*D22))
E23	=D23*$B$6–($B$14+($B$21*D23))
E24	=D24*$B$6–($B$14+($B$21*D24))
E25	=D25*$B$6–($B$14+($B$21*D25))
E26	=D26*$B$6–($B$14+($B$21*D26))
E27	=D27*$B$6–($B$14+($B$21*D27))
E28	=D28*$B$6–($B$14+($B$21*D28))
E29	=D29*$B$6–($B$14+($B$21*D29))
E30	=D30*$B$6–($B$14+($B$21*D30))
E31	=D31*$B$6–($B$14+($B$21*D31))
E32	=D32*$B$6–($B$14+($B$21*D32))
E33	=D33*$B$6–($B$14+($B$21*D33))
E34	=D34*$B$6–($B$14+($B$21*D34))
E35	=D35*$B$6–($B$14+($B$21*D35))
E36	=D36*$B$6–($B$14+($B$21*D36))
E37	=D37*$B$6–($B$14+($B$21*D37))
E38	=D38*$B$6–($B$14+($B$21*D38))
E39	=D39*$B$6–($B$14+($B$21*D39))
E40	=D40*$B$6–($B$14+($B$21*D40))
E41	=D41*$B$6–($B$14+($B$21*D41))

Either choose Accounting from the Formatting palette's Number Format drop-down list or use Format ⇨ Cells (⌘-1) to format the ranges from B6 to B21 and from E5 to E41 with the Accounting format (click the Number tab, choose Accounting in the Category list, and then click OK). To use the worksheet, enter your respective fixed and variable costs in the cells provided. In the QUANTITY INCREMENT cell, enter the quantity you want to use as a scale for the break-even analysis. For example, to see how many hundreds of units it will take to break even, enter **100** for a quantity increment. For a more detailed analysis, enter a smaller increment. You can extend the analysis to cover even more units by simply copying the respective formulas down the column past row 41. However, if you're not breaking even by row 41 of the worksheet, the analysis is trying to tell you that either your increment is too small or your pricing or manufacturing strategy has a serious flaw!

Using the IRA Calculator

An IRA calculator is a straightforward financial tool designed to plot the increasing value of an IRA (Individual Retirement Account). Four columns within the worksheet contain a beginning balance in the account, a yearly contribution, an interest rate, and an ending balance. A less complex worksheet would assume a standard interest rate and yearly contribution, but in real life, your yearly contribution may vary, and it is virtually impossible to plan for a standard interest rate. Keeping separate columns for these values for each year gives you the ability to insert each year's interest rate and the amount of the IRA contribution.

Figure 26-3 shows an example of an IRA calculator worksheet. In column C, you enter the beginning balance (starting with zero in the first row). Column D contains the yearly contribution, which in this example is $1,700 the first year, $1,850 the second, $1,900 the third, and assumed to be $2,000 per year afterward. Column E contains the interest rate, assumed to be 8.5 percent the first year, 7.25 percent the second year, 6.75 percent the third year, and 6.5 percent per year afterwards. Column F contains the formula that calculates the effect of the accumulating interest and the added yearly investment. The formula calculates on the basis of simple interest by adding the current balance to the yearly contribution and adding the result multiplied by the yearly interest rate to provide the new balance. Each year's new balance is then carried to the successive balance column.

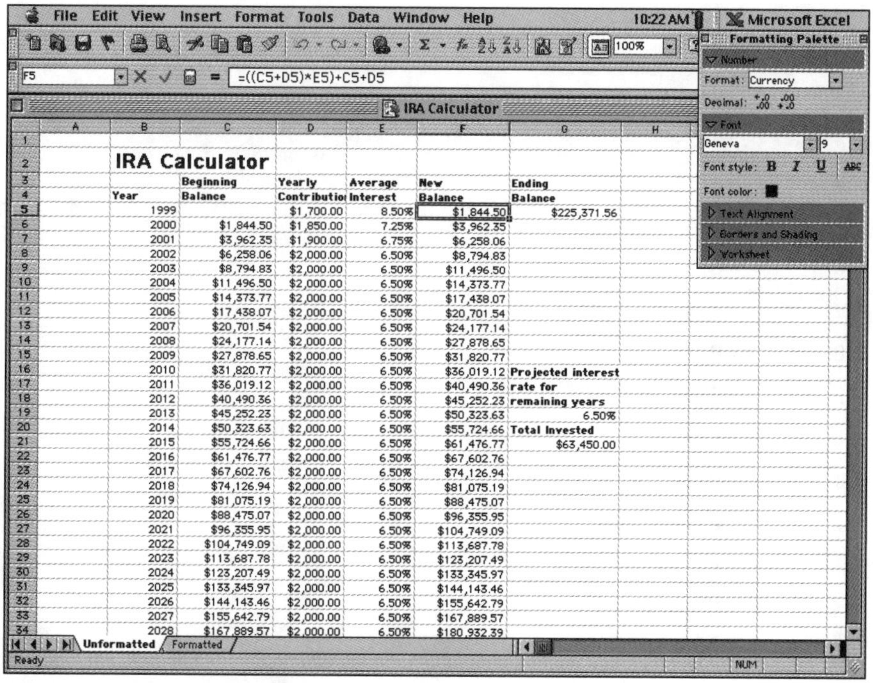

Figure 26-3: An IRA calculator worksheet

To build the worksheet, enter the following formulas into the cells shown:

Cell	Entry
B2	IRA Calculator
B4	Year
B5	1999
B6	=B5+1

To create the following formulas, select the range from B6 to B37. Then choose Edit ➪ Fill ➪ Down, or select B6 and, when the cursor is over the lower-right corner, drag down through B37 (this is called *drag-fill*).

Cell	Entry
B7	=B6+1
B8	=B7+1
B9	=B8+1
B10	=B9+1
B11	=B10+1
B12	=B11+1
B13	=B12+1
B14	=B13+1
B15	=B14+1
B16	=B15+1
B17	=B16+1
B18	=B17+1
B19	=B18+1
B20	=B19+1
B21	=B20+1
B22	=B21+1
B23	=B22+1
B24	=B23+1
B25	=B24+1
B26	=B25+1
B27	=B26+1

Cell	Entry
B28	=B27+1
B29	=B28+1
B30	=B29+1
B31	=B30+1
B32	=B31+1
B33	=B32+1
B34	=B33+1
B35	=B34+1
B36	=B35+1
B37	=B36+1

In column C of the worksheet, enter the following values and formulas:

Cell	Entry
C3	Beginning
C4	Balance
C6	=F5

To create the following formulas, select the range from C6 to C37. Then choose Edit ⇨ Fill ⇨ Down, or use the drag-fill technique.

Cell	Entry
C7	=F6
C8	=F7
C9	=F8
C10	=F9
C11	=F10
C12	=F11
C13	=F12
C14	=F13
C15	=F14

Continued

Cell	Entry
C16	=F15
C17	=F16
C18	=F17
C19	=F18
C20	=F19
C21	=F20
C22	=F21
C23	=F22
C24	=F23
C25	=F24
C26	=F25
C27	=F26
C28	=F27
C29	=F28
C30	=F29
C31	=F30
C32	=F31
C33	=F32
C34	=F33
C35	=F34
C36	=F35
C37	=F36

In column D of the worksheet, enter the following values:

Cell	Entry
D3	Yearly
D4	Contribution
D5	1700
D6	1850
D7	1900
D8	2000

To create the following entries, select the range from D8 to D37. Then choose Edit ➪ Fill ➪ Down.

Cell	Entry
D9	2000
D10	2000
D11	2000
D12	2000
D13	2000
D14	2000
D15	2000
D16	2000
D17	2000
D18	2000
D19	2000
D20	2000
D21	2000
D22	2000
D23	2000
D24	2000
D25	2000
D26	2000
D27	2000
D28	2000
D29	2000
D30	2000
D31	2000
D32	2000
D33	2000
D34	2000
D35	2000
D36	2000
D37	2000

In column E of the worksheet, enter the following values and formulas:

Cell	Entry
E3	Average
E4	Interest
E5	8.5%
E6	7.25%
E7	6.75%
E8	=$G$19

To create the following formulas, select the range from E8 to E37. Then choose Edit ⇨ Fill ⇨ Down, or use drag-fill.

Cell	Entry
E9	=$G$19
E10	=$G$19
E11	=$G$19
E12	=$G$19
E13	=$G$19
E14	=$G$19
E15	=$G$19
E16	=$G$19
E17	=$G$19
E18	=$G$19
E19	=$G$19
E20	=$G$19
E21	=$G$19
E22	=$G$19
E23	=$G$19
E24	=$G$19
E25	=$G$19
E26	=$G$19
E27	=$G$19

Cell	Entry
E28	=$G$19
E29	=$G$19
E30	=$G$19
E31	=$G$19
E32	=$G$19
E33	=$G$19
E34	=$G$19
E35	=$G$19
E36	=$G$19
E37	=$G$19

In column F of the worksheet, enter the following:

Cell	Entry
F3	New
F4	Balance
F5	=((C5+D5)*E5)+C5+D5

Select the range of cells from F5 to F37. Then choose Edit ⇨ Fill ⇨ Down to copy the formula into the successive cells, or use drag-fill.

In column G of the worksheet, enter the following values and formulas:

Cell	Entry
G3	Ending
G4	Balance
G5	=F37
G16	Projected interest
G17	rate for
G18	remaining years
G19	6.5%

Continued

Cell	Entry
G20	Total invested:
G21	=SUM(D4:D36)

Using Format ➪ Cells, select the ranges from C6 to C37, D5 to D37, and F5 to F37, one range at a time. Choose Currency in the Formatting palette's Number Format drop-down list to format these cells in the currency format. Also format cells G5 and G21 for the same type of display. Similarly, select the range from E8 to E37 and choose Percentage from the Formatting palette's Number Format drop-down list.

After you have entered the formulas, the worksheet displays the interest accumulation and yearly balances, as shown in Figure 26-3. You can change the interest rates and investment amounts to correspond to your desired investment rates.

Working with Mortgages and Amortization

The mortgage analysis worksheet has a straightforward design. It uses the PMT (payment) function to calculate the payments on a loan and displays an amortization schedule for the term of the loan. Figure 26-4 shows the worksheet.

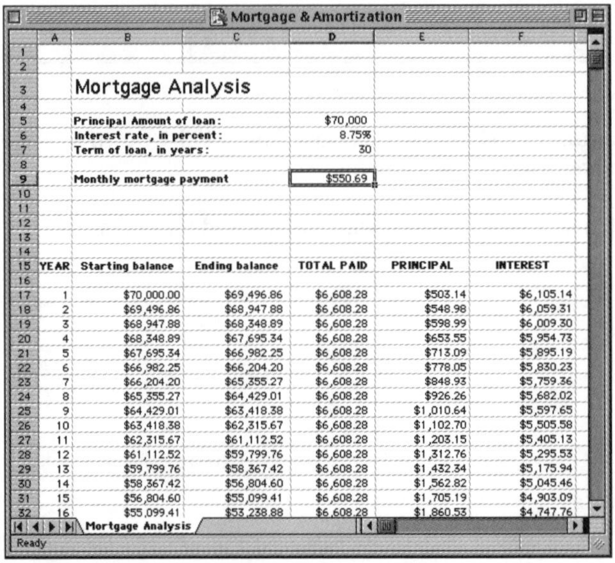

YEAR	Starting balance	Ending balance	TOTAL PAID	PRINCIPAL	INTEREST
1	$70,000.00	$69,496.86	$6,608.28	$503.14	$6,105.14
2	$69,496.86	$68,947.88	$6,608.28	$548.98	$6,059.31
3	$68,947.88	$68,348.89	$6,608.28	$598.99	$6,009.30
4	$68,348.89	$67,695.34	$6,608.28	$653.55	$5,954.73
5	$67,695.34	$66,982.25	$6,608.28	$713.09	$5,895.19
6	$66,982.25	$66,204.20	$6,608.28	$778.05	$5,830.23
7	$66,204.20	$65,355.27	$6,608.28	$848.93	$5,759.36
8	$65,355.27	$64,429.01	$6,608.28	$926.26	$5,682.02
9	$64,429.01	$63,418.38	$6,608.28	$1,010.64	$5,597.65
10	$63,418.38	$62,315.67	$6,608.28	$1,102.70	$5,505.58
11	$62,315.67	$61,112.52	$6,608.28	$1,203.15	$5,405.13
12	$61,112.52	$59,799.76	$6,608.28	$1,312.76	$5,295.53
13	$59,799.76	$58,367.42	$6,608.28	$1,432.34	$5,175.94
14	$58,367.42	$56,804.60	$6,608.28	$1,562.82	$5,045.46
15	$56,804.60	$55,099.41	$6,608.28	$1,705.19	$4,903.09
16	$55,099.41	$53,238.88	$6,608.28	$1,860.53	$4,747.76

Figure 26-4: A mortgage analysis worksheet

Cells D5, D6, and D7 of the worksheet contain the principal loan amount, interest rate, and term of the loan in years. In cell D9, the following formula supplies the rate, number of periods, and present value:

```
=PMT((D6/12),(D7*12),-D5)
```

The rate and the number of periods are converted to months, and the present value is shown as a negative value representing cash paid out.

Year one of the amortization schedule begins in row 17. The starting balance is derived from the amount entered in cell D5. To arrive at the ending balance in column C for the first year, use a formula containing the following variation of Excel's PV (Present Value) function:

```
=PV(($D$6/12),(12*($D$7-A17)),-$D$9)
```

Now calculate the remaining forms in the row. The total paid (column D of the amortization schedule) is the monthly payment (cell D9) multiplied by 12 to compute a yearly amount. The principal in column E is calculated by subtracting column C of the schedule (the ending balance) from column B (the starting balance).

You calculate the interest (column F) by subtracting the difference between the starting and ending balance from the total paid. As the formulas are duplicated down the worksheet, relative references are adjusted upwards for each successive row location.

Choose Format ➪ Column ➪ Width to change the width of column A to 5 spaces and the width of columns B, C, D, E, and F to 15 spaces. (You can also format any of the columns by dragging the right column border in the column header. As you drag, the ScreenTip reports the column width in spaces and hundredths of a space.)

To build the worksheet, enter the following formulas in the cells shown:

Cell	Entry
A15	YEAR
A17	1

To enter the rest of the year numbers, select the range from A17 to A46. Then choose Edit ➪ Fill ➪ Series. (Be sure to choose Edit ➪ Fill ➪ Series, not Edit ➪ Fill ➪ Down.) Click OK in the dialog box to fill the range. When you do so, cells A17 through A46 contain values from 1 through 30 representing 30 years of mortgage payments.

In column B of the worksheet, enter the following information:

Cell	Entry
B3	Mortgage Analysis
B5	Principal amount of loan:
B6	Interest rate, in percent:
B7	Term of loan, in years:
B9	Monthly mortgage payment
B15	Starting balance
B17	=D5
B18	=C17

In column C of the worksheet, enter the following information and formulas:

Cell	Entry
C15	Ending balance
C17	=PV(($D$6/12),(12*($D$7–A17)),–$D$9)
C18	=PV(($D$6/12),(12*($D$7–A18)),–$D$9)

In column D of the worksheet, enter the following values and formulas:

Cell	Entry
D5	70000
D6	8.75%
D7	30
D9	=PMT(($D6/12),(D7*12),–D5)
D15	TOTAL PAID
D17	=$D$9*12
D18	=$D$9*12

In column E of the worksheet, enter the following information and formulas:

Cell	Entry
E15	PRINCIPAL
E17	=B17−C17
E18	=B18−C18

In column F of the worksheet, enter the following information and formulas:

Cell	Entry
F15	INTEREST
F17	=D17−(B17−C17)
F18	=D18−(B18−C18)

When you have entered these formulas, select the range of cells from B18 to F46. Choose Edit ⇨ Fill ⇨ Down (or use drag-fill) to fill the successive formulas into the selected rows. To apply formatting to a range, select the range from B17 to F46. Choose Currency from the Formatting palette's Number Format drop-down list or choose Format ⇨ Cells (⌘-1) and click the Number tab in the Format Cells dialog box. Click Currency in the Category list and click OK. Apply the same formatting for D5. At this point, your worksheet should resemble the example in Figure 26-4.

The range in this example assumes a 30-year loan. However, if you enter a period of 15 years but leave the formulas intact for 30 years, you will get the interesting benefit of a nest egg that has been calculated as an increasing negative balance when the mortgage ends and the amortization schedule shows mortgage payments still being added. To avoid this situation, just adjust the range when you fill down to match the number of years for the mortgage. If you want to get fancy, you can record a macro that clears the range, takes the number of years from cell D7, selects a new range equivalent to that number of years, and performs a Fill Down command.

Summary

This chapter provided step-by-step instructions for creating various models that you may find useful in Excel. You learned how to create worksheets to do the following:

✦ Cash-flow management

✦ Break-even analysis

✦ IRA calculations

✦ Mortgage loan calculation and amortization

Where to go next

As these examples demonstrate, much of the basic work behind creating and using spreadsheets involves routine data and formula entry and simple to moderately complex formatting. For many spreadsheet users, these tasks are 90 percent of what they do in Excel.

✦ The next chapter answers common questions that arise when you use Excel.

✦ You can find tips and techniques that help ease the tedium of basic data and formula entry in Chapter 16.

✦ For the complete scoop on how you can format your Excel worksheets, see Chapter 17.

✦   ✦   ✦

The Excel Top Ten

◆ ◆ ◆ ◆

Excel users routinely find the same questions arising as they gain proficiency with the program. To save you time and effort, we've compiled the top ten Excel questions and their answers, based on inquiries to Microsoft Technical Support.

1. Can I set up a workbook to open when I launch Excel?

You can open a workbook each time you start Excel by placing the workbook in the Excel Startup folder. The full path to this folder is Microsoft Office 2001:Office:Startup:Excel. All the workbooks placed in this folder will open automatically whenever you launch Excel. These workbooks can include worksheets, chart sheets, Visual Basic modules, Excel dialog sheets, and older Excel macro sheets.

Caution

Normally, we do not recommend storing a worksheet anywhere within an application folder. This can be disastrous if someone unknowingly trashes the Microsoft Office 2001 folder to perform a clean reinstall. We *strongly* recommend you place an alias of the workbook in the Startup:Excel folder instead.

2. Can I change the folder Excel jumps to during an open or save? While I'm at it, can I change the default font?

Changing the default folder and the standard font are simple tasks in Excel 2001. To set these preferences for all workbooks, use the General tab of the Preferences dialog box, which appears after you choose Edit ⇨ Preferences. Follow these steps to change the default working directory:

1. Choose Edit ⇨ Preferences and click the General tab in the Preferences dialog box.

2. Click the Select button next to the Default file location text box. Use the resulting dialog box to select the folder you want Excel to jump to in all Open and Save dialog boxes.

3. Click OK when you've made all your preferences changes.

To change the default font for all new workbooks, follow these steps:

1. Choose Edit ➪ Preferences and click the General tab in the Preferences dialog box.

2. Click the arrows next to the Standard font list and select from the list of available fonts. Do the same with the Size arrows.

3. Click OK when you've made all your preferences changes.

While you're in the Preferences dialog box, you can also change the default number of tabs per workbook, if you want, or change any of the other default options.

3. How can I display more than one workbook at a time?

Each workbook you open is its own window. You can move each window around as you please. However, when you create a new workbook and then another, they open on top of one another. Follow these steps to view multiple workbooks simultaneously:

1. Open as many workbooks as you want to view. (Double-click to open a worksheet, use File ➪ Open, or open them any other way you prefer.)

2. Choose Window ➪ Arrange.

3. In the Arrange Windows dialog box that appears, choose tiled, horizontal, vertical, or cascade as desired, and then click OK to arrange the workbooks so you can see them all.

4. How can I prevent slashes or hyphens from being formatted as dates?

Excel automatically applies built-in number formats to values entered in an unformatted cell. Normally, the appearance of the value is not altered because the format is a general number format. However, Excel tries to help you with formatting, so if the entry contains a slash or a hyphen that separates values, Excel interprets the value as a date. If the entry contains a colon, Excel expects that the value represents a time value (hours, minutes, seconds, and so on). If you want to display the value exactly as it was entered—with slashes, hyphens, or colons—and don't want Excel to confuse the value with a date or time, you must format the value as a text value. To create a text value, simply precede the entry with a single quotation mark (') or follow these steps:

1. Select the cells in which you want to enter data.

2. Choose Text in the Number Format drop-down list in the Formatting palette.

Or, if you prefer to go through a dialog, follow these steps:

1. Select the cells in which you want to enter data.

2. Choose Format ⇨ Cells (⌘-1) and select the Number tab from the dialog box that appears.

3. In the Category list, select Text.

4. Click OK.

When you enter values in the selected cells, the values are displayed as you typed them. Remember that the cells must be formatted as text prior to entering your data.

5. What are some shortcuts for selecting cells and ranges?

Rather than clicking and dragging to select a range, you can use the Name list on the left side of the formula bar to select cells and ranges. This not only selects ranges on the active sheet — it selects ranges on other sheets within the workbook, too!

The Name list displays the cell reference or the cell name of the currently selected cell and provides a list of all the defined names in your workbook when you click the arrow to the right of the list box. When you click the arrow and select a name or enter a cell reference in this list box, Excel selects the specified cell or range, moving to the other worksheet if needed.

Tip   You can also use the Name list to define a name and insert the name into a formula. If you want to define a name for a cell or cell range so you can select it later or use it in a formula, select the cell or range, click in the Name list box, type a new name, and press Enter.

Table 27-1 contains a list of shortcuts for selecting cells and ranges.

Table 27-1
Shortcuts for Selecting Cells and Ranges

To Select	Do the Following
A named cell or range on the active or another worksheet	In the Name list box, type or select the name.
An unnamed cell	In the Name list box, enter the cell reference and press Enter.
An unnamed range	With your mouse, select the first cell in the range. If the last cell in your range is an unnamed cell, enter a cell reference and press Shift-Enter. If the last cell in your range is a named cell, press Shift as you select the name from the Name list.
Nonadjacent named and unnamed cells	With your mouse, select the first cell or range. To make subsequent selections, press the ⌘ key as you click in other cells, drag over a range of cells, select a name from the Name list box, or enter a cell reference in the Name list box.

6. How do I format characters in superscript, subscript, or a different font?

In Excel, you can add such character formatting as superscript, subscript, different fonts, styles, size, underlining, color, and so on to individual characters in a single cell. Table 27-2 contains a few examples of different kinds of formatting you can add to the characters in a cell.

Table 27-2 Formatting You Can Add to Characters in a Cell	
Formatting	*Example*
Italics	*4th Quarter*
Superscript	2³
Subscript	10₂
Different font	_(R-S)=_-1(S)

Note   The phi character (_) is a capital F in the Symbol font. (Use the Font list in the tool-bars to change to the Symbol font, and type **F**.)

You can format text just as you do in any word processor, except you select the text within the formula bar or in the cell (if you have in-cell editing turned on). To select individual text in a cell, select the cell, and then click in the formula bar and drag over the text. If you are using in-cell editing, you can double-click in the cell and drag to select the text you want to format. To select text in a text box, double-click in the text box and drag to make the selection you want. After the text is selected, you can use the Formatting palette or, for more variations, you can choose Format ⇨ Cells (⌘-1) or Control-click the selected text and choose Format Cells. In either of the latter two cases, you bring up the Format Cells dialog box. Select the Font tab and choose the options you want. The multiple-character formatting applies only to text.

To enter superscript and subscript, you must either enter the values as text by preceding the value with a single quotation mark (') or preformatting the cell as Text. For example, 2³ and 10₂ would be displayed as 23 and 102 if they are not entered as text.

7. How can I combine the contents of two cells into one?

If you have information in two separate cells that you want to combine into one cell, or if you want to combine text with a formula in a cell, use the CONCATENATE( ) function, which takes up to 30 arguments (the contents of up to 30 cells) and can consist of cell references, text, and formulas. Note that the text arguments must be enclosed in quotation marks.

Suppose someone's first name is stored in cell C1 and the last name is stored in cell D1. If you want to combine the text in those cells, enter the following formula in cell E1:

```
=CONCATENATE(C1, " ",D1)
```

The second argument in the formula is a space enclosed in quotation marks, so there will be a space between the first and last names. If you want to combine the text Amount Payable: $ with the sum of cells A1:B1, you could enter the following formula in cell E1:

```
=CONCATENATE("Amount Payable: $",SUM(A1:B1))
```

8. How can I define a worksheet area for printing?

To define a print area, choose File ➪ Page Setup and click the Sheet tab of the Page Setup dialog box. Place the insertion pointer in the Print Area text box and, on your worksheet, select the range or ranges you want to print. You can also enter references or names for the print area yourself. You may even want to add the Set Print Area button to a toolbar.

Another way to define a print area is to simply select your range, choose File ➪ Print, choose Microsoft Excel in the pop-up menu in the Print dialog box, and then click the Selection radio button and click Print.

And still another way to define a print area is to simply select the range(s) and choose File ➪ Print Area ➪ Set Print Area.

Cross-Reference   These options are explained in more detail in Chapter 20.

9. How can I make titles print on each page?

If you want to print titles on each page, choose File ➪ Page Setup and click the Sheet tab. Place your insertion pointer in the Rows to repeat at top box or the Columns to repeat at left box, and then select the rows or columns on your worksheet that you want to have print on each page. You may also enter references or names for the rows or columns in these boxes.

10. Can I open a spreadsheet created in ClarisWorks Office or AppleWorks 5?

The answer is yes . . . and no. A spreadsheet saved as a ClarisWorks document doesn't open as a spreadsheet in Excel 2001. However, ClarisWorks 5.0 and AppleWorks 5 comes with many filters. An AppleWorks or ClarisWorks user can easily do a Save As and select a format Excel can read. For example, the file can be saved as an Excel (for Mac) 5.0 file or as an Excel (for Windows) 5.0/7.0 file. When you receive the file, it will have the familiar Excel icon. Just double-click to open the file. By the way, ClarisWorks 5.0 and AppleWorks 5 use DataViz Version 9.7 translators (as of this writing, the current version is 12).

In addition, if you have upgraded to AppleWorks 6 from either ClarisWorks or AppleWorks 5, those DataViz translators will still work with AppleWorks 6, enabling you to save your files in the format of one of the earlier Excel versions.

Tip The MacLink Plus translators, from DataViz (www.dataviz.com), are an excellent investment if you will be dealing with documents from a variety of other products. The stand-alone MacLink Plus product will convert documents from one application format to another without requiring that either application be present.

Summary

This chapter covered the top ten Excel questions and their answers. This chapter concludes the Excel section of this book. The section that follows describes Microsoft PowerPoint, the presentation graphics package provided with Office 2001.

Where to go next

✦ If you have questions regarding formatting that aren't covered here, look in Chapter 17.

✦ Chapter 20, about printing and page setup, answers your printing questions.

PowerPoint

This part introduces PowerPoint, the Office 2001 presentation program. You'll begin with an overview of Power Point's menus and toolbars, and then work your way through creating a presentation. You'll also learn about macros and using PowerPoint to generate Web pages. And finally, you'll learn how to make your presentation sing and dance with animation.

Working with PowerPoint

This chapter teaches methods for moving your toolbars and palettes, saving presentations, aligning objects, rearranging a slide show, and changing the slide layout itself. Objects become more important in PowerPoint as you experiment with different layouts. You will also learn how to perform different tasks with the objects that you add to your presentation.

Discovering the Presentation Window

PowerPoint's presentation window is where you create slides and arrange them in your presentation—this is the bulk of the work that is done in PowerPoint. Familiarizing yourself with the PowerPoint window (see Figure 28-1) is very important for easy functioning in PowerPoint.

At the lower-left corner of the presentation window are the view buttons (see Figure 28-2), which enable you to switch among different views in the PowerPoint presentation window. The view buttons include, from left to right: Normal view, Outline view, Slide view, Slide Sorter view, and Slide Show view. You can also change views by choosing the appropriate commands from the View menu.

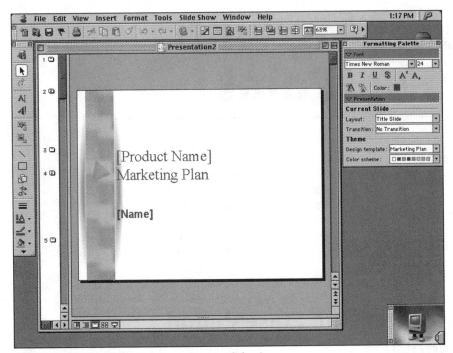

Figure 28-1: The PowerPoint window in Slide view

Figure 28-2: The view buttons (close up)

Click the Slide view button when you want only one slide to appear onscreen. Slide view is a WYSIWYG (What You See Is What You Get) representation of your slide. (Figure 28-1 shows Slide view.)

Click the Outline view button to show the slide in outline form so that you can move headings and other information by clicking and dragging text (see Figure 28-3). Outline view enables you to see the title and body text of all your slides simultaneously.

Click the Slide Sorter view button for a view of all the slides in a presentation so that you can quickly see their layout and sequence (see Figure 28-4).

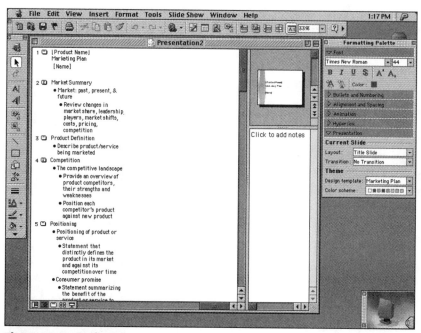

Figure 28-3: Outline view

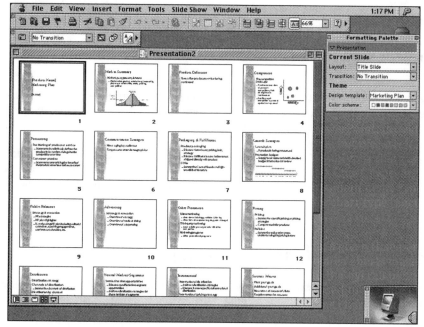

Figure 28-4: Slide Sorter view

One other editing view worth knowing about at this point is the Notes Page view. Choose View ➪ Notes Page to enter any notes that you may want to attach to the slide or to display any notes that you may have already written (see Figure 28-5).

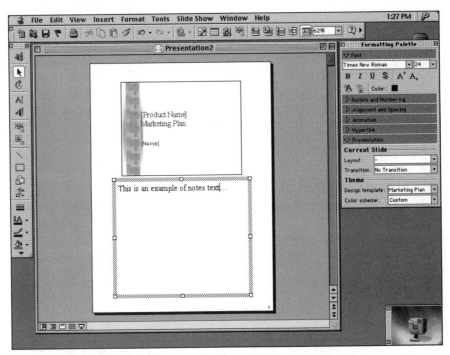

Figure 28-5: Notes Page view

Click the Slide Show button to run the slide show after you have completed the slides. Notice how the slide now fills the screen (see Figure 28-6). You can also view your slides as a timed presentation.

> **Tip** To end a slide show press either Escape or ⌘-Period, or Control-click and choose End Show from the contextual menu. You can also simply click while in the final slide of the presentation to return to the view you were in when you began the slide show.

Working with Shortcuts and Toolbars

Just as with other Microsoft programs, PowerPoint offers shortcut menus, shortcut buttons, and toolbars to make it as easy as possible to create a presentation.

Using shortcut menus

PowerPoint provides shortcut menus so you can perform different commands without using the pull-down menus. Shortcut menus, as the name suggests, can save lots of time. To activate any of the shortcut menus, move the pointer to the object that you want the command to act on, press and hold down Control, and click with the mouse. Figure 28-7 shows the shortcut menu that appears when you Control-click outside any objects in the Slide view.

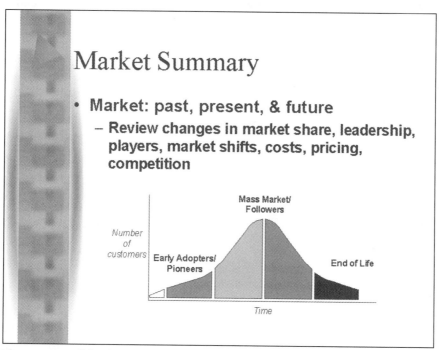

Figure 28-6: Slide Show view

Figure 28-7: A shortcut menu in a PowerPoint slide window

Using the toolbars and palettes

When you open the PowerPoint window and enter Slide view, you see the Standard toolbar and two palettes. The Standard toolbar appears at the very top of the screen (see Figure 28-8) to open presentations, to save, to print, or to insert objects and charts. At the right of the screen is the Formatting palette (see Figure 28-9), which is used to perform tasks related to formatting, such as applying different fonts and styles and changing the indentation of the presentation. At the left of the screen is the Drawing toolbar (see Figure 28-10), which is used to perform tasks related to controlling the appearance of shapes. You can draw shapes, rotate them, and control different aspects of their appearance onscreen.

Figure 28-8: The Standard toolbar

Figure 28-9: The Formatting palette

Figure 28-10: The Drawing toolbar

Tip Hold the cursor over any item on a toolbar without clicking and a "tip" will pop up and tell you what it is.

You can activate the other PowerPoint toolbars by choosing View ➪ Toolbars and selecting other toolbars from the list in the Toolbars submenu (see Figure 28-11), or you can Control-click the toolbar area of the screen and select the toolbars you want from the shortcut menu that appears.

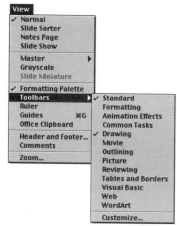

Figure 28-11: The Toolbars drop-down menu

Tip As with all Office toolbars, you can grab any or all of PowerPoint's toolbars and drag them to anywhere onscreen. Just click the dots on the left end or top, and drag. Moreover, you can change a toolbar's size and shape by clicking and dragging its lower-right corner.

Using PowerPoint's Default Presentations

By far, the easiest way to create a presentation in PowerPoint is to use one of the many default presentation templates that are provided with the software. The advantage of using a default template is that it already contains slides with content guidelines that you can follow to quickly build a presentation for a typical business need. PowerPoint provides one blank presentation, many presentation templates, and complete presentations.

The following is a list of a handful of the types of default presentation templates available in the Project Gallery dialog box. Some of the templates listed are only available after installing the additional templates found in the Value Pack folder.

✦ **Company Meeting** creates a presentation for a company meeting.

✦ **Financial Overview** creates a presentation that enables you to give a financial overview of your company.

✦ **Marketing Plan** creates a presentation that enables you to show a marketing plan for a company.

✦ **Project Overview** shows the progress of a company project.

✦ **Recommending a Strategy** offers a slide layout that is useful for determining a strategy.

✦ **Generic** creates a blank presentation—you have to provide all the formatting, layout, and content.

The last default presentation template is the new blank presentation option (File ⇨ New Presentation or ⌘-N), which enables you to create your own layout. As you gain experience using PowerPoint, you will feel more comfortable using this option.

To create a presentation by using a default presentation template, follow these steps:

1. Start a new presentation by choosing File ⇨ Project Gallery (⌘-Shift-P). The Project Gallery dialog box appears, as shown in Figure 28-12.

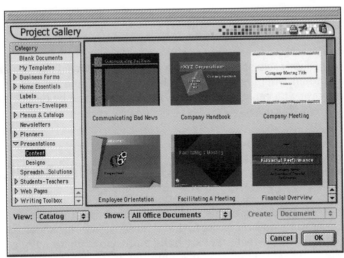

Figure 28-12: The Project Gallery dialog box

2. Click the Presentations: Content or Presentations: Designs category from the list on the left to display the default presentation template.

Tip The Content category contains complete multislide templates with content inserted for your convenience; the Designs category contains empty single-slide templates with no text or other content inserted. Which is a better choice? That depends upon the task at hand and user's the level of experience in creating presentations.

3. Click the desired presentation format on the right, and then click OK (or double-click the desired presentation template). PowerPoint loads the presentation template and the first slide of the presentation appears. Figure 28-13 shows the first slide of the Project Overview presentation template.

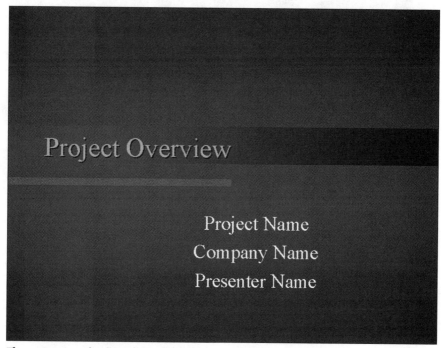

Figure 28-13: The first slide of the Project Overview presentation

After you use these steps to create a presentation, you can modify the text in the slides by clicking the text to select each item you see (titles, subtitles, or text within the presentation) and typing your desired text. You can use the Page Up and Page Down keys or click the Previous Slide and Next Slide buttons at the lower-right side of the window to move among the various slides of your presentation.

Each slide contains text in the form of suggestions that you can modify. Figure 28-14, for example, shows the second of 10 available slides in the Project Overview presentation. You can click the existing text and edit it as desired while in Slide view.

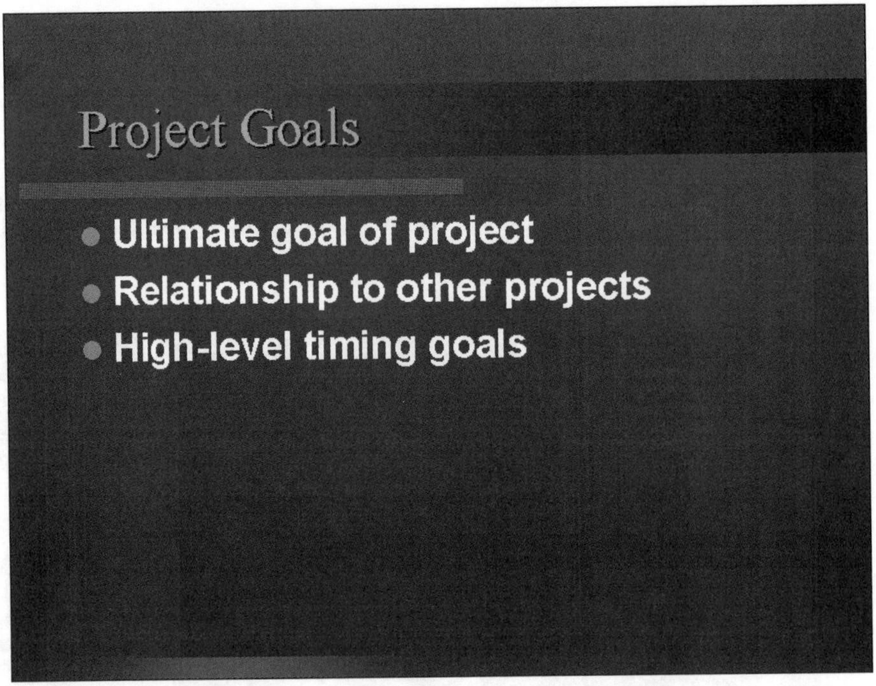

Figure 28-14: The second slide of the Project Status presentation

If you don't want one of the default slides in your presentation, just move to the unwanted slide and choose Edit ➪ Delete Slide. Or, if you're in any view but Slide Show, you can just click the outline item or slide and press Delete to get rid of it.

If you want to add a new slide to the presentation, move to the slide that you want the new slide to follow and choose Insert ➪ New Slide (⌘-M). The New Slide dialog box appears. Now choose your slide layout. Then click the boxes and type the desired text for the slide. (You learn more about adding slides and about adding items to slides later in this chapter.)

After you've finished adding the needed text to the pages of your presentation, save it by choosing File ➪ Save (⌘-S). When you save a presentation for the first time, the Save dialog box shown in Figure 28-15 appears. Enter a name for the file in the Save text box and, if you want, choose a different folder in which to save the file. Then click the Save button to save the presentation.

Tip   You might notice a new (in Office 2001) Append file extension checkbox. This is a nice new feature in all the Office applications that enables you to automatically append the extension (.ppt in this case, or .xls, or .doc) to the file name, based upon the type of file you're saving. This can be helpful when you have to exchange files with the technologically disadvantaged (for example, Windows users).

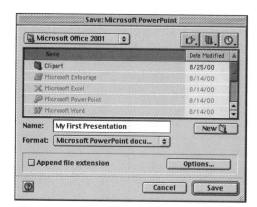

Figure 28-15: The Save dialog box

Cross-Reference

You can print your finished presentation by choosing File ➪ Print (⌘-P) to open the Print dialog box. Choose All if you want to print all the slides in the presentation or type numbers in the From and To fields to print only part of the presentation. After you make your selection, click OK to begin printing. You can print information in PowerPoint in several ways. A full description of printing and of the other options in the Print dialog box is found in Chapter 30.

When you're finished with the presentation, choose File ➪ Close (⌘-W) if you want to do other work in PowerPoint or File ➪ Quit (⌘-Q) to exit PowerPoint.

Working with Presentations

With the information that has been provided so far, you can easily start creating effective business presentations. However, you can do a lot more with PowerPoint, and the rest of this chapter gives you the basics.

Creating a new presentation

When you want to create a new presentation, choose File ➪ Project Gallery (⌘-Shift-P) to open the Project Gallery dialog box (refer to Figure 28-12). The dialog box contains a lengthy list of categories on the left side including many that are not designed for PowerPoint. To see only PowerPoint templates, choose PowerPoint Documents from the pop-up Show menu near the bottom of the window.

Click the first entry, Blank Document, and you'll have two options: the Blank Presentation or the AutoContent Wizard (see Figure 28-16). (See Chapter 29 for more on the AutoContent Wizard.)

Further down the category list you'll see Presentations. Click it, and then click one of its two subcategories: Content or Designs. A host of designs that can be used for your slide backgrounds (see Figure 28-17) will appear on the right.

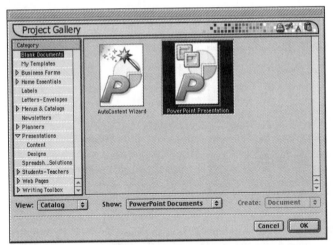

Figure 28-16: The Blank Document category in the Project Gallery dialog box

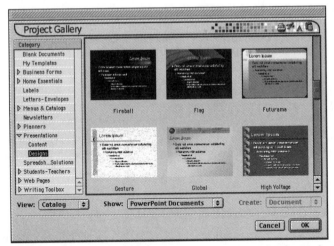

Figure 28-17: The Presentation: Designs category in the Project Gallery dialog box

Tip

At the bottom left of the Project Gallery window is a pop-up menu called View. The default view is Catalog. Choose List view from this View menu and you can see more templates at once (although you can only preview one at a time in List view).

After you have chosen the template for your presentation, click OK to begin filling out the template.

You can also create a template using the design of another presentation. Choose Format ➪ Apply Design Template and choose from the Open dialog box the presentation from which you want to borrow the design.

Saving a presentation

You save a presentation in PowerPoint the same way that you save a file in most Mac programs — by choosing File ➪ Save (⌘-S). If you have not previously saved the presentation, the Save As dialog box opens, and you are prompted to enter a name for the presentation. If you have already given the presentation a name, it is saved under that name.

You can also perform other tasks in the Save As dialog box. You can change the name of a presentation by entering a new name in the File Name text box. You can save files in a variety of formats including older versions of PowerPoint, PICT, JPEG, GIF, and Macintosh Scrapbook by choosing a new file type from the Save as type pop-up menu and then clicking OK to save the file. Remember that you need to save a presentation as a PowerPoint 4.0 file if you want to use it with PowerPoint 4.0.

When you have completed your work in PowerPoint and you want to exit the program, choose File ➪ Quit (⌘-Q).

Entering summary information

You can include summary information with the presentations that you save. You enter summary information — which includes a title, subject, and other key information to help you keep track of the presentations — in the Summary Information dialog box. To enter summary information for your presentation, follow these steps:

1. Choose File ➪ Properties. The Properties dialog box appears with the Summary tab open, as shown in Figure 28-18.

2. Enter the information you want in each of the following text boxes:

   - *Title*. Enter a name for the presentation.

   - *Subject*. Enter a brief description of the contents of the presentation.

   - *Author*. Enter the name of the author. The default name is the name that you entered when you installed Microsoft Office.

   - *Manager*. Enter a manager name, if you wish.

   - *Company*. Enter a company name, if you wish.

   - *Category*. Enter a category for the presentation if you wish to categorize it.

   - *Keywords*. Enter keywords that you associate with the presentation. These words can help you in a Find File search, if you need to use this command from the File menu. You can use the Copy and Paste commands from the Edit menu to insert the titles of your slides in the Keywords list box.

   - *Comments*. Enter any needed comments.

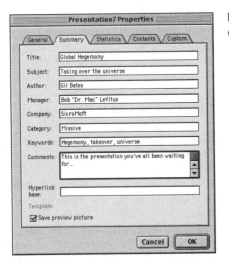

Figure 28-18: The Summary tab of the Properties dialog box

3. When you are finished entering the information, click OK to store the information.

4. The summary information can be viewed by choosing File ➪ Properties, which displays the properties for the presentation, and then choosing the Summary tab to display the summary info.

Entering and editing text

After you have opened a new presentation, it will not contain the text that you want to use, so you will have to add and edit your own text. This section teaches the basics of editing text in Outline view and Slide view. Later in the chapter, you learn how to add objects to your presentation.

Editing in Outline view

Outline view is excellent for editing text because it enables you to see the overall content of your presentation while you are editing the text. You can switch to Outline view by choosing View ➪ Outline or by clicking the Outline view button in the status bar. After you are in Outline view, you can edit text by simply clicking it and moving the cursor to the area you want to change. Use Delete or Backspace to delete characters that are to the left of the cursor. Figure 28-19 shows a slide in Outline view ready for editing.

Tip   When you select text in PowerPoint, the program automatically selects whole words by default. If you want to select individual characters, choose Edit ➪ Preferences. In the Preferences dialog box, choose the Edit tab. Next, uncheck the When selecting, automatically select entire word option and click OK to turn it off.

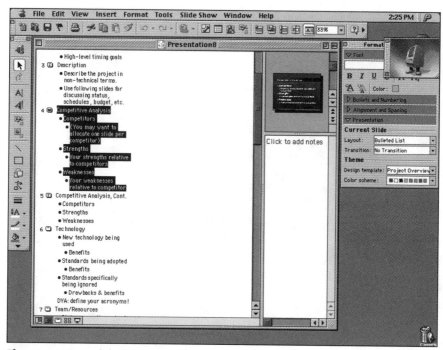

Figure 28-19: A slide in Outline view

Editing in Slide view

Slide view also provides an easy way to edit text, and it provides a good opportunity to see an individual slide's appearance. You can switch to Slide view by choosing View ➪ Slide or by clicking the Slide view button in the status bar. In Slide view, shown in Figure 28-20, you can edit either text or an object by clicking the text or the object to select it, clicking the space where you want the cursor to appear, and then making the changes.

Working with slides

Slide view is used to do most of your work with slides. Slide view lets you see each slide pretty much as it will appear in your presentation. It also lets you move between the slides in your presentations, and it lets you use click-and-drag to move the slide within your presentation.

Moving between slides

When you have more than one slide in a presentation, you must be able to move easily among the slides so that you can quickly work on all of them. (Remember that in all views except Slide Show, you can perform edits by double-clicking the slide.) How you move among the slides depends on the view that you are in at the time. Table 28-1 shows how you can move among slides in each of the views.

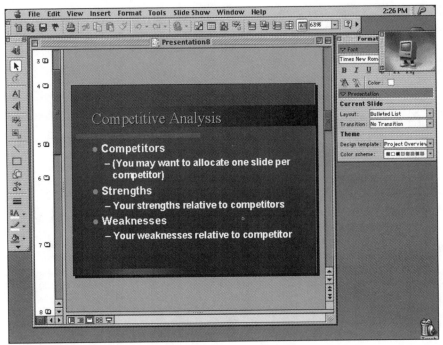

Figure 28-20: The same slide in Slide view

Table 28-1
Moving Among Slides in Different Views

View	How to Move Among Slides
Normal	Use the scroll bar to move to the slide, click the slide icon to the left of the slide's title, or click the text to perform the changes.
Outline	Use the scroll bar to move to the slide, click the slide icon to the left of the slide's title, or click the text to perform the changes.
Slide Sorter	Click the slide that you want to see. A border appears around the slide. Double-clicking the slide switches to Slide view where you can make changes to your slide.
Slide	Drag the scroll bar until the slide that you want appears, or press Page Up or Page Down.
Notes Pages	Drag the scroll bar until the slide that you want appears, or press Page Up or Page Down.

Inserting slides

As you build your presentations in PowerPoint, you may need to make changes to the presentation by inserting, deleting, and copying slides. To add a slide to a presentation, follow these steps:

1. In any view, choose the slide after which you want the new slide to appear.

2. Choose Insert ➪ New Slide (⌘-M).

3. The New Slide dialog box appears. Choose the slide layout you want and click OK to choose that slide layout.

To change the new slide's layout (or to create a slide layout), follow these steps:

1. In Slide view, Control-click the slide and choose Slide Layout from the shortcut menu or choose Format ➪ Slide Layout. The Slide Layout dialog box appears.

2. Choose the layout you want and click the Reapply button. (If you are creating a slide layout for the first time, the button is Apply.) The layout is then applied to the slide.

Tip Another way to add a new slide is by clicking the New Slide button on the Standard toolbar.

You can also add slides from a previous presentation to your current presentation. This shortcut is useful because it prevents you from taking the time to create an entirely new presentation when you already have slides that you can use from an old presentation. First, you must open the presentation to which you want to add the slides and choose the place where you want to insert the slides. The new slides will appear after the chosen slide. Second, choose Insert ➪ Slides from Files and find the previous presentation in the Open dialog box and click the Insert button. All the slides contained in that presentation will be inserted into the new presentation. The inserted slides take on the look of the presentation in which they are inserted. This prevents you from having to make any changes to the look of the imported slides.

Deleting slides

Deleting a slide is simple and can be performed in any view except Slide Show. Navigate to the slide and choose Edit ➪ Delete Slide to remove the slide or select the slide itself (in most views) and press Delete or Backspace. If you delete a slide by accident, choose Edit ➪ Undo (⌘-Z) or click the Undo button on the Standard toolbar to bring back the slide.

Copying and moving slides

You copy slides in PowerPoint the same way you copy items in other Mac programs by using the Copy and Paste commands from the Edit menu.

To copy a slide, follow these steps:

1. Switch to Slide Sorter view.

2. Choose the slide(s) you want to copy. To select more than one slide, press the Shift while you select the slides.

3. Choose Edit ➪ Copy (⌘-C).

4. Move to the slide after which you want to place the copied slide.

5. Choose Edit ➪ Paste (⌘-V).

You can use the same method to move a slide, except that you use the Cut command rather than the Copy command.

Rearranging slides

Occasionally you will need to change the order in which the slides appear in your presentation. PowerPoint provides for this need in Normal view, Slide Sorter view, and Outline view. In these views, you can use the drag-and-drop technique to move slides around.

To rearrange the order of your slides in Normal view or Outline view, follow these steps:

1. Click the icon for the slide that you want to move.

2. Drag the icon up or down in the outline.

You can also select just one piece of information on a slide and move it to another slide by clicking and dragging it to the desired place.

To rearrange slides in Slide Sorter view, follow these steps:

1. Select the slide you want to move to a new location.

2. Drag the slide to its new location. As you drag the slide, a vertical line marks the place where it will appear.

3. Release the mouse button to insert the slide in its new location.

Changing the slide layout

You can also change the slide layout after you have created a slide. To change a slide layout, follow these steps:

1. In Slide Sorter view, move to the slide that you want to change.

2. Choose Format ➪ Slide Layout.

3. In the Slide Layout dialog box, choose the layout that you want to apply to the slide and click Apply (see Figure 28-21).

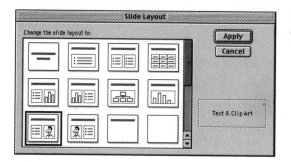

Figure 28-21: The Slide Layout dialog box

Working with objects

In PowerPoint, objects are the basic components that you use to construct a slide. An object can be the box in which you enter text, a picture brought in from another source, or the shape that you draw. You can have as many objects as you want on a slide.

Selecting and grouping objects

To select the object you want to work with, click it. After selecting the object, you can add text to it and change its orientation, shape, color, or pattern. You can also select multiple objects by holding down Shift as you select the objects. To deselect an object, simply hold down Shift and click the object again.

You can also group objects together, which is useful when you want to change the colors for a group of objects or align them horizontally. All the objects that you include in the group will act as one object. To group objects, select them and then choose Draw ⇨ Group from the Drawing toolbar. Thereafter, if you perform an action on one of the objects, the action will affect all the objects in the group. When you group objects, you can flip, resize, or rotate them. If you want to change the grouping, choose Draw ⇨ Regroup from the Drawing toolbar after the objects have been grouped and ungrouped. Remember that the Regroup command will affect only the objects that were included in the original group.

You can also select and deselect noncontiguous objects in PowerPoint by clicking the objects while pressing Shift.

Moving and copying objects

As you work out a presentation, you may need to move your objects around. Power-Point provides for this need nicely with two options: the cut-and-copy method or the click-and-drag method.

To use the cut-and-copy method to move objects to a different slide, follow these steps:

1. Switch to Slide view and select the object(s) that you want to move or copy.

2. Choose Edit ⇨ Cut (⌘-X) to move the object to a new location via the Clipboard, or choose Edit ⇨ Copy (⌘-C) to copy the object.

3. Move to the slide on which you want to place the information.

4. Choose Edit ⇨ Paste (⌘-V) to place the Clipboard information onto the slide.

Using the click-and-drag method to move objects around on the same slide is equally simple. To use this method, click the object and hold down the mouse button. Then move to the area where you want to place the object. Release the mouse button to place the object.

Sometimes you may find that you need to remove an object from a slide. To remove an object, select it and press Delete or choose Edit ⇨ Clear.

Cropping objects

In your quest to give your presentation a refined look, it may be necessary to crop the objects — both pictures and graphics — that you added to your presentation. Cropping is the trimming of an object to remove elements that you don't want from the picture. To crop an object, follow these steps:

1. After you add an object to a slide and the Picture toolbar appears, click the Crop button.

2. Place the mouse pointer over a selection handle. If you want to crop two sides simultaneously, use a corner handle. If you want to crop only one side, use a top or bottom handle. Figure 28-22 shows a cropped image and the Picture toolbar with the Crop tool selected. Click and drag the handle to do the cropping.

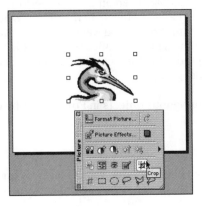

Figure 28-22: An image cropped in PowerPoint and the Picture toolbar with the Crop tool selected.

Aligning objects

When you create presentations, it is important that the objects have the same sort of alignment. Figure 28-23 shows a before and after shot of some objects on a slide in PowerPoint. As you can see, the slide with aligned objects has a better appearance than the slide in which the objects are not aligned. Aligned objects appear more organized than unaligned objects.

The Align command gives you a choice of alignment methods. You can select objects and then align them, or you can use the rulers available in the PowerPoint window. PowerPoint is equipped with a reference system for aligning objects on slides. The system uses a grid and guides. The invisible grid covers the slide with 12 gridlines per inch and 5 lines per centimeter. When the objects are drawn, their corners align on the nearest intersection of the grid, which is how PowerPoint helps you to align objects.

The guides that PowerPoint provides are two rulers: one horizontal and one vertical. When the corners or center of an object (whichever is closer) is close to the guide, it snaps to the guide, which is how you align the object. You can even align a group of objects.

To align an object, follow these steps:

1. Select the object(s) to align.

2. Choose Draw ➪ Align or Distribute from the Drawing toolbar, and then choose the alignment that you want from the submenu. You can choose from left, center, right, top, middle, or bottom.

If you want to align your objects automatically, choose Draw ➪ Snap ➪ To Grid from the Drawing toolbar. If the grid is on, you will see a checkmark beside the choice on the menu. The Draw ➪ Nudge choice enables you to align objects by moving the image in the direction you choose, a little at a time.

Tip

For aligning objects, the Customize dialog box has a number of helpful toolbar buttons. Choosing Tools ➪ Customize, or choosing Customize from most contextual menus (for example, when you Control-click), opens the Customize dialog box with the Toolbars tab chosen. Choose the Commands tab and other useful toolbar buttons appear. To add any of these buttons to your toolbar, click the name of the button you wish to add from the Commands box. Next, drag the name up to a toolbar. (Hint: If you like, first create a new toolbar.) The outline of a button appears and each of the dragged buttons is added to that toolbar. If you are not sure of what each of the buttons does, the box at the bottom of the tab gives a description of the selected button.

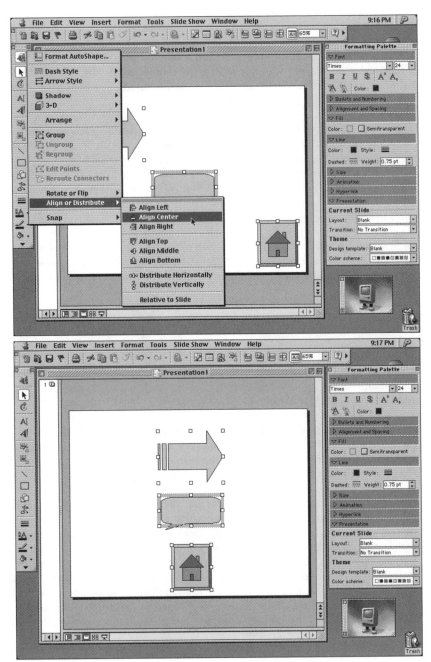

Figure 28-23: Objects before (top) and after (bottom) alignment.

Stacking objects

Sometimes you have to overlap objects to give them the correct effect. You may even want to change the order of overlapped objects. You can also stack groups of objects by moving a group of objects forward or backward. You can use the Tab key to navigate through the stacked objects.

Objects in a stack can be moved up or down one level at a time, or you can immediately send an object to the back or to the front. This feature prevents you from having to keep track of the objects as you draw them; in other words, you don't have to draw the bottom object first or the top object last, and so on.

To bring an object to the front or to the back of a stack, click the object that you want to move and choose Draw ➪ Arrange and either Bring Forward, Send Backward, Send to Back, or Bring to Front from the Drawing toolbar. Figure 28-24 shows the original positions of objects on a slide and how Bring Forward can change their positions.

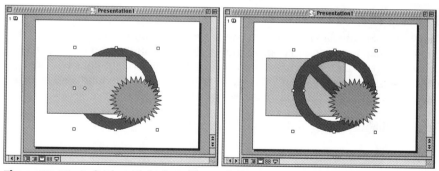

Figure 28-24: *Left:* The original positions of objects on a slide
Right: Changing the position of the objects with the Bring Forward command

Working with shapes

While working with PowerPoint, you may want to add your own shapes or art to the presentation. (Remember that these shapes are still considered objects by PowerPoint.) You can draw lines, arcs, rectangles, and ovals with the Drawing toolbar. Figure 28-25 shows some examples of shapes that you can create in PowerPoint.

You can also add different attributes to the lines and shapes that you create. For example, you can insert dotted lines, color the lines, fill in the shapes, and add arrowheads to lines. Remember that you can't add text to your shapes except by grouping.

Figure 28-25: Examples of shapes that you can create in PowerPoint

Drawing shapes

Many tools are available for you to use to perform your drawing tasks. On the Drawing toolbar, use the Rectangle tool to draw rectangles and the Line tools to draw lines (two Line tools exist — one called *line* for straight lines and another called *lines* for other types of lines, such as arrowhead, freehand, and so on). You can also use the AutoShapes tools to create shapes.

To draw shapes in your slides, follow these steps:

1. Switch to Slide view if you are not already there.

2. On the Drawing toolbar, click the button for the object that you want to draw. Click one of the Line tool buttons if you want to draw a line; click the Rectangle tool button if you want to draw a rectangle; and so on. You can also click the AutoShapes Button on the Drawing toolbar and select any of a variety of shapes.

3. Click the place where you want the shape to begin and drag to the place where you want the shape to end.

4. Release the mouse button.

Constraint keys are used to create shapes that are difficult to create freehand. The available constraint keys are:

✦ Hold down Shift to draw perfectly round circles and perfectly square squares.

✦ Hold down Option to expand the size of the object you're drawing.

Drawing freeform shapes

You may want to add a freeform shape, such as a flower or an ice cream cone, to a slide. You can create any kind of drawing that you want by clicking the (bottom) Lines button on the Drawing toolbar, and selecting the freeform button in the sub-menu that appears (see Figure 28-26). You draw the shape that you want by clicking and holding down the mouse button as you draw. Double-click to stop drawing.

You can also use the Freeform tool to draw a polygon, which is a series of points joined by lines. After you click the Freeform tool button, click the point where you want the first vertex of the polygon to appear and release the mouse button. Then you click the point where you want the second point to appear and release the mouse button. Continue to click the desired points and release the mouse button until you create the polygon shape you want.

Figure 28-26: Choosing the Freeform tool from the Lines menu

Changing the color and style of shapes

You can change the color or style of the lines in a shape. You can also apply a fill color to a shape. To change the color or style of a line in a shape, follow these steps:

1. Select the shape to change.

2. Choose Format ⇨ Colors and Lines to go to the Colors and Lines tab of the Format AutoShape dialog box shown in Figure 28-27. In the Line area, you can choose to change the color or style of the line in any shape. You also can add dashed lines and an arrowhead.

Tip   After making a change but before clicking OK, you can click the Preview button to see the effect of the change (you may have to move the Format AutoShape dialog box out of the way).

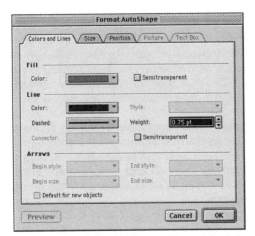

Figure 28-27: The Colors and Lines tab of the Format AutoShape dialog box

3. Clicking the Preview button applies the selected options to the slide so that you can see what they look like before making the changes. You may need to drag the dialog box out of the way to see the results because the box appears on top of the slide.

You may also want to add a fill color to a shape. Simply select the shape that you want to fill with color and choose Format ➪ Colors and Lines. In the Colors and Lines tab, select a color in the Fill list box and then click OK.

Tip   Another way to change colors and to change line attributes is to use the bottom four items on the Draw toolbar: Line Style, Font Color, Line Color, and Fill Color.

Rotating and sizing shapes

Rotating and changing the size of a shape is also a simple matter with PowerPoint. To rotate a shape on its center point, first select the shape. Then click the Free Rotate tool button on the Drawing toolbar. Now drag a handle of the shape to rotate it. Figure 28-28 shows the difference.

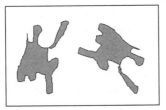

Figure 28-28: *Left:* A freeform object
Right: The same object rotated

To change the size of a shape, select the shape. Small black squares, called handles, appear around the shape. To resize the width of the shape, drag one of the side handles to the desired width. To change the height of the shape, drag a top or bottom handle. If you want to resize the shape proportionally, drag a corner handle while holding down the Shift key. A shape can also be resized from its center by holding down the Option key and dragging the handles.

Using AutoShapes and clip art

PowerPoint has many standard shapes and pieces of clip art. To activate the Drawing toolbar, if it's not already active, choose View ➪ Toolbars, and click Drawing. Click the AutoShapes button in the toolbar and choose the type of shape you want to add to your presentation. A submenu for each of them appears. Make your choice from the submenu. Next, move to the area of the presentation where you want to add the shape. Click to add the shape and then size it by using the resizing techniques. Remember that you can also add color to the shapes by choosing Format ➪ Colors and Lines, which brings up the Colors and Lines tab.

PowerPoint comes with a whole bunch of clip art, which is invaluable in creating presentations. The clip art comes in many different categories. To access the Clip Art Gallery, follow these steps:

1. Click the Insert Clip Art button on the Standard toolbar.

2. The Microsoft Clip Art Gallery dialog box appears.

3. Choose the category of clip art you want.

4. Select the clip art you want and click Insert. PowerPoint inserts it at the insertion point.

Summary

This chapter described many techniques for the everyday use of PowerPoint. With these skills, you can build presentations, enter the text you want, and choose the correct slide layout. This chapter discussed how to do the following:

✦ Use the convenient shortcut menus that make life easy and provide quick access to the commands you may need in Power Point.

✦ Experiment with the different methods for laying out new slides and editing text, including slides with placeholders for clip art and other slide layouts.

✦ Insert objects into presentations and edit the objects. Using objects makes for nicer presentations.

✦ Use the built-in templates and prefabricated presentations to make creating a presentation less time-consuming.

✦ Save your presentations and enter summary information that will help you find the presentations if you tend to forget where they are. This is quite useful if you create many presentations.

Where to go next

✦ Now that you have the tools to begin your work in PowerPoint, you can begin refining the presentations that you create. Chapter 29 gets you started.

✦ The obvious goal when you use PowerPoint is to produce a finished presentation from the slides you created with the software. Chapter 31 tells you how.

✦   ✦   ✦

Enhancing a Presentation

♦ ♦ ♦ ♦

In This Chapter

Using the AutoContent Wizard

Using the AutoLayout feature

Using the Slide Master

Working with lists and columns

Adding formatting and special effects

♦ ♦ ♦ ♦

PowerPoint provides many tools that enable you to give your presentation a more professional look. To help you along, PowerPoint provides several wizards, most notably the AutoContent Wizard, that provide simple ways to help you make your presentations look better. Creating columns and bulleted lists also helps you set up the information in a way that grabs the attention of your audience. Using different fonts and colors is another technique that can help your presentation take on a different look. This chapter discusses these methods and several others that will enhance the appearance of your presentation.

Using the AutoContent Wizard

PowerPoint includes the AutoContent Wizard to help you define your presentation's look and contents. To use the AutoContent wizard, follow these steps:

1. Launch PowerPoint. The Project Gallery window will appear. Choose Blank Document from the category list on the left, and then choose AutoContent Wizard from selections on the right.

   (If PowerPoint is already open, choose File ➪ Project Gallery or use the keyboard shortcut ⌘-shift-P. Choose Blank Document from the category list on the left, and then choose AutoContent Wizard from selections on the right.)

   This activates the AutoContent Wizard (see Figure 29-1).

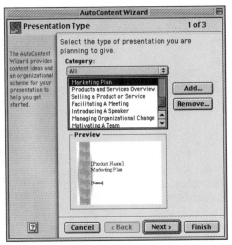

Figure 29-1: The first AutoContent Wizard
dialog box

2. The first AutoContent Wizard dialog box asks you to choose the type of presentation that you want to give. The choices are divided into several categories. Making a choice from the category menu makes all the choices for that category appear. The default is General; choose All (as shown in Figure 29-1) to show all the listings from all the categories.

After you choose the type of presentation that you want to create, click the Next button. You will see the second AutoContent Wizard dialog box, which is shown in Figure 29-2.

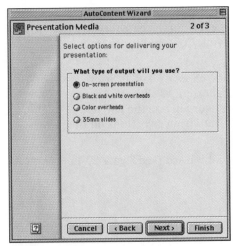

Figure 29-2: The second AutoContent
Wizard dialog box

The second dialog box (as shown in Figure 29-2) is used to choose the presentation output option. Under the type of output section, select the way your slides will be presented. You can choose from On-screen presentation, Black and white overheads, Color overheads, or 35mm slides.

After you have made your selection, click Next to go to the third window of the AutoContent Wizard, which is shown in Figure 29-3.

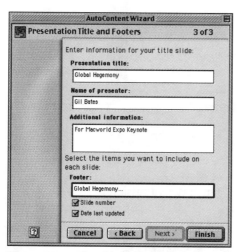

Figure 29-3: The third AutoContent Wizard dialog box

3. The third dialog box of the AutoContent Wizard (as shown in Figure 29-3) is used to set up your title slide. After you have finished making your entries, click Finish. PowerPoint will create the presentation using the settings you chose, as shown in Figure 29-4.

Now just go through the slides and replace the sample text with your own. It's that easy.

Tip   Remember that if you wish to change the layout of the slides later, you can do so by simply choosing the Apply Design Template command from the Format menu.

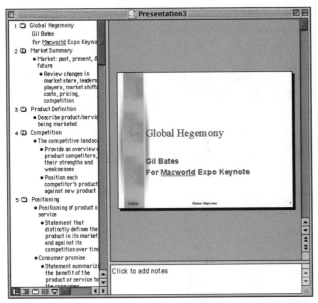

Figure 29-4: The result of our AutoContent Wizard session

Using the AutoLayout Feature

The AutoLayout feature provides a series of slide layouts that you can use to speed up the process of laying out a slide. The layouts vary greatly. Layouts can include graphs, clip art, and text. Figure 29-5 shows the Slide Layout dialog box. This is very useful when creating a presentation or when adding slides to an existing presentation.

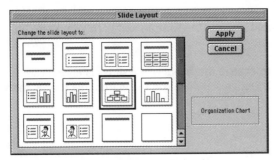

Figure 29-5: The Slide Layout dialog box

To use the AutoLayout feature, follow these steps:

1. After opening a presentation, move to the slide that you wish to change.

2. Choose Format ⇨ Slide Layout or click the Slide Layout button on the Standard toolbar.

3. In the Slide Layout dialog box, select the layout that you want to apply to the slide.

4. After selecting the layout, click the Apply button to apply the layout to the slide.

 The button will say Reapply until you make a new selection in the dialog box.

(This same AutoLayout dialog box also appears whenever you create a new slide in your presentation.)

Using the Slide Master

You can use the Slide Master to control the overall appearance and layout of each slide in a presentation. Editing with the Slide Master is very useful because you can change all the slides in your presentation, not just one slide at a time. You can add graphics or other layouts to the Slide Master, and they will automatically appear in all the slides in that presentation.

The Slide Master contains two important elements: a title area and an object area. The formatting in the title area is specific to the title of each slide in your presentation. The title area tells PowerPoint the font size, style, and color to use for the text. The object area contains the formatting for the remaining text on the slide. The object area also sets the specifications for bulleted lists, which include the indents for each of the lists, the font styles, and size of the fonts. Figure 29-6 shows the Slide Master.

Along with the usual text formats and object setups, you can use the Slide Master to include borders, page numbers, logos, clip art, and many other elements in the slides. To view the Slide Master, follow these steps:

1. Open a presentation and choose View ⇨ Master ⇨ Slide Master. The Slide Master appears, as shown previously in Figure 29-6.

2. Make any adjustment that you want to the Slide Master. To bring up a shortcut menu of available formatting options, Control-click the area outside the slide. You can access the Master Layout dialog box, the Background dialog box, the Color Scheme dialog box, and the Apply Design Template dialog box.

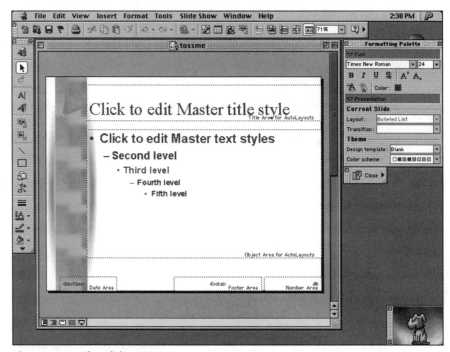

Figure 29-6: The Slide Master

3. When you finish adjusting the Slide Master, you return to your regular slide by choosing the Slides command from the View menu or by clicking the Slide view button at the lower-left corner of the PowerPoint window. The changes apply to all slides.

You can create a custom color scheme for your slides. Choose Format ➪ Slide Color Scheme, and then click the Custom tab in the Color Scheme dialog box (see Figure 29-7).

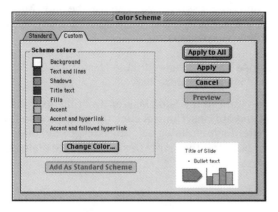

Figure 29-7: The Custom tab of the Color Scheme dialog box

In the Scheme colors area, click the box whose color you want to change and then click the Change Color button. A color picker dialog box appears. Repeat the process for each box whose color you wish to change. You can add your new color scheme to the standard color schemes available by clicking the Add As Standard Scheme button.

After you apply the editing in the Slide Master to all your slides, you can still edit and change individual slides in whatever way you want. You can even change the headings or the formatting that you added with the Slide Master. If you don't like the editing that you have done to a slide, however, and want to return it to its Slide Master state, just reapply the Slide Master formatting. To reapply the Slide Master formatting, follow these steps:

1. Move to the slide to which you want to reapply the Slide Master formatting.

2. Choose Format ➪ Slide Layout. The Slide Layout dialog box appears with the current layout selected.

3. Click the Reapply button to reapply the format. The slide reverts to the formatting of the Slide Master. This can be helpful if you've moved things around and become unhappy with your slide's layout.

Working with Lists and Columns

Columns and bulleted lists can be important parts of your slides. Putting columns and bulleted lists into your slides is easy with PowerPoint. This is another useful layout feature when creating slides.

Creating bulleted lists

In PowerPoint, indents are used to create bulleted lists. You can use this technique for objects (shapes you can add), too. Figure 29-8 shows a bulleted list in PowerPoint.

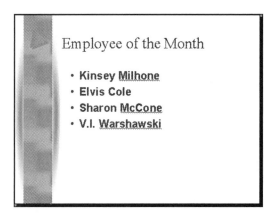

Figure 29-8: A bulleted list in PowerPoint

To create a bulleted list, follow these steps:

1. After opening a presentation, switch to Slide view and create a new slide (Select the New Slide button in the Standard toolbar, choose Insert ➪ New Slide, or use the keyboard shortcut ⌘-M). Then choose the Bulleted List layout from the AutoLayout dialog box.

2. Choose View ➪ Ruler so that the PowerPoint ruler is displayed onscreen.

3. Now enter the following names so you can get an idea of how the indent markers affect the text that you have entered on the bulleted list:

   Kinsey Milhone
   Elvis Cole
   Sharon McCone
   V. I. Warshawski

4. Click anywhere in your bullet list and drag the bottom indent marker in the ruler to the right. The bottom marker moves the text away from the bullets, and the top marker moves the bullets away from the text. You can use this technique to set indentations.

A text box can have up to five indent levels. To add an indent level, select the item to indent and click the Demote (Indent more) button on the Bullets and Numbering tab in the Formatting palette. You may find it easier to handle your indents in Outline view where you can create the headings by using the Demote and Promote buttons.

You can also change bullet characters. To do so, choose the paragraph with the bullet that you want to change. Then choose Format ➪ Bullets and Numbering to open the Bullets and Numbering dialog box, and then click the Bulleted tab. To change the bullet character, click the Character button at the bottom of the Bullets and Numbering dialog box.

Figure 29-9 shows the Bullet dialog box and the many different characters in PowerPoint that can be used as a bullet. From the boxes, select the character that you want to use as your bullet.

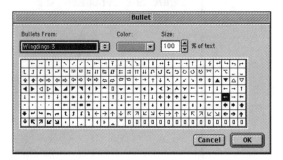

Figure 29-9: The Bullet dialog box

In the Bullets From pop-up menu, choose the font from which you want to select the bullet; remember that each font has a set of bullet characters that go with it. If you want to change the color or size of the bullet, you can do that here as well.

Creating columns

Columns are also useful organizational features that you can create in PowerPoint (see Figure 29-10). Most people have an easier time reading shorter lines of text, and columns are a good way to make lines of text narrower. This is why newspapers contain multiple columns. If you have a large amount of textual information to get across in your presentation, you can take advantage of columns to make the information easier to comprehend.

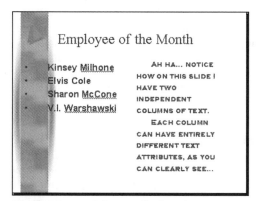

Figure 29-10: Columns displayed on a PowerPoint slide

To add columns to a slide, follow these steps:

1. Before entering the text, choose the Slide Layout button from the Standard toolbar and select 2 Column Text as the layout for the slide.

   This creates a two-column layout for this slide.

2. Click in either column and click the Left Alignment button in the Formatting toolbar.

Remember that you can perform the same procedure on the Slide Master if you want them to apply to all your slides.

Adding Formatting and Special Effects

When it comes to enhancing a presentation, fonts, styles, colors, and WordArt (an Office program for creating text in a variety of shapes) can be effective tools. PowerPoint also lets you embed Excel worksheets and Word tables in slides. Finally, the capability to add sound, slide animation, and action buttons can really bring your presentations to life. The following sections detail all these formatting enhancements.

Fonts, styles, and colors

Fonts, styles, and colors contribute to the look of a presentation. Just as with most Macintosh applications and the other Office 2001 applications, the Formatting palette and toolbar in PowerPoint makes it easy to change the font or to apply styles to the text in your presentation. Select the text that you want to change and click a button on the Formatting palette or toolbar to change the font or the point size, or to apply bold, italic, underlining, shadow, or color. The two font-sizing buttons enable you to change the font of the selected text painlessly by just clicking them. If you click a formatting button before you begin to type, the formatting is applied to all the text that you type until you click the button again.

Applying shadowing and embossing

Shadowing and embossing are techniques that you can use to add emphasis to text in a presentation. These techniques are extremely effective in making certain words or phrases stand out. They also add a more refined look to a presentation when you use them correctly.

Shadowing adds a drop shadow behind your text to emphasize it. This effect is useful in headings and best if not overused (see Figure 29-11 for what, in my opinion, is a nice effect). To add shadowing to text, select the text and click the Shadow button on the Formatting palette. To adjust the shadowing effect, click the More Buttons button on the Draw palette (the little down-pointing triangle at the bottom), and then click the Shadow button. Finally, choose Shadow Settings from the Shadow button's pop-up menu. A palette enables you to nudge your shadow and change its offset amount and color.

Embossing is similar to shadowing, but it adds a highlight rather than a shadow to words (shown in Figure 29-11). This effect gives the text the appearance of being slightly raised. To add embossing to your presentation, select the text and choose Format ➪ Font. In the Font dialog box, click the Emboss checkbox in the Effects area of the dialog box, and then click OK.

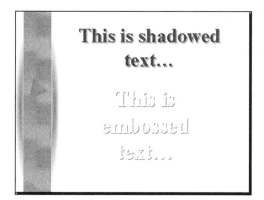

Figure 29-11: Examples of shadowed and embossed text

Applying superscript and subscript

You can also apply superscript and subscript to text in your slides. Choose Format ➪ Font.

Tip

You can also use the superscript and subscript buttons in the Formatting palette if you don't care about setting exact percentages (the buttons use the defaults of −25 percent for subscript and +30 percent for superscript).

In the Effects area of the font dialog box, you will see the two checkboxes for these options. After you click one of the options, enter a percentage by which to offset the text in the Offset box and click OK. Superscript looks like ^{this}; subscript looks like $_{this}$.

Special effects with WordArt

You can also enhance a presentation by using WordArt, a program in Office 2001 that lets you make text take on a variety of shapes. To use WordArt to change the shape of your text, follow these steps:

1. Highlight the text where you wish to apply WordArt. Choose Insert ➪ Picture ➪ WordArt.

2. The WordArt Gallery, shown in Figure 29-12, appears.

3. Choose the form you wish your text to take on. Click OK.

4. A window appears for you to enter your text. Do so. Click OK.

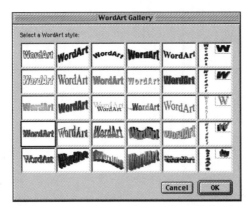

Figure 29-12: The WordArt Gallery dialog box

5. The text is then inserted into the slide. You can make any other changes to WordArt-created text with the WordArt toolbar that appears at the bottom of the slide window when your WordArt is selected (see Figure 29-13).

Figure 29-13: The WordArt toolbar and examples of WordArt

If you use WordArt frequently, you may want to set it as one of your active toolbars. You can do this by choosing View ➪ Toolbars ➪ WordArt. This will make the WordArt toolbar an active toolbar each time you start PowerPoint. Now simply dock the toolbar where desired on the screen, and it will be there for your use during each of your PowerPoint sessions.

After your WordArt toolbar is active, click the WordArt Gallery button and see the effects that WordArt offers (as shown earlier in Figure 29-12). Next, you can choose a different shape for your WordArt. To do so, press and hold down the WordArt Shape button on the WordArt toolbar. This displays the Shape options pop-up menu for your WordArt (see Figure 29-14). Slide the cursor over the one you like and release the mouse button to make your desired selection.

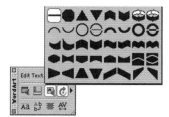

Figure 29-14: The WordArt Shape options pop-up menu

Table 29-1 explains the menu options available on the WordArt toolbar.

Table 29-1 WordArt Toolbar Options	
Button	**Function**
WordArt Gallery	Enables you to choose a style for the WordArt you are inserting. If you want to change the WordArt text after you have inserted it in the slide, double-click the text to activate the text box and make changes to it. Figure 29-13, earlier in this chapter, shows an example of text that was formatted with WordArt.
Format WordArt	Enables you to change the color and fill, size, and positioning for the WordArt.
WordArt Shape	Gives text the shape you select.
Free Rotate	Rotates the WordArt object to any degree.
WordArt Same Letter Heights	Changes all the WordArt letters to the same height.

Continued

Button	Function
Table 29-1 *(continued)*	
WordArt Vertical Text	Changes the WordArt text to a vertical appearance.
WordArt Alignment	Enables you to choose an alignment for the WordArt you have inserted in your slide.
WordArt Character Spacing	Opens the Spacing Between Characters pop-up menu shown in Figure 29-15, which lets you adjust the spacing between the characters.

Figure 29-15: The Spacing Between Characters pop-up menu

Excel Worksheets and Word Tables

Another strong feature of PowerPoint is that it enables you to embed Excel worksheets and Word tables in the slides. The following sections show you, step by step, how to do this.

Working Together

The capability to insert Excel worksheets and Word tables in your PowerPoint presentations saves a lot of time because you don't have to retype the information. You can use information that already exists.

It is important to explain the difference between the two methods that can be used to insert information into PowerPoint. One method uses Edit ➪ Copy and Edit ➪ Paste. The other method uses Insert ➪ Object. Although the two methods accomplish the same goal, they do work differently. If you want to insert a workbook, you need to use Insert ➪ Object. If you want to insert more than one worksheet, you need to use copy and paste. (To select the worksheets, Shift-click the worksheets that you wish to insert, or Command-click them if they're not contiguous; use File ➪ Copy to copy the worksheets; move to where you want to paste the worksheets; choose File ➪ Paste to place them there.)

Tip

You may not want to insert an entire worksheet because it may be too hard to see on a slide. It is often better to just paste in the table that you created in Excel.

Double-clicking the sheet after it is inserted activates Excel. Now you can also perform maintenance on the workbook or worksheet. Remember that the embedding principles that are explained here apply to all applications that support object linking and embedding (OLE).

Inserting Excel worksheets

To insert an Excel worksheet into a PowerPoint slide using Edit ⇨ Copy and Edit ⇨ Paste, follow these steps:

1. From Excel, choose the worksheet that you want to insert into your presentation.

2. Select the information by using the standard selection methods. Remember that you need to select just the area of the worksheet you wish to paste on the slide. This will let you size your insertion to fit the slide. If you don't do this, the worksheet will appear to flow off the slide.

3. Click the Copy button on the Standard toolbar or choose Edit ⇨ Copy.

4. Switch to PowerPoint and the slide in which you want to place the information.

5. Click the Paste button on the Standard toolbar or choose Edit ⇨ Paste.

6. Use the handles to resize the worksheet as you please.

Tip   You can also select cells in Excel and drag and drop them on a PowerPoint slide.

To add an Excel worksheet to a PowerPoint presentation by using Insert ⇨ Object, follow these steps:

1. From PowerPoint, choose Insert ⇨ Object to bring up the Insert Object dialog box shown in Figure 29-16.

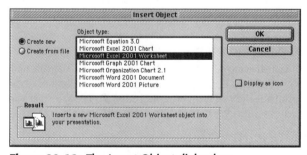

Figure 29-16: The Insert Object dialog box

2. Click the Create from file button or Create new button, and then choose Microsoft Excel 2001 Worksheet. If you choose Create from file, an Open File dialog box appears and you can choose your Excel worksheet. If you choose Create new, a new worksheet appears in your presentation.

   You can also use this dialog box to insert Microsoft Equation Editor documents, Excel charts, Graph charts, Organization charts, Word documents, or Word pictures.

Sound, slide animation, and action buttons

When it comes to enhancing a presentation, sound can also be an effective tool. If you have sound files (Mac OS sounds, .wav, .snd files, or any sound format supported by QuickTime, including AIFF and MP3) stored on your computer, you can place sound in your presentation. To add sound to your presentation, follow these steps:

1. Move to the slide to which you want to add sound.

2. Choose Insert ➪ Movies and Sounds ➪ Sound from File.

3. After finding the desired sound file, click OK. A small icon appears in the center of the slide.

You can use the usual selection techniques to drag the icon to a desired location on the slide. When you run the presentation, clicking the icon plays the sound.

Alternatively, you can choose Insert ➪ Movies and Sounds ➪ Sound From Gallery and choose a sound from those supplied with PowerPoint.

Tip   All the sounds are in the Value Pack; to use them, you'll have to install them if you haven't already.

Or, choose one of the other selections from the Movies and Sounds submenu and insert sound files from your hard disk (AIFF, MP3, QuickTime, and so on), an audio CD, or even a sound you record yourself.

Adding narration to a presentation

PowerPoint also offers you the capability to add narration for the slides in your presentation. This is very useful as a backup for presentation in case of absence, loss of voice, or other events that may occur unexpectedly. To record narration for a slide, first move the slide in Slide view and then follow these steps:

1. Choose Record Narration from the Slide Show menu and click OK. PowerPoint changes to Slide Show view and you can begin recording.

2. After recording, Control-click the screen and choose End show. You are asked if you want to save times for the slides or review time settings in Slide Sorter view.

3. Answer the question as desired and continue for subsequent slides in the presentation.

Tip   If you have a lengthy narration, it's best to break it into small segments rather than try to record it all in one take.

Slide animation

As you progress in setting up your slide show, you'll work with techniques that enable you to make truly professional slide shows. Along with the transition effects and timing settings that you can set using the Slide Transition dialog box, you can add animation to your presentation and function buttons to your presentation.

Animation effects can especially help hold the attention of your audience. PowerPoint offers some interesting animation effects. First, you need to activate the Animation Effects toolbar. To do so, choose Toolbars from the View menu and turn on the Animation Effects toolbar.

To animate the text of a slide, follow these steps:

1. Move to the slide in which you want to animate the title in Slide view.

2. Click the Animate Title button on the Animation Effects toolbar.

3. Choose from one of the effect buttons for the effect that you want applied to the title animation:

   • *Drive-in effect/out* causes the title to come in from the right side and exit from the left.

   • *Fly In effect* causes the title to come in from the left side.

   • *Camera effect* causes the title to appear with the click of a camera.

   • *Flash Once effect* causes the title to flash on the slide once.

   • *Fly Out effect* causes the title to exit to the right side.

   • *Laser Text effect* causes the letters of the title to appear one by one with the sound of a laser.

   • *Typewriter Text effect* causes the text to appear as if being typed with the sound of a typewriter.

   • *Reverse Text Order* causes bullets to appear from last to first rather than first to last.

   • *DropIn effect* causes the title to fall from the top of the slide.

   • *DropOut effect* causes the title to fall from off the bottom of the slide.

There's also a Custom button that brings up a dialog box in which you can create/define your own effect(s).

Adding action buttons to a slide

Action buttons are another way to enhance a presentation. PowerPoint has the capability to set a button to perform an action that you specify. This action can include sounds, links to Web pages, links to other slides in the presentation, or links to other files of any kind. One good use for an action button is if you need to show a worksheet in Excel that you cannot readily show on a slide. Another use for an action button is to link your presentation to a Web site page, which you can view with your default Web browser.

To add an action button to your presentation, follow these steps:

1. Move to the slide in which you want to place the button.

2. Choose Action Buttons from the AutoShapes menu of the Drawing toolbar.

3. Select the kind of button you wish to have represent your action.

4. As soon as you draw the button on your slide, the Action Settings dialog box is activated.

5. Choose either the Mouse Click tab or the Mouse Over tab, depending on the mouse action that you want to activate the hyperlink.

6. Click the Hyperlink To: radio button.

7. Specify the type of hyperlink that you want to create (to another slide, to a URL, or to another choice from the pop-up list).

8. If you wish it to run a program, choose the Run Program radio button.

9. After you have set up your button action, click OK.

Now, you are all set. Test the object you have linked to make sure that it works properly. To make any adjustments, simply repeat the steps and make the changes.

Summary

This chapter discussed techniques to enhance the appearance of a presentation, including the following:

✦ The different methods of formatting text

✦ How WordArt can be used to enhance text entries

✦ How the Slide Master can be used to apply universal options to your presentation

✦ How you can use the AutoContent Wizard to create a presentation

Where to go next

✦ Now that you have learned the steps to enhance a presentation, you will want to produce your work. Chapter 30 tells you how.

✦   ✦   ✦

Working with Charts in PowerPoint

Among PowerPoint's strong features is its capability to create charts you can include in your business presentations. Charts in PowerPoint are based on numeric data you enter into a spreadsheet-like window called a datasheet. The charts are generated by Microsoft Graph, a mini-application included with Office 2001.

Looking at a Typical Chart

Figure 30-1 shows an example of a typical chart in a PowerPoint presentation. (Note that charts are sometimes referred to as graphs; in fact, Microsoft uses the terms interchangeably.) Each chart consists of a series of markers, which represent the data you enter in the datasheet. The appearance of the markers varies according to the type of chart you decide to insert in your presentation. In a bar chart, the markers appear as a series of horizontal bars. In a column chart, the markers look like a series of vertical columns. Line charts use markers that look like a series of thin lines. In pie charts the markers are the wedges of the pie, and doughnut charts use markers that appear as slices of the doughnut.

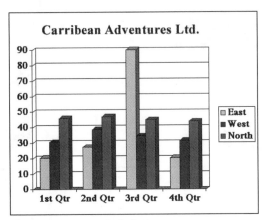

Figure 30-1: A typical chart

With the exceptions of pie charts and doughnut charts, all charts use at least two axes: a horizontal axis (also known as the category axis) and a vertical axis (also known as the value axis). With three-dimensional charts, you also have a third axis, called the series axis.

In addition to the markers aligned along the axes, charts can also contain titles and legends (which serve to identify the categories indicated by the various markers). Microsoft Graph, running from within PowerPoint, lets you customize any of these items in your charts.

Charts in Excel or in PowerPoint?

You can create charts in PowerPoint using Microsoft Graph and the techniques detailed in this chapter, or you can create charts in Excel using the techniques detailed in Chapter 19. Because Excel charts can be selected, copied, and pasted into a PowerPoint presentation, you have two ways of creating charts in PowerPoint. So, where should you create your charts?

If you don't mind the added complexities of a spreadsheet (maybe you're already an accomplished Excel user), you're probably better off creating your charts in Excel and then pasting them into PowerPoint. Why? Because Excel's charting capabilities exceed those of Microsoft Graph, and Excel has Chart Wizards that help you quickly design the precise kind of chart you need. Also, you can take advantage of Excel's capability to perform calculations on the data used as the basis of the chart. In contrast, the Microsoft Graph Datasheet window won't let you add two and two, much less perform any complex calculations.

On the other hand, if you're not an Excel user and have no desire to become one, stick with Microsoft Graph within PowerPoint to produce your charts.

Working with Chart Types

Microsoft Graph, the program used to insert charts in PowerPoint, provides area, bar, column, line, pie, doughnut, radar, XY scatter, surface, bubble, stock, cylinder, cone, and pyramid charts. Each chart type has optional subtypes that can also be chosen. You choose the chart type after choosing Chart ⇨ Chart Types in Microsoft Graph. The following descriptions identify the various standard chart types you'll find in the Chart Types dialog box (see the "Changing the chart type" section, later in this chapter, for details):

✦ **Area charts** show the significance of change during a given time period. The top line of the chart totals the individual series, so area charts make it visually apparent how each individual series contributes to the overall picture. Area charts emphasize the magnitude of change as opposed to the rate of change. (If you want to emphasize the rate of change, use line charts instead.)

✦ **Bar charts** use horizontal bars to show distinct figures at a specified time. Each horizontal bar in the chart shows a specific amount of change from the base value used in the chart. Bar charts visually emphasize different values, arranged vertically.

✦ **Column charts** use columns, much like bar charts, to show distinct figures over a time period. The difference is that the markers in column charts are oriented along a horizontal plane, with the columns running vertically up or down from a base value used in the chart.

✦ **Line charts** are perfect for showing trends in data over a period of time. As with area charts, line charts show the significance of change, but line charts emphasize the rate instead of the magnitude of change.

✦ **Pie charts** show relationships between the pieces of a picture. They also can show a relationship between a piece of the picture and the entire picture. You can use a pie chart to display only one series of data at a time, because each piece of a pie chart represents part of a total series. If you have a large number of series to plot, however, you are probably better off with a column chart because a pie crowded with slices is hard to interpret.

✦ **Doughnut charts** show relationships between pieces of a picture, as do pie charts. The difference is that the doughnut chart has a hollow center.

✦ **Radar charts** show the changes or frequencies of a data series in relation to a central point and to each other. (Every category has an axis value that radiates from a center point. Lines connect all data in the same series.) Radar charts can be difficult to interpret, unless you're accustomed to working with them.

✦ **XY Scatter charts** show relationships between different points of data either to compare trends across uneven time periods or to show patterns as a set of X and Y coordinates. These charts are commonly used to plot scientific data.

✦ **Surface charts** show trends in values across two dimensions in a continuous curve.

✦ **Bubble charts** compare sets of three values. In appearance, these charts are similar to scatter charts, with the third value interpreted by the size of the bubbles.

✦ **Stock charts** are also known as open-hi-lo-close charts. These charts are used to display the day-to-day values of stocks, commodities, or other financial market data. Stock charts require series containing four values to plot the four points (open, high, low, and close).

✦ **Cylinder charts** are column charts with the columns appearing as cylindrical shapes.

✦ **Cone charts** are column charts with the columns appearing as cone shapes.

✦ **Pyramid charts** are column charts with the columns appearing as pyramid shapes.

Inserting Charts

PowerPoint includes a mini-application, Microsoft Graph, that helps you create charts. Microsoft Graph displays a Datasheet window, in which you can enter the numeric data that will serve as the chart's basis. After you enter your data, Microsoft Graph translates it into professional-looking charts.

To insert a chart on a PowerPoint slide, follow these steps:

1. Choose Insert ➪ Chart or click the Insert Chart button on the Standard toolbar. A column chart appears in your presentation (this is the default type, but you can easily change it), and you're switched into Microsoft Graph, which launches automatically. A Datasheet window appears atop the chart, as shown in Figure 30-2 (with PowerPoint running in the background).

   Note that the menus and toolbar change to reflect the fact that Microsoft Graph is now the active application.

2. Enter your data directly into the Datasheet window. (See the "Entering Data and Editing Charts" section, later in this chapter, for more details.)

3. Choose Chart ➪ Chart Type to select the type of chart you want. After selecting the chart type you want, click OK. (You can also Control-click the chart and choose Chart Type from the shortcut menu that appears.)

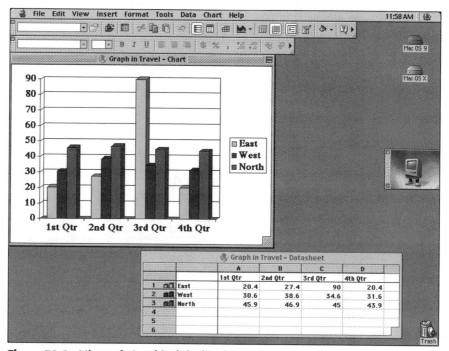

Figure 30-2: Microsoft Graph's default column chart and Datasheet windows

Tip There's a cool Press and Hold to View Sample button in the Chart Type dialog box. Choose a chart type, and then, instead of clicking OK, click and hold that button to see a larger example of that type of chart.

4. Open the Chart menu and choose Chart Options to use the various options to add titles, axes, gridlines, legends, data labels, and data tables. The Chart Options dialog box contains the following options (see Figure 30-3):

   • *Titles* displays chart title fields, which you can use to add titles to the chart or its axes.

   • *Axes* enables you to show or hide axes in the chart.

- *Gridlines* gives you the option to show or hide major and minor gridlines along any of the chart axes.

- *Legend* enables you to add legends to your chart.

- *Data Labels* enables you to add data labels to a data series or to all data points in the chart.

- *Data Table* enables you to show or hide a data table for your chart.

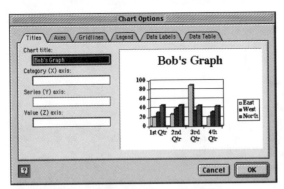

Figure 30-3: The Chart Options dialog box

5. When you're finished refining the chart, quit Microsoft Graph. You automatically return to PowerPoint, where the chart appears inside your presentation and the menus and toolbars revert back to those of PowerPoint.

If you later want to make more changes to the chart's design, you can double-click the chart to switch back to the Microsoft Graph application.

Note   You can move and size your completed chart as you would any other object in a presentation—either by dragging it to the desired location or by dragging its size handles.

Entering Data and Editing Charts

To enter data in the Datasheet window, just move to the desired cell and type the data. You'll also want to enter the names for each data series into the left-most column, and enter the labels for each category into the top row. (The default data that appears in the Datasheet window gives you a model to follow when you enter your own data.) When you enter text in the top row and the left-most column, Microsoft Graph assigns that text as category names and legend names in the resulting chart.

Legends and headings

The default data provided in the Datasheet window shown in Figure 30-4, and the text labels in the left-most column of the datasheet—East, West, and North—are automatically used for the legend that accompanies the chart. The headings entered in the top row of the datasheet—1st, 2nd, 3rd, and 4th Qtr—appear as labels for the markers in the chart.

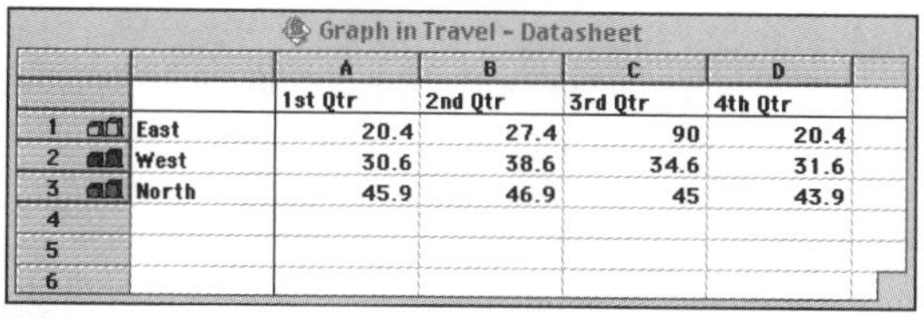

		A	B	C	D
		1st Qtr	2nd Qtr	3rd Qtr	4th Qtr
1	East	20.4	27.4	90	20.4
2	West	30.6	38.6	34.6	31.6
3	North	45.9	46.9	45	43.9
4					
5					
6					

Figure 30-4: The Datasheet window

Adjusting the column width

Navigate within the Datasheet window with either the mouse or the arrow keys. You can widen the columns if they're too narrow to display the numbers you enter. To widen the columns, either drag the column's right edge with the mouse or click in any cell in the column you want to widen, choose Format ➪ Column Width, and then enter a width for the column.

Excel Users May Prefer Excel Charts

If you're familiar with Excel, you may prefer using Excel's worksheet and charting techniques for producing charts to use in your PowerPoint presentations.

To add an existing Excel chart to a PowerPoint presentation, go into Excel, select the chart, and choose Edit ➪ Copy. Switch to PowerPoint, move to the slide on which you want to insert the chart, and choose Edit ➪ Paste. The Excel chart appears in the slide, and you can move and size it to your liking using the usual Mac moving and sizing techniques.

To add a new Excel chart to a PowerPoint presentation, go into PowerPoint and move to the slide on which you want to place the chart. Next, select Insert ➪ Object and then choose Microsoft Excel Chart from the list of objects to insert. PowerPoint then inserts a default Excel chart on the PowerPoint slide and launches Excel (memory permitting). You can then use Excel techniques (detailed in the Excel section of this book) to manipulate the data that produces the chart and to change the chart's appearance.

Number formats

When typing numeric data into cells, you can include dollar signs in front of the numbers to cause them to appear as currency values. When you do this, Microsoft Graph automatically includes the dollar sign with the values in the value axis in the chart. To apply a specific format by selecting a cell or group of cells in the datasheet, open the Format menu and choose Number. In the Number Format dialog box that appears, choose a desired number format and then click OK.

Tip   After the chart exists on a slide, you can bring up the Datasheet window at any time by double-clicking the chart to make it active and choosing View ⇨ Datasheet.

Editing charts

Changing circumstances may require the figures used to create a chart to change. When these figures change, you need to make adjustments to the chart's datasheet. At times you many also want to edit a chart for the sake of altering a presentation. To update figures used when you created a chart, choose View ⇨ Datasheet (in Microsoft Graph) and then make the necessary changes in the datasheet (using the customary methods of editing) then choose File ⇨ Update to update your presentation.

Changing the data series

In some cases you may want to swap the data series for a chart. For example, you'd want to swap if you had set up a chart to show total sales over four years for divisions of a company, and you wanted the columns — which represent years — to symbolize each division. Swapping the data series would fix that.

Tip   Remember you must be in Microsoft Graph to do this. If you're not, select the graph object in your presentation and choose Edit ⇨ Chart Object ⇨ Edit. That will switch you to Graph.

You can swap data series for a chart by choosing either Data ⇨ Series in Rows or Data ⇨ Series in Columns.

Alternatively, you can click the By Row or By Column buttons in the Standard toolbar while the datasheet is active. To see an example of the effects of the selection of data series, take a look at Figure 30-5, which shows a data series arranged by rows.

In contrast, note the same data shown in Figure 30-6. Here the data in the datasheet is arranged by columns in the resulting graph.

You can also change the actual display of the information. The most convenient way to do this is by using the shortcut menu that appears when you Control-click the bars, columns, lines, or pie slices of the chart. The shortcut menu that appears contains commands related to changes in the display of the chart information you clicked. The shortcut menu is shown in Figure 30-7.

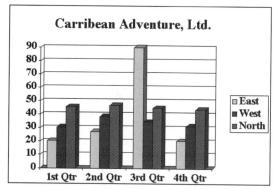

Figure 30-5: A data series arranged by rows

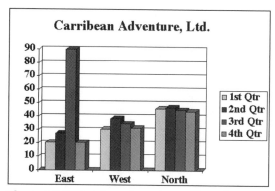

Figure 30-6: A data series arranged by columns

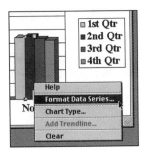

Figure 30-7: The shortcut menu for a data series

The shortcut menu includes the following commands:

✦ **Format Data Series** lets you add labels or change the color of the data series. When you choose this option, the Format Data Series dialog box appears, shown in Figure 30-8, with the Patterns tab visible. Using the Patterns tab, you can add a border to the data series by setting the options in the Borders portion of the dialog box. You can vary the border's style, color, and thickness by selecting what you want in the Style, Color, and Weights list boxes.

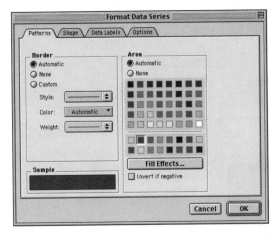

Figure 30-8: The Patterns tab of the Format Data Series dialog box

✦ **Chart Type** lets you change the chart type. When you choose this option from the shortcut menu, the Chart Type dialog box appears (see Figure 30-9). The options for this dialog box are discussed in the next section.

✦ **Add Trendline** adds trendlines to area, bar, column, lines, and scatter charts. This choice is not available for charts if it's inappropriate for that type of chart.

✦ **Clear** removes a data series, the actual markers related to that series of numbers.

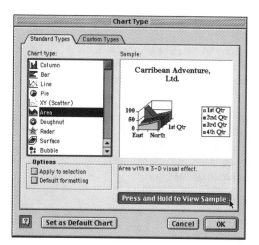

Figure 30-9: The Chart Type dialog box

Inside the Format Data Series Dialog Box

In the Area portion of the Format Data Series dialog box, you can change the color of the data series to your liking. You can select a color or turn on the Automatic option, which applies the document default. Choosing None makes the marker invisible. Turning on the Invert If Negative option in the dialog box reverses the foreground and background colors for a marker if the value is negative.

The Shape tab of the Format Data Series dialog box lets you choose the 3D shape you want for the selected data series.

The Data Labels tab of the Format Data Series dialog box (see the accompanying figure) lets you determine whether labels appear beside the markers to the data series. You can also have a legend appear next to the label—turn on the corresponding checkbox.

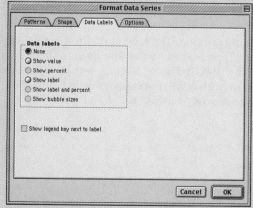

The Data Labels tab of the Format Data Series dialog box

Changing the chart type

After creating a chart, you can experiment to be sure you've selected the type that best represents your data. Microsoft Graph provides a range of chart types that can be viewed with a few mouse clicks. Table 30-1 lists these chart types.

Table 30-1 PowerPoint's Chart Types	
Two-Dimensional Charts	*Three-Dimensional Charts*
Column	3-D Column
Bar	3-D Bar
Line	3-D Line
Pie	3-D Pie
Area	3-D Area
Doughnut	
Radar	
Scatter	
Area	
Bubble	(XY) Scatter
Stock	
Cylinder	3-D Cylinder
Cone	3-D Cone
Pyramid	3-D Pyramid
Surface	3-D Surface

You can select chart types using different methods. The fastest method is to click the down arrow at the right of the Chart Type button on the Standard toolbar. This gives you a pop-up list of chart types, as shown in Figure 30-10. Select the chart you like and the values will be applied to it. As with many pop-up menus in Office 98, this one can be dragged off as a floating window or dragged onto a toolbar for easier access.

Figure 30-10: The Chart types available from the Chart Type button on the Standard toolbar

The other methods of changing the chart type include choosing Chart Type from the Chart menu, and Control-clicking the chart and choosing Chart Type from the shortcut menu. The Chart Type dialog box appears.

When you select a chart type, you can also click the Custom Types tab to use built-in custom chart types or user-defined chart types. The Custom Types tab contains many combinations of formatting, such as exploded pie charts, floating bars, and other chart types that can be useful for specialized chart needs.

Enhancing a Chart's Appearance

You can enhance the appearance of a chart in several ways. A few are simple, such as changes to fonts and colors. Others, however, are a little more involved, such as adding text boxes. All can make a difference in the appearance of the presentation.

Changing fonts

You can easily change the fonts used for text anywhere in your chart. These fonts include those used for titles, legends, or axes.

To change the fonts, Control-click the text you want to change. For example, if you want to change the fonts used for a legend, Control-click the legend. From the short-cut menu that appears, choose the Format Legend option. The dialog box contains three tabs (we discuss the additional ones shortly): Pattern, for making pattern changes to the chart; Font, for making font changes to the chart; and Placement, for controlling the placement of the object. Figure 30-11 shows the Font tab of the Format Legend dialog box.

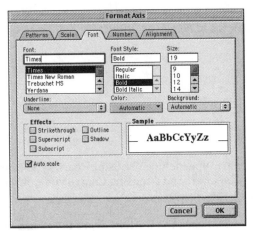

Figure 30-11: The Font tab of the Format Legend dialog box

Under the Font tab you'll see your options for setting the fonts used by the selected item. Choose a font, font style, and font size using the options displayed. You can also select underlining, color, and background, and you can turn on special effects such as strikethrough, superscript, and subscript. Under the Patterns tab you can change various options that control the style and color of the background pattern for the object.

Looks Aren't Everything, But . . .

As you work with fonts, colors, and other appearance-related aspects of a chart, remember the principles of good design by using fonts and colors wisely. It's easy to get carried away with fonts and colors and produce a chart so visually busy it distracts the reader.

You should rarely need more than two and never more than three fonts in the same chart. You'll probably need more colors, because each set of markers typically uses its own color — again, be judicious. Stick with complementary colors. PowerPoint does this automatically, but if you customize the colors, be sure to avoid clashing combinations such as bright pink against lime green. (Some designers argue strongly against using these two colors anywhere, anytime!) Keep colors elsewhere in the chart to a minimum. Before committing the chart to your presentation, step back and give it a critical, overall review for visual clarity and organization. Better charts in your presentations make for better overall presentations.

Changing chart colors

Creating and changing color schemes is another effective way to improve your chart's appearance. Color schemes are sets of colors designed to be used as main colors for presentations and to ensure that the presentations have a professional look.

Each presentation you open in PowerPoint has a default color scheme, but as you work with the program more and more, you'll want to create your own schemes. Chapter 27 discusses in detail what's involved in creating color schemes for an entire presentation. This section focuses on changing chart colors.

Changing the colors of your chart is relatively simple, thanks to shortcut menus. Follow these steps:

1. After choosing a chart and setting it up on your slide, double-click the chart to launch Microsoft Graph. Then Control-click the bar or section of the chart you want to change to open the shortcut menu shown earlier in Figure 30-7.

2. From the shortcut menu, choose Format Data Series. The Format Data Series dialog box opens with the Patterns tab visible, as shown earlier in Figure 30-8. This dialog box enables you to change the border settings, selecting from a range of line styles.

3. To change the color of the particular section of the chart you want to change, move to the Area portion of the Patterns tab and then click the color you want. You can also add patterns if you want by clicking the Patterns list box and then choosing a pattern from the list. When you're finished, click OK to accept the changes.

Adding titles

You may find it useful to add titles to your charts. Titles help an audience understand what a chart means, and they help you quickly find values you want to point out when giving your presentation.

To add titles to a chart area, Control-click the area to open the shortcut menu. Next, choose the Titles tab of the Chart Options dialog box, shown in Figure 30-12.

The Titles tab enables you to add a title either to your entire chart or to just one of the available axes. Turn on the option you want and then click OK; the cursor appears in a text box in which you insert the title. If you choose more than one area to receive a title, use the mouse and click the text boxes for each of the titles. To enter the titles, click in the text boxes and type the titles you want.

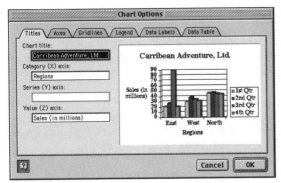

Figure 30-12: The Titles tab of the Chart Options dialog box

You can also format the text on a chart after the text has been entered. Double-click the text and choose the formats you want from the Format dialog box.

Changing axes

You can modify the axes used by your charts to emphasize the points you're trying to get across. You can change the line style, the font of the axes' text, the scale used by the numbers, and the alignment.

To change any of these formats, select one of the axes by clicking it. Next, either choose Format ➪ Selected Axis, Control-click the axis and choose Format Axis, or double-click the selected axis. The Format Axis dialog box opens, as shown in Figure 30-11. You can now select the options you want from the various tabs. Table 30-2 tells what you can accomplish with each of these tabs.

Table 30-2
Tabs of the Format Axis Dialog Box

Tab	Purpose
Patterns	Change axis formatting or choose tick mark types, both major and minor.
Scale	Control the scale settings for axis values. Logarithmic scales can also be set, along with reversing the order of the values and setting the Floor XY Plane (the floor of the chart) at a value other than zero.
Font	Change font settings for the axis.
Number	Control the number formats for the numbers used for the axis.
Alignment	Control the alignment of text used in the axis.

Changing borders

You can also change a chart by changing its borders. Control-click outside the chart's area and choose Format Chart Area from the shortcut menu. The Format Chart Area dialog box appears, as shown in Figure 30-13. This dialog box has two tabs, Patterns and Font. Make the changes you want and then click OK.

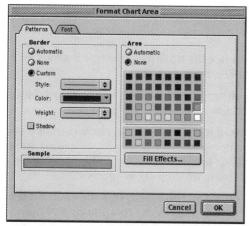

Figure 30-13: The Format Chart Area dialog box

Enhancing 3-D charts

Three-dimensional (3-D) charts are a popular variation of basic charts. Creating 3-D charts is simple in PowerPoint. When you choose Chart ➪ Chart Type, the Chart Type dialog box that appears (shown earlier in Figure 30-9) gives you the option of selecting a 2-D or a 3-D chart.

If you use 3-D charts often, it's good to know about the flexibility that Microsoft Graph offers for changing various aspects of the appearance of 3-D charts. You can change the elevation, the rotation, and the perspective used for the chart with the following steps:

1. Double-click the 3-D chart to activate it, and choose Chart ➪ 3-D View. (Alternatively, you can Control-click the area of the chart and select 3-D View from the shortcut menu that appears.) The 3-D View dialog box appears (see Figure 30-14). As you change the settings in this dialog box, the picture of a chart near the center of the dialog box reflects your changes.

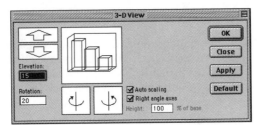

Figure 30-14: The 3-D View dialog box

2. To change the chart's elevation, click the up or down arrow buttons above Elevation or enter a value in the Elevation text box.

3. To change the chart's rotation, either click the left or right rotation buttons or enter a value in the Rotation text box.

4. To change the chart's perspective (if Right angle axes is not turned on), click the up or down arrow buttons above Perspective or enter a value in the Perspective text box. The Format 3-D View dialog box also contains options for Auto scaling, Right angle axes, and Height % of base, which work as follows:

   • *Right angle axes.* This option, when turned on, sets the chart's axes at right angles independent of what you set the rotation or elevation to. (If you want to see the axes in perspective, you must turn off this option.)

   • *Auto scaling.* If Right angle axes is turned on, this option is enabled. The Auto scaling option scales 3-D charts so they are closer in size to 2-D charts.

   • *Height % of base.* This option controls the height of the value axis and walls of the chart, relative to the length of the category axis (the base of the chart). For example, if you enter 300 percent in this box, the chart's height becomes three times the length of the base.

To see how your changes will affect your chart in PowerPoint, while leaving the dialog box open, click the Apply button. When you're finished making changes, click OK. You can use the Default button to undo your changes and return the settings to their defaults.

Creating Organizational Charts

Organizational charts are useful in a presentation for showing the hierarchy of an organization. You can create this type of chart from scratch, but PowerPoint provides an application called Microsoft Organizational Chart that greatly simplifies the process.

The following steps tell you how to create a simple organizational chart. (See Chapter 33 for an example of creating a more complex organizational chart.)

1. Choose Insert ⇨ Picture ⇨ Organization Chart.

   Note that you should select a slide layout with the organizational chart place-holder on it. Also remember that the chart you create will be significantly smaller when placed in the placeholder area; if you have a large chart, you may want to use a blank slide.

2. Microsoft Organizational Chart launches, and a window opens with a simple chart layout. You can proceed with this default layout if you want, adding boxes to the chart as needed. On the toolbar you'll see buttons for adding boxes for the different levels of an organization. Each of the buttons lets you add boxes for the respective level of the chart. Choose the button that corresponds to the level of organization you want, and then click next to the box you want to add the selection under or next to; the box is then added to the chart.

3. After creating your chart, you may want to edit it. First click the box containing the name or entry you want to change, and then make the changes. Afterward, be sure to update the presentation within PowerPoint by choosing File ⇨ Update or Quit and Return to (your document). Then if you want to save the changes to the presentation, choose File ⇨ Save from within PowerPoint.

4. If you prefer, you can create an organizational chart from scratch. Choosing Style from the menu bar gives you a selection of organizational chart types. As Figure 30-15 shows, you can lay out these charts several ways from the Styles menu.

Figure 30-15: The organizational chart Styles menu

After choosing a chart style, you can add boxes to it using the toolbar. Choose the level of the chart to which you want to add boxes and then click the box you want connected.

When the chart is placed in PowerPoint, you can size it to your liking by selecting the object and clicking the handles.

3-D Charts Can Lie (Or at Least, Greatly Mislead)

With 3-D charts, it's easy to get carried away with changing the various viewing angles by modifying the chart's elevation and perspective. Get too carried away and you can wind up with a chart that's so hard to interpret, it becomes meaningless. Get even slightly carried away and you can produce charts that distort the meaning of the underlying numbers.

For example, changing the elevation so that a chart is viewed from a high angle tends to overemphasize growth; presenting the chart as viewed from a low angle tends to minimize growth. (Could that be why many advertisements in business and financial magazines use 3-D charts viewed at high angles?) The example shown here is a 3-D chart with an elevation of 30, which severely distorts the visual growth represented by the chart.

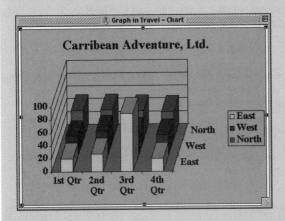

By comparison, the next example shows the same 3-D chart with a moderate elevation of 10, which avoids the visual distortion produced by the earlier chart.

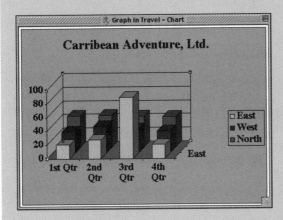

Be aware of the effects that such changes can have on your charts, and use them only when you intend to obtain such distorted results

Summary

This chapter showed you the different options for using charts in your PowerPoint presentations. The following topics were covered:

✦ You can add a chart to any slide of a presentation either by choosing Insert ⇨ Chart or by clicking the Insert Chart button on the Standard toolbar.

✦ When you add a chart, a Datasheet window appears in which you can enter the numeric information that serves as the chart's thesis.

✦ After adding a chart to a presentation, you can double-click the chart and then choose Chart ⇨ Chart Type to change the chart's type.

✦ You can Control-click any object in a chart and then choose Format from the shortcut menu that appears to display a dialog box that lets you change the appearance of the selected object.

✦ In addition to conventional charts, you can create organizational charts in PowerPoint.

Where to go next

✦ Now that you have completed charts in PowerPoint, you will want to produce your work. Chapter 30 has the story.

✦ If you want to produce more elaborate charts, use Excel's chart-making feature. Head straight for Chapter 19.

✦　　✦　　✦

Producing Your Work

◆ ◆ ◆ ◆

In This Chapter

Printing presentations

Producing onscreen slide shows

Adding speaker notes and handouts

Creating custom shows

PowerPoint for people without a copy of PowerPoint

◆ ◆ ◆ ◆

After you have created all the slides, you will want to prepare your work for presentation. This chapter covers the methods you can use to produce your work, including printing presentations, creating slide shows, and creating speaker's notes and audience handouts.

Printing Presentations

PowerPoint enables you to print slides, outlines, speaker's notes, and audience handouts. These items can all be printed on overhead transparencies or on paper. Slides can also be saved to a file or shipped to an outside graphics shop to create them. The printing process is basically the same, regardless of whether you are printing outlines, notes, or handouts: you open the presentation, identify what you want printed, specify the range of slides to be printed, and choose the number of copies.

Setting up your slides for printing

Before you print your presentation, you need to open the presentation and set it up for printing. Follow these steps:

1. Choose File ➪ Page Setup. The Page Setup dialog box appears, as shown in Figure 31-1.

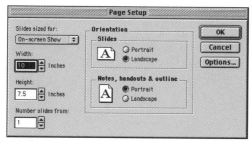

Figure 31-1: The Page Setup dialog box

2. In this dialog box, select the desired size for the slides. Note that, by default, PowerPoint is set up to create and print slides in Landscape orientation. Also remember that, by default, the slides are set up to print 10 inches wide by 7.5 inches tall. The Slides sized for pop-up menu is set at Custom, which lets you change the following settings:

- *On-screen Show* sets the width at 10 inches and the height at 7.5 inches with Landscape orientation.

- *Letter Paper (8.5 × 11 inches)* sets the width at 10 inches and the height at 7.5 inches with Landscape orientation. These measurements cause the slides to fill the page. Choose this option when you want to print on paper and fill the entire page.

- *US Ledger Paper (13.3 × 10 inches)* sets the width at 13.3 inches and the height at 10 inches with Landscape orientation. These measurements cause the slides to fill the page. Choose this option when you want to print on paper and fill the entire page.

- *A3 Paper (14 × 10 inches)* sets the width at 14 inches and the height at 10.5 inches with Landscape orientation. The slides then fill A3 (European size) paper.

- *A4 Paper (10.83 × 7.5 inches)* sets the width at 10.83 inches and the height at 7.5 inches with Landscape orientation. The slides then fill A4 (European size) paper.

- *B4 Paper (12 × 9 inches)* sets the width at 12 inches and the height at 9 inches with Landscape orientation. The slides then fill B4 (European size) paper.

- *B5 Paper (8 × 6 inches)* sets the width at 8 inches and the height at 6 inches with Landscape orientation. The slides then fill B5 (European size) paper.

- *35mm Slides* sets the width at 11.25 inches and the height at 7.5 inches. These measurements enable the contents to fill the slide area in Landscape orientation, ideal for reduction to a 35mm slide.

- *Overhead.* Use this option when you want to create transparencies. It makes slides fill the transparencies, making them easier to see when they are placed on an overhead projector.

- *Web Banner (8 × 1 inches).* Use this option to change the layout of your slides to a Web banner 8 inches wide by 1 inch high. This is both for printing and an onscreen presentation.

- *Custom* lets you set dimensions of your own choosing, either by entering values in the Width and Height boxes or by clicking the up and down arrows to enter the desired value.

3. In the Orientation portion of the dialog box, choose the desired orientation (Portrait or Landscape). Note that you can separately set the orientation for your speaker's notes, handouts, and outlines.

4. If you want to use a starting number other than 1 for your slides, enter a desired number in the Number slides from text box.

5. Click OK.

The Options button brings up a standard Mac OS Page Setup dialog box.

Printing parts of your presentation

After your printing dimensions have been set by means of the Page Setup dialog box options, you can choose File ➪ Print to reveal the Print dialog box (see Figure 31-2).

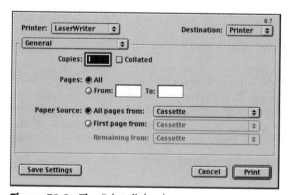

Figure 31-2: The Print dialog box

In this dialog box, you can choose what parts of the presentation you want to print. In the Pages area, choose All to print all slides, or choose From and To and type the starting and ending pages you desire. In the Copies box, you can enter the number of copies you want and have them collated if you like. Finally, you can choose a paper source for all pages or the first page, if your printer supports multiple paper sources.

If you click the pop-up menu at top left (it says General in Figure 31-2) and choose Microsoft PowerPoint, you'll see several additional choices (see Figure 31-3).

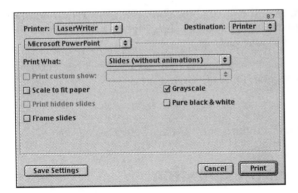

Figure 31-3: The Print dialog box after choosing Microsoft PowerPoint from the pop-up menu at the top left

Use the Print What pop-up menu to tell PowerPoint exactly which parts of your presentation you want to print. The choices you have from the Print What menu are as follows:

✦ **Slides** prints your slides on paper or on overhead transparencies with all of its contents.

✦ **Handouts.** You can print audience handouts that contain two, three, or six slides per page. Two slides per page is a good choice for a large image with great detail. Use three slides per page if you want to leave space for the audience to write notes. If you want to provide a presentation outline with the most information on each page of the audience handout, use six slides per page.

✦ **Notes Pages** prints the speaker's notes pages that correspond to the slides that you decide to print.

✦ **Outline View** prints the outline that appears onscreen in Outline view.

If any slides in the presentation have been hidden (by choosing Slide Show ➪ Hide Slide), the Print Hidden Slides checkbox becomes available in the Print dialog box (choose File ➪ Print), and you can click it to tell PowerPoint to include hidden slides in the printout. The Black and White option tells PowerPoint to optimize the printing of color slides when printed on a black-and-white printer. The Pure Black and White option is used to print the slides in black and white while printing on a color printer; this will change all the shades of gray to either black or white. (This option is useful only if you have a color printer and, for some reason, you don't want the presentation in color.)

The Frame Slides option frames the printouts so they best fit transparencies when they are reduced, and the Scale to Fit Paper option scales the printout to the paper you have loaded in the printer. Choose your desired printing options in the dialog box and then click OK.

Producing Onscreen Slide Shows

Slide shows are another strength of PowerPoint because you can create professional-looking slide shows without much hassle. You can create a slide show by accepting PowerPoint's defaults and then choosing the Slide Show command from the View menu. The Slide Show will then begin. If you wish to change the default settings, the time settings between each of the slides, and any transition effects you wish to add to the presentation slide, you first need to go to Slide Sorter view. In Slide Sorter view, follow these steps to change the timing settings to the slide presentation:

1. Select the slide for which you want to set timings or effects. Click the Slide Transitions button on the Slide Sorter toolbar or choose Slide Show and then Slide Transition. This will open the Slide Transition dialog box shown in Figure 31-4.

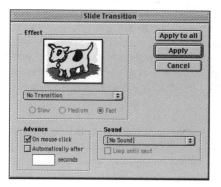

Figure 31-4: The Slide Transition dialog box

2. Choose the effects you want for the slide from the pop-up menu in the Effect area.

3. Move on to the Advance section to set your timings or choose the mouse as the signal to move to the next slide.

4. In the Sound area of the dialog box, you can add one of the default sounds or open another sound file that will play as you move to the next slide. Remember that all the effects you set are for the slide you currently have selected in Slide Sorter view unless you click Apply to all.

5. Move through your presentation, setting the effects you want for each of the slides (if you want them to vary).

Getting the Results You Want

Don't rush to print by clicking the Print button on the Standard toolbar or by immediately clicking the OK button in the Print dialog box to accept the defaults.

Because PowerPoint has so many options for what you can print and how you can print, you may not get what you want by fast clicking. Think of the Print dialog box and the Slide Setup dialog box as working in combination to give you exactly what you want. Be sure that you set the options correctly before you start printing.

Tip   Each of the effects you set in the Slide Transition box can also be set using the Slide Sorter toolbar or the Formatting Palette. The Slide Sorter toolbar is usually more useful. Its leftmost button opens the Slide Transition dialog box discussed earlier. Next to that is a Slide Transition Effects pop-up menu that allows for the setting of slide transitions. To the right of the Slide Transition Effects pop-up list is the Hide Slide button used to hide slides in a show. To the right of the Hide Slide button is the Rehearse Timings button, used to set and rehearse the slide show timings and set how long each of the slides is visible. The rightmost button is the Show Formatting button, which switches between showing the text and graphics for each of the slides and showing just the title (in Slide Sorter view, of course). You will find this toolbar very useful for quickly assigning settings to each of your slides for a slide show.

In the Advance area of the dialog box, choose On mouse click if you want to move from slide to slide manually during the show, or choose Automatically if you want the slides to advance automatically at timed intervals. (You'll learn how to change the intervals later.)

Creating progressive slides

Have you ever seen a presentation that included a slide that was nearly blank at first, but as the speaker talked, points seemed to appear on it magically? That savvy speaker used a progressive disclosure slide to create that effect. Progressive slides let your audience see your presentation develop and help them remember the most recent point you make. You may recall that "progressive slides" were "build slides" in earlier versions of PowerPoint because you progressively built the points of your presentation. You can create a progressive slide by following these steps:

1. Switch to Slide view and locate the text or text object you want to show up first in your progressive slide.

2. Control-click the text or object and choose Custom Animation from the short-cut menu (or click the Custom Animation button in the Animation tab of the Formatting palette). The Custom Animation dialog box appears, as shown in Figure 31-5.

Giving Slide Shows with Polish

Giving a good presentation isn't entirely a matter of mastering PowerPoint techniques. Most of what creates a presentation that captivates (rather than enslaves) your audience falls under the more general heading of "tips for better presentations."

Always, always, always, always (did we say that enough?) test your presentation on the hardware that you plan to use before the audience starts taking their seats. No matter how well things worked back in the home office and at the last 27 on-site presentations you've given, there's no guarantee that the hardware you're using at the 28th site is correctly set up or will behave as well as the rest.

Try not to spend too much time on a single slide. If a slide stays onscreen for five minutes or more, rethink your content. Believe it or not, five minutes is a long time when a speaker drones—this has put many an audience to sleep. The audience stays with you if you break up big chunks of information into two or three separate slides.

Add a blank slide (or a slide with nothing more than an attractive background) as the last slide in your presentation. Then when you finish, the audience has an attractive slide to look at, as opposed to being dumped back in Slide view of PowerPoint.

As you verbally emphasize points, you can use the mouse pointer as an onscreen pointer. (A commercial laser pointer is nicer, but it costs a lot more.)

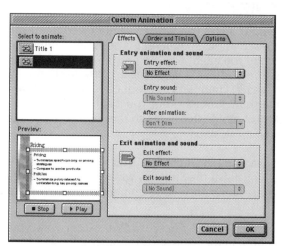

Figure 31-5: The Custom Animation dialog box

3. Click the Effects tab and choose the type of Entry and Exit animation effects you want for the text or object.

4. Click the Play button to preview the effect.

5. If you like it, click OK.

You just created the first animation in your progressive slide. Now let's fine tune it:

1. Click the Options tab of the Custom Animation box.

2. Click the appropriate item in the "Select to animate" section of the dialog box.

3. Make the appropriate selections from the pop-up Text enters and Text exits menus.

Repeat this process for each object — text or graphic — you wish to progressively animate. The Text enters and Text exits menus let you choose to have your text items enter or exit all at once, by letter, or by word. The Bullets grouped by pop-up menu lets you determine how many bullet points or objects appear each time you click.

You can make other changes to the animation order using the Order and Timing tab. In this tab, you can change the order in which objects on the slide animate and also choose to start the animation automatically after a given number of seconds or after the click of the mouse, depending on the radio button you activate. Again, use the Play button to preview your selections. When you get everything just the way you like it, click OK.

Hiding and unhiding slides

The capability to hide or unhide slides is another useful PowerPoint feature. You may want to give similar presentations to different groups but modify the content to fit each group. For example, you might want to present revenue data to each department in a company. For example, it might make sense to show detailed financial data to Sales but more general numbers to production workers. PowerPoint lets you use one presentation for both groups — but you can hide slides so they do not appear for one group and then unhide the slides so they appear for the other group. To hide a slide, follow these steps:

1. Display the slide you want to hide. In Slide Sorter view, you can select more than one slide by holding down the Shift key while you click each slide you want to hide. When you do this, the slide's number is marked with a line through it.

2. Choose Slide Show ⇨ Hide Slide. (If you are in Slide Sorter view, you can also click the Hide Slide button in the Slide Sorter toolbar.)

This option is a toggle, so you can unhide a hidden slide by selecting it in Slide Sorter view and choosing Slide Show ⇨ Hide Slide or you can simply click the Hide Slide button on the Slide Sorter toolbar again.

You can also unhide slides before you give a presentation. To do this, Control-click the slide in Slide Sorter view and choose Hide Slide from the shortcut menu.

Adding speaker notes and handouts

In PowerPoint, you can add two items to your presentation that help improve the presentation: speaker's notes and audience handouts. Each of the slides has a companion notes page that includes a small version of the slide and room for typed notes. You can print the notes and use them to recall the points you want to make for each slide. You can also print audience handouts. Audience handouts make it easy for the audience to follow your presentation and give the audience members something to take with them after the presentation is over. The handouts can contain two, three, or six slides per page.

To create speaker's notes for a presentation, follow these steps:

1. Select the slide to which you want to add a notes page. Choose View ➪ Notes Pages. The notes page appears, as shown in Figure 31-6.

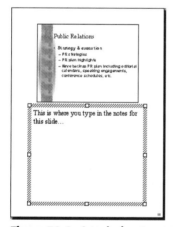

Figure 31-6: A typical notes page

2. At this size, you will have difficulty reading the notes you add to the notes page. Use the Zoom control on the Standard toolbar to increase the size of the notes page to 75 or 100 percent.

3. To enter the notes, click the box provided for notes and type your entry. After you have added speaker's notes to a presentation, you can print the notes by using the steps outlined in "Printing parts of your presentation" earlier in this chapter.

Tip

It's generally easier to see the text you type in the notes box if you change the default magnification. From the Zoom control pop-up menu on the Standard toolbar, zoom to 75 percent or larger.

You can create audience handouts by performing the following steps:

1. Choose View ⇨ Master ⇨ Handout Master. Your screen takes on the appearance shown in Figure 31-7. In the figure, the areas outlined by dotted lines represent where your slides will appear. Figure 31-7 shows six slides per page. To select the number of slides you want to appear per page, use the Handout Master toolbar.

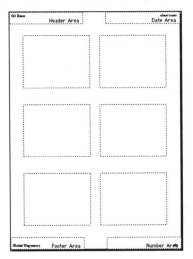

Figure 31-7: The Handout Master screen

2. Choose Insert ⇨ Text Box and click and drag the desired text box to the desired size. You can then type the desired text (see Figure 31-8).

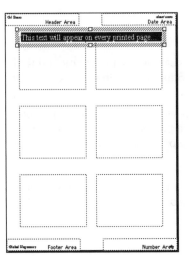

Figure 31-8: Adding a text box and text to the Handout Master

You can add the date and time or page numbers to text boxes in your handouts. To do so, place the insertion point where you want the text inside the text box, open the Insert menu, and choose the Date and Time or Page Number command. Then select the format you want in the dialog box that appears. To customize your header or footer, choose View ➪ Header and Footer.

Creating Custom Shows

PowerPoint 2001 offers you the flexibility of custom slide shows. These are basically variations of the same presentation. You can give the same presentation to different sections of a company, for example. Follow these steps to create custom shows:

1. From the Slide Show menu, choose Custom Shows. You then see the Custom Shows dialog box, as shown in Figure 31-9.

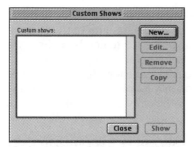

Figure 31-9: The Custom Shows dialog box

2. Choose the New button. This activates the Define Custom Show dialog box shown in Figure 31-10.

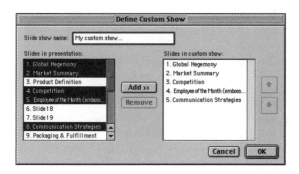

Figure 31-10: The Define Custom Show dialog box

3. In the Slides in Presentation area of the dialog box, choose the desired slides and click Add. (If you want to select multiple slides, hold the ⌘ key while clicking.)

4. Using the arrows beside the Slides in Custom Show box, move the slides to appear in the order you want.

5. Give the slide show a name and save it by clicking OK. The next time you invoke the Custom Shows dialog box, you'll be able to choose this show.

The Custom Shows feature comes in handy when making on-the-fly adjustments to a presentation, which is fairly common. This feature also provides you with a way to make a presentation more adaptable to the circumstances. Although at one time you may have had to create three presentations on the same topic, directed at different audiences with some slides in common, you can now create one presentation with several ways of running the presentation.

Tip   To see a preview of a custom show, select the name of the show in the Custom Shows dialog box and then Show.

Just before you run your slide show, you will want to select Slide Show and then Set Up Show, enabling you to make some final adjustments to the slide show. Figure 31-11 shows the Set Up Show dialog box. This dialog box offers you the option to select a type of show you want to give (for example, for browsing, where the presentation shows up in a window, or the typical slide show in full screen). You are also able to show the presentation in a looping manner or without the narration or animation. You can make these choices by clicking the corresponding checkboxes.

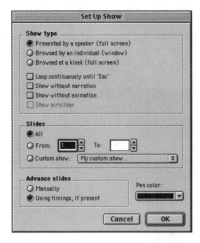

Figure 31-11: The Set Up Show dialog box

You can also specify which slides you wish to show in that particular session or whether you want to use one of your previously created custom shows. Finally, Pen Color and Advance slides options can be selected here.

PowerPoint for People Without a Copy of PowerPoint

What if you want to view a presentation with another computer that does not have PowerPoint installed, or e-mail a copy of your slide show to a friend that doesn't have PowerPoint? No problem. PowerPoint now has a Save as PowerPoint movie command that creates a QuickTime movie of your slide show.

Choose File ⇨ Make Movie. In the Save File dialog box that appears, you have two options: Use current settings or Adjust settings. If you choose Use current settings, click the Save button, and you're through. If you choose Adjust settings, the Movie Options dialog box appears, enabling you to change the settings before creating your movie.

Note Even if you think your slide show is fine the way it is, it's usually a good idea to visit the Movie Options dialog box at least once per slide show. In it you can, among other things, optimize the movie for size or quality as well as adjust transitions and add a soundtrack if you like.

Tip One last detail you might consider is that you can use QuickTime Pro and iMovie to convert the QuickTime movie to digital video, which can be shown on a TV or dubbed to a VHS tape.

The E-mail Connection

One other common option that you have for producing your presentation is the Send To command from the File menu. With this command, you can send the presentation to another person via electronic mail. This command requires that you have an e-mail client program—for example, Entourage, Outlook Express, or Eudora—installed and have set up your mail preferences.

Using the Send To Mail Recipient command creates a new e-mail message with your presentation attached in most e-mail clients, enabling you to send the presentation to the desired recipient easily.

Summary

As demonstrated in this chapter, producing your work in PowerPoint is not an incredibly involved process. This chapter showed you how you can print presentations and how you can use different methods to improve your slide presentations. The chapter covered the following points:

✦ You can print presentation slides by choosing File ➪ Print, but you should first set up your presentation for the type of printing you want. First choose File ➪ Page Setup and then select the desired options in the Slide Setup dialog box.

✦ You can produce onscreen slide shows by using Slide Show menu and selecting the desired options from the Slide Show dialog box.

✦ You can add transitions or builds to each slide to enhance the effects of an onscreen presentation.

✦ You can add speaker's notes or audience handouts to presentations. You can print these items separately for distribution to the speaker or the audience.

Where to go next

✦ The next chapter demonstrates how you can use macros within PowerPoint to automate various tasks.

✦ PowerPoint offers many ways to enhance your presentation. It's never too late to make a better presentation! See Chapter 28 for details.

✦   ✦   ✦

Working with PowerPoint Macros

Macros are combinations of keystrokes that automate many of the tasks that you normally perform with a program. Macros enable you to record a sequence of characters that you can then assign to text, or to a graphic on a slide, or to a button on a toolbar. Later, you can play back the character sequence by choosing a menu option used for running macros or by clicking the slide object or toolbar button assigned to the macro. When you run the macro, PowerPoint performs the steps as if you had just typed the characters, made the menu choices, or done whatever actions you recorded for that macro. If you must perform any repetitive tasks in PowerPoint, you can save many keystrokes and mouse option choices with macros.

Approaching Visual Basic

Unfortunately, Windows users have it better than us Mac folk when it comes to macros in Office 2001. They get a PowerPoint macro recorder that isn't available in the Mac version. Which is a pity because, as you'll soon see, creating a macro using Visual Basic is a lot like programming.

Note

If the idea of macros appeals to you, you'll get a lot more done in a lot less time with one of the commercial Mac macro programs—QuicKeys from CE Software (www.cesoft.com/products/quickeys.html) and OneClick from Westcode Software (http://westcodesoft.com) are the two most popular—than you will using Visual Basic. Still, because this is a "Bible," we'll show you how to create a simple macro as well as where (within Office, of course) to find help to create more sophisticated macros.

Each of the macros you create is stored in a new Visual Basic module and attached to the open presentation. Note that you should store your macros with your presentation and not with a PowerPoint template because macros that are stored in templates are not attached to the presentation.

Creating a Macro

In this section, you create a simple macro that changes the text contained in the title text box of slide 1 to 36-point Palatino italic.

Using the Macro dialog box

To begin creating your macro, open the desired presentation and choose Tools ➪ Macro ➪ Macros. The Macro dialog box appears (see Figure 32-1).

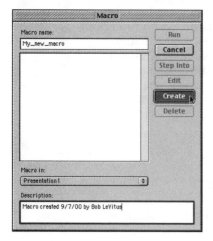

Figure 32-1: The Macro dialog box

To create a macro that changes the point size of the title text in slide 1 to 36-point Palatino italic, follow these steps:

1. Type **My_new_macro** in the Macro Name field. Note that you cannot use spaces in macro names.

2. Click the Create button. The Microsoft Visual Basic Editor window appears (see Figure 32-2).

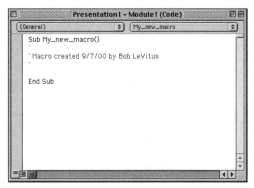

Figure 32-2: The Visual Basic Editor window

3. Click the blank line just above the words End sub and type the following:

```
With ActivePresentation.Slides(1).Shapes.Title.TextFrame.
TextRange
    With .Font
        .italic = True
        .Name = "Palatino"
        .Size = 36
    End With
End With
```

Be sure to type everything exactly as you see it or the macro won't work. Spaces, periods, and indenting all count. Also note that lines that begin with an apostrophe are considered comments and are ignored by Visual Basic when you run the macro. Finally, don't forget to type some text into the title block of slide 1 or you won't be able to see the effect of the macro when you run it.

When you're through typing the text, it should look like Figure 32-3.

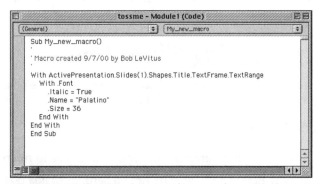

Figure 32-3: The Visual Basic Editor window with the text you typed

4. Choose File ➪ Close and Return to Microsoft PowerPoint, or use the keyboard shortcut ⌘-Q.

The Visual Basic Editor closes and you are returned to PowerPoint.

5. Choose Tools ➪ Macro ➪ Macros.

6. Click My_new_macro, and then click Run.

That's it. Assuming you did everything correctly and text exists in the title text box of slide 1 for the macro to work on, the macro changes that text to 36-point Palatino italic.

Getting help with Visual Basic

If you want to learn more about creating macros with Visual Basic, you must make sure that you installed VBA Help (in the Programmability section of the Value Pack Installer). If you didn't do so when you first installed Office, install the help files now.

After the help files are installed, follow these steps to learn more about Visual Basic:

1. Choose Tools ➪ Macro ➪ Visual Basic Editor.

2. Click the Office Assistant.

3. In the Assistant, type the method, property, function, statement, or object that you want Help on, or type a query.

4. Click Search, and then click the topic you want.

To browse through a list of all Visual Basic methods, properties, functions, and objects for PowerPoint in Visual Basic Editor, choose View ➪ Object Browser. In the list of libraries, click the library for PowerPoint. For help on an item, click the item, and then click the question mark button in the Object Browser dialog box.

To show help for Visual Basic Editor, choose Help ➪ Contents and Index.

Running Macros During Slide Shows

You can assign a macro to an object (such as text or a graphic) that's placed on a slide. This technique enables you to access the macro by clicking the object.

Follow these steps to attach a macro button to an object on a slide:

1. In Slide View, select the text or graphic that you want to use to run the macro.

2. Choose Slide Show ➪ Action Settings. The Action Settings dialog box appears, as shown in Figure 32-4.

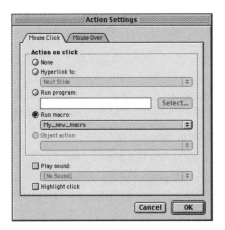

Figure 32-4: The Action Settings dialog box

3. If you want to run the macro by clicking the selected object during the slide show, click the Mouse Click tab. If you want to run the macro by moving the mouse pointer over the object, click the Mouse Over tab.

4. Click Run macro and then choose the desired macro in the pop-up menu.

5. Choose any other desired options in the dialog box.

6. Click OK, and the object in the slide takes on a highlighted appearance. When you click the object during a slide show, the macro will run.

Using action buttons

Another way to get a Macro on to your slide is by using an Action Button. An Action Button is nothing more than an Action Setting attached to an icon that you draw on your slide.

To create an Action Button, choose Slide Show ➪ Action Buttons, and then choose an action button from the submenu.

Your cursor will turn into a crosshair; you can now draw the Action Button on your slide. As soon as you release the mouse button, the Action Settings dialog box will automatically appear, configured to perform the action you choose.

Each submenu selection — First Slide, Last Slide, Next Slide, Previous Slide, and so on — creates a unique-looking icon that performs that particular action. Or choose Custom and configure the Action Settings to run a macro that you've created.

Assigning macros to toolbar buttons

You can assign macros to buttons on a toolbar, which is useful if you perform some tasks on a regular basis. The macro button to which the macro is assigned is usually a custom button, but you also have the option of assigning the macro to an existing button on the toolbar, which cancels the previous function. To assign a macro to a toolbar button, follow these steps:

1. Choose Tools ➪ Customize.

2. If the toolbar to which you want to add a button isn't visible, click the Toolbars tab of the dialog box and turn on the check box beside the toolbar name.

3. Click the Commands tab of the Customize dialog box.

4. Scroll down in the Categories list and click Macros to select it.

5. In the right half of the dialog box, click and drag the desired macro onto the desired toolbar. When you release the mouse button, a button appears on the toolbar for the macro.

Running the macro

After you create a macro, you can run it in different ways. After reading this section, decide for yourself which method is best for your needs.

One way to run a macro is to choose Tools ➪ Macro ➪ Macros. In the Macro dialog box, click the name of the desired macro and then click Run.

A second method for running macros is to click an object in a slide that you assigned to the macro.

You can stop a running macro at any time by pressing ⌘-. (period).

A Note About Macro Viruses

Macro viruses are computer viruses that are stored in macros within PowerPoint presentations. PowerPoint does not have the capability to scan a floppy disk, hard disk, or network drive for a macro virus and remove it. (You can obtain this kind of protection from antivirus software, which is available from your software retailer.) PowerPoint warns you about the possibility of viruses every time you open a presentation with macros, because the presentation may contain harmful macros. When you receive the warning, you are given the option of opening the presentation with or without the macros.

A good rule of thumb is if the presentation contains useful macros, you may want to open it with the macros, but if you don't know the source of the presentation (if it is attached to an e-mail, for example), you may want to open it without the macros; this will prevent you from running the risk of contamination.

If you want to avoid the warning, you can turn off the Always ask before opening presentations with macros checkbox. To turn off the option later, choose Tools ➪ Preferences, click the General tab, and uncheck the Macro virus protection checkbox. For more information on macro viruses, you can download virus protection information from Microsoft's Web site (www.microsoft.com).

One last detail: Most (but not all) macro viruses are Windows-only. Think of this as yet another way Mac users have it better than Windows users.

Deleting a macro

After you have created a presentation, you may want to eliminate the macros; this task that can be accomplished with ease. Follow these steps to delete a macro:

1. Choose Tools ➪ Macro ➪ Macros.

2. In the Macro dialog box, choose the name of the macro.

3. Click Delete.

When you perform these steps, the macro is removed from the presentation. (This if also useful when you mess up a macro and want to start over.)

About the macro code

Without knowledge of Visual Basic for Applications (VBA), you can't easily create new or edit existing macros. Unfortunately, an in-depth discussion of VBA is far beyond the scope of this book. If you'd like to learn more about programming in Visual Basic, take a look at *Microsoft Excel 2000 Power Programming with VBA* by John Walkenbach (IDG Books Worldwide, Inc.).

However, if you are familiar with the workings of VBA, you can make changes to an existing macro by editing the VBA code that lies at the heart of the macro. Choose Tools ➪ Macro ➪ Macros, select the desired macro in the Macro dialog box that appears, and click Edit. When you do this, the VBA code of the macro appears in a VBA Editor window. (Figure 32-3 shows the code for the macro you created earlier.)

Summary

This chapter covered the basics of using macros in PowerPoint. Now you have the tools you need to record macros efficiently and put them to work. We covered these points:

✦ Macros are created in Visual Basic for Applications (VBA) code, the underlying programming language of Word, Excel, PowerPoint, and Access.

✦ You can run macros by choosing the Macro command from the Tools menu and selecting the desired macro in the dialog box that appears.

✦ You can attach macros to objects on slides and to toolbar buttons, or create new Action Buttons that trigger a macro.

Where to go next

✦ The next chapter discusses how to use PowerPoint on the Internet and on intranets.

✦ Macros can take much of the repetitive drudgery out of formatting and printing tasks. For an explanation of the kinds of formatting tasks you can automate, see Chapter 29.

✦   ✦   ✦

PowerPoint and the Web

PowerPoint 2001 differs significantly from earlier versions. This version comes enabled with more specific features for producing presentation-quality Web pages for use with the Internet and with intranets than any prior version came with. PowerPoint 2001 enables you to attach hyperlinks to other Office 2001 documents or to Web sites. These hyperlinks let you easily jump to locations in other Office 2001 documents. Additionally, you can easily save PowerPoint slides as HTML pages that are ready to be published on the Web.

Getting Started

This chapter assumes a familiarity with the basics of Power Point. If you are familiar with the Web or with intranets but haven't yet learned to work with PowerPoint, you should consider reading Chapters 28 through 32 before proceeding with this chapter.

Exploring what's possible

PowerPoint 2001 enables you to perform a number of Net-related tasks as you work with presentations. You can insert hyperlinks at any desired location in a presentation to link to other Office 2001 documents or to Web sites. Or, you can insert hyperlinks that open and preaddress an e-mail message. When you click these hyperlinks while viewing a presentation, you can jump directly to that location in the other file, to a specified Web site, or to a preaddressed e-mail message.

You can also save PowerPoint slides as HTML (Hypertext Markup Language) pages, the publishing language of the World Wide Web. These topics are covered in further detail throughout this chapter.

Figure 33-1 shows a PowerPoint slide. This slide was saved as a Web page and pre-viewed using Microsoft Internet Explorer (see Chapter 37), the popular Web browser that is included with Office 2001.

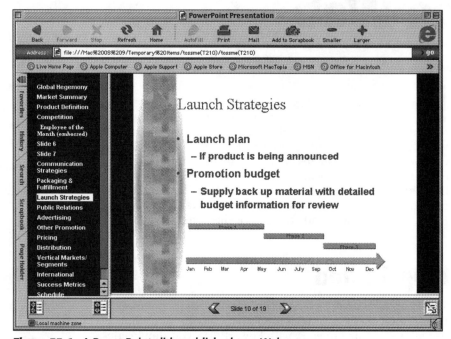

Figure 33-1: A PowerPoint slide published as a Web page

Note   Notice how PowerPoint creates an outline (see the left-hand frame in Figure 33-1), and "next slide/previous slide" buttons (bottom) for your Web-based slide show on the fly. Cool, eh? You learn how to publish your presentation as a Web page later in the chapter.

Connecting to a network

To accomplish most of the tasks described in this chapter, you need to be connected to a network. This connection can be a dial-up connection to the Internet by means of a commercial Internet service provider such as AT&T WorldNet, or EarthLink. Your connection can also be a direct connection through your organization's local area network, and you may be connected directly to a corporate intranet, in which case you're able to retrieve or publish data to your company's private network.

This chapter doesn't go into specifics on making a network connection, because that topic is an entire book in itself. If you need help in this area, look at *Web Design Studio Secrets* by Deke McClelland, Katrin Eismann, and Terri Stone (from IDG Books Worldwide, Inc.).

Defining Some Terms and Concepts

Because intranets and the Internet are newer concepts to many readers than presentations, a few explanations of terms may be in order. (If you're intimately familiar with the Internet, intranets, and the World Wide Web, you may want to skip this section and the next, and dive right into working with PowerPoint and the Web.)

The Internet

The Internet is a global collection of computers, linked together by means of telephone and microwave lines and accessible to the public by means of various connections in offices and in homes. The Internet grew out of a research project in the 1970s that originally linked university and government computers in the United States. Since its inception, the Internet has grown to encompass millions of computers spread throughout dozens of nations. Any Mac (or PC) user with an Internet connection can connect to the Internet (either by means of a phone line or by a direct hookup) and gain access to the volumes of information located there.

The World Wide Web

A major component of the Internet is the World Wide Web. The Internet has other parts, but the World Wide Web is the best known. The World Wide Web uses graphical software known as Web browsers and files stored as HTML. The computers on the Internet that store the HTML files are known as Web servers. When PCs connect to the Internet to retrieve this data, they use Web browser software, which converts the incoming information (encoded in HTML) to graphical pages displayed as a combination of text, graphics, and, in some cases, audio and video. Commonly used Web browsers include Microsoft Internet Explorer, Netscape Communicator, and the custom Web browsers built into the software provided by America Online and CompuServe.

Each site on the Internet has a unique address, commonly known as the Internet address (and less commonly known by the official name of URL, or Uniform Resource Locator). When you establish an Internet connection, open a Web browser, and enter an Internet address such as `www.whitehouse.gov`, you are entering the address for the Web server that provides the home page for the President's office in the United States. Web addresses such as these can be stored in PowerPoint slides and displayed as hyperlinks.

About intranets

Many Internet-related uses of Office 2001 involve making data available on intranets. An intranet is a private network of computers available only to the members of a specific organization. Intranets make use of World Wide Web technology — Web servers, network connections, and Web-browser software — to enable members of an organization to share information. Intranets are popular with corporations because they enable employees to share work-related information in a confidential manner.

About HTML

As mentioned earlier, HTML is the language used for publishing information to the World Wide Web and to intranets that use World Wide Web technology. HTML is a text-based language that makes use of special codes called tags. These tags are included in the text of the HTML documents, and they provide instructions to the Web browser software that determine how the data appears when it is viewed by the end-user. Although you don't need to know the nuts and bolts of HTML coding to work with PowerPoint and the Web, it's a good idea to at least be familiar with the concept of saving your data in HTML file format. To publish PowerPoint data on the Internet or on an intranet, you need to save that data in HTML format and upload it to your Web server. If you are dealing with a corporate intranet, your company's Webmaster can tell you how to upload the HTML files that PowerPoint produces to your company's Web server. If you are managing a Web site on the Internet or on an intranet, you already know how to do this; much of the rest of this chapter deals with getting that PowerPoint data ready for uploading to your server.

Using the Web Toolbar

As with all the major Office 2001 applications, PowerPoint provides the Web toolbar, a toolbar that helps you browse through the resources on an intranet or on the Web. Using the Web toolbar, you can quickly open, search, and browse through any document or through a Web page. You can jump between documents, and you can add favorite sites you find on the Web to the Favorites folder, enabling you to go back to those sites quickly at a later time.

In PowerPoint you can display the Web toolbar by choosing View ➪ Toolbars and then selecting Web from the submenu that appears, or you can click the Web toolbar button in the Standard toolbar. Figure 33-2 shows the Web toolbar.

Figure 33-2: The Web toolbar

You'll find the Web toolbar to be handy when you happen to be in PowerPoint and need to go to the Web (or to your company's intranet) for information. For example, you can click the Search the Web button to launch your default Web browser and search the Web, or you can click the Favorites button to open a list of your favorite Web sites. Refer to Chapter 11 for more specifics on the use of the Web toolbar.

Creating Hyperlinks in Documents

A significant feature of PowerPoint 2001 is its capability to use hyperlinks in documents. You can create hyperlinks to jump to other Office documents stored on your Mac, on your company's network, on a company intranet, or on the Internet.

Linking to Office documents with copy and paste

If you want to create a hyperlink to a Word document, in an Excel worksheet, or to another location in the PowerPoint presentation, the easiest way is to use the Copy and Paste Hyperlink commands of the Edit menu. In a nutshell, first select a location in the PowerPoint slide, Excel worksheet, or Word document to which you want the hyperlink to lead. Then choose Copy from the Edit menu. Finally, return to PowerPoint. At the point where you want the hyperlink to appear, choose Paste as Hyperlink from the Edit menu. In more detail, follow these steps to create a hyperlink from another Office document:

1. Open the document containing the location to which you want to link. (If the location is in PowerPoint, it can be in the same presentation or in a different presentation that's open. If the location is in an Excel or a Word file, it can be in any area of the worksheet or document.)

2. Select the portion of the document to which you want to link.

3. Choose Edit ⇨ Copy.

4. In PowerPoint, go into Slide view or Outline view and place the insertion pointer at the location you want to insert the hyperlink.

5. Choose Edit ⇨ Paste as Hyperlink.

When you perform these steps, PowerPoint inserts a hyperlink back to the original document at the selected location. When you view the presentation in Slide view mode, you can click the hyperlink to jump to the linked document.

Linking to Web sites, files, and preaddressed e-mail messages with Insert Hyperlink

If you need to establish a hyperlink from a PowerPoint slide to a Web site on an intranet or on the Internet, you can use the following steps. (Technically, you can use these same steps to link to another Office document, but it's easier to use the copy and paste methods described earlier.)

1. In Slide view or in Outline view, select the text in the slide that will serve as the hyperlink.

Note   If you don't select some text in Step 1, the rest of the procedure won't work.

2. Click the Insert Hyperlink button in the Standard toolbar, or choose Insert ⇨ Hyperlink. The Edit Hyperlink dialog box appears, as shown in Figure 33-3.

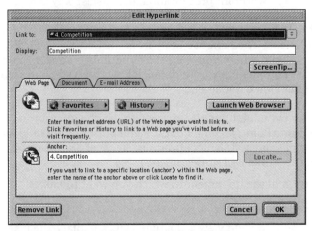

Figure 33-3: The Edit Hyperlink dialog box

3. Click the appropriate tab at the top of the Edit Hyperlink dialog box — Web Page, Document, or E-Mail Address. In the Link to text box, enter the Web address (or the path for the file) of the destination for the link.

   If you chose the E-mail Address tab in this step, then clicking the hyperlink will create a new mail message with the subject and address you specify in the Edit Hyperlink dialog box.

4. If you are establishing a link to a Web page or file and want to jump to a specific location on that page, enter that location in the Anchor file text box.

(The location can be a cell reference or named range in an Excel worksheet, a Word bookmark, or the name of another PowerPoint slide.) If you link to a file and leave this entry blank, the hyperlink jumps to the beginning of the file.

5. Click OK to establish the hyperlink.

Publishing PowerPoint Slides on the Web

The Save as Web Page option of the File menu enables you to save existing presentations as HTML files for Web publication. After you save a presentation as Web pages, you can upload the HTML files to your Internet or intranet Web server, using the procedures applicable to your server.

To save an existing presentation in HTML format, choose File ➪ Save as Web Page. A standard Save dialog box appears. Click the Web Options button to open the Web Options dialog box to configure specific Web options, as shown in Figure 33-4.

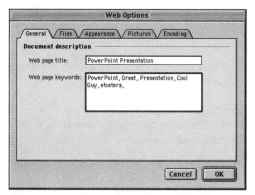

Figure 33-4: The Web Options dialog box

The Web Options dialog box has five tabs:

✦ **General.** Add a Web page title and/or keywords.

✦ **Files.** Save options and browser support.

✦ **Appearance.** Color and navigation button options.

✦ **Pictures.** Screen size and Use PNG as an output format.

✦ **Encoding.** Keyboard encoding options.

Tip

The only one that really requires your attention is the General tab, where you can add a page title and keywords for search engines. The stuff in the other tabs — Tiles, Appearance, Pictures, and Encoding — can be tweaked if you want, but you don't need to.

Using the Online Presentation Templates

Note that you can also create Web pages using PowerPoint's online presentation templates. Many of the presentations included with PowerPoint look great as online presentations, making their preparation for Web publication easy.

If you wish to use one of these presentations, simply choose File ➪ Project Gallery (Command-Shift-P), and then select the Presentations: Designs in the left-hand Category list. This enables you to see some of the presentations available for easy Web publication. Remember that if you don't find one that meets your needs, you can always alter the presentation using the techniques described in Chapters 28 and 29.

Tip You can see how your presentation is going to look if you save it as a Web page by choosing File ➪ Web Preview. Rather than saving your entire presentation, PowerPoint creates temporary files, and then displays them in your chosen browser.

Summary

This chapter detailed how to share your PowerPoint data with Internet/intranet users. Points covered in this chapter include the following:

✦ Hyperlinks can be added to PowerPoint slides, and you can store Web addresses, jump locations to other Office documents in PowerPoint slides, or create links to preaddressed e-mail messages.

✦ You can use the Save as Web Page option of the File menu to save existing PowerPoint slides as HTML files so that you can publish on the Internet or on an intranet.

Where to go next

✦ The next chapter demonstrates how you can put PowerPoint to work in real-world applications.

✦ PowerPoint is just one component of the Web-publishing capabilities provided by Office 2001. Excel and Word also offer Web publishing and Web-interaction features. For specifics on Excel and the Web, see Chapter 24; for Word and the Web, see Chapter 11.

✦   ✦   ✦

PowerPoint at Work

✦ ✦ ✦ ✦

In This Chapter

Creating an
organization chart

Creating a travel
presentation

✦ ✦ ✦ ✦

This chapter shows you a nifty trick—how to create organization charts in PowerPoint. Executive secretaries throughout the corporate world rejoice in this feature, because so many companies regularly play Musical Vice Presidents in these days of downsizing.

This chapter also walks you through creating a presentation for choosing a site for a convention. In this case, the presentation's contents are less important than the general ideas you learn—you can use these ideas to create any kind of presentation.

Creating an Organization Chart

PowerPoint's organization chart feature lets you create company hierarchy diagrams in a hurry. By way of example, follow these steps to create a chart for the fictitious ElvisCo (see Figure 34-1):

1. Create a new presentation in PowerPoint by choosing File ⇨ New Presentation.

2. The New Slide dialog box appears. Choose the Organization Chart layout (see Figure 34-2).

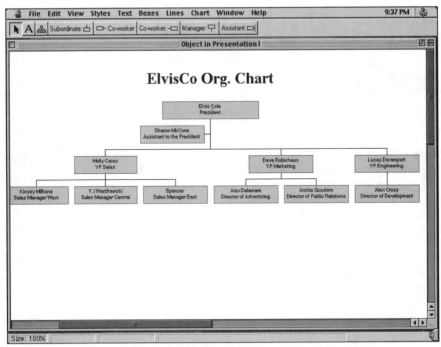

Figure 34-1: The completed organization chart in PowerPoint for ElvisCo

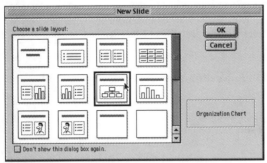

Figure 34-2: Choosing the Organization Chart
layout in the New Slide dialog box

3. Double-click the Organization Chart placeholder to activate the Microsoft Organization Chart application and to display a default chart. Organization Chart opens with the default chart shown in Figure 34-3.

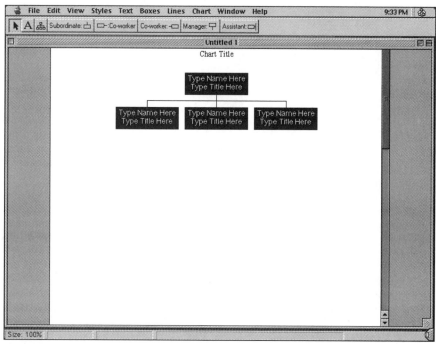

Figure 34-3: The default organization chart

4. Click in the first box of the chart. In the box type **Elvis Cole** for the name and **President** for the title (or enter a name and title of your own choosing). Use the Tab or down arrow key to move from the name to the title. If you want to add a comment in the chart box, simply move to the comment area and begin entering your information.

5. Next, add the administrative assistant. Click the Assistant button on the toolbar, and move the pointer and click in the President's box. Enter **Sharon McCone** for the name and **Assistant to the President** for the title (or enter a name and title of your own choosing).

6. Enter the following names and titles for the division managers (or names and titles of your own choosing) from left to right in the next level of boxes that appear below Administrative Assistant:

Molly Cates, VP Sales
Dave Robichaux, VP Marketing
Lucas Davenport, VP Engineering

7. Click the Styles menu to drop down its Group styles options. Click the upper-left icon shown in Figure 34-4 to create subordinate levels in the chart levels.

Figure 34-4: The Group styles menu

8. Click the Subordinate button on the Organization Chart toolbar and then click Molly Cates's box. Enter the following names and titles (or use names and titles of your own choosing). Remember that you need to click the Subordinate button for each of the subordinate entries you make:

Kinsey Milhone, Sales Manager West
V. I. Warshawski, Sales Manager Central
Spenser, Sales Manager East

9. Using the procedure in Step 8, enter names and titles underneath Dave Robichaux and Lucas Davenport's boxes:

10. Now choose File ⇨ Update Presentation to update your presentation and place the chart on the blank slide.

11. Choose File ⇨ Close and Return to return to PowerPoint to see the chart.

12. Choose File ⇨ Save to save the presentation. Save your presentation as **Chart**. Your finished chart should look more or less like the one shown in Figure 34-1.

Creating a Travel Presentation

Suppose you head the committee to choose the site for your company's annual convention this year. Your first meeting with the committee is right around the corner. It's PowerPoint to the rescue.

Applying a template

The following example applies a template to the presentation. The template gives the presentation's slides a consistent look. PowerPoint comes with many different templates that you can apply to your presentation; choose the one that works best for you. Follow these steps:

1. Choose File ⇨ New Presentation.

2. Choose Title Slide as the slide layout and then click OK. A slide appears without any formatting.

3. Enter the title **Convention Site Option for 2001**.

4. Control-click the PowerPoint window. In the shortcut menu that appears, choose Apply Design Template to open the Apply Design dialog box shown in Figure 34-5. Choose a template design you like and click Apply.

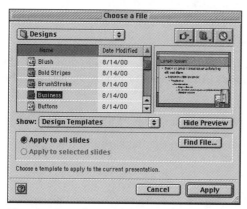

Figure 34-5: The Apply Design dialog box

Note   If you don't see a preview on the right, click the Show Preview button (which says "Hide Preview" in Figure 34-5).

5. Click the Insert New Slide button on the Standard toolbar and select Bulleted List as the slide layout. Enter **San Diego** as the title, and in the bulleted list, enter the following:

   Wide range of pricing regarding accommodations
   Excellent restaurants and entertainment
   Close to Mexico
   Beautiful scenery

6. Click the Insert New Slide button on the Standard toolbar and select Bulleted List as the slide layout. Enter **San Francisco** as the title, and in the bulleted list, enter the following:

   Excellent dining and attractions in Fisherman's Wharf area
   Proximity to sites of interest reduces transportation costs

7. Click the Insert New Slide button on the Standard toolbar and select Bulleted List as the slide layout. Enter **Cancun, Mexico** as the title, and in the bulleted list, enter the following:

   Favorable currency exchange rate maximizes dollar usage
   Outstanding water sports in close proximity to hotels

8. Click the Insert New Slide button on the Standard toolbar and select Bulleted List as the slide layout. Enter **San Juan, PR** as the title, and in the bulleted list, enter the following:

   **Excellent hotel and conference facilities with casino-based entertainment
   Spanish flavor to cultural attractions
   No need for passport/visa or currency exchange**

Applying a background

Now that you have applied the template to the presentation and entered the text, apply a background to all the slides in the presentation by performing the following steps:

1. Switch to Slide Master view by choosing View ⇨ Master ⇨ Slide Master.

2. Choose Format ⇨ Background to open the Background dialog box (see Figure 34-6).

Figure 34-6: The Background dialog box

3. Choose a light gray as the background color by clicking the arrow in the Background fill area to open the list box. Select gray from the submenu of colors that appears and click Apply To All.

Note Choose Fill Effects from the background fill list box to choose gradient, texture, pattern, or picture backgrounds instead of solid colors.

Adding notes and handouts

After you have created the presentation and applied a template to it, you can create a set of speaker's notes. Perform the following steps to create these items:

1. The notes page that appears onscreen corresponds to the slide you are currently working on. Therefore, switch to Slide view and move to the San Diego slide.

2. Choose View ⇨ Notes Page.

3. Click inside the notes box to make it active. You may need to use the Zoom control to see the text better. Click the Zoom control button on the Standard toolbar and choose a larger percentage to increase the size of the box.

4. Enter the following notes:

> **To Garfinkles/$75 and up a meal/two persons**
> **Broadway shows at San Diego Theater**
> **Venture to Tijuana to purchase authentic Mexican arts and crafts**
> **Genuine Mexican food available (not those so-called imitations)**

5. Move to the San Francisco slide and create a notes page by entering the following notes:

> **From Hilton/double occupancy/$200 per night**
> **To La Quinta/double occupancy/$75 per night**
> **From Fisherman's Wharf/$20-$75 a meal/two persons**
> **Down by the Sea Restaurant rated best in San Francisco, widest selection of seafood**
> **12 other wharf restaurants to choose from**
> **5 different options of transportation with low costs as opposed to cabs**

6. Move to the Cancun, Mexico, slide and create a notes page by entering the following notes:

> **5. pesos to a dollar**
> **Outstanding snorkeling and scuba diving**
> **Most hotels offer snorkeling gear onsite and are located on the beach**

7. Move to the San Juan, Puerto Rico, slide and create a notes page by entering the following notes:

> **ESJ Hotel facilities perfect for working vacation**
> **Many Puerto Rican art museums**
> **Puerto Rico is a commonwealth of the United States, so you need no special paperwork to visit there.**

Adding headers and footers

After creating the notes pages, you can add page numbers by choosing View ⇨ Header and Footer. The Header and Footer dialog box appears, as shown in Figure 34-7.

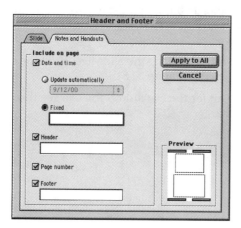

Figure 34-7: The Notes and Handouts tab of the Header and Footer dialog box

You can use this dialog box to include headers and footers on the slides and slide notes. (You can do this only from the Slide Master.) If you click the Slide tab, you can add the date, time, and slide numbers to your slides. While you're at it, you can exclude the title slide from getting these additions. Apply these items by clicking the corresponding checkboxes on the Slide tab.

You use the Notes and Handouts tab to apply these same elements to the notes pages and handouts that may be included with a presentation. The one additional option you have here is the addition of headers. You may need to add headers to identify your handouts or notes. You can click the Page number box to add page numbers to your speaker's notes. The Preview box shows you where the page numbers will appear.

Printing your notes pages

To print your notes pages, follow these steps:

1. Be sure your printer is ready (check to see if it is online).
2. Choose File ⇨ Print.
3. In the Print What pop-up menu of the Print dialog box, choose Notes Pages.
4. Click OK.

Adding transitions

Transitions are another feature you can add to the presentation. Transitions are visual changes between the slides. For example, one kind of transition makes one slide appear to dissolve into another. Transitions can make a presentation more appealing to an audience and can be a good special effect to add to a presentation. Perform the following steps to create a transition between two slides. You must perform these steps for each slide transition or select all (Command-A) in the Slide Sorter to apply the same transition to every slide.

1. Switch to Slide Sorter view by clicking its button on the left side of the status bar. Click the appropriate slide to select it; hold down the Shift key to select multiple slides.
2. Choose the slide transition you want by clicking the Slide Transition box on the Slide Sorter toolbar that appears (see Figure 34-8).
3. In the Effect list box, choose Box Out for the transition. You can see the effect of this transition in the Preview box.

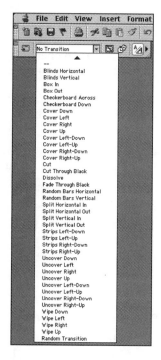

Figure 34-8: The Slide Transition list

You can also insert transitions using the Transition Effects list box on the Slide Sorter toolbar at the top of your screen. Use the arrow keys to move to the slide for which you want to set a transition. Then click the arrow of the list box and choose the effect you want to apply to the slide.

The benefit of using the dialog box is that you have a chance to preview the transition before it is applied, and to adjust the speed of the transition. However, you can click the Transition button on the Slide Sorter toolbar to open the Transitions dialog box. Here you can preview the transition by selecting it from the list of transitions.

Finally, save the completed presentation by choosing the Save command from the File menu. When asked for a name, you can call the presentation Travel 1. Run the presentation by clicking the Slide Show button on the left side of the status bar.

Summary

This chapter provided a step-by-step look at creating an organization chart and walked you through creating a presentation. The following key points were discussed in the chapter:

✦ You can use the Organization Chart layout in the New Slide dialog box to create organization charts.

✦ To apply a design to a presentation, Control-click any blank part of the Power Point window and choose Apply Design Template from the shortcut menu.

✦ While in Slide View, you can create notes pages that provide speaker's notes you can work from while giving your presentation.

✦ While in Slide Sorter view, you can use Tools ➪ Slide Transition to add transitions to your slides.

Where to go next

✦ The next chapter answers common questions PowerPoint users have.

✦ Now that you have created a presentation in PowerPoint, you may want to take some time to make it more visually appealing. Chapter 29 tells you how.

✦ You may also want to produce the presentation you created in this chapter. See Chapter 31.

✦   ✦   ✦

The PowerPoint Top Ten

In this chapter, you find questions and answers detailing the most common problems encountered by PowerPoint users. As usual, the answers are based on information we picked up from Microsoft Technical Support and the Microsoft forums on CompuServe.

1. How can I format titles and text for entire presentations?

Sometimes you will need to make formatting changes to an entire presentation, whether those changes are for the text or for the layout of your slides. Choose View ➪ Master ➪ Slide Master. When you make the changes in the Slide Master, they are applied to the entire presentation.

2. How can I group and edit objects as one?

To group objects, select them and choose Draw ➪ Group on the Drawing toolbar. This action groups the selected objects as one. If you want to edit the objects, use the editing techniques you learned in the PowerPoint section of this book.

3. How can I copy the formatting of one object to another?

First, highlight the object that contains the formatting you want to copy. Next, double-click the Format Painter button on the Standard toolbar. Finally, select the object(s) to which you want to apply the formatting, and the formatting is automatically applied.

4. How can I apply a PowerPoint presentation as a template?

Applying a PowerPoint presentation as a template is, in essence, creating a new template. First, create the presentation exactly the way you want it with all the formatting and objects. Next, choose File ➪ Save As. In the Save As dialog box, choose Design Template from the Format pop-up menu. The file is then saved as a template file that you can later use to create new presentations.

Tip

If you save it in the Templates folder, it'll be available in the Project Gallery along with all your other Design Templates.

5. How can I change a slide's layout without losing existing work?

If you decide to change the layout of your slide while you are working on it, first click the Layout button on the right side of the status bar to open the Slide Layout dialog box. From this dialog box, choose the desired slide layout. After you click OK, the layout is applied to the slide.

6. How can I preview all my slide transitions?

To preview all your slide transitions, switch to the Slide Sorter view by clicking its button on the left of the status bar. After switching to Slide Sorter view, click the transition icon underneath each slide to see the transition.

7. How can I view my presentations without installing PowerPoint?

Use the Make Movie command in the File menu. This creates a QuickTime movie of your presentation that can be viewed on any computer — Mac or PC — that has QuickTime installed.

8. How can I print slides in reverse order?

You can't. Actually, you can, but it's a lot of work. In the Slide Sorter view, rearrange your slides so the first is last and the last is first, and then print. (The Windows version does let you print in reverse order using the Print dialog box; Mac users aren't so lucky.)

9. How can I add and erase onscreen annotations?

Annotations are useful in a slide show to make different points in your presentation. To add annotations, switch to the Slide Show view and control-click any portion of the screen. In the shortcut menu that appears, choose Pointer Options ➪ Pen. The pointer then becomes a pen, enabling you to make the necessary annotations to your slide show. You can also change the color of the marks by using the same shortcut menu. Choose Pointer Options and then Pen Color. From the next menu that appears, choose the color of your choice.

If you want to draw a straight line with the pen cursor in Slide Show view, hold down the Shift key while you draw the line.

After you have made the marks you need, you can press the E key to remove them. Remember that all annotation marks are temporary. Or, Control-click and choose Screen ➪ Erase Pen.

When you advance to the next slide, all marks are automatically erased.

10. How can I create new slides without the New Slide dialog box?

If you want to create new slides without using the New Slide dialog box, you need to make an adjustment in the Options dialog box. To do so, choose Edit ➪ Preferences to open the Preferences dialog box. Click the View tab, and then turn off the Show New Slide Dialog check box. With this option turned off, you can add new slides without using the New Slide dialog box each time. PowerPoint adds a slide with a title box and text area each time you ask for a new slide.

Summary

This chapter has covered the top ten PowerPoint questions and their answers. The chapter also concludes the PowerPoint section of this book.

Where to go next

✦ Many of the common PowerPoint questions relate to working with presentation formats and layouts. Chapter 28 gives you specifics that will help you change your presentation's appearance.

✦ Producing finished presentations generates many questions, too. Chapter 30 takes you by the hand and leads you through it.

✦ ✦ ✦

The Internet Office

◆ ◆ ◆ ◆

◆ ◆ ◆ ◆

This part tells you about Microsoft Office 2001's Internet (and intranet) tools: Entourage and Internet Explorer. You'll learn how to use Entourage to read Internet newsgroups and send and receive e-mail. You'll also see how Entourage helps manage your personal information, such as your address book, calendar, and to-do lists in conjunction with using e-mail to schedule meetings and other events. In addition, you'll see how to use Internet Explorer to your advantage when surfing the World Wide Web.

Using Entourage

E-mail is where it's at these days. Type a message and send it, and in moments your message completes its trip across town or across the world to be read and addressed at the convenience of the recipient. With e-mail you can correspond several times a day, or have a message wait weeks to be read. This chapter familiarizes you with the newest member of the Microsoft Office for the Mac family — the Entourage 2001 Internet mail, news client, and personal information manager — and the benefits of using it as part of Office 2001.

Introducing Entourage

In response to e-mail's popularity, Microsoft introduced Outlook Express, which replaced Microsoft Internet Mail and News. Although Microsoft still provides Outlook Express, they have added significant *PIM* (Personal Information Management) functionality to it in Entourage. If you are already using Outlook Express for e-mail and possibly for newsgroups, those parts of Entourage will be just like home to you with no apparent changes. If you're using Netscape Communicator, Claris Emailer, Eudora, or Eudora Lite as your e-mail client, you might find Entourage's features and integration a compelling argument to switch.

How it works

Entourage enables you to send, receive, and store your e-mail. It also enables you to manage e-mail as it comes in to make reading it easier. Entourage can also handle your newsgroup mail. (A newsgroup is a list to which subscribers can send and receive each other's messages. Each newsgroup covers a specific topic, and you subscribe to a group because of its topic.) So far, that is the same functionality that you have in Outlook Express, in the exact same interface. Entourage goes one step further, however, by integrating PIM tools, such as a calendar, task (to-do) lists, a note pad, and an address book. These PIM tools are shared with the other Office 2001 applications: Word, Excel, and PowerPoint.

Probably most exciting (and controversial) is the ability to view your e-mail not only as plain text but also in HTML format, enabling your messages to be fully creative—with active links and formatted text. Usenet and Internet purists object (strenuously) to HTML-formatted e-mail and news postings. Using HTML increases the size of the message, clogging the servers with more data than is necessary, and is awkward for recipients who do not use an HTML-capable mail/news program.

Looking at the window

The Entourage window consists of three sections with a toolbar at the top. Figure 36-1 shows you this window, as it first appears when you launch Entourage and read your first e-mail—the welcome letter.

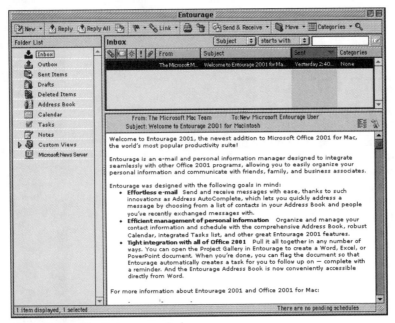

Figure 36-1: The Entourage window

The toolbar

As with each of the Office applications and most software these days, Entourage has a toolbar that makes common tasks easier, without demanding that you memorize keyboard shortcuts. Two clues help you identify the function of each button: a representative icon (often, but not always, including a text label) and a ScreenTip, which appears when you rest your mouse over the button (without clicking) to offer a description of each button. You have control over the option to show the ScreenTips. To turn this option on or off, choose Edit ⇨ Preferences ⇨ General (⌘-;), select the General tab, and uncheck the Show ToolTips box. If you prefer not to use the toolbar(s), you can uncheck that box here as well.

Creating More Folders

The Folder list is, in effect, your filing cabinet. If all your mail remained in your inbox, you'd never find anything. Therefore, you can create as many other folders as you want. If your mail is being downloaded to your hard drive for storage and handling, each folder you create appears below the Drafts folder. If you are using an IMAP account, your online folders will appear as subfolders of your server icon, but you can also create folders on your hard drive.

It is common to create a new folder for each project you are working on, each list you subscribe to, or for any other category by which you want to file your messages. To create a new folder, select File ➪ New ➪ Folder (⌘-Shift-N). You can also add subfolders within any folder. Click the folder you want the subfolder to land in, and then select File ➪ New ➪ Subfolder. These commands are also available via the New button's drop-down menu on the toolbar. For more about folders, see "Filing your messages" later in this chapter.

The Folder list

For lack of a better name, the area to the left of the Entourage window is called the Folder list. Actually, this area also lists your Address Book, Calendar, Tasks, Notes, and the servers you are set up to connect with—perhaps you can stretch your imagination just a bit and consider these as folders. (Good thing Mac users are used to custom icons on folders.) Clicking any icon in this section reveals the corresponding information, and, in the case of the Accounts (the server-type icons), ultimately initiates the corresponding connection. This section provides the lowdown on the Folder list contents.

The first items in the Folder list are folders. Each of these folders holds messages that are actually on your hard drive. Each of the following default folders serves a different purpose. Soon you'll learn how to make all the folders you want so that you can file your mail as desired. You can drag messages from any Message list that appears on the right side of the Entourage window to any message folder in this area. The folders appearing in the default Folder list are:

✦ **Inbox.** Your incoming messages land in this folder unless you set up an Inbox Rule that tells Entourage to take other action for a message. The Inbox name appears in bold when unread messages are waiting. Additionally, the number of unread messages appears in parentheses beside the Inbox name. Clicking the Inbox icon displays a list of its contents in the area to the right. (If you are a corporate user accessing e-mail from an IMAP server, note that only mail you transfer to your hard drive lands here.) In Figure 36-1, the Inbox is the selected folder.

✦ **Outbox.** All messages within this folder are sent when you issue the command to send your e-mail. When you compose a message, it is stored in the Drafts folder automatically, unless you click the Send button in the message composition window to move the message to the Outbox. To view and/or edit this mail, click this folder. Its contents will appear in the messages list.

✦ **Sent Items.** Messages are filed in this folder after you send them, unless you set your preferences to do something else to the messages. You can choose not to have messages move here by choosing Edit ⇨ Preferences ⇨ Mail & News (⌘-Shift-;), selecting the Compose tab, and then unchecking the action. To review your sent mail, click this folder. You'll see its contents in the messages list.

✦ **Drafts.** This folder is where all newly composed messages are stored. A new outgoing message remains in this folder until you decide it is ready to send and move it to the Outbox. To view and/or edit your drafts, click this folder. Its contents appear in the messages list.

✦ **Deleted Items.** This folder, whose icon looks like a trash can next to a folder, is where you drag any message that you wish to delete. (You drag them from other items in the Folder list.) Alternatively, you can select an item and click the Delete button. Sometimes the Deleted Items trash can's label appears in bold, with a number beside it in parentheses. This number indicates how many unread messages you have in the folder. (If you are using an IMAP server, your messages aren't on your local hard drive, so this folder is not used. It is only for downloaded messages.)

✦ **Address Book.** The Address Book includes your addressees and their e-mail address, as well as phone numbers and street addresses. When you click the Address Book, your entire list of contacts is revealed to the right of the Folder list. After you create mailing lists, a disclosure triangle appears beside the Address Book icon. Just like the Mac's Finder, clicking the arrow reveals the lists. (See the section later in this chapter on the Address Book ("Dealing with Contacts") for more information.)

✦ **Calendar.** The Calendar helps you better organize your schedule and manage your time, much like a DayTimer does. You can view your schedule by day, week, or month at the same time in the Tri-Pane View. Because Entourage is *iCalendar*-compliant (iCalendar is a format for meeting requests and responses sent over the Internet), you can receive meeting invitations via e-mail, accept or decline the invitation, and have it added to your schedule without having to retype any of the information. You can also save the Calendar as a Web page, optionally hiding information designated as private.

✦ **Tasks.** The Task List, with its built-in reminder functionality, helps you keep track of your appointments and chores. The Task list is also integrated with the Calendar, so you can check your tasks from inside the Calendar as well.

✦ **Notes.** Here you can create notes that are stored with other personal information, such as that in the Address Book, Calendar, and Task list. You can also link these notes to other files.

✦ **Custom Views.** Microsoft starts you out with a number of custom views into your data, and you can create more. Custom views are filtered searches of your messages, contacts (people and companies in your Address Book), Calendar events, Tasks, and Notes.

Below your Custom Views folder you'll find your Accounts — identified by their server-type icons — shown in the following list. Microsoft starts you out with an account for the Microsoft News Server. You set up these servers by selecting Tools ➪ Accounts and then selecting News from the tabs in the window. The name you enter in the Account name field appears in the Folder list area in the main Entourage window. Back in the main Entourage window, when you click a server icon, the server information appears to the right.

Note

In Outlook Express, you would find Directory Services, such as Four11, Yahoo! People Search, and WhoWhere in the folder list. These are now accessed by choosing Tools ➪ Directory Services to bring up a Directory Services window very similar in appearance to the main Entourage window but customized for searches.

✦ **E-mail server.** If you have an IMAP server (or, for some reason, you've set up your POP account to allow online access), clicking this icon connects you to your mail server and provides a live view into the messages waiting there. Your messages appear in the right side of the Entourage window.

Before you click this icon to connect, hide your Preview pane (View ➪ Preview Pane). If the Preview pane is showing, Entourage assumes you want to download your messages, and it sends all of them to your hard drive.

When you delete a message from this list, Entourage deletes the message from the server, not from your hard drive. When you double-click a message here or drag a message from this list to a folder, you tell Entourage to download it to your hard drive. See "Working with E-mail Accounts" for more information.

✦ **Microsoft News Server.** This is a preset link to the news lists hosted by the Microsoft News Server. (Newsgroups are covered in detail later in this chapter.) You can change this server or add another one.

Tip

If you use a dial-up account (your phone line) to access the Internet, an application has to be allowed to initiate your PPP connection. To give Entourage this permission (and all other Web-based applications), open your PPP control panel, click Options, select the Connections tab, and then check Connect automatically when starting TCP/IP applications. Also go to your TCP/IP control panel, click Options, and check Load only when needed, or your Mac will mysteriously try to connect every time you start it.

Entourage and Exchange

If you're part of a large company that uses Exchange to handle its corporate e-mail, having Macs in the system may have been problematic in the past. Good news: Mac users can now interact with Exchange (if your company is running Exchange 5.5).

In case you're wondering why, read on.

First, as of Exchange 5.5, IMAP is fully supported and Entourage also provides IMAP support. Next, Entourage takes care of the user authentication issue by providing the secure logon protocol used by Exchange. Therefore, Mac users can connect to the Exchange server, send their passwords, and be online along with any PC user.

For full interoperability, such as integration into automated notification and routing services, you still need the Outlook Mac client for Exchange Server, which is available for download from Microsoft's Web site.

The Message list

When you click an item in the Folder list, its contents appear to the right in the Message list. Depending on what you are viewing, clicking or double-clicking an item in this list reveals the item's contents. If you are viewing a mail folder, clicking a message once reveals the message in the Preview area below, while double-clicking the message reveals the message in a new, separate window. If you are viewing your Address Book, you see a bit of information in the columns shown, but you must double-click the contact to see all the contact information or edit the contact. When viewing the Calendar, you get a Tri-Pane View, with Today in the upper-left pane, two months in the upper-right pane, and a desktop-planner variety of views in the lower pane. If an account is selected in the Folder list, the Folder list area provides the pertinent account information in list form; again, double-clicking reveals more information. This list cannot be turned on and off in the View menu. In Figure 36-1, one message exists in the Inbox, thus one message appears in the Message list. That message was clicked once and is selected.

The Preview pane

This area is only available when viewing your e-mail, your Address book, or reading a newsgroup. The Preview pane lets you easily view the contents of the message selected in the Message list by clicking the message once, as shown earlier in Figure 36-1. In case you prefer more room to see the contents of your folders, you can resize the space given to the Folder list and Preview pane or turn off the Preview pane.

To change the size of the Preview pane, move your pointer over the divider line between the two areas so your pointer becomes a double-headed arrow, and then click and drag to size. To turn off the Preview pane, choose View ⇨ Preview pane and remove the checkmark.

What Internet Services Can I Access?

Entourage supports many common Internet standard protocols, such as SMTP, POP3 (for e-mail), NNTP (for newsgroups), IMAP4 (for message server access), iCalendar (for electronic scheduling), vCard (for exchanging contact information), and LDAP (for accessing directories such as Four11). If an Internet service complies with any one of these protocols, you can access it using Entourage. The best way to know if a service supports one of these standards is to check the service's Web site, or ask the service provider, or just try.

At the time of this writing America Online (AOL) doesn't support an Internet standard, so you can't access AOL accounts from Entourage. If AOL changes its protocol or works with Microsoft to create an interface, this may change. If it does change, chances are the Microsoft Office Web site (www.microsoft.com/macoffice) will announce it, so check there from time to time.

Working with E-mail Accounts

You have two ways to access your e-mail: downloading it to your hard drive for handling, or keeping your mail on the server and connecting to the server to access and handle your messages.

If you are a normal home user or small business user, chances are you use Post Office Protocol (POP). By default, this method downloads your mail to your hard drive for storage and handling. That way your Internet service provider (ISP) doesn't have to provide tons of hard drive space storing your messages, and you can handle your mail on your own time without having to remain connected for long periods of time, driving up the cost of Internet access.

If you are accessing a corporate server, you may be using Internet Message Access Protocol (IMAP). IMAP servers keep your e-mail on the server, so you must connect to the server to read and handle your messages. IMAP is handy in business because you can access all your e-mail from anywhere. IMAP server-based folders can be shared by a group of people for collaboration or set up as private. If you are using IMAP, chances are your network administrator will set up your account and explain how to use it. Just in case, however, we discuss the basics of IMAP usage here, too.

Entourage can handle multiple accounts, so it is possible to have both POP accounts and IMAP accounts, simultaneously.

Regardless of how you access your e-mail, composing it and sending it is the same. In fact, most of what you do in Entourage is the same. Some details, however — such as where your mail filing folders are located and appear in Entourage, and how mail is deleted — can be different. We point out those differences as we go along.

Tip

If you are on the road, you'll love this feature: Entourage can extend the capabili-ties of POP to let you use your POP account by connecting to the server and work-ing directly on the server instead of having your mail transferred to your hard drive. To do this, choose Tools ➪ Accounts, double-click the account on the News tab (or select it and click the Edit button), click the Options tab, and check the box to leave a copy of each message on the server. This gives you the best of both worlds. Instead of always connecting and downloading unwanted messages, you can con-nect this way, read the subjects and sender information, and then download only the messages you want and delete the rest from the server. You can also select View ➪ Columns ➪ Size to see the message size in the Message list. That way you can elect not to download a message if it will take too long or is too large. More details about this are scattered throughout this chapter.

Setting up your e-mail account

To set up an e-mail account, you enter the information needed to connect to your mail server. You do this by telling Entourage the name of your account and the server your mail comes into and goes out of. When you first launch Entourage, a message comes up, inviting you to set up your account. If you click Yes, the neces-sary dialog box boxes open, so you are, in effect, taken directly to Step 3 in the fol-lowing steps. Follow these steps to set up your e-mail account:

1. Select Tools ➪ Accounts.

2. Click the Mail tab to indicate that you're working with e-mail accounts.

3. Click the New button at the top to invoke the Account Setup Assistant. You can either continue with the Assistant or (as we'll describe) click the Configure account manually button, bringing up the New Account dialog box, shown in Figure 36-2.

Figure 36-2: The New Account dialog box. You can return to the Assistant by clicking the Assist Me button.

4. Choose either POP, IMAP, or HotMail from the pop-up menu and click OK, pre-senting the Edit Account dialog box shown in Figure 36-3. Enter a descriptive name for your account. This name is not an official name; it is only for your own use so you can identify the account in the Folder list and in menus.

5. Enter your first and last name in the Name field. (If you have already set up a default account, your name automatically appears there.) Enter your name as you want people to see it.

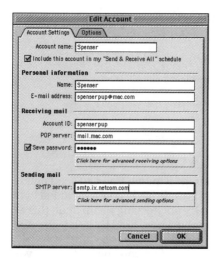

Figure 36-3: Completed New Account preferences

6. Enter your e-mail address in the E-mail address field. This is the address that you want the world to see. It's the one used when someone clicks Reply to respond to your message. Therefore, this address should be your exact e-mail address. For example, in Figure 36-3 the address people would see and respond to is spenserpup@mac.com.

7. Enter the name of your mail account in the Account ID field. You select this part of your e-mail address when you sign up with your ISP; it is how your ISP identifies you during sign-in. Unless your ISP tells you differently, this name is the same as the part of your e-mail address that goes in front of the @ sign.

8. Enter the name of your incoming mail server in the POP server box. (Again, your ISP provides this name. It is usually the same as the SMTP address.)

9. Now you set up how your mail will be sent, which is via SMTP (Simple Mail Transport Protocol). Enter the name of your outgoing mail server in the SMTP server field. (When you sign up with an ISP, your outgoing mail server is one of the pieces of information your ISP gives you.)

10. To avoid having to enter your password every time you connect, click the Save password checkbox. Then enter your e-mail password. This is a password that you set up with your ISP when you signed up. If other users have access to your Mac, you may prefer to keep this checkbox blank and enter the password when you connect.

11. *(Optional)* You can click the Click here for advanced sending options (and/or the Click here for advanced receiving options) button to set up more specific preferences shown in Figure 36-4. Your ISP or mail server administrator determines some of these preferences; others are up to you.

Figure 36-4: Advanced receiving options

For example, from the main Entourage window, you can send and receive mail from all your accounts. If you don't want this account included in that mass mail exchange, you can exclude it by unchecking the Include this account in my "Send & Receive All" schedule checkbox, directly below the Account name text box. Another option that you might change is to have your ISP leave all your collected messages on the server after you collect them — you can do this on the Options tab. This is not commonly done because it takes up room on the server, but while traveling you may want to do this. If you do, you'll also want to select the next option so that you don't keep receiving the same e-mail over and over. If you want the account to give you access to messages on the server without downloading them to your Mac, click the Allow Online Access checkbox on the Options tab; this will also list the account in the Folder list as a server.

Some servers provide a secure connection in which your messages are encrypted to prevent interception and reading. Another advanced option allows retrieval from a secure server. If your account doesn't support a secure server connection and you enable this option, you will probably receive an error when you try to receive your mail. However, if you do require a secure connection, check This POP service requires a secure connection in the Advanced receiving options, and/or check This SMTP service requires a secure connection in the Advanced sending options. If you are told your secure connection is on a different port, check Override default port and enter the port number. (Your ISP should help you with these options.)

If you've set up a POP account and want to give yourself online access to it, check Allow online access. Your mail server appears in the Folder list, which is where you initiate the online connection.

13. By default, one account (address) will be used when you send your mail or post to a newsgroup. If this is the account you wish to have as the default, click Make Default. The default account is always the one used to post to newsgroups, but you can send a message from any of your other accounts by selecting another address from the Mail From menu.

The account is now ready to send and receive from. It appears under the Tools ⇨ Send & Receive submenu from the Entourage main window.

Dealing with contacts

To send an e-mail message, you need to address the message to the recipient. This is where the Address Book comes into play. You can address a note to someone without placing the name in your Address Book, but unless you'll never write to that person again, it's more efficient to enter the names.

Creating contacts

To create a new contact while you are in the Address Book (it's selected in the Folder list), click the New Contact button or press ⌘-N. To create a new contact while in another folder, select File ➪ New ➪ Contact. Alternatively, you can open the Address Book by clicking the Address Book button, or you can Control-click anywhere (other than the Preview pane or a list) in the Entourage window, select Address Book from the shortcut menu, and then click the New Contact button. All these methods open a new, empty Create Contact window so you can enter your contact information (see Figure 36-5).

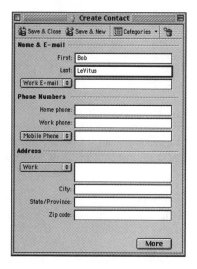

Figure 36-5: The Create Contact window as a contact is being entered

Enter information in the Create Contact window as you would in any other window. Type, paste, or drag the data into the appropriate field. Press Tab to move to the next field or Shift-Tab to move backward. Of course, you can also click in any field to enter information into it. You can also select text to copy or delete it.

The Create Contact window is fairly straightforward. Pop-up menus provide options at times. Click in any pop-up menu to select your best choice. Click the More button to present the Address Book entry, positioned to the Name & E-mail tab, as shown in Figure 36-6. The E-mail Address area bears some explaining, however. This area is capable of storing several e-mail addresses for one person. The first time you tab or click here, a checkmark appears along with a text box with an insertion point. Just type your address as normal. To add another address, either click the Add button or click below the existing address. When you have more than one address, you must choose one to be the default. Click the desired address and click Make Default, or, as a shortcut, just click in the checkmark area of the desired address.

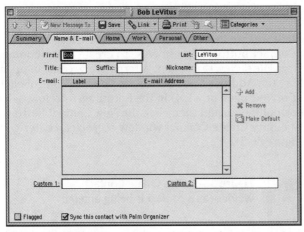

Figure 36-6: The Name & E-mail tab for the contact you're creating

When you're finished entering new contact information (or editing an existing contact), you can click the Save button or use ⌘-S to save the contact before closing the window. However, in case you don't remember, a dialog box will ask if you want to save your information or changes.

Tip   If you are entering your contacts manually, as opposed to importing them, just enter the ones to which you are sending a message right away. That way you can wait until you receive e-mail from your other contacts and add them the easy way. As you receive each e-mail, if you want to add the sender to your contact list, click the message in the Message list and then choose Tools ➪ Add to Address Book (⌘-=). The sender is invisibly added to your Contact list. Alternatively, you can Control-click any message and select Add Sender to Address Book from the shortcut menu.

Importing contacts

If you are already using an e-mail application, you probably have a ton of e-mail addresses already listed. Rather than entering all that information again, you can import those addresses into Entourage. Follow these steps:

1. Open your current e-mail application.

2. Export your contacts per that application's export method. (For example, from Claris E-mailer select File ➪ Export Addresses.)

If you are exporting from a regular address book, export the file as text. If you have the ability to control the order in which the fields are exported, match the order to that of Entourage.

3. Select File ➪ Import, and then select the list you just exported. As you import, if Entourage comes across a name that already exists, you are asked if you'd like to add this redundant name or replace the one already in Entourage.

Entourage also provides the capability to directly import information (including contacts) from a variety of applications, in addition to importing it from a text file. If you choose to import directly, the other application must be present so that Entourage can communicate with it.

Caution

If you are about to import any significant amount of information from another application, particularly a database of messages, be sure to provide Entourage with sufficient memory. To import a 22-MB database of messages and contacts from Claris Emailer requires a 40-MB memory partition for Entourage.

Viewing contacts

You have two ways to see your Address Book (see Figure 36-7):

✦ Click Address Book in the Folder list on the left of your window. Your list of contacts opens in the Entourage window.

✦ Choose Window ➪ Address Book (⌘-2). This opens the same list, but as a separate window.

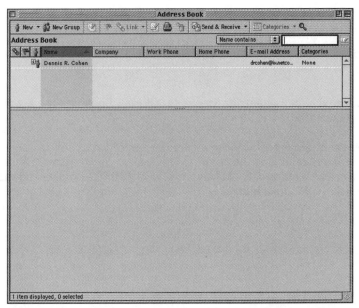

Figure 36-7: Viewing contacts within the Address Book window

Deleting contacts

Click the contact and click the Delete button (which looks like a trash can). A dialog box message asks whether you really want to delete the message. Click Yes. To avoid the confirmation message, press Option as you click the Delete button.

Creating mailing list groups

One of the most powerful (and simple) tasks you can do in Entourage is create a group (it was called a mailing list in Outlook Express). A group is simply a selection of your contacts that are grouped together for whatever reason you may have. Rather than individually adding the names of tons of people as message recipients, you just enter the group name.

Another advantage of using a group is the optional ability to suppress the recipients' names when you send your message. That way you don't publicize recipients' addresses. There's another benefit, too. Have you ever been one of several recipients and had to endure a bombardment of unwanted messages and complaints when one recipient failed to respond to the sender only and responded to every original recipient? By suppressing your recipient's names, any replies come back only to you.

The same contact can be part of many lists. Names can be added or deleted at any time, and the cool part is that it's almost all done by dragging.

To create a mailing list, follow these steps:

1. Select File ➪ New ➪ Group. An Untitled Group window opens.

2. The default group name (Untitled Group) is preselected, so you don't have to click anywhere. Just type a short descriptive name for your list.

3. Click the Add button and starting typing the contact information. Entourage will display a list of all matches while you're typing and you can select from it at any point.

4. Alternatively, you can drag entries from your Address Book into the list area of the group's window.

The names in the group are actually aliases. Therefore, you can remove a name from a list without really removing the contact. The easiest way to remove a name is to select it — from the mailing list, not from the "real" Address Book — and then press Delete or click the Remove button.

What Are These Categories?

Categories are organizational labels that you can apply to Entourage items such as messages, contacts, and events. They are similar in some ways to Labels in the Finder in that they color-code the item, enable you to sort by the category, or filter by it. Unlike Finder labels, however, you can add your own categories to the ones Entourage provides. Additionally, you can place an item in more than one category, although one category needs to be designated as primary and, while a filter will find nonprimary category matches, the color-coding and sorting will be based upon the primary category.

If you assign one of your regular correspondents to a category, such as putting your sister in the Family category, any messages you receive from that user will automatically be similarly categorized.

Most of the custom views provided with Entourage are category-based, providing you with quick built-in filters for such options as family member contacts, or tasks and events that are work-related. Of course, using these views requires that you first go to the effort to categorize your contacts and other Entourage items.

Working with Messages

Your messages can take either of two forms: plain text or HTML. Plain text is just that; it has no fancy formatting—only spaces and characters. Plain-text messages can be read by anyone on any computer, old or new, with any e-mail software. HTML format provides the capability to use text formatting, color, and such, as with the Web pages that have made the World Wide Web so popular. Entourage does its best to give you the best of both worlds. You can create your messages using HTML formatting, as is done in Figure 36-8. When the message is received, most e-mail software reads and presents the HTML formatting or presents a plain-text version (perhaps attaching the HTML version). In case you don't want to risk the recipient's capability to recognize HTML formatting or to switch to plain text, you can switch off HTML prior to sending the message by choosing Format ⇨ HTML and removing the checkmark if it is present, or by clicking the Use HTML button in the message window.

Creating a message

Creating a new e-mail message is almost just like creating any new document. Simply select File ⇨ New and then, because you also have the option of creating new contacts or folders, slide over to Mail Message. Alternatively, you can press ⌘-Option-N. If you're viewing the contents of a folder, you can also use the ⌘-N keyboard shortcut.

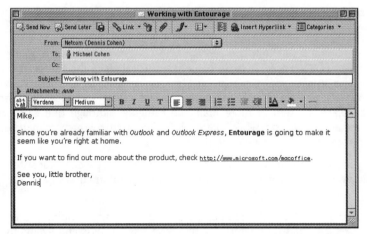

Figure 36-8: An HTML message in the message-creation window

Don't forget to save your work as you create it. You can press the Save button in the message composition window's toolbar, or you can select File⇨Save (⌘-S). All begun but unsent messages are stored in the Drafts folder when you save them. You can come back to work on any message in this folder until you send it.

Addressing a message

Reflecting the common style of sending business letters, Entourage lets you send your message to (To) a person or persons, send a (carbon) copy (Cc) to a person or persons, and send a blind (carbon) copy (Bcc) to others still. As demonstrated in Figure 36-8, each new message window has an area to enter all these recipients. When a message is a blind carbon copy, the other recipients don't see the Bcc recipient's name or address in the recipient list.

You have several ways to enter the e-mail addresses of your recipients:

✦ You can type the address if you have it handy and feel like typing. This way is best if your contact with the recipient(s) is a one-time effort.

✦ If you have entered your recipient in your Address Book, you can begin typing the recipient's name. As Entourage matches the letters you type, it provides a menu of choices that match what you've typed so far. If you see the match, stop typing and select it from the menu. If not, keep typing. Entourage will continue refining the list.

✦ If you have created a group, begin typing the group's name. Entourage will probably offer it as a choice before you finish typing. (Remember the benefit of suppressing the recipient list: easy addressing, respect of recipients' privacy, and prevention of readers from replying to the entire group along with a response to you.)

✦ If you have entered your recipient in your Address Book, you can also view the Address Book in a pane to the right and drag the contact from that pane into the To, Cc, or Bcc area of your message.

✦ You can use drag-and-drop to drag a name and/or address from the body of another e-mail or other document into place on your new message. (When you select the name or address to be dragged, your cursor turns into a hand. When you click the mouse to drag, the hand "grabs" the text to drag it.)

✦ You can copy the address from any other source and paste it into the appropriate addressee field.

✦ To begin your new message and address it to the primary recipient(s) at the same time, select your contact(s) or mailing list and then click the Mail To button.

Tip   If you are still using another organizer, such as Palm Desktop or Now Contact, click the appropriate icon in the organizer and let it address your e-mail for you. In fact, you won't need to start your e-mail message in Entourage because the organizer application will start the message for you as well as address it automatically.

In each of the previous cases, if you have more than one recipient to send To, Cc, or Bcc, type a comma or semicolon between each recipient.

Tip   After you define a mailing list, you can create a message and address it to everyone on the list with just two clicks. Simply control-click the list name in the Address Book and select New Message To, or click the list name once in the Address Book and click the New Message To button.

Formatting your message

By sending your messages in HTML, you can create appealing, emphatic, or even decorative messages. Formatting your message is easy. If you've already used Word or just about any other word processor on the Mac, you already know how. All you need to do is select the text to be formatted, and then click the formatting buttons at the top of the message window or choose the formatting commands from the Format menu.

Note   If you don't see buttons you are in plain-text mode. To switch, select Format ⇨ HTML, click the Options button in the Toolbar and choose HTML, or click the Use HTML button on the left above the text box.

Entourage's HTML enables all the standard text document formatting: font, font size, bold, italic, underline, teletype (otherwise known as monospaced text), align text left, center text, and align text right. You can also create a numbered or bulleted list, modify indentation, and change text and background color. Additionally, as this is actually an HTML document after all, you can add what is known in Web page design as a horizontal rule (a line drawn horizontally across the page), and you can apply text emphasis by using HTML headers.

Caution   If your recipient's e-mail program doesn't read HTML-formatted e-mail, the document should appear in plain text, perhaps with the HTML code as an attached file. However, sometimes an Internet gateway or the e-mail reader can't handle the HTML version and doesn't discriminate to display the plain text version. In that case, the recipient may end up viewing the raw HTML code. If you're not sure whether your recipient's e-mail program can appreciate an HTML-formatted e-mail, perhaps it's not a good idea to send it in this format. You might want to try a test among friends and associates.

Figure 36-8 showed you a message in HTML. Figure 36-9 shows a message with HTML deselected.

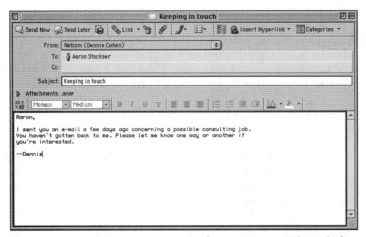

Figure 36-9: A plain-text message in the message-creation window

Attaching files to a message

An attached file is a document that is sent along with your message. For example, while writing this book, we wrote each chapter as a Word document and sent one or two chapters (usually with a number of separate graphic files) at a time as attachments via e-mail. You have two ways to attach a file:

✦ Open the folder that contains your attachment and drag it onto the message window. You can select multiple items and drag them all at once, too.

✦ Click the Add Attachment button in the message window, and then navigate to the document, select it, and click Choose. If you want to attach the entire contents of a folder, select that folder and then click Choose. If you attach a folder, Entourage will alert you that compression needs to be turned on for this message and that it has done so.

If you decide you don't want to send the attachment, click it once in the message window to select it, and then click Remove. To select all the attachments, click one, choose Select All (⌘-A), and then click Remove.

When you send your message, all attachments are encoded and prepared for transit. Several types of such encoding can be used. By default, the encoding used is Apple-Double, the method preferred when you aren't sure the recipient is on a Mac. If you know that the recipient is using a Mac, you might be better placed to use BinHex. The method that you use is set in Preferences. You can check this or change it by choosing Edit ➪ Preferences ➪ Mail & News, selecting the Compose tab, clicking the bevel button under Attachments, and then clicking in the pop-up window for the Attachment encoding you desire. You can select a different encoding for a specific message by clicking the bevel button telling you the current encoding and selecting new options in the pop-up window.

Cross-Reference

You can send a Word, Excel, or PowerPoint document from within that application. With the document open, select File ➪ Send to ➪ Mail Recipient. Entourage launches, starts a new outgoing message, and attaches your document automatically. (You'll see its icon in the attachments section of the message window.) All you need to do is address the message and compose the message body text as normal, and then send it.

Adding a signature

To create your signature, select Tools ➪ Signatures, click the New button in the Signatures window, name the signature, and then type or paste your signature text into the large text area at the bottom of this preference window. Click Save and close the window. If you want your signature added to each new message from a given account by default, choose Tools ➪ Accounts, double-click the account, switch to the Options tab, and select the signature from the pop-up menu. If you prefer not to always add the signature, you can add your signature to any message by clicking the Signature button and choosing from the pop-up menu. Figure 36-10 shows you a message that has a signature. When the recipient views this message, the e-mail address and Web site will be live links. These live links would also show in the Preview pane if the sender previewed this outgoing message.

Entourage uses and supports the Internet Control Panel (or Internet Config, if you're using a version of the MacOS earlier than 8.5). With the Internet Control Panel, you can have multiple signatures and generate them at random. However, the Internet Control Panel and Internet Config are beyond the scope of this book.

Quoting another message or other text

In the world of e-mail it has become common practice to quote the text of the message to which you are responding, and then respond to each line, sentence, topic, or such below the quoted text. That way, your recipient is reminded of the conversation you two are having and can consider your responses in context. The common quote character of the day is >, so a quoted sentence and its response might look like this:

```
>Hi, Uncle Dennis. This is Allie. We're coming down to the Bay
Area for a vacation. Would Saturday be a good day to come see you?
That's a great idea. Tell your dad to bring Jake and Astro to play
with Spenser!
```

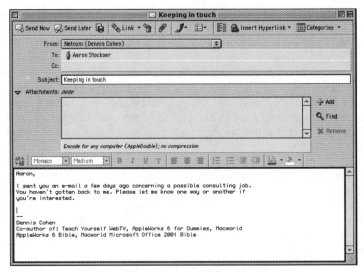

Figure 36-10: An outgoing message with a signature

The quote indicator is also set in the Internet Control Panel. If you don't have one, the default is a greater than sign (>) followed by a space.

You have two ways to apply your quote character to text. One is to select that text in an e-mail message before you click Reply. The other is to copy text from any source, and then place your insertion point in your outgoing message and select Edit ➪ Paste As Quotation (⌘-'). See "Replying to a Message" for more details.

Sending a message

After you compose your message, you can click the Send button at the top of the toolbar while you're in the message composition window. If you are composing and responding to several messages, you may opt to save the message first and then connect and send all your messages at the same time when you're finished composing. All saved unsent messages are stored in the Drafts folder by default. They remain there until you click the Send button in the message composition window.

Rather than sending each message as you complete it, you can send all your outgoing messages at the same time. Select Tools ➪ Send & Receive ➪ Send All (⌘-Shift-K). Another option is to receive your new incoming e-mail at the same time you send your outgoing messages. Either click the Send & Receive button on the toolbar or select Tools ➪ Send & Receive ➪ Send & Receive All (⌘-M). We discuss this option further in the next section.

As you send or receive messages, a Progress dialog box (choose Window ➪ Progress, or press ⌘-3) is available to let you know what's happening, as shown in Figure 36-11.

It informs you when it logs on, checks for messages, gets messages, sends messages, and so on; otherwise, you can get basic progress information in the status area in the area below the Folder List.

Figure 36-11: The Progress dialog box as a message is sent

Receiving and reading messages

Depending on whether you have a regular POP account (which is typical for the home user and nonbusiness user) or an IMAP account (which is common in large businesses), you will either download your messages or read them on the server. We cover both procedures in the following sections; you can read only the section that pertains to you.

With a POP account

If you have a POP account, you will be connecting to your ISP only long enough to download your messages (and send any outgoing messages, too). You can disconnect after you've downloaded your e-mail. That way, you can read your mail, respond at your leisure, and then connect again when you're ready to send your reply (and download any new messages that have come in for you).

To send your outgoing messages and receive your new incoming e-mail at the same time, just click the Send & Receive button on the toolbar. Or, if you prefer, choose Tools ⇨ Send & Receive and then choose an option from the Send & Receive submenu. If you have only one account, both options are the same. If you have multiple accounts, you may prefer to exchange your messages from only one account at any time. The Tools menu provides this flexibility. Choose Tools ⇨ Send & Receive, and then choose one specific account from the bottom part of the Send & Receive submenu. (All your accounts appear under this submenu.)

Perhaps you have more than one account but like to check only one of the accounts. To make life easier, you can exclude any account(s) from the Send & Receive All command. Select Tools ⇨ Accounts, and then select your account and click Edit. Remove the checkmark next to Include This Account in My Send & Receive All Schedule on the Account Settings tab. By selecting this preference, you can use the Send & Receive button to collect mail on a regular basis, and the Tools menu command to check mail at the excluded account(s) on demand.

Another option is to send your messages without receiving any. Select Tools ⇨ Send & Receive ⇨ Send All. This sends all your messages from all your accounts.

Caution   If you take advantage of this option, be sure not to abuse it. Leaving all your mail on the server causes the ISP to need more servers and drives up the cost of service for everyone. Your ISP may limit the amount of space you can use for storing your messages on the server, or it may ask you to purge them from time to time.

After you've downloaded your messages, you can read them. Unless you've set up a mail filter (Inbox Rule), your messages land in the Inbox. You can tell you have unread mail when the folder name appears in boldface and the number of unread messages appears in parentheses next to the name. Click the Inbox folder to reveal the headers of each message in the message list to the right of the window. You have two options for viewing any message. If you click the message in the message list to select it, the message appears in the Preview pane (if the pane is showing). See Figure 36-12, which shows an HTML message, marked as high priority. If you prefer to view a message in a larger area, double-click the message in the message list. The message opens in its own window. If you've opened the message as a separate window, click the close box the same as you would to close any Mac window when you're finished looking at it.

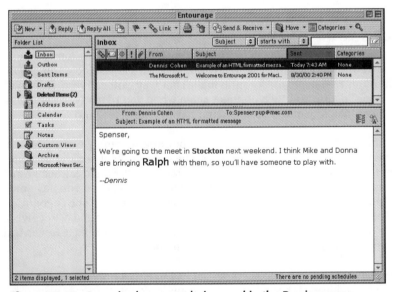

Figure 36-12: A received message being read in the Preview pane

With an IMAP account

If your e-mail is on an IMAP server, you don't download your messages to read them. Instead, you deal with messages completely while connected to the server and read the messages directly from the server. Entourage merely caches the message to your hard disk. (A cache is a temporary file. You have no control over when it will be replaced, and when the message the cache pertains to is deleted from the server, it is gone.)

Keeping the Original Message

By default, when you download a message, it is deleted from your ISP's mail server so that it doesn't use up space unnecessarily. In some cases, however, such as when you are checking your e-mail from someone else's computer, you may want to keep the original message on the server so you can download it again later and have it on your own Mac.

Choose Tools ⇨ Accounts, select your account, and click Edit, and then select the Options tab. Place a checkmark next to Leave a copy of each message on the server. Remember that you don't want to set this preference on your own Mac. Set them on the computer you are borrowing to check your e-mail.

Before you can view your e-mail, you have to subscribe to the folders that you have the option of seeing. There's a good chance your MIS person will do this for you or show you how, providing company-specific instructions. Basically, you click the server icon after setting it up. This connects you to the mail server and automatically provides a complete list of available folders. Click any unsubscribed folder to which you want access, and then click the Subscribe button in the toolbar. The full list of folders appears in the list on the right, while currently subscribed folders appear in the Folder list on the left.

Note
You can update your list of available folders at any time. Click the server icon to connect to the mail server, and then choose View ⇨ Get Complete Folder List to get the list of available folders.

To view your e-mail, click the account's icon in the Folder list. (If you have access to more than one folder on the server, click the arrow next to the account's icon to reveal those folders. Then click the folder you want to view.) Your connection to the server opens (if it's not already open), and you see the subject of each message on the right side of your window. To read a message in the Preview pane, click the subject once. To see it in a larger, separate window, double-click the message subject.

While you are connected, more new messages may arrive. To check, click the folder to select it and then choose View ⇨ Refresh Folder Messages.

Caution
It is important to realize that messages that you read from the server are not on your hard drive. If a message is important to you, you must save it to your own server-based folder or your hard drive, or the message can disappear without warning. To save a message to your own server-based folder, drag it from the message list to your own folder, which appears in your Folder list. To save a message to your own hard drive, drag it from the message list into a folder you've created on your hard drive. Folders on your hard drive appear after Custom Views and before your server icons. Folders on your server appear under your server icon when you click the triangle next to the server's icon.

From a POP account online

Entourage provides the capability to set up online access for POP accounts so that you can access them from any computer without having to download the messages. More accurately, you can view the subject, from, sent, size, date, to, and account information — or message headers. To actually read the message you must download it. This type of access, however, saves you from unnecessarily downloading messages that aren't of interest at that particular time. It also enables you to delete any unwanted messages from the server without ever downloading them.

To connect online, choose Tools ➪ Accounts, select your account, click Edit, and select the Options tab. On the Options tab, check the box next to Allow Online Access (shows account in folder list). An icon for that account now shows up as a server in your Folder List and you can click it to access your mail.

To refresh your message list in case any new messages have arrived while you were online, select View ➪ Refresh Message List (⌘-L).

To read any message of interest, double-click the message in the message list. A full message window opens and downloads the message.

Tip   If you're curious as to what route a message took to get to you or when it was sent, you can reveal its Internet header. If you always want to see these headers, set your preferences. Choose Edit ➪ Preferences ➪ Mail & News (⌘-Shift-;) and then select View and check Show Internet headers. If you are just curious about one message here and there, while the message is being viewed, choose View ➪ Internet Headers (⌘-Shift-H). This menu option is only available in a message window, not in the Preview pane.

Making attachments

When a document contains an attachment, the word "Attachment" will appear above the message with a disclosure triangle beside it. Click that triangle and double-click the attachment that you want to view. The attachment automatically opens if your Internet preferences already name the necessary file helper. (Several helpers are set by default.) If Entourage doesn't know which file helper to use, it offers you the opportunity to select an application (via a dialog box). Otherwise you can save and file the attachment for later, or you can save the message so that you can open or save the attachment later.

When QuickTime-readable images (and movies) are sent to you as attachments, they should automatically appear in your message. If they don't, choose Edit ➪ Preferences ➪ Mail & News, click View, and then check the option Show attached pictures and movies in messages. This feature uses Apple's QuickTime, so you need to have the QuickTime extension turned on for it to work. Figure 36-13 displays a plain-text message sent with a TIFF attachment as the message is viewed in the Preview pane.

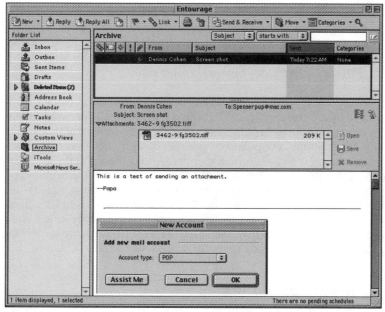

Figure 36-13: A received plain-text message with a TIFF image attached

About file helpers

File helpers are actually regular software programs. They are simply applications elected to be automatically called into play when the associated file type is called on — for instance, when you click the arrow next to the paper clip (see Figure 36-14) and select an attachment to view. To assign a file type to a file helper, choose ⌘ ⇨ Control Panels ⇨ Internet, select the Advanced tab and then click Helper Apps in the list. If you have an application that works as a helper, it appears in full color in the list. If you don't have the default application, that default is grayed out. You can assign your own helpers by clicking Add, and you can change a helper by clicking Change. Click Delete to delete a helper. If the Advanced tab isn't available, you need to set the User Mode to Advanced (choose Edit ⇨ User Mode or press ⌘-U).

Figure 36-14: Selecting an attachment for viewing or saving

When you click the disclosure triangle next to Attachments and select the attachment, if the Open button is not enabled as a choice, you don't have a File Helper assigned to that file type.

Saving file attachments

As you are viewing a message, either in the Preview pane or in its own window, you can save any attachments that came along with the message. Simply select Message ⇨ Save All Attachments. As with any saving you do on the Mac, you should navigate to the target folder before clicking Save.

Attachments are typically compressed and encoded in order to travel the Internet. Entourage decodes your attachments. (That takes care of the mysterious .hqx extension on the filename.) Entourage continues to decode your document unless it is stuffed with Aladdin's StuffIt, a popular compression program. In that case, Aladdin's freeware decompression utility—StuffIt Expander—does the job (taking care of the .sit or .sea part of the filename). Depending on the options you set in StuffIt Expander, the document unstuffs and lands in the same folder as the download, or it requests your attention and asks where you want the file to decompress. StuffIt Expander is also available from www.aladdinsys.com. Just place it on your hard drive, and Entourage will recognize it as a helper. StuffIt Expander is a must-have for all Mac owners and Mac BBS or Internet users.

Printing a message

You can print a message while it is open in its own window or while it is simply selected (clicked) in the message list. The latter offers the advantage of enabling you to print more than one message at a time because you can select more than one message at a time in the message list. Press Shift to select a range of messages, or press ⌘ to select messages that are not next to each other in the list. After making your selection(s) (or with a single message window open), select File ⇨ Print or press ⌘-P as usual. Entourage will display a dialog box with some print formatting options: header, footer, whether pictures print, and so on. From there, it's printing as normal.

Saving a message

When you file a message in any folder in your Folder List, you save it. You can only read messages in these folders, however, when you have Entourage open. Sometimes you'll want to save a message as a SimpleText document so that you can pass it along to others. Open the message in the Preview Pane by clicking it (or in its own window by double-clicking it) in the message list. Then select File ⇨ Save As. Navigate to the destination folder (or click Desktop), make sure SimpleText text document is chosen in the Format pop-up menu, name your document, and then click Save.

Replying to a message

To reply to a message you just click Reply and type your response, and then you handle it the same as any other outgoing e-mail. As stated previously, the common practice with e-mail, however, is to "quote" the message you receive and add your response beneath the quoted text. That's the e-mail equivalent to having a conversation and addressing each subject as it is talked about. The common quote character of the day is the greater-than symbol (>), which is located on the same key as the period.

Entourage uses the quote character/style established in your Internet control panel (a > by default) and adds the capability to visualize quotes and quotes of quotes in color. Check the Color Quoting area of your Mail & News Preferences' View tab to discover your options.

A message that has gone back and forth a couple of times will show a trace of the previous exchanges. When you reply to a message, you will "quote" the text you received, and it will appear with one quote character, because this text is being sent back to the sender and he or she had the most recent new text. Where a double quote character exists at the start of a paragraph, the sender is quoting the previous person who is quoting the sender of the message before that. The newest words are on the lines that have no quotation marks. Remember that you have the option of seeing not only double greater-than symbols but also color-coding.

You should also consider whether your correspondent's e-mail program recognizes HTML formatting or at least knows to discard the HTML message and deliver the plain-text version. This is discussed in the "Working with Messages" section. One step that you can take to ensure smooth e-mailing is to select Edit ⇨ Preferences ⇨ Mail & News, select Reply & Forward, and then check Reply to messages in the format in which they were sent. Entourage will then look at the incoming message and respond in kind.

When you respond, you may want to quote the entire letter to which you're responding, or to just a part of it. If you've set up a quote character, when you click the Reply or Reply All button, the entire message is quoted in your new reply. If you select specific text, only that text will be quoted. There's a trick you can use if you want to quote noncontiguous sections of text. Select the first section and click a reply button. After the new outgoing document opens, return to the incoming message and select and copy the next section to be quoted. Then click back in the outgoing message, place the insertion point, and choose Edit ⇨ Paste as Quotation (⌘-'). You can do this as many times as you like. You can also use the Paste as Quotation command to paste in text you copy from anywhere on your Mac.

You may notice two reply buttons: Reply and Reply All. If your incoming message was sent only to you, it doesn't matter which button you click. If the message was sent to several people, however, you definitely want to be sure you reply only to the sender—unless you really want all other recipients of the incoming message to see your response. If the message sent to you says Recipient list suppressed, you can simply reply to the sender or to all, and the other recipients should not receive your response. It is usually better to be safe than sorry, however, and you should get into the habit of replying wisely. We recommend that you click Reply when you want to reply only to the sender. Should the message come from a list (which is a group correspondence), watch the results of clicking Reply. This may address your message to the sender, but it may also address it to the entire list. Instead of clicking buttons, you can use the Message ⇨ Reply to Sender (⌘-Option-R) or Message ⇨ Reply to All (⌘-Shift-R) commands or their keyboard equivalents, as noted in the menu.

When you use either Reply button to create your response, the subject of the incoming note is copied to your response and Re: is appended to it. This creates a thread and helps you identify your messages. Some e-mail software enable users to follow the thread via buttons, as Entourage does with Newsgroups. It is considered impolite to rename a message to which you are replying. If you change the topic within the body of your reply, however, you might change the subject line so people can see that the original discussion has changed direction. It is common to place the original subject in brackets ([ ]) after the new subject. For example, "Re: Sugar made Champion [was Cow Palace Dog Show]." Get used to e-mail and notice proper practices before you begin renaming responses.

Note   When you reply to a message, any attachments that came with the original message are removed, so they are not unnecessarily bandied back and forth.

Forwarding a message

After you read a message, you may want to send it to another person. This is called forwarding the message. To forward a message, click the Forward button in the toolbar or select Message ⇨ Forward. A new message window opens, complete with the entire message; the From, Date, To, and Subject information; and any attachments included originally. The insertion point waits for you in the new To field so that you can address the message. The Subject line is automatically filled in with the original message name preceded by FW:, which indicates that the message is being forwarded. You can change the subject if you like. In the message body, a dotted line is added one line down. This line enables you to place the cursor in the blank top line and to compose a note to the recipient. When you're ready, send the new message the same way that you send any other message.

Note   By default the body of a forwarded message appears in its original form. Some people prefer to have quotation marks appear to designate that they didn't compose the message. If you want quotation marks, select Edit ⇨ Preferences ⇨ Mail & News (⌘-Shift-;), click Reply & Forward, and then check Use quoting characters when forwarding.

Deleting messages

It's not always necessary to keep a message. After a while even the largest hard drives get crowded, so we thought we'd better tell you how to get rid of some of your messages.

From your hard drive

If your messages are on your hard drive, you have several ways to delete them. You can click any message in the Folder List and then either choose Edit ⇨ Delete Message, press ⌘-D, click the Delete button, or press the Delete key. Each method moves the message to the Deleted Items folder without confirmation. You can also drag any message or messages from the Folder List pane to the trash can, which is labeled Deleted Items and is located in the Folder List. To provide feedback about what you are deleting, if the trash can holds any unread messages, its label appears in boldface and the number of unread messages to be deleted appears next to it in parentheses.

Messages remain in the Deleted Items folder until you Control-click the trash icon in the Folder List and select Empty Deleted Items, or you choose Tools ⇨ Run Schedule ⇨ Empty Deleted Items Folder to empty this folder. For an extra measure of safety, you must confirm this action. You can also set the trash to empty whenever you quit Entourage by selecting Tools ⇨ Schedules, selecting Empty Deleted Items Folder, clicking Edit, and then choosing On Quit from the pop-up menu in the When area. Make sure that the Enabled checkbox is marked, then click OK, and then close the Schedules window.

If you decide you don't want to delete a message after all, and the message is still in the Deleted Items folder, you can open that folder (click it) and drag the message to any other folder. After you empty the Deleted Items folder, the message is not retrievable.

From an IMAP server

If you are accessing your message from an IMAP server, you don't actually delete the message immediately; instead, you rather mark the message for deletion. To mark a message, select the message in the message list and click Delete (trash can) or use any of the other deletion methods previously mentioned. The marked message appears with a line struck though it. If you select Hide deleted IMAP messages in the General area of Preferences, messages marked for deletion do not appear at all. The number at the bottom of the window indicates how many deleted messages exist.

If you are accessing your messages live on the server and you've marked one for deletion, you can change your mind by selecting the message and choosing Edit ⇨ Undelete. If you've already deleted the message, however, it's gone and you're out of luck.

When you are certain that you absolutely don't want to keep messages any longer, you can purge them from the server. You purge folder by folder or the entire account, rather than message by message. Click the account icon or the folder you want to purge. Then choose Edit ⇨ Purge Deleted Items.

While online with a POP server

If you have a POP server and are viewing your messages online, click any message in the list to select it and then either choose Edit ➪ Delete Message, press ⌘-Delete, click the Delete button, or press the Delete key. Unless you've disabled deletion warnings, a dialog box asks whether you want to delete the message and reminds you that this deletion can't be undone. When you click Yes, Entourage sends the command directly to the server and the message is removed immediately.

Filing your messages

The first step to organizing your messages is to create folders. As with the file cabinets in your office or home, or with the folders on your Mac, use whatever filing system works best for you. Typically, users organize files by project, category, or topic. You may even file news list messages into a folder along with "regular" e-mail if the topic matches.

You can create a new folder at any time — it's never too late — by selecting File ➪ New ➪ Folder (⌘-Shift-N). It's a good idea to begin by giving yourself a few basic folders, so you may want to try that now to get the hang of it.

To create a new folder on your hard drive, follow these steps:

1. Select File ➪ New ➪ Folder (⌘-Shift-N) or Control-click any existing folder (Drafts or Inbox are your choices to start with) and select New Folder from the shortcut menu. This method is shown in Figure 36-15. The new folder appears in the Folder List. Just as in the Mac Finder, the new folder is named untitled folder and the name is preselected so you can easily name it.

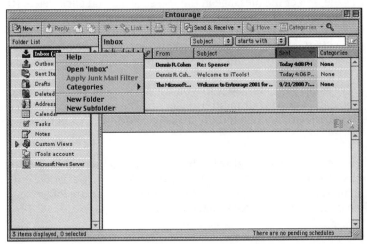

Figure 36-15: Control-clicking to create a new folder on the hard drive

The Entourage window does not have to be open to choose File ⇨ New ⇨ Folder (⌘-Shift-N), but it is less confusing to have it open when you do.

2. Without clicking anywhere, type the name for your new folder. As in the Mac Finder, the name you type replaces the words untitled folder. When you finish typing, press Return or Enter to set the name, or click anywhere but on the folder's name.

To create a new subfolder within a folder, Control-click the folder you want the subfolder to land in and select New Subfolder from the shortcut menu. Alternatively, click the folder you want the subfolder to land in and then select File ⇨ New ⇨ Subfolder. The subfolder appears with the generic name preselected just like a main-level folder. Type the new name and press Return or Enter to set the name, or click anywhere but on the folder's name.

As with the Mac's Finder, you can easily rename a folder at any time. You do this the same way you do in the Finder — click the folder's name to select it and then type the new name.

After you have begun to create folders, you can begin to file your mail. Filing is easy. All you do is click a message and drag it to the folder of choice. Files can be moved from any folder to any other folder at any time. How's that for flexibility? Simply view a folder's contents so you see the message's name, and then drag the message to the new folder. Your messages can also be set up for automatic filing based on a set of criteria. Entourage calls these criteria Rules.

If you are creating folders on your IMAP server, you will see an extra dialog box in which you name your folder (as opposed to naming the folder as you name any other Mac folder). If you are unsure whether your folder has landed on the server or your hard drive, note its location. If the folder is on the server, it appears below the server icon. If the folder is on the hard drive, it appears between the Custom Views folder and the server icons.

Automating your incoming mail

Some people find life easier when certain mail is filed automatically. For example, if you subscribe to a list about magic but it's just a hobby, it's easier to have all those list messages go directly into a folder called Magic. Then, when you have time, you can click the Magic folder and read the messages. Meanwhile, the messages are out of the way, rather than clogging up your Inbox, preventing you from easily noticing more important messages, or, at least, more timely messages. Then, perhaps you want to keep other important messages in the Inbox to make sure you act on them. As your Inbox gets full, however, you may find it difficult to notice this important mail among your numerous, plain-black messages. Maybe you even have some not-so-timely mail you'd like to identify. To accommodate easy mail identification, you can assign a color code to your messages. For example, messages about your current work project can be assigned a bright red, while notes from your family and friends can be made light blue. These are called Categories.

Before you can set up an automatic message filter, you need to identify some characteristics with which to filter your mail. For example, if all messages from Linda Turnowski are about your current project, you can use the name Linda Turnowski as a criterion (see Figure 36-16). If all messages from your client's domain name are about the project, use the domain name as the filter (shown in Figure 36-16). If you're really lucky, all of you involved with the project have agreed to place a word or project code in the subject line, so that's all you need for the criteria.

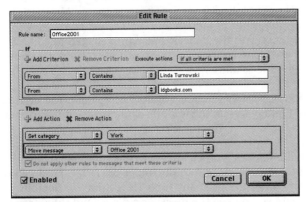

Figure 36-16: The Define Inbox Rule dialog box

When you have some criteria in mind, you can set up the filter by following these steps:

1. Choose Tools ⇨ Rules to open the Rules window.

2. Click the New Rule button at the top of the window. The Edit Rule dialog box opens with the new rule displayed by default.

3. The Rule name field is preselected, so begin by typing a descriptive name for your rule.

4. The top part of the dialog box contains criteria settings. You can apply up to five filtering criteria to refine your selection. Use the first pop-up list to select the part of the message you are scanning for your criteria. If necessary, click Add Criterion and use the second pop-up to narrow your filter. In the text box enter (or paste) the text by which you are filtering. For example, for this book we might have set up a filter that said From contains @idgbooks.com.

   To apply more filter actions, click the Add Criterion button, and then set that line's criterion. Do the same for more criteria, if desired.

5. In the Execute actions pop-up, tell Entourage whether to apply your actions only if all the criteria are met, if any of the criteria are met, if none of the criteria are met, or unless at least one criterion is met.

6. You can apply up to five actions. Determine what the first action should be, and then select that action from the first Actions pop-up menu. When you select an action, pop-up menus and text boxes appear to the right so you can enter the rest of the action's details.

Continue to set your criteria in the order you want the actions processed and carried out.

7. To activate the filter, click OK. This rule now appears in the Rules window.

Place the rules in the order in which you want them performed. Click a rule to select it, and then click the Move Up or Move Down buttons to arrange your priorities.

At times you may not want to apply a rule. You can temporarily disable any rule by returning to the Rule window and unchecking the Enabled checkbox for that rule.

When a rule is no longer needed, choose Tools ➪ Rules to open the Rules window. Click the rule to select it and then click the Delete Rule button.

If you already have an Inbox full of messages that you want to run through one or more of your mail filters, select the messages in the message list, and then select Message ➪ Apply Rule and choose the desired rule or All Rules from the submenu.

Sorting messages

Messages can easily be sorted to make it easier to identify the newest or oldest message, a message from a specific person, or a message about a specific topic. As with the Mac's Finder and most Mac software, click any column heading to sort by that column's criteria. Click the triangle in that column to switch the sort from ascending to descending, or vice versa.

If you are looking for a specific message, sometimes filtering the message list helps. See "Searching for Messages" for more information.

Searching for messages

If you're trying to locate a message(s) containing specific words or characters, you can perform a Find. Sometimes that's more than you need, however. For example, at times you may need to view all messages within a specific folder whose subjects, senders, or recipients contain a word or name. This is more of a filter than a search.

When you're not sure where to look or you want to be sure to find all pertinent messages, use the Find command. Choose Edit ➪ Find (⌘-F) and then enter the text you seek into the Find field. You can narrow your search by searching for this text in a specific area(s) of your messages. Either click More Options to present the Advanced Find dialog box or, if you know ahead of time, choose Edit ➪ Advanced Find (⌘-Option-F) instead of Edit ➪ Find. Create criteria to search only From, To, Subject, and/or Body. Next, tell Entourage to search the current message only, all of your Entourage mail folders, or a specific folder and whether to limit the search to just messages. Finally, click Find or press Return or Enter (because Find is the default button).

When you just need a clearer view of a folder's contents or you pretty much know where you want to look, use the message list's filtering capability. Click the folder in the Folder List so you are viewing all messages within that folder. Then select a field to search by choosing it from the pop-up menu at the top of the list's column headers. Finally, enter the text you are searching for. Only messages that meet your filtering criteria will appear in the message list. This viewing filter remains in effect until you delete the text from the criteria field.

Working with Multiple Users

If several people share your Mac, you can set up Entourage so all users can share the same copy of the program. Each user has his or her own folders and contacts, so mail is not confused among users. You can also maintain privacy by creating a password for each user. Additionally, Entourage is Mac OS 9 Multiple Users-aware, which means that each user defined in your Multiple Users control panel will have his or her own mailbox(es), subscriptions, and personal information..

Setting up multiple users

To set up multiple users, follow these steps:

1. Choose File ➪ Switch Identity (⌘-Shift-Q). A dialog box asks you to confirm that you want to change users, warning that you will be closing the current user's folders and connection. Click Yes and you're presented with a dialog box that handles your user accounts, as shown in Figure 36-17.

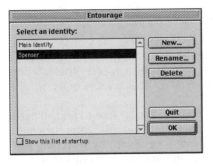

Figure 36-17: The dialog box for creating new users and renaming or selecting existing users

2. Click New. The New Identity dialog box opens, as shown in Figure 36-18.

Figure 36-18: Naming a new user

3. By default, the User Name is something like Identity 1. This field is preselected, so you can type your new user's name immediately.

Tip   When you have more than one account, it will be helpful to rename your first
account if it is still called Main User. This is a good time to do so because you're in
the right place. Click the Main User name and then click Rename. Type the new
name and click Save.

4. The Entourage Setup Assistant now runs through its paces, exactly as it did
the first time you ran Entourage.

5. Setting up any new user is the same, whether it's the first user or the third.
See "Setting Up Your E-mail Account" at the beginning of this chapter if you
need guidance in setting up the new user's preferences. Customize the new
user's settings to reflect the user's e-mail address, username, and password.
Click OK when you're finished.

When you set up a new user account, it remains as the open account until you
switch identities. You can tell which account you are in because the username
appears as part of the window name.

When you create a new user, a folder with the user's name is created within the
Office 2001 Identities folder in the Microsoft User Data Folder, which is in the
Documents folder on your hard disk. Each user's folder contains a file for messages,
rules, signatures, mailing lists, as well as their database. You can take advantage of
this knowledge — and the fact that Entourage recognizes aliases within these folders — to transfer a user from one Mac to another, to have multiple users share a
Mac, or to carry your e-mail with you to access your account and manage your
messages from any Mac. This is power user stuff — and it's all covered soon.

Switching between users

If you have more than one user, the last user to have used Entourage at quitting time
is the active user upon relaunch. To switch users, select File ⇨ Switch Identities
(⌘-Shift-Q).

Tip   You may prefer to have Entourage let you select an identity whenever it starts
up. Choose File ⇨ Switch Identity, and then check Show This List On Startup. (This
is Step 1 under "Setting Up Multiple Users.") The dialog box in which you select
an identity upon startup (or when switching identities anytime) is shown in
Figure 36-19.

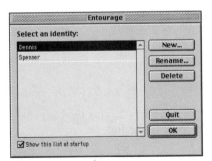

Figure 36-19: The identity selection dialog box

Deleting a user

Deleting an identity is easy. Just select the identity in the dialog box shown in Figure 36-19, and click Delete. Confirm that you really want to delete the identity and it is gone as are all its folders and files in the Office 2001 Identities folder hierarchy.

Transferring users from Mac to Mac

When you don't intend to have a user access mail from your Mac any longer, you can give that user his or her identity folder for transfer to another Mac that runs Entourage. Open the Office 2001 Identities folder (which is in the Microsoft User Data folder in the Documents folder). Drag the user's entire folder to a removable disk. Then go back to Entourage and delete the identity (yes, you could just trash the identity from the Finder). Later the user can copy his or her folder to the Office 2001 Identities folder on another Mac. If your Mac is directly connected to the other Mac's hard drive (over a network), instead of copying to a removable disk, you can drag the identity folder directly to that other drive.

Taking It with You

What if you are in business and need your e-mail with you, but you move from office to office? What if multiple students/employees share your Mac, but you don't want all their mail on the hard drive. Perhaps you have a Mac and want to access, read, and respond to your e-mail but don't have steady net access from where you're living. All of these situations are possible. This definitely is power user stuff, however, and is not commonly necessary. If you don't fit one of the user profiles just mentioned, don't bother with this stuff.

The bottom line is that Entourage recognizes alias-to-mail folders, so you can store your mail on any removable medium, such as a Zip or a Jaz disk, and then access your account from any copy of Entourage, downloading your mail to—and uploading mail from—the disk rather than the hard drive on which Entourage is installed. The key to carrying mail with you is having a disk to carry it on, so you or each user must have a removable disk, such as a Zip or a Jaz, to begin with.

To carry your own mail (or to have your users carry their own mail), follow these steps:

1. On the removable disk, create a new folder the same way you create any normal folder—using the File ⇨ New Folder (⌘-N) command. Give that folder the name you want your account to have.

2. Insert the disk into the Mac where mail will be accessed.

3. Open the folder called Office 2001 Identities, which is in the Document folder's Microsoft User Data folder.

4. Press ⌘-Option as you click the user folder (on the removable disk) and drag that folder into the Office 2001 Identities folder on the hard drive.

   The alias on the removable disk can be copied to another Office 2001 Identities folder on any hard drive over and over, or it can be trashed. A user can place an alias of his folder in multiple Macs—and should place an alias on any machine from which the wants to access his or her mail.

5. Restart Entourage before continuing use of the program if it was running.

The next time you select a new identity (see "Switching Between Users"), the aliased user appears as a choice, looking just like any other identity. When you select that identity, however, a dialog box asks you to insert the disk that contains the identity's folder. (By the way, the dialog box asks for the disk by name, so changing the disk's name is not a good idea.) If you are not that user and don't have that disk, or if the user doesn't have the disk handy, click Cancel. Otherwise, insert the disk. The dialog box disappears and the account opens. From there, use the account normally.

With this setup the user doesn't have Entourage on his disk. He must use his disk with a Mac that has Entourage installed.

As a portable user, to be able to read or compose mail while away from the Mac that provides your link to the net, Entourage must be installed on the removable disk. If that disk happens to contain the Mac's System folder, you can perform a normal install of Entourage onto that disk while it is the startup disk for the Mac to which it's attached.

Working with Newsgroups

A newsgroup is like a community bulletin board where the board addresses one specific issue. A newsgroup is a folder set up on a computer somewhere, to which anyone can post and read messages others have posted. A list may have hundreds of messages posted at one time. To read the messages within a newsgroup, you must subscribe to the list. Of course, it wouldn't be logical to have all these messages download to your hard drive, so newsgroups function with their own protocol, NNTP, rather than POP3 or IMAP4. This protocol enables all subscribers to access the messages live over the Net. Thousands and thousands of newsgroups are scattered all over the Internet. Chances are your ISP hosts thousands of them. If so, you received the news server's address when you signed up.

After you subscribe to a newsgroup, you read and respond to its messages the same as with an e-mail message. This section gets you started.

Setting up a news account

Setting up a news server account has two parts. First, you tell Entourage what server to call into. Then you view the available newsgroups and subscribe to the ones in which you are interested.

Defining a news account

Setting up a news account is much like setting up an e-mail account. Follow these steps:

1. Choose Tools ➪ Accounts and select the News tab and click New.

2. In the Account Setup Assistant that opens, tell Entourage which e-mail account to use as the reply-to account and, optionally, provide an organization. Click the right arrow or press Return.

3. Enter the address for your news server (which was probably provided by your ISP) in the News (NNTP) Server text box, as shown in Figure 36-20.

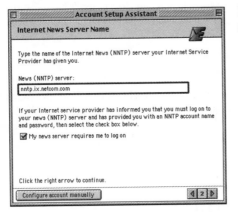

Figure 36-20: Setting up a news server in the Account Setup Assistant

4. If your ISP requires a password to allow access to this server, you have already been told so and have already chosen a username and a password. In that case, check the box to tell Entourage the server will ask for authentication, and then enter the username and password you and your ISP agreed on.

5. Name the account and click Finish to close the Account Setup Assistant.

Subscribing to a newsgroup

After you designate your news server, it appears in the Folder List, as shown in Figure 36-21 (where Netcom, a part of EarthLink, provides the news server).

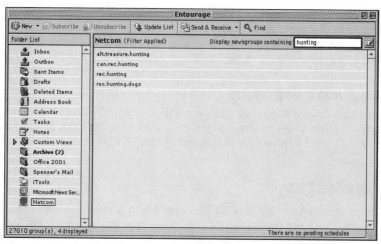

Figure 36-21: Subscribing to the alt.travel newsgroup list on the Westworld server

Now it's time to connect to the server, get the listing of available newsgroups, and subscribe. Follow these steps:

1. Click the server's icon in the Folder List. The server's name appears in the right side of the Entourage window, and a connection indicator appears at the lower right of the window.

2. Entourage will ask whether you want a full list of Newsgroups. This can take quite a while — most general news servers have over 30,000 newsgroups at this time.

   Remember that if you are using a modem to access the Internet, you need to set your PPP access to permit applications to make connections. Otherwise you need to open the PPP control panel and connect manually to access the news server, or you'll receive an error message.

3. To subscribe to a list, click the list's name and then click the Subscribe button in the toolbar, as shown in Figure 36-21. The list's name appears below the server name in the Folder list. (An arrow appears beside the server name so you can hide or reveal the lists, just as in the Mac's Finder).

   Your list of available newsgroups may contain thousands of group names, making it hard (not to mention tedious) to find the lists that interest you. Use the window's filter to make this search easier. Enter a key word to act as a filter. See Figure 36-21, where only groups with the word hunting are displayed.

   You can subscribe to as many newsgroups as you like. Simply select each list and click Subscribe. Changing the words you filter by doesn't affect your connection.

You can connect to the news server at any time to check whether any new newsgroups are available. Rather than repeat the entire listing, click your news server and select View ➪ Get New Newsgroups. That way only new groups will appear in the list on the right side of the window.

Unsubscribing from a newsgroup

To unsubscribe to a newsgroup, click the server icon in your Folder List. Choose View ➪ Subscribed Only. Then, in the group list on the right, click the newsgroup to select it and click the Unsubscribe button, or choose Edit ➪ Unsubscribe.

Viewing messages

To view the messages in a newsgroup, all you have to do is click the name of the newsgroup. (If you don't see the names of your subscribed lists in your Folder List, click the arrow beside the server name so it points downward and reveals the folder's contents.) Entourage automatically connects to the server and displays the newsgroup's messages. Click once to view a message in the Preview pane. (If it's not open choose View ➪ Preview pane.) Double-click a message to have it open in its own window.

When viewing messages in a separate window, the window gains two new buttons (with attached menu arrows) to help you move through the messages. To help you understand these buttons, we should explain that a thread is a subject. When someone posts a message and someone else replies, the reply receives the same subject name. This reply becomes the second message in that thread. When viewing the messages in a separate window, you can't see the subject headers in the list; consequently, instead, you use the pop-ups attached to the up arrow (or down arrow) to choose Previous Thread (or Next Thread) to move from subject to subject. To view a message's replies, you click the Next button to move to the next message for that subject. Likewise, click Previous to move to the previous message (if any exist) that has to do with the subject (thread). You can also choose the next/previous unread message or thread, and specify that it be deleted.

If you are viewing messages in the Preview pane in the main Entourage window, rather than clicking buttons to move from subject to subject, use the scroll bars and then click any message to read it. An arrow beside a message indicates that responses exist. Click the arrow to point it downward and reveal the responses. Then click any response to read it (see Figure 36-22).

After you've read some of the messages in the newsgroup list, you have the option of filtering out the ones you've read. To filter messages, select View ➪ Unread Only.

Sometimes so many messages have arrived that the server shows you only a few hundred at a time. You'll know by viewing the status report at that bottom left of the window. To see the next bunch of messages, select View ➪ Get More News Messages.

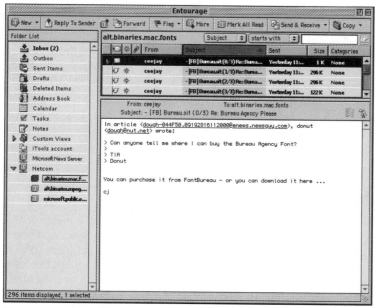

Figure 36-22: Reading a newsgroup message

You can also select View ⇨ Refresh Message List (⌘-L) to reconnect to your news server and view any new articles for that newsgroup.

Caution   Entourage (and its smaller sibling, Outlook Express) has one problem in dealing with newsgroups. It is very common for attachments in newsgroups to be *multipart* — that is, spread across multiple messages. Entourage usually has problems with multipart binary postings, retrieving only the first part and then letting the Helper application complain that the download was bad. If you are going to frequent binary-oriented newsgroups, we would recommend that you keep another newsreader (such as the free YA-NewsWatcher or MT-NewsWatcher) to deal with these groups, at least until Microsoft rectifies this deficiency.

Keeping messages

Remember that the messages you are reading in a newsgroup are on the news server or another computer feeding the server, not on your hard drive or in your e-mail folders, wherever they may be. If you want to keep a message, you need to transfer it to your own drive. You have two ways to transfer a message: by keeping a message in its e-mail form or by saving it as a standalone document. To keep the message as e-mail, drag the message from the message list into the folder in which you want it stored. To save the message as a document, click the message in the message list and then select File ⇨ Save (⌘-S). If you're viewing the message in its own window, you can also select File ⇨ Save (⌘-S).

Working Offline

Suppose you have a PowerBook and are spending time in transit. With the Work Offline feature, you can keep up with your newsgroup, IMAP-served or POP-served messages. While connected to the server, when you click a newsgroup message, IMAP-served or POP-served, the message is cached to your hard drive.

Later, select File ⇨ Work Offline. When you click the News Server icon to look at the messages, Entourage won't attempt to connect to the server.

Automating actions

Rather than wading through tons of newsgroup messages to find a message that interests you, you can set up Newsgroup Rules to search the messages. When messages meeting your criteria are found, you can have Entourage set them to a certain color and/or download and file them for you. Entourage can also mark the message as read if you want. If you've read the section "Automating Your Incoming Mail," you will find this procedure familiar. To filter newsgroup messages, follow these steps:

1. Choose Tools ⇨ Rules to open the Rules window and select the News tab.

2. Click the New button at the top of the window. The Edit Rule window opens with the new rule displayed.

3. The Rule name field is preselected, so begin by typing a descriptive name for your rule.

4. The top part of the dialog box contains criteria settings. In the first pop-up menu, tell Entourage whether the rule applies to All Newsgroups or just what the newsgroup name should contain or not contain, be or not be, and start with or end with by selecting one of these options from the pop-up menu and then entering the text you are interested in. The example shown in Figure 36-23 searches newsgroups whose subject contains the word travel.

   Use the first pop-up list to select the part of the message you are scanning for your criteria. Use the second pop-up to narrow your filter. In the text box, enter (or paste) the text you are filtering by. In Figure 36-23, we search the subject for the words Rome or London.

   To apply a second filter action, click the Add Criterion button and set the criterion in the new line. Do the same for up to three more criteria if desired.

5. In the Execute actions if pop-up menu, tell Entourage whether to apply your actions only if all the criteria are met, if any of the criteria are met, unless all are met, or unless at least one is met.

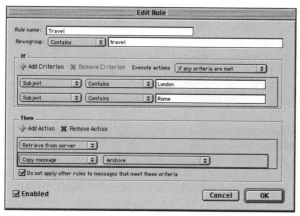

Figure 36-23: Setting up a Newsgroup Rule

6. In the Actions area, tell Entourage what to do when the criteria are met. Check Do Not Show Message if you want Entourage to filter out the messages that meet your criteria. Check Set Category if you want to categorize them. If you want these messages to be marked as already read, check that option. To have Entourage download these messages and file them in any one of your Entourage folders, check Move, and then select the folder in which you want the messages filed. In Figure 36-23, we have all travel messages about Rome or London downloaded to the Archive folder.

7. Click OK to activate the filter. This rule now appears in the News tab of the Rules dialog box.

Posting to a newsgroup

Composing a new message for a newsgroup is just like composing a regular e-mail message — perhaps just a tad easier. While you are viewing the newsgroup list or a newsgroup message, click the New (Message) button. The new message window that opens is preaddressed to the newsgroup you are currently in. You can cc the message to another recipient if you want. Give your message a subject and then type your message. To send the message, click the Post Now button. You can also add attachments and sign it, just like any other e-mail message. If you are not ready to post the message, click Post Later to place it in the Outbox folder until you are ready to post it. If you aren't sure you've completed it, click the Save as Draft button to store it in the Drafts folder until you are ready to complete and post it.

Replying to a message

When responding to a newsgroup message, you can send your response to the newsgroup for the entire group to see, or you can send it to the author only. What's most important is to pay attention to whom you are sending your message.

Otherwise, the results can be embarrassing, or you may be posting personal information to (potentially) the entire world.

To reply only to the sender, with the message being responded to as the active message, click the Reply To Sender button or select Message ⇨ Reply To Sender (⌘-Option-R). The message window you are presented with is a regular e-mail message window because you are sending a regular e-mail message.

To send your reply to the newsgroup for public viewing, with the message being responded to as the active message, click the Reply to Newsgroup button or select Message ⇨ Reply. The outgoing message window is similar to a regular e-mail message window except that you'll see a Post button in lieu of a Send button, and the addressing is to a news server and a newsgroup instead of to a person. By default, newsgroup messages are in plain text. You can change this under the Composition area of Preferences.

Keeping Your Calendar

As we stated earlier, the primary distinction between Entourage and Outlook Express is that Entourage includes PIM tools that are not present in Outlook Express. Foremost among these added tools is the Calendar. The Calendar, shown in Figure 36-24, presents a tri-pane view. The top two, side-by-side panes present a view of Today (the date reflected by the Mac's System clock) and a modifiable (by the scroll arrows) two-calendar-month presentation. The lower pane shows your choice of a month, week, workweek, or a single day view.

Tip   If you want to display a specific date range in the View pane, you can select it in the two-month pane. The range shown can be from one to six days or one to six weeks.

Matching the calendar to your work schedule

As delivered, the calendar assumes that the workday runs from 9:00 a.m. to 5:00 p.m., that the week starts on Sunday, and that the workweek is Monday through Friday. If these parameters don't match your life, you can easily change them by choosing Edit ⇨ Preferences ⇨ General (⌘-;) and selecting the Calendar tab, shown in Figure 36-25.

If you want the calendar to start weeks on a day other than Sunday, choose that day from the First day of week pop-up menu. If your workweek isn't the traditional five-day, Monday through Friday grind, check (and uncheck) the Calendar workweek checkboxes to reflect the days you work. Set the start and end times of your workday in the Work hours text boxes, either by typing or using the up and down arrows.

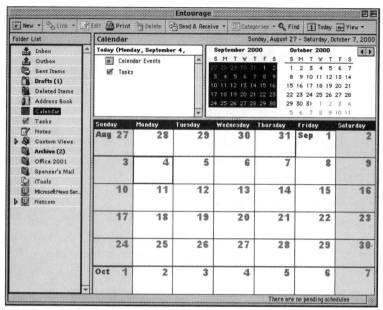

Figure 36-24: The Entourage Calendar, showing a month view

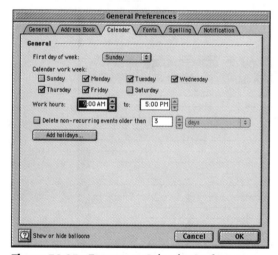

Figure 36-25: Entourage Calendar Preferences

Entourage comes with holiday schedules for a great many countries. You can add the holidays you recognize from one or more countries by clicking the Add holidays button and checking the countries whose holidays you wish to include in the Add Holidays to Calendar dialog box, as shown in Figure 36-26.

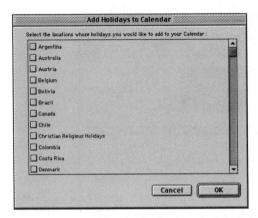

Figure 36-26: The Add Holidays to Calendar dialog box

Holidays will appear in bold type in the two-month pane, in red in the Today pane, and in a banner in the View pane. Figure 36-27 shows an example of this.

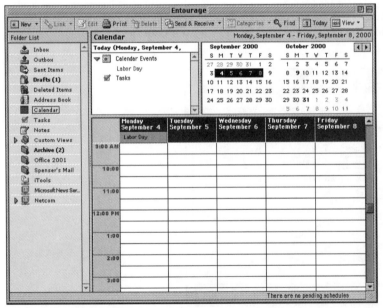

Figure 36-27: Labor Day, 2000 showing up as a holiday in all three panes

Many of us employ a personal calendar as much for a record of what we did and when as we do for a reminder of what we have scheduled. If you don't fall into that camp and don't care about history, you can check the box to Delete nonrecurring events older than and then set the threshold period—the default is three days.

The Holidays File

The Holidays file that you are offered is the one that comes with Office 2001. However, it is just a text file that follows a specific format. A line prefaces each country's holidays with the country name in brackets, a space, and the number of lines that follow for that country. Each holiday line has the name of the holiday, followed by a comma and the date (in yyyy/mm/dd format). The holiday lists provided cover the years 2000 to 2005 and the holidays are listed in alphabetic order.

Because you are not constrained to use the Office-provided Holidays file, or just the one file, you can also create your own ancillary files and import them.

Scheduling calendar events

You can schedule a number of events in the Calendar: meetings, conferences, vacations, birthdays, appointments, and so forth. As you'll see later in this chapter, tasks will also appear in your Calendar.

To place an event on the Calendar, follow these steps:

1. With the Calendar showing (if it isn't, click it in the Folder List), click New.

2. In the Subject text box, type the name or other identifying information about the event.

3. *(Optional)* If you have a place that you want to specify for the event, type it in the Location text box.

4. To specify a date or time, enter the information and select the options that you want.

5. *(Optional)* If you wish to be reminded before the event, click the Reminder checkbox and set how early you want the reminder. You can also include estimated travel time.

Caution

For these reminders and for Task reminders, which are discussed later, you need to be aware that they are only displayed if Entourage is running. If you intend to make use of the reminder feature, it is imperative that Entourage run at all times.

6. *(Optional)* If this is a party or a meeting to which you wish to invite other people, click the Invite button in the window's toolbar. You are presented with an e-mail dialog box with a pop-up window to address the invitations, as shown in Figure 36-28.

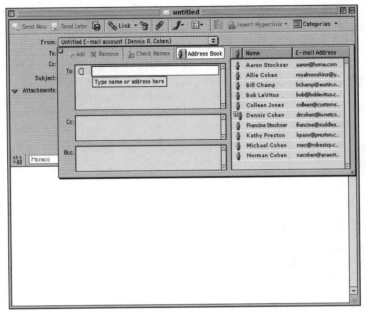

Figure 36-28: Invite participants using this dialog box

When invited to an event, open the e-mail containing the invitation and click the Accept button if you agree to attend, Decline if you don't agree, and Tentative if you intend to decide at a later time. Unless you decline, the event will be added to your calendar.

Note   If you change your mind later, you can reopen the message and click a different button.

Publishing your calendar

You can choose File ➪ Save as Web Page to publish your Calendar in HTML format, viewable with any recent Web browser. Thus, you can display it on an internal or external Web site or send it in an e-mail. An option exists to exclude any activities categorized as private when publishing the Web page.

Setting Tasks

The Tasks list is your to-do list. While you can enter activities in the Calendar, as described earlier, you can also build a list of activities in the Tasks list. A short example of a task list can be seen in Figure 36-29.

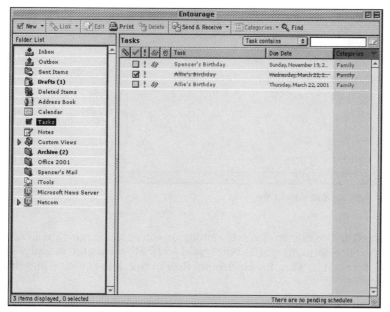

Figure 36-29: A short list of tasks, one of which is completed

Tasks are also displayed in your Calendar, so you don't have to worry about entering them in two places to make sure that they show up.

The only substantive difference between the Task List and Calendar events is that you don't have an Invite option available for tasks and you can display them sorted by name, due date, or category in one place, whereas the Calendar has only a temporal display and is limited to six weeks at a time, with a lot of white space. In either case, you can categorize the item, prioritize it, and set reminders.

Taking Notes

Notes are just what the name implies. While not visually similar to the ubiquitous Post-It notes, they serve the same purpose. Notes created in Entourage can be linked to other files and stored with your other personal information in the Address Book, Calendar, and Task List.

To create a Note, select Notes in the Folder List and click New. You will be presented with a window very similar to the bottom half of a message window, as shown in Figure 36-30.

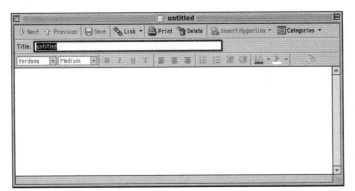

Figure 36-30: A new Note window

The text in the Title box is preselected, waiting for you to name the note. Do so, and then create the note, formatting it as you would an HTML-formatted message. The button on the far right, next to the Horizontal Rule button lets you date and time-stamp the note.

Linking Entourage Items

Entourage presents you with a way to link any Entourage item (message, contact, calendar event, task, or note) to any other item or file. This feature enables you to collect disparate information quickly and easily when reviewing material or creating a synopsis.

To link an Entourage item to a file, follow these steps:

1. Create and save the item you wish to link. If the item hasn't been saved, Entourage will not let you link it.

2. Click the arrow next to the Link button and choose Link to Existing ⇨ File from the menu which appears.

3. Navigate to and select the file in the Open dialog box that appears.

Now, when you display the window for that message, task, event, note, or contact, you can click the arrow next to the Links button and either choose Files from the menu that descends to see which files are linked or you can choose Open Links to present the Links To window, as shown in Figure 36-31.

To link an Entourage item to another Entourage item, follow these steps:

1. Select the item you wish to link to another Entourage item.

2. Click the menu arrow next to the Links button and choose the type of item to which you wish to link from the Link to Existing submenu.

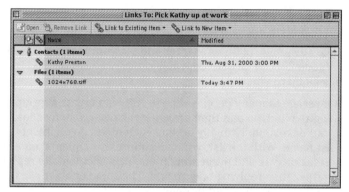

Figure 36-31: The Links To window, showing an item's links

3. Find the item to which you want to link, and drag it to the Link to area of the Link Maker palette, shown in Figure 36-32.

Figure 36-32: The Link Maker palette

4. *(Optional)* Create additional links by repeating Step 3.

5. Click the Create Links button in the Link Maker.

You can also create a new item to link to by choosing the item type from the Link to New submenu instead of the Link to Existing submenu in Step 2.

Summary

This chapter familiarized you with Entourage — Microsoft's Internet mail and news client/Personal Information Manager. We covered these points:

✦ Whether you have a POP dial-up account or an IMAP corporate server, Entourage can handle your e-mail with ease.

✦ Multiple users can share the same copy of Entourage, each maintaining separate access, files, passwords, and so on.

✦ The Folder List is your filing cabinet. You can create as many other folders as you want and store messages by topic or by any organizational method.

Folders residing on your hard drive appear below the Custom Views folder. IMAP account folders appear as subfolders of your server icon.

✦ You can take advantage of Rules to filter and file your incoming messages for you. Unwanted mail can be deleted, while other mail can be filed by topic or content. It's all up to you.

✦ To send a message to many people at once, you can create a group simply by clicking the group button and then dragging the desired names into the group list. Then, rather than individually adding each message recipients, you just enter the list name. With the list, you can suppress recipients' names, keeping their addresses private and preventing them from accidentally replying to all recipients rather than replying only to you. The same contact can be part of many lists. Names can be added or deleted at any time.

✦ Outgoing messages can be sent with color and styles or in plain-text format.

✦ Newsgroup messages can also be handled in Entourage, almost exactly like regular e-mail.

✦ You can keep an electronic calendar and to-do list, and have automated reminders. Events created in the Calendar let you invite others electronically and, when you accept such an invitation, the activity is automatically entered in your Calendar.

✦ Any Entourage item can be linked to any other Entourage item or to any file on your disk.

Where to go next

✦ Need to compose the documents to be enclosed with your e-mail? Check out Part I: Word, Part II: Excel, and Part III: PowerPoint.

✦ Ready to cruise the Web? Check out Chapter 37 for information on using Internet Explorer.

✦   ✦   ✦

Overview of Internet Explorer

Internet Explorer's main function is to enable you to visit the World Wide Web and view today's Web pages in their fullest glory. Today's Web makes it easy to seek out a page on any topic, and some Web sites even bring their content to you by enabling you to subscribe to the page or to set up a channel. Internet Explorer 5.0 supports these new technologies and makes it easy for you to take advantage of the technologies. Because the Internet also includes newsgroups and e-mail, some browsers have concentrated too hard on these features. Happily, Internet Explorer has opted not to go in this direction. Instead, Internet Explorer does the Web and nothing but the Web, while giving you easy access to your newsgroups and e-mail with the click of a button.

Internet Explorer's sister application, Outlook Express, is designed specifically to handle news and mail. As we saw in Chapter 36, Entourage 2001 is an Outlook Express superset and is included as part of Office 2001. By default, when you click Internet Explorer's Mail button, you are taken to your Internet Preferences selection for a default mail client — Entourage if you answered affirmatively when asked if you wanted it to be your default. However, it is very easy to change this preference to open E-mailer, Outlook Express, Mailsmith, or Eudora if you prefer to use one of them to handle your e-mail or news (see "Reading Mail and News" later in the chapter).

At the time this book is being written, Internet Explorer 5 is the current version and is the version included on the Microsoft Office 2001 CD-ROM. Microsoft releases new versions of Internet Explorer separately from Microsoft Office and it is possible that a different (newer) version will be included on the CD-ROM at a later date or available separately from www.microsoft.com.

Looking at the Window

The first time you launch Internet Explorer, you may be taken to a preset page. After that, you can set Internet Explorer to take you to the page of your choice, called your home page, or to leave the browser window blank. Figure 37-1 illustrates a blank window.

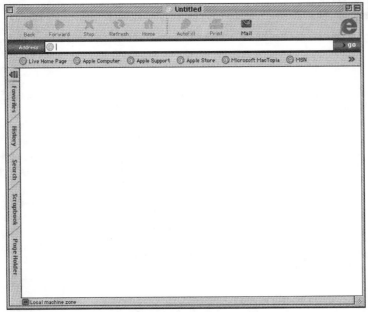

Figure 37-1: A blank Internet Explorer window—no page is loaded

The Internet Explorer window begins with the title bar, as does any Mac program. The name in the title bar usually reflects the Web page you are on. The page's creator determines that title. No page exists in Figure 37-1, so the title is untitled. The title bar also contains the standard Mac close box, size box, and windowshade button.

Below the title bar is the Internet Explorer toolbar, also called the Button Bar. Starting with Internet Explorer 5.0, the Button Bar is customizable and Microsoft includes a number of buttons as well as two button sets which you can add either by choosing View ➪ Customize Toolbar or by Control-clicking in the toolbar and choosing Customize from the shortcut menu.

Next, you find the address bar. This is where you type the URL, or address, of the page you want to visit. Alternatives to hand-entering an address are clicking a favorite (sometimes called a bookmark in other applications), clicking a link — which appears in another page or in any document that contains live links — or using Apple's Data Detectors to Control-click a destination and go there. As you enter a site's address, or just part of it, a feature called AutoComplete searches all addresses you've visited before that contain that address or word you entered. Click the arrow in the address bar to display the list of matching addresses, and then select any address from this list to go to that page. (See "Using the Address Bar" later in this chapter.)

The next strip of buttons is the Toolbar Favorites bar. Don't confuse this with the list of preferred Web sites that you build for yourself. Each of these buttons is a link to a page Microsoft has set up to provide information about and provide links to areas that may be of interest to you. You can add to or remove items from the Toolbar Favorites, as we'll discuss later in this chapter.

Along the left side of the window is the Explorer bar — another tool designed to make your Internet travels easier and more efficient. You'll see five tabs: Favorites, History, Search, Scrapbook, and Page Holder. These tabs hang out quietly on the side trying not to encroach on the Web page until you click one of them to call it into action. When you're done with the information in the tab, click the tab again and it slides back to the side. This is an alternative to selecting an item from a pop-up list or opening a separate window.

At the bottom of the window is the status bar. This is where you are kept informed of what Internet Explorer is doing, where a link will take you, whether the page you are accessing is from the Web or from your hard drive, whether it is secure (a padlock is shown), and so on. For example, while a page is loading, the status bar tells you as it retrieves each component and what percent of the download is complete.

Next to the status bar is the scroll bar and arrows when applicable. The right side of the window also has a scroll bar and arrows as needed. And, of course, you can always click in the bottom-right corner and drag to custom-size your window.

Completing the picture in the Internet Explorer window, smack dab in the center, is the reason you're in Internet Explorer in the first place — the Web page you are visiting.

In more detail, here's how each part of the Internet Explorer window can serve you.

Changing the Window's Look

Each of the bars — the button, address, favorites, Explorer, and status bar — can be turned on and off by default or per session. To affect the default, choose Edit ➪ Preferences (⌘-;) or, if you've added it to the toolbar, click the Preferences button, and then click Browser Display and check or uncheck each bar. To turn one on or off temporarily, select the bar in the View menu, removing the checkmark. (The View menu is a toggle.)

When you rest your mouse over any button, a balloon appears to tell you about that button's function. This is called a ToolTip. You can turn ToolTips on or off by checking or unchecking Show ToolTips in the Browser Display page of the Preferences dialog box.

Unlike the toolbars in the core Office 2001 applications or in previous versions of Internet Explorer, you cannot rearrange the order in which the toolbars appear. You can only Hide/Show them or change their color.

Using the button bar

The button bar performs an action with a single click. Table 37-1 lists the function of each button on the default button bar.

<table>
<tr><td colspan="2" align="center">Table 37-1
The Functions of the Button Bar</td></tr>
<tr><td>*Button*</td><td>*How It Works*</td></tr>
<tr><td>Back</td><td>With each click, the Back button takes you back one page through the pages you've visited in this browser window. To move back several pages at a time, click the Back button and hold the mouse button until a list of all sites visited in this browser window appears, and then select a site's address from the list. If you have two browser windows open, use the History tab to return to a site you visited in another browser window.</td></tr>
<tr><td>Forward</td><td>Each click moves you forward through the pages you've visited during this session in this browser window. Hold the mouse down to jump several sites forward at once by selecting an address from the pop-up list. (See Back for more details.)</td></tr>
<tr><td>Stop</td><td>Stops the current page that's being downloaded from continuing. Refresh reinitiates the loading of the page you stopped.</td></tr>
<tr><td>Refresh</td><td>Reloads the Web page currently designated in the address bar. If you've deleted the last URL, it will reappear and reload. Refresh is handy when a page fails to load properly, hangs up, or may have newer information than the last time you loaded it. If you stop a page, Refresh continues the load.</td></tr>
</table>

Button	How It Works
Home	Takes you to the page you designate as your home page. When you set a home page, Internet Explorer also accesses it upon each launch.
AutoFill	Completes forms on the currently displayed page using settings you've stored.
Print	Prints the currently loaded page or, if held down, displays a pop-up menu enabling you to choose Page Setup, Print Preview, or Print.
Mail	Opens your mail reader for you to read your mail, create a new message, or send the current URL within a new message. It also lets you read your news. For each of these actions, your designated mail or newsreader opens.

Using the Explorer bar

The Explorer bar is like a windowshade that conveniently rolls out the left side of your window and then folds back when you're done. To access the Explorer bar, click the tab that you want and the bar will pull out; this has the effect of pushing the Web page to the right. Clicking the tab again scrolls it back in and pushes the Web page back to the left.

Favorites tab

Cyberspace is vast and so easy to move around in that you are bound to forget where you've been. Placing a site's address in your Favorites list makes the site easier to return to. Organizing your Favorites list into logical folders makes it even easier. (Your list will grow and grow — believe us!) This organization is usually done in a separate Favorites window, but it can also be accomplished in the Favorites tab. See the section on marking your favorite sites, later in this chapter.

One at-sign (@) icon appears for each site you bookmark as a favorite. If you've organized your favorite sites into folders, click the triangle beside the folder to reveal its contents. As you click a folder, any previously open folder automatically closes. Each site usually has a name attached to it. The page's designer assigns the site's name. At times, the name can be helpful; at other times, it may just say index or something equally vague. You can see where a site actually leads by resting your mouse over the icon until the ToolTip pops up and displays the site's URL. You can also rename the item in the Favorites list. You can also edit the URL, for those favored sites whose addresses change. To learn how, see the "Marking Favorite Sites for Easy Return" section later in this chapter.

To visit a site, click the icon or name of the site. (You can also return to a site by selecting it from the Favorites menu.) The tab won't automatically disappear, as you may want it again. To give your page more room onscreen, remember to click the Favorites tab.

To rearrange items in your Favorites list, click the item (icon or name), hold the mouse a moment, and then drag. After you move the item a bit, its outline appears, along with a black bar. The black bar shows you where the icon will land when you release the mouse. You can move an item anywhere in the Favorite tab — between other icons, into a folder, or from folder to folder — just as in the Finder. (Favorites can also be rearranged from within the Favorites window, as discussed in "Marking Favorite Sites for Easy Return.")

To remove an item from your Favorites list while in this tab, drag the item to the Mac's Trash folder, or Control-click the item and choose Delete from the shortcut menu.

Another task that you can do with Favorites is to *subscribe* to them. If you choose Favorites ⇨ Subscribe, that site is added to your Favorites list and will be checked for changes on the schedule you set in your Web Browser Subscriptions preferences. If you don't want to use your default settings for one of your subscriptions, press the Customize button in the alert box which appears when you choose Favorites ⇨ Subscribe. You can also override the schedule and tell Internet Explorer to update all subscriptions by choosing Favorites ⇨ Update Subscriptions (⌘-U). To determine the status of the subscription, either choose Favorites ⇨ Organize Favorites to open the Favorites window, or click the Favorites tab in the Explorer bar. If the subscription is up-to-date, there will be a small newspaper icon to the left; if the subscription has been updated since it was last viewed, there will be a blue star icon; and, if Internet Explorer was unable to check the site, there will be a Caution icon (an orange triangle with an exclamation point inside).

Tip   If the Caution icon appears, double-click it, and then click the Subscribe tab in the dialog which appears for an explanation.

History tab

This tab tracks all the pages you visit in your travels on the Web. Whether you work within one browser window or open several browser windows in a session, they are all tracked in this tab and show in the History tab or any browser window. Histories don't begin and end with one Web session; they are carried over from one session to the next. This means if you visit a site on Monday, and then close your connection and/or quit Internet Explorer, the sites you visited are still in the History list when you connect on Wednesday and open a new browser window. To make your exploration history even more clear to you, Internet Explorer creates a folder for each day's travels.

Note   You can control how far back History records in Preferences, in the Web Browser ⇨ Advanced page. The default is to record the last 300 pages visited.

One at-sign (@) icon appears for each site you visit, each time you visit that site. The name you see on each icon is the page name assigned by the page's designer. To see a site address, rest your mouse over the icon until the ToolTip pops up.

To revisit a site, click the icon or name of the site. If you plan to visit a site again, rather than keeping it in the History tab, designate the site as a favorite. To do so, click the icon of the site (your cursor becomes a hand) and drag it, resting your mouse over the Favorites tab. In a moment, the Favorites tab becomes the active tab. Continue dragging until the site's icon lands where you want it; it can land in a folder or between any other existing favorites icons. A black line indicates where the icon will land when you release the mouse.

You can remove a site from your History list. (A great feature if your boss may see it.) Just drag the site's icon to your Mac's Trash, or Control-click and choose Delete from the shortcut menu. (You can't click the icon and select Clear because clicking the icon in the tab initiates a connection.)

To switch to another tab, click the desired tab. If you are finished using the Explorer bar and want it to roll back to the left side of the window, click the History tab.

Tip   In addition to learning the address of a site in your History list, you can also learn the date you first visited and last visited the site. To see this information, open the History list as a separate window by selecting Window ➪ History (⌘-3). In the History window, click the site to select it and choose File ➪ Get Info (⌘-I), as in the Finder. If you click and hold on an item or Control-click the item, you can also choose Get Info from the shortcut menu that appears.

Search tab

This tab (see Figure 37-2) is a miniature one-stop shop for quick and easy searches. To use this tab, you must be connected to the Internet so that Internet Explorer can load its search assistant page from the Microsoft Web site. At the top of the tab's area, a pop-up list (labeled Next) automatically cycles through several providers (or search engines) and offers you the provider of the day. You can use that provider or select your preference from the pop-up list.

Taking Control of Your History

Internet Explorer's history of your Web page visits is finite. At some point, the memory of a visited site drops off the list. By default, Internet Explorer recalls approximately 300 pages; however, you can change the number of recorded visits.

To do so, choose Edit ➪ Preferences, and then select the Advanced preference pane under the Web Browser category. The first option in this pane determines the number of pages that are remembered by your History list. After that, the older pages are dropped from the record (which is a good reason to add pages to your Favorites list). To change the number of pages tracked, enter a new number and click OK to close the Preferences window and effect the change.

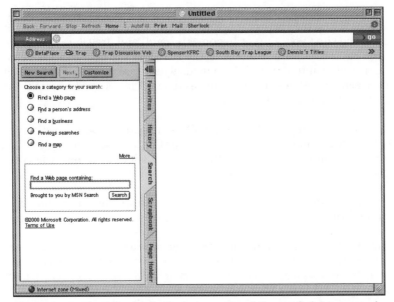

Figure 37-2: The Search tab displays results while one link is accessed

You can also click the Customize button and have a Customize Search Settings –
Web Page dialog window appear, where you can specify your preferences for various types of searches.

Before You Visit the Web

To access a Web site, you need to be able to connect to the Web. If you are using your Mac
at home, you are probably using a modem and your phone line to create a PPP connection
via a local Internet service provider (ISP). If you don't yet have an ISP, we recommend
checking with your local Macintosh User's Group for recommendations. You want to find an
ISP with a good modem-to-user ratio, reliable lines, knowledge of the Mac (for good
technical support), and a good reputation. Other faster connections, such as an Integrated
Services Digital Network (ISDN), Digital Subscriber Lines (DSL), or cable connections are
also possible to have at home, although they are more expensive and therefore less
common. The Mac OS comes complete with all the software you need to initiate your
Internet connection.

If you are accessing the Internet from a corporate office, your company most likely provides
your connection via its company network. In that case, you may be connected all the time.
Office setups may include a *firewall,* which acts as a protective buffer, and your setup may
include a *proxy server,* a computer that acts as a gateway between a network protected by
a firewall and other networks. Your network administrator or MIS personnel most likely
handle these setups in your company, and will make sure you are properly configured.

A small text field is the next item of interest. Here you enter the text you are seeking information on from the Web. Enter your text, and then click the Search button—whatever it might be labeled. In a few moments, you have a list of sites that met your criteria (contained your text) listed below in the Search tab. Each found site contains a link to the found site. Clicking any returned link takes you to that site. To view a site in a larger window, click the Search tab; this rolls back to the left side of the window. Your current Web page slides over, too. To check out another found link, click the Search tab again. The information from your search remains intact until you search again. Therefore, you can look through each found site while looking at the other options simultaneously. See the section "Searching Web Sites" for more on searches.

When you are completely done with the Explorer bar, click the last tab you used to roll it back. If you click a different tab from the tab you are in, you switch tabs but do not roll back the Explorer bar.

Scrapbook tab

The Scrapbook tab is new to Internet Explorer 5. It enables you to collect Web pages, such as news articles and e-commerce receipts, for future reference. The Internet Scrapbook provides a snapshot in time, so even if a Web page changes, you still have a record of the page. Figure 37-3 shows a Web page that has been stored in the Internet Scrapbook.

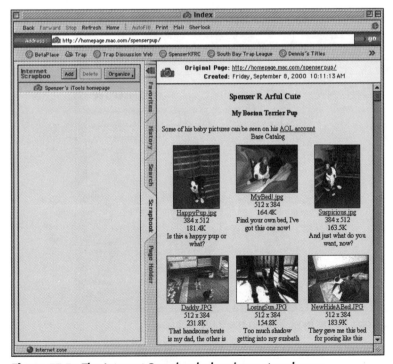

Figure 37-3: The Internet Scrapbook showing a stored page

To add a page to the Scrapbook, load it in your browser window, click the Scrapbook tab to reveal the Internet Scrapbook, and click the Add button.

Use the Organize button to create dividing lines and organizational folders to separate your Scrapbook pages from each other.

If you wish to delete a page from your Scrapbook, select it and click Delete.

When you display a Scrapbook page, you'll see a small camera icon to the left of the URL in the Address bar and a descriptive banner across the top of the page in the content area as shown in Figure 37-3, which tells the URL and the date the page was added to the Scrapbook.

Because many pages have less-than-descriptive names (witness "index" in Figure 37-3), you can Control-click the entry name and choose Edit Name from the shortcut menu.

Page Holder tab

The Page Holder tab makes it easy to browse any page that contains a lot of links. Load the page, click the Place Holder tab, and click the Add button, and you will see the page displayed in the Page Holder area. If you click the Links button, the page will be replaced by a list of all the links on that page, as shown in Figure 37-4, and you can click any of them to browse the page's links, freeing you from repeatedly clicking the Back button to return to the main page.

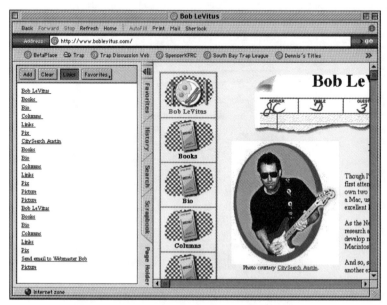

Figure 37-4: Bob's home page links in the Page Holder

You can use the Favorites button to add pages to your Page Holder Favorites. Page Holder Favorites are a folder within your Favorites, similar to Toolbar Favorites. If you open the Page Holder Favorites window (click the Favorites button and choose from the pop-up list) you are presented with a window enabling you to use the Favorites menu to further organize your Page Holder Favorites by grouping them into folders, adding dividing lines, or just reordering them by dragging them into a different order.

Working with Web Pages and Sites

A Web page is a document written with HTML tags, which make the document deliverable to the Web. In the earlier days of the Web, most people posted one page of any length and used hyperlinks to take you from one part of that page to another. These days, people tend to create Web sites, rather than post single pages. A Web site is a collection of HTML pages that link together. As with the hyperlinks that take a user from one part of a page to another, hyperlinks (called links in everyday language) take visitors from one page to another. The same hyperlinks also take a user from one Web site to another.

Rather than create redundant page parts, such as strips of buttons along the side or top of page after page, some people have moved toward using frames. Frames are sections of a browser window. A small frame across the top of a page may contain a banner ad, while another frame along the side contains navigational buttons. The rest of the window is reserved for the page that displays the actual information. Because that's the section visitors are most likely to be interested in, that's the frame they have to click in to print the desired information or save the address of the page as a favorite.

Web pages are not actually solid pages; they are really text documents that contain references to graphics, movies, sounds, other pages, or e-mail addresses. As any page loads into your browser, watch the status bar at the bottom of the screen and you'll see messages whizzing by, telling you as Internet Explorer calls for a page, then a graphic, and then another graphic. For each call, there is a request, a download, and more. The status bar is quite entertaining to watch at times. The status bar also informs you of any problems that the host site may be having if, for example, Internet Explorer makes a request and no response comes for a long period of time.

Visiting a Web site

Web pages appear within the Internet Explorer window, which is called a browser window. When Internet Explorer is launched, one browser window opens automatically. At times, links from pages you visit may open additional browser windows. This enables you to view the information contained in both windows at the same time, rather than switching pages by reloading them. You can also create additional windows at any time by selecting File ➪ New Window, or by clicking and holding the mouse button down (or Control-clicking) in the browser window and selecting Open

Page in New Window from the contextual menu that appears—we call this a *clone*. Both methods enable you to use one of the windows to move on to another site while also viewing the current site. A clone takes the new window to the same site as the current window. New Window either takes you to your home page or to a blank page, depending on your preference settings under Home/Search. If you plan to follow a link from your current page, Open Page in New Window is your best option other than using the Place Holder tab. Otherwise, New Window is faster (if you've deselected the option to have every new window take you to your home page).

Getting to a site

Web surfers have basically two ways to arrive at a Web page the first time: by entering its address (URL) into the address bar and pressing Enter or Return, or by clicking a link that takes you there. This link could be in a Web page or other document that supports hyperlinks, or it could be an Internet Location document on your Desktop. After you've been to a site once, you can return to it in several ways—and you can also come across links in several places. The option to subscribe to a site adds to the number of ways by which you can get to a site—or how a site can get to you. This section covers getting to a Web page.

Remember that while you're at the site, you can mark that site as a favorite site, and then return to it by clicking that favorites icon later. After you leave a site, you can seek it in the History list and return to it by clicking that site's icon.

Using the address bar

As we just mentioned, you can visit a site by clicking in the address bar's text field, typing in the address, and then pressing Enter or Return. This submits the request to the Web and soon your page is sent to you.

To enter an address, you can have Internet Explorer automatically type the `http://www` part of the address by pressing Control and the right arrow. Alternatively, you can type the address manually—make sure you enter the address correctly. Another way to enter an address is to type only the domain part of the address. For example, type **Apple** and Internet Explorer changes it to `http://www.apple.com/`. Technically, with this method, Explorer first attempts to find a local intranet site with this name before looking for it out on the Internet, but this doesn't take much time.

Tip   Some addresses don't include `www` but use other text instead. If the URL you enter doesn't locate the desired site, look closely at the address, edit it if needed, and then press Enter or Return to resubmit the request.

If you have already visited a site, as you begin to enter a site's address, Auto Complete jumps into action, searching your Favorites and History lists for all addresses that contain the address. If AutoComplete finds what it thinks may be the URL you are typing, it suggests that URL by automatically entering it. If this URL is indeed your desired destination, simply press Return or Enter to go there.

If AutoComplete guessed wrong, keep typing. AutoComplete will try again, and again, until you accept its guess or type your own.

AutoComplete is actually a full automatic search. As you enter a site's address, or just part of it, Internet Explorer searches your Favorites and History lists for all addresses that contain the address or word you entered. The results of this search appear in a pop-up list below the address bar. If you drag down to select any address from this list, you are taken to that page. The cool thing here is that you can enter only part of an address and Internet Explorer lists all matches for that word. For example, if you know you once visited a site about balloons, just begin typing **balloons**. By the time you type **bal**, AutoComplete may already fill in the first balloons site you've visited. If there was more than one, the arrow also becomes active so that you can click the arrow to see the complete list of balloon sites you've been to. By selecting any one of those balloon sites from the list, you are returned to that site.

Note AutoComplete can be turned off or on by clicking the Preferences button, selecting the section called Browser Display, and clicking the checkbox to place a check or remove a check by the Use Address AutoComplete option.

When You Can't Get Through to a Site

When the server you are accessing has a problem, it sends Internet Explorer a message. Internet Explorer should display that error message. If the message isn't being displayed, perhaps you have turned off this capability. To check or change this, choose Edit ⇨ Preferences (⌘-;) and then click Advanced. You want to have Show Server Messages checked.

One message you might receive is, "The specified server could not be found." In this case, you've most likely mistyped the URL, the URL was given to you incorrectly, or it is no longer a valid address. Try entering it again or use a search site to verify the address. Some Web servers are case-sensitive, so it is always a good idea to make sure that the capitalization matches. If you are accessing the Web from a corporate work site, you may be behind a firewall and have the proxy server setting wrong. In that case, check with your computer personnel.

Another message you might receive is, "The attempt to load 'http://www.something.com' failed." In case you typed the URL incorrectly, try retyping it. While you're at it, check that you entered the right addressing protocol (for example, `http://`, `http://www`, or `ftp://`). Also try deleting any extra path information — the text after the domain name that is divided by slashes — and see if you can get to the main page. If you are using a modem to connect to the Web, and Internet Explorer initiated the connection (started Remote Access and dialed the modem) when you entered the address, the connection may not have gone through. Open your Remote Access control panel, disconnect and reconnect, and then try the URL again. There's also a chance that the site's server is down or busy. In that case, try again later.

Using the Open command

Another way to visit a page is to choose File ⇨ Open Location (⌘-L). Internet Explorer will select the text in the Address bar and wait for you to type, or begin to type, the address.

Using Apple's Data Detectors

Apple's Data Detectors intelligently extract Internet-related data from bodies of text, and offer you various appropriate actions. For example, if you have a sentence that contains a URL, you can select the sentence, and then Control-click it to reveal contextual menu (or shortcut menu) of actions from which to choose. With the Internet Data Detectors installed, you can launch Internet Explorer and be taken to the address noted in your text.

Using the History tab

The History tab retains a complete list of the sites that you've visited. As days pass, sites are automatically filed into folders according to the day they were visited. You can click any address in the History tab to return to that site. See the section on the History tab for details.

Using the Favorites tab

If you think that you might want to return to a site, it's a good idea to designate that site as a favorite. You fully control what sites are listed here, what order they appear in, what folder (if any) a site appears in, where dividing lines are placed, and so on. See the section on the Favorites tab for details.

Using the Place Holder tab

Just as with the Favorites tab, you can use the Place Holder tab (and Place Holder Favorites) to facilitate access to sites you visit frequently. These pages can also be HTML files on your disk. See the section on the Place Holder tab for details.

Clicking links

More than anything else, you're most likely to use links to get around the Web. Regardless of how you get to the first page you visit, links are what take you to the subsequent pages within a site. By the way, buttons or graphics that you click within a page are also links. As often as not, links lead you out of your original site and into another, and another. . . . In the earlier days of the Web, you probably arrived at your first destination by entering an address. These days, links can be found in any Office 2001 (Mac) or Office 2000 (Windows) document, in any AppleWorks 6 (Mac or Windows) document, in e-mail from Outlook Express or Entourage, and in several other types of documents. Clicking any of these links connect you to the Web and take you to their destinations (as long as your Mac has an Internet connection or allows connections). The process is very straightforward: click and go.

Speeding Up Your Viewing Time

We have written about you visiting a Web page, but actually, the page visits you. When you view a page, that page is downloaded to your Mac. Although it appears to you as one page, it is not one element. Often a page is composed of several elements—and that requires several separate downloads from the page's host to your own computer. That's why you see the text appear first (as the text is downloaded), and then a graphic appears (as it is downloaded), and then another graphic appears (as it is downloaded), and so on. By enabling Internet Explorer to make several concurrent connections, several elements can download simultaneously.

By default, Internet Explorer is set to allow four simultaneous connections, as the Internet Explorer programmers found this most efficient when downloading one page from one server. You can check or change this option by choosing Edit ➪ Preferences, and then clicking Advanced. The Support Multiple Connections box should be checked. The Max Connections number should be 4. You can set this number as high as 8, but any number over 4 will only be a benefit if you are downloading many files from several servers simultaneously. If you have a fast Mac with a fast connection, you might as well set the number higher.

You can tell you're at a link when your cursor changes from an arrow to a pointing hand icon. Unless you're in a frame, you can also tell where the link leads to by looking in the status bar (at the bottom-left of the browser window).

Normally when you click a link, the new page replaces the one you're in within your current browser window. If you prefer to open a link within a new window, instead of clicking quickly on the link, either Control-click or keep the mouse pressed a bit longer until a shortcut menu appears, and then select Open Link in New Window.

Stopping a page

If a page is taking too long to appear, or if you decide that it's not of interest to you, click the Stop button, choose View ➪ Stop Loading, or press ⌘-. (period) (the Mac's universal stop command).

Subscribing to a site

Subscriptions can either be like the ones that bring newspapers to your home (by bringing a Web site to you) or they can simply bring you the notification that a Web site has changed, so that you can return to the site and check out the new information. You can subscribe to any site and handle each one differently. There is no cost or registration process. It's totally up to you to tell Internet Explorer how often to check the site for changes and what to do when the site does change.

If you have not yet marked a site as a favorite, you can subscribe to it and add it to your Favorites list at the same time. To do so, while at the site, select Favorites ➪ Subscribe. This opens the Subscribe alert box shown in Figure 37-5. To use the default notification and scheduling, simply click Subscribe. Click Customize to open the Get Info dialog box and set unique scheduling and notification for this site. If you click Customize, you are presented with the set of tabs shown in Figure 37-6.

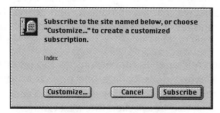

Figure 37-5: The Subscription dialog box

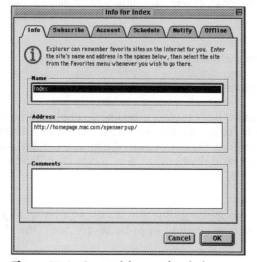

Figure 37-6: Customizing a subscription

If the site you want to subscribe to is already one of your favorites, the fastest way to subscribe is to click in the column to the left of the site's icon (either in the Favorites tab or in the Favorites window). When you do, a subscription (newspaper) icon appears to mark it as subscribed and the default subscription preferences go into effect. Double-click the subscription icon to customize these settings in the Get Info dialog box.

A longer route to subscribing to one of your favorites is to click the Favorites button (or choose Favorites ➪ Organize Favorites), click the site to select it, and then choose File ➪ Get Info. In the Get Info dialog box, click the Subscribe tab, and then check the Check This Site For Changes box.

Across-the-board subscription preferences can be changed any time. To change them, select Edit ⇨ Preferences (or press ⌘-;), and then click Subscriptions. First, click a radio button to tell Internet Explorer how often you want it to check for updates (manual updates only, check each time Explorer is launched, or check every *x* minutes, hours, or days — you determine *x*). Then tell Explorer how to inform you of the change. This can be by sound, an alert, flashing the Explorer icon, by sending an e-mail, or by some combination of the preceding methods.

Caution   If you tell Explorer to check a subscription's content at a specific time interval, Explorer checks that site at that interval when it is running. This means that if you use a modem to dial into the Internet and have set Remote Access to start when an application needs it, Remote Access will automatically dial up your account and connect. This can be bothersome if you are working on something at the time.

Icons help keep you informed about the status of your subscriptions, as demonstrated in Figure 37-7. The newspaper icon indicates that your subscription is up-to-date. The light blue star icon tells you that the page has changed since you last visited. The Caution alert icon — an exclamation point in an orange triangle — informs you the page could not be checked for updates. Double-click this icon to learn more about the alert.

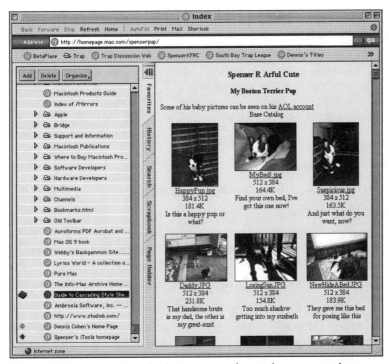

Figure 37-7: Three subscribed sites — two changed, one up to date

You can check for updates manually by choosing Favorites ⇨ Update Subscriptions (⌘-U), which is handy if you need to check for updates between Internet Explorer's designated checks. You'll also need this if, for some reason, you elected not to have an icon or other notification tell you about a site change.

When you no longer want to subscribe to a page, simply click the subscription icon to turn it off. Alternatively, you can double-click the subscription icon and uncheck the option to check the site for changes.

Tip   If you prefer to have the site's contents delivered to you as an archive that you can read while offline, you can do so in the Get Info box for that site. This feature works the same for a subscription as it does for a channel; it's basically an automatic archive feature. (See "Browsing Offline" for more information on archives.) By selecting the offline option in the Offline tab, you tell Explorer to archive the site to your hard drive. While you're there, designate a folder to have the site downloaded into. By clicking Options, you can set the components to download. Use this tab in conjunction with the default timing options or the Schedule tab to control the frequency and time of your downloads. Don't forget that if you set the download for the middle of the night, your Mac must be on. You can use the Energy Saver control panel along with this option to turn your Mac on for downloading or off after downloading.

Tracking auctions

Similar to subscribing to a site, Internet Explorer 5 added the capability of tracking online auction involvement for you, freeing you to visit other Web pages without having to repeatedly return to the auction site.

To track an auction, perform these steps:

1. Load the page of the auction that you want to track

2. Choose Tools ⇨ Track Auction

3. If you are registered with the auction site, type your ID in the User ID box.

4. Do one of the following:

   • If you want to specify custom scheduling or notification for this auction, click the Customize button and select the option you want from the dialog which appears.

   • If you are satisfied with the default settings in your Preferences, click Track.

Caution   If Internet Explorer is unable to ascertain when an auction is due to close, choose Tools ⇨ Auction Manager and enter that information in the Auction Close area on the Description tab for that auction.

The Auction Manager window will now appear with your tracked auction(s) listed, as shown in Figure 37-8.

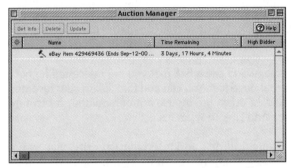

Figure 37-8: The Auction Manager window tells you about your tracked auctions.

Marking favorite sites for easy return

Cyberspace is vast — and incredibly easy to take exciting detours in as you follow links from one page to another. As you come across a page you are interested in, you may want to note its location so that you can return to it later. In Internet Explorer, this bookmarking is called adding an address to your list of favorites.

Some people go wild marking every site they come across as a favorite site. Others explore several pages within a site or as the result of a search, and then return to the one of most interest and only add that one. The History tab tracks your travels as you explore, enabling you to relax and enjoy the trip. You can then look over your History list later, and move sites of interest into the Favorites tab or Place Holder tab. This has a downside, though, as the titles of each page may not be enough to remind you which pages were worthy of your return. In that case, you need to Control-click the title, choose Edit Name from the shortcut menu, and give it a new name that will better remind you of what it is.

If you don't mark a site in your Favorites list, you might still find it another way. You may opt to save e-mail messages with links (of course, you'd have to return to that e-mail to find the link). And you can always perform a search by keyword(s) to return to sites of interest.

One thing is certain, however: You will find yourself with an ever-growing list of favorites as you spend more time in cyberspace.

Adding a favorite

You have several ways to add a page to your list of favorites, depending on what you're doing, where you are, or what you've done. Because Place Holder Favorites are saved in your Favorites, all of the following applies to them as well.

The most obvious time to add a page to your Favorites list is while you are visiting the page. The easiest way to add a page is to Control-click within the page/frame, or to click within the page/frame and hold the mouse until the shortcut menu appears. Then drag down to the Add Page to Favorites command and release the mouse button. Another option is to select Favorites ⇨ Add Page to Favorites. (You could use the keyboard equivalent, ⌘-D, but because that's usually the Delete command in Mac software, we don't recommend you get in the habit of using it.)

Tip   At times you may be on a page and see a link that you are interested in, but you may not have time to visit that page first. You can add that link to your favorites list by clicking that link and holding down the mouse button until the shortcut menu pops up, and then selecting Add Link To Favorites.

If you've already visited the page, but didn't add it to your Favorites list, you can open the History tab and drag it from the History tab into the Favorites tab. Because the Favorites tab is not open, move the icon over the Favorites tab and rest it there until the Favorites tab becomes active. Then release the mouse when the icon will land where you want it. A black line indicates where the icon will land when you release the mouse.

Note   There's another way to move an item from the History to the Favorites list. Click the Favorites tab so that it is showing. Then choose Window ⇨ History (⌘-3) and drag an icon from the History window into the Favorites list. A black line indicates where the icon will land when you release the mouse.

Adding a folder

To make a folder, choose Favorites ⇨ Organize Favorites ⇨ New Folder. Your Favorites list opens in a separate window and the new folder appears there. Naming a folder works the same as naming a folder in the Finder; it is preselected so that you can type a name for it immediately. To rename a folder, click the folder's title to select it and enter a new name. As in the Finder, you can click any favorite in the Favorites window and drag it into any folder. You can also move a folder into a folder. Better than in the Finder, you can move folders into any position in the list.

Renaming a folder or favorite

As we've mentioned, the page designer determines the name that a site is given when you mark it as a favorite — and not all designers are savvy. By renaming a page and giving it a name that you can recognize, you'll make it much easier to find later when you want to return to the site. To rename a site in your Favorites list, choose Favorites ⇨ Organize Favorites to open the Favorites window. While you're in the Favorites window, you can rename items the same way you do in the Finder. Control-click the name, or click the name, keep the mouse button pressed for about two seconds, and choose Edit Name from the shortcut menu. Type a new name or click to place the insertion point, and then edit the item's name.

Adding a divider

Dividing lines can do a lot to make your list easier to use. To add a dividing line, select Favorites ➪ Organize Favorites ➪ New Divider. The Favorites window automatically opens and a new dividing line appears. Click the line and drag it into place between any favorites or folders. As you drag the divider, a black line appears to show you where the line is due to land when you release the mouse. After you've added a few lines, you can move favorites and/or folders into any order between the dividers.

Deleting a favorite

Deleting is easy — another reason that marking a site as a favorite is better than not marking it and trying to find it again later. When you no longer want to save a favorite, choose Favorites ➪ Organize Favorites to open the Favorites window. Then drag the item to the Trash as you do with any file in a Finder window. You can also Control-click the item and choose Delete from the shortcut menu. This removes the item without placing it in the Trash.

Controlling how you see Web sites

You control much of how you — a visitor to a site — see the pages delivered to your Mac. You can select colors, turn images, videos, and sounds on or off, and more. Distributed among the various panes of the Preferences dialog box are the many changes you can make (see Figure 37-9 for one set of them). In many cases, you may be happy with the default. However, it's worth a visit to this dialog box to see what your options are. For page-viewing options, check out the Web Content, Browser Display, and Language/Fonts panes.

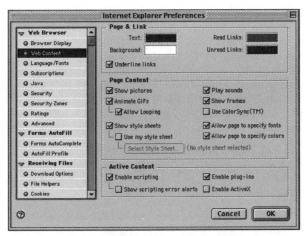

Figure 37-9: The Web Content pane and its options

Fonts

Fonts play a large role in how we perceive a message. However, a Web page is not like a printed page, as a Web page designer has no control over what fonts viewers have on their hard drives. It is quite possible for a viewer to select any font and make it any size. One option is to make messages into images, therefore protecting the look of the text. However, a viewer can turn off image loading to speed up delivery of information over his or her modem. That means the viewer doesn't get the message the image contained. If the designer is savvy, alternate image tags may present at least part of the image's text message, but it's not the same as seeing the works nicely laid out. To address this issue, HTML now includes something known as style sheets (the first bullet point). Among the choices you can make within the Web Content pane are the following:

✦ **Show Style Sheets.** Style sheets are similar to the styles you can set up in Word to predefine the look of a body of text. With style sheets, a Web page designer can control margins, line spacing, text placement, text colors, font faces, font sizes, and graphics placement. Designers have to worry about style sheets; all you have to do is take advantage of them. You, as the viewer, have the ability to recognize the use of style sheets or not, although you have no real reason not to. To make sure style sheets are recognized, choose Edit ➪ Preferences, and then select the Web Content pane, and check the Show Style Sheets box. If you are savvy enough with style sheets, you can point Internet Explorer at your own style sheet.

✦ **Allow page to specify colors.** Designers work hard to make their pages look good, but if the colors don't work for you or if you're color-blind, you can take control of the colors you see by turning this option off in the Web Content pane.

✦ **Allow page to specify fonts.** As with colors, you can use what is sent to you or choose to override them by unchecking Allow page to specify fonts in the Web Content pane. This forces the page to use the fonts you select. (See the next point. Yes, we know it's also about fonts, but it's a different preference.)

✦ **Font.** If you find pages hard to read, choose Edit ➪ Preferences, and then click Language/Fonts and choose a font(s) that is easier on your eyes. You can designate two (one serif, one sans serif) for display of all proportional text and one for fixed-width text. Most fonts on your Mac are proportional. Common sans serif fonts include Helvetica and Arial, while Times and Palatino are common serif fonts. The two common fixed-width fonts are Courier (the typewriter font) and Monaco.

✦ **Font Size.** If the text on Web pages appears too small or too large, select Edit ➪ Preferences and then Language/Fonts. At the top of the Fonts and Size section, select a font size from the pop-up menu. When you return to your current page, it will reload to reflect the change.

✦ **Language.** You can select the language selected by default in cases in which a site offers its pages in more than one language. English is the default if you have an English version of Office 2001. To change the language, choose Edit ➪ Preferences and then Language/Fonts.

Working with Cookies

Since their inception, there has been a lot of controversy over *cookies*. A spy doesn't sneak a cookie into your computer to steal data. A cookie is just a bit of information a Web page's server sends to a file on your computer. Later, when you revisit that page or site, the information in that cookie is returned to the Web site so it can recognize you. Don't worry—a cookie doesn't have your social security number or any such thing; a cookie is usually a randomly generated number. Databases often rely on cookies to make sure the information that you request gets back to you.

You have full control of the cookies on your Mac. To see for yourself and to review your options, click the Preferences button, and then select the Cookies pane (under Receiving Files). The following controls are offered:

✦ Use the When Receiving Cookies pop-up menu to select the option with which you are most comfortable. Perhaps you want to decide on a site-to-site basis, or maybe you don't mind accepting any cookie. If you choose Ask for each site, you can predetermine whether you accept a site or not. To do so, click the cookie in question, and then click the button that pertains to your options. For example, if you previously had your preference set to Always accept cookies, and then switch to Ask for each site, the option you have for each cookie is to Decline.

✦ You can view the information within a cookie by selecting the cookie and clicking the View button.

✦ You can delete a cookie by selecting the cookie and clicking the Delete button. If you delete a cookie, the next time you visit that cookie's site, a new cookie downloads.

Other page content

As we mentioned, you have the option to turn off each of the special effects available. You'll find many in the Web Content pane of the Preferences dialog box, but you can change other effects as well. If speed is an issue, you can try turning off sound, video, and/or pictures. If you feel you need to see any or all of the pictures while viewing a site, you can. Click the image-missing icon for any single image, and then click and hold while you select Load Missing Image. Or, choose View ⇨ Load Images to view them all.

Note   The Mac can do some incredible tricks thanks to QuickTime, QuickTime VR, and QuickDraw 3D/VRML. These are all extensions that come with your system installer. We recommend that you install them and keep them on if you really want to take advantage of the Mac. (Actually, this technology has become the standard, so everyone will have it soon.)

Plug-ins

A plug-in is a small program that adds extra functionality to a browser. If a page designer has created a page that calls for a certain plug-in, you must download and install that plug-in before you can see that page properly. Sometimes you can still enjoy a page without the plug-in; at other times, the entire page depends upon the plug-in. You will most likely be alerted when a plug-in is required. You will also be given the opportunity to download the plug-in. To install a plug-in, you need to place it in the Plug-ins folder inside your Internet Explorer 5 folder — probably after decompressing it. You also need to relaunch Internet Explorer. Plug-ins share RAM with Internet Explorer, so as you add plug-ins, you may need to allot more memory to Explorer.

Searching Web sites

The Web is full of information just waiting to be discovered. Knowing how to search for it is the key to finding it. Internet Explorer provides several search options.

Using search engines

While Internet Explorer provides several ways to search, it's the search engines on the Web that do the actual searching. Internet Explorer simply makes the pages of the search engines easily accessible. To search, you visit — download — the search engine's search page. In the fields provided, you enter your search criteria. Then you click Search (or something to that effect) and your request is processed, returning a results page to you. A results page always contains some sort of brief description of the sites found and a link to each site found.

To access the search engines, use one of these methods:

✦ **The Search tab in the Explorer bar.** The Search tab of the Explorer bar provides quick access to several search engines. Click the Search tab, and then either use the provider of the day, which is automatically chosen as a special search page set up by Microsoft, or select the provider of your choice from the pop-up list. (If the Explorer bar is not showing, choose View ➪ Explorer Bar, or press ⌘-T.) One excellent benefit to this tab is you can see the results of your search in the tab while you click the resulting links to see where they lead.

✦ **The address bar.** Internet Explorer's AutoSearch enables you to search directly from the address bar without going to a specific search page first. Click in the address bar and type **go** or **?** (a question mark), and then a space, followed by the word you want to search for. Then press Enter or Return, as you do whenever you enter an address in this field. Internet Explorer does the rest, taking you to a special search page provided by Microsoft that displays your results.

Searching for text

As in a regular document, you can search for specific text within a Web page. The command is the same as it usually is on the Mac — Find and Find Again. To find text, select Edit ⇨ Find (⌘-F).

In the Find dialog box, enter the text you are seeking. Check Match Case if you want only the same pattern of capital and lowercase letters to be found. Leave it unchecked if you don't care about capitalization. In the example in Figure 37-10, we are searching for Chocolate, but only for occurrences of the word with a capital C. To begin your search from wherever your cursor is, leave the Start From Top option unchecked. To start your search at the top of the page, check Start From Top, as we did in our quest for Chocolate.

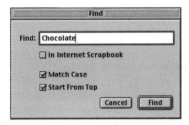

Figure 37-10: The Find dialog box — searching for Chocolate with a capital C

After entering your criteria, click Find to locate the first occurrence of the text you seek. To find subsequent occurrences of that text, select Edit ⇨ Find Again (⌘-G). ⌘-G is easier to use. Keep pressing ⌘-G and each occurrence of your desired text appears highlighted on the Web page.

To search beyond the current page and check an entire Web site, you need to use a search engine.

Browsing offline

Internet Explorer provides a few features that make it possible to review Web content without being connected to the Internet. This is a terrific feature if you want to work while commuting, access the Web at school but not at home, or if you pay for your connection time. To check a site on a regular basis, subscribe to the site and set it to download for offline browsing.

While you are still online, visit each site in which you are interested, but instead of reading it, archive it. An archive is a single file that can contain every graphic, sound, movie, and link, in addition to all the site's text. By double-clicking the file, the archive opens and you have, in effect, the entire Web site, complete with working links. That way you can read the site at your leisure — even when you're not connected to the Internet.

When you create your archive, you set the option to save any number of links that connect from the site. While viewing offline, eventually, you may get to a link that is beyond what you elected to save. (After all, the Web keeps going and going.) If you click a link that was not included in your archive, you see a message, as shown in Figure 37-11. While offline, click Cancel.

Figure 37-11: The offline alert asking to connect

For more on saving a site as an archive, see "Downloading and Saving Files."

When you subscribe to a site (see "Subscribing to a Site"), rather than accepting the default options, click Customize to bring up the Get Info window. In this window, be sure to select the Offline tab, as shown in Figure 37-12 and check the Download This Site for Offline Browsing option as shown. As with archiving, click Options to determine which accompanying files will be downloaded.

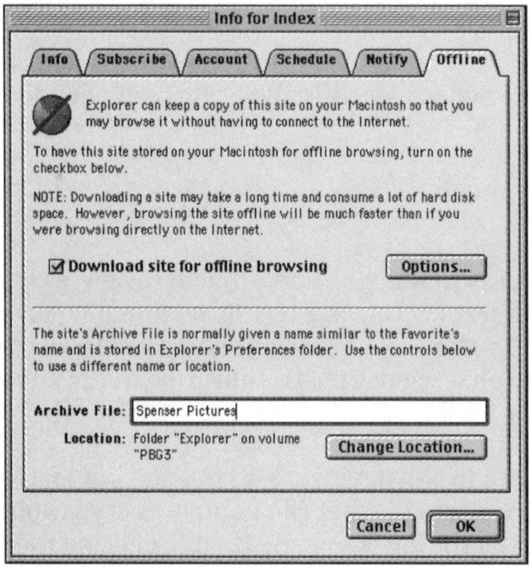

Figure 37-12: Automatic delivery of a site archive is set in this tab.

Even though you have access to the Internet, there may be times when you do not wish to connect. In that case, be sure to select File ➪ Work Offline. That way, when you click links that would otherwise attempt a Web connection, they will not do so.

Downloading and Saving Files

You have several ways to save the information found on the Web and keep it for your own reference. This section covers your options. Please remember that material on the Web was created by people who may have worked very hard on it and the creators of the material retain the rights to the material. (Just because it's easy to copy material doesn't make it legal to copy it.)

Copying

The easiest way to transfer text from a Web page is to copy it, and then paste in into your Notepad, organizer, document, and so on. Simply drag over the text to select it and choose Edit ➪ Copy (⌘-C) the same way you select text and copy it in any Mac document. Then paste the text into your destination document.

Links can be tricky to copy by selecting. Try starting at the end of the link text, rather than the left side. The easiest way to copy a link is to either Control-click the link or click the link, and then hold the mouse button down until the shortcut menu pops up. From the menu, select Copy Link to Clipboard. Then paste as normal.

To copy an image for pasting, click the image, holding the mouse button down until the shortcut menu pops up, and then select Copy Image. Paste this copied image as normal.

Tip   Some images also serve as links. Similarly, some images are collections of links (these are called *image maps*). When you Control-click one of these, the shortcut menu will be longer and you have the choice of either the link or the image. Choose the one you want.

Saving a file

While you are viewing a Web page, you can save it as plain text, as HTML code, or as an Internet Explorer archive. All of these are done via the File ➪ Save As command.

✦ Saving as Plain Text is easiest if you want to show someone the content of the page. You'll be able to open the document in SimpleText or in a word processor. However, images and formatting are lost this way.

✦ Saving as HTML Source enables you to see the page as it was created. It's a great way to learn how to create your own Web pages. This method doesn't download the images, however.

✦ Saving as an archive saves the entire site, not just the page you are on. Saving as an archive can also download the page's images, sounds, movies, and/or links at the same time. (Click the Options button to determine what will be downloaded.) You can also choose how many links deep you want to go — up to five. Archiving a site, or page enables you to read it offline. To view an archived site, double-click it in the Finder.

Choose File ➪ Save As, and then click the Format pop-up menu to select Plain Text, HTML Source, or Web Archive. As your download takes place, the Download Manager window reports its progress. To learn more about the downloaded item, double-click the item in the window. See "Reviewing Your Downloads."

Note   To preserve the look of text, it has been common for designers to use graphics that contain text, rather than using plain text. Therefore, if you save a site without saving the graphics, you may be missing important information. When saving as HTML, you need to be sure to save each important graphic as a separate save. The easiest solution is to save the site as an archive, remembering to click the Options button and to make sure you are saving the images and any other components that are important to your appreciation of the site.

Downloading

Downloading a file, text, link, or image creates a new file on your hard drive (as does the Save As command but not the Copy command). This file can be opened later and handled however you want.

Tip   For easy access to your downloads, make the folder you elect to collect your downloaded files easily accessible. You might make an alias of this folder, and then place that alias in the Apple menu, or in a folder within that menu. Another possibility is to make it a pop-up folder so that its tab will be readily accessible at the bottom of your screen.

Decoding Files

To travel through cyberspace, files must be encoded and often compressed to make transfers faster. Aladdin's StuffIt Deluxe is the de facto standard for compression on the Mac. Aladdin provides a free decompressor called StuffIt Expander (also available for Windows as Aladdin Expander). You'll know these files by the extension .sit (for StuffIt), .bin, or .hqx (which stand for an encoding process called BinHex — Versions 5 and 4, respectively). At present, StuffIt Expander is not installed by Internet Explorer or by any of the other Office 2001 programs, but it is automatically installed in your Internet folder when you do an OS install. We highly recommend that you download this application if you don't already have StuffIt Deluxe. StuffIt Expander is freeware and is available at www.aladinsys.com. After StuffIt Expander is installed, you can drag any .bin, .hqx, or .sit file onto the program's icon to decode and expand the file. Current versions of StuffIt Expander will also decompress .zip (the Windows standard) archives.

To download an image, either Control-click the image or click the image and hold the mouse button down until the shortcut menu pops up, and then select Download Image To Disk from the shortcut menu.

Sounds, and sometimes videos, are not actually in the Web page but are links the page retrieves at the user's request. Therefore, to download sounds, select Download Link To Disk from the shortcut menu. (Clicking quickly on a sound link plays the sound instead of presenting the menu, so be sure to either Control-click or hold the mouse button down when you click the sound's link or icon.)

If a movie has been embedded in the page, the shortcut menu offers Save Movie As, rather than the Download Link To Disk command. To download an embedded movie, select Save Movie As. In this case, the Download Manager won't track the download.

In each case, as when you save any file, you must choose a folder in which to save the file, and then name or rename the file and click Save.

Note　The truth is that images are also not actually in a Web page; they are referred to by the page and downloaded separately. It just so happens that the command to save them to disk is a different one from the command to download a sound or movie link.

To download an entire page if you are already there, select the URL in the Address box and press Option-Return. This opens the Download Manager window so that you can watch the progress, as shown in Figure 37-13. It's okay to continue working in Internet Explorer as a file downloads. Internet Explorer works in the background.

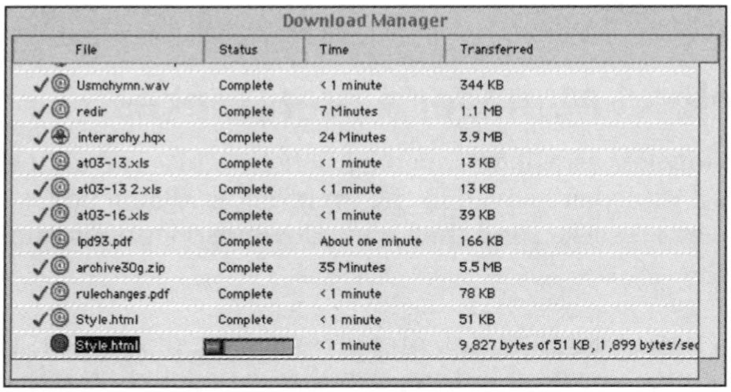

File	Status	Time	Transferred
✓ 🔘 Usmohymn.wav	Complete	< 1 minute	344 KB
✓ 🔘 redir	Complete	7 Minutes	1.1 MB
✓ ⊕ interarohy.hqx	Complete	24 Minutes	3.9 MB
✓ 🔘 at03-13.xls	Complete	< 1 minute	13 KB
✓ 🔘 at03-13 2.xls	Complete	< 1 minute	13 KB
✓ 🔘 at03-16.xls	Complete	< 1 minute	39 KB
✓ 🔘 ipd93.pdf	Complete	About one minute	166 KB
✓ 🔘 archive30g.zip	Complete	35 Minutes	5.5 MB
✓ 🔘 rulechanges.pdf	Complete	< 1 minute	78 KB
✓ 🔘 Style.html	Complete	< 1 minute	51 KB
🔘 Style.html	▭▭▭	< 1 minute	9,827 bytes of 51 KB, 1,899 bytes/sec

Download Manager

Figure 37-13: The Download Manager tracking a download's progress

Stopping a download

To stop a file from downloading once you've started the download, select View ➪ Stop Loading (⌘-.). This file will be listed as Canceled in the Download Manager.

Reviewing your downloads

If you can't recall where you saved a file or aren't sure the file downloaded success-fully, check with the Download Manager, shown previously in Figure 37-13. To open the Download Manager, select Window ➪ Download Manager or Tools ➪ Download Manager (⌘-M). When a file is downloaded successfully, a green checkmark appears beside it and `complete` appears in the Status column. You can sort the list by any column header by clicking that header. Therefore, you can sort by filename, status, the time it took to download, or the size of the file transferred. To resize a column for easier reading, move your mouse pointer over the crosshatched area in the header until your pointer becomes a hand. Then click and drag the column to size. Double-click a filename to reveal information about the file, such as the folder that file landed in. The file in Figure 37-14 was successful and was stored in the Downloads folder of the disk Spenser.

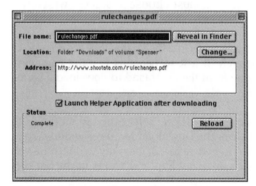

Figure 37-14: Details of a download

Setting the Download Manager's preferences

You can determine where downloads will be saved by default. This, and all the other Download Manager's settings are saved in the Preferences dialog box, so choose Edit ➪ Preferences, or press ⌘-;, and then click Download Options under Receiving Files.

The currently selected location is noted in the top portion of the dialog box. To change folders, click the Change Location button, and then navigate to the folder you want your downloaded files to land in. If you always want your files to land in that folder, click the radio button for this option. The alternative is to let files go to folders that the appropriate helpers send files to. For example, if you use StuffIt Expander to translate and decompress files, and you've set StuffIt Expander to decompress to a folder called InBox, then a downloaded unstuffed file would land in the InBox rather than in the folder designated by the Download Manager. In gen-eral, this location is the one specified in your Internet control panel preferences on the Web tab.

You can control how many files you can download at one time by choosing a number from the pop-up box labeled Maximum number of concurrent downloads.

If the Download Manager does not list the files that you download, select the radio button marked Immediately remove items after they have been downloaded. Otherwise, keep the default, which is to track all downloads and enter the maximum number of downloads you want tracked in the list. By the way, you can always delete a listing from the Download Manager's window by dragging it from the window to the Mac's Trash folder, or by Control-clicking and choosing Delete from the shortcut menu.

Automatic decoding of files is very handy and makes the Internet less confusing. Keep the two decoding options checked.

Printing Web Pages

Web pages are printed just like any other document. Go to the page, and then select File ➪ Print or ⌘-P. Frames are the only tricky thing to print. To print the page contained within a frame, click inside the frame before you give the print command. If you want images to print, be sure to turn them on in Preferences first. If you see images on your screen, they are on. If they are off, you see a red circle and white X.

Dealing with Security Concerns

To make your exchanges on the Web as secure as possible, Internet Explorer supports various security standards, which are described as follows.

Site certificates

When a Web site wants its users to be confident of the site's security, it can apply for a certificate. These certificates are not given out lightly. They are costly and the site is rigorously tested to make sure it meets the demands of the issuer. Internet Explorer is set up to recognize trusted certificates. You can choose which ones you want to accept or ignore by checking or unchecking each one in the Security pane of the Preferences dialog box.

Security zones

Security zones are a set of four zones, set by you, each bearing a security level. You then assign any site to a zone. As you call on a site, Internet Explorer notes the zone and checks the security setting for that site's zone. You can always tell which zone you are accessing by looking in the status bar.

The four zones are as follows:

✦ **Local Intranet.** Assigned a Medium security level by default. These are the addresses on your company or group's intranet, placed there by your system administrator. This administrator can also add new addresses to this zone.

✦ **Trusted Sites.** Assigned a Low security level by default, which is probably all that is needed here. These are the sites that you trust. They feel safe to download or run files from.

✦ **Restricted Sites.** Assigned a High security level by default, which is probably needed here. These are the sites that you aren't sure of. They may be fine, but you have no way of knowing whether accessing files from these sites is safe.

✦ **Internet zone.** Medium-level security is assigned here. This is the rest of the Internet. You've weeded out and marked the sites that you don't trust, and marked the sites you do trust. You know your intranet and your own hard drive are safe. This is everything else. You don't assign every single site in existence to a level; this is the catchall for that.

Each zone is preset with a set of permitted actions and alerts. You can use these or customize your own permissions for each zone. For example, you can allow full access—running and downloading—of files in your intranet zone; therefore setting security to Low. For sites in the restricted zone, you can prevent any active exchange—no running of scripts, no downloading, no active content.

The first step is to determine which security level you want for each zone. To do so, choose Edit ➪ Preferences, and then click Security Zones, as shown in Figure 37-15. Select the zone that you want to effect from the Zone pop-up menu, and then click one of the four radio buttons to set a security level.

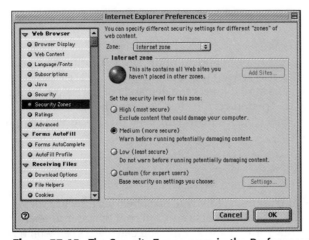

Figure 37-15: The Security Zones pane in the Preferences dialog box

The next step is to assign each Web site to a security zone. To do so, choose Edit ⇨ Preferences, and then click Security Zones. Only the system administrator sets up the Local Intranet zone, and the Internet zone is all the sites that are otherwise not assigned. That leaves the Trusted Sites zone and the Restricted Sites zone for site assignment, so choose one of these from the Zone menu. When you do, the Add Sites button becomes active. Click Add Sites to open a sites list dialog box. Click the next Add button, and then enter a URL for the Web site you are assigning to that zone and click OK. For example, in Figure 37-16 we show the addition of bighit.com into our zone. Figure 37-17 shows the sites in our Trusted sites list.

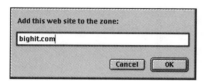

Figure 37-16: Adding a site to a zone

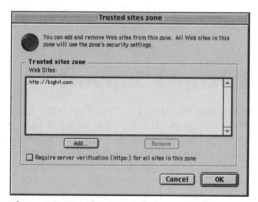

Figure 37-17: The Trusted sites zone list

Security alerts

Security alerts are warnings that appear when you attempt to access, submit, or download items that are potential security risks. An alert may be helpful to remind you — or the users of the Mac in use — that a site is not secure. It may help users think twice before sending such details as account or client information.

To display security alerts, choose Edit ⇨ Preferences, and then click Security. This brings up the Security pane, as shown in Figure 37-18. Add or remove checks to activate or deactivate the alerts you want in effect.

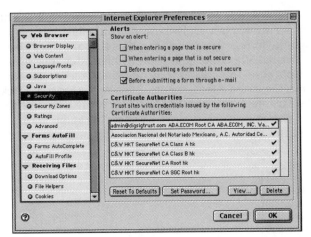

Figure 37-18: Security alerts and certificates settings

Tip   Besides relying on alerts, it is helpful to train yourself and users to notice the lock icon (or lack thereof) in the status bar.

Working with Internet Ratings Support

In case you have family or business members accessing the Internet from your Mac, Internet Explorer provides the capability to control the types of content that your computer can access on the Internet. By turning on Internet Ratings and by password protecting your settings, you can ensure that only the content that meets your criteria is accessed and viewed.

To set up your content screening, click the Preferences button, and then click Ratings to select the Ratings Preferences pane, as shown in Figure 37-19.

Then, follow these steps:

1. By default ratings are turned off, so click Enabled to turn them on.

2. Ratings screening doesn't mean much if anyone can change the settings. By default no password is necessary, so click Change Password and enter a password in the New Password field — not the top field. To make sure you've entered the desired word correctly, you must type it again.

   Notice that you can change your password at any time. But no matter what — remember your password! You will need it to change the ratings.

3. Use the pop-up menu by each of the four categories: Violence, Sex, Nudity, and Language to tell Internet Explorer the level you are comfortable with for each of them. Figure 37-20 demonstrates the types of choices you can make for Sex.

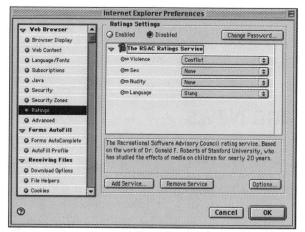

Figure 37-19: Preparing to set up ratings screening

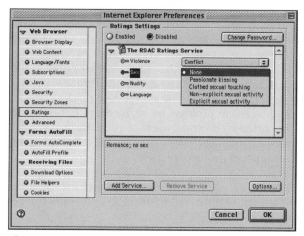

Figure 37-20: Setting up ratings screening

4. *(Optional)* You can allow users to have access to sites that are unrated. To do so, click the Options button, and then check User Can View Sites that Have No Rating.

5. *(Optional)* You can opt to set up Internet Explorer so you can enter your password at any time and give your users access to all restricted sites. To do so, check the option that says Supervisor Can Type a Password to Allow Users to View Restricted Content.

6. *(Optional)* If you want to use a Ratings Bureau, enter the name of the bureau in the Ratings Bureau text field.

Tip   The default rating system is that of the Recreational Software Advisory Council (RSAC) at www.rsac.org. If you prefer, you can elect to choose from other rating services instead. To do so, download these services. Then click Add Service in the Ratings Preferences pane and select the new service.

Reading Mail and News

From Internet Explorer, you can read your e-mail or read your news. You can also send a new e-mail message or even send a new message that automatically includes the URL of the page you are currently on. To do either of these tasks, click and hold the Mail button, which is actually a pop-up menu, and then make your selection. By default, any of these selections opens your default application for that activity. If, when you launched Entourage you agreed to have it be your default client for news or e-mail, then it is the one that will be opened. You can change this so the button opens another program. In fact, you can have one program selected to handle e-mail and another to handle news.

To change your Mail and News program, select Edit ➪ Preferences, and then click Protocol Helpers. Click mailto in the Helpers list, and then click the Change button. In the Protocol Helper Editor that opens, click Choose Helper. Navigate to your e-mail program of choice and click Open. You see the chosen helper noted in the Protocol Helper Editor dialog box. Click OK. Next click news in the Protocol list and repeat the steps to elect your preferred helper—you should also do the same for nntp, as news links can be invoked by either protocol name. By default, the protocols and the helpers available are sorted by protocol (as shown by the underline). To sort by application, click the word Application. These changes are reflected in the Advanced tab of your Internet control panel protocol helpers.

To create a new message and have the body of the message list the URL you are at, go to the Web site you want to note, and then select Send Link from the Mail button's pop-up menu.

Getting More Help

To access Internet Explorer's Help, go to Help ➪ Internet Explorer Help. This Help is a system of linked Web pages presented in frames via Internet Explorer. You can print the pages and change their look the same way that you change any other Web page—just remember to click in the correct frame. If you have disabled frames in your preferences, you will see a window telling you to turn them back on.

Tip   As with most Web pages, the colors the designer set up work well. If you have altered your colors and are having trouble seeing the information, click the Preferences button, click Web Content, and then check Allow Page To Specify Colors.

Click Index to view the Index and select your topic from there. After each topic is a list of related topics. Each related topic is a link, so you can click it to follow it immediately. As with all links, the color changes after you follow it so you can tell where you've already been.

Reference Information is a good place to pick up not only tips and tricks, but also menu command definitions.

The Glossary will help you understand terms you may be unfamiliar with.

An entire newsgroup is also dedicated to using Internet Explorer for the Macintosh. Because it's a newsgroup, its subscription and message exchanges are handled by Entourage — or another newsgroup client, if you have another one that you prefer. Please refer to Chapter 36 to learn about Entourage and newsgroups. You can subscribe to the Internet Explorer for Macintosh list at `microsoft.public.inetexplorer.mac`.

Finally, at `www.microsoft.com/ie/mac`, you find updated announcements about Internet Explorer and possibly more help, tips, and so on.

Summary

This chapter provided an overview of Internet Explorer, Microsoft's Web browser. Points covered in this chapter included the following:

✦ Marking a site as a favorite enables you to revisit it easily.

✦ You can have Internet Explorer notify you when a site's content changes by subscribing to that site.

✦ As you visit sites, Internet Explorer keeps a history of those sites. (You can limit the number of sites tracked by setting this in the Advanced section of your Preferences under Web Browser.)

✦ The Search tab of the Explorer bar makes it easier than ever to seek out Web sites by content. You can do your search within the Explorer bar and continue to view the search results while visiting the found sites.

✦ Internet Explorer supports several security standards. It recognizes site certificates, enables you to set up security zones, and uses security alerts to warn users they are entering an unsecured Web site. It also enables you to use the standardized ratings to help you restrict access to sites by content.

Where to go next

✦ Are you considering placing your own documents on the Web? Chapter 11 covers Word and the Web; Chapter 24 covers Excel and the Web; and Chapter 33 covers PowerPoint and the Web.

✦ Wondering how to send and receive e-mail or access newsgroups? Chapter 36 is standing by to help you do so with Entourage 2001.

✦   ✦   ✦

Installing Microsoft Office 2001

◆ ◆ ◆ ◆

In This Appendix

Getting started

Making a custom installation

Working with the Value Pack

Installing Internet Explorer

◆ ◆ ◆ ◆

The Microsoft Office 2001 CD-ROM includes two installation options — basic and custom — for installing the core Office 2001 applications: Word, Excel, Entourage, and PowerPoint. In addition, Microsoft provides several extras for Office 2001 and an Internet browser.

Getting Started

The basic installation is incredibly easy. You simply drag the Microsoft Office 2001 folder to your hard drive. (This is covered in Chapter 1.) This basic installation may well include all you need — or even more than you need (in which case, you may prefer a custom install).

The Office custom install is an alternative to the standard drag-install, enabling you to install only portions of the standard Office software. It may also contain functions that are not part of the drag-install, but those options are likely to also be available in the Value Pack Installer, which you are more likely to use. The Value Pack folder provides more Office software that complements the standard install. In the Value Pack section of this appendix, we explore each of the options and what it provides for you. The Internet Explorer 5 folder provides Microsoft Internet Explorer, a browser, and support files.

Making a Custom Installation

When should you use the custom installer?

+ If you don't need all the programs and options that the basic Office installation offers, you can choose to do a custom install instead, opting to install only part of the full offering.

+ If you've installed Office 2001 and find you need to reinstall part of the program, a custom install may be your solution.

+ If you have installed only parts of the Office installation and later decide to install other components, use the custom install.

To perform a custom install, follow these steps:

1. Insert the Microsoft Office 2001 CD-ROM and scroll down in the window to display the Microsoft Office Installer icon.

2. Double-click the Microsoft Office Installer to launch this installer application.

3. The Microsoft Office Installer dialog box should be familiar to you if you have ever performed a software installation on the Mac. At the top of the dialog box is a pop-up menu. Click and drag to the option of your choice: Easy Install or Custom Install. Figure A-1 shows the first installer dialog box with Custom Install being selected.

Figure A-1: The Microsoft Office Installer dialog box

• **Easy Install** is the equivalent of the drag-install: it places the same applications and components. If you want this option, select it in the menu and skip to Step 5.

• **Custom Install** is the option you most likely want. If so, check out the next steps.

4. If you choose the Custom Install option, you are presented with another dialog box in which you select the software you want to install. As you click the arrows beside folders in the Finder, you reveal smaller components to install. An X beside a software category indicates that all components within the category will be installed. A horizontal line means not all but some parts will be installed. Check or uncheck each part you want to install or not install. In Figure A-2, the wizards and all the templates will be installed, but only part of the Proofing Tools.

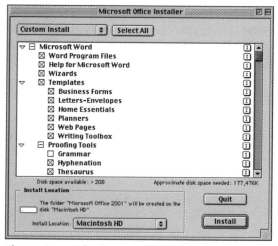

Figure A-2: Selecting software to install

5. Select an install location from the pop-up menu at the bottom of the dialog box. In Figure A-2, Hard Drive is the location where Office will be stored.

You can also choose to select a folder into which Office, or the installed components, will be installed. In Figure A-3, this option is being selected. When you choose Select Folder, you see an open dialog box in which you can navigate to the folder you want, and then click.

Figure A-3: Selecting a new destination for the custom installation

Regardless of where you install, a folder called Microsoft Office 2001 is created — unless you elect to install into an existing Microsoft Office 2001 folder.

6. Click Install (or Remove).

Working with the Value Pack

The Value Pack is one of two places to go for items that will enhance your Office productivity. (The other place to go is www.microsoft.com/macoffice—a site that has new and useful files and tips.)

Installing Value Pack

To install any part of the Value Pack, follow these steps:

1. Insert the Office CD-ROM and double-click the Value Pack folder to open it. (Press Option as you open the folder to close the Microsoft Office 2001 CD window automatically.)

2. Double-click the Value Pack Installer to launch it. (Again, pressing Option as you do will automatically close the Value Pack folder.)

3. The Value Pack Installer dialog box has the same install interface common to most Mac programs—except no Easy Install exists and you are taken directly to the Custom Install with no pop-up menu at the top. Figure A-4 shows the first screen of the Value Pack Installer dialog box.

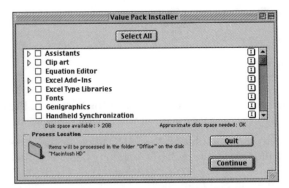

Figure A-4: Value Pack Installer dialog box

4. Check each part you want to install and uncheck what you don't want to install. If an option has more than one component, it has a disclosure triangle beside it (similar to the Finder). Click the triangle to reveal the components. When all components within the category are to be installed, an X appears beside the option. A horizontal line means some, but not all, parts will be installed. In Figure A-4, nothing is set to be installed. To learn a bit more about an option, click the I (Information) button to its right.

As you select items to install, the installer reports the space it will require and lets you know how much space you have available. If you want to install the entire Value Pack, click Select All at the top of the dialog box. Select All is also handy if you want to install most components; it checks everything so all you have to do is uncheck what you don't want. To see your options better, you can make the box longer by dragging the sizing corner at the bottom right.

5. Click Install.

Cross-Reference

To learn more about the Value Pack and its components, double-click Guide to the Value Pack.htm — a Help file inside the Value Pack folder on the Microsoft Office 2001 CD-ROM. This HTML file will launch Internet Explorer by default and uses the support files in the ValuePackGuideSupport folder. You'll get better performance if the guide file and the support folder are copied to your hard disk.

Value Pack contents

To help you decide which Value Pack items are right for you, here's an overview of what each item does.

Assistants

If you have already launched Word, Excel, or PowerPoint, you have probably met the default Office Assistant, Max. He's cute and entertaining, but he's not your only Assistant. By clicking the arrow next to Assistants in the Value Pack Installer, you reveal several more Assistants. Each has its own personality, as described when you click the Information (I) button to its right.

After you do the Value Pack installation, you can give Max a rest and change Assistants at any time. To do so, call up your Assistant, and then click Options in the Assistant's dialog box. Next, click the Gallery tab. Then click the Next and/or Back buttons to check out all your installed Assistants. When you arrive at the one you want, click OK.

Clip art

Clip art, which is discussed in Chapter 10, is predrawn artwork that you may use to spice up your documents or presentations (within the limits of copyright law and the software license agreement). Office 2001 provides plenty of clip art, movies, photos, and animated GIFs, divided into categories. Click the triangle by the check-box to reveal the various libraries of art you can install and use.

Equation editor

Into mathematical equations? If so, this is for you. This application is specifically designed to enable you to create any kind of equation. If you're using such formulas (and don't already own a full-blown version of an Equation editor), this is a must-have.

Excel add-ins

The following is a list of the various Excel add-ins that come with the Office 2001 Value Pack:

+ Analysis Toolpak is a set of statistical and engineering functions.

+ Analysis Toolpak VBA lets you access the Analysis Toolpak functions from Visual Basic for Applications.

+ HTML Add-in provides backward compatibility for Excel 98 worksheets that used the HTML Convert function.

+ Lookup Wizard helps you create formulas to locate data in lists/databases.

+ Report Manager is, as it sounds, an aid in creating reports. After installation, you can access it from View ➪ Report Manager. Report Manager is a simple interface that enables you to add reports with a click of a button.

+ Set Language enables you to set the proofing language to be used by the spelling and grammar checkers.

+ Solver calculates solutions to your what-if scenarios. You'll find Solver in the Tools menu if it has been installed.

+ Update add-in enables you to convert links to functions from previous versions' add-ins that are now built into Excel.

Excel type libraries

Do you have old Excel 5 worksheets (Office 95 for Windows or Office 4.2.1 for the Mac) with VBA routines written in other languages? If so, these worksheets provide localized support for converting those macros to Excel 97–2001 format.

In case you are using VBA macros written in a language other than English, you can install other language type libraries. Language support is there for Danish, Dutch, French, German, Italian, Japanese, Norwegian, Portuguese, Spanish, and Swedish. Excel type library files are stored in the Type Libraries folder inside the Extensions folder in your System folder.

Fonts

Want more fonts to jazz up your documents? Check out these fonts. You have 53 TrueType fonts to explore.

Tip   If you're going to load up on fonts, you might want to try Font Reserve (www. fontreserve.com) by DiamondSoft; that way you don't have to install all the fonts into your system, but you have easy access to them. Another possibility is Suitcase (www.extensis.com) from Extensis.

Genigraphics

After you've created your terrific presentation materials, you may want to have them professionally prepared as slides, overheads, or such. Genigraphics has long been an expert in such materials creation. This file is actually a wizard that assists you in preparing and sending your documents to Genigraphics.

Handheld synchronization

This addition enables Entourage to sync with devices running PalmOS.

Microsoft Query

Microsoft Query lets Office 2001 applications access ODBC-compatible databases. It does not include the specific ODBC drivers for any databases or the driver manager.

Microsoft Works 4.0 Converter

This text converter lets Microsoft Word 2001 open Microsoft Works 4.0 documents.

Proofing tools

Proofing tools consist of the Hyphenation files and the Spelling and Thesaurus dictionaries. They come in nine languages in addition to English. These tools are stored in the Proofing Tools folder, which is in the Shared Applications folder inside the main Microsoft Office 2001 folder. Of course, if you are using an English version of Office, English tools are installed by default.

Programmability

If you're into automation, you'll want these files; you'll find some macros for Word and some macros and VBA code for Excel. In addition, you'll find sample files for Solver and the Help files for VBA.

Templates

Here you can choose to install extra templates and wizards for Word, Excel, or PowerPoint. In Chapter 2, we list the Word templates and wizards that come with Office 2001 and let you know which ones are part of this install. Numerous Excel spreadsheet solutions exist, as do a ton of presentations and a whole lot of presentation design elements.

Text Encoding Converter

The Text Encoding Converter (TEC) enables you to convert between multiple script systems (such as Japanese, Greek, and English). This is Apple software and is included with Mac OS 8 and 9, but it is provided for convenience.

Unbinder

Windows Office has a feature called the Binder. With it, users can create a Binder into which they can place one or more Word, Excel, or PowerPoint documents. If you receive a file that's a Binder, you'll need to be able to open it. That's when the Unbinder comes in handy.

Word 97–2001 converter

This extension is for you to give away to others running older versions of Word (Word 5.1 and Word 6) so that they can open documents created in Word 2001 (and Word 98) on the Mac or Word 97 or 2000 on Windows. You do not need to install it and the Value Pack Installer does not do so.

WordPerfect 5 converters

These files enable you to open and save files created with WordPerfect 5 and 5.1. The Value Pack Installer does not install these text converters. You must drag them manually from the Text Converters folder inside the Shared Applications folder of the Value Pack folder to your Text Converters folder.

Installing Internet Explorer

Internet Explorer 5 is a separate installation process from the core applications (Word, Excel, Entourage, and PowerPoint) that you are used to getting with Office.

To install Internet Explorer 5, drag the Internet Explorer 5 folder from your Microsoft Office 2001 CD-ROM to your hard disk (the Internet folder is a good place for it). You should probably check first to see whether you already have Internet Explorer 5 (or a newer version) installed there as Internet Explorer is included with your OS installation.

✦   ✦   ✦

Word Quick Start

This appendix provides a fast-paced overview of Word 2001 basics, particularly the details of the Word menus and document window. It also introduces text editing for beginners. If you've never used Word, start here.

Launching Word

You can launch Word several ways. If you've done the simplest install — by dragging the Microsoft Office 2001 folder to your hard drive and letting Word do the installation for you — you can launch Word as you launch any program on your Mac. Word is located directly in the Microsoft Office 2001 folder, which is either immediately on your hard drive, or within a folder such as Applications, depending upon where you've placed it. The icon for the actual Word program is a blue W; this is the icon you double-click to launch Word. Rather than having to open the hard drive, and then open the Microsoft Office 2001 folder every time you launch Word, we recommend that you place an alias of the Word icon under your Apple menu.

In Chapter 1, we discuss launching all Office applications.

Learning About the Screen

Each time you launch Word, you are presented with the Project Gallery where the thumbnail for a new Word document is highlighted. Press Return or Enter, and a new blank document is automatically started for you to begin entering text. Figure B-1 shows the different parts of the screen. Menus, located in the white strip at the top of your screen, are one of the founding principles of all Macintosh applications.

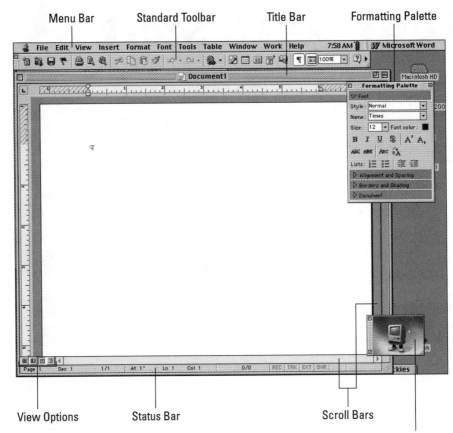

Menu Bar   Standard Toolbar   Title Bar   Formatting Palette

View Options   Status Bar   Scroll Bars

Office Assistant covers the Previous, Select Browse Object, and Next buttons in the figure

Figure B-1: The Word window

The rest of your screen area, your desktop, is where Word's toolbars, palettes, and document windows reside when active. At the top of your desktop, immediately below the menus, you find Word-specific tools. Word's default setup is to show you its Standard toolbar (top) and the Formatting palette (below). The numerous buttons on the toolbar may seem daunting at first, but move your mouse pointer (cursor) over any button and let it rest a moment (without clicking). Notice a yellow box appears, telling you what that button does. These are called ScreenTips. ScreenTips can also list the key combinations you can press if you prefer not to use the mouse. The presence of ScreenTips is a preference you can set (covered in Chapter 1). Now that you know Word will tell you what each button does, you needn't worry about memorizing the buttons. Some of the buttons, especially the ones on the Formatting palette, are clearly depicted for you. For example, the button with the lines all to the left represents left-alignment.

When you're working with a document, the document appears onscreen in its own free-floating window (as do all Mac documents). When you're not working with a document, you just see your desktop (unless you've set your Mac to hide the desktop). The document window appears below the toolbars. Word's document window is the same as any other Mac application's — but with a few more controls. You can resize it or move it at any time. The top of the window has stripes going across it and a name in the center. This is the title bar for your document window. The name there is the name of your document ("Document" followed by a number, if unsaved). To move your document around onscreen, click in the title bar area and drag. This is a basic Mac function. (If you're coming to the Mac from a Windows background, the title bar is in a new location for you, as are the close window and windowshade boxes.) Everything on the title bar is standard on the Mac; however, Word introduces a few of its own window controls: view controls at the bottom left (discussed in Chapter 2); the Status Bar below the view controls and horizontal scroll bar; and Next, Previous, and Select Browse Object controls on the right side.

By default, Next and Previous jump the onscreen view of your document to the top of the next or previous page. In addition, they jump your text insertion point to the top of the page you are viewing. Select Browse Object is a pop-up menu that enables you to jump through your document, landing at the next or previous object of the type you select. These objects include fields, comments, and other such Word features. Whatever object is selected in this pop-up menu is the object that the Next and Previous buttons jump to.

Below the title bar, if it is showing, is the ruler. The ruler lets you use the mouse to change paragraph indents, adjust page margins, change the width of columns, and set tab stops. See Chapters 2, 3, and 5 for more information on these topics. If you don't see a ruler, you can turn it on by selecting Ruler from the View menu. A check mark tells you it's on.

Figure B-2 shows the toolbar that, by default, appears when you launch Word: the Standard toolbar. Table B-1 describes the Standard toolbar's buttons. Table B-2 briefly describes the Formatting palette's buttons for the four panes present when dealing with text. Figure B-3 shows the Formatting palette with the panes available when you create a new document or are entering/editing text. For detailed information on how to format documents with the Formatting palette, see Chapter 3.

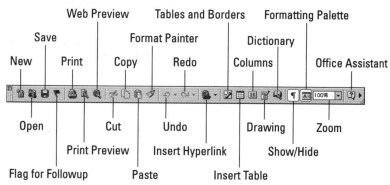

Figure B-2: The Standard toolbar

Table B-1
Standard Toolbar Buttons

Button	Button Name	Description
	New	Opens a new document using the default page settings
	Open	Opens the Open/Save dialog box so you can open an existing document
	Save	Saves the current document under its present name; if no name exists, the Save As dialog box appears so you can provide one
	Flag for Followup	Creates a task in Entourage and sets a reminder that will alert you on the date and time you specify (if Entourage is running) to follow up on whatever you have left undone
	Print	Opens the Print dialog box to print the current document
	Print Preview	Lets you see what your current document will look like when printed and lets you make layout changes
	Web Page Preview	Saves a temporary HTML copy of your document and displays it in your default Web browser
	Cut	Removes a section of selected (highlighted) text and places it on the clipboard
	Copy	Makes a copy of the current section of text and places it on the clipboard
	Paste	Pastes the contents of the clipboard into the document at the insertion point
	Format Painter	Copies formatting characteristics from one selection of text to another

Button	Button Name	Description
	Undo	Reverses the last action; the arrow lets you choose the action that you wish to undo
	Redo	Redoes the last action that was undone; the arrow lets you choose the undone action that you wish to redo
	Insert Hyperlink	Inserts a link to a URL or another file in Word
	Tables and Borders	Activates the Tables and Borders toolbar, and enables creation of tables (for more information on tables, see Chapter 5)
	Insert Table	Inserts a table in your document (Chapter 5 tells you all about tables)
	Columns	Formats the current selection or section into columns
	Drawing	Shows or hides the Drawing toolbar
	Dictionary	Displays the dictionary so that you can look up words to check spelling and definition
	Show/Hide ¶	Shows or hides all nonprinting characters
	Formatting Palette	Shows or hides the Formatting palette
100%	Zoom Control	Lets you zoom in closer to your document so text and symbols appear closer. Also enables you to zoom out so more of your document fits onscreen. This doesn't affect the actual characteristic of the text — only its appearance onscreen. (8-point Helvetica, zoomed so it's larger, is still 8-point Helvetica.)
	Office Assistant	Activates the Office Assistant, which provides general help

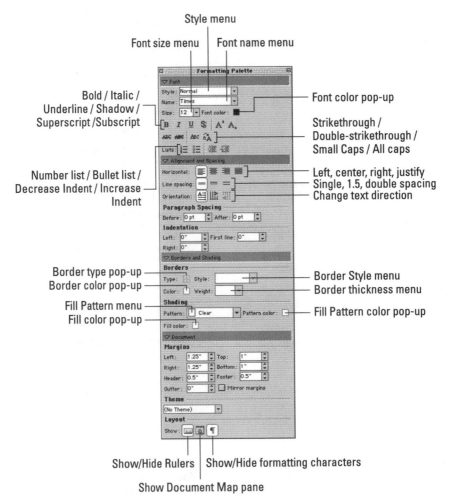

Figure B-3: The Formatting palette with the four default panes open

Pane	Button	Name	Description
Font	Normal ▼	Style	Lets you choose a style for your text
Font	Times ▼	Name	Lets you choose a font for your text
Font	12 ▼	Size	Lets you choose a size for your text's font

Table B-2
Formatting Palette Buttons

Pane	Button	Name	Description
Font	Font color : ■	Font Color	Lets you choose a color for the text
Font	**B**	Bold	Applies or removes boldface from text
Font	*I*	Italic	Applies or removes italics from text
Font	U	Underline	Applies or removes underlining from text
Font	S	Shadow	Applies or removes shadowing from text
Font	A²	Superscript	Applies or removes superscripting from text
Font	A₂	Subscript	Applies or removes subscripting from text
Font	ABC	Strikethrough	Applies or removes strikethrough from text
Font	ABC	Double strikethrough	Applies or removes double strikethrough from text
Font	ABC	Small Caps	Applies or removes small caps styling from text
Font	A	All Caps	Applies or removes all caps styling from text

Continued

Table B-2 *(continued)*

Pane	Button	Name	Description
Font		Lists:Number	Applies or removes list numbering from text
Font		Lists:Bullets	Applies or removes list bulleting from text
Font		Decrease Indent	Decreases the amount text is indented from the left margin
Font		Increase Indent	Increases the amount text is indented from the left margin
Alignment and Spacing		Horizontal: Left	Aligns text to the left margin
Alignment and Spacing		Horizontal: Center	Centers text between margins
Alignment and Spacing		Horizontal: Right	Aligns text to the right margin
Alignment and Spacing		Horizontal: Justify	Aligns text to both the left and the right margins
Alignment and Spacing		Line Spacing: Single	Single space text
Alignment and Spacing		Line Spacing: 1.5	1.5 line spacing
Alignment and Spacing		Line Spacing: Double	Double-space text
Alignment and Spacing		Orientation: Left to right	Change text direction
Alignment and Spacing		Line Spacing: Top to bottom	Rotate text 90 degrees clockwise

Pane	Button	Name	Description
Alignment and Spacing		Line Spacing: Bottom to top	Rotate text 90 degrees counterclockwise
Alignment and Spacing	Before: 0 pt	Paragraph Spacing: Before	Specify the amount of white space to precede a paragraph
Alignment and Spacing	After: 0 pt	Paragraph Spacing:After	Specify the amount of white space to appear after a paragraph
Alignment and Spacing	Left: 0"	Indentation: Left	Specify how much text will be indented from the left margin
Alignment and Spacing	First line: 0"	Indentation: First Line	Specify by how much text will be indented from the left margin for the first line of a paragraph.
Alignment and Spacing	Right: 0"	Indentation: Right	Specify by how much text will be indented from the right margin
Borders and Shading		Borders:Type	Lets you apply borders for your text
Borders and Shading	Style:	Borders: Style	Lets you specify the thickness and style of the line(s) used for the text border specified in Type
Borders and Shading		Borders: Color	Specify the color to be used for the border

Continued

Table B-2 *(continued)*

Pane	Button	Name	Description
Borders and Shading	Weight: 1/2 ▼	Borders: Weight	Specify the weight (thickness) of the border
Borders and Shading	☐ Clear ▼	Shading: Pattern	Specify a pattern or opacity to use as a shading/ background
Borders and Shading	▣	Shading: Pattern color	Specify the (foreground) color to use in the shading
Borders and Shading	▢	Shading: Fill color	Specify the background color to use in the pattern
Document	1 " ▲▼	Margins: Left	Specify the size of the document's left margin
Document	1 " ▲▼	Margins: Top	Specify the size of the document's top margin
Document	1 " ▲▼	Margins: Right	Specify the size of the document's right margin
Document	1 " ▲▼	Margins: Bottom	Specify the size of the document's bottom margin
Document	1 " ▲▼	Margins: Header	Specify the distance from the top of the page to the top of the header area
Document	1 " ▲▼	Margins: Footer	Specify the distance from the bottom of the page to the bottom of the footer area

Pane	Button	Name	Description
Document	1 "	Margins: Gutter	Specify a extra area to the outside or top of a page to provide room for binding
Document	Mirror margins	Margins: Mirror margins	Make left (even) and right (odd) pages mirror images of each other in terms of the preceding margin settings
Document	(No Theme)	Theme	Specify a collection of font, style, background, and other ornamental settings for your document.
Document		Layout: Show:Ruler	Hide/show the text ruler
Document		Layout: Show: Document Map	Activates (or hides) the Document Map pane (for more information, see Chapter 5)
Document	¶	Layout:Show: Show/Hide ¶	Show or hide formatting characters

Starting at the top of the Formatting palette, you first see the Font section open. In it are, from the top, the Style menu, which lets you apply any of Word's styles to a selection (or the paragraph where the insertion point is placed). Next comes the Name menu, which lets you change the appearance of selected characters by choosing different typefaces. Below the Name menu is the Size menu, which lets you change the size of the selected characters. Next are the ten character-formatting buttons in two rows: **Bold**, *Italic*, <u>Underline</u>, Shadow, Superscript, Subscript, Strikethrough, Double Strikethrough, Small Caps, and All Caps. Below the character formatting buttons are the buttons to create numbered or bullet lists and to decrease or increase a line's indent.

The Alignment and Spacing pane comes next, followed by the Borders and Shading pane, and the Document pane—all of which are initially closed.

Each component of the Formatting palette is discussed in detail in the corresponding section.

Opening New or Existing Documents

Each time you launch Microsoft Word, the Project Gallery automatically appears, ready for you to select Word Document to create a new blank document. This automatic document is the "default." In Chapter 2, you learn how to adjust its margins, font, and so on by changing your preferences. If you are starting a new document from scratch, this document is usually the best starting place; it's the document you work with in Chapter 2 as you become familiar with the basics of word processing with Word.

Creating new documents

As you use Word, the chances are you'll create more than one document in one session. It's common to create one document, close it when done, and then start another. To create more documents, simply choose File ⇨ New (⌘-N), click the New Document button on Word's Standard toolbar, or choose File ⇨ Project Gallery (⌘-Shift-P). You can create new documents any time Word is the active application. If you choose File ⇨ New, press ⌘-N or click the New Document button, you get the same default document. If you choose File ⇨ Project Gallery, you see what's called the Project Gallery dialog box. To open a new default page, you locate the thumbnail called Word Document, click it to select it, and then click OK (or just double-click the thumbnail). If you want to begin with a specific style document, find and click your desired template once, and then click OK. Templates are discussed in Chapter 2.

 Tip Rather than selecting the document and then clicking OK, you can simply double-click the document. This is possible because OK is the default option (that Word assumes you'll want), and a black line surrounds the OK button.

Opening existing documents

To open an existing document, either click the Open icon on the toolbar, choose File ⇨ Open, or press ⌘-O. If the Project Gallery is open, click its Open button. The Open dialog box appears. When you see the name of the desired document in the immediate list, simply double-click it.

Tip   To open an existing document, you can also go to the desktop, open the folder that contains the document, and double-click the document. This action launches Word if it's not already running.

If you do not immediately see the desired document, you need to navigate to the folder that contains it. The pop-up menu at the top of the Open dialog box states the folder, disk, or hard drive that you are currently viewing. The list box shows you the contents of that folder, disk, or hard drive. By clicking the pop-up menu, you can travel from the current folder to any location between that folder and your desktop. To get to another disk, return to the desktop so you can view the contents of the desktop by choosing Desktop from the Shortcuts button menu or press ⌘-D. Double-click any folder, disk, or hard drive in the list box to open it. Click the pop-up menu at the top to travel back out of the current folder. You can select the folder, disk, or hard drive you want to see. You can peruse your entire hard drive and all connected volumes from here. For more understanding of the Open or Open and Save dialog box, see your Macintosh manual.

Entering and Editing Text

If you already have text in your computer, you can copy and paste it into your new document or use drag and drop to place it there. Otherwise, the common way to get text into your document is to type it. Assuming you are starting with the blank new document Word provides when you launch Word, you see a flashing line at the top of your new document page. That line, called the insertion point, shows you where your typed or pasted text will be entered. If you're completely new to Word, practice by typing the following text. Humor us on this; we use this example again later, and it will help if you've already typed it:

```
Choices, choices, choices
```

It seems you always have at least three ways to do anything on the Mac. Margins and indents are no exception. If you're a visual person, you'll love using the ruler so you can see where you're moving the text to. More numerically based? You'll prefer opening dialog boxes or using the Formatting palette and entering numbers to set indents and such. If you're a bit of both, you can use the ruler, but double-click any ruler element any time to call up the dialog box.

Basic navigation

Now that you have some text in your new document, you can practice some basic navigation skills. To place text, you need to have the insertion point (that flashing line) at the place you want your text to appear. You can use the arrow keys to move the insertion point in the direction of the arrow you press. However, this can be tedious. The standard way to move your insertion point on the Mac is to use your mouse. When your mouse pointer is in the text area of a page, the pointer turns into an I-beam. Click this I-beam in your document to place the insertion point there. To move from page to page within your document, use the scroll bars on the side of your document window.

If you prefer not to take your fingers off the keyboard, you can use the built-in key combinations to move through chunks of text, and so on. Table B-3 lists keystrokes that move you around your documents. You can learn the keystrokes if you like; however, you don't have to learn any of them.

Table B-3 Navigation Keystrokes	
Keystroke	*Function*
Arrow keys	Move the insertion point around in your document
⌘-↑	Moves the cursor up one paragraph
⌘-↓	Moves the cursor down one paragraph
⌘-←	Moves the cursor one word to the left
⌘-→	Moves the cursor one word to the right
Page Up key	Moves the cursor up one screen page
Page Down key	Moves the cursor down one screen page
Home key	Moves the cursor to the beginning of the current line of text
⌘-Home key	Moves the cursor to the beginning of the document
End key	Moves the cursor to the end of the current line of text
⌘-End key	Moves the cursor to the end of the document

Note Depending upon your keyboard (for example, if you're using a PowerBook), you might have to press an addition (fn) key to access some of these, such as Page Up, Page Down, Home, and End.

The scroll bars move you through a document, too. You have four ways to scroll with the scroll bar: click the arrows incrementally, hold down the mouse button on the scroll arrow, drag the scroll bar box, or click in the gray area above or below the scroll bar.

Basic text editing

Text editing has two basic rules. First, as already mentioned, you can type or paste text at the insertion point. Second, any text that is selected can be changed.

To try adding text, return to the second line of the "Choices" document you typed earlier (or any practice document). Move your I-beam until it's in front of the first line of the text you just typed, and then click to place the insertion point there. Now type **Wow**. Wow lands in front of the word *Choices*. In some word processors, this is known as Insert mode. (The term Insert mode is used in Word for Windows but isn't common on the Mac.)

To try deleting text, with the insertion point flashing after Wow, press the Delete key. Press once and the *w* is removed. Press again and the *o* is removed. As the insertion point travels backward over text, via the Delete key, it removes the text and the existing text moves back over. Now try deleting an entire word: double-click the middle word, *choices*. With the word *choices* selected, press Delete. The selected text (*choices*) is gone, and the insertion point is left flashing in the space. You can type a new word there if you'd like. For now, type **many**. Pressing Delete isn't necessary, however. Whenever text is selected, it is automatically replaced by whatever is typed at the time it is selected. In other words, if you select text, and then type, the selected text is deleted and the new text is entered in place of it. This is standard for the Mac.

Word provides another editing feature that non-Mac word processor users may already be familiar with. In Overtype mode, text you type replaces existing text, letter for letter. Overtype mode is not the default. You enter Overtype mode by double-clicking the letters OVR in the status bar at the bottom of your window. If OVR appears in black letters, you're in Overtype mode; if it's dimmed, you're in the normal Insert mode. When you are in Overtype mode, the cursor moves forward as normal and enters your new text. However, it erases your existing type as you type the new text. To see the effect, double-click OVR in the status bar (if it's not on yet), and then go back to the first line you typed and place your insertion point in front of the *m* in *many*. Now type the letters **oh**. Notice your word is no longer *many*, but is now *ohny*. You typed two letters so two letters were deleted. Overtype mode replaces all text until you stop typing, so be careful not to overwrite what you want to keep. Rather than overtyping, it is more common on the Mac to select the text you don't want and then type new text in its place.

Tip The status bar is on by default, but it may be turned off. To do so, choose Edit⇨ Preferences, click the View tab, and then click in the box next to Status bar. A check means the status bar is showing; no check means it's off.

Saving Documents

When you create a document, it exists only in the temporary memory of your computer. When you turn the power off, or a power outage turns it off for you, your document is lost—unless you've saved it. Saving is the act of writing the document to the hard drive or disk. Once the document is saved, you can open it again later. Word provides a variety of save options. You can save a file under a new name or an existing one. You can save files in Word's own file format, or you can save them in the formats of other popular word processors.

Using the Save command

To save a file, go to the File menu and choose Save, or press ⌘-S—the keyboard equivalent. Word also provides a Save button you can click in the Standard toolbar. The first time you save a document, Word displays the Save As dialog box (see Figure B-4). Enter a filename, select the folder you want to save it to, and then click Save. You can save to your hard drive or to any removable disk. When you do subsequent saves, Word saves the file without prompting you for any information. It's a good idea to save often.

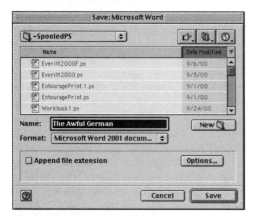

Figure B-4: The Save dialog box

If you created the example document "Choices," save it now by following these steps:

1. Choose File ⇨ Save. Because you have never saved this file, the Save As dialog box appears.

2. Word gives you a head start on naming the document by taking the first few words of your first page and automatically placing them in the Save Current Document as field. In this case, the name field probably already says "Choices." You can select the entire name or any part of it, or enter any name you'd like.

3. Click the pop-up menu at the top of the dialog box and navigate to the disk or folder to which you want your document saved. If you are not yet comfortable with navigating folders this way, just press ⌘-D or choose Desktop from the Shortcuts button (the one with a pointing finger). That way the document will be saved to the desktop and you can drag it to a folder later.

4. Click OK. You now have a document named "Choices."

Caution   When you quit Word, you are asked if you want to save any documents you have not yet saved or have made changes to since your last save. It is not a good idea to get dependent on that dialog box, however. It is much better to save your document each time you make a change you want to keep. Developing the ⌘-S reflex will save you a lot of grief.

Using the Save As command

At times you will find that you like a document you created but want to try another version of it. This is where Save As comes in. The Save As command silently and invisibly makes a copy of your document, safely putting your original away. Word then presents you with a new Save As dialog box (the same as the one shown earlier in Figure B-4) so you can give the copy a new name and even select a new location to save it to. Save As is also handy when you've finished your document and need to create a copy of it in another file format (for example, when you need to give a document to a friend who uses an older version of Word or Word for Windows or another word processing program).

When you do a Save As, the original name of the file appears in the Name field (if the document has ever been saved). On the Mac, two files within the same folder cannot have the same name. If you don't give your new document a different name, you are asked if you want to replace the original. You can save the file with the same name if you save it to another location, but it is very confusing to have two files with the same name. To avoid confusion, give this document a new name.

New Feature   New in Office 2001 is a checkbox in the Save As dialog to Append file extension. If you check this box, Word will use the Windows-convention 3-character filename extension appropriate to that file type to the name. This is very handy if you are going to be sharing documents with people using Windows or even other Mac users so that their File Exchange preferences can invoke an appropriate application for the document.

If you are using File ⇨ Save As to save a document in the format of another word processor, in addition to naming your new copy, you need to choose the new format. Click the arrow of the Format pop-up menu to reveal the installed formats in which you can save your document (see Figure B-5). Drag up or down to the format you desire, and then release the mouse button.

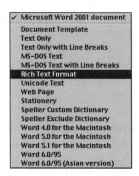

Figure B-5: The Format pop-up menu

Note that the available formats depends on what converters you've installed. If you need a popular file format and you don't see it in the pop-up menu, the Value Pack Installer may provide it. Microsoft may also provide other format converters from time to time. If so, the converters will be on the Microsoft Web site for you to download and install (www.microsoft.com).

Word enables you to set certain preferences for your saving pleasure. You can see and change these preferences by selecting Edit ⇨ Preferences or by clicking the Options button in the Save dialog box. Your options include: Always Create Backup Copy, Allow Fast Saves, Prompt for Document Properties, Prompt to Save Normal Template, Save Data Only for Forms, and Save AutoRecover Info every *x* Minutes. The following sections cover the most basic options for saving files.

The Always Create Backup Copy option

In case your original document somehow becomes corrupted, you'll be happy to have a backup copy of your document. When the Always Create Backup Copy option is on, Word creates a backup file every time you save. The backup file will have the name "Backup (or Bkup) of document name." The backup is saved to the folder where the original document is stored. You can open the backup file the same way you open any document.

The Allow Fast Saves option

Some of Word's behavior when saving files depends on how much editing you've done to the file since it was saved last.

Word saves files using either of two methods: a fast save or a full save. When you save, Word saves your file using the method indicated by the circumstances. Normally, Word performs a fast save, where your changes are appended onto the end of an existing file. With a full save, Word saves the entire document, including unchanged parts, as if you were saving the file for the first time. The first time a document is saved, Word performs a full save. After that, Word usually performs a fast save whenever you save updates to your document. (If you make extensive changes, Word may perform a full save automatically.)

Operationally, you'll see no difference between the two methods other than speed. Full saves take somewhat longer than fast saves; exactly how much longer varies greatly depending on the speed of your hardware. Fast-saved files become larger as all changes are included. To turn fast saves on or off, go to the Save tab of the Preferences dialog box or click the Options button from the Save dialog box, and check or uncheck the Allow Fast Saves checkbox.

Tip   It is generally a good idea to do a full save on a document you are going to transfer to someone else, particularly via e-mail or on the Web. Fast-saved copies are larger and can contain information from previous versions that you don't wish others to see.

The Prompt for Document Properties option

The Prompt for document properties option shows the Summary tab of the Properties dialog box the first time you save a document. This tab lets you store general information about the document, such as title, subject, or author.

The Save AutoRecover Every *x* Minutes option

AutoRecover may help you recover your document in the case of a power outage or system crash. You determine how often AutoRecover makes a copy of your document by entering a time interval in the Preferences Save tab. The recovery files are temporary. They are erased when your document is saved and are deleted when you close the file. Recovery files come into play after a freeze and are automatically opened when you restart and relaunch Word.

Printing Your Documents

This section quickly shows how to print to the printer you've chosen in the Chooser. (Printing is covered in detail in Chapter 4.)

To print a document, choose File ⇨ Print (or press ⌘-P). The Print dialog box appears, as shown in Figure B-6.

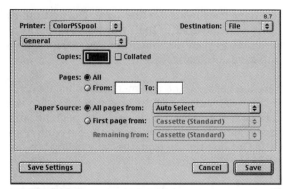

Figure B-6: The Print dialog box

Choosing the printer and number of copies

Check that the printer name that appears at the top of the dialog box is the printer to which you want to print. If it's not, use the Chooser, the pop-up menu at the top of the Print dialog box, or switch to the Finder (if using Desktop Printers) to select the correct printer and try again. The default options in the dialog box assume you want one copy of the document and that you want all pages in the document printed. The Copies field is preselected so you can easily type a different number of copies.

After reviewing or selecting the options you want, click Print.

Printing part of a document

You can also enter a specific page at which to begin printing (in the From box), a specific page to end printing (in the To box), or a page to begin with and end with (by entering a number in each box). You can print several ranges of pages by entering the range in the Microsoft Word section of the Print dialog box. You can even print a selected portion of a document by highlighting the selection and choosing File ➪ Print, going to the Microsoft Word section of the Print dialog box, and checking Print Selection. This is all covered in detail in Chapter 4.

You can even print a document without opening it. Just locate the document in its folder and drag it to your desktop printer icon. Your Mac launches Word, opens the document, prompts you for a number of copies (and other options), and then quits Word when done.

✦　　✦　　✦

Excel Quick Start

APPENDIX

This appendix provides a fast-paced overview of Excel 2001 basics, particularly the details of the Excel menus and workbook window. If you're new to Excel, start here.

Getting Started

You can launch Excel the same way you launch any Mac program — by double-clicking the application's icon or alias, or selecting it from the Apple menu (if you've placed it there).

Understanding spreadsheets

A spreadsheet is an electronic version of bookkeeping tools: the ledger pad, pencil, and calculator. Excel spreadsheets, called worksheets in Microsoft terminology, can be likened to huge sheets of ledger paper. Each worksheet measures 65,536 rows by 256 columns — realistically, more size than you should ever need on a single page. Each cell is made up of the intersection of a row and column. Therefore cells are identified by their column (letter or letters) and row (number) coordinates. A1 is the cell in the upper-left corner of the worksheet, and IV256 is the cell at the lower-right corner. When you click any cell to select it, the row and column that cell is in become highlighted in the row and column headings to help you identify where you are. In addition, as you drag across a cell, a yellow ScreenTip is likely to report that cell's address to you so you know where you're going.

Dealing with data

Data you enter in a worksheet can take the form of constant values or of variables that are based on formulas. Constant values, such as a number (13) or a name (Dennis Cohen), do not change. They are the data you enter to track your information. Values are the information Excel calculates for you. They are the result of formulas you place in cells. Behind the scenes is the formula (which shows in the formula bar). In the spreadsheet, the result of the formula shows so you can do your work. Formulas most often refer to other cells in the worksheet to get their data and do their calculations. For example, a cell might contain the formula C5+C6+C7 or SUM(C5:C7), which adds the contents of those three cells.

Note   Excel's worksheets can display data in a wide variety of formats. You can display numeric values with or without decimals, currency amounts, or exponential values. You can also enter text, such as the name of a month or a product model name. And you can store and display date and time-of-day data in worksheet cells.

Introducing calculations and formulas

Calculations are what nearly all spreadsheet models are about. Formulas can be as simple as the addition of cells or be highly intricate. Excel helps you with formulas by providing a rich assortment of functions, which are special built-in formulas that provide a variety of calculations (the average of a series of values, for example, or the square root of a number). Excel provides functions for mathematical, statistical, financial, logical, date and time, text, and special-purpose operations.

Note   At first glance, Excel can be scary and seem to appeal only to people who must manage numbers on a daily basis. However, if you give it a chance, you may find Excel easy to use and quite handy. In addition to tracking numeric-based information, Excel can build you some excellent charts and graphs. Excel 2001 also includes rich graphics capabilities to jazz up documents for presentations. Furthermore, Excel 2001 includes new List Manager tools making it easier than ever to use Excel to manage databases (see Chapter 21).

Understanding the Excel screen

By default, Excel provides one toolbar when it launches — the Standard toolbar — directly below the menus. Some toolbar buttons may be familiar to you if you've used another version of Excel or used Word or PowerPoint. Below the toolbar, you'll see the workbook, which you can move and resize as you can with any Mac document. At the bottom of your window is the status bar. If you've used other Microsoft products, you are probably familiar with status bars. Previous versions of Excel presented the formula bar by default. Excel 2001 does not display it automatically, you need to turn it on by choosing View ⇨ Formula Bar.

Figure C-1 shows what Excel looks like when first opened; you'll see a new workbook with the title "Workbook1."

The components of Excel's workbook window are explained in Chapter 15.

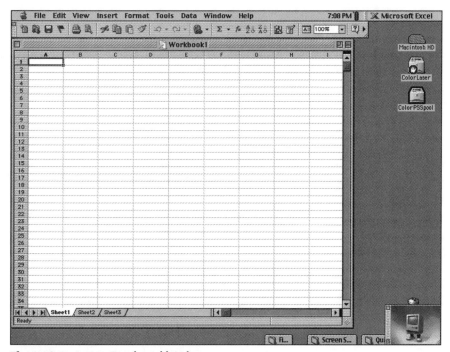

Figure C-1: A new Excel workbook

Excel's toolbars

Toolbars are customizable sections of buttons. Each button, when clicked once, performs a function. Some buttons provide pop-up selections you drag to and click instead. This section describes Excel's toolbars. Although each button has an icon that attempts to convey its function, some can be rather mystical. You can always tell what a button does by bringing your mouse over the button and pausing there; after a moment a ScreenTip appears presenting the name of the button. (More later on ScreenTips.)

Note   Excel—and the other core Office applications—makes good use of ScreenTips. You'll see them appear occasionally to provide various bits of information.

Figure C-2 shows Excel's Standard toolbar. Table C-1 shows its buttons.

Figure C-2: The Standard toolbar

Table C-1
Standard Toolbar Buttons

Button	Function	Name
	New	Opens a new workbook
	Open	Opens a workbook file
	Save	Saves a current workbook; if it has not been saved before, you are prompted to enter a name for the workbook
	Flag for Followup	Creates a task in Entourage and sets a reminder as you specify so that you can come back and finish or update the workbook, as appropriate, at a later date
	Print	Opens the Print dialog box for printing
	Print Preview	Shows you what the workbook will look like when printed
	Cut	Cuts the selected information and places it on the clipboard
	Copy	Copies selected text and places it on a clipboard
	Paste	Pastes selected text in the document at the insertion point
	Format Painter	Copies text formatting from one area to another
	Undo	Reverses last action; the arrow lets you choose the action that you wish to undo
	Redo	Redoes the last action that was undone; the arrow lets you choose the undone action that you wish to redo
	Insert Hyperlink	Inserts a link to another file or to a Web site on the Internet or on an intranet
Σ	AutoSum	Invokes the SUM function, which adds a column of numbers; the arrow lets you choose a function other than SUM
f_x	Paste Function	Activates the Function Wizard, which quickly locates a desired function for use in a formula

Button	Function	Name
$\begin{smallmatrix}A\\Z\end{smallmatrix}\downarrow$	Sort Ascending	Sorts list information in ascending order
$\begin{smallmatrix}Z\\A\end{smallmatrix}\downarrow$	Sort Descending	Sorts list information in descending order
(icon)	ChartWizard	Activates the Chart Wizard, which creates a chart based on worksheet data
(icon)	Drawing	Displays the Drawing toolbar, which contains various tools that can be used to draw graphic shapes in a worksheet
A	Formatting palette	Shows or hides the Formatting Palette window
100% ▼	Zoom Control	Controls the size of a document's appearance onscreen
?	Office Assistant	Activates the Office Assistant Help system
▶	More buttons	Gives you a selection of other buttons that do not fit in the space available for the Standard toolbar, such as Spelling, Web Toolbar, Office Clipboard, PivotTable Wizard, Dictionary, and Insert Comment. If you add buttons to the Standard toolbar, buttons to the right will be pushed off into this "More Buttons" pop-up menu.

Figure C-3 shows Excel's Formatting Palette with the mouse resting over a button, revealing a ScreenTip. Table C-2 explains the visible Formatting Palette buttons.

Figure C-3: The Formatting Palette with a ScreenTip revealed

	Table C-2	
	Formatting Palette Buttons	
Button	**Name**	**Function**
General ▼	Format	Pop-up menu of data formats, showing the one currently applied to the selected cell(s)
+.0 .00	Decrease Decimal	Decreases the number of digits shown after the decimal point in the selection
.00 +.0	Increase Decimal	Increases the number of digits shown after the decimal point in the selection
Geneva ▼	Font	Displays list of fonts
9 ▼	Font Size	Displays available font sizes
B	Bold	Changes the selected text to boldface
I	Italic	Changes the selected text to italics
U̲	Underline	Underlines the selected text
A̶B̶C̶	Strikethrough	Changes the selected text to strikethrough style
■	Font Color	Displays a Font Color palette, which can be used to apply a font color choice to the current selection

Note   Additional buttons are available under the other, closed panes.

Understanding the workbook concept

Workbooks were introduced to Excel with Version 5.0, so if you discuss Excel with someone using Version 4.0, the concept of workbooks may be new. In a nutshell, a workbook is a collection of worksheets. Each of the worksheets consists of columns and rows that form cells. A tab appears at the bottom of each of sheet so you can click a tab to go to that sheet. The tabs can be easily renamed so you can know what information is on each sheet.

The advantage of using workbooks is you can keep more than one spreadsheet in a file. This is especially useful when you have a series of worksheets that track time-related data, such as sales or expenses for a series of months. Instead of storing several files, you can place all the worksheets in the same workbook—a single file.

Opening and Using Workbooks

The following sections cover the basics of opening and navigating within Excel files: workbooks and worksheets.

Opening an existing file

You can open an existing (previously saved) workbook the same way you open any file on the Mac—by double-clicking the document's icon or alias, or using the Open dialog box via File ⇨ Open. Another option is the File menu, if the file has been recently opened. Opening files is discussed fully in Chapter 1, and opening workbooks is discussed briefly in Chapter 15.

Workbook and worksheet navigation

This section teaches the basics of navigation within a worksheet and workbook. As always, you can use either the mouse or the keyboard, depending on your preference.

Navigating in the workbook window

When you launch Excel, a new workbook opens and takes you to the first worksheet. If you launch a workbook, it opens to the worksheet that was in front when the worksheet was last saved. To switch to another worksheet, just click the tab of the desired worksheet. You can see the tabs in Figure C-1, but Figure C-4 shows a close-up of a workbook's worksheet tabs. (If you can't see the needed tab, use the four arrows—which are scroll buttons—at the lower left or the use the workbook window scroll bar.)

Figure C-4: The tabs of an Excel workbook

You can also move from worksheet to worksheet by pressing ⌘-PgDn to move to the next sheet or ⌘-PgUp to move to the preceding sheet.

Navigating in a worksheet

After selecting your worksheet, you'll want to move around within it. (Remember that the part of the spreadsheet you see onscreen is only a small section of the entire worksheet.) This section introduces four navigation methods.

To make a cell active, just point your cursor at the center of the cell and click. If the desired cell isn't in view, use the scroll arrows to move sideways or up and down until you can see it. You can use the arrows or the scroll box to move through your worksheet. Click any arrow quickly to move a bit or keep the mouse pressed longer to move it farther. Or drag the scroll bar box any distance — note the ScreenTip that tells you what row or column you're on. A less accurate but sometimes faster way to move long distances is to click in the gray area above or below the scroll box. The farther away from the box you click, the farther you'll move within the spreadsheet.

If you prefer to keep your hands on the keys, you can use the key combinations noted in Table C-3 to move around in any Excel worksheet. (This table also appears in Chapter 15.)

Table C-3	
Keys and Key Combinations for Navigating in a Worksheet	
Keys	*Function*
Arrow keys	Move the cursor in direction of the arrow
Control-↑ or Control-↓	Moves the cursor to the top or bottom of a region of data
Control-← or Control-→	Moves the cursor to the left-most or right-most region of data
Page Up or Page Down	Moves the cursor up or down one screen
Control-Page Up or Control-Page Down	Moves the cursor to the preceding or the following worksheet
Home	Moves the cursor to the first cell in a row
Control-Home	Moves the cursor to the upper-left corner of the worksheet
Option-End	Moves the cursor to the last cell in a row which contains data
Control-End	Moves the cursor to the last cell in the used area of a worksheet
End-Enter	Moves the cursor to the last column in a row containing data

Using the Go To command

Yet another option for moving is with the Go To command. You can move to a specific cell on a worksheet by selecting Edit ⇨ Go To or pressing F5. Both moves open the Go To dialog box, as shown in Figure C-5. The text insertion point should be waiting for you in the Reference box or the box will be preselected. Just enter the cell address you want to move to, and then click OK to go directly to that cell. If the insertion point is not awaiting you in the Reference box and it's not preselected (highlighted), click in that cell to place the cursor there, and then type.

Figure C-5: The Excel Go To dialog box

Using the Name box

The last method for moving to a cell or area of your worksheet becomes available after you begin to assign names to your cells or to ranges of cells. (Naming cell ranges is covered in Chapter 16.) If any ranges are defined in your worksheet, they appear in the pop-up list when you click the arrow next to the Name box in the formula bar. (The Name box is farthest left in formula bar.) Even thought the formula bar is not showing by default in Excel 2001, we recommend that you use it — you can do just too many things that are easier to do from the formula bar than by direct in-cell editing. By dragging down to a name in this list and clicking, you move to this range. At the same time, the entire range will also become selected. The uniqueness of this method is if the named range is on a different worksheet in your workbook, Excel jumps you to that other worksheet.

Entering and Editing Data

Cells can contain text, numbers, or combinations of both. This data lands in whatever cell is currently selected. If a range of cells is selected, the data lands in the top-left cell of that range. Just move to any cell and start typing. When done with your entry, you must tell Excel you are done entering data and want that data to be entered into that cell. Until you do, you remain in an entry mode and are adding data to your cell or to your formula. We go into detail about how to enter and edit data in a moment.

Two kinds of data can be entered into a worksheet: values and formulas.

  ✦ **Values** are data, such as dates, time, percentages, scientific notation, or text; values don't change unless the cell is edited.

  ✦ **Formulas** are sequences of cell references, names, functions, or operators that produce a new value based on existing values in other cells of the worksheet.

Formulas can be tricky so Excel provides some coaching to make them easier. (This is covered in detail in Chapter 16.)

Figure C-6 shows a typical worksheet containing both values and formulas.

	A	B	C	D
			Western Region	
2	This represents sales data from Q1FY2000			
3		January	February	March
4	Walnut Creek	$123,440.00	$137,000.00	$89,900.00
5	River Hills	$248,700.00	$256,750.00	$302,500.00
6	Spring Gardens	$97,000.00	$102,500.00	$121,500.00
7	Lake Newport	$346,300.00	$372,300.00	$317,500.00
8				
9	Total Sales	$815,440.00	$868,550.00	$831,400.00
10				
11				

Houses.xls — Houses / House Sales+Chart / House Graph (2) / Ho

Figure C-6: A typical worksheet with values and formulas stored in cells

Entering data

Excel 98 introduced an alternative to the traditional spreadsheet data-entry method. You could enter data directly into the cell, which may be more comfortable for you. You simply double-click in the cell into which you want to enter data. The insertion point flashes directly in the cell and, as you enter your data, the data appears right there in the cell. Actually, it also appears in the formula bar. (In-cell editing works for editing as well as initial data entry.) Excel 2001 adopts this procedure as the preferred method, not even showing the formula bar unless you request it.

Tip In-cell editing is turned on by default. If double-clicking in a cell doesn't place the insertion point in the cell, in-cell editing may not be turned on. To check, or to turn it on, select Edit ⇨ Preferences, and then click the Edit tab and check Edit directly in cell.

Whether you enter your data into the formula bar or directly into the cell, after you've entered it, you must tell Excel to accept your data. You have a few ways to do so, as follows:

  ✦ You can click the green check mark in the formula bar or press Enter. Both methods store the data in the cell but don't move you out of that cell.

✦ Another option is to accept the data and move to another cell at the same time. To do so, you can press Return or Tab or use the arrow keys. The arrow keys move you the next cell to the left, right, up, or down, depending on the direction of the arrow you pressed. You control the effect of pressing Return in your Excel Preferences. (Select Edit ⇨ Preferences, and then click the Edit tab.) By default, Excel moves you down the column to the next cell, but it can move you left, right, or up instead. If you prefer, you can uncheck the option and have Return act the same as Enter. Pressing Tab moves you one cell to the right.

If you decide you don't really want to enter the data you typed, click the Cancel button in the formula bar (the red X, as shown in Figure C-7) or press Esc. If you've already entered the text and told Excel to accept it, you can undo your entry or changes with the Undo command by selecting Edit ⇨ Undo, pressing ⌘-Z, or by clicking the Undo button on the Standard toolbar.

Figure C-7: The Cancel button of the formula bar

Editing data

As you enter text, you'll sometimes want to edit it. After you select your cell or place your insertion point, editing data is the same as entering it.

Follow these steps to edit existing data in cells using the traditional formula bar entry technique:

1. Move the cursor to the cell containing the data you want to edit. As you select any cell, the data or formula it contains appears in the formula bar.

2. Move the mouse pointer over the formula bar. (As you do so, the pointer becomes an I-beam — as used in text entry.)

3. Click the I-beam at the location where you want to start editing, just as you do to edit text in word processing. (The flashing insertion point in the formula bar indicates where your editing will occur.) Edit as in word processing, and then tell Excel to accept the changes using one of the same methods you use when you originally enter data (most commonly by pressing Return or Enter).

To edit existing data using in-cell editing, follow these steps:

1. Move the mouse pointer over the cell you want to edit and double-click. The insertion point appears in the cell and the pointer becomes an I-beam while over that cell.

   With practice, you can even control where the insertion point lands within the cell. (It lands at the left edge of the vertical part of the fat cross.)

2. Click the I-beam at the location where you want to start editing, or use the arrow keys to move the insertion point, just as you do to edit text in word processing. (The flashing insertion point indicates where your editing will occur.) Edit as in word processing, and then tell Excel to accept the changes using one of the same methods you use when you originally enter data (most commonly by pressing Return or Enter).

Caution   If you have data in a cell, be careful. It is quite possible to click a cell, enter new data, and accept it. This replaces the existing data or formula with the new entry. If you mean to edit the contents of a cell, be sure to place your cursor within the contents of that cell before typing and accepting the change.

If you decide you don't like your changes, click the Cancel button (the red X, as shown earlier in Figure C-7) in the formula bar or press Esc. If you've already told Excel to accept changes, you can undo your changes with the Undo command by selecting Edit ➪ Undo (⌘-Z) or by clicking the Undo button on the Standard toolbar.

Numbers

By default, cells are formatted with the General Number format. This causes Excel to display numbers as accurately as possible using the integer, decimal fraction, and — if the number is longer than the cell — scientific notation. You can easily format any cell or group of cells to take on any number format (or make the cell text format). However, you don't always have to format cells, as Excel tries to do it for you. As you enter your data, you can give Excel clues to assign the correct format. If you enter a dollar sign before the number, the number is assigned a currency format. If you enter a percent sign, the number is assigned the percent format.

Sometimes your number will be larger than the default column width. When the number is too large to fit in the column, Excel displays a series of # symbols. To see the entire number, simply widen the column. The fastest way to make the column wide enough to fit the entire number is by double-clicking the column's right border in the column header.

At times you may want to enter numbers as text, as may be the case with zip codes. To do this, you can format the column as text, or, as you enter each zip code, you can tell Excel to format the numbers as text and left-align them by entering a single quotation mark (') before the number.

You can enter numbers in your worksheet using any of the numeric characters along with any of the following special characters:

```
+ - ( ) , / $ % . E e
```

Dates and times

Dates and times are common in spreadsheets. Excel provides several standard date and time formats, as shown in Tables C-4 and C-5. In addition, you can create your own custom formats. (Chapter 16 tells you how.) If you use any of Table C-4 and C-5's formats to enter dates and times, the dates and times revert to that format automatically. Otherwise, you can enter the dates or times in any format, select the cells, and choose a format any time. You can also always change a format.

Table C-4 Date Formats	
Format	**Example**
D/M	3/5
D/M/YY	1/1/99
DD/MM/YY	01/01/99
D-MON	1-Apr
D-MON-YY	3-Aug-63
DD-MON-YY	03-Aug-63
MON-YY	Apr 98
MONTH-YY	April 98
MONTH-D-YYYY	February-3-1989
D/M/YY H:MM 24-hour	3/4/95 14:30 PM
D/M/YY H:MM AM/PM	5/12/93 2:30 PM (This defaults to 24 hour until you reformat it.)

Table C-5 Time Formats	
Format	**Example**
HH:MM	10:30
HH:MM AM/PM	02:30 PM
HH:MM:SS	10:30:55
HH:MM:SS (24-hour)	14:30:55
HH:MM:SS AM/PM	01:30:55 PM
HH:MM.n (with tenths)	02:30.7
D/M/YY H:MM (12 or 24-hour)	3/4/95 2:30

Text entry

To enter text in Excel, select the cell and type. You can type up to 32,000 characters in a cell. Entries can include text and numbers and, as mentioned earlier, numbers can also be entered as text.

You may want to format large amounts of text in a way that presents an attractive display. Rather than using the method of typing a single quote in front of the text, it is easier to format the cell properly. To do this, choose Format ⇨ Cells (⌘-1) to bring up the Format Cells dialog box shown in Figure C-8. In the Number tab, select Text.

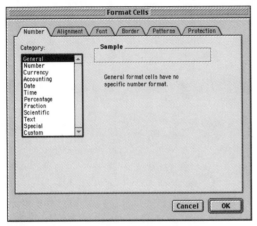

Figure C-8: The Format Cells dialog box

To accommodate a long display of text, you can set text wrap. This makes text wrap within the width of the cell (regardless of the cell width), therefore preventing long strips of text from overflowing into other cells. Instead, you will have multiple lines of text in your cells and the cell will grow to the height necessary to accommodate the number of lines.

To activate text wrap, click the Alignment tab in the Format Cells dialog box and click in the box next to Wrap text. You can change the column width any time and the text will wrap accordingly.

Building Formulas

The whole point of spreadsheets is to manipulate the numbers: Add them. Multiply them. Calculate their cosines, if the numbers measure angles and you're trigonometrically inclined. You use formulas to do this. You build a formula by indicating which values should be used and which calculations should apply to these values.

For example, if you wanted to add the values in cells B1 and B2 and then display the results of that calculation in cell B5, you could place the cursor in cell B5 and enter the simple formula =B1+B2. The equal sign tells Excel this cell will be calculating a result based on a formula. Formulas always start with an equal sign.

A formula calculates a value based on a combination of other values. These other values can be numbers, cell references, operators (+, –, *, and /), or other formulas. Formulas can also include the names of other areas in the worksheet, as well as cell references in other worksheets.

Math operators produce numeric results. Besides addition (+), subtraction (–), multiplication (*), and division (/) symbols, Excel accepts as math operators the exponentiation (^) and percentage (%) symbols. A number of other types of characters can be used in formulas for manipulating text and numbers. Chapter 16 covers formula entry in detail.

Printing Your Worksheets

For the most part, you print an Excel worksheet the same way you print any other document on the Mac — by choosing File ⇨ Print (⌘-P). This brings up the Print dialog box. Here you enter the number of copies, select a paper tray if applicable, and then click Print.

This prints the active worksheet by default. However, other options exist, such as printing a part of a page, printing an entire workbook, printing several worksheets within a workbook at once, and even printing several disconnected cell ranges. (Chapter 20 covers printing options in detail.)

Saving Your Worksheets

Although we didn't mention it in this appendix, we highly recommend saving your worksheet periodically. Even before it's complete? Yes! Definitely. Doing so reduces the possibility of losing large amounts of information due to a freeze or power failure. The commands used for saving worksheets — Save, Save As, and Save Workspace — are found in the File menu.

The Save and Save As commands save worksheets to disk. Save saves the worksheet under the existing name (after it has been saved once). Save As enables you to save a second copy of your workbook by prompting you for a new filename.

Save As is handy when you need to make a second copy so you can alter one without ruining the original. It also lets you save files in formats other than Excel's normal format. You can save the data in many other database and spreadsheet file formats. You can also save your worksheet as a Web Page for publishing on the Internet or on an intranet.

To save your worksheet, choose File ⇨ Save (⌘-S). When you do this the first time, the dialog box shown in Figure C-9 appears. This enables you to name your workbook and select the folder to which the file is saved.

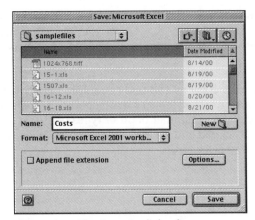

Figure C-9: The Save As dialog box

In Figure C-9, the file is being saved with the name Costs. It will land in a folder called Houses_files when the user clicks Open and then Save. (The Open button turns into a Save button once you are in a folder.) If you wish to make certain that the file will be openable by a Windows Excel user, check the Append file extension box and the file's name will be changed to Costs.xls. (You can always move the file later, after closing it, but that's an extra step that can be avoided by paying attention to where you save to initially.) Saving is covered in detail in Chapter 15.

✦   ✦   ✦

PowerPoint Quick Start

This introduction to PowerPoint covers basic PowerPoint skills and is designed to familiarize readers who have never worked with PowerPoint. In this introduction, you learn how to create presentations with and without the aid of the wizards, how to enter and edit text, how to add clip art to slides, and how to print your slides. You also learn some basic terminology that applies to using PowerPoint. When you feel familiar with the basics, you'll find the more advanced details of PowerPoint in Chapters 28 through 35.

Understanding PowerPoint

As you work with PowerPoint, you'll encounter some common terms. Being familiar with these terms will maximize your effectiveness in using PowerPoint. Look over the following list and familiarize yourself with these common PowerPoint terms:

+ **Presentation.** A presentation is the container holding all the individual slides, text, graphics, drawings, and other objects that make up your presentation. PowerPoint stores each presentation in a separate file on your hard disk.

+ **Template.** A template is a kind of formatting model. You use templates to apply a chosen group of styles, colors, and fonts to the slides you are working with. PowerPoint comes with over 150 different templates.

+ **Slides.** Slides are the individual screens or pages that you see within your presentation.

+ **Slide masters.** Slide masters are master documents that control the appearance and layout of the slides you create. If you make a design change to a slide master, the same change is reflected in all the new slides that you create based on that master.

+ **Layout.** This term refers to the overall appearance of a single slide. You can change the layout for any slide on an individual basis without affecting other slides in the presentation.

Creating Presentations

To create a new presentation, choose File ⇨ Project Gallery (⌘-Shift-P) to open the Project Gallery dialog box shown in Figure D-1.

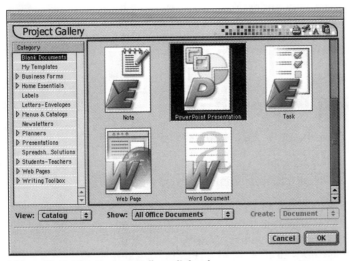

Figure D-1: The Project Gallery dialog box

When the Project Gallery dialog box opens, Blank Document is selected in the Category list (on the left). To create a new blank presentation, click OK. But that's probably the hardest way. Instead, start with a template or use the AutoContent Wizard. To start with one of Office 2001's prebuilt templates, click the triangle next to the word Presentations in the Category list. Now click either

+ **Content.** This tab contains two dozen prepopulated templates, with ideas for slide titles and content already in place. Among the canned presentations are Project Post-Mortem, Business Plan, Company Meeting, and more. All you need to do is replace its canned text and pictures with your own. If one of the Content Templates suits your need, it can be a timesaving place to begin.

or

✦ **Designs.** This tab contains empty templates that help you create presentations from scratch. PowerPoint contains 61 template designs — some beautiful, some less so. If nothing else, a Design Template is a good place to start.

After you choose a template, click OK. Using templates is discussed in greater detail
later in this chapter.

Or, if you'd prefer more handholding, try the AutoContent Wizard. The Wizard, discussed next, asks you questions to help determine the layout and content of your
presentation. When you are finished answering the questions, the basis of your presentation appears onscreen, and you can edit it as you see fit.

Using the AutoContent Wizard

To use the AutoContent Wizard, open the Project Gallery (File ⇨ Project Gallery or
⌘-Shift-P) and select Blank Document in the Category list. Now select AutoContent
Wizard from the documents available on the right side of the window (you may
have to scroll to select it) and click OK.

The first AutoContent Wizard dialog box appears, as shown in Figure D-2.

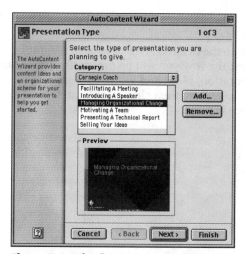

Figure D-2: The first AutoContent Wizard
dialog box

The wizard asks you to choose the type of presentation you want to create. You
have choices divided into several categories. Choosing the desired category from
the Category pop-up menu makes all the choices for that category appear in the list
below. The default is General: Generic. Choose the All category to see every one of
the choices.

After you choose the category and type of presentation you want to create, click the Next button; you see the second AutoContent Wizard dialog box, as shown in Figure D-3.

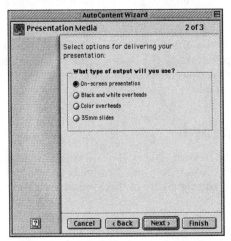

Figure D-3: The second AutoContent Wizard dialog box

The second dialog box is used to choose the desired style of your presentation. Under the type of output section, select the way you will be presenting your slides. You can choose from On-screen presentation, Black and White overheads, Color overheads, or 35mm slides. Make your selection then click Next to go to the third window of the AutoContent Wizard (see Figure D-4).

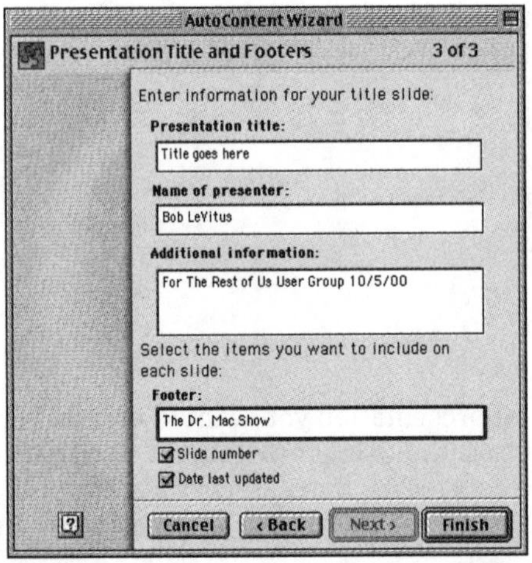

Figure D-4: The third AutoContent Wizard dialog box

This third dialog box to the AutoContent Wizard is used to set up your title slide. Here, you enter a title for your first slide. After entering a title, you may want to include your name. If so, enter it in the Name of Presenter field. The wizard also provides space for any additional information that you wish to add to the title slide of the presentation. After you have completed making your choices, click Finish to complete the presentation.

Using a template

To use a template, choose File ⇨ Project Gallery, and then click the triangle next to the word Presentations in the Category list. Now click Designs to choose from the 61 templates.

Choose the desired template and click OK. Next, you see the New Slide dialog box, as shown in Figure D-5.

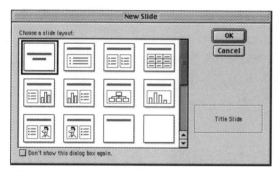

Figure D-5: The New Slide dialog box

After you choose one of the layouts shown in the dialog box, click OK. PowerPoint creates a presentation that uses the style and layout you have specified. You can then add text and graphics to the slide and insert additional slides into the presentation.

Starting a blank presentation

The Blank Document option is suited to PowerPoint users who are familiar with the package. This option assumes you want to handle all the design and content decisions on your own. After you choose the Blank Document option from the Category list of the Project Gallery and click OK, the New Slide dialog box appears. After you select the layout you want, click OK. The result is a blank presentation containing a single slide. If you accepted the default layout, it will look similar to the one shown in Figure D-6. You can add text and slides as desired.

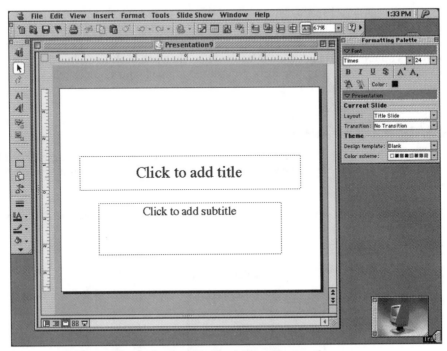

Figure D-6: The result of selecting the Blank Document option

Opening, Saving, and Closing Presentations

You can open an existing presentation by choosing File ⇨ Open or by clicking the Open button on the Standard toolbar. Either method results in the appearance of the Open dialog box. Choose the presentation you want and click OK. You can open and work with multiple presentations simultaneously. As you open each presentation, its name is added to the bottom of the Window menu.

PowerPoint uses the standard Mac methods to save files. When you choose File ⇨ Save or click the Save button on the Standard toolbar, PowerPoint saves the presentation to a file. If you are saving the presentation for the first time, a Save As dialog box appears, where you provide a filename for the presentation. You can save an existing presentation under a different filename by choosing File ⇨ Save As and entering the new name for the presentation.

To close a presentation, choose File ⇨ Close, or click the close box in the top-left corner of the presentation's window.

Using PowerPoint's Views

As you work with your presentations, you can switch between any one of five different views: Normal, Outline, Slide, Slide Sorter, and Slide Show.

Each of these views provides you with a different way of looking at the same presentation. To switch between the available views, click the appropriate view button at the lower-left corner of your screen. You can also choose the corresponding view from the View menu. Here is a description of the available views:

✦ **Normal view.** A combination of the Outline and Slide views, this is a convenient view and the view many users choose while working on a presentation. Figure D-7 shows a sample presentation in Normal view.

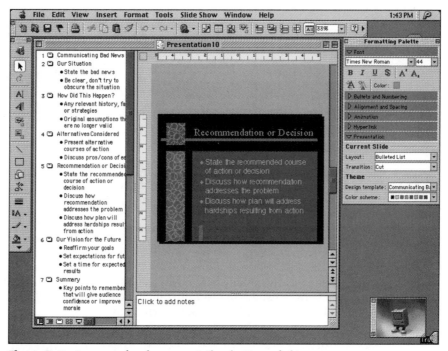

Figure D-7: An example of a presentation in Normal view

✦ **Outline view.** Provides a view of the overall organization of the text in your presentation. In this view, it's easier to see a large portion of your presentation's contents. Although you can't change the slide layouts or modify graphics in this view, you can add and edit the slide titles and the main text. Figure D-8 shows an example of a presentation in Outline view.

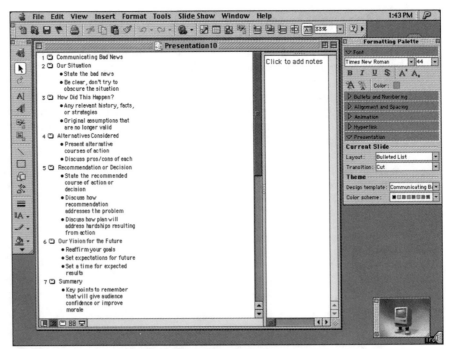

Figure D-8: An example of a presentation in Outline view

✦ **Slide view.** Fills the window with a view of the current slide. In this view, you can add and edit text and graphics or change the layout of the slide. Figure D-9 shows an example of a presentation in Slide view.

✦ **Slide Sorter view.** Provides a window containing multiple slides, each in reduced form. This view is best when you want an overall view of your presentation or when you want to see the overall appearance of the text and the graphics. You can't edit text or graphics in this view, but you can reorder the slides. When you are working with electronic slide shows, you can also add transitions between slides and set the timing in this view (see Chapter 30). Figure D-10 shows an example of Slide Sorter view.

✦ **Slide Show view.** Fills the screen with a view of one slide at a time. In this view, you also see the effects of any transitions and timing that you have added to the presentation. Figure D-11 shows an example of Slide Show view.

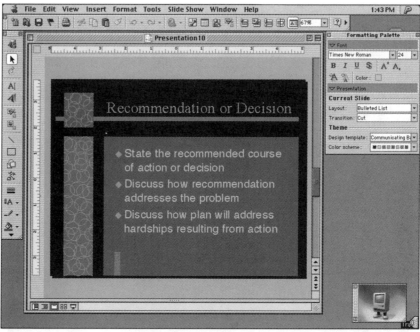

Figure D-9: An example of a presentation in Slide view

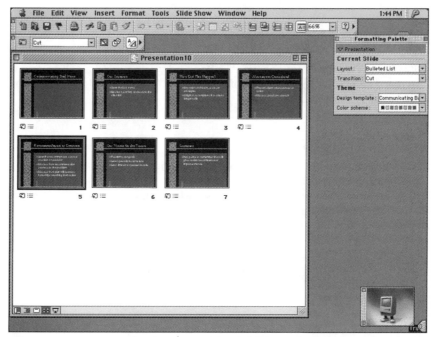

Figure D-10: An example of a presentation in Slide Sorter view

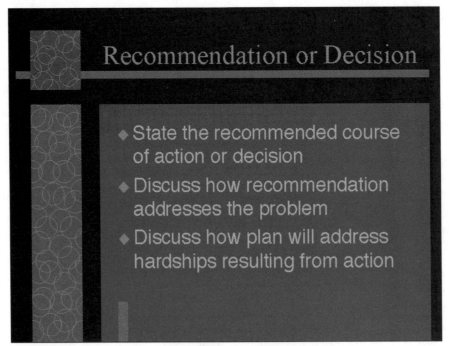

Figure D-11: An example of a presentation in Slide Show view

Working with Slides

If you use PowerPoint much, you'll often find yourself adding slides, moving among slides, and editing the contents of your slides. The following sections cover these eventualities in brief.

Adding slides

To add a slide to your presentation, follow these steps:

1. In any view, choose Insert ⇨ New Slide. (You can also use ⌘-M as a shortcut.) The New Slide dialog box appears.

2. Choose the layout you want for the new slide and click OK.

The slide is then added directly after the slide you're currently viewing; it has the same design as the other slides in your presentation.

Moving among slides

Most presentations have more than one slide, so you must be able to move among slides to work on your whole presentation. How you move among slides depends on which view you're in. Table D-1 shows the different methods for moving around within the different slide views.

Table D-1 **Methods of Moving Among Slides**	
View	*How to Move Among Slides*
Normal View	Drag the scroll box to display the desired slide. Click the slide icon to the left of the slide's title to select the slide. Or click anywhere within the slide's text to edit it.
Outline view	Drag the scroll box to display the desired slide. Click the slide icon to the left of the slide's title to select the slide. Click anywhere within the slide's text to edit it.
Slide view	Drag the scroll box until you reach the desired slide number or click the Previous Slide or Next Slide button at the bottom of the vertical scroll bar.
Slide Sorter view	Click the desired slide.
Slide Show view	Click the mouse or use the left and right arrow keys.

Editing a slide's contents

If you've created a presentation based on a blank slide, you must enter all the required text. If you used an AutoContent Wizard, you've got a fair amount of text in your presentation already, but it's probably not precisely what you want. In either case, you need to add or edit the text you want in your presentation. This section details how you can add or edit text in Normal view, Slide view, or Outline view.

Editing text in Normal or Slide view

In Normal or Slide view, you see your text along with any graphics you have added to the slide, and you can edit any object in the slide by clicking the object. To add text, click in the placeholder labeled Click to add title and type the text, as shown in Figure D-12. To edit existing text, click the text to select it and then edit as you normally would. If you're working with a bulleted list of topics, you can add a new topic by placing the insertion point at the end of an existing topic and pressing Enter.

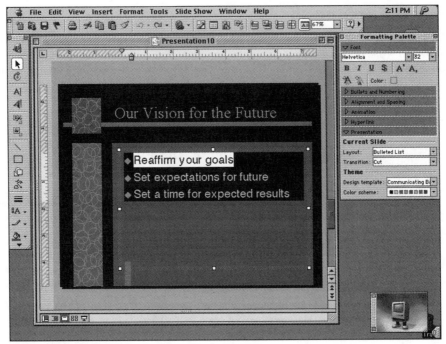

Figure D-12: Editing text in Slide view

Editing text in Outline view

Outline view provides an easy way to edit text because you can view much of your presentation at one time. To edit text, just click to place the insertion point where you want it and type the desired text, as shown in Figure D-13. You can use the Delete or Backspace keys to remove unwanted text.

As you work with text in Outline view, remember that you can use the Promote, Demote, Move Up, and Move Down buttons on the Outlining toolbar to the left of the screen to change the levels or the locations of the items with which you are working. Simply place the insertion point anywhere inside the desired entry and then click the appropriate button. The outlining buttons perform the following tasks:

✦ **Promote (Indent less).** Click this button to remove an indent and move the entry one level higher (in importance) within the list. The item moves to the left, and in most cases, the font size increases.

✦ **Demote (Indent more).** Click this button to add an indent and move the entry one level lower (in importance) within the list. The item moves to the right, and in most cases, the font size decreases.

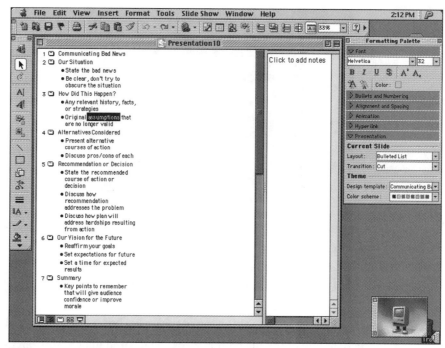

Figure D-13: Editing text in Outline view

✦ **Move Up.** Click this button to move the entry up in the list by one line.

✦ **Move Down.** Click this button to move the entry down in the list by one line.

Adding Clip Art

PowerPoint comes with hundreds of clip-art images that you can easily add to your presentations to add pizzazz to your slides. Note that before you can insert clip art, you must have installed the ClipArt Gallery along with PowerPoint. You can add clip art by following these steps:

1. Switch to Slide view and display the slide where you want to add the clip art.

2. Choose Insert ➪ Picture, and then choose Clip Art or click the Insert Clip Art button on the Standard toolbar to open the Microsoft Clip Gallery dialog box, as shown in Figure D-14.

Note

If you're inserting clip art for the first time, you may see a dialog box warning you that the process may take some time because PowerPoint has to organize the files first.

Figure D-14: The Microsoft Clip Gallery dialog box

3. In the categories list box at the top of the dialog box, click the desired category.

4. In the right half of the dialog box, click the desired image. You can use the scroll bar at the right side of the dialog box to see additional images.

5. Click the Insert button to place the clip art in the slide.

After the clip art appears in the slide, you can click it to select it. Then hold down the mouse button while you drag the clip art to the location you want. You can resize the clip art by clicking one of the sizing handles (the small rectangles that surround the clip art when you select it) and dragging it until the clip art reaches the desired size.

You may often want to add clip art to an area that has existing text, but by default, any clip art you add covers the existing text. To solve this problem, go into Slide view and select the clip art by clicking it. Then choose the Send to Back command from the Draw menu to place the clip art underneath the text, which makes the text visible.

Printing Your Presentation

You can print various parts of your presentation or all of your presentation. To print your presentation, choose File ⇨ Print or click the Print button on the Standard toolbar. The Print dialog box appears, as shown in Figure D-15.

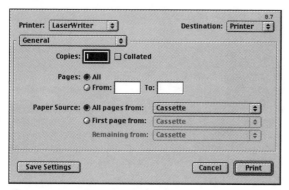

Figure D-15: The Print dialog box

You learn more about the Print dialog box in Chapter 30, but for now, the most important point is to select exactly what you want to print. First, choose Microsoft Power Point from the pop-up menu (it says General when you first open the dialog box and has a downward-pointing arrow on it). Then, in the Print What list box, you can choose Slides, Note Pages, Handouts, or Outline View. Finally, choose General from the pop-up menu and choose the pages you want to print (the default option is All). Select any other desired options in the dialog box and click OK to begin printing.

✦   ✦   ✦

Entourage Quick Start

This introduction to Entourage covers basic Entourage skills and is designed to familiarize readers who have never worked with Entourage or its older sibling, Outlook Express. In this introduction, you learn how to create e-mail accounts, subscribe to newsgroups, manage your address book, keep your calendar, and set up reminders for tasks. When you feel familiar with the basics, you'll find the more advanced details of Entourage in Chapter 36.

Getting Started with Entourage

The first time you launch Entourage, it will present the Entourage Setup Assistant, as shown in Figure E-1, to guide you through establishing your e-mail and newsgroup accounts. If you already have the information for your ISP (Internet Service Provider) in your Internet control panel settings from another application, those values will be presented as the default entries whenever appropriate.

```
┌──────────────── Entourage Setup Assistant ─────────────────┐
│ Welcome                                             /E      │
│                                                            │
│ Welcome to Microsoft Office 2001. Before you begin, Office │
│ needs to know who you are. This information is used to     │
│ customize Office with your personal data such as name,     │
│ company, mailing address, e-mail address, and phone        │
│ numbers.                                                   │
│                                                            │
│ Please type your name.                                     │
│                                                            │
│    First name:    [Dennis R.]                              │
│    Last name:     [Cohen]                                  │
│                                                            │
│                                                            │
│                                                            │
│ Click the right arrow to continue.                         │
│                                              ◁ 1 ▷         │
└────────────────────────────────────────────────────────────┘
```

Figure E-1: Welcome from the Entourage Setup Assistant

After providing your name, either click the right arrow or press Return to move to the next screen, where Entourage requests your home address and phone number. When you've entered that information, either click the right arrow or press Return and provide your work address and related information. You should be in the swing of advancing screens by now, so next comes a request for whether you have data to import from another program (such as Outlook Express, Emailer, Eudora, Now Contact, or Palm Desktop), as shown in Figure E-2. If you wish to import the data, the program that created it must still be present on your machine, because Entourage will use AppleEvents (application-to-application messaging) to retrieve the information.

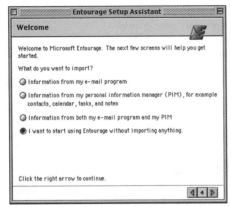

Figure E-2: Entourage asks you if you have information to import.

The next screen will request that you tell it the first program from which to extract information.

Caution   It is crucial, if you have a large amount of data in the other application, that you allocate sufficient memory to Entourage. For example, to import a 20MB Emailer database of messages and contacts, I had to allocate almost 45MB to Entourage (it would hang with 40MB).

After importing your data, you are presented with a request for the name you would like to have appear in the From area of outgoing messages. The following screen will request your existing e-mail address or solicit you to create a Hotmail account. If you wish to create a Hotmail account, you will need to have a connection available to the Internet and have a Web browser designated. Assuming that you are using an established account, you will be presented with a screen querying whether your server is POP or IMAP, and a request for the incoming and outgoing mail server addresses. The following screen will ask for your log-in information. The Account ID is usually the part of your e-mail address preceding the @. If you wish to have Entourage automatically send your password, provide it in the text box and check the Save password box.

Caution   If you are the only one with access to your Mac, having Entourage automatically send your password is probably a reasonable thing to do; however, if others have access to your Mac, they could launch Entourage and masquerade as you, downloading and sending messages.

Next comes a screen asking you to give a name to this account—the default is "Untitled E-mail account." The account name is solely for display and organizational purposes, so you can call it anything you like. Common choices are the name of the ISP, Home, or Personal. Click the Finish button when you are ready to go.

At this point, the Assistant has finished its chores and the main Entourage window is in front, with your Inbox selected, as shown in Figure E-3.

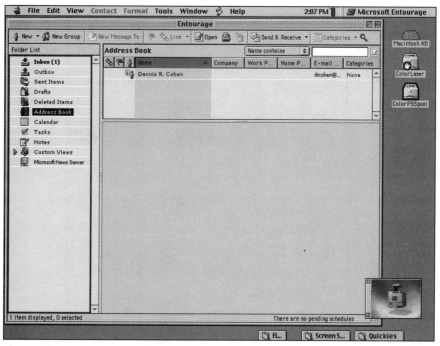

Figure E-3: Entourage's main window

You have a toolbar across the top, a Folder List on the left and display panes on the right. The number of display panes will vary depending upon what you have selected in the Folder List.

Managing Addresses

Entourage manages the Address Book shared among all the Office 2001 applications. This is the home port for the addresses you use in Word when addressing correspondence or performing data merges, for example. Each item in your Address Book is a *contact*.

When you select Address Book in the Folder List, you will be presented with two panes on the right: a list on top and a preview pane beneath it. If you select an entry (such as the one you created when you entered your personal information during setup, as described previously), your window will look something like that shown in Figure E-4; the data will, however, be yours.

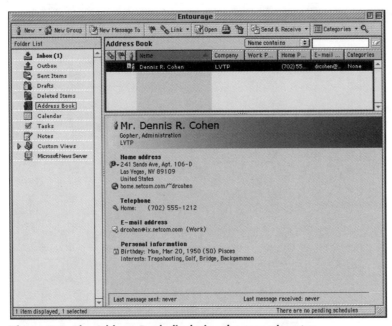

Figure E-4: The Address Book displaying the owner's entry

Creating a contact

You add contacts to your address book by clicking the New button in the toolbar and filling out the fields in the Create Contact dialog box, as shown in Figure E-5.

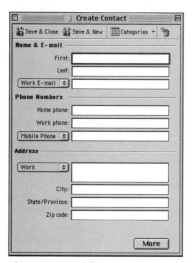

Figure E-5: Adding a contact to the Address Book

Grouping contacts

Frequently, you will find it convenient to create mailing lists for e-mail correspondence. Entourage provides for this with its Groups feature. Groups consist of contacts and other groups. A contact can be in as many groups as you wish. Thus, when you send e-mail to a group you don't have to worry about forgetting to include someone, nor do you have to make as many entries in the address fields as you would if you entered them individually. In fact, you can tell Entourage to not include the names of the group members in the address information—thus, your recipients receive a shorter message and, if they choose to reply to the e-mail, they don't reply to everyone in the group by mistake.

Sending and Receiving E-mail

Sending and receiving e-mail is probably what Entourage is used for most. Incoming mail goes into the Inbox by default and outgoing mail is in the Outbox until it is waiting to be sent. Incomplete outgoing messages are stored in the Drafts folder. The Sent Items folder holds those messages you've sent unless you turn that setting off in the Compose tab of your Mail & News Preferences (choose Edit ⇨ Preferences ⇨ Mail & News or press ⌘-Shift-;) as shown in Figure E-6.

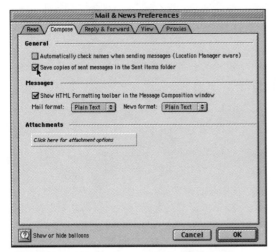

Figure E-6: The Compose tab in Mail & News Preferences

The Compose tab has a couple of other interesting settings. Entourage provides the capability to send your e-mail messages and news postings as HTML files. Although this enables you to add stylistic variation to your electronic correspondence, much of the Internet-using world does not use mail or news clients that handle HTML directly. Additionally, HTML-formatted messages are larger than plain text messages. You will note in Figure E-6 that the default for outgoing messages is Plain text. You can change that to HTML, but then you run the risk of having unhappy recipients. It is not at all uncommon for people to filter out all HTML-formatted e-mail as junk mail and not bother to read it. Additionally, most newsgroups (newsgroups are discussed later in this appendix) are populated by people who will either filter people who send HTML-formatted postings into their *kill-files* (lists of posters they tell their news clients to ignore) or will go so far as to send you nasty e-mail responses to your post simply because you used HTML. Unless you are absolutely certain that your audience is willing to receive HTML messages, you should send the messages as plain text. You can override this preference setting on a case-by-case basis in the message composition window, as we'll discuss next.

Composing a new message

When you click the New button to create a new e-mail message, you are presented with an Untitled message composition window, with a subwindow present for you to address the message, as shown in Figure E-7. The three address areas are To (for principal recipients), Cc (carbon copy), and Bcc (for blind carbon copy). Bcc recipients' names and addresses do not show up in the e-mail header information sent to any other recipients.

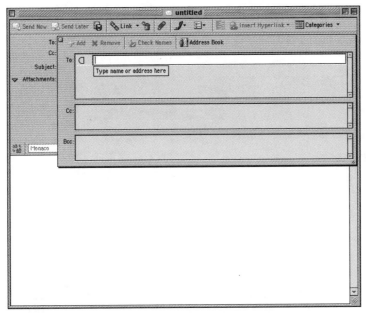

Figure E-7: The message composition window, awaiting your recipient information

If you click the Address Book button in the subwindow, the subwindow will change appearance to include a list of your Address Book entries (shown in Figure E-8) from which you can pick and choose.

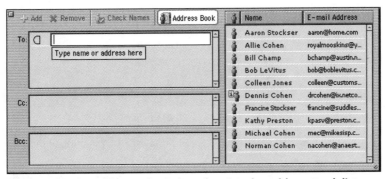

Figure E-8: The address subwindow showing the Address Book list

Double-click any name in the list to include that addressee. You can also go through the list, ⌘-clicking various entries and dragging them to the address area of your choice, as shown in Figure E-9.

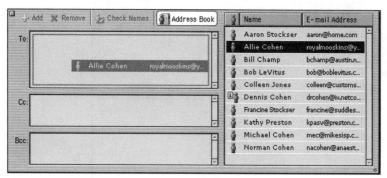

Figure E-9: Drag contacts into the address boxes.

Back in the main message window, give your message a Subject and then click in the main message area or tab to it. Above this large text box, you'll see a row of dimmed buttons. The one on the far left enables you to turn HTML-formatting on and off. This is where you can override the preference setting for individual messages. When you click the Use HTML button, the row becomes enabled, as shown in Figure E-10.

Figure E-10: The HTML formatting buttons

Table E-1 describes each of the HTML formatting buttons shown in Figure E-10.

Table E-1 HTML Formatting Buttons		
Button	**Name**	**Meaning**
ab↵ ↳ab	Use HTML	Turns HTML formatting of the message on and off
Monaco ▾	Font	Select the font to be used. You should use fonts that your recipient is likely to also have; otherwise their mail client will perform a substitution and your formatting can be affected.
Medium ▾	Font Size	Select from five font sizes: Largest, Larger, Medium, Smaller, Smallest

Button	Name	Meaning
B	Bold	Set the font style to bold
I	Italic	Set the font style to italic
U	Underline	Set the font style to underline
T	Teletype	Set the font to teletype style (will change the font to a monospaced font, such as Monaco or Courier)
≡	Align Left	Left justify the text
≡	Center	Center align the text
≡	Align Right	Right justify the text
≣	Numbering	Create a numbered list
≣	Bullets	Create a bulleted list
⇤≣	Decrease Indent	Decrease the indent by one tab stop
⇥≣	Increase Indent	Increase the indent by one tab stop
A ▾	Font Color	Set the color for text: the arrow enables you select from a list of alternatives, the button will set the text color to the color of the underline
⬧ ▾	Background	Set the background color: the arrow enables you select from a list of alternatives. Clicking the button sets the background to the color in the underscore.
—	Horizontal Line	Create a horizontal line to separate parts of your message

After you've composed your message, click Send Now if you want to send the message immediately (or as soon as a connection has been made to your ISP), Send Later if you want the message saved in your Outbox to be sent at your next connection, or Drafts if you wish it to be saved for later modification before sending.

A number of other options are available to you, and these are discussed in Chapter 36.

Reading News

As with e-mail, newsgroups (sometimes referred to as Usenet) have been a part of the Internet since long before the advent of the Web. Newsgroups harken back to the days of the Bulletin Board Systems (BBS) and provide a format for non-real-time chat groups. Usenet has a number of *hierarchies* (organizational groups), but the most common are as follows:

✦ *alt:* alternative, nonmoderated, free-form discussions — not all servers carry these groups

✦ *biz:* business-oriented groups

✦ *comp:* related to computers and computer software

✦ *rec:* recreational groups

✦ *soc:* social and societal discussions

✦ *talk:* topical debates — these frequently get a bit heated

For most of these groups (well over 30,000 exist at the time of this writing, and the number grows daily), Entourage will function quite well, albeit a bit slowly in some cases, compared to a dedicated newsreader program. If you happen to become interested in a group that includes multipart binary attachments for your downloading pleasure, you will probably need to get a dedicated newsreader program. Fortunately, two very fine, free newsreader programs are available for Mac users: YA-Newswatcher and MT-Newswatcher. Both of these programs are based on the original Newswatcher code by John Norstad and are updated regularly. Either can be found through www.versiontracker.com.

Microsoft provides a default news server for you to use: Microsoft News Server. Unfortunately, the selection of newsgroups is limited and only pertains to Microsoft and its products — none of the standard hierarchies are included. You can, however, create a news-server entry for the news server provided by your ISP by choosing Tools ➪ Accounts, selecting the News tab in the Accounts window that opens, and clicking the New button to produce the Account Setup Assistant set to create an Internet News Account as shown in Figure E-11. Step through the screens of the Assistant, and you'll have a new server on the News tab of the Accounts window and in your Folder List. The first time you select the server and each time until you answer affirmatively, your Office Assistant will ask whether you would like a full download of the server's newsgroup list, as shown in Figure E-12. This can take awhile because of the huge number of newsgroups, though not all servers carry all groups.

Figure E-11: Set up an Internet News Account
with the Account Setup Assistant

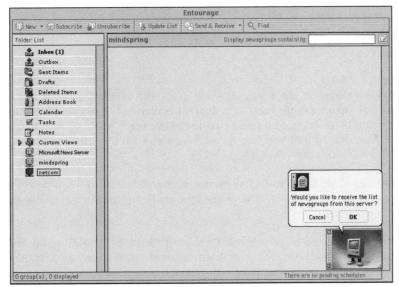

Figure E-12: Max asks whether you want to download a complete list of
groups from the server.

After you have the list of newsgroups, you can use the Display newsgroups containing text box to filter the list down to a more manageable size, showing only those
groups whose names include the string for which you're searching: for example,
you could type **.mac** to limit the display to only those groups in a Macintosh sub-
hierarchy. You can then select groups that you wish to peruse on a regular basis

and click Subscribe. This will add those groups as subordinate items to the news server icon in your Folder List, as shown in Figure E-13, and enable you to quickly select the group to check for what's new.

Figure E-13: Subscribed groups appear under the server in the Folder List

When you select a newsgroup, Entourage will query the server for you and bring down a list of all the messages (up to the limit specified in the Account's Options tab, which defaults to 300) and display that list in the upper-right pane. Unread messages are boldfaced, but you can speed things up a bit by choosing View ⇨ Unread Only (⌘-Y) for each newsgroup.

Tip   Choose View ⇨ Threaded to display messages grouped with the responses to that message in the message list. When messages are threaded, you can follow a discussion more easily.

Internet newsgroups are a huge subject. Check out Chapter 37 for more information, and browse the Web if you want to learn more about the history, organization, netiquette, and politics of newsgroups.

Keeping a Calendar

One of the new *Personal Information Manager (PIM)* features added to Outlook Express to create Entourage is the Calendar. Entourage's Calendar is an easy-to-use planner and scheduler that helps you keep track of your commitments.

You can use the Calendar to do the following:

✦ **Plan events.** Use the Entourage Calendar just as you do a planner notebook or wall/desktop calendar to plan and schedule activities. You can arrange an all-day or multiday event, such as a birthday or a vacation, or an event of shorter duration, such as a doctor's appointment or an automobile service. Events can appear in the Calendar just once or can recur.

✦ **Set reminders.** You can set a reminder to appear at a specified time or date prior to the event.

✦ **Send and receive invitations.** Schedule an event and invite others to attend. If your invitee's e-mail program supports Internet Calendaring (the iCalendar protocol), you will receive a response that indicates whether they accepted or declined the invitation. You can also receive invitations from other people. Unless you decline the invitation, the event is automatically added to the Calendar.

✦ **Add holidays.** Entourage comes with a number of holiday collections for various nations and religions. You can add holidays for any (one or more) of these to the Calendar.

✦ **Save as a Web page.** You can save the Calendar in Web format to share it with others. When you do this, Entourage creates an HTML file and saves it on your computer, along with a folder that contains all of the other HTML files and graphics needed to display your Calendar. You can then post the files on a Web site or attach them to a message. You have the option of designating certain activities as Private and having those excluded from the generated Web page.

✦ **Customize the Calendar.** You can specify the Calendar's appearance—for example, which day starts the week, which days compose a workweek, and the hours in a workday.

Viewing and organizing information

When you first click the Calendar in the Folder List, you see three panes on the right—this is called a *tri-pane view*. The upper-left pane contains a list of calendar events and tasks (covered later in this appendix) for the current day. The upper-right pane will display one or more months (depending upon your window's size) of the calendar where you can select the day(s) to be displayed in the bottom pane, which defaults to a one-month view, reminiscent of a wall calendar. You can view the events in this bottom pane in a variety of formats: by the day, week, workweek, or month, or as a list by choosing from the View menu or Control-clicking and choosing from the shortcut menu (you can't choose a List view from the shortcut menu). The default appearance of this window is shown in Figure E-14. The dates displayed in the view pane are highlighted in the upper-right pane and the current date is framed in red.

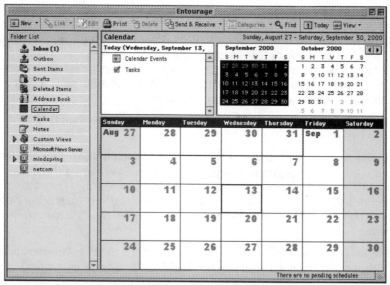

Figure E-14: Entourage's default Calendar view

Scheduling an event

Scheduling an event, such as a meeting, is quite straightforward. Follow these steps:

1. Choose File ⇨ New ⇨ Calendar Event (⌘-N) or Control-click a date and choose New Calendar Event from the shortcut menu. An Untitled event window, as shown in Figure E-15, appears.

2. Type a subject and location for the event in the text boxes. Specify a start and end time and date for the event. The date initially displayed will reflect the selection you made when performing Step 1—you can change this if you wish the event to be on a different day. If the event is to be an all-day event, check that box and the start and end times will adjust to reflect your workday settings.

3. *(Optional)* If the event is to recur on a regular basis, click the recurrence button to display the Recurring Event dialog box, shown in Figure E-16. Make your settings for this meeting and click OK.

4. If you wish to have Entourage remind you beforehand of the event, set the number of minutes, hours, or days of warning you desire. You can also estimate the time you'll need to travel to the meeting in the Add travel time box. If you check Add travel time, Entourage will send the reminder at the interval that includes the time you'll need to travel.

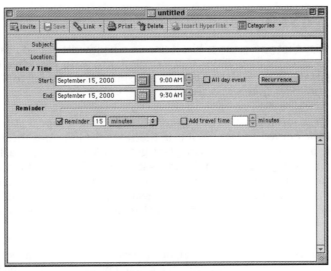

Figure E-15: A new, untitled event window

Figure E-16: The Recurring Event dialog box

5. If you wish to invite others to attend, click the Invite button in the toolbar, and a bevel button will appear above the Subject box telling you to click there to add recipients. When you click, a pop-up windoid appears where you add recipients just as you do for e-mail (described earlier). An Attachment area also appears, where you can include additional material, such as an agenda.

Specifying Tasks

Tasks are activities that you manage like items on a handwritten to-do list. You can specify a due date for completion and a reminder to warn you when the task is approaching its deadline. Finished tasks can be marked as complete. Overdue tasks appear in boldface in the Task list.

Some tasks, such as turning in a weekly summary of activities, repeat at set intervals. An icon of two curved arrows circling in the Tasks list indicates these recurring tasks. When one occurrence of a recurring task gets marked as complete, the next occurrence automatically appears on the Tasks list with a due date at the specified interval. You can specify the interval between occurrences in two ways: absolute and relative. An *absolute* interval would be, for example, each Friday at 1:00 p.m., whereas a *relative* interval would be something like five days after completion of the previous instance.

When you flag a document in Word, Excel, or PowerPoint, it also creates a Task that is entered in your Task list. All tasks due on a given day are displayed in the Today pane of the Calendar, as described earlier.

✦   ✦   ✦

Customizing Toolbars and Menus

This appendix is your one-stop shop for the lowdown on customizing Microsoft Office toolbars and menus.

About Toolbars

Toolbars are strips of buttons you click to perform certain common tasks. Toolbars are a great way to accomplish an action with as few motions as possible. While buttons are helpful, you don't need every button all the time, so each Office application has a standard toolbar you can keep on all the time, as well as several function-specific toolbars you can turn on as needed. Office even turns on some of these function-specific toolbars for you when appropriate. (You can turn them off if you want.) In Office 2001, toolbars can also contain menus. This feature means you can place a menu in a toolbar.

Note   There's only one main rule to remember: You have to be in an application to work with its toolbars, so remember to launch your Office application before you try to do any of these customizations.

Turning Toolbars On or Off

Turning a toolbar on or off is very easy. You have several ways to do so:

✦ Choose View ➪ Toolbars, and then choose the toolbar you wish to turn on or off from the submenu. A check mark in the menu indicates the toolbar is on. (Of course, you can also, usually, see the toolbar onscreen.)

✦ Control-click any blank part of any visible toolbar. This brings up the list of toolbars. Checks indicate which toolbars are active. Click any toolbar to open or close it.

✦ Choose Tools ⇨ Customize, and then click the Toolbars tab. Check or uncheck any toolbar.

✦ Click the More Buttons arrow at the end of any visible toolbar and choose Customize from the pop-up menu. Then, check or uncheck any toolbar.

Repositioning Toolbars

Rather than keeping toolbars at the top of the screen, you may prefer to move a toolbar to the left or right edge of your monitor or have it float freely as a palette. Simply click the rows of dots at the left side of the toolbar, or any edge of a toolbar, and drag. If you drag to an edge of the monitor, the toolbar docks there; if you drag to the middle of your screen, the toolbar floats freely. (When the toolbar docks, that means that it is in a fixed position, stacked in rows at the top of the screen and aligned to the left edge of the screen.) To move a toolbar back to the top or to redock the toolbar, drag it back up into the toolbar area until your mouse overlaps the toolbar you want it to fall below. When you dock a toolbar, any open document windows will resize and move so as to not overlap (or be overlapped by) the toolbar.

A toolbar has the standard Mac window features: a close box, a title bar (which might or might not show the toolbar's name), and a resize corner (bottom right). As with any window, you can drag this palette anywhere onscreen and resize it. Resizing the palette doesn't add a scroll bar; instead it reshapes the toolbar and rearranges the buttons. When a toolbar is shaped (or reshaped) to display more than one row or column of buttons, it acquires a windowshade box, which goes away if you resize back to a single row or column.

Customizing Toolbars

To customize a toolbar, launch the application for the toolbar you want to customize. Then Control-click in any blank spot on the toolbar and choose Customize (or choose Tools ⇨ Customize, or choose Customize from the More Buttons pop-up menu). The Customize dialog box appears. Notice it has three tabs and a Keyboard button; these are your keys to making all sorts of changes to the toolbars. It's a good idea to explore the Commands tab of the Customize dialog box, just to discover some the possibilities available to you. Figure F-1 shows you the Customize dialog box with the Commands tab chosen.

Figure F-1: The Commands tab of the Customize dialog box

Adding or deleting a button (or menu)

To add or remove a button from a toolbar, the Customize dialog box must be open. Select Tools ➪ Customize from the menus or Control-click any toolbar and select Customize from the shortcut menu.

Adding a button is easy—you just drag it to the toolbar. Follow these steps:

1. Select the Commands tab of the Customize dialog box so you can locate the command (button) you want to add.

2. In the Categories list, click a category. On the right, you see a list of all commands within that category. (To make it easier for you to find a command, all commands are categorized.) You will also see All Commands, which, of course, lists every command available.

   To add a menu, choose Built-in Menus from the Categories list.

3. Scroll through the Commands list until you locate the desired command. To learn exactly what a command does, click it, and then look in the Description area.

4. To add the button to the toolbar, click the command and drag it into place on the toolbar. As you drag it to the toolbar, a black bar shows you where the button will land. When it is where you want, release the mouse button. Toolbars grow to accommodate a new button, so beware that you don't grow the toolbar so long that you can't grab the resize handle. If the button doesn't land where you want, you can drag it to the desired location. (If the toolbar you want to add the button or menu to is not showing, first click the Toolbars tab, and then check the appropriate box to turn on any toolbar. Then proceed with this step.)

You may notice that some commands have an image on their left while others don't. If a command has an image, this image will be shown on its button. If not, the command name (text) appears on the button. You can change this later (read on to learn how).

To remove a button from a toolbar, select Tools ⇨ Customize, and then simply click the button and drag it off the toolbar. While the Customize dialog box is open, clicking a button doesn't issue a command. You'll notice that when you click the button and begin to drag it, your cursor gets an X at the end of it.

To move a button off the main portion of the toolbar into the More Buttons pop-up menu, control-click the button and choose Hide Command from the shortcut menu. To move a button from the More Buttons pop-up back to the main portion of the toolbar, click the More Buttons arrow, and then Control-click the button in question and choose Show Command from the shortcut menu.

To restore a toolbar, select Tools ⇨ Customize, and then select the Toolbars tab. In the Toolbars list, click the toolbar to select it and then click the Reset button.

Customizing a button icon

After you add a new button, you may want to change its icon. You can assign the button a predrawn image, paste in your own image, or draw your own image with the Button Editor.

Adding an existing image

To give your button an existing image, follow these steps:

1. Control-click the button to be changed to bring up the shortcut menu. (After you Control-click, you can release the Control key.)

2. Choose Properties from the shortcut menu, click the arrow next to the button's icon and choose the image of your choice from the pop-up menu. Figure F-2 shows the images menu.

Figure F-2: Selecting a predrawn image for your button

3. If your button contains text, the icon appears along with the text. To remove the text from the button, choose Text Only (in Menus) in the View pop-up menu of the Command Properties dialog box.

4. Close the Command Properties dialog box by clicking OK (or Cancel, if you decide against the change).

Pasting an image from another source

A cool way to give your new button an image is to copy an image from another source and paste in into your button. To paste an image from another source onto your button, follow these steps:

1. Open the program that contains the image you want to use, select the image, and copy it to the clipboard. To achieve the best look for your button, the copied image should be ×16 pixels.

2. Control-click the button to be changed and choose Properties from the short-cut menu.

3. In the Command Properties dialog box, click the arrow next to the button's icon, and then choose Paste Button Image from the pop-up menu.

4. Click OK to close the Customize Properties dialog box.

Drawing your own image

You can draw your own button icon by using the Button Editor — a miniature paint program for drawing buttons. As a shortcut, you can assign an already-created image, as explained previously, and then use the Button Editor to make changes to that image. To give your button your own image, follow these steps:

1. Control-click the button to be changed and choose Properties from the short-cut menu. This brings up the Command Properties dialog box. Click the arrow next to the button's icon and choose Edit Button Image from the pop-up menu to display the Button Editor, as shown in Figure F-3. The existing button image appears in the Picture section of the Editor. A preview of your button appears in the Preview box.

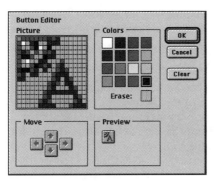

Figure F-3: The Button Editor dialog box

2. To edit the existing image, keep the image in the Picture section. To start fresh, click Clear. Click any color from the Colors section to choose it. Then bring your cursor over to the picture and click in any square to place the color in that square. You can keep your mouse button pressed and drag your mouse to draw. Click the Erase "color" to remove any color from a square.

3. To see your new button appear on the toolbar, click OK to close the Button Editor dialog box. After that, either finish or choose Edit Button Image in the Command Properties dialog box to edit it again.

It's common to misjudge size or dimensions as you draw. To make this less of a problem, you can move your image within the button by clicking the arrows in the dialog box.

Customizing the text on a button

The text that appears on your button is actually the name of your button. To change the text that appears, follow the directions in the next section.

Naming buttons

Follow these two steps to give a button a name:

1. Control-click the button to be changed and choose Properties from the shortcut menu. Type the new name in the Name text box of the Command Properties dialog box that appears. (You can see this field in Figure F-2.) Click in that field to place an insertion point in the field, and then edit the name text as you would any text. (Use an ampersand [&] to create a space in this field.)

2. Click OK to enforce the change.

Creating a New Toolbar

You can create a new toolbar easily by following these steps:

1. Control-click in any blank spot on a toolbar and select Customize (or select Tools ⇨ Customize). When the Customize dialog box appears, click the Toolbars tab.

2. Click the New button. In the New Toolbar dialog box, name your new toolbar.

   In Word, you can also set where you want that toolbar to be available. For each toolbar, you can choose the open document or template in which you want it stored from the Save in pop-up menu at the bottom of the Customize dialog box. By default, the toolbar is saved to the Normal template. (See Chapter 2 to learn about templates.)

That's it. Behind or near the dialog box, a new, empty floating toolbar appears, ready for you to add buttons to it.

Customizing Menus

Office's menus are also very flexible. You can add or remove commands (including styles, AutoText entries, and macros) to make the menus most efficient for your use. To customize a menu, launch the application containing the menu you want to customize.

Customize commands in an existing menu

To customize the commands in an existing menu, follow these steps:

1. Control-click any blank spot on a toolbar and select Customize (or select Tools ➪ Customize). When the Customize dialog box appears, click the Toolbars tab.

2. In the Toolbars list, check Menu Bar (Word and PowerPoint), or Worksheet Menu bar or Chart Menu bar (Excel). This brings up a customizable copy of the menu bar you are altering. You'll find this customizable menu bar at the top of your screen, below the docked toolbars.

3. Click the Commands tab (of the Customize dialog box).

4. In the Categories list, select the category of the command you wish to add.

5. Scroll to the command you want. If you don't see the command you want, try another category or click All Commands.

6. Click the desired command in the Commands box and drag it over the customizable menu bar. The menu drop downs and reveals a list of its commands, and your cursor gains a field and a plus sign. Move your cursor (pointer) to the exact location on the menu where you want the new command to fall. A horizontal black line shows you where it is due to fall as you release the mouse button. Release the mouse button when the command is in place.

To remove a command from a menu, repeat Steps 1 and 2. Then, in the customizable version of the menu bar, click the menu that contains your command. This reveals all of that menu's commands. Click the command you want to remove and drag it off the menu. (You can stop dragging as soon as it's off the menu area.)

You can also change the order of commands on your menus or move them to another menu. In the customizable version of the menu bar, click the menu that contains your command. When the menu's commands appear, click the command you want to reorder and drag it to a new position on that menu. To move the command to another menu, drag the command on top of that menu's name, and move it into place when the menu's contents appear.

Adding your own menus

You can even add your own menu. This is a great option if you're hesitant to alter the standard menus. If you are using Office in an office environment, you should consider creating task or job-specific menus. To do so, follow these steps:

1. Control-click in any blank spot on a toolbar and choose Customize (or choose Tools ⇨ Customize or choose Customize from any toolbar's More Buttons pop-up menu). When the Customize dialog box appears, click the Toolbars tab.

2. In the Toolbars list, check Menu Bar (Word and PowerPoint), or Worksheet Menu bar or Chart Menu bar (Excel). This brings up a customizable copy of the menu bar you are altering. You'll find this customizable menu bar at the top of your screen, below the docked toolbars.

3. Click the Commands tab (of the Customize dialog box).

4. In the Categories list, select New Menu.

5. Click New Menu in the Commands list and drag it over the customizable menu bar. The menu drop downs and reveals a list of its commands and your cursor gains a field and a plus sign. Move your cursor (pointer) to the exact location between existing menus where you want the new menu to fall. A vertical black line shows you where the menu is due to fall as you release the mouse button. Release the mouse button when it's in place.

Tip

For more information about customizing Office 2001's menus and toolbars, check out the Help within each application. Go to Help ⇨ Contents and Indexes. In Word, select Customizing Microsoft Word, and then select Customizing Command Bars for a plethora of choices; in Excel, click Customizing Excel, and then click Customizing Menus and Toolbars; in PowerPoint, see Customizing Menus and Toolbars under Customizing PowerPoint.

Renaming menus or menu items

To rename any menu command or menu name, follow Steps 1 and 2 under "Customizing Menus."

If you want to change a menu name in the customizable menu, click that menu name. If you want to rename a command, click the menu name, and then Control-click the command you want to rename and choose Properties from the shortcut menu. In the Command Properties dialog box, edit the text in the Name text box.

Restoring menus

After you've customized the built-in menus for an Office application, you can restore the original settings — their look, commands, and submenus — at any time.

Caution If you are in an office and inheriting your Mac from another employee, restoring menus is a good way to make sure you are working with the default settings. However, you should check with your Mac manager first to make sure the menus weren't specifically customized for your office or position.

To restore your menus, follow these steps:

1. As with many menu or toolbar customizations, the Customize dialog box must be open. Select Tools ⇨ Customize (or Control-click a toolbar and select Customize). In the Customize dialog box that appears, click the Toolbars tab.

2. In the Toolbars list, check the Menu Bar check box (or the Worksheet Menu bar or Chart Menu bar in Excel). This displays the customizable copy of the menu bar below docked toolbars.

3. Select the menu you want to restore, and click the Reset button.

4. Close the Customize dialog box.

If you completely removed a built-in menu, go to the Commands tab of the Customize dialog box and select Built-in Menus from the Categories list. From the Commands list, drag the desired menu name into place on the customizable menu bar (which is below the normal menu bar).

Changing Word's Keyboard Shortcuts

By default, Office's applications provide you with keyboard command (shortcuts) that you can press to invoke a command without going to the menus and/or dialog boxes. In Word (but only in Word), you can change these shortcuts. For example, if you are used to a certain key combination from another program, you can assign that combination to the parallel command in Word.

To alter (or just to discover) a keyboard combination, launch the application containing the commands you want to customize. Then Control-click in any blank spot on a toolbar and choose Customize, or choose Customize from any toolbar's More Buttons pop-up menu (or choose Tools ⇨ Customize). When the Customize dialog box appears, click the Keyboard button to open the Customize Keyboard dialog box. Select the category the command falls under (or select All Commands), and then click the command in the Commands list. If a shortcut already exists, it appears in the Current keys list. In Figure F-4, the command selected has two shortcut combinations already.

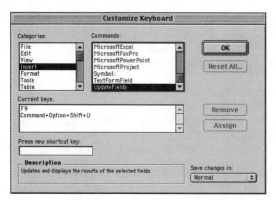

Figure F-4: The Customize Keyboard dialog box

To add a key combination, after selecting the command from the Commands list, click in the box that aptly says Press new shortcut key, and then press your new combination. A message appears in the dialog box, telling you if this combination is available or already taken and, if so, what command uses it. If these keys are already assigned to something you want to keep, use the Delete key to delete your combination, and then try a new one. When you are happy with a new key combination, click Assign. You can also specify where to save these changes from the Save changes in pop-up menu — the default is to save in the Normal template.

Note   A word about locating commands in the Commands list: Built-in menu commands are represented by the name of their menu, attached to the name of the command, rather than the name of the command. For example, the Save command isn't under S for Save, but under F for FileSave.

✦   ✦   ✦

Index

Continued

Continued

Continued

Continued

my2cents.idgbooks.com

Register This Book — And Win!

Visit **http://my2cents.idgbooks.com** to register this book and we'll automatically enter you in our fantastic monthly prize giveaway. It's also your opportunity to give us feedback: let us know what you thought of this book and how you would like to see other topics covered.

Discover IDG Books Online!

The IDG Books Online Web site is your online resource for tackling technology — at home and at the office. Frequently updated, the IDG Books Online Web site features exclusive software, insider information, online books, and live events!

10 Productive & Career-Enhancing Things You Can Do at www.idgbooks.com

- Nab source code for your own programming projects.
- Download software.
- Read Web exclusives: special articles and book excerpts by IDG Books Worldwide authors.
- Take advantage of resources to help you advance your career as a Novell or Microsoft professional.
- Buy IDG Books Worldwide titles or find a convenient bookstore that carries them.
- Register your book and win a prize.
- Chat live online with authors.
- Sign up for regular e-mail updates about our latest books.
- Suggest a book you'd like to read or write.
- Give us your 2¢ about our books and about our Web site.

You say you're not on the Web yet? It's easy to get started with IDG Books' *Discover the Internet*, available at local retailers everywhere.